MW01626024

Degas

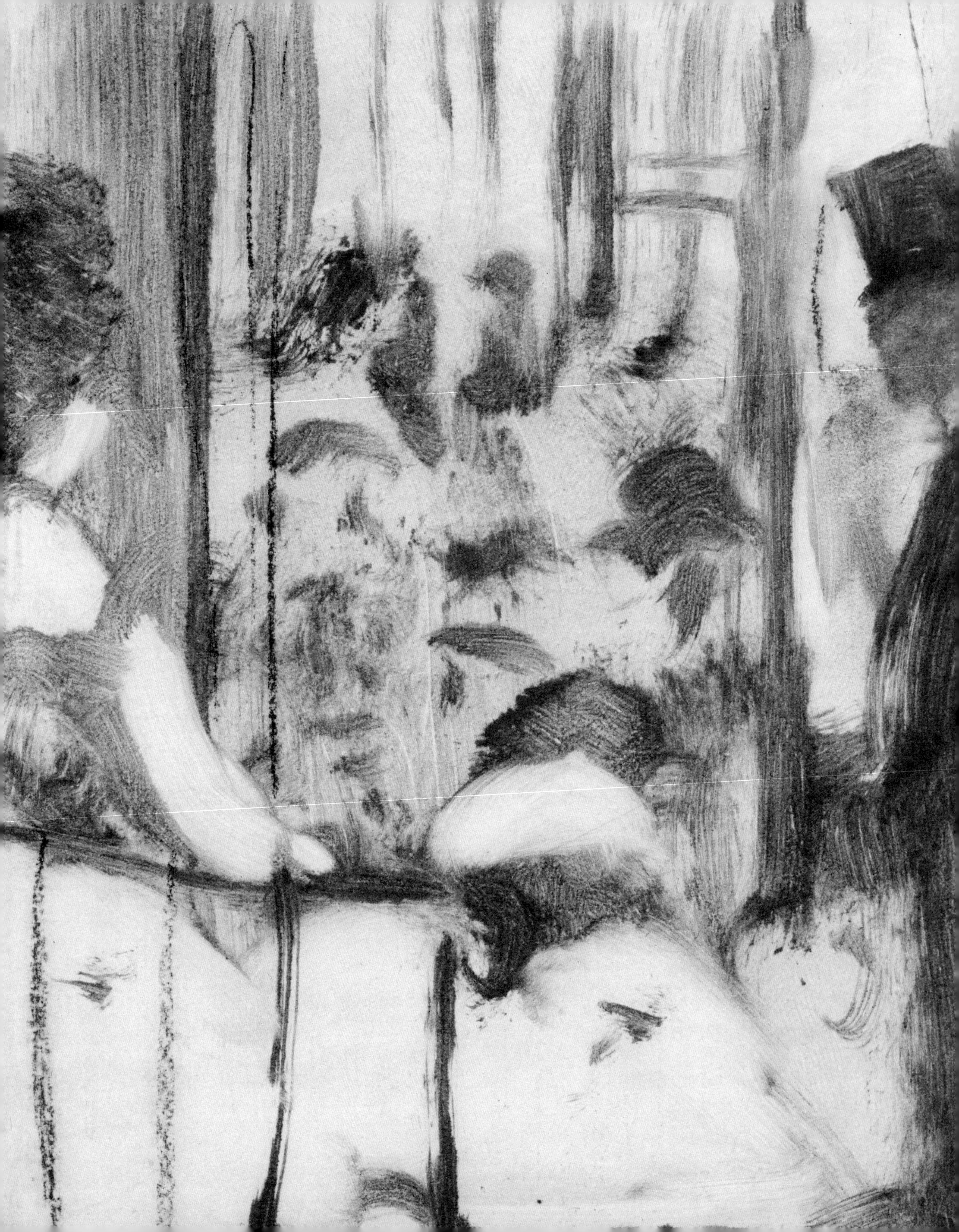

Degas
A Strange New Beauty

Jodi Hauptman

With essays by Carol Armstrong, Jonas Beyer, Kathryn Brown, Karl Buchberg and Laura Neufeld, Hollis Clayson, Jill DeVonyar, Samantha Friedman, Richard Kendall, Stephanie O'Rourke, Raisa Rexer, and Kimberly Schenck

The Museum of Modern Art, New York

Published in conjunction with the exhibition *Edgar Degas: A Strange New Beauty*, at The Museum of Modern Art, New York, March 26–July 24, 2016, organized by Jodi Hauptman, Senior Curator, Department of Drawings and Prints, with Richard Kendall

Lead sponsor of the exhibition is The Philip and Janice Levin Foundation.

Major support is provided by the Robert Lehman Foundation and by Sue and Edgar Wachenheim III.

Generous funding is provided by Dian Woodner.

This exhibition is supported by an indemnity from the Federal Council on the Arts and the Humanities.

Additional support is provided by the MoMA Annual Exhibition Fund.

This publication is made possible by the Riva Castleman Fund for Publications in the Department of Drawings and Prints, established by The Derald H. Ruttenberg Foundation.

Produced by the Department of Publications, The Museum of Modern Art, New York

Christopher Hudson, Publisher
Chul R. Kim, Associate Publisher
David Frankel, Editorial Director
Marc Sapir, Production Director

Edited by David Frankel
Designed by Tsang Seymour
Production by Matthew Pimm
Printed and bound by Brizzolis, S. A., Madrid

Jonas Beyer's essay was translated from the German by Russell Stockman.

This book is typeset in Monotype Ionic and Franklin Gothic. The paper is 120gsm Munken Polar Rough.

Library of Congress Control Number: 2015960601
ISBN: 978-1-63345-005-9

Published by The Museum of Modern Art
11 West 53 Street
New York, New York 10019
www.moma.org

Distributed in the United States and Canada by ARTBOOK | D.A.P., New York
155 Sixth Avenue, 2nd floor, New York, NY 10013
www.artbook.com

Distributed outside the United States and Canada by Thames & Hudson ltd
181A High Holborn, London WC1V 7QX
www.thamesandhudson.com

Cover: Hilaire-Germain-Edgar Degas. *Factory Smoke* (*Fumées d'usines*). 1877–79. Monotype on paper, plate: 4 11/16 × 6 5/16 in. (11.9 × 16.1 cm), sheet: 5 13/16 × 6 13/16 in. (14.7 × 17.3 cm). The Metropolitan Museum of Art, New York. The Elisha Whittelsey Collection, The Elisha Whittelsey Fund. See plate 47

Frontispiece: Hilaire-Germain-Edgar Degas. *Dancers Coming from the Dressing Rooms onto the Stage* (*Et ces demoiselles frétillaient gentiment devant la glace du foyer*). c. 1876–77. Proposed illustration for *The Cardinal Family* (*La Famille Cardinal*). Pastel over monotype on paper, plate: 8 3/8 × 6 1/4 in. (21.2 × 15.8 cm). Schorr Collection. See plate 78

Endpapers: Hilaire-Germain-Edgar Degas. *Green Landscape* (*Paysage vert*; detail). 1890. Monotype in oil on paper, plate: 11 3/4 × 15 5/8 in. (29.9 × 39.7 cm), sheet: 12 3/8 × 15 7/8 in. (31.4 × 40.4 cm). The Museum of Modern Art, New York. Louise Reinhardt Smith Bequest. See plate 127

Printed in Spain

Contents

Foreword

In a notebook dating from around 1879, Edgar Degas lists subjects for works of art on the theme of smoke: "smoke of smokers, pipes cigarettes,/cigars/smoke from locomotive, from high chimneys/of factories, of steam boats, etc./squishing of smoke under bridges/ steam." Some of these ideas found their way onto paper and canvas—the image on the cover of this book is one example—but the significance of the list goes beyond the works it generated to its evidence of Degas's visual imagination, his perpetual quest for new topics, new techniques, new materials. Whether concerning strategy or subject, these notes convey the impression of an artist bursting with ideas and willing to take risks. This inventiveness is palpably visible in the corpus that is this exhibition's subject: Degas's monotypes.

Edgar Degas: A Strange New Beauty explores the artist's experimentation in monotype and offers something of an adventure. We watch Degas's introduction to this medium in the mid-1870s, then follow his journey as he assesses and probes, learning its strengths and weaknesses, understanding its many promises, and developing his own course. We also see the impact of these lessons on his approach to painting and other kinds of drawing and printmaking. Degas's foray into monotype reveals an artist who is always testing, whether wresting new possibilities from available techniques, imagining new subjects, or proposing a new kind of artwork that is less about completion than about an inexorable search for variations in form.

Providing an opportunity to experience rarely seen and lesser-known works, the exhibition also tackles the sweeping changes of Degas's time. The way he addressed transformations in modern life, the expansion in the availability of images via mechanical reproduction, the representation of the body, and the possibilities of abstraction will resonate with twenty-first-century viewers who face a similar proliferation of images, proving the ongoing relevance of modernism's foundational figures for the art of today.

To understand Degas's practice, our curatorial team partnered with colleagues in MoMA's Department of Conservation, Karl Buchberg, Senior Conservator, and Laura Neufeld, Assistant Conservator, to delve into Degas's process and materials, affording visitors the opportunity to share the artist's discovery of monotype in a tangible way. The Museum of Modern Art is a leader in such collaborative work, and its record in technical art history makes it well-suited to this project. I am especially indebted to Jodi Hauptman, Senior Curator, Department of Drawings and Prints, for organizing this exhibition and for her outstanding research into Degas's working methods.

Many have contributed. We are indebted to private individuals who have enthusiastically participated, graciously lending precious works. Our counterparts at other museums have been equally supportive, allowing us to closely study key examples and making exceptional loans. Scholars, curators, and conservators have shared their knowledge and expertise; we are fortunate that a number of them have agreed to publish here, including Richard Kendall, who also served as a curatorial consultant. Here at MoMA, we relied on the Museum's senior staff, including Ramona Bannayan, Peter Reed, James Gara, Todd Bishop, and Patty Lipschutz and their talented teams.

Bringing together important works from around the globe requires significant resources. We are profoundly grateful to our lead sponsor, The Philip and Janice Levin Foundation, and to the Robert Lehman Foundation, Sue and Edgar Wachenheim III, and Dian Woodner for their support. Our thanks go to the generous donors to the MoMA Annual Exhibition Fund. Finally, an exhibition of this scale and ambition could not be mounted without the support of the Federal Council on the Arts and Humanities and the very generous indemnity they have granted.

—Glenn D. Lowry
Director, The Museum of Modern Art

Acknowledgments

Degas, some said, could be solitary and severe, but the many who value his art are wonderfully collaborative and, above all, curious—about a body of work that close to a century after his death remains enigmatic. Countless colleagues, scholars, and enthusiasts have contributed to our efforts to understand some of these mysteries.

Our first and greatest debt is to the exhibition's lenders, private individuals who warmly welcomed us and performed many acts of generosity. We thank: Mrs. Martin Atlas, James Bergquist, Judith and Bernard Briskin, André Bromberg, Marty de Cambiare, the Larry Ellison Collection, Ann and Gordon Getty, Wendy and Leonard Goldberg, the Haroche Collection, Frederick Iseman, Chunhui Zhao-Lecomte and Bernard Lecomte, Collection Marcel Lecomte, Ursula and R. Stanley Johnson, William I. Koch, the Henry and Rose Pearlman Foundation, the Schorr Collection, the John and Marine van Vlissingen Foundation, and many others who wish to remain anonymous.

Colleagues at institutions have been true collaborators, studying these works with us, sharing their resources (many of those mentioned here are Degas specialists with expertise developed in exhibition and collection research), and ultimately making exceptional loans possible. Many people helped us at each museum, from curators to registrars to image and rights providers, and we especially acknowledge: at the Ackland Art Museum, University of North Carolina at Chapel Hill, Peter Nisbet and Scott Hankins; at The Art Institute of Chicago, Douglas Druick, Suzanne Folds McCullagh, Nancy Ireson, Marc Pascal, and Emily Ziemba; at the Baltimore Museum of Art, Jay Fisher, Rena M. Hoisington, Melanie F. Harwood, and Nicole Simpson; at the Bibliothèque nationale de France, Jocelyn Monchamp, Thierry Grillet, Valérie Sueur-Hermel, Vanessa Selbach, and Isabelle Georjon; at the British Museum, Neil MacGregor and Hugo Chapman; at the Cantor Arts Center at Stanford University, Connie Wolf and Katie Clifford; at the Carnegie Museum of Art, Lynn Zelevansky; at the Clark Art Institute, Michael Conforti, Jay Clarke, and Teresa O'Toole; at the Cleveland Museum of Art, William M. Griswold, Debbie Gribbon, and Jane Glaubinger; at the Courtauld Gallery, Deborah Swallow, Karen Serres, and Barnaby Wright; at the Fondation de l'Hermitage, Sylvie Wuhrmann and Aurélie Couvreur; at the Fitzwilliam Museum, University of Cambridge, Tim Knox and Lucilla Brown; at the Fine Arts Museums of San Francisco, Richard Benefield; at the Harvard Art Museums, Thomas Lentz, Miriam Stewart, Casey Kane Monahan, and Francine Flynn; at the High Museum of Art, Michael Shapiro and Randall Suffolk; at the Kunsthalle Bremen, Christoph Grunenberg; at the J. Paul Getty Museum, Timothy Potts; at the Kunstmuseum Wintherthur, Dieter Schwarz and Ludamilla Sala; at the Los Angeles County Museum of Art, Michael Govan and Leslie Jones; at The Metropolitan Museum of Art, Thomas Campbell, Nadine Orenstein, Freyda Spira, Susan Stein, Dita Amory, Manus Gallagher, Emily Foss, Liz Zanis, and Allison Rudnick; at the Morgan Library and Museum, Colin Bailey, Peggy Fogelman, and Jennifer Tonkovich; at the Musée d'art et d'histoire, Neuchâtel, Renée Knecht and Lucie Girardin-Cestone; at the Musée d'Orsay, Guy Cogeval, Xavier Rey, Elise Dubreuil, Claire Bernardi, and Leïla Jarbouaï; at the Musée Picasso, Paris, Laurent Le Bon and Sarah Lagrevol; at the Museum of Fine Arts, Boston, Matthew Teitelbaum, Malcolm Rogers, and Helen Burnham; at the National Gallery, London, Gabriele Finaldi, Shona Connechen, and Anne Robbins; at the National Gallery of Canada, Marc Mayer and Kate Beresford; at the National Gallery of Art, Washington, D.C., Earl A. Powell III, Judith Brodie, Ginger Hammer, Lisa M. MacDougall, and Andrew Robison; at the National Museum of Art, Architecture and Design, Oslo, Audun Eckhoff and Stine Hoel; at the National Trust, Mottisfont Abbey, Paul Cook and Fernanda Torrente; at the Norton Simon Museum, Pasadena, Walter Timoshuk, Carol Togneri, Emily Beeny, Lisa Escovedo, and Jacqui Chambers; at the Ny Carlsberg Glyptotek, Flemming Friborg and Line Clausen Pedersen; at the Philadelphia Museum of Art, Timothy Rub, Innis Howe Shoemaker, and Shelley Langdale; at the Portland Museum of Art, Mark Bessire, Andrew Eschelbacher, Karen Sherry, and Erin Damon; at the Princeton University Art Museum, James Steward; at the Reading Public Museum, John Smith and Ashley Hamilton; at the Saint Louis Art Museum, Brent R. Benjamin, Elizabeth Wyckoff, and Simon Kelly; at the Scottish National Gallery, Edinburgh, Michael Clarke; at the Staatliche Kunsthalle Karlsruhe, Dr Pia Müller-Tamm, Alexander Eiling, and Rieke Friese; at the Staatsgalerie Stuttgart, Christiane Lange, Anna Marie Pfäfflin, and Annette Blattmacher; at the Städel Museum, Frankfurt am Main, Max Hollein and Dr. Jutta Schütt; at the Statens Museum for Kunst, Copenhagen, Mikkel Bogh; and at the Yale University Art Gallery, Jock Reynolds, Lisa Hodermarsky, and L. Lynne Addison.

For crucial assistance in facilitating these loans we thank Nicholas Acquavella, Alexander Apsis, Jean-Luc Baroni, Kate Brown, Jean Edmonson, Eric Gillis, Dr. Kuno Fischer, Armin Kunz, Marc Rosen, Manuel Schmit, Susan Schulman, Martin Schwander, and Nicholas Stogdon. At Christie's we thank Cyanne Chutkow, Vanessa Fusco, Amy Indyke, Sharon Kim, and Maria Los; and, at Sotheby's, Campbell Mobley, Takako Nagasawa, Kathryn Solomon, Christina Williams, Yin Zhao, and Mark Best. Others who assisted include Matthew Armstrong, Kelly Baum, Bojana Borić-Brešković, Mr. and Mrs. Michael von Brentano, Cynthia Burlingham, Aisha Burtenshaw, Connie Butler, Alison Chang, Ann Dumas, Sophia Elze, Scott Gerson, John and Paul Herring, David E. Little, Maura Lynch, Nannette V. Maciejunes, Peter Parshall, Anne-Sophie Kofoed Rasmussen, Sylvie Ramond, Jeff Rosenheim, Karen Roswell, Lara Smith, Margaret Stuffmann, Patty Tang, Richard Thomson, Makiko Yamada, Martina Yamin, and, at the Bibliothèque de l'Institut national d'histoire de l'art (INHA), Collections Jacques Doucet, Antoinette Le Normand-Romain, Fabienne Queyroux, and Nathalie Muller.

For their exceptional efforts we recognize with immense gratitude Erika Abad, Paola Aeschlimann-Rebstein, Brenna Cothran, Bertrand Dumas, Evelyne Ferlay, Irene Foster, Deborah Anne Hatch, Mimi Haas, Tracy Hamilton, Diana Howard, Philip Isles, Elise Johnson, Natasha Khandekar, Teresa Krasny, Elizabeth Kujawski, Vlasta Odell, Marie-Anne Krugier-Poniatowski, Lea Raffl, Marie-Pierre Salé, Margo Schab, Farrah Spot, Lara Smith, Christine Stauffer, Verane Tasseau, and Jaime Toporovich.

This exhibition is indebted to the vast scholarship on Degas. Research on the monotypes is detailed in this volume's bibliography; of those efforts we acknowledge with veneration the volume on Degas's monotypes by Eugenia Parry Janis, which remains the required reference. We are most grateful to Richard Kendall, who agreed to play the role of consultant, sharing experience gained from years of engagement with Degas's work. His essay here details the arc of the artist's practice in monotype. The voices of the other scholars who agreed to write for our publication expand the story in important ways: Carol Armstrong links Degas's monotypes to his experiments in photography; Stephanie O'Rourke identifies the roots of Degas's interest in repetition and variation; Kimberly Schenk connects the monotypes to other kinds of printmaking; Hollis Clayson identifies Degas's read on illumination in modern Paris; Kathryn Brown shares recent research on *The Cardinal Family*; Jonas Beyer focuses on time in the landscapes; and Jill de Vonyar extends her study of the ballet.

For excellent guidance on all things Degas we are profoundly indebted to Theodore Reff and Barbara Divver, who, in the midst of deadlines for a highly anticipated volume of Degas's correspondence, welcomed questions and shared their unparalleled knowledge. George Shackelford thoughtfully discussed the exhibition's goals. Others were essential interlocutors: I am deeply grateful to Dominique Fourcade, who so generously shared his own book on the monotypes and his profound understanding of their power; Maria Gough, a vital sounding board; Stephan Wolohojian, who offered advice and encouragement at crucial moments; and Matthew Affron, Kathy Fuld, Ewa Lajer-Burcharth, Jill Moser, Avril Peck, and Jeffrey Weiss.

This exhibition's focus on Degas's materials and methods was given form and substance by conservators and exceptional partners Karl Buchberg and Laura Neufeld. Here in our own labs we were immeasurably enriched by Jim Coddington, Lee Ann Daffner, and Lynda Zycherman. Our team benefited enormously from conversations with conservators, often as we studied works together: at The Art Institute of Chicago, Harriet Stratis and Antoinette Owen; at the Baltimore Museum of Art, Tom Primeau; at the Fine Arts Museums of San Francisco, Debra Evans and Victoria Binder; at the Harvard Art Museums Straus Center, Penley Knipe and Anne Driesse; at The Metropolitan Museum of Art, Marjorie Shelley; at the Morgan Library and Museum, Margaret Holben Ellis and Reba Fishman Snyder; at the National Gallery of Art, Washington, D.C., Daphne Barbour, Marian Dirda, Michelle Facini, Kimberly Schenk, and Shelley Sturman; at the Philadelphia Museum of Art, Nancy Ash and Scott Homolka; at the Saint Louis Art Museum, L. H. Shockey; and Antoinette Dwan, conservator in private practice. Andrew Mockler, publisher of Jungle Press, opened his studio to us, inviting us to join him and his colleague Evan Bellantone in making monotypes, the better to understand Degas's methods and results. The experience was thrilling—and fun!—and demonstrated for us the simplicity and the complexity of the process. We were able to capture it on film, and we so appreciate Andrew's willingness to participate. Here at MoMA we thank Fiona Romeo and Eva Kozanecka for producing this instructive film for our audiences, as well as Chiara Bernasconi, Shannon Darrough, Mike Gibbons, Aaron Harrow, Maggie Lederer, and Aaron Louis for the digital initiatives that bring Degas's practice to life.

I am humbled by the exceptional efforts made on behalf of this project by my colleagues at MoMA. Almost a decade ago, MoMA's director, Glenn D. Lowry nudged me toward Degas in a conversation about the artist's sketchbooks and the way he captured the modern experience. I am grateful for his support since then—as well as for the ready assistance of Diana Pulling, Madeline Casella, and Jesse Parsons. Ramona Bannayan, Senior Deputy Director, Exhibitions and Collections, advises on every aspect of the exhibition process and her good counsel is evident in the project's result. Peter Reed, Senior Deputy Director for Curatorial Affairs, offered sage advice at key moments—as did Patty Lipschutz and Nancy Adelson, General Counsel, who tackled challenges with aplomb. Other members of MoMA's senior staff who made significant contributions include James Gara, Chief Operating Officer, Kathy Halbreich, Associate Director, and Jay Levenson, Director of the Museum's International Program.

An exhibition of this scale and ambition can only be realized with significant resources, and we depended on Todd Bishop, Senior Deputy Director for External Affairs, and his team, including Lauren Stakias, Kayla Dryden, Claire Huddleston, Blair Shoemaker, Bobby Kean, and Anna Luisa Vallifuoco. I join them and our Director in thanking our extraordinarily generous donors: The Philip and Janice Levin Foundation, lead sponsor; the Robert Lehman Foundation and Philip Isles; Sue and Edgar Wachenheim III; and Dian Woodner. The expert Communications and Marketing team of Margaret Doyle, Sara Beth Walsh (the project's publicist), Paul Jackson, Rebecca Stokes, Wendy Olson, Jason Perse, and Jocelyn Meinhardt, led by Kim Mitchell, Chief Communications Officer, brought out Degas's radicality for our visitors. MoMA's talented graphics staff found visual ways to reflect Degas's inventiveness: Ingrid Chou, Claire Corey, Elle Kim, and Vanessa Lam. To expand the experience within the galleries and continue the thinking outside them, we relied on our dedicated educators, led by Wendy Woon and including Sara Bodinson, Cari Frisch, Pablo Helguera, Sarah Kennedy, Elizabeth Margulies, Jenna Madison, and Jess Van Nostrand, as well as those from Antenna, including Sofie Andersen, Emma Lunbeck, and Miranda Smith. We also enjoyed the collaboration of our colleagues in MoMA's Retail Department, especially Emmanuel Plat, Karen Hernandez, and Emily Greer.

Given the vast scholarship on Degas, we were regulars in the Museum's library. Our work was facilitated by Milan Hughston, Chief of Library and Museum Archives, and Jennifer Tobias and David Senior, as well as Michelle Elligott, Chief Archivist. We relied on the CEMS staff to keep us organized, often calling on Leslie Davis and Allison LaPlatney. Erik Landsberg, Robert Kastler, and Roberto Rivera, our colleagues in the Imaging and Visual Resources Department, generated new photography and supplied existing images for the project. As always we received crucial assistance from colleagues in Special Events, including Maggie Lyko, Pamela Eisenberg, and Pamela Duncan; Facilities and Security, led by Tunji Adeniji; Human Resources, especially Laura Coppelli; and Membership and Visitor Services, including Meagan Johnson, Sonya Shrier, Jean-Mary Bongiorno, and Kaitlyn Klimetis.

Bringing 180 works to the Museum from nearly 100 lenders around the world is no easy feat, but Susan Palamara, Registrar, managed this task with absolute precision and with sensitivity both to the material and to the curators. We were fortunate that she was joined by Victoria Manning. Carlos Yepes oversaw lenders' queries and contracts as well as our complex indemnity application with great care. We are grateful to Erik Patton and Jennifer Cohen for their steady advice and involvement. The in-house transportation and installation of artwork was smoothly handled by Rob Jung, Sarah Wood, Tom Krueger, and their team. It has been a true pleasure to collaborate with Betty Fisher, exhibition designer, whose engagement with the subject matter of the exhibition and whose sense of space and how visitors navigate it are unmatched. Peter Perez, who designs our frames, brings his wisdom to every work he examines, knowing exactly how to make each look its best.

Producing this volume has been a group effort and I appreciate the dedication of my colleagues in the Museum's Department of Publications, led by Christopher Hudson, Publisher, and Charles Kim, Associate Publisher. This book offered the opportunity to work with the superb editor David Frankel, whose erudition enhanced the content on every page. Matthew Pimm managed all aspects of the book's production, skillfully ensuring that the images look their very best. Patrick Seymour of Tsang Seymour, with the assistance of Hector Sos, designed the book with great sensitivity to its potential readers. Production Director Marc Sapir was a key sounding board for the project, advising on all aspects, big and small. The exhibition provided an occasion to produce a children's book; in *What Degas Saw*, Samantha Friedman, Assistant Curator, brings Degas's approach to the younger set with insight and beauty, a story wonderfully illustrated by Christina Pieropan and thoughtfully edited by Emily Hall. I appreciate the input of Hannah Kim and Cerise Fontaine on both titles, and Maria Marchenkova edited the gallery texts with consummate calm and care.

Crucial sustenance and sociability were provided by my colleagues in the Department of Drawings and Prints. I feel lucky every day for their warmth and good cheer, for what they teach me, for their willingness to pitch in when needed. My boundless appreciation goes to each member of our crew, and especially to Christophe Cherix, The Robert Lehman Foundation Chief Curator of Drawings and Prints, for his unwavering support and clear-eyed intelligence, and my fellow curators Esther Adler, Kathy Curry, Starr Figura, Luis Perez-Oramas, David Platzker, Christian Rattemeyer, and Sarah Suzuki, our former colleague Judy Hecker, as well as preparators David Moreno and Jeff White. Words are not enough to thank John Prochilo, for his open door and excellent counsel, and LJ McNerney, for patiently keeping me on track. Emily Cushman and Ingrid Langston stepped in at crucial moments, as has Anna Blaha, the Louise Bourgeois 12-Month Intern, who has persevered with focus and determination in searching for answers to daily questions.

As an exhibition that foregrounds a hybrid medium—a combination of drawing and printmaking—this project has the strong encouragement of the Museum's Committee on Drawings and Prints. Many in MoMA's curatorial departments advised on both practical and conceptual matters: Chief Curators Quentin Bajac, Stuart Comer, Rajendra Roy, Martino Stierli, Ann Temkin; and Lily Goldberg, Sarah Meister, Cora Rosevear, Lynn Rother, and Anne Umland.

I have had the great good fortune to work with an amazingly talented team. Research on the monotypes began in earnest with two now-former staff members, Curatorial Assistant Katie Hanson and Mellon Research Consortium Fellow Stephanie O'Rourke, who mapped out the exhibition's key themes. Hillary Reder intrepidly compiled the book's bibliography while superbly completing a host of other projects for the exhibition. Ever enthusiastic and dedicated, Laura Neufeld, Assistant Conservator at MoMA, lent incisive eyes to this project; what we understand about Degas is deepened by her thoughtful approach. Even in the midst of other projects, Samantha Friedman has graciously participated in every aspect of this one; her clear thinking and resonant writing are essential contributions. Over the course of the exhibition's development, Heidi Hirschl played a number of roles, from investigating questions around Degas's printmaking to interfacing with lenders; soon—lucky for us!—she was available to work on the exhibition full time. Since then she has been the hub of the project, managing every detail with outstanding dedication and inspired intelligence, a model of grace under pressure.

My closest collaborator has been Karl Buchberg, whose acumen, keen eyes, and good judgment have been a vital part of understanding this difficult artist. Our decade-long conversation has taught me much about the crucial import of an artist's materials and techniques. What I have learned has impacted all of my endeavors, a debt that is impossible to repay.

Finally, an exhibition about relentless experimentation has a broader message about persistence and invention—a refusal to accept things as they are. Those at home—Greg, Benjamin, and Julia, and our extended family members and dear friends who provided all manner of sustenance—indulged my choice of this tenacious path, always offering needed respite and unyielding support.

—Jodi Hauptman
Senior Curator, Department of Drawings and Prints

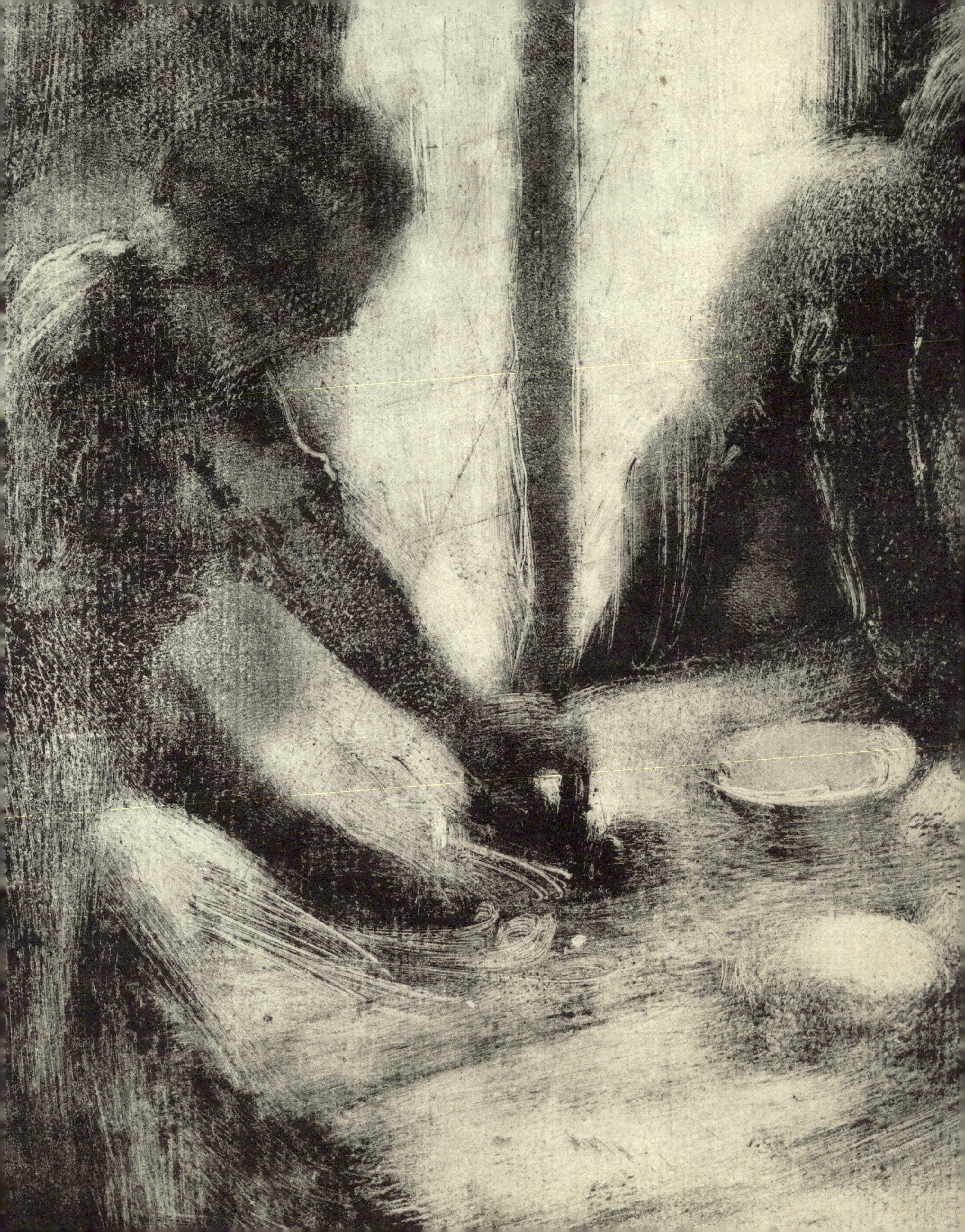

Introduction

Jodi Hauptman

In a letter of July 1876, the etcher Marcellin Desboutin described Edgar Degas's new mania for monotype. Degas, Desboutin wrote in scandalized incredulity, "is no longer a friend, a man, an artist! He's a zinc or copper plate blackened with printer's ink, and plate and man are flattened together by his printing press whose mechanism has swallowed him completely! The man's crazes are out of this world. He now is in the metallurgic phase of reproducing his drawings with a roller and is running all over Paris, in the heat wave—trying to find the legion of specialists who will realize his obsession. He is a real poem! He talks only of metallurgists, lead casters, lithographers, planishers!"[1]

The lines are richly evocative, offering a sense of how Degas looked—black ink to his elbows, staining his suit, dripping onto his shoes—as well as of how he acted: dashing in the summer sun to all manner of print specialists, from publishers to scientists to suppliers, to gather advice. For Desboutin, in immersing himself in monotype, Degas had vacated his humanness, his agency, his very self, in favor of materials, implements, processes.

The poet Paul Valéry addressed Degas's absorption in his materials in an extraordinary essay published in 1936. For his title Valéry found a clever alliteration—"*Degas danse dessin*" (Degas dance drawing)—to suggest an equivalence between the artist, his drawing, and one of his most renowned subjects, the ballet.[2] Valéry's sense of Degas's working methods—his "labor"—is of someone contaminated by his materials: surrounded by "bottles, flasks, pencils, bits of pastel chalk, etching needles, and all the nameless odds and ends that may come in handy one day," Degas exhibits an "untidy intimacy with his tools." By invoking in the same breath Degas's singularity, his "working in his own room" and "following his own homemade empirical methods," with "his eyes intent on what is in his mind, blind to his surroundings," Valéry defines this intimacy as something studio-based, intensely private, deeply personal, and vaguely illicit. But it is also inventive, allowing Degas to make productive use of whatever "comes to hand": "broken pots, kitchenware, any old castoffs."[3] This physical contiguity of hand to materials and tools—and, by implication, the *extension* of the hand by the implements of making—make possible a profound knowledge of their potential. Having this deep understanding of his materials, Degas was able to submit to their possibilities, but he was also their master, transgressing their limits and using his preferred mediums and methods in unorthodox ways. It is this combination of submission and transgression that constitutes his "untidy intimacy," this relationship between creator and what he uses to create that fuels his production. Nowhere is this intimacy more apparent or more important than in his monotypes.

Hilaire-Germain-Edgar Degas. *Ironing Women* (*Les Repasseuses*). c. 1877–79. Detail of plate 55

Best known as a painter and sculptor, Degas was also an inventive printmaker, mixing techniques with abandon and sharing recipes with other artists for unconventional effects.[4] Probing the possibilities of printmaking without the benefit of either academic training or an apprenticeship in the craft, he experimented with a range of processes that included etching, drypoint, aquatint, and lithography. More than all of these, however, it was monotype that captured his restless imagination.[5]

To create a monotype, the artist draws in ink on a metal plate, which is then sandwiched with a damp sheet of paper and run through a press.[6] The method typically produces a single impression, which reverses the composition from what the artist has rendered on the plate. Where most printmaking processes fix the image on the matrix—carving it into wood or metal, or chemically bonding it to a lithographic stone—monotype remains unfixed and manipulable up until the very instant of printing. Its promise of spontaneity and malleability, its reliance on tone and tactility, its productive inversions, its refusal of precision—these qualities captivated Degas. Having been introduced to the process in the mid-1870s by his artist friend Ludovic-Napoléon Lepic, he immersed himself in it with enormous enthusiasm, making over 300 works during two discrete bursts of activity. The first lasted from the mid-1870s to the mid-1880s, a near-decade in which he worked with black printers' ink and composed contemporary urban subjects; the second was a shorter campaign in the early 1890s, when he used pigmented oil paint to depict real and imaginary landscapes in images that verge on abstraction.

The monotype expanded Degas's capacity for representing a diversity of subject matter: ballerinas in motion, the radiance of electric light, meteorological effects in nature. The malleable ink also allowed him to twist and contort bodies into unusual and even impossible poses, to venture into caricature, and to create dramatic relationships between dark and light. The ability to move pigment freely on the slick plate right up to the last minute encouraged him to abandon the precise rendering of his youth, when he had worked under the influence of Jean-Auguste-Dominique Ingres, and led him to invent wholly new modes of drawing.

The monotype process had been known since the seventeenth century and was of renewed interest during Degas's time, when etching underwent a revival. In response to new technologies of reproduction such as photography, artist etchers sought to distinguish their work from rapidly proliferating, industrially made, mass-produced images by emphasizing the singularity of their expression and craft; by deploying handwork, especially variable inking, on the plate; by printing on different papers to create unique impressions; and by producing their work in small editions.[7] The prints of Rembrandt, with their wide-ranging variations, served as an important model for these artists, who formed groups, opened galleries, and published journals to share their ideas.[8] The etching revival's spontaneous-feeling and gestural hand-inking opened up the possibility of manipulating ink on the plate—the essence of the monotype—as a separate process from the etching of the image. And Degas took this possibility to new and radical ends.[9]

To the writer Arsène Alexandre, writing not long after the artist's death, "his monotypes represent the area of his work in which he was most free, most alive, and most reckless . . . not hampered by any rule."[10] Indeed, it is in the monotypes that Degas is at his most modern—capturing the spirit of urban life, depicting the body in new and daring ways, debating the singular and the copy, liberating mark-making from tradition, and boldly engaging the possibilities of abstraction.

It is significant that when Degas was called on to describe these works he used a phrase, "drawings made with greasy ink and put through a press," that emphasizes process and materials.[11] The print is something made; that making demands a course of action, with one step taken after another; the medium is a greasy kind of ink—in fact a printers' ink, though Degas does not acknowledge it as such; and the root of the print is in drawing. Since that pursuit is tied to the properties of the hand, Degas's phrase emphasizes the "mono-" or unique quality of the monotype while obscuring any reference to the multiple "-type" of mechanical reproduction. In all of his printed work, including his later foray into photography, he was less interested in the medium's reproductive potential than in the ways it could be made to produce variations.[12] Process defining product—or, really, process *as* product: that principle pervades Degas's career-long approach and interests (note, for example, his description of drawing as "not the same as form [but] a way of seeing form").[13] It is especially evident in his monotypes, where each work is an index of the act of making: the implements deployed, the gestures of the hand, the force of the press. "Nothing could be more modern," Valéry writes, than "taking for an end what can only be a means."[14]

Degas used his brush and ink in traditional ways on the printing-press plate, but he also experimented with a range of strategies to develop a new vocabulary of mark-making. Laying a curtain of ink down on the plate, for example, he would draw by removal, conjuring an image out of darkness by wiping the ink away with a rag, a card, or his own hand. Wiping is a step in etching, a way to remove the pigment from the surface of the plate once the ink has been pushed into the crevices carved into it; Degas applied this technique to a new kind of gestural rendering. He also broadened his tool kit, using brushes with dry, hardened bristles instead of soft ones to create striated patterns, a hard-pointed implement—probably the brush's wooden handle—to incise into the ink, sponges or cloths to dab or smoothly move the ink around, his hands to sculpt his subjects, his thumb and palm prints to impress texture, and his fingernails for contour.[15] Wiping, dabbing, fingerprinting, scratching, and incising, deployed in combinations of the additive and the subtractive, are the principal terms of his vocabulary. In addition, the impact of the press's rollers on the plate and the paper, and the transfer of pigment from one to the other, produce a flat surface that looks quite different from the dimensionality of ink or paint applied directly to the page.

A painting or drawing is an accumulation of marks made over time, a process that the viewer may be able to decipher or that the artist may emphasize. The layering of the image visualizes temporality as unfolding, in process, almost geological. A monotype, though, is printed at a particular moment in the development of the image on the plate.[16] The artist must work relatively quickly, before the medium dries, and can make wholesale changes right up until the plate goes through the press; as an index of that final instant, the resulting impression is a kind of arrest, a way of freezing the gestures of making in time.[17] It is interesting in this context to recall Degas's later interest in photography, and also his strategies, throughout his different kinds of image-making, to capture the instant: the crops where characters in his urban dramas move in and out of the picture's boundaries, the juxtapositions in which the inherent movement of ballet contrasts with the split-second pose of a dancer en pointe, or, in a kind of proto-futurism, the smudges and smears that indicate motion.[18] Because Degas "enshrin[es] his impression" of a subject "in prolonged study," Valéry explains, "the instantaneous [is] given enduring quality by the patience of intense meditation."[19]

Degas, then, "is visibly aligned and even identified" with the building blocks of his art, as Ewa Lajer-Burcharth says of Jean-Antoine Watteau.[20] Such identification, Lajer-Burcharth observes, undoes the sense of the hand as a direct sign of authorship and of the individual authority of the maker, offering it instead as "an instrument of the medium. . . . This submission to or identification with the medium [demonstrates a] capacity not only to mobilize but also to think *through* the materials."[21] For Valéry, materials and tools affect comprehension and vision. He pointed out, "There is a tremendous difference between seeing a thing without a pencil in your hand and seeing it while *drawing* it."[22]

The relinquishment of self to materials also exposed Degas to chance.[23] Whether using printers' inks or oil paints, he balanced control against accident. This kind of acceptance of happenstance is an inherent part of the transfer process of printmaking, in which there is always an element of surprise in what comes out of the press—an absolute predetermination of the final result is impossible. And just as Degas balanced control against accident, he also balanced a keen understanding of the properties of his tools and materials against a constant push beyond their supposed limits, demanding that they do things "that they were not designed to do."[24] Those limits were provocations or dares, calls to arms. "Degas," Valéry wrote admiringly, "rejected *facility*, . . . create[d] difficulties," and would always "shrink away from any shortcut."[25] Where for some artists "obstacles are the ambiguous signs that prompt despair, . . . they only convince [Degas] that there is something beyond," something "worth understanding." It was by feeling through the "recalcitrance and rebelliousness of the medium," Valéry insisted, that Degas would find "the very mystery and essence of our art."[26]

The obstacles Valéry refers to here concern Degas's

poetry—around 1888–89, he tackled the sonnet—but in his visual art, too, we often see him undoing the basic character of his materials and tools, from mixing pastels with water, or steaming them to turn their chalky, friable substance into a thickened wet paste, to leeching the oil out of oil paint to create a dry, pastel-like medium.[27] Degas's notebooks and letters are full of recipes for and advice about mixing materials—think of his "*pastel-savon*" ("pastel soap"), for example, or of his replacement of turpentine with lavender oil—and of speculations on the potential of unorthodox implements, such as the use of a light filament as an etching tool.[28] His eccentric approach to materials extended beyond mixing concoctions in his studio (which at times was more like a laboratory, as Theodore Reff has noted)[29] to physical engagement. According to Pierre-Auguste Renoir, Degas once laid a drawing on the floor, covered it with a board, and stamped on it "to grind the pastel into the support."[30] He also often expanded his compositions by adding strips of paper to them, surpassing the limits of the sheet. These lateral expansions were echoed by his vertical layering of pastel, which he applied in encrustations or sediments, exceeding the flatness of the support. Valéry claims that Degas lived by Emile Zola's definition of art (a version of a phrase of the philosopher Francis Bacon's): "*homo additus naturae*," a motto that has been translated as "nature seen through a temperament" and might also be understood as "nature provides the material and man has to do something with it."[31] As much as Degas resisted the idea of relying on a particular way of working—"Fortunately for me, I have not found my method, that would only bore me"[32]—this doing something to materials, an "experimental approach to media and techniques," became, Jeffrey Weiss argues, a method in itself.[33]

Degas's most significant challenge to the monotype was aimed at its singularity. Instead of accepting its production of unique works, he used it to make variations: after printing an impression, he would often put the plate through the press a second time, pulling another print. Because much of the ink would have been transferred to the first sheet during the plate's initial run through the press, the second impression, called a "cognate," would be a much lighter version of the first print, an image both the same as and different from it. Degas often then applied a layer of pastel (sometimes with gouache) on top of this lighter image, using it as a tonal map of the original composition to create a new work that was both a repetition and a transformation of it—"as if," Stephanie O'Rourke writes, "one needed to break the image *down* in order to produce the linear refinements, shaded contours, and formal clarity that characterize his pastel cognates."[34] The ambiguities of the monotypes in black ink—the enigmatic and mutable forms emerging out of shadow, the contrasts of luminosity and darkness—are often resolved by pastel, made readable and evenly lit.

There are many of these cognate pairs, a black monotype and its pastelized double (e.g., plates 100, 101). Sometimes, though, Degas went even farther, creating still more variant images. To make the first impression of *Woman Reading* (*Liseuse*, c. 1880–85; plate 106), for example, Degas slid a rag and brush across and through the greasy ink on the plate, rendering the figure and the interior by removing the pigment. He bent, twisted, and flattened her torso and limbs and curved the edges of the tub and chaise into illuminated and undulating paths, creating a body and a space as malleable as the monotype medium itself. Then, having made a print from this plate and while that print was still wet, he made a counterproof by sandwiching the damp paper against a second sheet and running the two through the press together, creating a mirror reflection of the first print (plate 107). Since the first impression reversed the image Degas had drawn on the plate—an inescapable effect of the printing process—the counterproof returned to the same orientation as this original drawing. On the back of the counterproof, Degas printed a second impression from the ink left on the plate, a lighter version of the first (plate 108). Finally, he pulled from the plate a third time and used that print to make a work in pastel.[35] From a process that typically yielded one impression, Degas extracted four linked but different works. And in a brainteaser of relationships, the figure's shape shifts back and forth, reversing and reversing back. Degas was interested in mining the countless possibilities of a single image, including the many ways a body can be twisted and contorted through repetition and reversal.

This drive to generate many variants from one may have emerged from Degas's understanding that a transfer process always involves related but different images:

the initial drawing—whether in etched lines, cut wood, or any of the other methods of printing—is both the same as and different from the result. In composition, the print is reversed; in feel, it bears the reticulations particular to the pressured encounter between pigment and plate. Thus the monotype displays in a double the roots of extended iteration. Degas took this duality inherent in the monotype process to new realms of multiplicity. In this context it is useful to be reminded of his instructions to younger artists: "make a drawing, begin it again, trace it, begin it again, and retrace it."[36]

Degas's conviction that something singular can spark multiple variations, that an image can always be reworked, revised, and recrafted, is rooted in the logic of the monotype and pervades his particularly relentless approach to the study of form: an unceasing pursuit and modification of key motifs across mediums.[37] For Valéry, that ruthless rigor found an analogy in the author's own occupation: "He is like a writer striving to attain the utmost precision of form, drafting and redrafting, canceling, advancing by endless recapitulation, never admitting that his work has reached its *final* stage."[38] The essential qualities of monotype—repetition and transformation, mirroring and reversal—and his methods of harnessing them, particularly by creating cognate pairs, triples, and quads, reappear in his subsequent work through different means. Techniques like tracing, counterproofing, and copying allowed him to continue to play with difference and similarity in painting and drawing.[39] Degas traced, inverted, and recombined figures in multiple arrangements, layering pastel or charcoal on paper, or oil paint on canvas, to further transform his subjects. The results are chains of images—of ballerinas and bathers, alone or in ensembles—each both the same as and different from others in the group, proving that Degas saw iteration as an end in itself rather than a step toward something final or finished. "For Degas," Valéry tells us, "a painting was the result of a limitless number of sketches—and of a *whole series of operations*."[40] In this way Degas's efforts in monotype sparked the emergence of a new, acutely modern conception of the artwork as unfixed, self-referential, and recursive, accumulated and dispersed across diverse mediums and materials.

In *Degas danse dessin* Valéry emphasizes the "operative"—the strategies Degas adopted, the mediums he harnessed—and showcases his process. He highlights the artist's "tactical images and solutions," his "method of practical speculation," while discouraging readers from seeing "things merely by their names."[41] But as much as Degas's work, and his monotypes in particular, foreground material invention and experimentation, these strategies are in the service of representation. In fact Degas continually wedded strategy to subject, demonstrating that new topics demand new means. His monotype's loose brushwork turned out to be a perfect vehicle for capturing both ballerinas in motion and the bustle of city life—and that relaxed linearity was well-suited for his foray into caricature, including suggesting the financial exchange at the heart of prostitution. Degas's method of incising into the greasy pigment offered a way to render the artificial lighting that was not only illuminating Paris in new and exciting ways but changing vision itself.[42] Liquid ink could mimic both the new factories' wafting smoke and the complicated ornament of the period's fashion. Transparent washes of oil paint alluded to the natural world while undermining any sense of the earth as solid and stable. And the ink's pliant viscosity stimulated Degas to twist and contort female bathers into seemingly impossible poses, demonstrating the malleability of flesh.

Degas made his most daring application of the monotype medium in depicting these female subjects. The private acts of bathing and grooming became an opportunity to portray bodies in unusual and awkward positions—bones and muscles stretched, heads and limbs obscured—and to dramatically illuminate their environs.[43] Refusing an idealized image, Degas's renderings are pliable and tactile, rough and unresolved. More formless than formed, their ambiguous contours undo distinctions between body and environment as the figure melts into water, is wrapped in firelight, or is absorbed into wallpaper or upholstery. Degas's process is pointedly allied to the activities of his subjects. Wiping, for example, is both subject and technique, what the woman in the image is doing (*s'essuyer*) and how Degas renders her by manipulating the ink on the plate (*essuyer*). Valéry's phrase "untidy intimacy" again seems appropriate here: coined in reference to Degas's physical proximity to and familiarity with his tools and materials, it also captures this close alliance of process and subject (and even the way one contaminates the other), describes the imbrication of Degas's figures in cramped and object-filled private and personal spaces, and insinuates the way he sculpted these bodies with his own fingerprints, making the monotype function as an index of his touch. In the wake of these works in monotype and with lessons learned, Degas created similarly liberated, improvisational, and tactile effects in pastel and oil, rendering bodies, fabrics, and wallpaper with his fingers.

"His hands," Valéry writes, were always "groping for form."[44] The monotypes reveal both the importance of the hands' labor—their touch—to his inexorable probing and the endlessness of his quest.[45] Degas's touch reflected his deep understanding of the properties of ink and oil paint, his responsiveness to them as he worked on the metal plate, and his alertness to the press's pressure, while his embrace and extension of the medium's generative logic resulted in a new kind of artwork that was less about completion than about boundless iteration. Whether visual or tactile, Degas's investigations represent his experimental spirit. In 1876, when he was on the cusp of immersing himself in monotype, his friend Stéphane Mallarmé articulated his restlessness, noting that although the artist was already a "master of drawing," he nonetheless still sought "delicate lines and movements exquisite or grotesque."[46] The result of this search—of this groping, this immersion, this variation, this submission to and transgression of materials and method—is, Mallarmé tells us, "a strange new beauty."[47]

This exhibition and publication rely on the vast scholarship on Edgar Degas, beginning with contemporary commentators, through those who began to give the work shape after the artist's death, to a number of remarkable assessments closer to our own time. The latter include the magisterial *Degas* (1988), the catalogue of an exhibition seen in Paris at the Galeries Nationales du Grand Palais, in Ottawa at the National Gallery of Canada, and in New York at The Metropolitan Museum of Art, by Jean Sutherland Boggs, the General Editor, with the collaboration of Henri Loyrette, Michael Pantazzi, Gary Tinterow, and Douglas W. Druick, as well as Theodore Reff's important *Degas: The Artist's Mind* (1976). I have benefited from the work of too many extraordinary individuals to name them here; many appear in this book's Bibliography, which details publications on the monotypes, and in its Acknowledgments, which thanks many friends of this project who shared expertise and advice. Above all, however, any voyage into the world of Degas's monotypes is guided by the extraordinary scholarship of Eugenia Parry Janis, who took on the subject of the monotypes at Harvard in the 1960s and produced a catalogue raisonné of them (the book was also a catalogue of her exhibition of 1968) that remains indispensable today. Her documentation is an essential part of the field and her thinking remains foundational.

1. Marcellin Desboutin, letter to Giuseppe de Nittis, Dijon, July 17, 1876, in Mary Pittaluga, *De Nittis* (Milan: Bramante, 1963), p. 359, Eng. trans. in Sue Welsh Reed and Barbara Stern Shapiro, *Edgar Degas: The Painter as Printmaker*, exh. cat. (Boston: Museum of Fine Arts, 1984), p. xxix.
2. Paul Valéry, *Degas danse dessin* (Paris: Ambroise Vollard, 1936), Eng. trans. as "Degas Dance Drawing" in Valéry, *Degas Manet Morisot*, vol. 12 of *Collected Works of Paul Valéry*, Bollingen Series XLV, trans. David Paul (Princeton: Bollingen Foundation and Princeton University Press, 1960, repr. in paperback 1989), pp. 1–102.
3. Ibid., p. 19.
4. Theodore Reff makes a compelling case for Degas's expansive experimentation in *Degas: The Artist's Mind* (New York: The Metropolitan Museum of Art and Harper and Row, 1976). See especially chapter VII, "The Artist as Technician," pp. 270–303; Reff describes Degas's "recipes and projects scattered through his notebooks" on pp. 273–74. My sense of Degas's inventiveness is rooted in Reff's pioneering scholarship as well as in Richard Kendall's crucial book *Degas: Beyond Impressionism* (London: National Gallery Publications Limited, 1996).
5. The indispensable source on Degas's printmaking outside of monotype is Reed and Shapiro, *The Painter as Printmaker*. On his printmaking in the context of the work of his artist colleagues see Michel Melot, *The Impressionist Print*, trans. Caroline Beamish (New Haven: Yale University Press, 1996). On his work in monotype see Janis, *Degas Monotypes: Essay, Catalogue & Checklist* (Cambridge, Mass.: Fogg Art Museum, Harvard University, 1968) and Kendall's essay in the present volume. See also Kendall's compelling essay "The Impromptu Print: Degas' Monotypes and Their Technical Significance" in Mikael Wivel, *Degas Intime* (Copenhagen: Ordrupgaard, 1994), n.p.
6. Here and throughout this essay my understanding of the monotype process is based on an ongoing dialogue with Karl Buchberg and Laura Neufeld, Senior Conservator and Assistant Conservator at MoMA and my partners in this project. See their essay in this volume. Sarah Suzuki, Associate Curator in the Museum's Department of Drawings and Prints, articulated for me the mutability of the monotype and its relationship to other forms of printmaking.
7. On the etching revival see Melot, *The Impressionist Print*.
8. See Melot's discussion, for example, of the formation of the Society of Etchers (Société des Aquafortistes), in ibid., chapter 11, pp. 49–51. Members of the group included Félix Bracquemond, Alfred Cadart, Auguste Delâtre, Maxime Lalanne, Edouard Manet, and Théodule Ribot.
9. On Degas and the etching revival see Reed and Shapiro, *The Painter as Printmaker*, especially part II. On the long history of the monotype see Shapiro, *The Painterly Print: Monotypes from the Seventeenth to the Twentieth Century*, exh. cat. (New York: The Metropolitan Museum of Art, 1980).
10. Arsène Alexandre, "Degas: Graveur et Lithographe," *Les Arts* XV, no. 171 (1918):18–19. Trans. Stephanie O'Rourke.
11. Degas used this phrase in the catalogue of the Impressionist exhibition of 1877, the first occasion on which he exhibited monotypes. See page 6 of that catalogue, which is reproduced in Charles Moffett, *The New Painting: Impressionism 1874–1886*, exh. cat. (San Francisco: Fine Arts Museums of San Francisco, 1986), p. 204. See also Richard R. Brettell, "The 'First' Exhibition of Impressionist Painters," in ibid., p. 199, and Ruth Berson, *The New Painting: Impressionism 1874–1886*, vol. 1: *Documentation*, and vol. 2: *Exhibited Works* (San Francisco: Fine Arts Museums of San Francisco, 1996), p. 118.
12. On Degas's photography see Malcolm Daniel, *Edgar Degas, Photographer*, exh. cat. (New York: The Metropolitan Museum of Art, 1998); Douglas Crimp, "Positive/Negative: A Note on Degas's Photographs," *October* 5 (Summer 1978):89–100; and Elizabeth C. Childs, "Habits of the Eye: Degas, Photography, and Modes of Vision," in Dorothy Kosinski, *The Artist and the Camera: Degas to Picasso*, exh. cat. (Dallas: Dallas Museum of Art, 1999), pp. 73–87.
13. Degas, quoted in Valéry, "Degas Dance Drawing," p. 82.
14. Ibid., p. 20.
15. See Buchberg and Neufeld's essay in the present volume.
16. My thanks to Jill Moser for explicating this aspect of the monotype's temporality.

17. Degas would have had more time to work on his monotypes in oil, which stays wet longer than ink. See Buchberg and Neufeld's essay in the present volume.
18. See Jill DeVonyar and Kendall, *Degas and the Ballet: Picturing Movement* (London: The Royal Academy, 2011), and Kirk Varnedoe, "The Artifice of Candor: Impressionism and Photography Reconsidered," *Art in America* 68, no. 1 (January 1980):66–78, and "The Ideology of Time: Degas and Photography," *Art in America* 68, no. 6 (Summer 1980):96–110.
19. Valéry, "Degas Dance Drawing," p. 55. Valéry also explains that both arrest and flux are central to the dance: "In ballets there are moments of immobility when the grouping of the whole ensemble offers a picture, stilled but not permanent, a complex of human bodies suddenly arrested in their postures, giving a singular emphasis to the impression of flux." P. 16.
20. Ewa Lajer-Burcharth, "Drawing Time," *October* 151 (Winter 2015):20. Lajer-Burcharth makes a case for "an authorial performance of a particular kind" in the drawings of Jean-Antoine Watteau, in which the artist "is visibly aligned and even identified with the draftsman's tools and materials."
21. Ibid.
22. Valéry, "Degas Dance Drawing," p. 36.
23. Again in relation to Watteau, Lajer-Burcharth notes the way that "submission to or identification with the medium . . . is symptomatic of a specific way of thinking that opens itself to chance." Lajer-Burcharth, "Drawing Time," p. 20.
24. Stephanie O'Rourke, "Images, Unmade: Degas and the Monotype," paper presented at the College Art Association annual conference, New York, February 15, 2015.
25. Valéry, "Degas Dance Drawing," p. 6. Valéry goes on, "He wanted nothing but what he considered the most difficult thing to require of himself."
26. Ibid., p. 63.
27. See Anne Maheux, "Looking into Degas's Pastel Technique," in Boggs and Maheux, *Degas Pastels* (New York: George Braziller, 1992), pp. 19–38. While some of these strategies were known, Degas pushed them farther or deployed them less for a particular pictorial goal than to see what would happen.
28. See ibid., pp. 19–38, and Reff, *The Artist's Mind*, especially chapter VII. For the "carbon filament from an electric light bulb" see Reff, p. 292. See also Denis Rouart, *Degas: In Search of His Technique*, trans. Pia C. DeSantis, Sarah L. Fisher, and Shelley Fletcher (New York: Rizzoli, 1988).
29. Reff writes "While Desboutin, [Camille] Pissarro, and most of their Impressionist colleagues were working with conventional techniques, Degas was converting his studio into a kind of attic laboratory." Reff, *The Artist's Mind*, p. 271.
30. See Maheux, "Looking into Degas's Pastel Technique," p. 31. Maheux cites Jeanne Baudot, *Renoir. Ses amis, ses modèles* (Paris: Editions littéraires de France, 1949), p. 102.
31. See Valéry, "Degas Dance Drawing," p. 83.
32. Degas, quoted in Reff, *The Artist's Mind*, p. 270. The original is in A. Vollard, *Degas (1834–1917)* (Paris: Les Editions G. Crès, 1924), p. 80.
33. Jeffrey Weiss, "State of the Art," *Artforum* 48, no. 7 (March 2010):210.
34. O'Rourke, "Images, Unmade."
35. Buchberg and Neufeld have considered the possibility that the third pull covered with pastel could have resulted from an accidental offset. When Degas ran the sheet through the press, which already had the counterproof on one side, he would have needed a piece of paper to protect the felts on the press from getting stained with the wet ink. The image could have offset onto that paper, producing yet another impression—something productive emerging from the practical. It should also be noted that we cannot know which imprint was made first on the two-sided sheet, the counterproof made from the first pull or the second pull from the plate.
36. Degas, quoted in Kendall, *Beyond Impressionism*, p. 81. See also Jacques-Emile Blanche, *Propos de peintre. De David à Degas* (Paris: Emile-Paul frères, 1919), p. 295, and Paul Lafond, *Degas*, 2 vols. (Paris: H. Floury, 1919), 1:20. This phrase bears a striking relationship to Jasper Johns's widely quoted "Take an object. Do something with it. Do something else with it." Quoted from Book A, p. 42, c. 1963–64, in Kirk Varnedoe, ed., *Jasper Johns: Writings, Sketchbooks, Notes, Interviews* (New York: The Museum of Modern Art, 2002), p. 54. Degas also advised Paul-Albert Bartholomé, "It is essential to do the same subject over again, ten times, a hundred times." Quoted in Kendall, *Beyond Impressionism*, p. 81. See Kendall's discussion of Degas's tracing in ibid., pp. 77–87. Richard Thomson writes that "by 1879–80 the procedure of making a cluster of drawings which were variants on a particular pose became habitual in Degas's studio practice. Such repetition seems restrictive, but it was, in fact, one element in a series of experimental initiatives designed to challenge both his skills as a draftsman and the accepted norms of drawing, to keep draftsmanship challenging, up to the mark, modern." See Thomson, *Waiting*, Getty Museum Studies on Art (Malibu: J. Paul Getty Museum, 1995), p. 6.
37. See O'Rourke's essay in the present volume for the dialogue in Degas's work between repetition in traditional drawing practice and the monotype.
38. Valéry continues, "From sheet to sheet, copy to copy, he continually revises his drawing, deepening, tightening, closing it up." "Degas Dance Drawing," p. 39.
39. This interest in mining, repeating, transforming, and extending motifs can be seen in the work of Paul Gauguin, another artist whose engagement with printmaking fueled his experimentation. This was the focus of Starr Figura's extraordinary exhibition *Gauguin: Metamorphoses*, at The Museum of Modern Art in 2014, and of its catalogue (New York: The Museum of Modern Art, 2014), especially her essay "Gauguin's Metamorphoses: Repetition, Transformation, and the Catalyst of Printmaking," pp. 14–35. Figura quotes Gauguin sounding uncannily like Degas on the generative possibilities of a single drawing: "He traces a drawing, then he traces this tracing, and so on till the moment when, like the ostrich, with his head in the sand, he decides that it does not resemble the original any longer. Then!! He signs." P. 18.
40. Valéry, "Degas Dance Drawing," p. 50. The italicized phrase also appears on p. 6.
41. Ibid., pp. 64, 66, 101.
42. See Hollis Clayson's essay in the present volume.
43. See Carol Armstrong's essay in the present volume, and her *Odd Man Out: Readings of the Work and Reputation of Edgar Degas* (Chicago: at the University Press, 1991), esp. chapter 4, pp. 157–209. For other takes on Degas's brothel and bather monotypes see Clayson, "In the Brothel," *Painted Love: Prostitution in French Art of the Impressionist Era* (New Haven: Yale University Press, 1991), chapter 2, pp. 27–55, and Anthea Callen, *The Spectacular Body: Science, Method, and Meaning in the Work of Degas* (New Haven: Yale University Press, 1995), esp. her chapter "The Invisible Man: Voyeurism and the Narratives of Sexual Conquest," pp. 71–110.
44. Valéry, "Degas Dance Drawing", p. 99.
45. In a wonderful essay on the monotypes, Peter Parshall points out Degas's "immediate engagement with the physical qualities of the materials he was using," revealing the links between touch in these prints and in his sculpture. In his wax sculpture—where the pliable wax was squeezed and shaped, the artist's fingerprints being left visible from this pressing, forming, and building up of small pieces to create cascading layers—we see a parallel tactility to the monotypes: the hand's role as an instrument of the medium. See Parshall, "Degas and the Closeted Image," in Pedersen, *Degas' Method*, pp. 153–72. See also Parshall's publication *The Darker Side of Light: Arts of Privacy, 1850–1900* (Washington, D.C.: National Gallery of Art in association with Lund Humphries, 2009). Armstrong explicates the role of touch in "Degas in the Studio: Embodying Medium, Materializing the Body," in Martin Schwander and Fondation Beyeler, *Degas: The Late Work*, exh. cat. (Ostfildern: Hatje Cantz, 2012), pp. 23–33. On Degas's wax sculpture, see Suzanne Glover Lindsay, Daphne S. Barbour, and Shelley G. Sturman, *Edgar Degas Sculpture* (Princeton: at the University Press, 2010).
46. Stéphane Mallarmé, "The Impressionists and Edouard Manet," *Art Monthly Review and Photographic Portfolio* (London) 1 (1876):121.
47. Ibid.

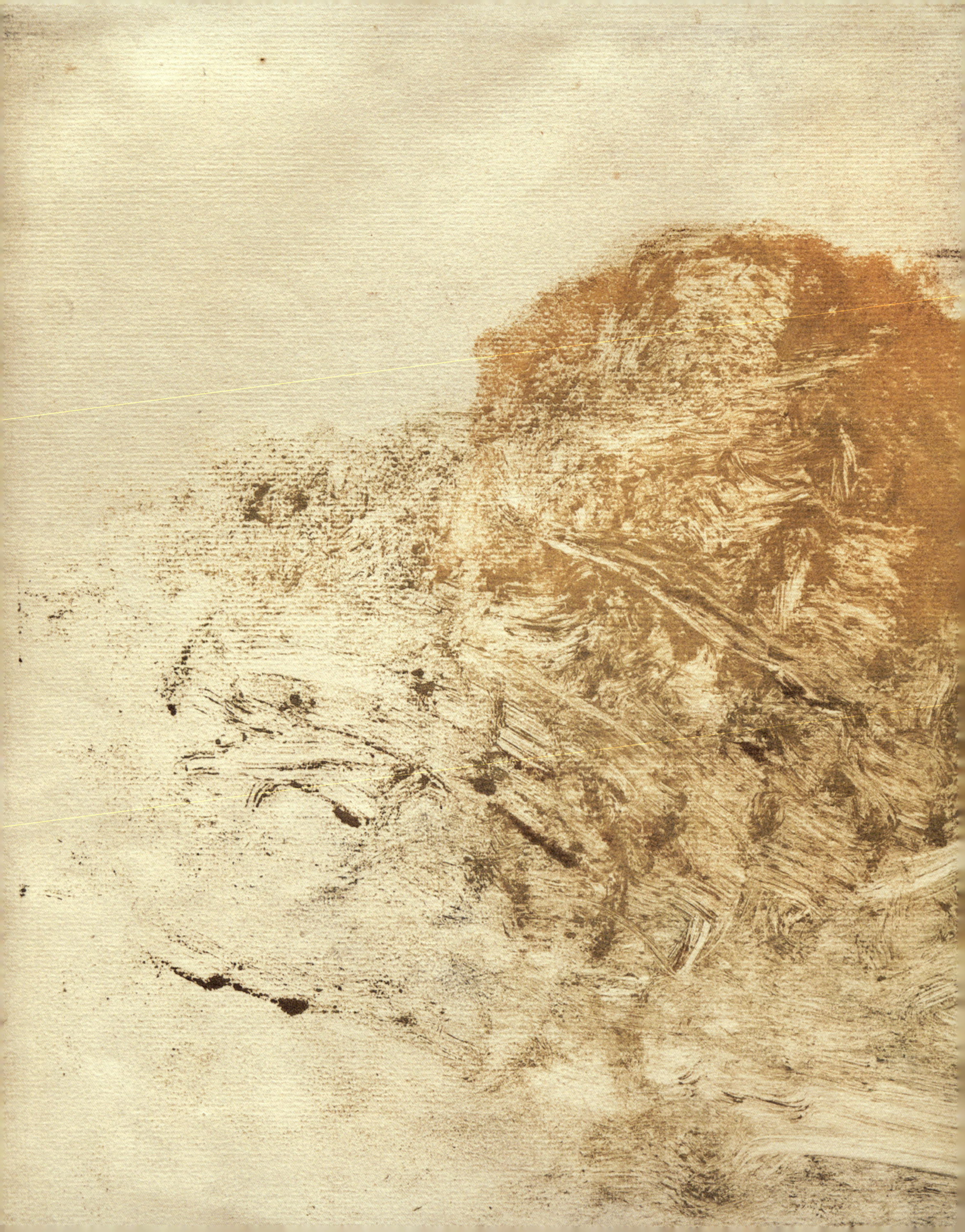

An Anarchist in Art: Degas and the Monotype

Richard Kendall

One of the more unexpected remarks made about Edgar Degas and his art appears in a letter written by Camille Pissarro to his son Lucien in 1891. Pissarro had long struggled with art dealers reluctant to show his work, attributing this to his well-known engagement with anarchism. Noting that Degas greatly admired his pictures, he then added, "He who is such an anarchist! In art, of course, and without knowing it!"[1] Surprising though it is, Pissarro's observation deserves to be taken seriously for several reasons. The two men had known each other since the 1860s and in the following decades had been among the most prominent organizers of the historic series of Impressionist exhibitions, as well as the most loyal participants in these events. More significant still in the present context is the fact that during these same years Pissarro had established a close relationship with Degas the printmaker, sometimes working alongside him on radical new techniques.

The notion of Degas as an anarchist of any kind is tantalizing but problematic. The son of a banker, he grew up in Paris in bourgeois surroundings and enjoyed a leisurely youth and an extended education. In late adolescence he began drawing from approved works of art, among them an engraving based on a Raphael fresco that he copied in a small sketchbook (fig. 1).[2] After a period at the renowned Ecole des Beaux-Arts, he left for Italy to study pictures by Renaissance and earlier masters, staying there for several years before finally settling in the French capital. Works on paper made at this time, such as *Female Nude Crouching* (c. 1860–62; fig. 2), show his continuing respect for the past and an aptitude for disciplined and refined draftsmanship in the traditional mode. During the Impressionist phase he was often recognized for such skills while experiencing strong criticism for his scenes of scantily clad ballerinas and dissolute drinkers. When speaking about his own work, the mature Degas continued to stress its historical roots, often citing the aphorisms of the classicist Jean-Dominique Ingres, whom he had met in the latter's old age: "Draw lots of lines, either from memory or from nature," Ingres advised the aspiring painter, and famously proclaimed elsewhere that "drawing is the probity of art."[3] As Degas emerged among the leading Impressionists he continued to make drawn studies for most of his pastels and paintings. Known for his hard work and professionalism, he was described by one acquaintance as "labor incarnate" and remembered by another for his insistence that art resulted from "a series of operations."[4] Personally, he clung to social formality throughout his career; portraits of the artist in public invariably show him wearing a suit and hat (fig. 3). In later life Degas became more and more reclusive, while his fame spread

Hilaire-Germain-Edgar Degas. *The Ochre Hill* (*Effet de montagne*). 1890. Detail of plate 135

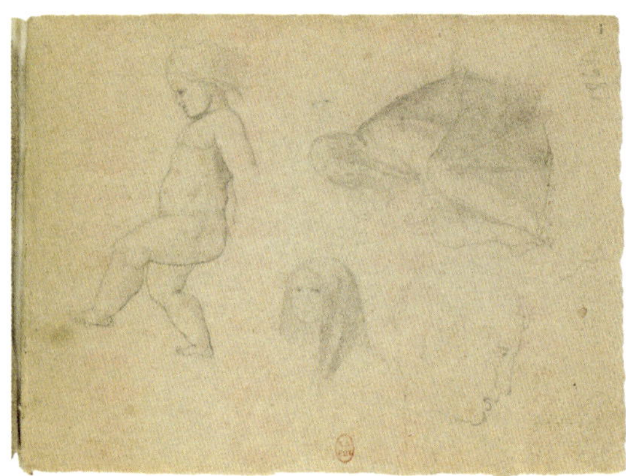

1. Hilaire-Germain-Edgar Degas. Sketchbook 14 (*Carnet 14*), p. 1. 1853. Pencil on paper, 4 7⁄16 × 6 1⁄8 in. (11.2 × 15.5 cm). Bibliothèque nationale de France, Paris

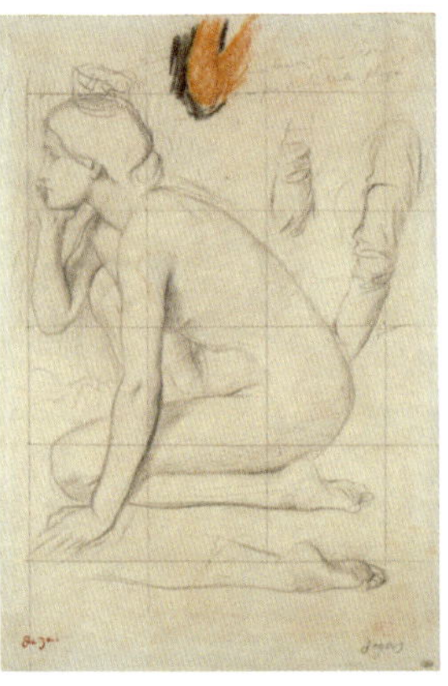

2. Hilaire-Germain-Edgar Degas. *Female Nude Crouching*. Studies for *Semiramis Building Babylon* (*Femme accroupie. Etudes pour "Sémiramis construisant Babylone"*). c. 1860–62. Pencil and pastel on paper, 13 7⁄16 × 8 13⁄16 in. (34.1 × 22.4 cm). Musée d'Orsay, Paris

through Europe and to the United States. During these same years his right-leaning politics were increasingly evident and he ultimately parted company with liberal friends, including Pissarro, during the Dreyfus Affair.

Degas's association with prints began early and was revisited intermittently over the years, a pattern followed by some of his colleagues in Impressionist circles. It is often overlooked that all but one of the eight group exhibitions that took place between 1874 and 1886 featured prints of some kind—among them etchings, lithographs, monotypes, and engravings on copper and wood—sometimes in considerable numbers and in a wide range of styles. In 1874, for example, Félix Bracquemond showed more than thirty etchings that included portraits of contemporary figures, landscapes, and studies from past masters, all executed in a relatively conventional manner. Degas would soon reveal a similar versatility, while also asserting himself as an audacious technical pioneer and encouraging others—notably Pissarro and Mary Cassatt—to follow suit. Prints had many virtues in this context: they were quicker to make and cheaper to sell than oil paintings; they potentially appealed to the already numerous middle-class print-collectors of France and elsewhere; and the medium itself was often associated with quotidian imagery and events, a frequent source of subject matter within the group. The Impressionists were also well aware that several renowned predecessors—among them Honoré Daumier and Paul Gavarni—had used lithography to reflect the contemporary world of Paris and its turbulent politics, and that both of them enjoyed enormous popular recognition. When Pissarro later called Degas an "anarchist," he was conscious that current political factions exploited printed graphic imagery, caricatures, and scenes of corruption to sway voters, while commercial printing presses were sufficiently feared at this time to be subject to police control. Whether or not such issues lay behind Pissarro's 1891 description, several colleagues demonstrably chose to make prints for their vernacular appeal and as an appropriate medium for their most experimental and sometimes provocative imagery. In Degas's case, some of his printed works would take him so far beyond existing visual and moral conventions that he felt unable to exhibit them.

Degas's own beginnings as a printmaker consisted of a group of small etchings that he made during his youthful sojourn in Italy. One of the earliest of these, his *Self-Portrait* (*Autoportrait*) of 1857 (plates 1, 2), is somber but notably skillful and was among several that revealed his admiration for the richly shadowed prints and paintings of Rembrandt. Following long-established practice, Degas's initial image was made by using acid to etch a series of fine lines into a copper plate, a technique closely analogous with traditional drawing and thus within the competence of the young artist. This plate was then covered with oil-based ink, thoroughly wiped, and printed on paper in a press. Several states of this print survive, with indications that Degas was already adding further modifications to his image and exploring different applications of ink. Even at this stage, it seems, he was inclined to push the

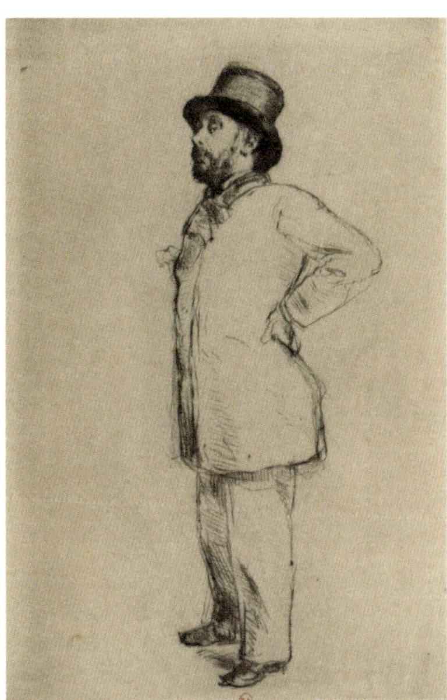

3. Marcellin Desboutin. *Edgar Degas* (*Degas au chapeau*). 1876. Drypoint, 8 ¾ × 5 ¾ in (22.8 × 14.5 cm). Bibliothèque nationale de France, Paris

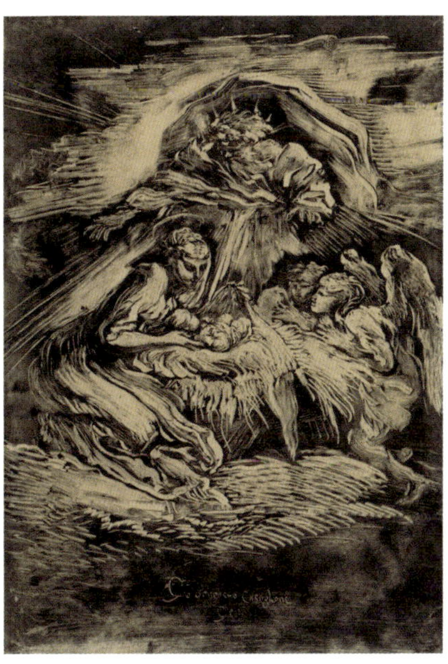

4. Giovanni Benedetto Castiglione. *The Nativity with Angels and God the Father* (*Nativité avec Dieu le Père*). Mid-1650s. Monotype on paper, 14 ⅞ × 9 ¹⁵⁄₁₆ in. (37.8 × 25.2 cm). Bibliothèque nationale de France, Paris

boundaries of the centuries-old craft. The dramatic settings of Rembrandt's portraits were again evoked in *The Engraver Joseph Tourny* (*Le Graveur Joseph Tourny*; plates 4–6), for which Degas used another plate that has historical claims as the basis of his first experience with monotype. In the sequence of prints made from this plate, it is clear that additional ink has been freely added to the surface and then manipulated with cloths or brushes before it was printed. These maneuvers involved no further etching and more closely resembled painting in the way that they turned the light-filled room into a shadowy, even ominous space. Perhaps the most remarkable feature of this print is the passage at upper right, where a dark rectangular form is bounded by a paler vertical that was clearly created when the artist's finger was pulled downward through recently added black ink. Crude but effective, this gesture summarizes both the technical advantages and disadvantages of monotype: the dark form was a powerful addition to the scene but would survive in two or three successive prints at most, the later proofs being inevitably paler or even indecipherable, as most of the ink had already been transferred from the plate to the earlier prints.

Over the centuries, variations on the monotype principle had been devised by several artists, notably by Rembrandt's Italian contemporary Benedetto Castiglione, who created complex and expressive scenes by vigorously manipulating black ink on a plate and then printing them (fig. 4).[5] The medium was subsequently rediscovered or reinvented in France in the 1860s and '70s, when two artists, Adolphe Appian and Ludovic-Napoléon Lepic, independently developed technical versions of their own. One sequence of Lepic's panorama-like hybrid prints with monotype additions shows a flat, almost featureless landscape and demonstrates the characteristic qualities and drawbacks of the monotype (plate 16). Here Lepic used conventional etching methods to define the horizon and certain details in the foreground, as well as a distinctive slender tree to the right of center. Because these features are etched into the metal, they recur in all subsequent printings, although in several versions they are almost obliterated by additional effects of light and weather, or by a dense cluster of large shadowy trees, created by manual additions of ink to the plate surface. The whimsical or even arbitrary aspect of monotype printmaking is much in evidence, notably when Lepic titled successive images *Rain*, *Snow*, and *Sunrise* after darkening or lightening the same expanse of plate, or when he introduced a burning building and a huge plume of smoke to another variant and called it *The Mill Fire*. By 1876, Degas knew at least some of these prints, since Lepic had

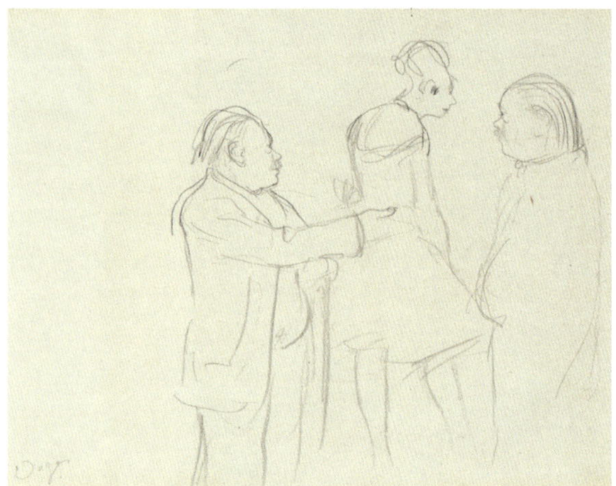

5. Hilaire-Germain-Edgar Degas. Sketches of a ballet master from an album of pencil sketches. c. 1877. Pencil on paper, 9 ¾ × 13 in. (24.8 × 33 cm). The J. Paul Getty Museum, Los Angeles

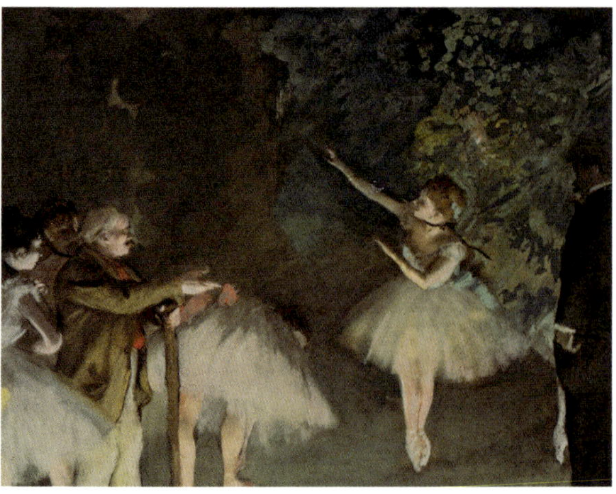

6. Hilaire-Germain-Edgar Degas. *Rehearsal of the Ballet* (*Répétition de ballet*). c. 1876. Opaque watercolor and pastel over monotype on paper, sheet: 21 ¾ × 26 ¾ in. (55.2 × 67.9 cm). The Nelson-Atkins Museum of Art, Kansas City, Missouri. The Kenneth A. and Helen F. Spencer Foundation Acquisition Fund

exhibited one example in the second Impressionist exhibition that year and Degas seems to have learned how to make such monotypes from him.[6]

Degas's First Monotypes

The paths of Degas and Lepic also crossed at the Paris Opéra, where the city's finest ballet company performed and where the subject of Degas's earliest "pure" monotype is implicitly located. Both men attended performances at the Opéra and were sufficiently well connected to go backstage and watch ballet instruction taking place. Clearly relating to one such real or partly contrived occasion is the ghostly-seeming composition known today as *The Ballet Master* (*Le Maître de ballet*, c. 1876; plate 17), which shows the celebrated former dancer Jules Perrot directing a young soloist on the Opéra stage itself. A hasty sketch of Perrot in one of Degas's notebooks (fig. 5) suggests that the artist took drawing equipment with him on this occasion.[7] The monotype itself was signed in the wet ink at upper left by Degas and Lepic, and may well have been Degas's first substantial foray into this unfamiliar medium. As was typically the case, the initial print was darker and clearer than the second made from the same plate, which registered only the thinner layer of ink left on the surface after the first image had been printed. In this case, the version of the print known as *Rehearsal of the Ballet* (*Répétition de ballet*; fig. 6) was allowed to dry and then enhanced with brilliant strokes of pastel and applications of colored gouache, to make a vivid, mixed-media masterpiece that obscures the monotype beneath. There seems to have been no precedent for Degas's hybrid pastel-over-monotype technique, which almost immediately became central to his creative activity at this formative moment in his burgeoning career. Numerous other works that are now seen as fundamental to his Impressionist period were also carried out in the same manner, a major shift in Degas's practice that was never explained by the artist himself and still remains largely unarticulated today. For the history-conscious Degas, the monotype medium inevitably represented a dramatic departure from—even a repudiation of—the assumptions that had informed his art since the Italian years. Even in the paintings that launched his name in Paris in the 1860s and '70s, and the works on paper that accompanied them, he had remained faithful to the principle that a white canvas or a blank sheet of paper was the primary arena for creativity. In this arena, lines were drawn or brushed onto the white surface as a subject took shape and was gradually defined as a portrait, landscape, still life, or other motif. While minor variations within this broad practice existed, the value-laden progression from blankness to articulated form was common to most of the two-dimensional arts and had acquired an unmistakable moral resonance in European culture over the centuries. After identifying himself strongly with this practice throughout his early life, Degas now chose to explore its exact opposite. Around his fortieth year, he inverted all these priorities when making his first monotypes, now spreading a continuous layer of black ink across a metal surface and then gradually wiping some of it away with cloths, fingers, and various implements until the composition was resolved to his satisfaction. Largely abandoning traditional drawing in these works, he banished the darkness in order to create light in an almost God-like manner, while definitively separating himself from his former idol Ingres. In Ingresque terms, this new departure represented heresy and rebellion of the worst kind.

Degas himself never explained or attempted to justify this new departure and was on the contrary invigorated by it. In July 1876, the printmaker Marcellin Desboutin, a friend and fellow exhibitor at the first Impressionist show, reported that he was "no longer a friend, a man, an artist! He's a zinc or copper plate blackened with printer's ink!"[8] As Lepic, Appian, and now Degas had realized, monotype seemed to invite experiment and improvisation as ink was freely added, subtracted, or variously manipulated in the studio. Lines could be instantly erased or modified as he progressed and were no longer necessary to mark boundaries or privilege certain forms and spaces. The artist was also able to modify or even completely transform his composition as he progressed by simply wiping ink away. Because a printing press was typically used, most monotypes were made at a distance from their ostensible subjects, and this again encouraged a freer, more creative approach to composition and execution. Monotypes tended to be relatively small and lent themselves to rapidly composed scenes that at their simplest might take minutes rather than hours or days to complete; Lepic's own term for the process, "*eau-forte mobile*" (mobile etching), captures this quality vividly. If *Rehearsal of the Ballet*, the pastel-enhanced cognate of *The Ballet Master*, was manifestly the product of "a series of operations" and of protracted labor, Degas's three-inch-high monotype *Heads of a Man and a Woman* (*Homme et femme, en buste*, c. 1877–80; plate 49), of approximately the same date, was probably dashed off spontaneously. Its composition is artless, and signs of haste are everywhere in the blurring of lines and facial features as Degas evoked a commonplace glimpse of two unremarkable figures on the street. In this same year, his writer friend Edmond Duranty observed in a manifesto-like essay titled "The New Painting" (*La Nouvelle Peinture*) that some of the Impressionist artists were actively aspiring to evoke fleeting sensations as they engaged with the energy of the modern city and the "hustle and bustle of passersby," a phrase that summarizes *Heads of a Man and a Woman* almost uncannily.[9] Here the medium's physical mobility is in some way complicit with the blurred image of two figures in actual movement, whereas the more formal scene in *The Ballet Master* demanded greater stability and refinement for its complex group of figures in a formal setting. The versatility of monotype now allowed Degas to differentiate in his visual language between two quite different encounters, one lasting just a few seconds as he walked through Paris and the other elaborately contrived from an experience on the Opéra stage, but both eloquent of the extremes of modern life. Revealing in a parallel sense is the fact that the smaller monotype was apparently not exhibited or sold in Degas's lifetime, remaining in his portfolios while *Rehearsal of the Ballet* was soon bought by Louisine Elder (later Louisine Havemeyer) and featured in the third Impressionist group show, in 1877. Ignored at this event by most critics, who were perhaps confused by its haphazard composition and strangely mixed technique, *The Ballet Master* was nevertheless judged by one brave voice to be "among the strongest and most interesting" works in the exhibition.[10]

For Degas the monotypist, traditional drawing and firsthand observation had now become options to be considered, not solemn duties or invariable routines but possibilities to be set aside at will in favor of spontaneous modes that were more appropriate to his current enthusiasms. It may have been such radical images as *Heads of a Man and a Woman* and the shadowy, unpastelized version of *The Ballet Master* that first alerted Pissarro to the subversive nature of Degas's technique, at a period when the two men were in contact and knew each other to be involved in printmaking. Degas's letters and notebooks make no reference to this breach with the past and to some extent he kept the evidence out of public view.

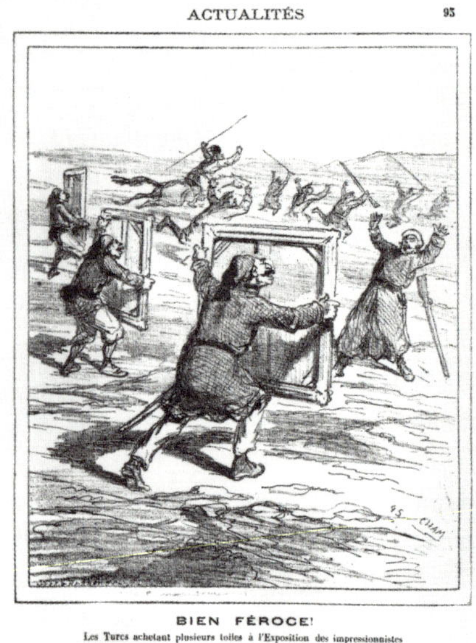

7. Cham (Amédée Charles Henri de Noé). "*Bien féroce!*" Cartoon in *Le Charivari*, April 28, 1877. Lithograph. Bibliothèque nationale de France, Paris

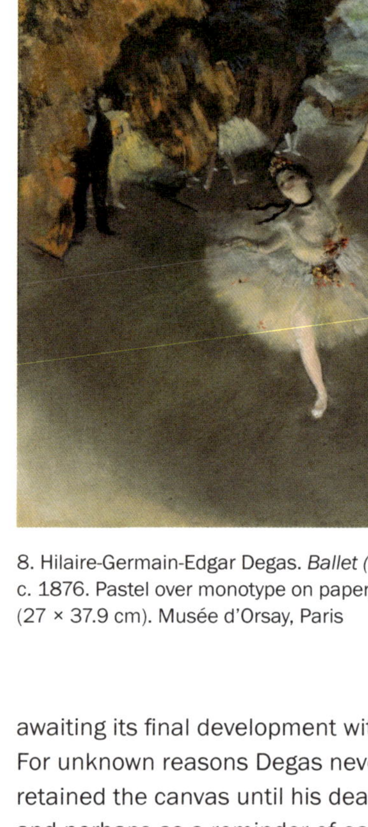

8. Hilaire-Germain-Edgar Degas. *Ballet (The Star)* (*L'Étoile*). c. 1876. Pastel over monotype on paper, plate: 10 5⁄8 × 14 15⁄16 in. (27 × 37.9 cm). Musée d'Orsay, Paris

While an important group of purely black-and-white monotypes was exhibited in the 1877 Impressionist exhibition and another example in 1881, Degas seems to have treated the medium itself as semiprivate in later years.[11] The fact that he did show and sell many pictures that were developed in pastel on an original black-and-white monotype is open to several interpretations. In one sense we might deduce that the artist was using the print in place of a preliminary drawing, with the advantage that tonal as well as linear structure were established in advance, before color was added. This would echo certain traditional practices in which a painted composition was "laid in" using neutral grays or browns before the final layers of color were added. Some of Degas's own monochrome works on canvas of this kind survive from these same years, among them the broadly brushed *Lady with a Parasol* (*Femme à l'ombrelle*, c. 1870–72; plate 51) and the more refined *Ballet Rehearsal on Stage* (*Répétition de ballet sur la scène*, 1874; Musée d'Orsay, Paris), which Degas chose to exhibit in this state in the Impressionist exhibition of 1874. An even more arresting example of the same phenomenon is *Nude Woman Drying Herself* (*Femme au tub*, c. 1880–85; Brooklyn Museum), one of the largest canvases of Degas's maturity, and one that can be imaginatively understood as an enormous monotype-like first draft awaiting its final development with appropriate hues. For unknown reasons Degas never took this step, but retained the canvas until his death in its present state and perhaps as a reminder of earlier ambitions. Yet it also resonates with several monotypes from around 1880 in which he explored horizontal rather than vertical formats and the interplay of bodily contours with surrounding cushions, tubs and lamps (e.g. plates 100, 101, 113, 114). These works all point to a complex interaction among the wide range of media that Degas came to use, where the humblest might influence the grandest and vice versa.

Examples of Degas's monotype-based works seem to have been shown in public for the first time at the third Impressionist exhibition, held in Paris in April 1877, when—by accident or design—he and several colleagues chose to present themselves at their most abrasive. Gustave Caillebotte unveiled his seven-foot-high *Rue de Paris, temps de pluie* (*Paris Street on a Rainy Day*, 1877), with its stark perspective and psychologically remote pedestrians; Claude Monet chose some of his Gare Saint-Lazare canvases that feature trains veiled in smoke and steam; and Pissarro presented several canvases in which tangled trees willfully obscure country dwellings. Unsurprisingly, the exhibition resulted in waves of commentary in the press that far exceeded coverage of the group's

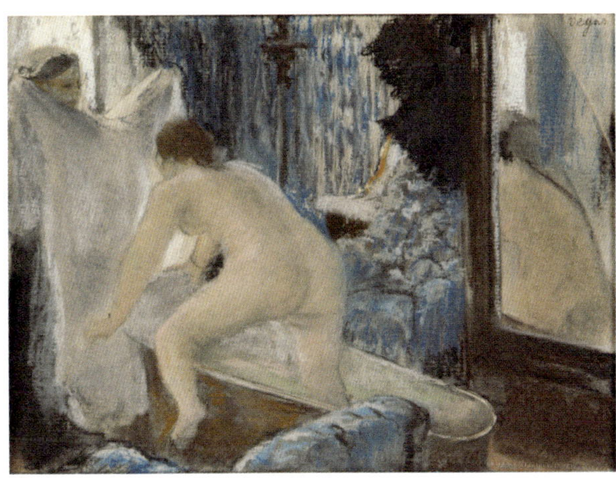

9. Hilaire-Germain-Edgar Degas. *Woman Getting Out of the Bath* (*Femme sortant du bain*). c. 1876–77. Pastel over monotype on paper, 6 ¼ × 8 ½ in. (15.9 × 21.6 cm). Norton Simon Art Foundation

earlier shows and included articles by many noted critics, among them the controversial young novelist Emile Zola, writing for the *Sémaphore de Marseilles*. Referring to Degas, Zola wrote of the "astonishing truth" of his cabaret pictures, while the prominent cartoonist known as Cham published a series of facetious drawings of exaggerated violence that mocked the idea of Impressionism's threats to the populace (fig. 7).[12] While many such responses were comic or hostile, others were now written by journalists who attempted to offer a balanced viewpoint as they became more accustomed to the new art. In general, Degas was treated more respectfully than others, and his skills and versatility were widely acknowledged. Among his approximately twenty works on view were at least eight that were executed in pastel over monotype. In most of these works the layer of pastel concealed much of the original print, which was thus unnoticed and uncommented upon by visitors. Critics also failed to draw attention to this feature and were perhaps oblivious to it, concentrating instead on Degas's role as a "historian of contemporary scenes" who was capable of "frightening realism."[13] As these writers and other visitors realized, the subjects now chosen for Degas's pastel-over-monotype works were also among the most provocative that he had revealed to date: ballerinas shown from above and from close quarters (fig. 8); nude women clambering in and out of bathtubs (fig. 9); and perhaps most shocking of all, a cluster of gaudily dressed prostitutes awaiting customers in a Parisian café (fig. 10). It is impossible to overlook the sense of challenge in such pictures, even in a city where scenes of this kind were commonplace or could be experienced for a price. While several of the monotype and pastel compositions in question were small, measuring around six inches in height, others reached the scale of modest oil paintings and were discussed by critics at commensurate length. Whatever the size, there seemed little doubt that Degas's art had taken a dramatic new turn, now dealing unflinchingly with the raw facts of urban life and using ingenious and unfamiliar combinations of media to express them appropriately. In an important and arguably career-changing sense, monotype also seems to have offered Degas the possibility of new kinds of drawing and new ways of making pictures, which in turn prompted engagement with subjects that had previously been outside the realm of art. A comparison with the clamorous arrival of Pop art in the 1950s and '60s is not altogether fanciful: in both cases, brash new colors and fragmentary compositions both shocked and delighted, while subjects chosen from the coarser side of city life and extremes of modern behavior startled many traditional art-lovers.

For Degas the fervent admirer of Ingres's neoclassical line, the shift to monotype had been transformative in many fundamental ways. Over the next decade he would divide his practice between ambitious, finely wrought oil paintings and pastels and smaller, print-based images that he made rapidly and sometimes even more freely than in the past. In the Impressionists' group shows, such images reinforced the sense that Degas was the leading innovator in miniature views of modern experience, as reviewers of the 1877 exhibition proposed; "Monsieur Degas is an observer not a caricaturist," a commentator noted approvingly, before explaining that he was also "an invaluable historian of contemporary scenes."[14] For the artist himself and perhaps for some of his colleagues and admirers, this sense of topicality seemed to resonate with the immediacy of monotype, as figures glimpsed briefly in a café or onstage at a theater were quickly summoned up on a metal plate in the studio and printed on his own press. *Three Ballet Dancers* (*Trois danseuses*, c. 1878; plate 21) was surely made in this way after one of Degas's frequent visits to the Paris

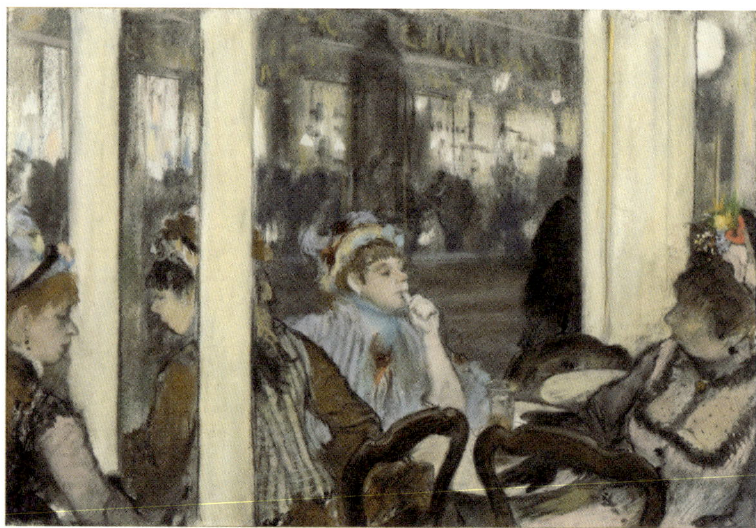

10. Hilaire-Germain-Edgar Degas. *Women on the Terrace of a Café in the Evening* (*Femmes à la terrasse d'un café le soir*). 1877. Pastel over monotype on paper, 16 ⅛ × 23 ⅝ in. (41 × 60 cm). Musée d'Orsay, Paris

Opéra, where he would watch the same production repeatedly and yet was rarely seen to make firsthand sketches during performances.[15] Evidently relying on his celebrated powers of recollection, Degas began this monotype in characteristic fashion by covering the entire plate with black, oil-based ink. Some of this ink was then wiped away to create the specterlike ballerinas against a dark stage, two of whom appear to be leaping into the air in a virtual embodiment of transience. The resulting image was signed by Degas in the still wet ink and also inscribed to a close friend, Alphonse Cherfils. Following the artist's newly established practice, the inked plate was then printed twice, resulting in a dramatically dark first version and a paler second one. When the paler sheet had dried, it was vigorously developed with bright pink, yellow, and green pastels, which may record costumes seen by the artist on the Opéra stage. Brash and dynamic, such works should again be considered against wider developments in contemporary Parisian culture, among them the first publication in these same months of high-speed photographs of animals and humans in movement.[16]

Vivid in a very different way is the pastel on monotype that is known to have featured in the 1877 exhibition, *Women on the Terrace of a Café in the Evening* (fig. 10). Again Degas had chosen a characteristic sight in nineteenth-century Paris, a group of young women who were immediately recognizable as prostitutes. Distinctively dressed in flamboyant outfits that would catch the eye of potential clients, the women are depicted as evening descends and the nightlife of the city begins. As Degas would have known well, artist-predecessors such as Constantin Guys had made a specialty of representing such prostitutes in prints more than two decades earlier, and Guys had prompted admiration from the poet Charles Baudelaire for his perspicacity. Where Guys's black-and-white lithographs of posturing women in interiors had appeared in the city's ephemeral journals, Degas now chose to exhibit his gaudily colored figures in a conspicuous, public art exhibition on the centrally located rue Le Peletier. Almost as bold as the work's subject is the dynamic nature of the scene, where pale pillars slice through several figures and fracture the street behind, while a tangle of chairbacks impedes the observer's view and the distance is little more than a blur. Social cohesion is similarly disrupted by the poses and expressions of the women, none of whom faces the others and all express boredom or indolence. This is the antithesis of bourgeois behavior as well as a mockery of artistic convention, replacing clarity with confusion and composure with vulgarity. Even more than in *Three Ballet Dancers*, the choice of monotype for this work is laden with significance. Comparable scenes of imminent or actual vice are largely absent from Degas's canvases and his more substantial works in pastel, as if the qualities or perhaps the implications of his newly devised prints belonged to a different visual language

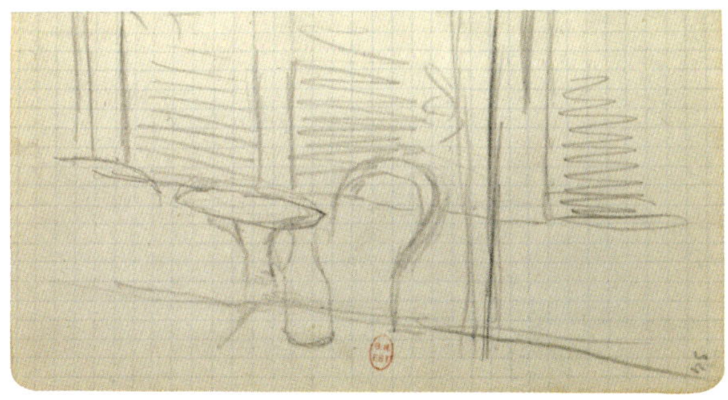

11. Hilaire-Germain-Edgar Degas. Sketchbook (*Carnet 7*). 1875–77. Pencil on paper, 5 ⅝ × 3 ⅞ in. (14.3 × 9.8 cm). Bibliothèque nationale de France, Paris

and a novel medium, as well as to an alternative social world. Journalists suggested as much when they noted the "frightening realism" of *Women on the Terrace of a Café in the Evening*, or even claimed that Degas's picture had "hurled a challenge at the philistines," though one lonely voice acknowledged that it was also "an incomparable page from the book of contemporary life."[17]

Monotype as Fantasy

Such works point to other distinctive qualities in Degas's monotypes at this period. It is not often noted, for example, that he made several practical distinctions between his approach to monotypes and his more conventional studio procedures. As in the early years, he continued to make observational drawings and compositional drafts for many of his paintings and pastels, generally preserving these works on paper in portfolios when the larger task was complete. This process could also involve hiring models, such as professional dancers, to pose in his studio, presumably when complex positions or specific expressions were required. With his monotypes, however, there is remarkably little evidence of preliminary drawing of this kind for the vast majority of Degas's prints. This is largely the case with *Women on the Terrace of a Café in the Evening*, where a single hasty notebook sketch records the rudimentary setting in the café without indicating any of the human protagonists (fig. 11). Lost or destroyed material may of course account for the lack of appropriate figure studies, and some censorship of erotic material from Degas's studio is said to have been carried out after the artist's death. Yet for the great majority of his monotypes of all kinds, which range over cityscapes and landscapes, portraits of individuals and complex figurative scenes, no preliminary drawings of any kind have been found. One explanation may have been Degas's strong aversion to working in public; he famously mocked plein air painters such as Monet and Pissarro who would boldly set up their easels in full view of passersby; "Painting is not a sport!" he once protested to his dealer friend Ambroise Vollard.[18] This self-consciousness about artmaking in front of others was also witnessed by friends who visited Degas at home, where they were rarely received when he was in the act of drawing, painting, or working on a sculpture. Similarly, most of his sketchbooks seem to have been a private matter, compiled for his own use and rarely displayed to others. Family censorship apart, the lack of a demonstrable origin in such sketches for many of these monotypes appears to point to a different conclusion. A young colleague who traveled through the countryside with Degas in his later years marveled at his retentive memory, which allowed him to re-create in monotype a distinctive landscape that he had seen earlier in the day without having stopped to study and record it.[19] Remote from his Paris experience as that was, it seems that Degas also relied on memory to reassemble or reimagine figures encountered on the streets and elsewhere, then incorporated them into monotypes, pastels, and paintings. In an important and little-explored sense, such improvised prints also opened the way to free invention and fantasy, territory largely unknown to him in his previous life as an artist.

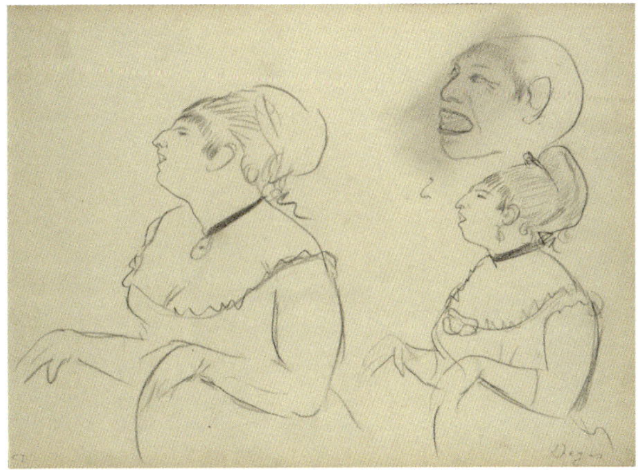

12. Hilaire-Germain-Edgar Degas. Sketches from an album of pencil sketches. c. 1877. Pencil on paper, sheet: 9 ¾ × 13 in. (24.8 × 33 cm). The J. Paul Getty Museum, Los Angeles

In a situation of this kind the survival of even a few sketches related to well-known monotype compositions is unusually instructive. A vivid case involves a group of rapidly executed drawings in the same

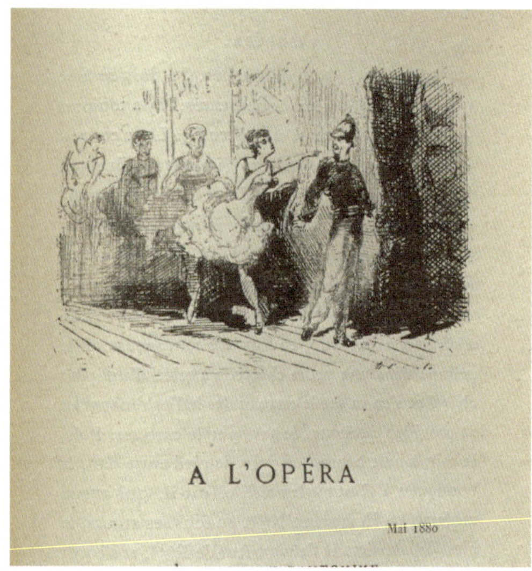

13. Henri Maigrot. Illustration for Ludovic Halévy's *Les Petites Cardinal*. Paris, 1880

large notebook that includes the study of Monsieur Perrot. In at least two of them we can also identify the cabaret singer Thérèsa in action (fig. 12), looking as if she were drawn on the spot when the artist was under the spell of a voice that he was briefly entranced by and described to a friend as "spiritually tender."[20] Degas manifestly consulted these sketches when he made the pastel over monotype known as *The Song of the Dog* (*La Chanson du chien*, c. 1876–77; private collection), integrating precise details of Thérèsa's dress, hairstyle, and gloved hands, while perhaps glamorizing her facial expression with a potential buyer in mind. Other cabaret artistes were also hastily or partially drawn in action on successive pages of the same notebook, some of them again familiar from Degas's known monotypes and lithographs. Yet few if any on-the-spot studies exist for entire series of other monotype prints, notably the three most substantial thematic groups in his entire print oeuvre. These represent brothel scenes and related female nudes; episodes from Ludovic Halévy's stories; and various rural landscapes, which together amount to around three-quarters of Degas's known monotype output. This absence is startling on such a scale and points to a new departure in his creative activity. When he made most of this large body of prints—perhaps the majority—it seems that Degas departed from a life-long practice by working from memory and imagination rather than direct observation. This was inevitably the case with the Halévy monotypes, which were exceptional in Degas's oeuvre in several respects. Based not on specific personal encounters or experiences, as most of his mature art was, these prints represent both fictional and real characters in a succession of episodes that refer loosely to happenings backstage at the Paris Opéra, some spelled out by Halévy himself in his tales. Halévy was well-known in Paris as a popular novelist and man of the theater, who compiled a sequence of verbal sketches based on the imaginary Madame Cardinal, the mother of two girls, Pauline and Virginie, who dance in the Opéra's corps de ballet. Under the title *Madame Cardinal*, these stories were first serialized in the periodical *La Vie Parisienne* in 1870 and became a wild popular success, soon appearing in book form.[21] Later in the decade and in unknown circumstances, the same tales prompted Degas to create his series of monotypes of backstage life, including many of near-identical size made from the same metal plate. These images are broadly rather than literally linked to Halévy's tales, and it remains unclear whether the prints were conceived as illustrations for a forthcoming publication or were simply inspired by the artist's delight in his friend's text.

Degas's enthusiasm for this project is evident in drawings of Halévy himself, which prepared the way for several monotypes showing the author backstage and in the glamorous Opéra foyer. Less expected are works in which the real Halévy is shown conversing with the fictional Mme Cardinal (plate 74), a step into imaginative territory of a kind that has rarely been associated with Degas himself. Halévy ultimately settled for more pedestrian illustrations to his books, by such artists as Henri Maigrot and Edmond Morin (fig. 13). The mixture of fact and fiction in some of Degas's prints was perhaps considered confusing, while the considerable graphic license in scenes such as *Dancers Coming from the Dressing Rooms onto the Stage* (*Et ces demoiselles frétillaient gentiment devant la glace du foyer*, c. 1876–77; plate 78) would have taxed most of the artist's and writer's peers. Here Degas went to extreme lengths to evoke a melée of activity among the excited young women, in a blur of tutus and barely coherent limbs, with only the familiar dark silhouette of Halévy to bring some coherence to the scene. In this monotype Degas laid ink over much of the plate with a brush, then wiped away the pigment in certain areas to convey highlights and added ink to the composition to render more precise details. Once the impression was printed, he enhanced it with strokes of pastel to suggest light, shadow, and human presences. A print of this kind would probably have been unacceptable in any current publication and possibly in most artistic circles of the time as well. As with the monotype *Heads of a Man and a Woman* but now on a more extensive scale, Degas again seems to delight in flirting with incoherence as he responds to an implicitly unstable motif, and thus to an experience beyond most conventions in late-nineteenth-century art. Traditional drawing has little or no role in most of the Halévy scenes, which play with a new language of human mobility and fleeting sensation that goes far beyond the period's notions of realism.

In the 1877 Impressionist exhibition catalogue, three groups of Degas's entries were listed as "*dessins faits à l'encre grasse et imprimé*" (drawings made with greasy ink and put through a press), or what we know today as monotypes.[22] In his review of the exhibition, the novelist and critic Jules Claretie identified these works as illustrations to the Halévy stories, which thus became the first pure monotypes by Degas known to have been shown in public.[23] There were no further comments on them in the press, despite Halévy's celebrity, and the monotypes were presumably returned to the artist when the exhibition closed and remained with him into old age. Apparently undaunted, Degas continued to use the monotype technique for more than a decade and persisted in seeing it as a primary medium for visual and thematic experimentation of a sometimes extreme kind. By this date his paintings and pastels were in demand from collectors, some bought by colleagues and fellow-artists such as Caillebotte and Henri Lerolle, or by a friend with advanced taste such as Jean-Baptiste Faure. Yet financial problems inherited from his family dogged Degas and his brothers, putting the artist under pressure to support himself while maintaining a modest apartment and studio in Paris. It may thus have seemed to be in his interest to push certain ideas and projects further, in situations that would raise his profile and draw public attention to works that he was currently producing. A case in point was perhaps the substantial sequence of monotypes devoted to brothel interiors that he now began to make, which were evidently based on the artist's personal knowledge of such establishments. Few details have survived about this private activity of Degas's, though Paris had long been known for its association with prostitution of various kinds and at various levels of discretion and squalor. In later years the artist was frank about anticipating the pleasures of Andalusian brothels when he traveled there with the Italian painter Giovanni Boldini and specified that they should take "a good quantity of condoms" with them.[24] No doubt fact and fantasy were again mingled in the works he now made in the late 1870s and early 1880s, as he pursued his latest project with characteristic energy and wit, and occasional solemnity.

The monotypes of brothel scenes can be divided into two loose categories, where those close in scale and facture to the Cardinal scenes are assumed to have been made around the same date and at least some were apparently printed from the same plates. This latter group, represented by the euphemistically titled *Two Young Girls* (*Deux jeunes filles*, c. 1877–79; plate 88), is explicit about the brothel settings and their customers, who are here shown in light-filled rooms and in situations that are mundane rather than crudely sexual. Such works have clear visual echoes of Halévy-related works such as *In the Green Room* (*Le Foyer*, c. 1876–77; plate 81) and *M. Cardinal About to Write a Letter* (*Je ne comprends pas, dit M. Cardinal*, c. 1876–77; plate 84), which are similarly illuminated and generally airy. While the perspective in the Halévy prints tends to be conventional, that in *The Bath* (*Le Bain*, 1879–83; plate 94) is frankly distorted as a misshapen tub seems to rise of its own accord toward the upper center of the scene. This work far exceeds most of the Halévy compositions in sheer graphic energy and visual force as the diagonal tub meets the vertical folds of the curtain and the chaotic heap of clothing sets off the sinuous naked body. Degas's growing enthusiasm for the graphic potential of the monotype is palpable here and in other works of a similar kind that seem to have broadened his creative horizons. This included adding complex layers of pastel to some of these intimate scenes, such as *Woman Getting Out of the Bath* (*Femme sortant du bain*, c. 1880–85; plate 124), a vivacious image that prompted him to reassert a kind of innocent domestic realism. Comparable pastel-over-monotype works of this kind, such as *Waiting for the Client* (*Attente d'un client*, c. 1877–79; plate 89), seem to evoke experiences in more glamorous brothels where colorful carpets and furnishings are brightly illuminated and several tantalizingly half-clad women display themselves for a customer who is discreetly indicated by a slender black form at the left edge. We can only guess whether Degas made sketches in any of these circumstances or was obliged to rely on his "memory strong like iron" when making the monotypes in question.[25] What is clear is the extreme vividness and inventiveness of the imagery that resulted, which took Degas far away from his roots in standard observational drawing and toward a new kind of flowering as an artist of recollection and free invention.

His extraordinary ability to compartmentalize the current output of his studio was perhaps at its height during the late 1870s. At the fourth Impressionist exhibition, in April 1879, Degas presented almost thirty substantial new pastels and oil paintings that ranged over portraits and dance classes, scenes of opera performances and cabarets, and even a group of decorated fans. Many of them were notably complex in structure and subtle in finish, and—as in *Miss La La at the Cirque Fernando* (*Miss Lola au Cirque Fernando*, 1879; fig. 14), a vertiginous scene of a trapeze act—frankly audacious as works of art. Entirely absent from this display was the monotype medium, both on its own terms and as the foundation for works in pastel. Yet paradoxically this was also a high point in Degas's career as a printmaker and as an advocate of the medium in Impressionist circles. He and his friends had proposed that the group should publish a journal to be called *Le Jour et la nuit* (Day and night), consisting largely of original prints made by this circle of artists. Bracquemond, Cassatt, and Pissarro were soon enlisted in the project, and less familiar names such as Jean-Louis Forain, Jean-Marius Raffaëlli, and Henri Rouart also showed active interest. But Degas was "the driving force behind the enterprise," in the words of Jean-Paul Bouillon, envisaging it as a way to promote their etchings, drypoints, and lithographs as well as their larger pictures to a public that was slowly adjusting to the "New Painting."[26]

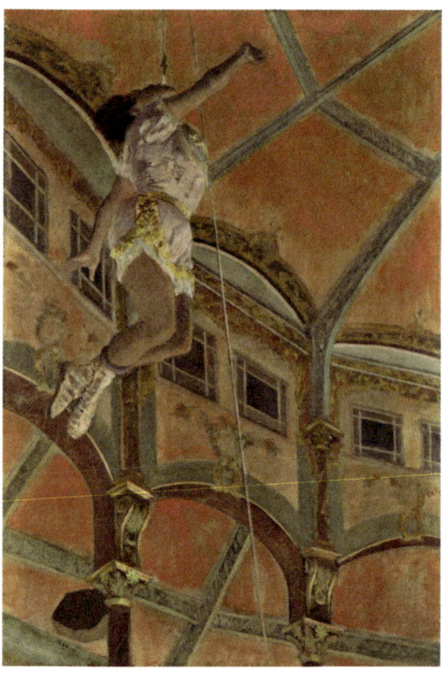

14. Hilaire-Germain-Edgar Degas. *Miss La La at the Cirque Fernando* (*Miss Lola au Cirque Fernando*). 1879. Oil on canvas, 46 ⅛ × 30 ½ in. (117.2 × 77.5 cm). The National Gallery, London

After much labor, confusion, and delay, the proposed journal was abandoned, but only after it had stimulated Degas's own print production and extended his co-operation with several fellow printmakers. Initially the most important of these had been his collaboration with Bracquemond, who was soon replaced by Pissarro as a colleague and fellow experimenter. Pissarro was still living outside Paris in rural Pontoise, but they met and exchanged letters about the journal and a variety of technical issues relating to prints. A common interest at this point was colored inks and the possibility of introducing different hues into varying states of a print and even into parts of a composition by means of "light copper" shapes that restricted coverage of the areas in question.[27] Such possibilities took them close to the cutting edge of printmaking technologies and resulted in works that have been described by Richard Brettell as "without precedent in the visual arts."[28] Significant in a different way is that the two men sometimes worked together on Degas's press in his Paris studio, experimenting with various modes of printing and reprinting from the same plate. Degas would also make trial proofs from plates sent to him by Pissarro, who at that point had no press of his own. Despite profound differences in background, social status, and ways of life, the two men established an increasingly warm relationship that lasted over the years and was for a long time unaffected by their politics. Degas was frank in his admiration for some of Pissarro's etchings, such as *The Cabbage Field* (*Le Champ de choux*, 1880; fig. 15), if a little ironic about differences in their tastes; in the same letter he signed off with a compliment on "the quality of the art of your vegetable gardens."[29]

Again beginning at an unknown date, Degas subsequently chose to move in a quite different direction with a second suite of monotypes of female nudes. Here he opted for much more somber territory, plunging most of his subjects into deep gloom and situating them in unidentifiable, even ominous spaces. Typically these prints show one or more heavily built women who are barely discernible as they rest on vast sofas or beds, or sit in massive tubs. Presumably prostitutes displaying themselves for the benefit of clients, they make no eye contact but calmly wash themselves, read, or stare into space. Most of these prints are significantly larger than the earlier series and some achieve an unexpected sculptural monumentality that is hardly characteristic of either the Halévy-related series or the lighter monotypes of nudes. Such images again represent a willed act of extreme distancing from Degas's earlier career, not just from academic figure drawing and his much more recent monotypes but from most of the norms associated with any kind of art at this time. In one sense *The Fireside* (*Le Foyer [La Cheminée]*, c. 1880–85; plate 102) can be seen as a larger and more ambitious variant on *The Bath*, with a subject that is now deeper in surrounding shadow and consequently more difficult to discern. In *The Fireside* spatial niceties have been set aside in favor of stygian blackness, almost denying coherence to the seated figure at left. Comparisons have been made between such splayed bodies and the engravings of mentally disturbed women published by Dr. Paul Richer in Paris at almost precisely this moment, in 1881, though here the individual at left in Degas's print seems to be enjoying the warmth of a fire.[30]
A work such as *Woman Reading* (*Liseuse*, c. 1880–85; plate 106), however, is both grim and unambiguous, with little to relieve the gloom or the sense of animal ponderousness. As with many other figures in the

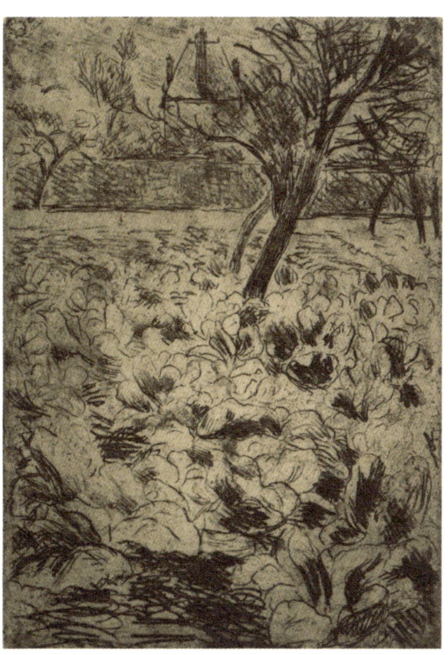

15. Camille Pissarro. *The Cabbage Field* (*Le Champ de choux*). 1880. Softground etching on laid paper, state II of II, plate: 9 ¾ × 6 ⅝ in. (24.7 × 16.8 cm), sheet: 12 ⅝ × 9 7⁄16 in. (32 × 23.9 cm). The Metropolitan Museum of Art, New York. The Elisha Whittelsey Collection, The Elisha Whittelsey Fund

approximately twenty works in this distinctive group, the woman's face is obscured and no attempt has been made to glamorize a body that seems incongruous among apparently grand furniture. Perhaps most ironic of all is the fact that she is shown reading, her back toward the customer or spectator. Some prints from this wider series were taken a stage further and partially returned to domesticity by the application of color. In *Female Nude Reclining* (*Femme nue couchée*, c. 1888–90; plate 101) Degas extended the pastel beyond the plate marks (and thus the original printed composition) to produce a sensuous composition of light and shadow, warmth and touches of cooler hue. Here the sexual significance of the composition is disarmingly frank rather than merely hinted at. Tellingly, this work and most of the series are unsigned, indicating that the artist failed to interest a dealer or collector in them or simply chose to keep the entire suite in his studio. Nothing prevented Degas from showing them to friends or colleagues, however, especially those who were themselves involved with printmaking and the new possibilities of the craft. More even than the earlier brothel series, these haunting prints seem to take us into the artist's imaginings as much as his mundane experiences in the city.

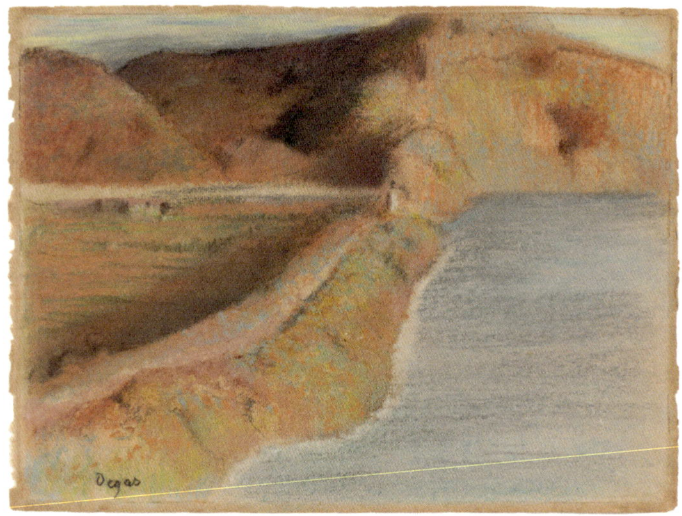

16. Hilaire-Germain-Edgar Degas. *Rocky Coast* (*Côte rocheuse*). 1890–92.
Pastel over monotype on paper, 12 × 16 in. (30.5 × 40.6 cm). Museum Ludwig, Cologne

The Last Monotypes: Whimsy and Abstraction

Despite a considerable outlay of time, creative energy, and personal self-revelation, neither series of monotype nudes seem to have been substantially exhibited in Degas's lifetime. By unveiling such works as the sculpture *Little Dancer Aged Fourteen* at the 1881 group show, and the majestic suite of pastels representing female nudes in 1886, Degas was able to remind the world of his continuing evolution and attainment, even as his printmaking came to a virtual standstill. Echoes of the repeated and reversed imagery associated with his prints certainly resound in paintings such as *Frieze of Dancers* (*Danseuses attachant leurs sandales*, c. 1895; plate 153), while his acquired mastery of tonal drama paid dividends in such majestic late canvases as *The Bath* (*Le Bain*, c. 1895; plate 171) and *After the Bath, Woman Drying Herself* (*Après le bain, femme s'essuyant*, c. 1896; plate 170). Even the handling of printing ink seems to have left its mark in the massed fingerprints that characterize several canvases of this and later periods. The main exception to this pattern was as whimsical yet startling as any of his previous departures. In the fall of 1890, Degas visited his younger friend Georges Jeanniot in the heart of rural Burgundy and announced that he wished to create a series of monotypes of landscapes he had just passed through. Though rarely associated with rural views then or now, Degas had tackled the Italian landscape as a youth, the Breton coast in his mid-thirties, and varied terrain as backgrounds to his equestrian scenes over the decades. The Burgundy suite is exceptional for its extent, its seriousness, but most of all for its extreme originality. Most surprising of all is the fact that Degas began many of these works with bold sweeps of color on a copper plate almost sixteen inches wide, to produce some of the largest prints of his career.[31] Now he deliberately encouraged chance effects, apparently made with rollers, cloths, and haphazard waves of diluted greens, ochers, and purples, some of them with visible fingerprints and coarse wipings that have little or no precedent in his own art or that of his peers.

While some of the prints, such as *Cap Hornu near Saint-Valery-sur-Somme* (*Le Cap Hornu près Saint-Valery-sur-Somme*, c. 1890–93; plate 138), were coaxed into plausible geographic forms, many—among them *Autumn Landscape* (*L'Estérel*, 1890; plates 136, 137) and *Twilight in the Pyrenees* (*Le Crépuscule dans les Pyrénées*, 1890; plate 128)—were retained in their original state. Second pulls were made in several cases and examples of each category were developed in pastel, many but not all acquiring greater cogency as scenes of farmland, rocky prominences, or distant hills. In this simple but exhilarating context Degas took the monotype to new and entirely unexpected levels, not least in a subgroup of these prints that toyed with anthropomorphism. *Cap Hornu near Saint-Valery-sur-Somme* can be seen as a land mass beside a lake or ocean, but also as a vestigial human body. Clearly intrigued, Degas made rocks look like teeth and promontories like legs (fig. 16), reminding us of a lighter, human side to his art that had occasionally surfaced throughout his career. After returning to Paris, Degas felt sufficiently emboldened by the project to mount an exhibition of his latest monotypes in 1892 at the gallery of Paul Durand-Ruel, currently the leading dealer in Impressionist art. Some visitors were perplexed and others exhilarated, reaching for Symbolist language to compare them to "tapestries hung in secret boudoirs" and "precious sapphires in velvet jewelry boxes."[32] Pissarro wrote to his son Lucien that they were "colored impressions," "curious" but "really delicate," and perhaps recalled a past when he and Degas struggled with color prints for *Le Jour et la nuit*.[33] Though separated now by politics, they had both witnessed the birth and maturity of the monotype, and its incursions into the most advanced art of their times.

1. Camille Pissarro, letter to his son Lucien, 1891, *Correspondence de Camille Pissarro*, ed. Janine Bailly-Herzberg (Saint-Ouen-l'Aumône: Editions du Valhermeil, 1991), 3:61. Author's trans.
2. Edgar Degas, *The Notebooks of Edgar Degas*, ed. Theodore Reff (Oxford: Clarendon Press, 1976), 1:39.
3. See Paul Valéry, "Degas Dance Drawing," in *Degas, Manet, Morisot* (New York: Pantheon Books, 1960), p. 35, and Henri Delaborde, *Ingres. Sa vie, ses travaux, sa doctrine* (Paris: H. Plon, 1870), p. 123.
4. Daniel Halévy, *Pays Parisiens* (Paris: B. Grasset, 2000), p. 93; Valéry, "Degas Dance Drawing," p. 6.
5. See Timothy Standring and Martin Clayton, *Castiglione: Lost Genius*, exh. cat. (London: Royal Collection Trust, 2013), pp. 131–43.
6. See Ruth Berson, *The New Painting: Impressionism 1874–1886* (San Francisco: Fine Arts Museums of San Francisco, 1996), 2:40, II–137, and Ludovic-Napoléon Lepic, *Comment je devins un graveur à l'eau-forte* (Paris: Cadart, 1876).
7. See Degas, *The Notebooks of Edgar Degas*, 2:41, notebook 28.
8. Marcellin Desboutin, letter to Léontine De Nittis, July 17, 1876, quoted in Eng. trans. in Jean Sutherland Boggs, *Degas*, exh. cat. (New York: The Metropolitan Museum of Art, and Ottawa: National Gallery of Canada, 1988), p. 258.
9. Edmond Duranty, *La Nouvelle Peinture* (Paris, 1876), trans. in Charles Moffett et al., *The New Painting*, exh. cat. (San Francisco: Fine Arts Museums of San Francisco, 1986), p. 45.
10. *Le Bien public*, April 7, 1877, p. 2, repr. in Berson, *The New Painting*, 1:190.
11. See Berson, *The New Painting*, 2:74, nos. III-58–60, and 2:180.
12. Ibid., 1:191.
13. G. Rivière, "Explications," *L'Impressioniste*, April 21, 1877, pp. 3–4, repr. in ibid., 1:187; Alexandre Pothey, "Beaux-Arts," *Le Petit Parisien*, April 7, 1877, p. 2, repr. in ibid., 1:173.
14. See ibid., 1:187.
15. See Henri Loyrette, "Degas à l'Opéra," in Musée d'Orsay, *Degas inédit* (Paris: Documentation française, 1989), pp. 47–63.
16. See Richard Kendall and Jill DeVonyar, *Degas and the Ballet: Picturing Movement*, exh. cat. (London: Royal Academy Books, 2011), chapters 3 and 4.
17. See Berson, *The New Painting*, 1:173, 157.
18. Degas, quoted in Ambroise Vollard, *Degas: An Intimate Portrait* (New York: Dover Publications, 1986), p. 56.
19. Georges Jeanniot, "Souvenirs sur Degas," *Revue Universelle* LV (October 15, 1933):153.
20. Degas, *Degas Letters*, ed. Marcel Guérin (Oxford: Bruno Cassirer, 1947), p. 76.
21. See Michael Pantazzi, "Degas, Halévy, and the Cardinals," in Boggs, *Degas*, p. 280.
22. Berson, *The New Painting*, 2:74, nos. III-58–60.
23. Ibid., 1:141.
24. Musée d'Orsay, *Degas Inédit*, p. 418.
25. Giovanni Boldini, quoted in Pantazzi, "The Event of the Season: Monsieur Degas Exhibits," unpublished lecture, 1989.
26. Jean-Paul Bouillon, *Félix Bracquemond, le réalisme absolu* (Geneva: Skira, 1987), p. 152.
27. See Degas, *Degas Letters*, p. 58.
28. Richard Brettell and Eric Gillis, *Degas and Pissarro. Alchimie d'une rencontre*, exh. cat. (Vevey: Musée Janisch, 1988), p. 34.
29. Degas, *Degas Letters*, p. 58.
30. See Xavier Rey, "The Body Exploited," in George T. M. Shackelford and Xavier Rey, *Degas and the Nude*, exh. cat. (Boston: Museum of Fine Arts, 2011), p. 91, n. 41.
31. See Kendall, *Degas Landscapes* (New Haven: Yale University Press, 1993).
32. Gustave Geffroy, "Historie de l'impressionisme. Edgar Degas," in *La Vie artistique* (Paris), troisième série, 1894, p. 176.
33. Pissarro, letter to his son Lucien, October 2, 1892, *Correspondence de Camille Pissarro*, 3:261–62.

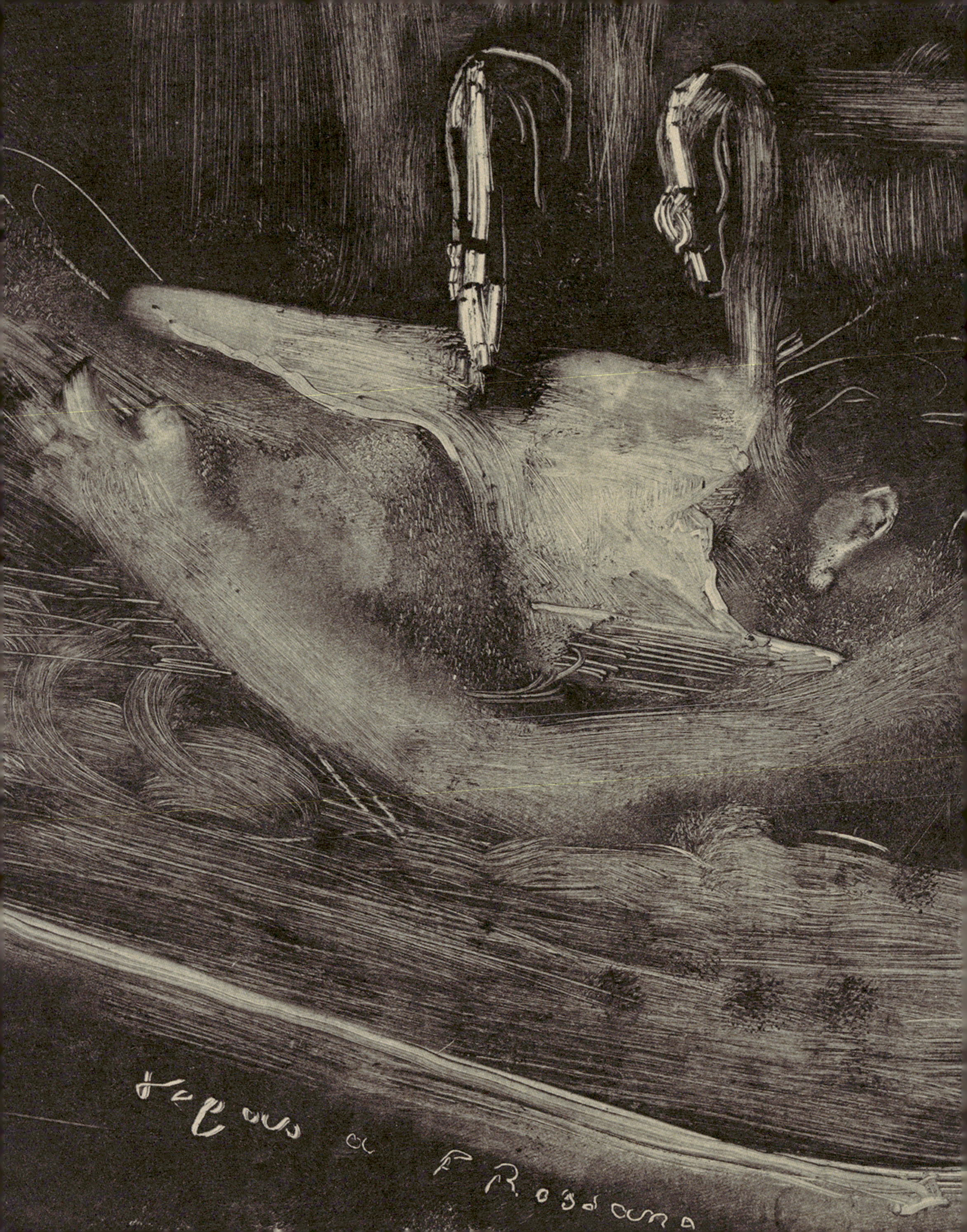

Degas in the Dark

Carol Armstrong

Degas's intense interest in the dark, and in what happens in the dark, took place in two different mediums at two different moments in his career: in his experimentation with the so-called "dark-ground" monotype in the period roughly between 1876 and 1885, and in his brief hands-on investigation of the photograph around 1895.[1] In those different moments and mediums, he first investigated what it meant to make an image subtractively—by removing ink from a surface covered with it ("dark ground") rather than by applying ink to an empty surface ("light ground")—and then what it meant to photograph indoors and at night, when there was little light. At the same time, he also pursued the somatic relations among sleep, nocturnal blindness, and unseeing acts of self-touching; the tactile and the sub-optical; and the reflexive animal physicality that lies underneath the specular aspect of the human body. In this essay I want to explore these uses of the dark-ground monotype, and the relations between darkness in the monotype and darkness in the photograph, from both a technical and a thematic point of view.

The first impressions of Degas's dark-ground monotypes produced very dark images indeed, since the plates were almost covered with ink. If he made a second impression, though, it would be lighter, since much of the ink had been removed on the first pass through the press, and he often used these second impressions as foundations to which to add pastel, or a mix of pastel and gouache. Many of his earliest essays in monotype took this double form, and by 1883, toward the end of his most intensive period of work with this kind of print, his use of the dark foundation beneath pastel, paired with a first, darker impression of the print without that supplement, was pointedly concerned with views of the female body in immediate physical contact with itself.

One such pastel is *Woman in Her Bath, Sponging Her Leg* (*Femme dans son bain s'épongeant la jambe*, c. 1880–85; plate 114), one of the series Suite of Female Nudes Bathing, Washing, Drying, Wiping, or Combing Themselves (*Suite de nus de femmes se baignant, se lavant, se séchant, s'essuyant, se peignant ou se faisant peigner*). When the series was exhibited in the last Impressionist exhibition, in 1886, J. K. Huysmans deemed it an "insulting adieu," and he and other critics saw it as a group of variations on a theme of female bestiality—a final gesture of what Leo Steinberg would later call "devenustation."[2] Huysmans wrote of Degas's toppling of the "idol . . . woman, whom he debases as he depicts her, in her tub, in the humiliating poses of her intimate activities," a savage summary of the strategies he saw in the series as a whole.[3] The version of *Woman in Her Bath* . . . that Huysmans would have seen in the

Hilaire-Germain-Edgar Degas. *Woman in a Bathtub* (*Femme au bain*). c. 1880–85. Detail of plate 113

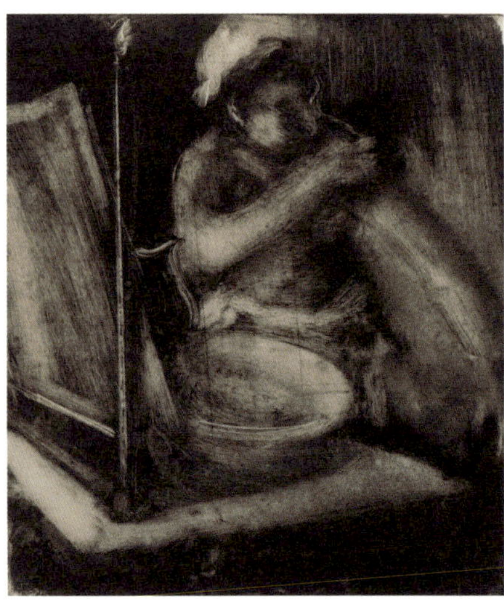

1. Hilaire-Germain Edgar Degas. *The Toilette* (*Arms*) (*La Toilette [Les Bras]*). c. 1880–85. Monotype on paper, plate: 12 5⁄16 × 10 5⁄16 in. (31.3 × 27.8 cm). UCLA Grunwald Center for the Graphic Arts, Hammer Museum. Given through the UCLA Art Council by B. Gerald Cantor

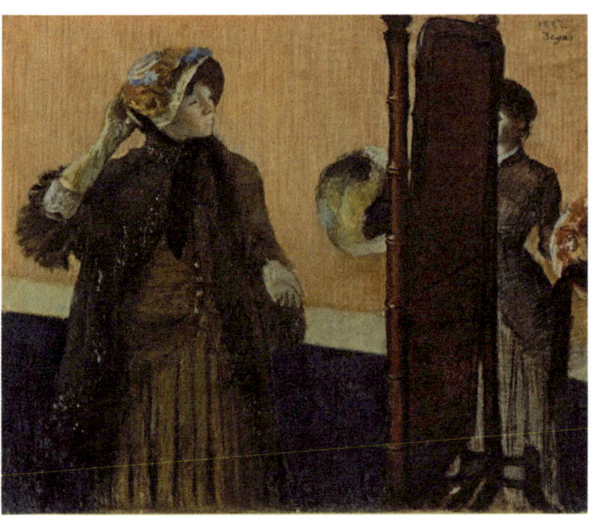

2. Hilaire-Germain-Edgar Degas. *At the Milliner's* (*Chez la modiste*). 1882. Pastel on pale gray wove paper, 30 × 34 in. (76.2 × 86.4 cm). The Metropolitan Museum of Art, New York. H. O. Havemeyer Collection, Bequest of Mrs. H. O. Havemeyer

show was actually the colored, pastel version, which pretties up its first-impression corollary. But he might just as well have been speaking of the murkier, more mordant, much franker world of the first-impression, dark-ground monotypes, minus the layer of pastel that makes the Suite of Female Nudes . . . rather more palatable.

The first-impression version of *Woman in Her Bath . . .* , *Woman in a Bathtub* (Femme au bain; plate 113), monotype contrasts with its pastel counterpart not only in the unalleviated darkness of the scene, which reads like a kind of *contre-jour* negative, but in other important respects as well. The simian aspect of the woman's profile (a *profil perdu*, turned away from the viewer to mainly show the roundness of the cheek), her outsized and highlighted ear, the enlarged clumsiness of her foot, the clawing gesture of her hand on the sponge, and the exaggerated fragmentation of the whole all combine to render her a caricature. The unmitigated inkiness of the image also yields a bath of dark grease for the she-creature to bathe in, and the technical production of the print by wiping and scratching away ink is conflated with her gestures of sponging and scraping at herself. Her pastel other, meanwhile, is dressed up by decorous redrawing in color. The dark-ground woman is in all ways a negative to the pastel's positive; we might also say that she is the pastel's "optical unconscious."[4]

In other dark-ground bather monotypes of the same period Degas was even more brutally blunt about the ablutionary and other activities of the faceless women he depicted—women who use bidets and chamber pots, who bend over with their backsides to the viewer, whose legs are splayed, whose hastily limned gestures may be masturbatory, whose bodies are upended in abandon or oblivion. All decorum is relinquished, all sublimation renounced, all inhibition surrendered, in favor of the netherworld of the guttersnipe girl, uncompromisingly delivered. Like *Woman in a Bathtub . . .* , many of these monotypes have counterparts in which pastel is layered over the dark ink as a kind of cosmetic, protecting and deflecting the gaze, at least a little, from the earthy uncouthness beneath the applied color, with its hints of sewer and scatology, its ob-scene body language, and its rude laying bare of the nocturnal secrets of the flesh.

One more dimension of difference between the first impression and the second impression with pastel overlay should be noted: in the first impression the figure is one with the ground. The ground refuses to become a background or surround for the figure; each is inextricable from the other. The pastels may mimic this effect through the array of fabric and furniture surfaces that they set around their bathing women, but they cannot quite duplicate or excavate it from beneath their top layer. In some ways a photographic negative operates similarly to the first-impression monotypes, partly as a function of its reversal of the relation between light and dark, which makes it harder for the eye to parse. But unlike the photographic negative, Degas's first-impression monotypes have a lubricious materiality that insists on its own opacity, and on the physical imbrication of figure and ground—indeed on the primacy of ground over figure, rather than the other way around.[5]

What this means for the image of the female body is that it falls back into its own base materiality, which cannot be transcended, or sublimated into a language of form and gesture, any more than the figure can rise out of its ground. Likewise, the act of drawing, which in Degas's case always identifies itself with the activities of the figures that it creates, remains resolutely mired in the brute stuff in which it takes place and of which it is made. Just as the bathing figure is sullied rather than cleansed by her bath, so drawing is debased rather than elevated into the figural realm of clear contour and readable, signifying gesture. The pastel *Woman in Her Bath . . .* reconstitutes the figural realm that the first-impression print undoes. Further, by laying down another stratum on top of the second-impression foundation, which is always paler than the first impression, it also returns the underlayer to where it belongs: properly *underneath* the image.

There are reversals aplenty in the monotype, and in Degas's use of it. A reversal of the image of course is innate to printmaking. There is also a tonal inversion, a consequence of the dark-ground method. The fact that the print is a monotype, a singular image, and that the image fades in all impressions after the first one, paradoxically contradicts the principle of mechanical reproduction that again is a function of printmaking. All of these reversals are exaggerated by Degas's idiosyncratic use of the medium. In his contrarian way, he also drove toward a figural dead end, undoing the binaries out of which the figure and its gestures arise.

Furthermore, in moving between the light- and the dark-ground monotypes Degas pursued a peculiarly antinarrative agenda, the light-ground works being much more illustrational and anecdotal than his dark-ground efforts. The artist's brothel scenes, in which the bodily themes of the dark-ground work often arise, tell stories about the daily lives of the Parisian sex-workers who worked in *maisons closes*, describing the rooms and salons in which they woke and slept, bathed and (un)dressed, and awaited and received clients (occasionally alone, often in groups). Sometimes these images indicate particular sexual practices, or include the presence of the madams who owned and ran the houses in which the women plied their trade.[6] These works imply narrative, and in fact the Cardinal Family (*Famille Cardinal*) series (1880–83; plates 72–84), which fell close in time to the brothel monotypes and tied the world of the prostitute to that of the dancer, was of course intended to accompany a set of stories by the writer Ludovic Halévy—it was an illustrational project, then, albeit a failed one that strained against the rules of illustration much more than it obeyed them.[7] In short, the light-ground monotypes stay close to the themes of novels and novelettes such as Guy de Maupassant's "The Tellier House" ("*La Maison Tellier*," 1881), and similar works of the period, functioning much like visual *romans*. Yet while the vulgar, chaotic poses, and the constitution of those poses out of coarse, blunted lines, smudges and smears, and thumb- and fingerprints, were much the same in both kinds of monotype, the dark-ground monotypes utterly undermine the legibility of the light-ground images through their virtual unintelligibility, and their insistence on the nocturnal rather than the diurnal aspects of the world they represent.

Many of these works share a curious feature: the presence of mirrors reflecting nothing but a sporadic blot here and an indistinct mark there. Mirrors appear in dark-ground monotypes such as *The Toilette (Arms)* (*La Toilette [Les Bras]*, c. 1880–85; fig. 1) as explicitly as they do in pastels such as *At the Milliner's* (*Chez la modiste*; fig. 2), from around 1882 and shown, like *Woman in Her Bath . . .*, in the Impressionist exhibition of 1886. As in *At the Milliner's*, the *Toilette* monotype shows a mirror from the back, so we cannot see the image reflected on its surface, but we nonetheless know that it is a mirror and it points to all the other mirrors present in the dark-ground monotypes: for example, in another contemporaneous monotype, *Woman at Her Toilette* (*A sa toilette*, c. 1885; Collections Jacques Doucet, Bibliothèque de l'Institute national d'histoire de l'art, Paris) in which a woman washes herself at a basin on a dresser in front of a mirror, this one turned toward us (though we see noth-

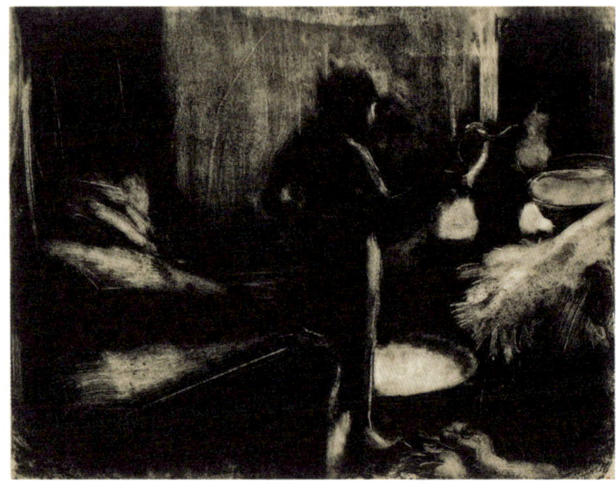

3. Hilaire-Germain-Edgar Degas. *The Tub (Le Tub),* 1876–77. Monotype on paper, plate: 16 9/16 × 21 5/16 in. (42 × 54.1 cm). Bibliothèque de l'Institut national d'histoire de l'Art. Collections Jacques Doucet

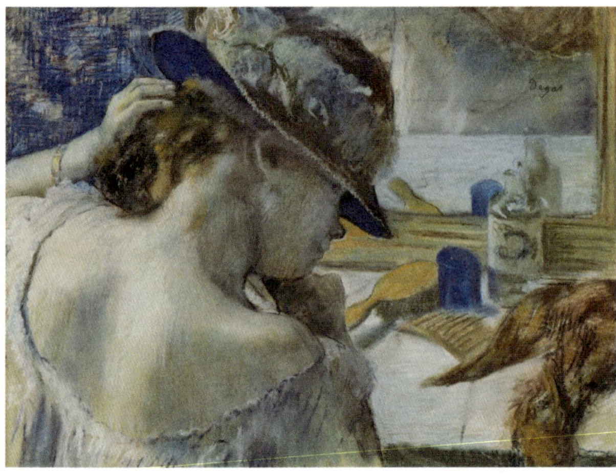

4. Hilaire-Germain-Edgar Degas. *In Front of the Mirror* (*Devant le miroir*). 1889. Pastel on paper, 19 5/16 × 25 3/16 in. (49 × 64 cm). Hamburger Kunsthalle, Hamburg

ing but a dark splotch mirrored in it), in *The Tub* (*Le Tub*, c. 1876–77; fig. 3), and in *Woman by a Fireplace* (1880–90; National Gallery of Art, Washington, D.C.) and *Woman Reading* (*Liseuse*, c. 1880–85; plate 106) as well.[8] Mirrors also appear in certain light-ground brothel monotypes, especially those featuring male clients, sometimes peering greedily at unclothed women.[9] And mirrors—never with much in the way of informative reflections—were a continuous theme for Degas throughout his career: they are found, for instance, in paintings such as *The Bellelli Family* (*La Famille Bellelli*) of 1867, *The Interior* (*Intérieur*)—otherwise known as *The Rape* (*Le Viol*)—of 1869, the early-1870s dance pictures, the 1877 *Dancer at the Photographer's Studio* (*Danseuse posant chez un photographe*), and *In Front of the Mirror* (*Devant le miroir*; fig. 5) of 1889, which picks up its mirror theme from the milliner series of 1882.[10]

Again, what looks like no more than murk in dark-ground versions of some of the monotype scenes with mirrors is fleshed out in their pastel-over-monotype corollaries. In *Woman Drying Herself after the Bath* (*Femme à sa toilette*, 1876–77; fig. 5), the pastelized cognate of the Doucet *Tub*, the boudoir vanity dresser is replete with pitcher, basin, cosmetic bottles, and of course a mirror in which they are reflected. In the first-impression monotype the mirror is a dark empty space, much like the somewhat sinister open doorway on the left. It does include a quick rendering of the pitcher's reflection, which turns the pitcher from dark to light, as if a photographic negative had been printed positive; otherwise the mirror shows nothing. Why then did Degas repeatedly include these mirrors? Why show mirrors that show almost nothing, repeatedly positioning them, as in *The Toilette (Arms)*, in counterpoint to unseeing acts of self-touching, as if to replace reflection with gestural reflexivity, vision with touch? Perhaps I have begun to answer my own question.

I have written elsewhere about the phenomenology of touch in the various mediums in which Degas involved himself, and of his identification with acts of touching (whether by dancers, bathers, or milliners) and more particularly with the reflexive touch—"*se toucher touchant*," as Maurice Merleau-Ponty put it—so insistently announced in the title of Suite of Female Nudes Bathing. . . .[11] What I would like to suggest here is that in addition to the monotypes' focus on darkness and the blindness that comes with it, the presence of dark mirrors counterpoises one kind of "reflexion" to another, negating the Lacanian "mirror stage" and its inauguration of the body's libidinal entrance into the order of the imaginary—the world of images—and substituting for it a regressive, tactile reflexivity that ties the body back to its own physical ground, the somatic ground of and prior to its emergence into sight.[12] It is in this pre-imaginary order of being that the ground of the dark-ground monotype does its work as well.

Other dark-ground monotypes render this somatic dimension of the body even more directly, none more forcefully than *Sleep* (*Le Sommeil*, c. 1880–85; plate 121). The pose of the female body here recalls some of Degas's sketches for his earliest history paintings, like those for the naked female corpses in the foreground of *Scene of War in the Middle Ages* (*Scène de guerre au Moyen Age*; fig. 6), from the mid-1860s, where the battlefield seems scattered with sculptural fragments rather than with the actual dead. The evocation of such poses underlines the crucial transformation in Degas's thinking about the human body—the *female* human body—in the intervening years. The implicit narrative and the figural elegance of the representation of the dead and dying in history painting, which was endorsed by a canon and carried a high pedigree, had already been undermined by the ambiguity of the poses he gave to the nude, and by his curious dispersal of the compositional devices of the tradition, such that the scene's disarray seems a consequence more of belatedness in art history than of war. But by the time of the monotype experiments, Degas had spent time in the twilight of the backstage, the boudoir, and the brothel, and he had gone much farther in returning the body to its presignifying ground of physical materiality and in submitting the narrative regime once occupied by history painting to the libidinal economy of the fleshly body. *Le jour* had been replaced by *la nuit*, semiosis by soma.[13]

Sleep brings all this to the fore in the context of the figural illegibility of the dark-ground method: are we looking at two heaving breasts or at a breast and a shoulder? Where is the second arm? Is the head turned toward us, into the pillow made by a swipe, or away? In doing so it ties that method to the somatic world of sleep and dream—or is it onanistic self-abandonment? In its close attention to a single, fairly decontextualized body, *Sleep* also zeroes in on the indeterminate constitution of that body through Degas's process of wiping, scratching, and rubbing out, a physical "denegation" in which what remains is the materiality of the ink that was laid down in the first place and then transferred to paper from the metal plate. This is one of a small group of such images—including the stunningly executed *Woman Reclining on Her Bed* (*Femme étendue sur son lit*, c. 1879–83; plate 100), the darker and lighter impressions of *The Toilette (Reading after the Bath)* (*La Toilette [La Lecture après le bain]*, c. 1880–85; plate 120), and *Woman Reading*, another treatment of the latter subject, this time in vertical format and with the woman's back turned—all of which zoom in on a single body in the dark, whether sleeping or reading, in a similar pose, and all of which resemble those early sketches for *Scene of War in the Middle Ages*.

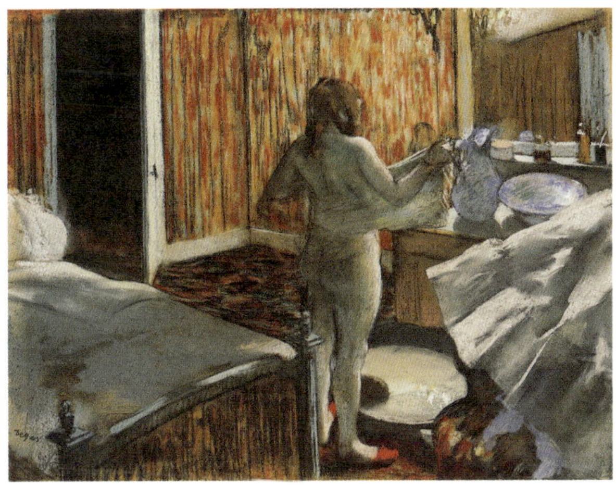

5. Hilaire-Germain-Edgar Degas. *Woman Drying Herself after the Bath* (*Femme à sa toilette*). 1876–77. Pastel over monotype on paper, 18 × 23 ¾ in. (45.7 × 60.3 cm). The Norton Simon Foundation

The figure in *Woman Reclining on her Bed* actually seems to have fallen asleep while reading, judging from the illuminated gas lamp on the left and, toward the right, the open page of the book or newspaper that seems to have fallen from her unconscious grasp. For some, the fact that the lamp has a dramatically phallic shape would irresistibly suggest a Lacanian reading—the phallocentrism of language—but I think it does something more persuasive: not only does it place the somatic body overtly under the sign of sex, it also sexualizes the transformation of dark into light and vice versa, and signals the inverting and doubling of one sex into the other—the single readable shape of the lamp into the doubled form of the woman's breasts and splayed legs, and the general undecidability of the apparently headless figure's contours.[14] Even more obviously and simply, the presence of the lamp and the fallen reading material sets reading and sleeping, light and dark—the light of the lamp and the page and the dark of the slumbering body—in explicit relation to one another. It is as if it were Degas's almost conscious intention to do just that.

From the beginning, Degas's experiments with monotype printing had been tied back to the materials and practices of photography: the copper and zinc plates that he used to print with were borrowed

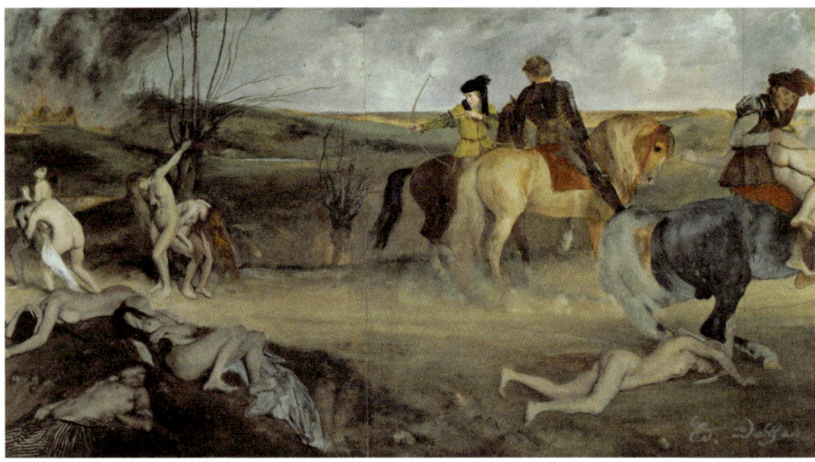

6. Hilaire-Germain-Edgar Degas. *Scene of War in the Middle Ages* (*Scène de guerre au Moyen Age*). c. 1865. Oil and petrol on paper glued on canvas, 33 7/16 × 57 7/8 in. (85 × 147 cm). Musée d'Orsay, Paris

not only from etching but from the daguerreotype.[15] When he actually turned to photography for a year or so around 1895, shortly after the medium's transformation by Kodak roll film and light, hand-held cameras, he chose to work with outmoded photographic materials that made the process more arduous and darkroom bound.[16] He did so with the help of his friend Louise Halévy (the wife of Ludovic), who did a lot of this darkroom work and who also appeared in a number of his photographs. Indeed, she seems to have agreed to figure darkness for him: the attachment of photography not only to the *camera obscura*—literally the dark room—but also to other things that took place in the dark, such as sleeping and reading by lamplight. Said Degas, "Daylight is too easy. What I want is difficult—the atmosphere of lamps or moonlight."[17] Louise Halévy helped him to play out that difficult desire.

Degas posed other people in the dark, including other members of the Halévy family.[18] It was Louise, though, whom he photographed not only sitting by lamplight in the antimacassar-decorated easy chair in which her son Daniel too sat to be photographed, and then sitting at a table with Degas, apparently reading to him from a newspaper that offers the only highlight in the scene (the lamp between them seems to be extinguished), but also asleep on a chaise longue, with possibly the same newspaper forgotten and lying loosely clasped in her hand, in a much more demure version of the indecorous *Woman Reclining on Her Bed*. While all three of these photographs focus on the difficult viewing conditions—seeing in the dark—that Degas preferred, and while *Louise Halévy Reading to Degas* (*Louise Halévy faisant la lecture à Degas*, 1895; fig. 7) implicates Degas's own growing eyesight problems in the scenario of having to be read to, *Louise Halévy Reclining* (*Louise Halévy allongée*, 1895; fig. 8) points directly to the somatic nature of what happens in the dark. In doing so it ties Degas's photographic practice back, equally directly, to the themes of his dark-ground monotypes.

Degas, remarkably, had drawn naked prostitutes with reading materials; it is much less surprising that Louise Halévy, an educated *haute bourgeoise* and a friend of his since childhood, should be shown reading.[19] There is certainly no whiff of an intention on his part to tie this friend of good family to the sexual topic of the brothel monotypes, but the photograph of Louise asleep in the dark, with the flare of lamplight to the right illuminating her extended arm and newspaper, nonetheless returns to several of the obsessions explored in the dark-ground monotypes: not only to the somatic realm of the darkened chamber—as if to extend the earlier opposition between dark and light, soma and semiosis, into a new contrast between the automatism of what takes place in the photographic dark and the waking intentionality of reading the lamplit page—but also to the darkness of another dark-ground medium. For the nocturnal photographs—none more so than *Louise Halévy Reclining*—stress the struggle of light to emerge from shadow, and specifically the emergence of a light figure out of an overall field of dark.[20]

Degas was one of a number of artists of this

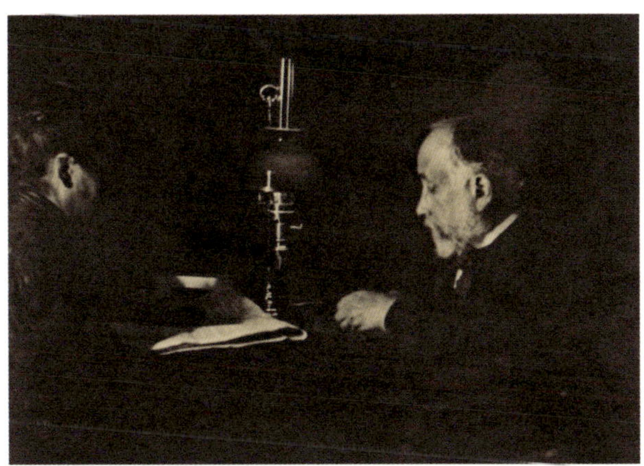

7. Hilaire-Germain-Edgar Degas. *Louise Halévy Reading to Degas* (*Louise Halévy faisant la lecture à Degas*). 1895. Gelatin silver print, 11 5⁄16 × 15 5⁄8 in. (28.7 × 39.7 cm). The J. Paul Getty Museum, Los Angeles

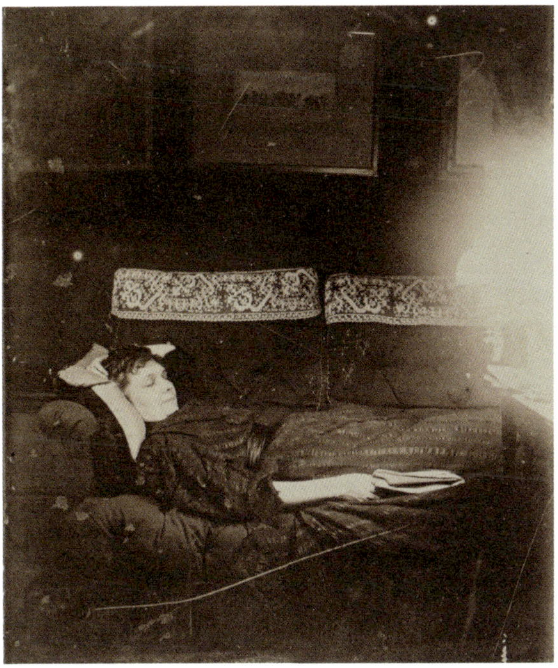

8. Hilaire-Germain-Edgar Degas. *Louise Halévy Reclining* (*Louise Halévy allongée*). 1895. Gelatin silver print, 3 3⁄4 × 3 1⁄16 in. (9.6 × 7.8 cm). The J. Paul Getty Museum, Los Angeles

period—Georges Seurat was another—who seems to have been struck by the phenomenon of the photographic negative, as well as by the negative-positive tonal system of the photograph, and to have learned from it in his drawing and printing practice.[21] But he was the only painter/draftsman to have experimented with that phenomenon and that system in the making of actual photographs, each of which was more or less, like the monotype, paradoxically a one-of-a-kind effort (or at most two or three of a kind). Indeed, several of his photographs of dancers explore the unstable chemistry of light-sensitive photographic emulsion as it shifts between positive and negative to produce proto-solarization effects (figs. 9, 10); he (and Louise Halévy) clearly embraced the experimental consequences of photographic chance, accident, and automatism, not to mention the photographic imbrication of light and dark and the mutual inextricability of figure and ground in photographs. While that experimentation yielded results that were specific to photography, it also demonstrated continuities between the handmade and the camera-made printed image.

Not the least of those continuities, insofar as Degas pursued them, was the interest in the optical doubling of the mirror reflection. The mirrors so prevalent in Degas's work in oil, pastel, and monotype made their way into his photographs as well. And they were often darkened, blinded mirrors, as in those suggested in the backgrounds of *Self-Portrait with Bartholomé's "Weeping Girl"* (c. 1895) and possibly of *Nude Drying Herself* (1896).[22] But the photograph in which the mirror appears most prominently and least ambiguously is the famous portrait *Pierre-Auguste Renoir and Stéphane Mallarmé* (1895; fig. 11).[23] One of the three positive enlargements of Degas's negative was inscribed by the poet Paul Valéry with the following note: "This photograph was given me by Degas, whose ghostly reflection and camera appear in the mirror. Mallarmé is standing beside Renoir, who is sitting on the sofa. Degas inflicted on them a pose for fifteen minutes, by the light of nine oil lamps. . . . In the mirror can be seen the shadowy figures of Mme. Mallarmé and her daughter."[24]

Degas, "whose ghostly reflection and camera appear in the mirror," often inflicted long poses by lamplight on the subjects of his photographs, and sleeping was one way of holding still for upward of fifteen minutes. Nobody has fallen asleep in the portrait of Renoir and Mallarmé, but what that photograph shows in the mirror so indistinctly—the glass eye of the camera, which is both doubled *by* and the double *of* the glassy glare of the mirror; the dark cloth over the hidden body of the artist-photographer; the blaze of light; and the smudges that denote two female heads—announces the same deep relation to the world of nocturnal darkness that is explored in Degas's monotypes, and not only in the fact that

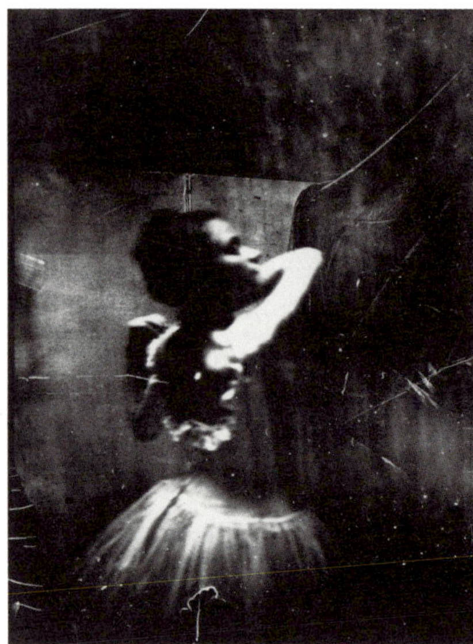

9. Hilaire-Germain-Edgar Degas. *Dancer Adjusting Her Shoulder Strap* (*Danseuse ajustant sa bretelle*). 1895–96. Modern print from gelatin dry-plate negative, 7 ¹⁄₁₆ × 5 ⅛ in. (18 × 13 cm). Bibliothèque nationale de France, Paris

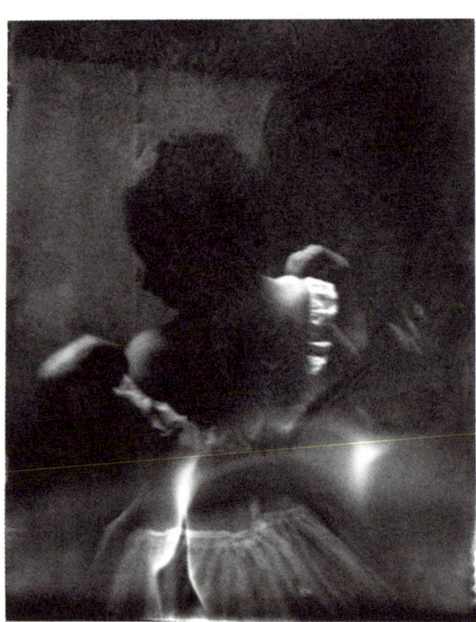

10. Hilaire-Germain-Edgar Degas. *Dancer Adjusting Her Two Shoulder Straps* (*Danseuse ajustant ses deux bretelles*). 1895–96. Modern print from gelatin dry-plate negative, 7 ¹⁄₁₆ × 5 ⅛ in. (18 × 13 cm). Bibliothèque nationale de France, Paris

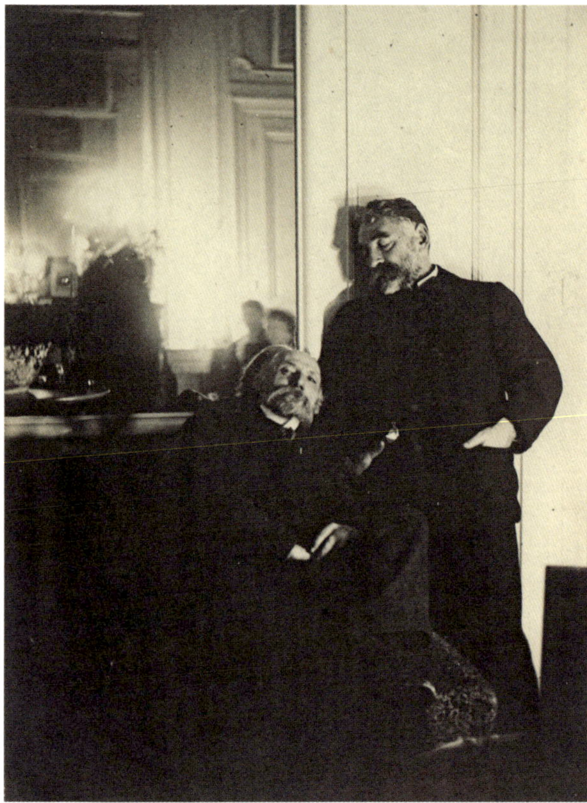

11. Hilaire-Germain-Edgar Degas. *Pierre-Auguste Renoir and Stéphane Mallarmé* (*Pierre-Auguste Renoir et Stéphane Mallarmé*). December 1895. Gelatin silver print, 15 ⅜ × 11 ³⁄₁₆ in. (39.1 × 28.4 cm). The Museum of Modern Art, New York. Gift of Paul F. Walter

this photograph was taken at night. For the flare of light that shows nothing but itself is intertwined with the darkness adjacent to it. And together with the dark field of clothed male bodies, painter and writer merging into one another, in the shadowy foreground that makes up so much of the image, that blinding flash of light/dark declares the image to be as much skiagraph as photograph, dependent on darkness as much as on light, on somatic obscurity as much as on illuminated night. Reflecting back on the dark-ground monotypes, it also suggests a kinship with a kind of handmaking in which no conscious gesture is free of the unconscious substrate, at once material, corporeal, and psychic, out of which it is born.

1. Edgar Degas's first monotype, *The Ballet Master*, executed in the dark-ground manner, was made in c. 1876; his last were executed around 1893. My focus is on the dark-ground treatment of the nocturnal subject of the nude bather. On the monotypes see especially Eugenia Parry Janis, Degas Monotypes: Essay, Catalogue & Checklist (Cambridge, Mass.: Fogg Art Museum, Harvard University, 1968); Jean Adhémar and Françoise Cachin, *Degas: The Complete Etchings, Lithographs and Monotypes,* trans. Jane Brenton (London: Thames & Hudson, 1974); and Richard Kendall, "The Impromptu Print: Degas's Monotypes and Their Technical Significance," in *Degas Intime* (Copenhagen: Ordrupgaard, 1994), n.p. See also Theodore Reff, "The Technical Aspects of Degas's Art," *Metropolitan Museum Journal* 4 (1971):141–66.

2. On the term "de-venustation" see Leo Steinberg, "The Algerian Women and Picasso at Large," *Other Criteria: Confrontations with Twentieth-Century Art* (Oxford: at the University Press, 1972), pp. 125–234.
3. Joris Karl Huysmans, *Certains* (Paris: Tresse & Stock, 1889), p. 23, quoted here from my own *Odd Man Out: Readings of the Work and Reputation of Edgar Degas* (Chicago and London: The University of Chicago Press, 1991), p. 181.
4. The term "optical unconscious" comes from Walter Benjamin's essay "A Small History of Photography," 1931, in *One-way Street and Other Writings*, trans. Edmund Jephcott and Kingsley Shorter (London: New Left Books, 1979), pp. 240–57. See Rosalind Krauss, *The Optical Unconscious* (Cambridge, Mass., and London: The MIT Press, October Books, 1993).
5. See Wolfram Pichler, "Zur Kunstgeschichte des Bildfeldes," in Gottfried Böhm and Matteo Burioni, eds., *Der Grund. Das Feld des Sichtbaren* (Munich: Wilhelm Fink Verlag, 2012), pp. 440–72.
6. On Degas and the subject of prostitution see Charles Bernheimer, *Figures of Ill Repute: Representing Prostitution in Nineteenth-Century France* (Cambridge, Mass.: Harvard University Press, 1989), and Hollis Clayton, *Painted Love: Prostitution and French Art of the Impressionist Era* (New Haven and London: Yale University Press, 1991). Degas exhibited some of his monotypes in the 1877 Impressionist exhibition, and one critic identified at least one as a brothel subject, but for the most part they remained clandestine works; see Kendall, "The Impromptu Print."
7. On the *Famille Cardinal* and the brothel monotypes see my *Odd Man Out*, pp. 65–72, 151–56, and Kathryn Brown's essay in the present volume.
8. On *Woman Reading* and other dark-ground monotypes see George T. M. Shackelford and Xavier Rey, *Degas and the Nude*, exh. cat. (Boston: Museum of Fine Arts, 2011), pp. 69–119.
9. I am referring here to several light-ground monotypes made between 1877 and 1880, including *Admiration*, *Femme nue se coiffant*, and *Le Tub*. See Janis, *Degas Monotypes*, nos. 184, 185, and 189.
10. On *Devant le miroir* see my "Degas in the Studio: Embodying Medium, Materializing the Body," in Martin Schwander, ed., *Edgar Degas: The Late Work* (Basel: Fondation Beyeler, 2012), pp. 23–31.
11. See Maurice Merleau-Ponty, "L'Expérience du corps et la psychologie classique," in *Phénoménologie de la perception* (Paris: Gallimard, 1945), pp. 106–13, Eng. trans. as "The Experience of the Body and Classical Psychology," *Phenomenology of Perception*, trans. Colin Smith (London and Henley: Routledge and Kegan Paul, 1962), pp. 90–97. On p. 93 of the English edition, Merleau-Ponty speaks specifically of "double sensations," of hands alternating between the function of "touching" and "touched": "The body catches itself from the outside engaged in a cognitive process; it tries *to touch itself while being touched*, and initiates 'a kind of reflection' which is sufficient to distinguish it from objects" ("Le corps se surprend lui-même de l'extérieur en train d'exercer une function de connaissance, il essaye de *se toucher touchant*, il ébauche 'une sorte de réflexion' et cela suffirait pour le distinguer des objets"; my emphasis), cited in my "Degas in the Studio," pp. 26, 31.
12. See Jacques Lacan, "The Mirror Stage as Formative of the Function of the I in Psychoanalytic Experience (1949)," *Ecrits: A Selection*, trans. Alan Sheridan (New York: W.W. Norton, 1982), pp. 1–6.
13. In 1879, Degas planned but did not realize a journal evocatively titled *Le Jour et la nuit*. See Marc Rosen and Susan Pinsky, "The Medium as Muse: Innovations and Intersections in Printmaking," in Kimberly A. Jones et al., *Degas/Cassatt*, exh. cat. (Washington, D.C.: The National Gallery of Art, and New York: Prestel Publishing, 2014), pp. 100–11.
14. See Lacan, "The Signification of the Phallus," in *Ecrits*, pp. 215–22. See also Luce Irigaray, *Ce sexe qui n'en est pas un* (Paris: Edition de Minuit, 1977), Eng. trans. as *This Sex Which Is Not One*, trans. Catherine Porter (Ithaca: Cornell University Press, 1985).
15. See Kendall, "The Impromptu Print," on Degas's use of the daguerreotype plate for some of his monotypes, as well as Karl Buchberg and Laura Neufeld's essay in the present volume.
16. See Malcolm Daniel, *Edgar Degas, Photographer*, exh. cat. (New York: The Metropolitan Museum of Art, 1998), p. 32, 136. See also Antoine Terrasse, *Degas et la photographie* (Paris: Denoel, 1983), and Dorothy Kosinski, *The Artist and the Camera: Degas to Picasso*, exh. cat. (Dallas: Dallas Museum of Art, 1999).
17. Degas, quoted in Daniel Halévy's journal for November 4, 1895. See Daniel Halévy, *Degas parle* (Paris: Editions de Fallois, 1995), p. 140, quoted in Daniel, *Edgar Degas, Photographer*, p. 24. On Degas's growing difficulties with his eyesight, which went all the way back to the Siege of Paris during the Franco-Prussian war, see Michael F. Marmor, *Degas through His own Eyes: Visual Disability and the Late Style of Degas* (Paris: Somogy Editions d'Art, 2002). See also my review of the Metropolitan Museum's show *Edgar Degas, Photographer*, in which I raise questions about eyesight, not as the determinant of Degas's photographs or late style, but rather as part and parcel of their content: "Edgar Degas," *Artforum* 37, no. 5 (January 1999).
18. On the Halévy family see Henri Loyrette, ed., *Entre le théâtre et l'histoire. La Famille Halévy, 1790–1960*, exh. cat. for Musée d'Orsay, Paris (Paris: Fayard/RMN, 1996). See also my "The Art of Unlearning," in *A Degas Sketchbook*, (Los Angeles: The J. Paul Getty Trust, 2000), pp. 1–65.
19. The fact that Degas depicted prostitutes as literate is one piece of evidence, among others, that runs counter to the frequent charges of misogyny that have been leveled against him and that in many respects seem to be supported by the brothel monotypes more than any others of his works. On the subject of women reading see Linda Nochlin's essay "Mary Cassatt's Modernity," in her *Representing Women* (London: Thames & Hudson, 1999), pp. 180–215.
20. On these photographic portraits see Douglas Crimp, "Positive/Negative: A Note on Degas's Photographs," *October* 5 (Summer 1978): 89–100.
21. On Seurat's dark-ground conte-crayon drawings see my "Seurat's Media, or a Matrix of Materialities," in *Grey Room* 58 (Winter 2015):6–25.
22. See my "Degas in the Studio: Embodying Medium, Materializing the Body," in Schwander, ed., *Edgar Degas: The Late Work*, esp. pp. 29–30.
23. On Degas's photographs and the mirror stage see the last chapter of my *Odd Man Out* ("The Myth of Degas," pp. 211–44), as well as my "Reflections on the Mirror: Painting, Photography and the Self-Portraits of Edgar Degas," *Representations* 22 (Spring 1988):108–41.
24. The inscription appears on the mount of the print in the Bibliothèque Littéraire Jacques Doucet, Paris, inv. 79. Quoted in Daniel, *Edgar Degas, Photographer*, p. 130.

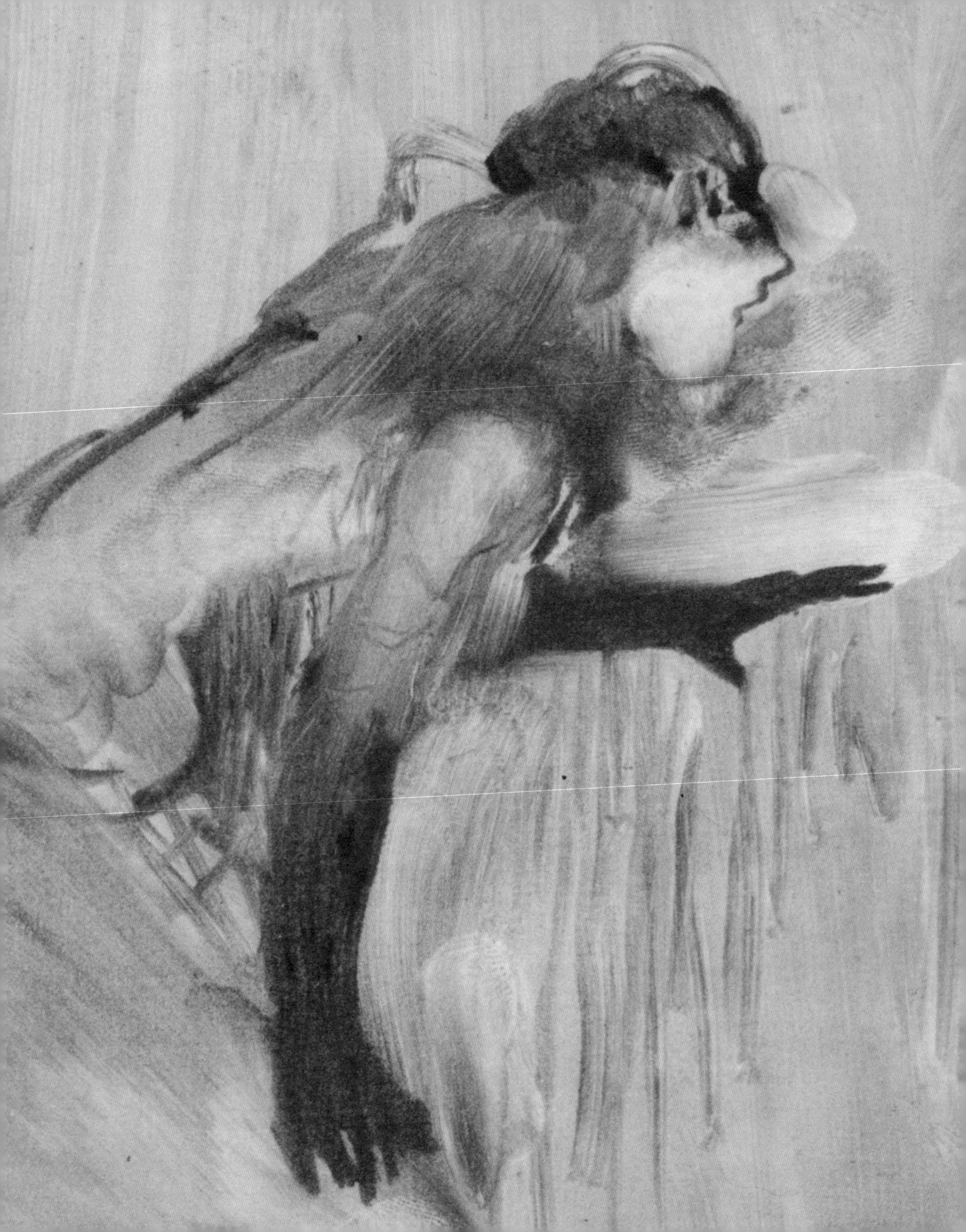

Indelible Ink: Degas's Methods and Materials

Karl Buchberg and Laura Neufeld

Degas used the phrase "drawings made with greasy ink and put through a press" to describe the process that we now term monotype.[1] What might seem from his description to be a simple medium led to a complex body of work. Two materials, ink and paper, combined to form many of his most daring monotypes. Once he had printed an image he could complicate that process by layering pastel over the black ink, transforming a monochrome impression into a multilayered colored world. Later on, he would print with oil paint rather than ink, sometimes once again enhancing the result with pastel.

Monotypes are produced by applying printing ink or oil paint to a clean unmarked printing plate. Degas used both a brush and a dabber, a traditional intaglio printing tool comprising a thick roll of fabric with a flat edge, to apply the media.[2] A sheet of damp paper is placed over the plate, and the image is transferred through pressure as the plate and paper are passed between the flat metal bed and adjustable roller of an etching press.

Intaglio print techniques create permanent marks physically cut or chemically bitten into the plate to hold ink, but a monotype's ink rests only on the plate's surface. As a result, a plate will typically yield just one strong print. A second or third print can be made, however, with diminishing image intensity, from residual ink on the plate. Prints pulled from the same plate are called "cognates." A second print can also be taken directly from the first print while the ink is still wet. This technique produces a "counterproof," and the composition will be a mirror image of the first print. When ink or oil paint is added to the plate between the first and second pull, each is then termed a "state."

Plates

Degas produced monotypes from four types of plate: copper, zinc, daguerreotype plates, and celluloid. Copper and zinc plates are traditionally used for intaglio printmaking and both are mentioned in accounts of Degas's studio practice.[3] A zinc monotype plate holding dried ink depicting a brothel scene was found in Degas's studio after his death and is now in the collection of the Bibliothèque nationale de France, Paris (fig. 1).

Daguerreotype plates are composed of a thin layer of silver adhered to a copper substrate.[4] Degas's use of daguerreotype plates was first identified by Janet Buerger and Barbara Stern Shapiro, who noted the appearance of manufacturer's stamps on several café-concert, brothel, and bather prints.[5] The corners of daguerreotype plates were often bent slightly backward when the plates were inserted into a vice to be polished. This process left crimps in the corners, and the crimps in turn left marks visible in many of Degas's monotypes (see, e.g., plate 77).

Hilaire-Germain-Edgar Degas. *Café-Concert Singer* (*Chanteuse de café-concert*). c. 1877. Detail of plate 36

Degas's inscriptions on two monotypes, *Fantasy* and *Fantasy, Nude Woman* (*Fantaisie*, c. 1880–85; plate 122), indicate that he printed them from celluloid.[6] A synthetic compound derived from nitrocellulose and camphor, celluloid was patented in 1870 and was initially used as a replacement for ivory in products such as billiard balls. Photographers tested celluloid sheets as a substitute for glass-plate negatives and the material was later used in the production of flexible roll films for cameras.[7] Degas may have been interested in the material for its transparency, which would have allowed him to produce an image on the plate by tracing, a method he often used to resolve compositions of his paintings. A transparent plate would also have allowed him to look at the verso and see the image in reverse before it was printed. His use of celluloid was limited, however, suggesting that despite these potential advantages it was not a preferred printing matrix for him.

Degas produced monotypes using two distinct, seemingly opposite techniques. In the dark-field or subtractive method, ink is applied to the whole plate and the image is created by selectively removing it from the surface. Working from dark to light, this method can produce dramatic tonal compositions (see plate 102). In the light-field or additive method the image is made by drawing with ink directly on the plate, often with a brush (see plate 57).

Cognate pairs exist in both dark-field and light-field images when a second impression was made. Degas could elaborate either impression but usually chose the second; sometimes he worked on both. Many monotypes exist only as a single impression: a second pull may not have been made, may not be understood as related to a first pull, may have been lost, destroyed, or is simply undiscovered.

Two trends in plate size are apparent in Degas's monotypes. Dark-field works, particularly those of dancers, nudes, and bathers, were printed from larger-scale rectangular plates, probably copper or zinc. The largest plate, measuring 22 ⅜ by 28 ⅜ inches (58 by 72 cm), was used for Degas's first monotype, *The Ballet Master* (*Le Maître de ballet*, c. 1876; plate 17), which he made with his friend and fellow artist Ludovic-Napoléon Lepic. Given its shared plate-mark dimensions, *The Dancing Lesson* (*La Leçon de danse*, c. 1877; plate 18) may

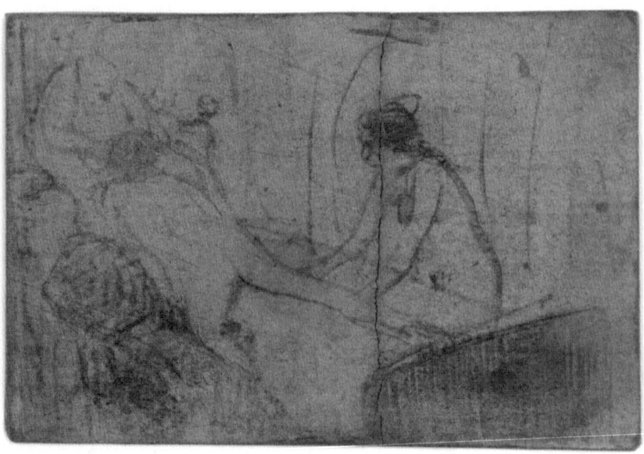

1. Zinc plate with inking for Degas's monotype *Brothel Scene* (*Scène de maison close*). 4 ¼ × 6 ¼ in. (10.8 × 15.9 cm). Bibliothèque nationale de France, Paris

also have been composed on this plate. The two prints also share a planisher's stamp—a stamp embossed on the back of a copper or zinc plate, identifying the firm that produced it—reading "H. GODARD, RUE DE LA HUCHETTE 27, PARIS," in the upper-right corner. *The Ballet Master* shows a second identical stamp at the lower left, absent from *The Dancing Lesson*, but this could be due to the removal of all ink in that area during the wiping process. The occurrence of planisher's stamps indicates that the monotypes were executed on the back side of the plate; perhaps there was already an etched image on the front of the plate and the plate was being reused. These early monotypes may have been made on a plate provided by Lepic, and the large scale, not seen in later monotypes, may be indicative of his influence and instruction.

Degas's general selection of larger plates for dark-field monotypes reflects the physical demands of the technique. The manipulation and removal of ink with bulky tools like wide brushes, rags, and fingertips is facilitated by a larger format. Conversely the light-field monotypes depicting brothels and scenes of modern life, as well as Degas's illustrations for Ludovic Halévy's Cardinal-family (*Famille Cardinal*) stories, were mostly printed from intimately scaled plates approximately 6 5⁄16 by 8 7⁄16 inches (16 by 21.5 cm) or 4 ¾ by 6 5⁄16 inches (12 by 16 cm). These respectively correspond to the standard dimensions of full- and half-size daguerreotype plates.[8] At about 4 ¼ by 6 ¼ inches (10.8 by 15.9 cm), the zinc plate in the Bibliothèque nationale is similarly proportioned. The use of two plate types in a similar size suggests a preference for this format, but the smaller scale may also correspond to Degas's intentions for the images: the brothel scenes were private works that he did not widely share and the Cardinal Family series were intended as illustrations for Halévy's book. Common plate-mark dimensions in prints from different series of monotypes suggest that Degas kept a stock of different plates in his studio, basing his selection of format in part on the image to be made. The frequency of a certain plate size within a group of monotypes suggests a serial working method in which the same plate is used repeatedly: since the plate is not marred in the printing process, it only requires cleaning before the next use. In the brothel and Cardinal Family series this notion is reinforced if the monotypes are viewed sequentially, when the repetition of the figures may suggest a narrative.

Degas's final series of monotypes were landscapes in oil colors. The majority of these works were printed in a horizontal orientation from a plate measuring 11 13⁄16 by 15 ¾ inches (30 by 40 cm), a plate size that is unique to this series. These works may have been executed while Degas was visiting his friend and fellow printmaker Georges Jeanniot on a trip to Diénay in the Côte d'Or. After Degas's death Jeanniot wrote an exuberant account of Degas's visit and production of landscape monotypes that elucidates our understanding of the process.[9]

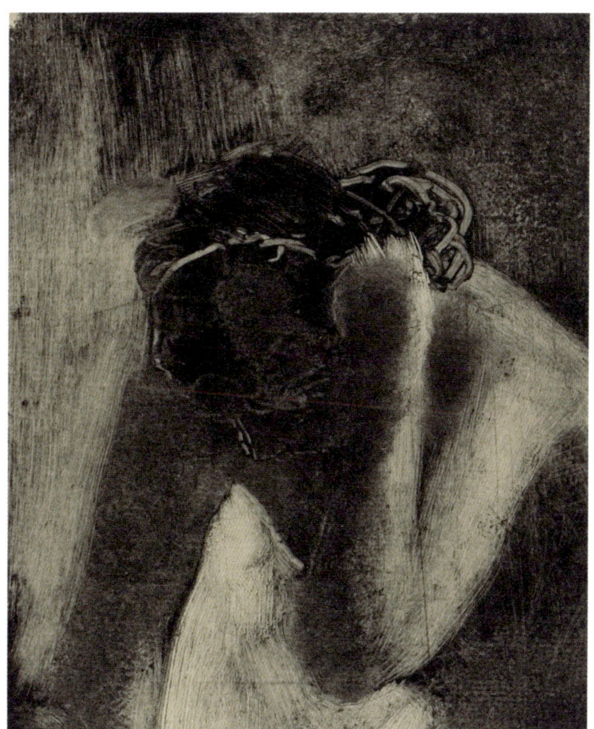

2. Hilaire-Germain-Edgar Degas. *The Bath* (*La Toilette [Le Bain]*). c. 1880–85. Detail of plate 112

Media, Tools, and Manipulation

Monotype is a deceptively simple technique in that the application of ink to plate can be done quickly and requires few specialized tools. Etching ink is composed of ground pigment mixed with boiled linseed oil.[10] Common pigments used to color black etching ink in Degas's time were lamp black, a color made from the soot of burned fat, oil, or tar resin; Frankfurt black, which was produced by charring wine lees and grape vines; and bone black, made from burned animal bones. The black inks used by Degas vary in both tone and consistency. Black ink was made warmer or cooler by adding small amounts of brown earth or blue pigments.[11] When viewed under low magnification, the ink in some monotypes appears coarse and grainy, probably as a result of insufficient grinding of the pigment when the ink was prepared. In second impressions this graininess is sometimes visible to the naked eye, as the coarsest particles of pigment continue to print darkly even though the surrounding ink is faint. Degas's landscape monotypes were printed with oil colors, identical, it is assumed, to artists' oil paints.[12] Colored printers' inks existed at the time; Degas must have consciously decided not to use them. Oil paints were readily available in an enormous variety of colors and his use of them for monotypes was an innovation.

The transfer of the image from plate to paper always included an element of chance and unpredictability. The viscosity of the printing ink needed to be adjusted by adding oil or solvent to achieve individual effects. Dark-field monotypes required a stiffer ink that would retain the marks made in it; fine details and highlights, which Degas made with a pointed tool such as the blunt end of a brush (fig. 2). For the light-field monotypes, which started with a blank plate rather than with a plate covered in a layer of ink, Degas worked with brushes but also with his fingers and hands. The ink was diluted in order to be effectively applied by brush and also for a variety of visual effects, mostly painterly (fig. 3).[13] Printing ink was formulated with a thick viscosity in order to transfer to

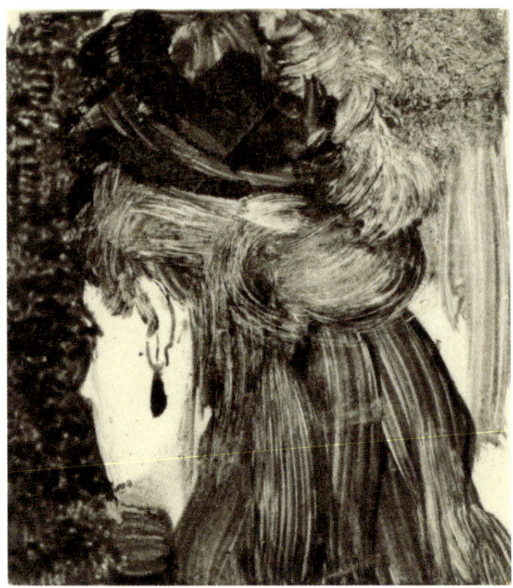

3. Hilaire-Germain-Edgar Degas. *The Jet Earring* (*Profil perdu à la boucle d'oreille*). 1876–77. Detail of plate 56

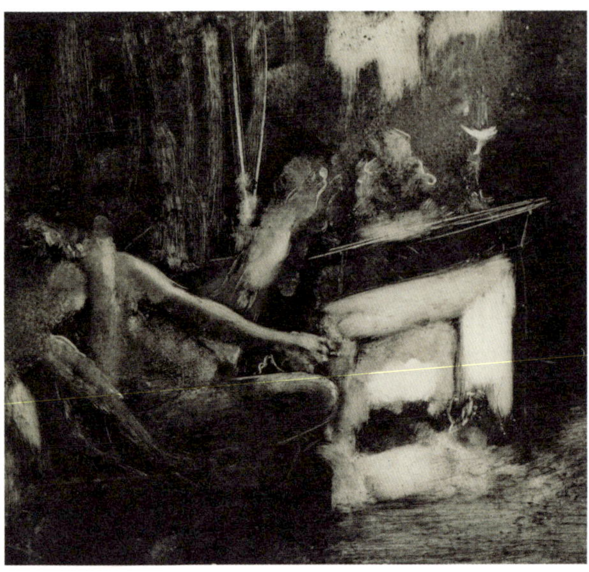

4. Hilaire-Germain-Edgar Degas. *The Fireside* (*Le Foyer [La Cheminée]*). c. 1880–85. Detail of plate 102

the dampened paper without smearing. Oil paints, on the other hand, flattened and ran under the pressure of the press, creating unexpected effects noticeable in Degas's landscapes. He could heighten these effects by varying the thickness of the application. Over time, the oil medium has leached into the paper to create "haloes," a hallmark of oil applied to paper (see plate 126). In the landscape monotypes Degas seems to revel in experimenting with a new combination of medium and technique.

Degas's ink-removal techniques varied widely and experimentally. He used a variety of tools to make marks in the ink, including stiff-bristled brushes, rags, sponges, the wooden end of a brush, and, again, his own hands and fingers (fig. 4). He might also manipulate the consistency of the ink, applying solvent, probably turpentine, to the plate with a brush to produce watery effects. His technique was delicate and sometimes suggested the decorative patterns on wallpaper and textiles (see plate 97).

Scholars have tended to group Degas's monotypes into the broad categories of dark field and light field, but many were a sophisticated combination of the two. A close examination of *Song of the Scissors* (*Chanson des Ciseaux*, c. 1877–78; plate 37) reveals a dark-field monotype with light-field additions. The plate was covered overall with black ink, slightly thinned to give it a "silvery grey" color.[14] The plate was then selectively wiped clean of ink, at left to create the white globes of light, at right around the sitter's head and shoulders, and at the lower left and center. The highlights of the sitter's face were modeled with either a rag or the artist's fingers (fig. 5). Some remaining areas were reworked with a brush, most noticeably her hat. Her bracelet, fingers, proper-right shoulder line, V-shaped garment opening, and the darks on the scissors were added with a stiffer black ink applied by brush. A thin wash of black ink was then added at the upper right, lower left, and just below the light globes, areas that had initially been wiped clean of ink. The white line of the scissor was made with the back end of a brush. Reticulation—graininess—in some areas may have been caused by incomplete mixing of ink with the solvent. The bottom edge of the plate was fed into the press first; as it moved through the rollers this inadequately mixed ink, visible as dark spots, produced vertical streaks. The pooling of ink along the top edge was created as the plate exited the press rollers.

Pauline and Virginie Conversing with Admirers (*Pauline et Virginie Cardinal bavardant avec des admirateurs*, c. 1876–77; plate 77) is an example of a work begun in the light-field manner and then augmented using subtractive techniques. The male figures and the architectural setting were brushed onto the plate, with different dilutions of ink for different intensities of black. The background is predominantly thin washes to achieve the very light gray, applied over

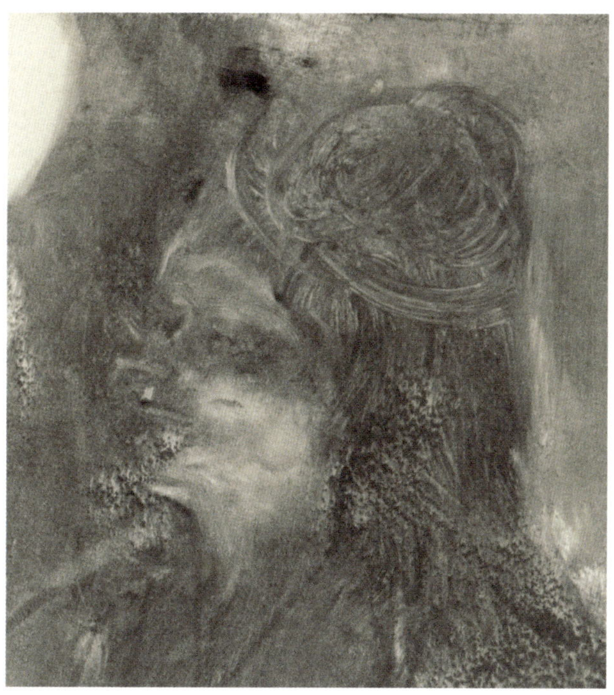

5. Hilaire-Germain-Edgar Degas. *Song of the Scissors* (*La Chanson des ciseaux*). c. 1877–78. Detail of plate 37

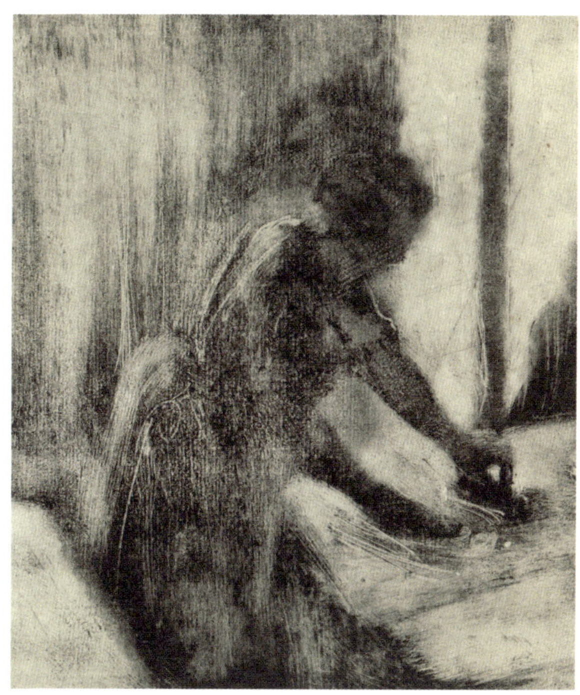

6. Hilaire-Germain-Edgar Degas. *Ironing Women* (*Les Repasseuses*). c. 1877–79. Detail of plate 55

some existing brushed line work. The door openings and light pools were then wiped. The area between the two main male figures at the center and the three at the left was selectively removed, defining both the lower front of one male figure and the lower part of the ballerinas' tutus. The women's bodies were then defined with brushwork. The top hats of the two center figures and one figure's clasped hands were further defined with the end of a brush.

Paper

Degas used a variety of paper for his monotypes: Western laid papers, Western wove papers, China papers, and much more rarely Bristol board (or cardstock). One work made on a blue-colored Bristol board has faded and now appears off-white, likely because of light exposure but also perhaps from the acidity in the paper affecting unstable colorants. This opens the possibility that other works were originally executed on colored papers.[15]

Before Degas began making monotypes, he used three main categories of paper for printmaking, laid, wove, and Asian, apparently with no clear preference between them.[16] This is in contrast to the papers chosen for monotypes. There is a relationship between image and paper choice. Laid paper has a pronounced texture produced during the paper-making process. Wet pulp is deposited on a screen made of thin parallel bars held in place by perpendicular rows of stitching, which creates in the finished sheet the laid lines, from the bars, and chain lines, from the stitching. In the monotype *Ironing Women* (*Les Repasseuses*, c. 1877–79; plate 55) this pattern is revealed by the way the ink sits on the surface, and is analogous to the way stick media, such as charcoal, exploit the surface of laid paper (fig. 6). Degas's application of dry pastel also retains the distinctive texture of the paper (fig. 7). In contrast, the smooth surface of wove paper, cast on a finely woven wire mesh, allowed for a meticulous transfer of ink from the plate to the paper sheet. Degas also used a thin, Asian-style paper identified in the monotype literature as "China paper," "a descriptive term characterizing a soft, thin, absorbent paper, relatively opaque and pearl grey to ivory white in colour."[17] China paper was highly absorbent, which allowed it to accept an ink impression extremely well. Degas used it for many of the light-field monotypes, where it translated the delicacy of the brush-applied ink with maximum effectiveness.[18]

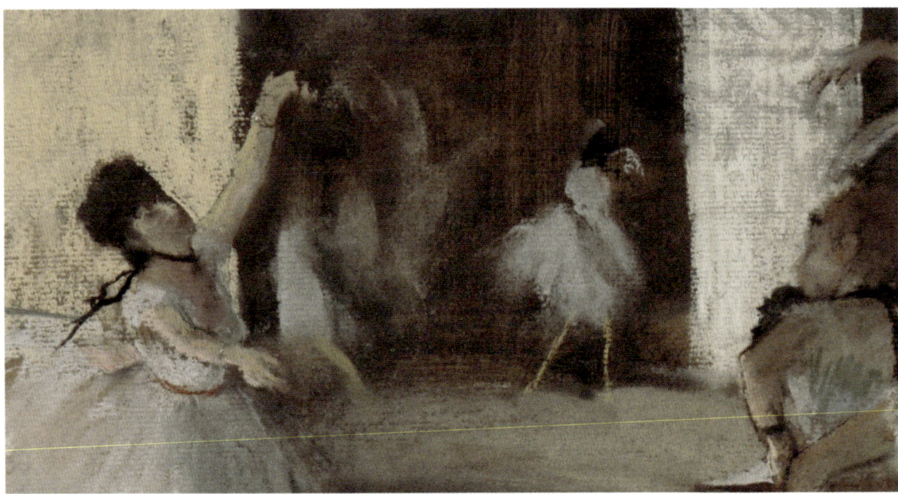

7. Hilaire-Germain-Edgar Degas. *The Dance Lesson* (*La Leçon de danse*). c. 1876. Detail of plate 19

Applied Media

Degas added media—watercolor, charcoal, oil paint, gouache, distemper, and predominantly pastel—to the printed monotypes. In some works small areas of pastel could be applied to locally accentuate a composition, as in *The Name Day of the Madam* (*La Fête de la patronne*, c. 1877–79; plate 85). In others a complex layered structure of pastel would allow him to totally obscure the monotype underneath, a strategy that could alter the printed composition either subtly or significantly.

The printed image functioned as an underdrawing that Degas would elaborate. In addition, the monotype provided a dark ground as a foil for subsequent media layers. Pastel sits differently over monotype ink than over bare paper. In *Female Nude Reclining* (*Femme nue couchée*, c. 1888–90; plate 101), for example, Degas extended the composition above and below the printed area. Here the paper fibers were not compressed by the pressure of the plate and the pastel appears more diffuse.

As one of the greatest of all pastel artists, Degas summoned a wide range of techniques of application and manipulation. The most basic method of application was using the commercially available pastel in its most familiar format, the stick. Stroke size and shape could be adjusted by using a pastel stick that had been formed into a point, or conversely a broader stroke using the side of the pastel. This dry pastel could be left as distinct strokes or, once on the paper, could be manipulated with a stump—a pointed rolled paper—to blend adjacent colored strokes, or with a wet brush for a more painterly mixing. On the paper, pastel could also be locally moistened with steam or boiling water, and then manipulated with a brush to translate fluffy pastel passages into a denser painterly layer. Degas also used his fingers directly on the sheet to apply, blend, and remove pastel, imparting a highly tactile quality to the image. He scored a layer of pastel with a pointed implement such as the back end of a brush, exposing an underlying layer or color and creating visual emphasis and excitement.

Another device was to dip the pastel stick into either water or a solvent such as turpentine before applying it to paper, creating a denser application, less fluffy than untreated pastel. More complex was the mixture of pastel with other media. Degas utilized and experimented with the following traditional pastel techniques, although he often pushed them to their limits. A paste made from crushed pastel and water was called *pastel à l'eau* and was applied with a brush. A mixture of crushed pastel and an adhesive made of either casein or animal glue created a combination called *détrempe à pastel*, which created a stronger, less flaky layer that would not be affected by subsequent applications of pastel. Pastel was also mixed with *essence*, a nonaqueous medium made by leaching most of the oil medium out of oil paint and then adding turpentine to the remaining paint. The resulting combination could be more or less opaque depending on the amount of solvent.[19]

To prevent a later application of pastel from disturbing the one below, Degas would fix the earlier one. He is known to have used steam and water mist to secure dry pastel particles; he is also thought to have employed other fixatives, and technical studies show that one of these might have been a casein adhesive.[20] Passages of pastel in the final layer were locally left unfixed to exploit the optical difference between the compacted fixed and the particulate unfixed pastel.

Degas's monotypes began with the exploration of a simple technique. The exploration became more important than the technique. Degas's physical interaction with the ink created powerful monochrome impressions. From a single layer of ink, the monotypes expanded to encompass the various media that Degas used to such great advantage. The investigation of each of these various media elucidates Degas's technical facility without ever fully demystifying the magic of this body of work.

Our understanding of Degas's monotype technique rests on past scholarship. A landmark 1968 publication by Eugenia Parry Janis first fully introduced these works and remains the standard reference: Janis, *Degas Monotypes: Essay, Catalogue & Checklist*, exh. cat. (Cambridge, Mass.: Fogg Art Museum, Harvard University, 1968). Denis Rouart covers the full range of the artist's methods in *Degas à la recherche de sa technique* (Paris: Floury, 1945), Eng. trans. as *Degas in Search of His Technique*, trans. Pia C. DeSantis, Sarah L. Fisher, and Shelley Fletcher (Geneva: Editions d'Art Albert Skira, 1988). Rouart's grandfather, Henri Rouart, was a friend of Degas's and the book is based on his accounts. Anne F. Maheux has published extensively on Degas's pastel technique: see Jean Sutherland Boggs and Maheux, *Degas Pastels* (New York: George Braziller, 1992); Maheux, *Degas Pastels*, exh. cat. (Ottawa: National Gallery of Canada, 1988); and Maheux and Peter Zegers, "Degas Pastel Research Project: A Progress Report," in *Preprints of Papers Presented at the Fourteenth Annual Meeting, Chicago, Illinois, 21–25 May 1986* (Washington, D.C.: The American Institute for Conservation of Historic and Artistic Works, 1986). Publications by Marjorie Shelley and Thea Burns contributed to our understanding of pastel techniques: Shelley, "American Pastels of the Late Nineteenth & Early Twentieth Centuries: Materials and Techniques," in *American Pastels in the Metropolitan Museum of Art* (New York: The Metropolitan Museum of Art, 1989), and Burns, *The Invention of Pastel Painting* (London: Archetype Publications, 2007). Richard Kendall incorporates technical issues in his extensive research on Degas: see particularly his *Degas Landscapes*, exh. cat. (New York: The Metropolitan Museum of Art, in association with Yale University Press, New Haven, 1993). Degas's choices of papers are detailed in Douglas Druick and Zegers, "Degas and the Printed Image, 1856–1914," and Roy L. Perkinson, "Degas's Printing Papers," both in Sue Welsh Reed and Barbara Stern Shapiro, *Edgar Degas: The Painter as Printmaker*, exh. cat. (Boston: Museum of Fine Arts, 1984). pp. xv–lxxii and 255–58 respectively, as well as in Kimberly Schenck, "The Role of China Paper in Nineteenth-Century French Printmaking," in *Looking at Paper: Evidence and Interpretation* (Ottawa: Canadian Conservation Institute, 1999), pp. 32–40.

1. Edgar Degas, quoted in Maheux, "Looking into Degas's Pastel technique," in Boggs and Maheux, *Degas Pastels*, p. 29. Degas's phrase is "dessins fait à l'encre grasse et imprimés"; the original source is *Catalogue de la 3e Exposition de peinture*, the exh. cat. for the third Impressionist exhibition (Paris, 1877), p. 6.
2. "I must ask you for a piece of cloth to make a dabber suited to my particular purpose." Degas, quoted in Rouart, *Degas in Search of His Technique*, p. 103.
3. "Do you have copper or zinc plates?" Degas, to his host the artist Georges Jeanniot, in ibid.
4. See Lee Ann Daffner, Dan Kushel, and John Messinger, "Investigation of Surface Tarnish Found on 19th Century Daguerreotypes," *Journal of the American Institute for Conservation* 35, no. 1 (1996):9–21.
5. See Janet Buerger and Shapiro, "A Note on Degas' Use of Daguerreotype Plates," *The Print Collector's Newsletter* XII, no. 4 (September–October 1981): 103–6. Using the numbering system in Janis's *Degas Monotypes*, the article identifies the following monotypes as having visible manufacturer's stamps: cat. nos. 11, 16, 20, 28, 40, 46, 48, 49, and checklist nos. 212, 213, and 214.
6. *Fantasy* is inscribed on the sheet "sur celluloid" and *Fantasy* (*Nude Woman*) is inscribed "Vignette No. 6 sur celluloid." See Janis, *Degas Monotypes*, nos. 183 and 246. The latter inscription suggests that at least six monotypes may have been made on celluloid. Plate marks show that the celluloid sheet was approximately 3 1/2 × 6 3/4 inches (8.9 × 17.2 cm). Based on plate size, appearance, and handling of the ink, *The River* (*La Rivière*, c. 1877–79; plate 61) and *Dancer Seen from the Back Adjusting Her Bodice* (Janis, *Degas Monotypes*, no. 17) may also have been printed from celluloid.
7. See John Hannavy, ed., *Encyclopedia of Nineteenth-Century Photography* (New York and London: Routledge, 2008), 1:1207.
8. See Buerger, *French Daguerreotypes* (Chicago and London: University of Chicago Press, 1989), pp. 196–97.
9. Originally published in Jeanniot, "Souvenir de Degas," *La Revue Universelle* no. 11 (November 1, 1933), and trans. in Janis, *Degas Monotypes*, p. xxv.
10. See Louis Edgar Andés, *Oil Colours and Printers' Inks*, 1889 (rev. ed. London: Scott, Greenwood and Son, 1918), p. 205.
11. See E. S. Lumsden, *The Art of Etching* (New York: Dover Publications, 1962), pp. 85–86.
12. "In this case, he did not draw his plate entirely in black ink but used many tints which were either colored inks or, what is more probable, oil paints." Rouart, *Degas in Search of His Technique*, p. 101.
13. "Later on, rather than ink the entire plate and lift the highlights and halftones with a brush or cloth pad, Degas drew his subject in brush with black diluted with spirits." Rouart, in ibid., p. 101.
14. Janis, *Degas Monotypes*, checklist no. 11.
15. Firsthand examination of the verso of *Landscape* (*Paysage*, 1892; plate 125) at The Metropolitan Museum of Art revealed that the monotype was printed on colored Bristol board: the recto has faded, the verso still retains a blue color.
16. "But his disregard for the papers used in printing suggests a difference in intention that sets him apart from *cuisiniers* like Félix Buhot, for whom the materials and the process seemed to count as much as the product." Druick and Zegers, "Degas and the Printed Image, 1856–1914," p. xxxiii.
17. Schenck, "The Role of China Paper in Nineteenth-Century French Printmaking," p. 32. Rouart quotes Degas saying of Jeanniot, "'He has China paper! Let's see this paper.'" Jeanniot then "deposited a majestic roll on the corner of the table." Rouart, *Degas in Search of His Technique*, p. 104.
18. "However, Degas's choice of paper for his monotypes reveals a distinct bias to certain supports for certain subjects; while the majority of the pastelized monotypes were printed on a medium-to-heavy-weight laid paper, other subjects that were rarely colored or heightened, like the brothel scenes, were executed on smooth, thin sheets of china paper." Maheux, "Looking into Degas's Pastel Technique," p. 22.
19. Boggs and Maheux, *Degas Pastels* p. 29.
20. See Fletcher and Pia Desantis, "Degas: The Search for His Technique Continues," *The Burlington Magazine* 131, no. 1033 (April 1989):256–65.

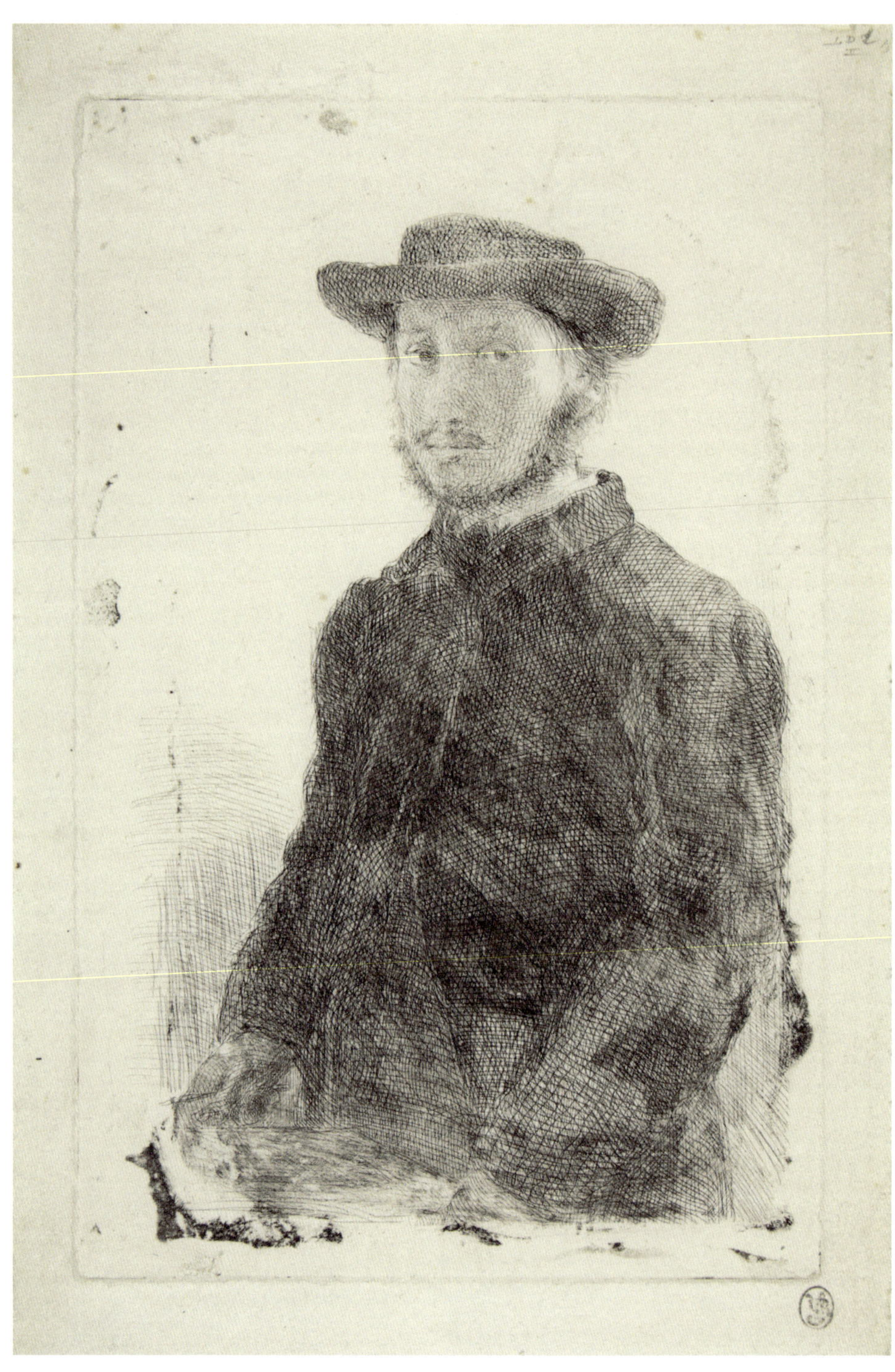

1. *Self-Portrait* (*Autoportrait*). 1857
Etching and drypoint on paper, state II of IV
Plate: 9 1⁄16 × 5 11⁄16 in. (23 × 14.4 cm), sheet: 10 3⁄8 × 6 3⁄4 in. (26.3 × 17.2 cm)
The Metropolitan Museum of Art, New York. Jacob H. Schiff Fund

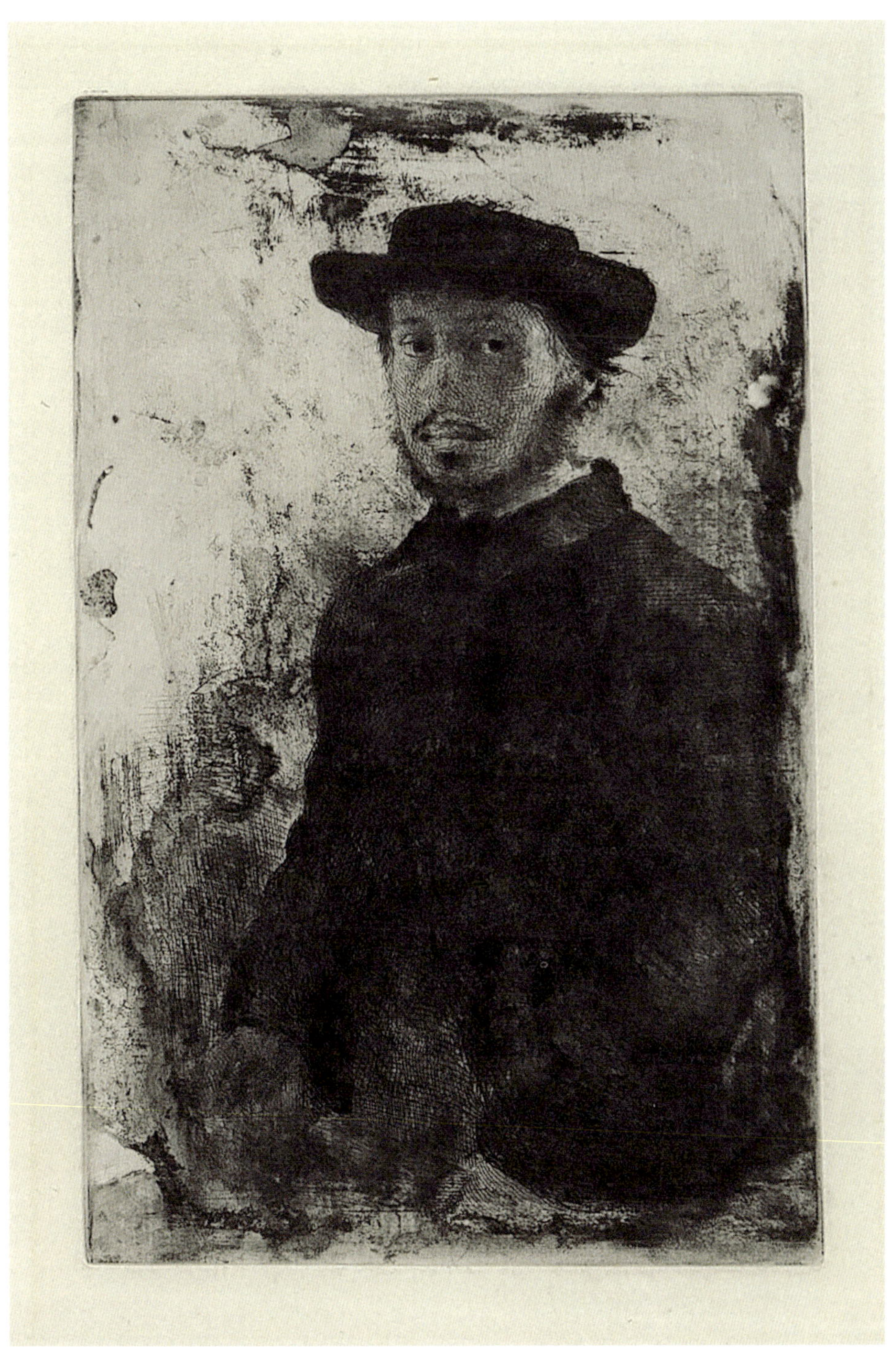

2. *Self-Portrait* (*Autoportrait*). 1857
Etching and drypoint on paper, state III of IV
Plate: 9 1/16 × 5 11/16 in. (23 × 14.4 cm), sheet: 20 ½ × 13 ¾ in. (52 × 35 cm)
Private collection. Courtesy C. G. Boerner, New York

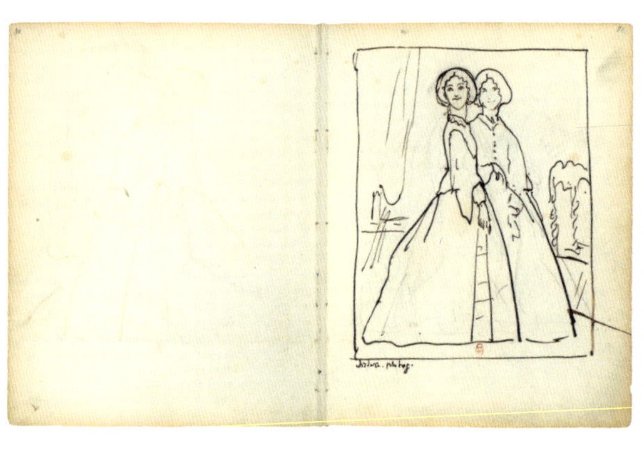

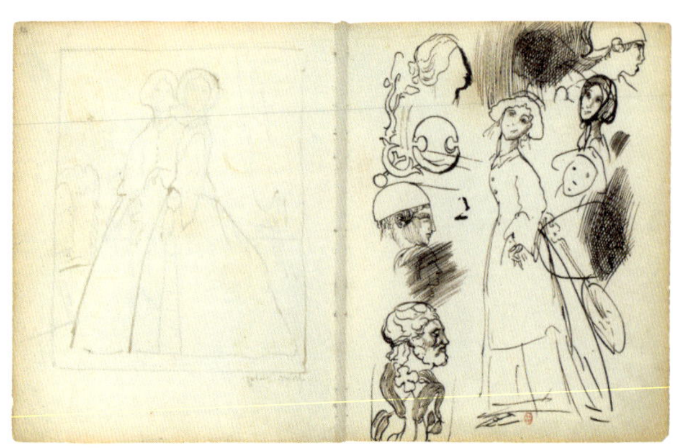

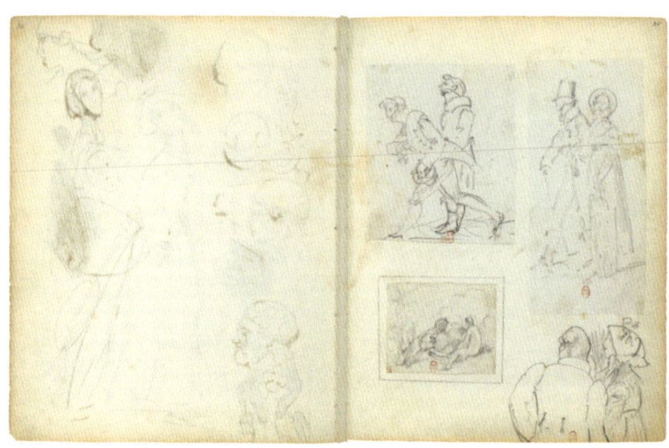

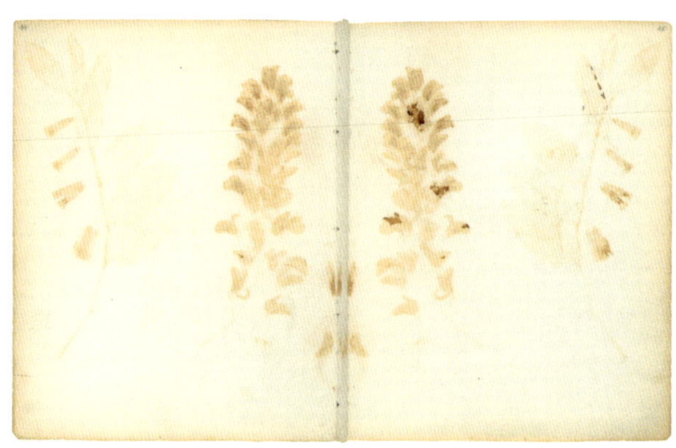

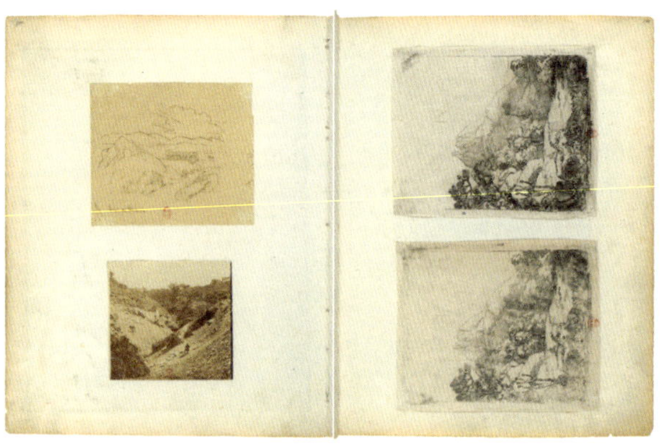

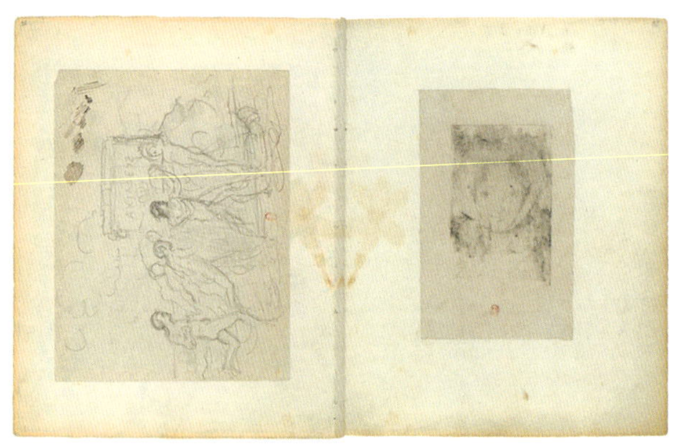

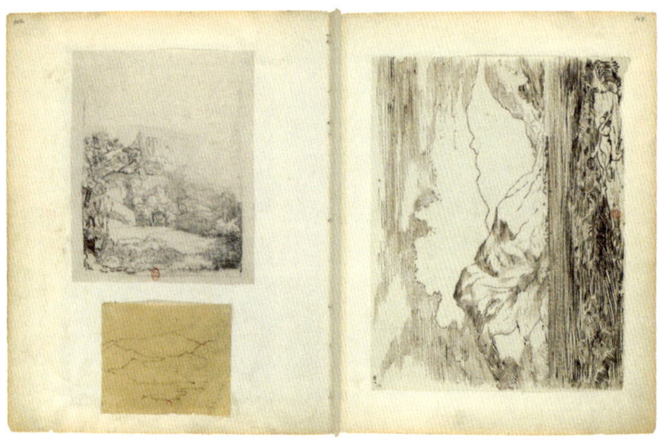

3. Sketchbook (*Carnet I*). 1859–64
Ink, graphite, charcoal with scrapbook additions including photographs, intaglio printing and pressed flowers
10 × 7 11⁄16 in. (25.4 × 19.5 cm)
Bibliothèque Nationale de France, Paris. Département Estampes et photographie

The Singular Multiple

Stephanie O'Rourke

The sketchbook that Degas used from roughly 1859 to 1864, today known as *Carnet I*, is one of the largest of his career and attests to the stunning diversity of the young artist's formal and technical interests.[1] On its pages we find loosely drawn sketches in pencil and more finely rendered ones in pen, some of them deepening and blooming under layers of translucent pigment, with pasted alongside them experimental etchings, photographs, tracings, and even pressed flowers. *Carnet I* is of particular interest in its documentation of the artist's long-standing concern with various forms of reproduction, and of his predilection for exploring and subverting some of the terms by which reproduction was understood in the mid-nineteenth century. These operations would become essential to his later monotypes. Years before he turned to that medium, he was already using *Carnet I* to examine the relationship between unique and multiple, original and copy, and repetition and transformation.[2]

In recent years, art historians have come to recognize that mechanical reproduction meant many different things in nineteenth-century France.[3] It encompassed an ever-growing body of commercial prints, book and journal illustrations, and photographs, but it also included forms of manual reproduction that had been employed in artists' workshops for centuries. Replicas, variations, copies, and imitations proliferated in this context, with each type of reproduction having its own artistic and monetary value.[4] As *Carnet I* attests, Degas was working during a period in which these modern and traditional forms of reproduction were densely entangled.

Degas affixed some of his earliest prints to the pages of this notebook, including three trial impressions of a single etching, *Rocky Landscape* (*Paysage rocheux*, c. 1856). On one sheet, of the print in its first state, Degas used pencil and ink to draw in the changes he would make for the second state (plate 3, left col., bottom, image at upper left). On the recto of the same page he included two variant second-state prints, a crisply inked impression on top and a fainter, blurred impression below (plate 3, left col., second from bottom). By pasting them together in the notebook, Degas showed the three prints as multiple stages within a single working process.

Another etching in the notebook is a copy of Jean-Auguste-Dominique Ingres's portrait *Jenny de Lavalette*, from 1817 (fig. 1). Fittingly, Ingres was an artist for whom copying was of profound importance: "Is not a good copy," he once asked, "worth more than a bad but original painting?"[5] Unlike the three impressions of *Rocky Landscape*, Degas's etching of *Jenny de Lavalette* is blotchy with surface tone and marred by cancellation lines (plate 3, right col., bottom, right). In these early experiments in printmaking he followed the example of artists such as Rembrandt van Rijn, who famously executed variant prints that darken and metamorphose through multiple states. Simultaneously, though, Degas confronted a modern marketplace of industrially produced imagery, emerging in high volume and exerting a considerable pressure on traditional forms of printmaking.[6] Yet his etchings differ emphatically from mass-produced, largely identical prints, an insistence quite visible in the selection he preserved in *Carnet I*—indeed he seems to have valued these works for the ways in which they do *not* resemble one another.

Degas's early etchings are "singular multiples." The implicit contradiction in these terms points to an underlying tension between originality and reproduction in nineteenth-century printmaking.[7] Although reproductive mediums such as engraving ostensibly generate identical copies of a single image, artists were increasingly drawn to forms of printmaking that produced nonidentical copies—prints that became unique works in their own right. In this context, printmaking did not actually "reproduce" a composition—it *altered* it. The means by which printmaking transforms an image would preoccupy Degas for decades, and would become central to his monotypes: as he pursued a given composition through several pulls, re-inkings, counterproofs, and pastel-covered cognates, the act of reproducing an image was made inseparable from the act of changing it.

Much of the reproduction seen on the pages of *Carnet I* belongs to a long tradition of copying that became a cornerstone of artistic education at Paris's Académie des Beaux-Arts in the seventeenth and eighteenth centuries.[8] This pedagogical model was rigidly sequential and hierarchical. Students began by copying simple line engravings, then increasingly complex ones, after which they could move on to drawing from plaster casts and paintings and eventually to drawing from live models. Although Degas studied at the Ecole des Beaux-Arts only briefly, he was committed to this method. Over forty years after his time at the Ecole, the art dealer Ambroise Vollard asked him how an artist should learn to paint, and received the reply, "You must copy and recopy the masters . . . only after having provided every proof of being a good copyist could one reasonably allow you to do a radish from nature."[9]

Even before enrolling at the Ecole, in 1855, Degas had replicated its pedagogical model on his own: he had begun to make copies from prints in the Bibliothèque Impériale and from paintings in the Musée du Louvre in 1853.[10] He also soon began to draw copies of contemporary paintings; *Carnet 1* includes one from Eugène Delacroix's *Ovid among the Scythians* (*Ovide chez les Scythes*), which he would have seen at the Salon of 1859. Many such copies fill the pages of the notebook, from an elaborate drawing of a sixteenth-century Flemish tapestry to a simple tracing from a print of *Le Concert champêtre* (c. 1509) in the Louvre, a painting long attributed to Giorgione but now given to his assistant, the young Titian (plate 3, left col., second from top).

This latter tracing testifies not only to Degas's respect for the Beaux-Arts tradition of the *copie* but to the flourishing mid-nineteenth-century print market that enabled old master paintings to circulate in unprecedented ways. On the notebook page, Degas drew a frame around the pasted tracing and added two spectators, who seem to be looking at the image as if it were the original painting in the Grande Galerie of the Louvre.[11] An engraving that reproduced a painting was roughly and partially reproduced a second time, as a tracing. Through these layers of mediation, much of the content and all of the masterful facture of the

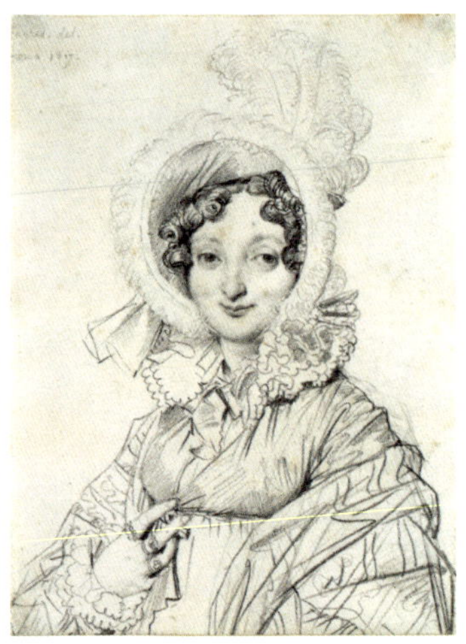

1. Jean-Auguste-Dominique Ingres. *Jenny de Lavalette*. 1817. Pencil on paper, 6 5⁄16 × 4 ½ in. (16.1 × 11.5 cm). National Museum of Western Art, Tokyo

original image were lost—yet Degas, flipping copy and original, affixed the result to an imagined museum wall in place of the work that it so poorly copied. And copies, even poor copies, could provide opportunities for envisioning new works. When Degas turned to the monotype, over a decade later, the act of breaking down an image (through the ink loss inherent to the monotype process when a print is pulled more than once) became a starting point from which new forms could be created. This offered yet another challenge to the traditional understanding of reproduction: rather than preserving a composition, printmaking could bring about its destruction.

Alongside his Beaux-Arts copies Degas placed examples of a novel and relatively young reproductive medium: modest landscape and portrait photographs (plate 3, left col., second from bottom). A more important engagement with photography, however, takes place in the form of a drawing. On page 31, a large sketch in pencil and brown ink depicts two women within a rectangular frame (plate 3, left col., top). An inscription to the lower left reads "Disdéri photog." This caption defines the drawing as a copy of a photograph by André-Adolphe-Eugène Disdéri, who attained great success with *cartes de visite*, calling cards featuring a small portrait photograph of the bearer (fig. 2).[12] The forms of the two women are conjoined; their heads face out toward the viewer while their bodies are at angles to each other. They are paired but distinct.[13]

Degas outlined this scene in decisive lines of brown ink that bled through the paper and on the other side—page 32—produced a faint copy that reversed the composition (plate 3, right col., top).

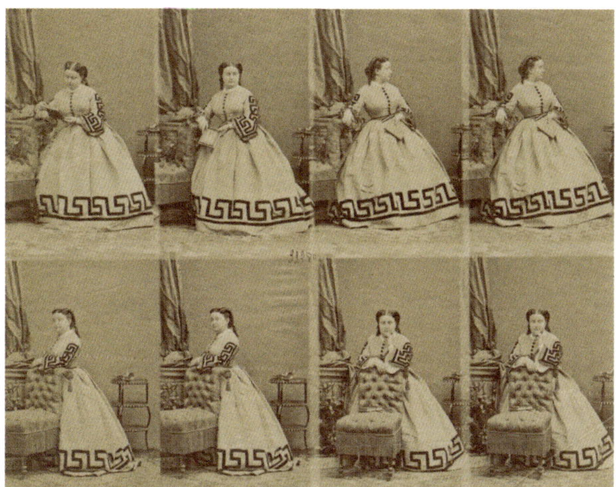

2. André-Adolphe-Eugène Disdéri. Portraits of Princess Gabriella Buonaparte. c. 1860–65. Albumen print sheet of uncut *cartes de visite*, 7 13⁄16 × 9 5⁄16 in. (19.8 × 23.7 cm). Harry Ransom Center, The University of Texas at Austin. Gernsheim Collection

This copy appears to have inspired a new drawing directly across from it, on page 33, the right side of the spread. Here, at the center of a page littered with smaller pictures, Degas drew a woman in profile, her pose and dress resembling one of the subjects Disdéri photographed—not as she appears on page 31, though, but reversed, in imitation of the faded composition that has bled through to page 32. This new drawing gave Degas the opportunity to exaggerate the bend of her head and the swoop of her torso. He probably first copied the photograph as an aide-memoire, a way to preserve the image for future reference, but in the process of translating it into a sketch, then inverting that sketch and copying it in a second one, it gave him a way to explore the possibilities of repeating and reversing an image. He also subtly registered the effect of emerging industrial processes on traditional artistic media such as drawing. Despite his evident interest in photography, however, Degas did not try his own hand at the medium until around 1895.[14]

Carnet I reminds us that the radical formal and technical experiments that Degas undertook in his monotypes grew out of his enduring fascination with the changing terms of reproduction in the nineteenth century. In this context, even the simple flowers preserved between its pages echo the printing press's exertion of flattening pressure. The diverse works preserved in the notebook demonstrate that copying an image can also mean transforming it; that in Degas's time traditional Beaux-Arts practices lay adjacent to a rapidly modernizing marketplace of images; and perhaps also that, in the words of the art historian Michel Melot, for Degas, "in printmaking as in painting, there is no such thing as reproduction."[15]

1. Theodore Reff, whose catalogue *The Notebooks of Edgar Degas* (Oxford: Clarendon Press, 1976) remains the definitive source on Degas's notebooks, dates most of the drawings to between 1859 and 1861, but he identifies one that cannot have been made before 1864. See 1:6 in his book.
2. For more on the rise of originality as a privileged concept in nineteenth-century art, see Richard Shiff, "The Original, the Imitation, the Copy, and the Spontaneous Classic: Theory and Painting in Nineteenth-Century France," in *Yale French Studies* no. 66, *The Anxiety of Anticipation* (1984):27–54, and Rosalind Krauss, *The Originality of the Avant-Garde and Other Modernist Myths* (Cambridge, Mass.: The MIT Press, 1985).
3. One of the most important contributions here is Stephen Bann's *Distinguished Images: Prints in the Visual Economy of Nineteenth-Century France* (New Haven: Yale University Press, 2013).
4. The terms and their definitions are drawn from Patricia Mainardi, "The 19th-century art trade: copies, variations, replicas," *Van Gogh Museum Journal* (2000):62–73.
5. Jean-Auguste-Dominique Ingres, *Écrits sur l'art*, ed. Raymond Cogniat (Paris: La Jeune Parque, 1947), 24:80. On Ingres and copying see Patricia Condon, Marjorie B. Cohn, and Agnes Mongan, *In Pursuit of Perfection: The Art of J.-A.-D. Ingres*, exh. cat. (Fort Worth: Kimbell Art Museum, 1983). Krauss explores some theoretical implications in "You irreplaceable you," in *Retaining the original: multiple originals, copies, and reproductions* (Washington, D.C.: National Gallery of Art, 1989; Studies in the history of art 20):XX.
6. One of the most recent contributions to this field is Anne Higonnet's "Manet and the Multiple," *Grey Room* 48 (Summer 2012):102–16. In addition to the other sources cited in this essay, see also Trevor Fawcett, "Graphic Versus Photographic in the Nineteenth-Century Reproduction," *XXX* 9, no. 2 (June 1986).
7. As Sue Welsh Reed and Barbara Stern Shapiro have observed, *Carnet 1* reveals that the boundaries "between reproductive and original print were less strictly drawn than the publicly advanced positions would suggest." Reed and Shapiro, *Edgar Degas: The Painter as Printmaker*, exh. cat. (Boston: Museum of Fine Arts, 1984), p. xxii.
8. See Albert Boime, *The Academy and French Painting in the 19th Century* (New Haven: Yale University Press, 1986).
9. Ambroise Vollard, *Degas* (Paris: G. Crès, 1924), p. 64. Author's trans.
10. See Jean Sutherland Boggs, *Degas*, exh. cat. (New York: The Metropolitan Museum of Art, 1988), p. 71, and Henri Loyrette, *Degas* (Paris: Fayard, 1990), pp. 35–50.
11. See Reff, "The Pictures within Degas's Pictures," *Metropolitan Museum Journal* 1 (1968):126.
12. As Reff has noted, Degas could have seen Disdéri's works exhibited at the Société française de Photographie on the rue Drouot in the winter of 1861. *The Notebooks of Edgar Degas*, 2:93. See also Reff, "The Pictures within Degas's Pictures," p. 126.
13. Ailene Loucheim discusses Degas's use of this compositional strategy in her essay "Degas's Double Vision," *Artnews* 46, no. 1 (March 1947):26–29, 61–62.
14. See Richard Kendall and Jill DeVonyar, "Eye and Camera: The Late Years," in *Degas and the Ballet: Picturing Motion* (London: Royal Academy of Arts, 2011). Also valuable is "Some Documented Links between Degas and Photography," pp. 256–59.
15. Michel Melot, *The Impressionist Print*, trans. Caroline Beamish (New Haven: Yale University Press, 1996), p. 45.

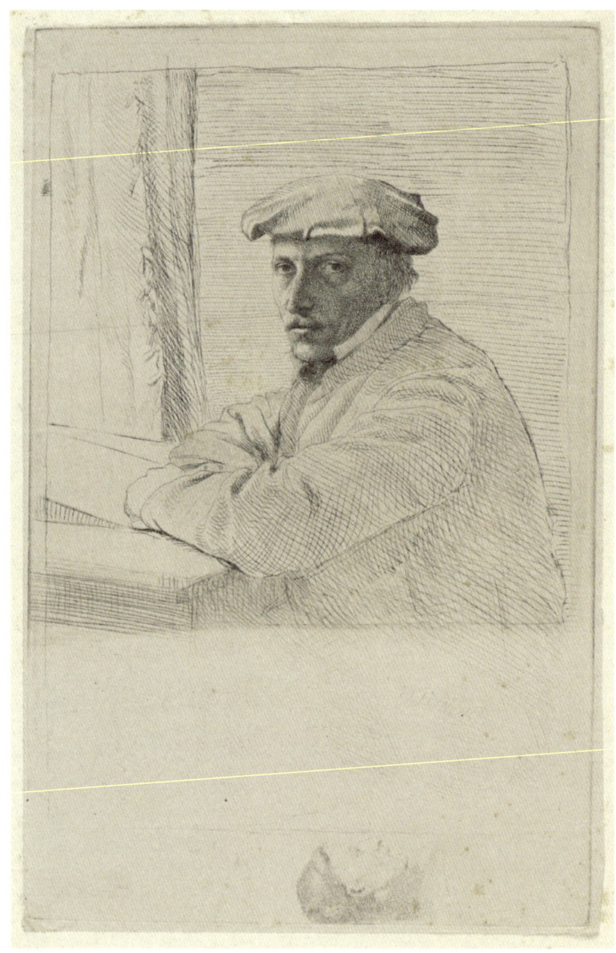

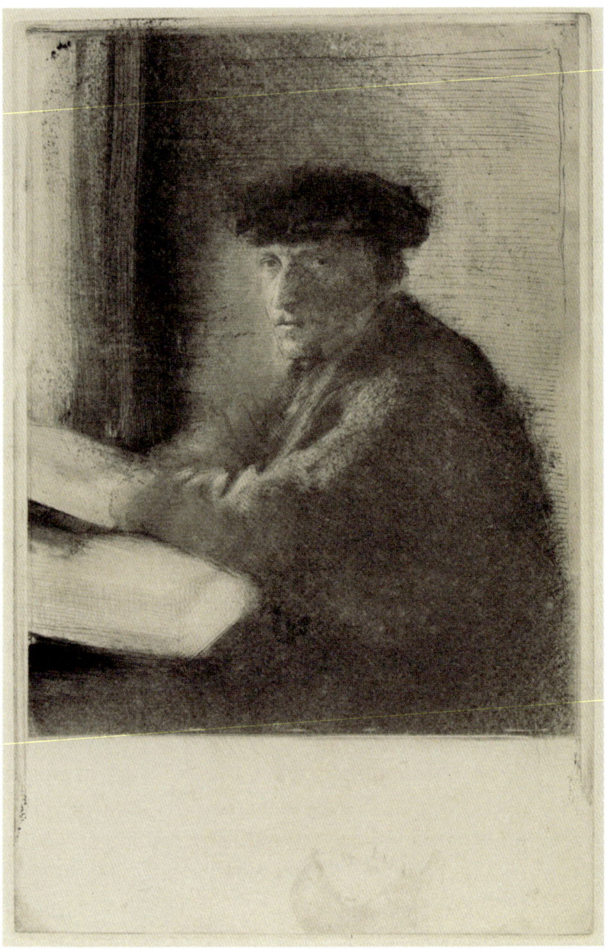

4. *The Engraver Joseph Tourny* (*Le Graveur Joseph Tourny*). 1858
Etching on paper
Plate: 9 1⁄16 × 5 11⁄16 in. (23 × 14.4 cm)
Princeton University Art Museum. Gift of James H. Lockhart, Jr., Class of 1935

5. *The Engraver Joseph Tourny* (*Le Graveur Joseph Tourny*). c. 1865
Etching on paper, only state
Plate: 9 1⁄16 × 5 11⁄16 in. (23 × 14.4 cm), sheet: 18 7⁄8 × 12 3⁄8 in. (48 × 31.5 cm)
Staatliche Kunsthalle, Karlsruhe

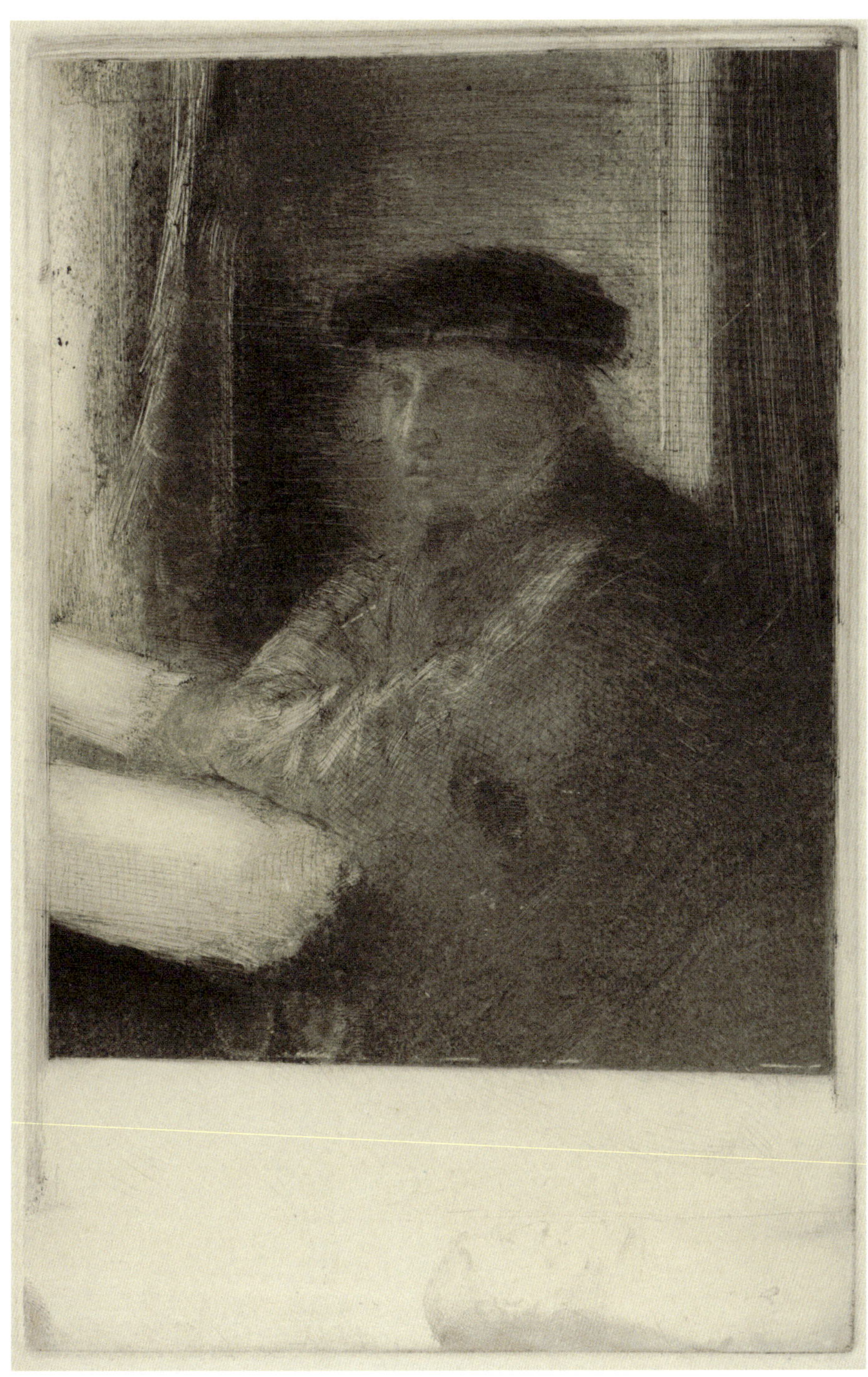

6. *The Engraver Joseph Tourny* (*Le Graveur Joseph Tourny*). 1857
Etching on paper
Plate: 9 1⁄16 × 5 11⁄16 in. (23 × 14.4 cm), sheet: 18 15⁄16 × 13 13⁄16 in. (48.1 × 35.1 cm)
The Metropolitan Museum of Art, New York. Harris Brisbane Dick Fund

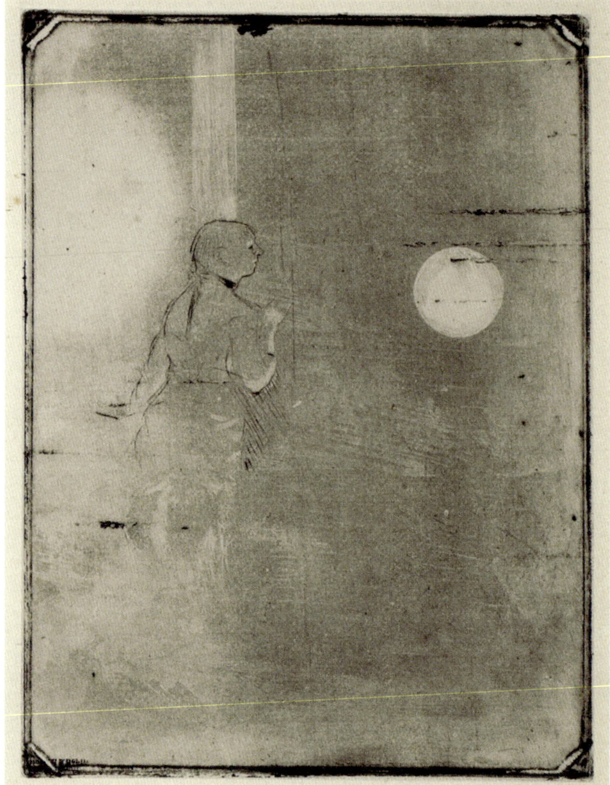

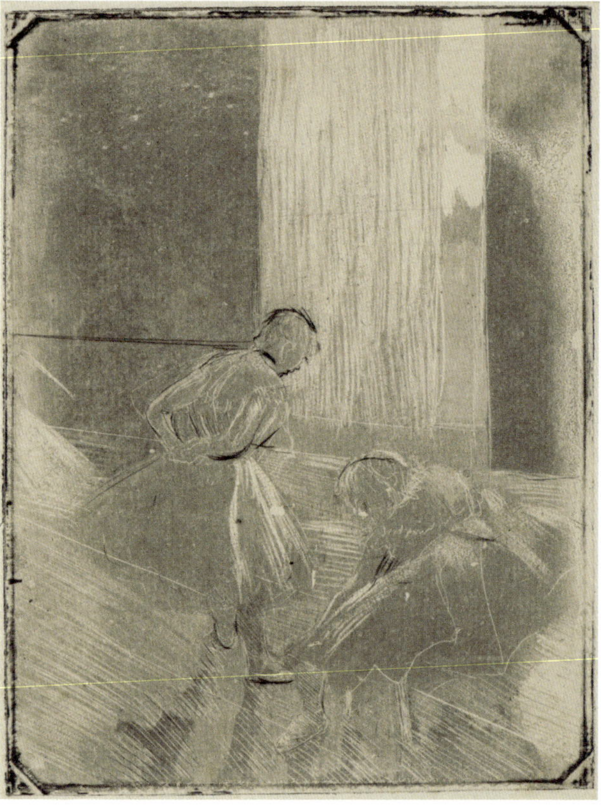

7. *A Café-Concert Singer* (*Derrière le rideau de fer*). 1877–78
Aquatint and drypoint on paper, only state
Plate: 6 ¼ × 4 5⁄16 in. (15.9 × 11 cm), sheet: 9 5⁄16 × 7 ¼ in. (23.6 × 18.4 cm)
Ursula and R. Stanley Johnson Family Collection

8. *Two Dancers in a Rehearsal Room* (*Deux danseuses*). 1877–78
Aquatint and drypoint on paper, only state
Plate: 6 3⁄16 × 4 9⁄16 in. (15.7 × 11.6 cm), sheet: 11 13⁄16 × 8 7⁄16 in. (30 × 21.4 cm)
Lent by James Bergquist

Defined by Light

Kimberly Schenck

Two Dancers in a Rehearsal Room (*Deux danseuses,* 1877–78; plate 8) is one of two etchings by Edgar Degas in which much of the design was made by scraping light marks into a flat field of darkened aquatint.[1] In the foreground of the print Degas depicts ballerinas preparing for rehearsal, one standing and one seated adjusting her slipper. The background is divided into panels of light and shadow, with a bright curtained window to the right of a dark wall equipped with a ballet barre. Like his monotypes, Degas's print is a monochromatic image in gradations of grays, and was made with both additive and subtractive techniques. He sometimes used a similar approach in his early charcoal drawings, building up layers of charcoal to create darks and removing them to establish lights. Degas saw printmaking and drawing as ways of exploring ideas, light, and form, and he was highly inventive and experimental in the use of his tools and materials.

Degas produced several etchings and monotypes, including *Two Dancers in a Rehearsal Room*, that show the crimped corners and embossed manufacturer's stamp characteristic of daguerreotype plates. The manufacturer's stamp, "Schneider . . . Berlin," is printed in reverse at the top-right corner. Made of copper electroplated with silver, daguerreotype plates have a highly polished, mirrorlike surface. Though it is unclear why Degas used them, it has been suggested that the reflective light-colored silver facilitated his ability to make images featuring a range of tones.[2] He may also have been attracted to their extremely smooth surface, especially when producing prints with fine-grained aquatint grounds.

Two Dancers in a Rehearsal Room was made using drypoint, aquatint, and scraping. Fine indistinct lines in the print, partly obscured by the aquatint, suggest that Degas may first have lightly indicated the figures in drypoint.[3] He then poured liquid aquatint onto the entire plate and applied a resist on specific areas to stop the action of the acid at different stages during biting. He created the white contours of the figures and the striped patterning in the curtain and floorboards by abrading or polishing away the bitten aquatint with a metal scraper and burnisher. The chatter pattern of the scraper blade is seen in the standing figure's skirt, whereas the smoother marks made by the curved burnisher are evident in the subtle highlights of the seated dancer's shoulder. Degas accentuated parts of the composition with bolder, darker drypoint lines. Displeased with the white lines marking his initial placement of the standing figure's bent left arm, he redrew it and then clarified the new position in drypoint. The pentimenti of the earlier placement of the figure's torso and arms record his refinement of her pose.

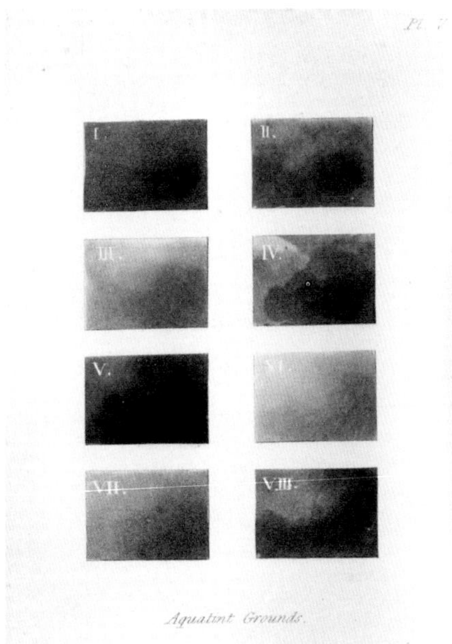

1. "Aquatint Grounds." Plate V from T. H. Fielding. *The Art of Engraving* (London: M. A. Nattali, 1844). The National Gallery of Art Library, Washington, D.C.

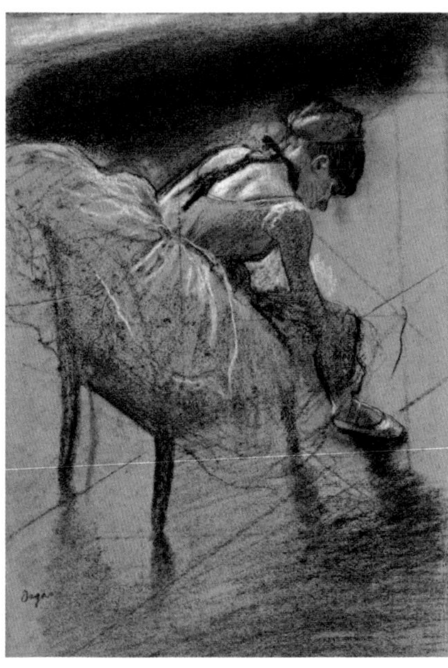

2. Hilaire-Germain-Edgar Degas. *Seated Dancer Rubbing Her Leg (Danseuse se chaussant).* c. 1878. Charcoal with white and dark brown pastel on gray-brown laid paper, 17 ⅝ × 12 ¼ in. (44.8 × 31.1 cm) irreg. Norton Simon Art Foundation

The aquatint grains of *Two Dancers in a Rehearsal Room* are slightly larger than the fine pattern observed in *A Café-Concert Singer* (*Derrière le rideau de fer*, 1877–78; plate 7), also made by scraping lines into an aquatint layer. This subtle distinction may indicate that Degas was experimenting with different recipes as well as refining his application technique. Nineteenth-century etching manuals discuss liquid aquatint recipes that include resins of pitch, mastic, turpentine, or frankincense mixed in alcohol;[4] the solution is poured onto the plate and left for the alcohol to evaporate, when tiny particles of resin form on the surface. The granulation pattern and grain size of these resin particles vary with the quantity and type of resin, and this affects the appearance of the bitten tone once the plate has been printed (fig. 1). Liquid aquatint can produce fine-grained, elegant tonalities but it can also lead to unpredictable effects. Minor accidents in the application of the ground in *Two Dancers in a Rehearsal Room* illustrate the serendipity of printmaking, which Degas seemed to appreciate: the aquatint ground puddled along the right edge, creating an ambiguous light area in the design, but instead of covering this area with lines or bitten tone, he added even more scraped white lines to the bottom corner.

The general evenness of the aquatint layer, and Degas's straightforward inking of the plate, resulted in a flat gray reminiscent of the toned papers he often used in his charcoal drawings of the period. He worked on papers both in neutral shades, such as tan and blue-gray, and in the stronger colors of pink and green. An overall midtone, whether supplied by a field of gray aquatint or by a colored paper, enabled him to easily develop darks and lights in a composition. In the drawing *Seated Dancer Rubbing Her Leg* (*Danseuse se chaussant*, c. 1878; fig. 2), for example, on gray-brown paper, Degas combined black charcoal with white and dark brown pastels. For an effect similar to the scraped pale lines in *Two Dancers in a Rehearsal Room*, he used white pastel to outline layers and folds of the dancer's tulle skirt, to add strong highlights on her back, and to accent her foot, neck, and hair.

The use of subtractive techniques in *Two Dancers in a Rehearsal Room* relates closely to Degas's work in other media, particularly monotype.[5] What may have been his first attempt at monotype, *The Ballet Master* (*Le Maître de ballet*, c. 1876; plate 17), made with Ludovic-Napoleón Lepic in Lepic's studio, exhibits different methods used to manipulate black ink applied to an unincised plate. The ballet master's stick and the outline of his coat are drawn into the ink with a slender, blunt instrument, possibly the end of a brush. A clean rag was pulled through the ink to make patches of lighter tonalities in the figures and

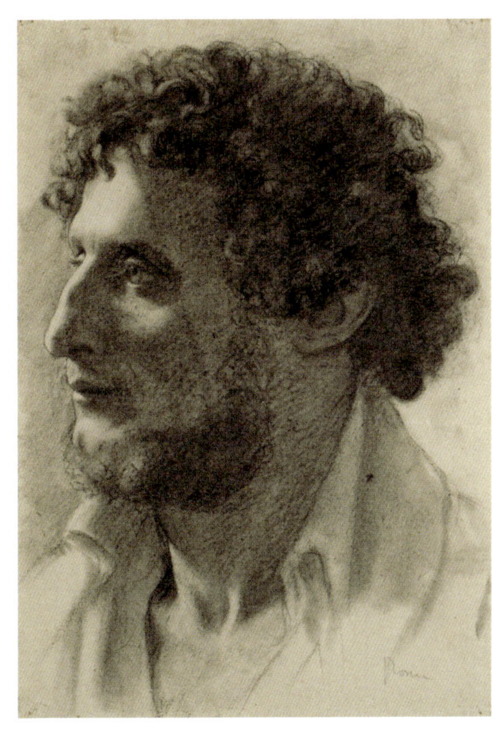

3. Hilaire-Germain-Edgar Degas. *Italian Head.* c. 1856. Charcoal, with stumping, heightened with touches of white chalk, on ivory wove paper, 15 ⅛ × 10 ⅝ in. (38.4 × 26 cm) irreg. The Art Institute of Chicago. Margaret Day Blake Collection

setting. Degas's techniques in both *Two Dancers in a Rehearsal Room* and *The Ballet Master* involved the removal of material, whether bitten aquatint or a film of ink, to create lines and highlights.

Charcoal also lends itself to the use of additive and subtractive techniques. Lines can be made with the tip or side of a charcoal stick and then modified with rolled paper stumps, brushes, or even fingertips. To produce broad areas of different shades of gray, the paper can be rubbed with a charcoal-rich chamois or stump. By selectively removing media from these midtones with a clean rag, the artist can create highlights. Fresh charcoal marks help to build deeper shadows and accentuate forms. Degas's skill in the use of such techniques is evident from the range of grays in *Italian Head* (c. 1856; fig. 3), made shortly after he left the Paris Ecole des Beaux-Arts, while he was living in Italy. He would also have been familiar with the highly finished, fully developed drawings in charcoal or black chalk displayed at the Salon or other exhibitions.[6]

Two Dancers in a Rehearsal Room shows a clear technical correlation with Degas's monotypes and charcoal drawings in the use of additive and subtractive techniques. It also has a similar directness, simplicity, and freshness commonly found in monotype and charcoal but not always present in the artist's heavily worked etchings. This print typifies Degas's experimental approach to making images and his ability to grasp practices possible in one medium and successfully interpret them in another.

1. Sue Welsh Reed and Barbara Stern Shapiro, *Edgar Degas: The Painter as Printmaker* (Boston: Museum of Fine Arts, 1984), pp. 100–101.
2. See Janet Buerger and Shapiro, "A Note on Degas' Use of Daguerreotype Plates," *The Print Collector's Newsletter* 12, no. 4 (September–October 1981):103–6.
3. This observation differs from the sequence offered by Reed and Shapiro, who believe that Degas started the plate with aquatint. But an abbreviated indication of the composition in drypoint would have helped Degas to block out the different shades of aquatint and later to scrape in the white lines and highlights. See Reed and Shapiro, *The Painter as Printmaker*, p. 100.
4. See T. H. Fielding, *The Art of Engraving* (London: M. A. Nattali, 1844), pp. 40–41.
5. In addition to more obvious connections of etching to monotype and charcoal drawing, a lithograph can also be worked both additively and subtractively to enhance tonalities and texture. This comparison was pointed out to me by Jonathan Bober, Curator of Old Master Prints, National Gallery of Art, Washington, D.C.
6. Fully developed tonal drawings in charcoal and black chalk, called *dessin à l'estompe*, were exhibited in the Salon by the 1840s. Théodore Caruelle d'Aligny exhibited *Pastorale*, a large landscape developed with different kinds of charcoal, at the Exposition Universelle in 1855. Jay McKean Fisher, William R. Johnston, Kimberly Schenck, and Cheryl Snay, *The Essence of Line: French Drawings from Ingres to Degas* (Baltimore: The Pennsylvania State University Press, 2005), pp. 65, 77, 146.

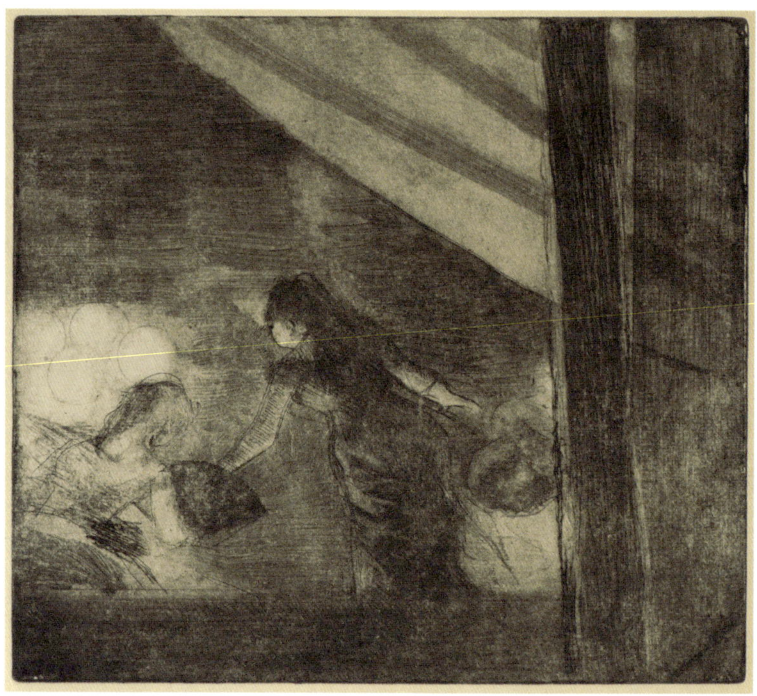

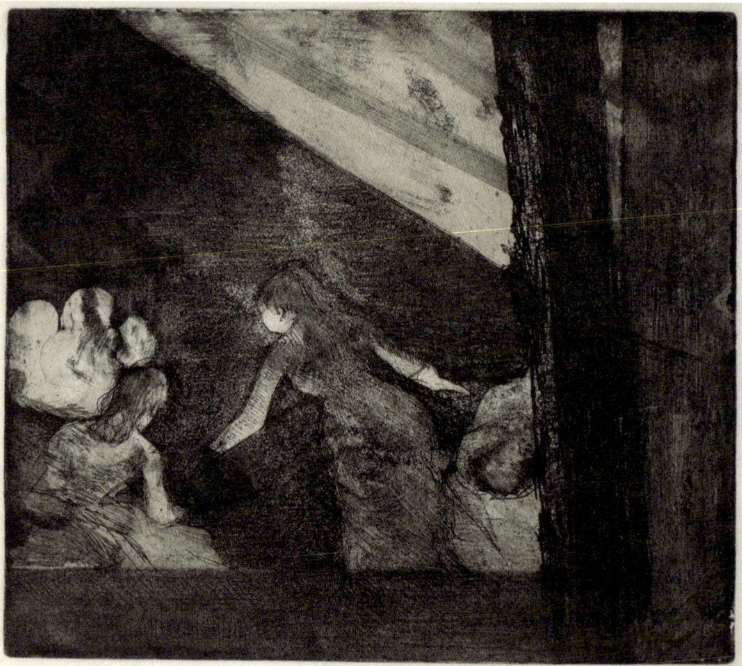

9. *At the Café des Ambassadeurs* (*Aux Ambassadeurs*). 1879–80
Etching, softground, drypoint, and aquatint on paper, state III of V
Plate: 10 ½ × 11 ⅝ in. (26.6 × 29.6 cm), sheet: 16 ⅛ × 12 ⅜ in. (41 × 31.5 cm)
Sterling and Francine Clark Art Institute, Williamstown, Massachusetts

10. *At the Ambassadeurs* (*Aux Ambassadeurs*). 1879–80
Etching, softground, drypoint, and aquatint on paper, state V of V
Plate: 10 ½ × 11 ⅝ in. (26.6 × 29.6 cm), sheet: 12 5/16 × 17 11/16 in. (31.3 × 44.9 cm) (irregular)
National Gallery of Canada, Ottawa. Purchase

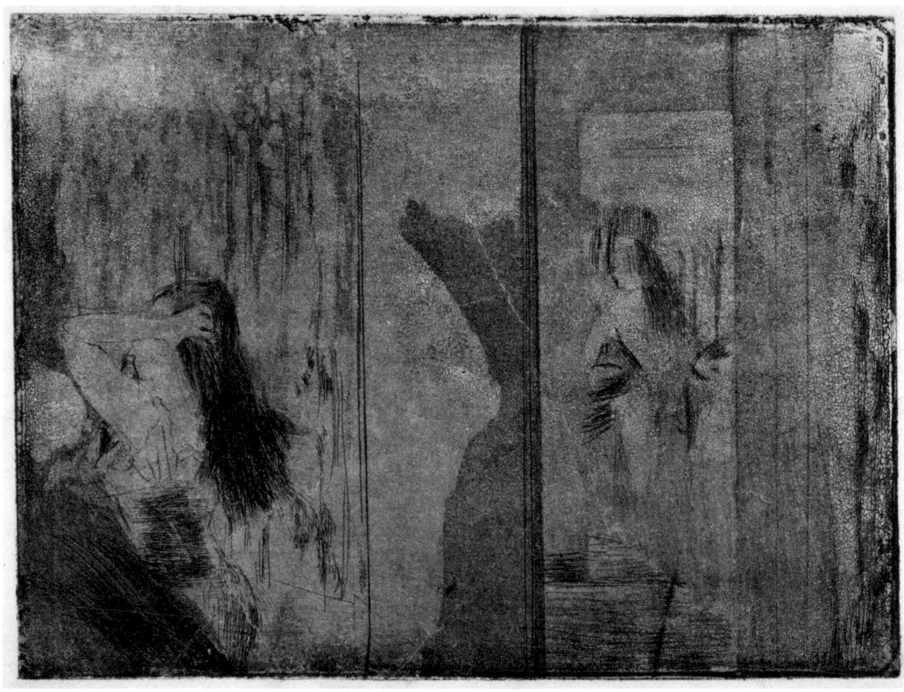

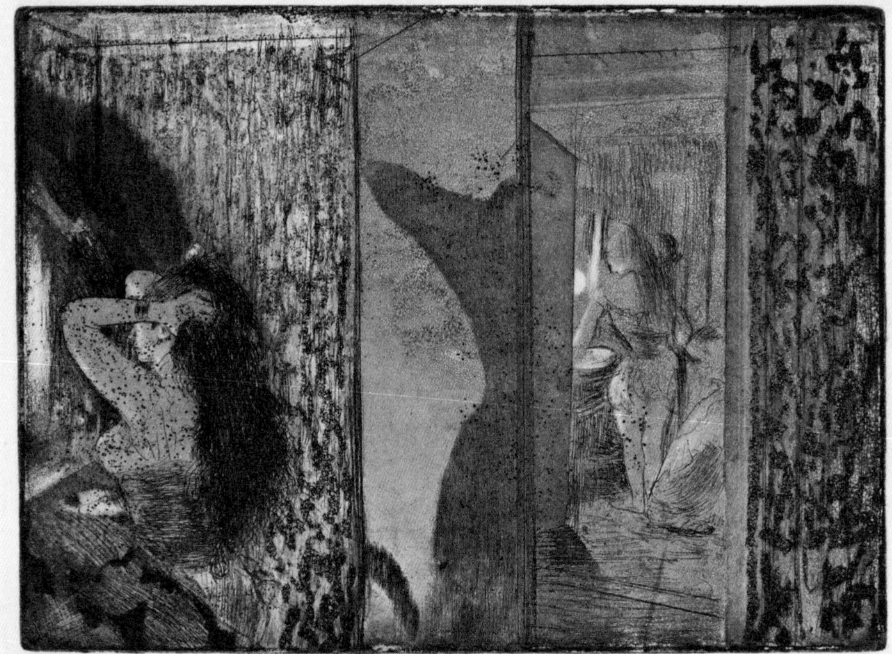

11. *Actresses in Their Dressing Rooms* (*Loges d'actrices*). 1879–80
Etching and aquatint on paper, state I of V
Plate: 6 5⁄16 × 8 3⁄8 in. (16.1 × 21.3 cm), sheet: 7 5⁄8 × 10 1⁄4 in. (19.3 × 26 cm)
Kunsthalle Bremen. Kupferstichkabinett–Der Kunstverein in Bremen

12. *Actresses in Their Dressing Rooms* (*Loges d'actrices*). 1879–80
Etching and aquatint on paper, state V of V
Plate: 6 5⁄16 × 8 7⁄16 in. (16 × 21.5 cm), sheet: 6 11⁄16 × 9 5⁄8 in. (17 × 24.5 cm)
Cantor Arts Center at Stanford University. Gift of Marion E. Fitzhugh and Dr. William M. Fitzhugh, Jr., in memory of their mother, Mary E. Fitzhugh

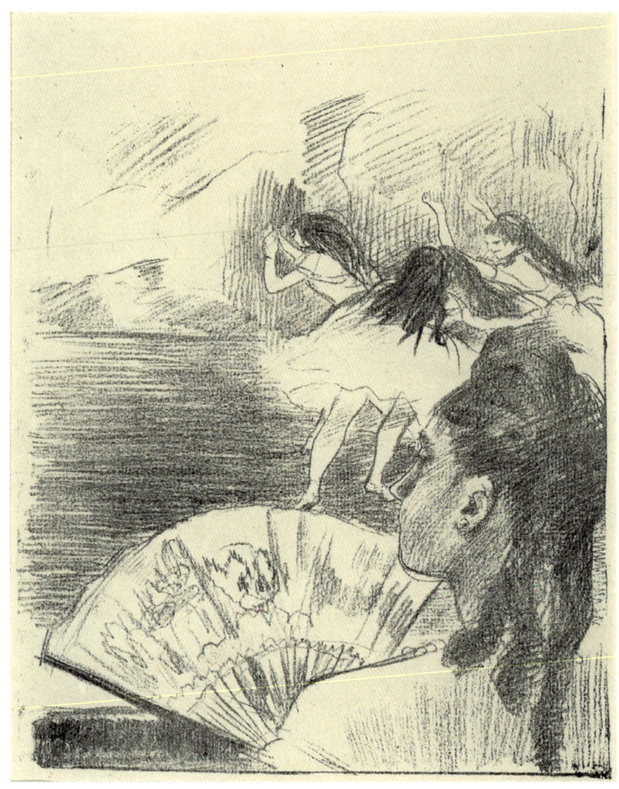

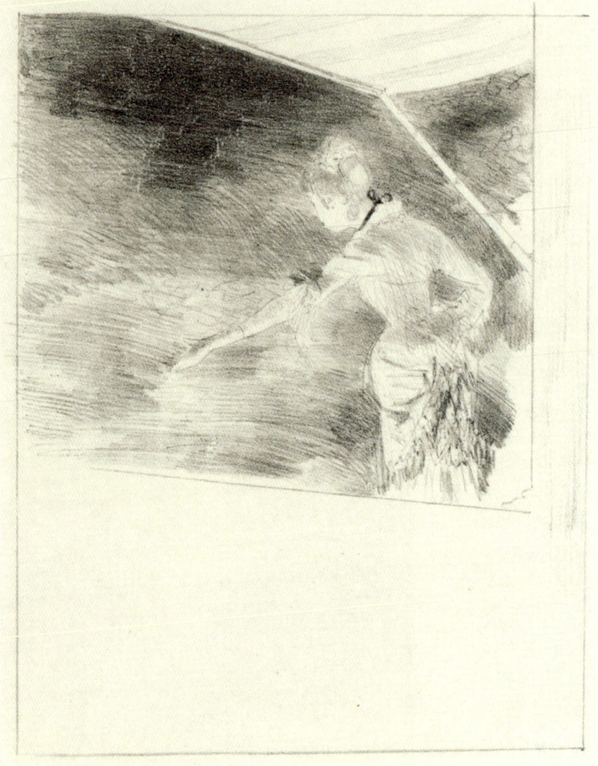

13. *At the Theater: Woman with a Fan* (*Femme à l'éventail, ou loge d'avant-scène*). 1878–80
Lithograph on paper, from transfer paper, only state
Composition: 9 ⅛ × 7 ⅞ in. (23.2 × 20 cm), sheet: 13 ¾ × 10 ⅝ in. (35 × 27 cm)
Private collection

14. *Singer at a café concert* (*Chanteuse de café concert*). 1875
Lithograph on paper, only state
Composition: 10 1⁄16 × 7 9⁄16 in. (25.6 × 19.2 cm),
sheet: 13 11⁄16 × 10 11⁄16 in. (34.8 × 27.2 cm)
The Museum of Modern Art, New York. Gift of Abby Aldrich Rockefeller

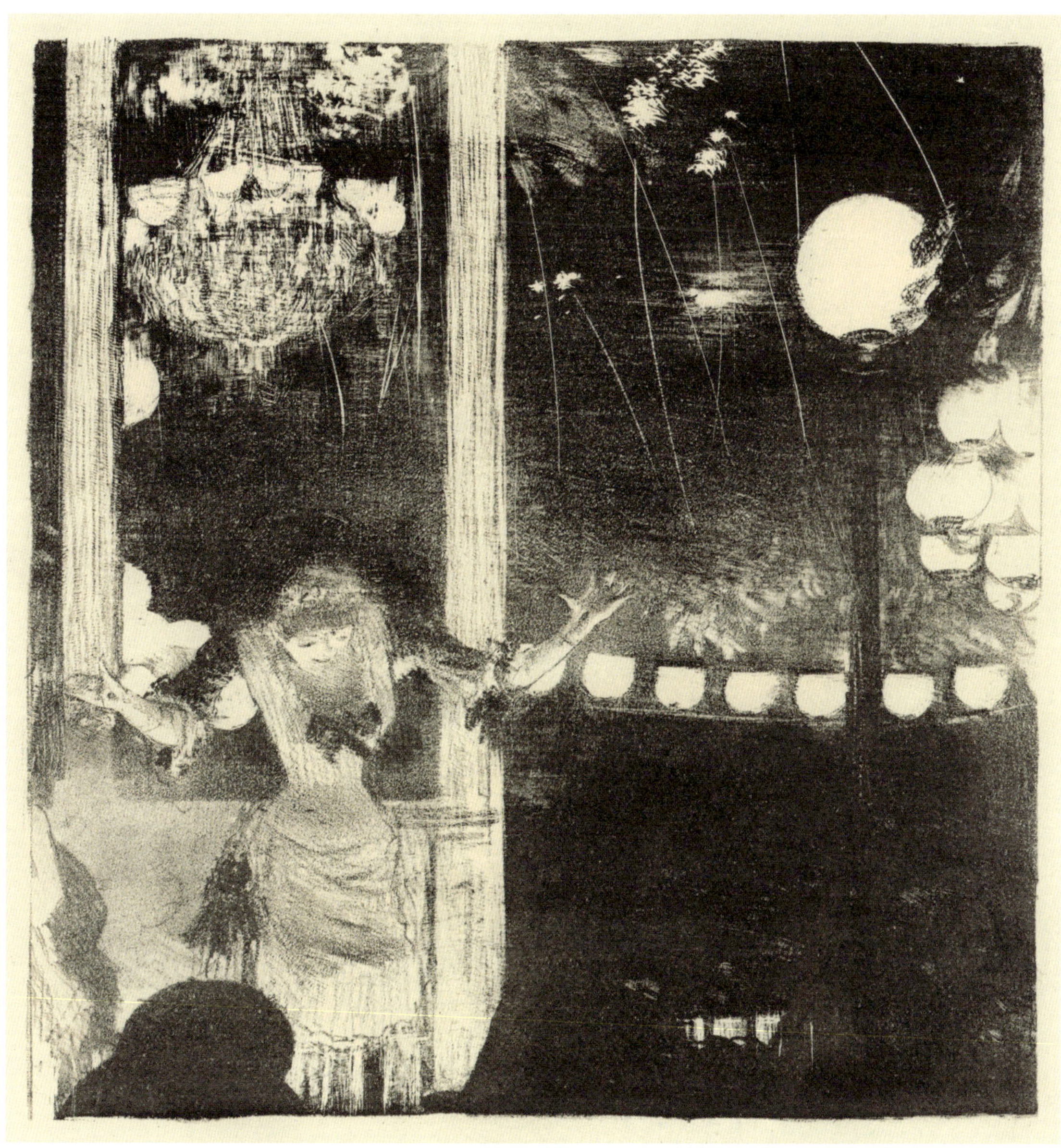

15. *Mademoiselle Bécat at the Ambassadeurs* (*Mademoiselle Bécat aux Ambassadeurs*). c. 1877
Lithograph on paper, only state
Composition: 8 ⅛ × 7 ⅝ in. (20.6 × 19.3 cm), sheet: 13 ½ × 10 ¾ in. (34.3 × 27.3 cm)
The Museum of Modern Art, New York. Gift of Abby Aldrich Rockefeller

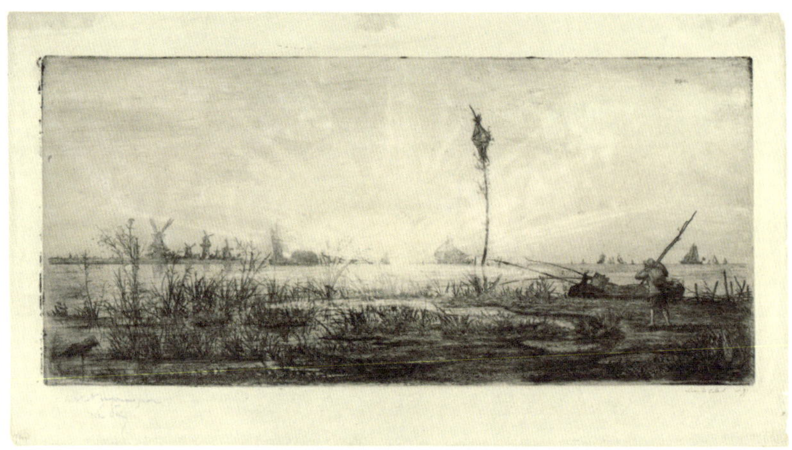

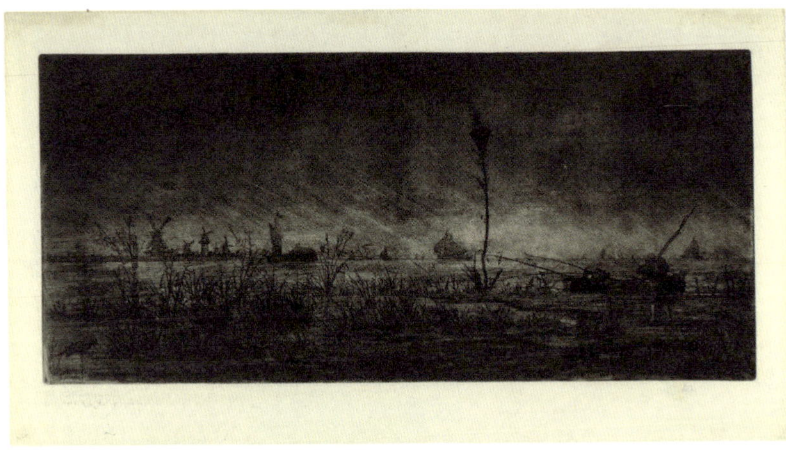

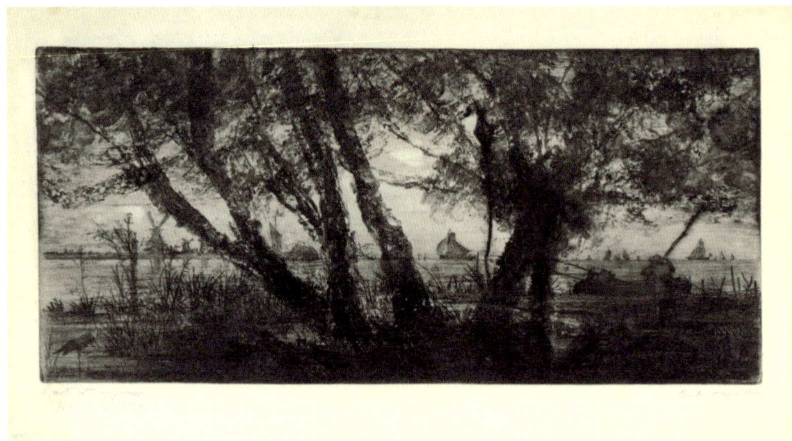

16. Ludovic-Napoléon Lepic
Views from the Banks of the Scheldt (*Vue des bords de l'Escaut*)
Six works from the series. Top to bottom, above: *Sunrise* (*Lever du soleil*), *Rain* (*La Pluie*), *Willows and Poplars* (*Saules et peupliers*). Top to bottom, opposite: *The Mill Fire* (*L'Incendie du moulin*), *Snow* (*La Neige*), *The Moon through the Willows* (*Lune dans les saules*). c. 1870–76
Etching with variable inking on paper
Plate: 13 ½ × 29 5⁄16 in. (34.3 × 74.4 cm), sheet: 17 11⁄16 × 31 7⁄8 in. (45 × 81 cm), each
The Baltimore Museum of Art. Garrett Collection

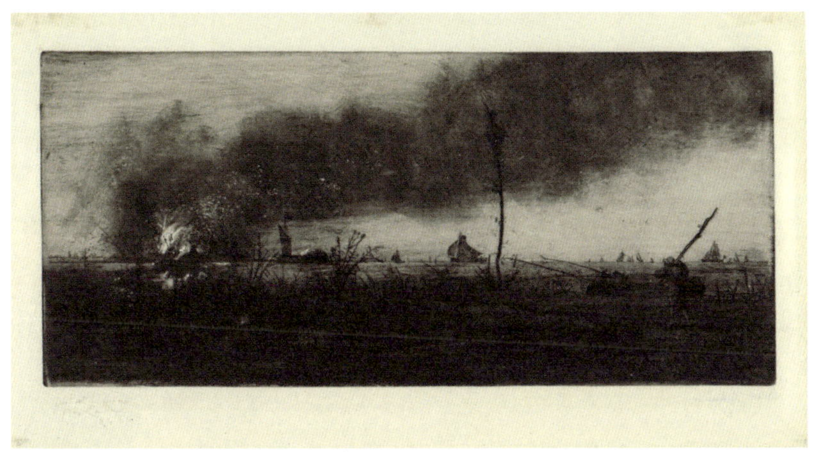

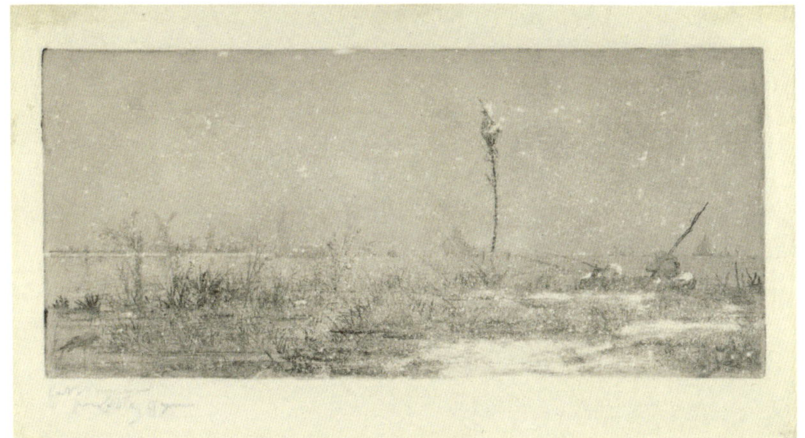

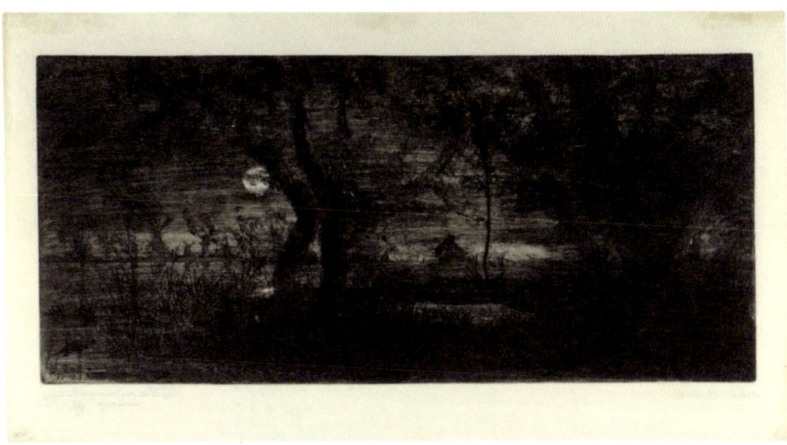

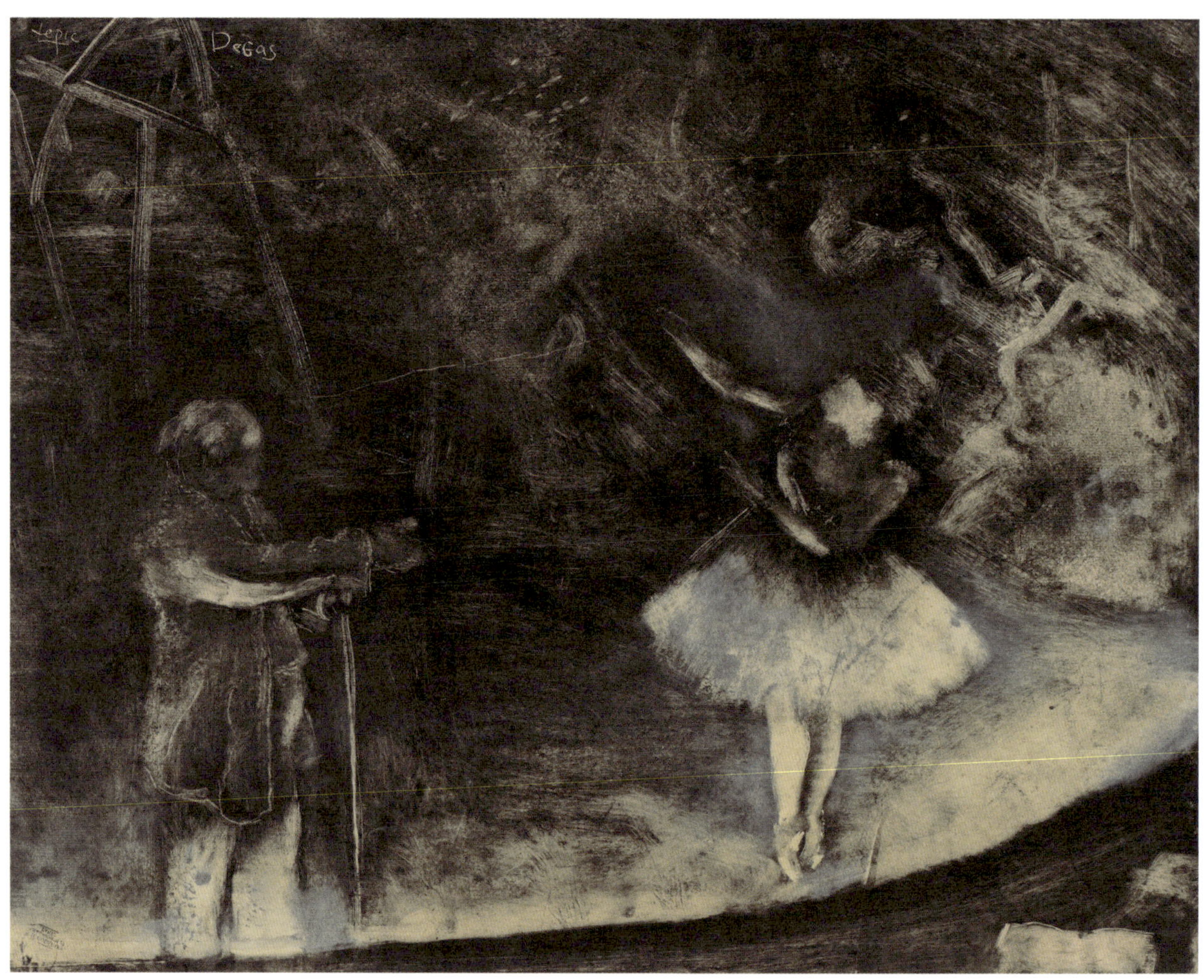

17. *The Ballet Master* (*Le Maître de ballet*). c. 1876
White chalk or opaque watercolor over monotype on paper
Plate: 22 ¼ × 27 9/16 in. (56.5 × 70 cm), sheet: 24 7/16 × 33 7/16 in. (62 × 85 cm)
National Gallery of Art, Washington, D.C. Rosenwald Collection

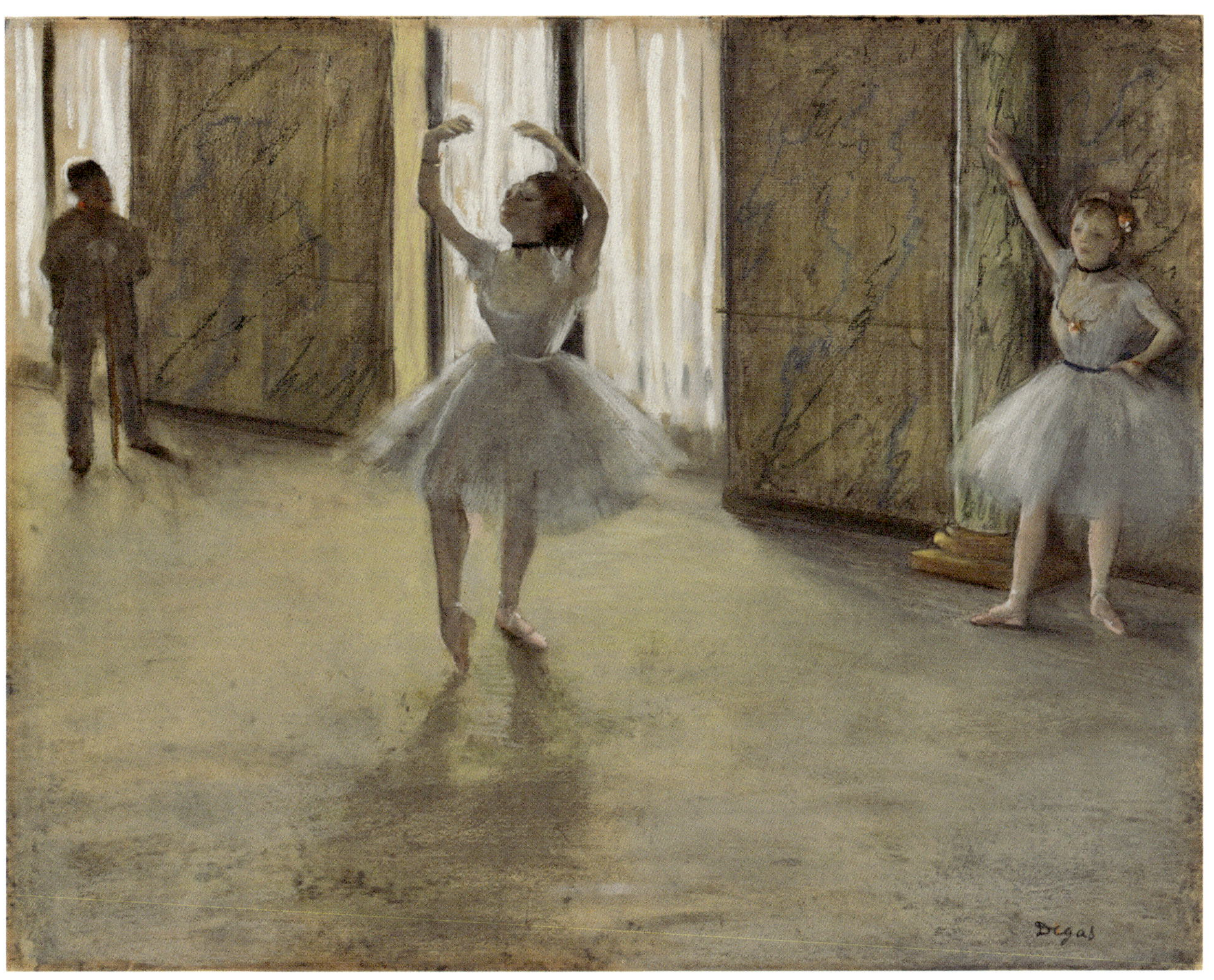

18. *The Dancing Lesson* (*La Leçon de danse*). c. 1877
Pastel over monotype on paper
Plate: 23 × 28 ⅝ in. (58.4 × 72.7 cm)
The Joan Whitney Payson Collection at the Portland Museum of Art. Gift of John Whitney Payson

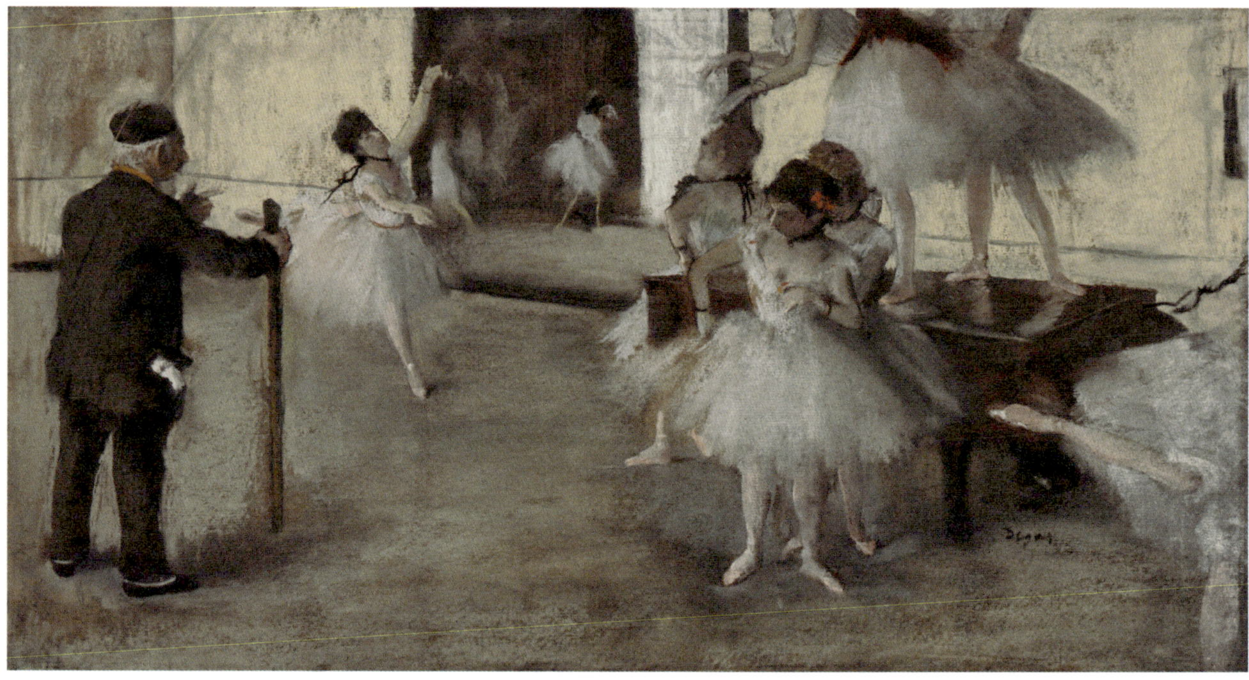

19. *The Dance Lesson* (*La Leçon de danse*). c. 1876
Pastel over monotype on paper mounted on board
Plate: 18 ⅕ × 31 ⅕ in. (43.6 × 79.2 cm)
Private collection

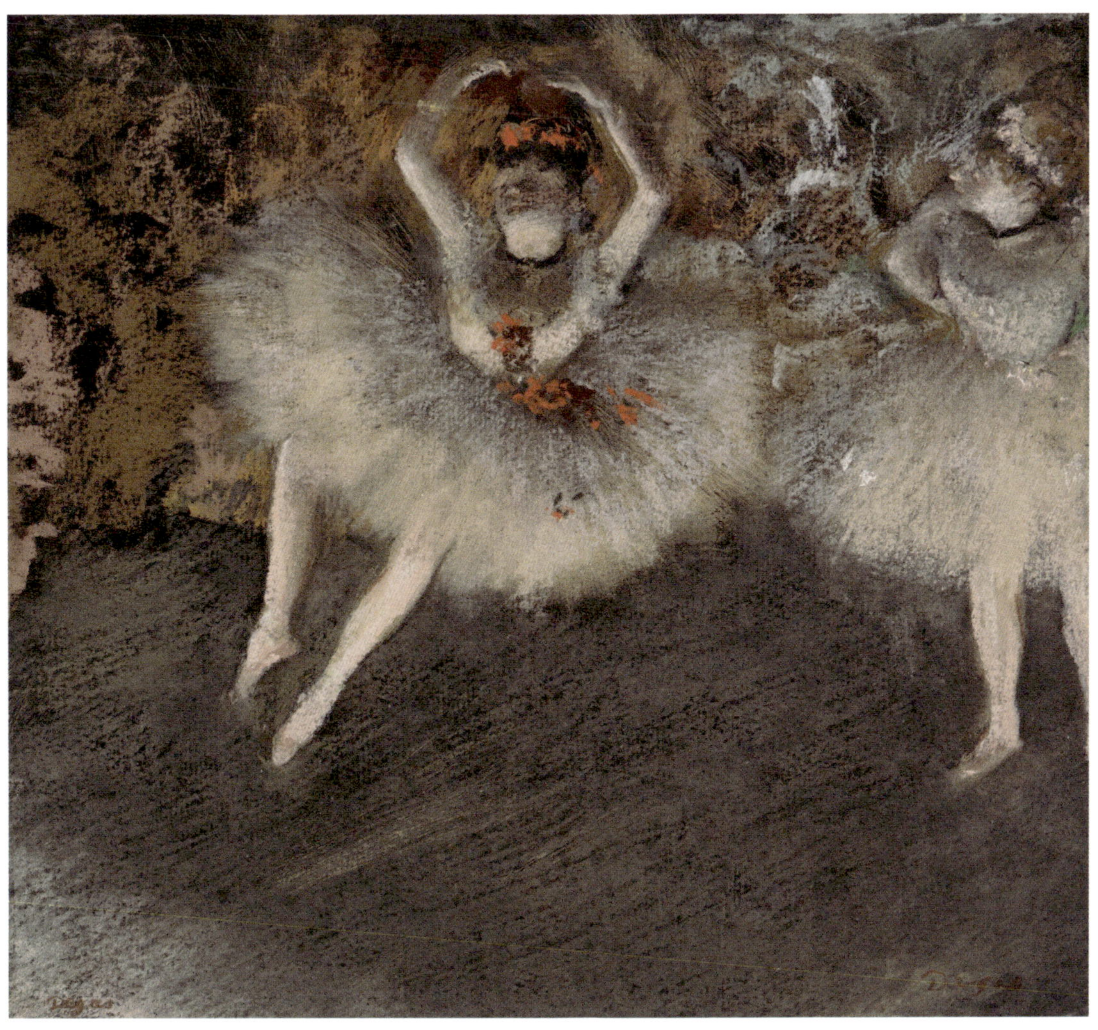

20. *Pas battu*. c. 1879
Pastel over monotype on paper
10 ¾ × 11 ⅝ in. (27.3 × 29.5 cm)
Private collection

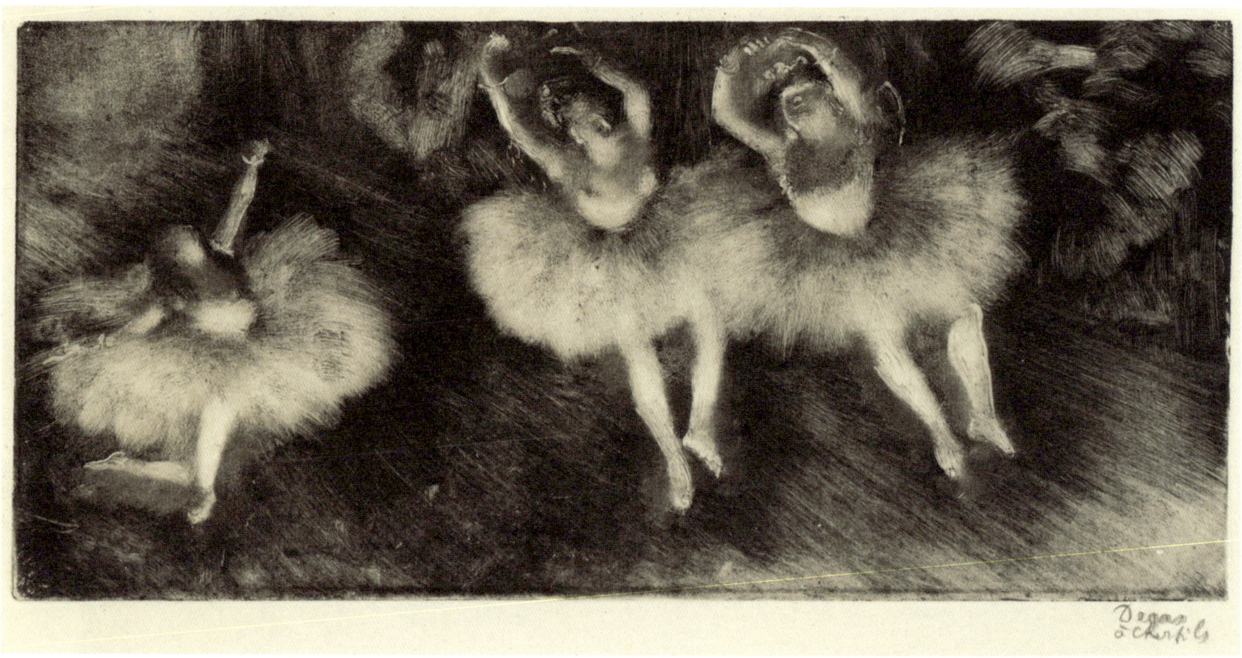

21. *Three Ballet Dancers* (*Trois danseuses*). c. 1878
Monotype on paper
Plate: 7 13⁄16 × 16 3⁄8 in. (19.9 × 41.6 cm), sheet: 14 × 20 3⁄16 in. (35.6 × 51.3 cm)
Sterling and Francine Clark Art Institute, Williamstown, Massachusetts

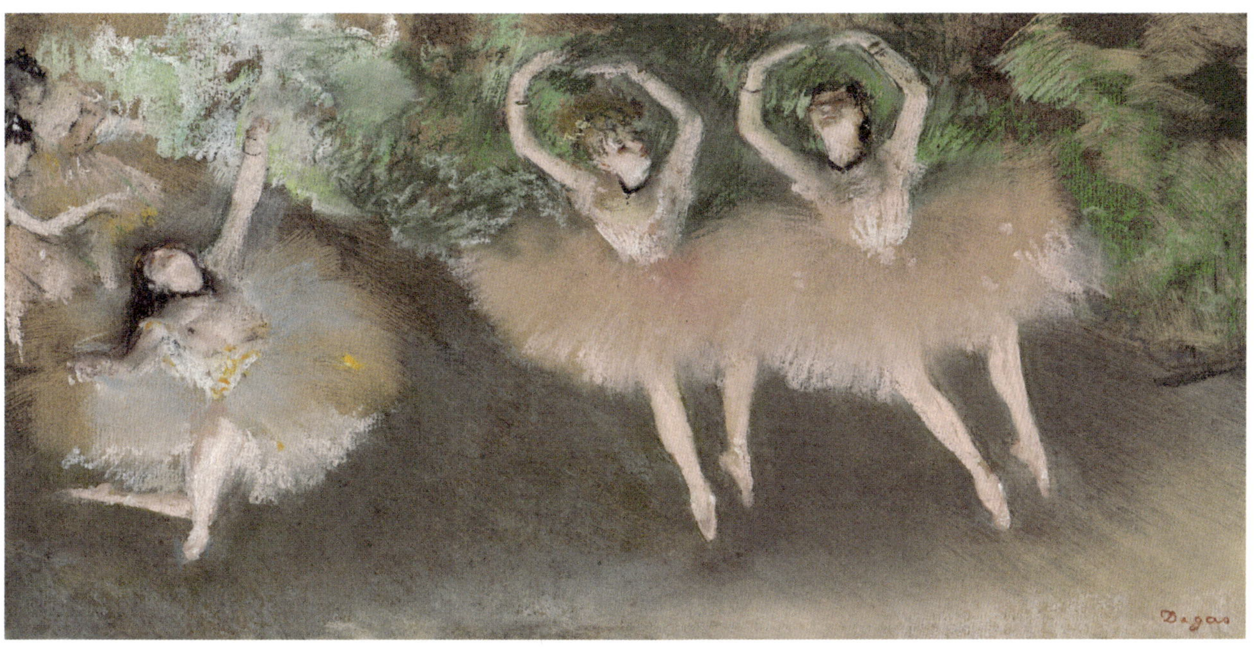

22. *Ballet Scene* (*Scène de ballet*). c. 1879
Pastel over monotype on paper
Plate: 8 × 16 in. (20.3 × 40.6 cm)
William I. Koch Collection

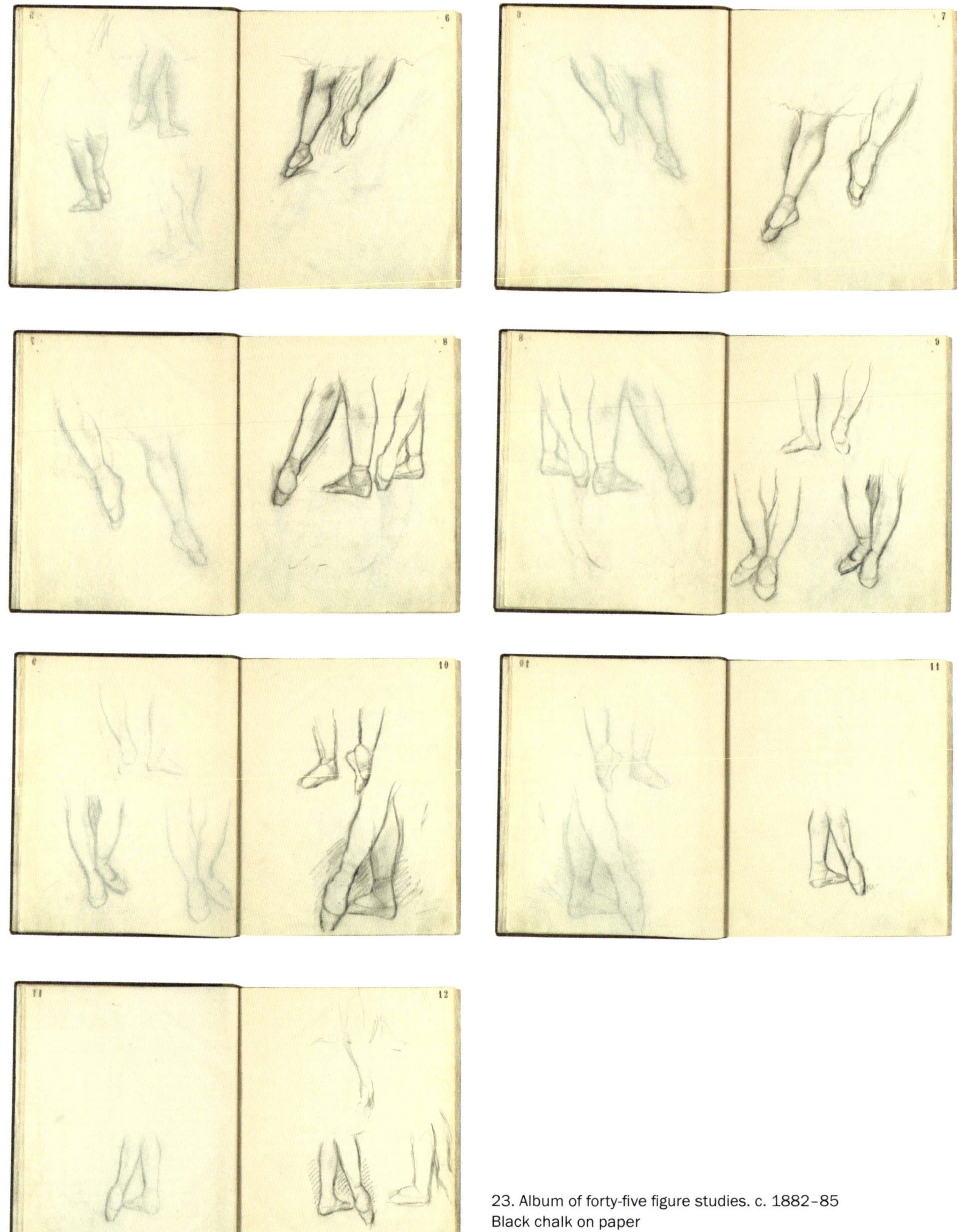

23. Album of forty-five figure studies. c. 1882–85
Black chalk on paper
Sheet: 10 $\frac{9}{16}$ × 8 $\frac{5}{8}$ in. (26.8 × 21.9 cm)
The Metropolitan Museum of Art, New York. Fletcher Fund

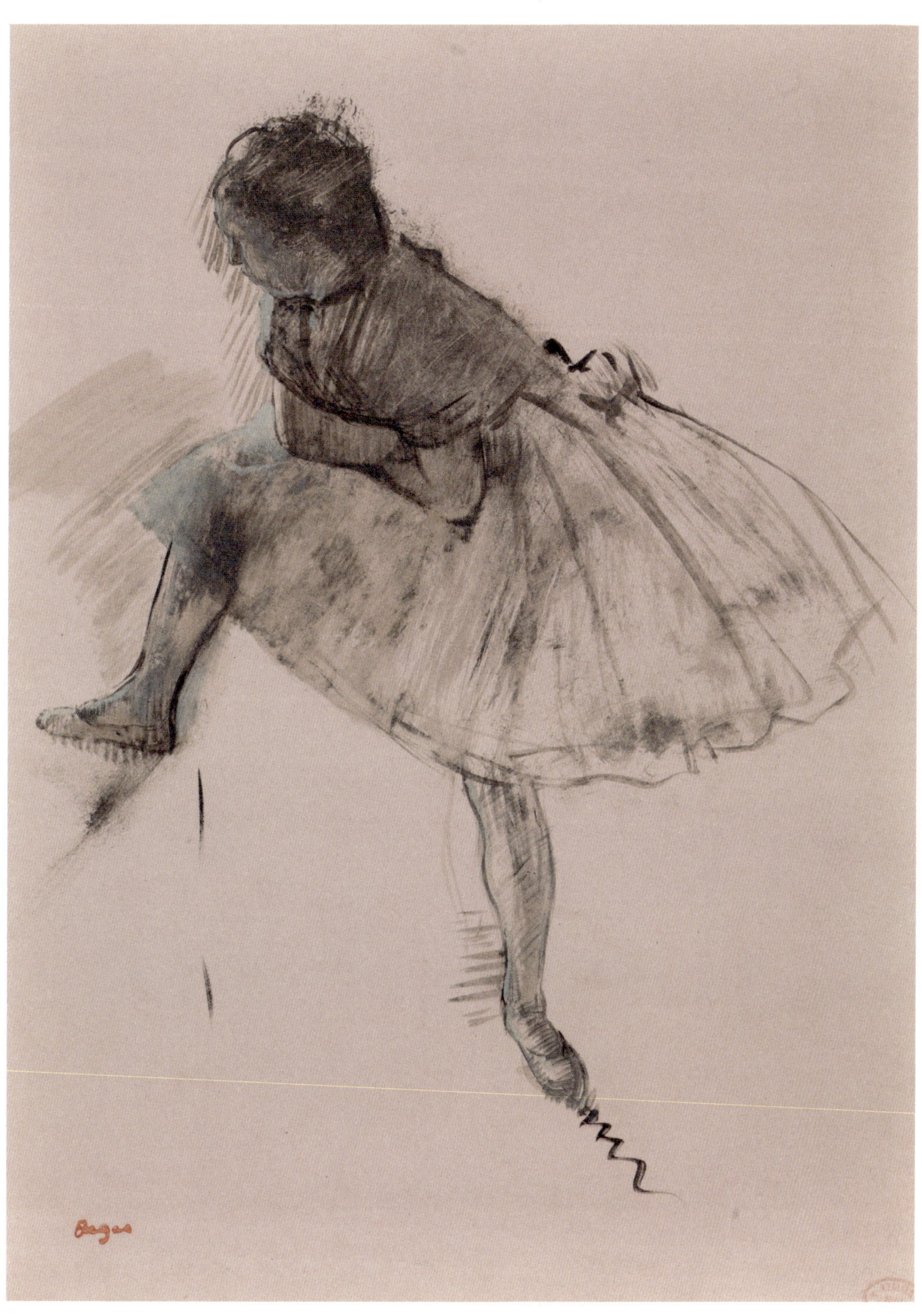

24. Study of a ballet dancer (recto). c. 1873
Oil with opaque watercolor on prepared pink paper
17 ½ × 12 ⅜ in. (44.5 × 31.4 cm)
The Metropolitan Museum of Art, New York. Robert Lehman Collection

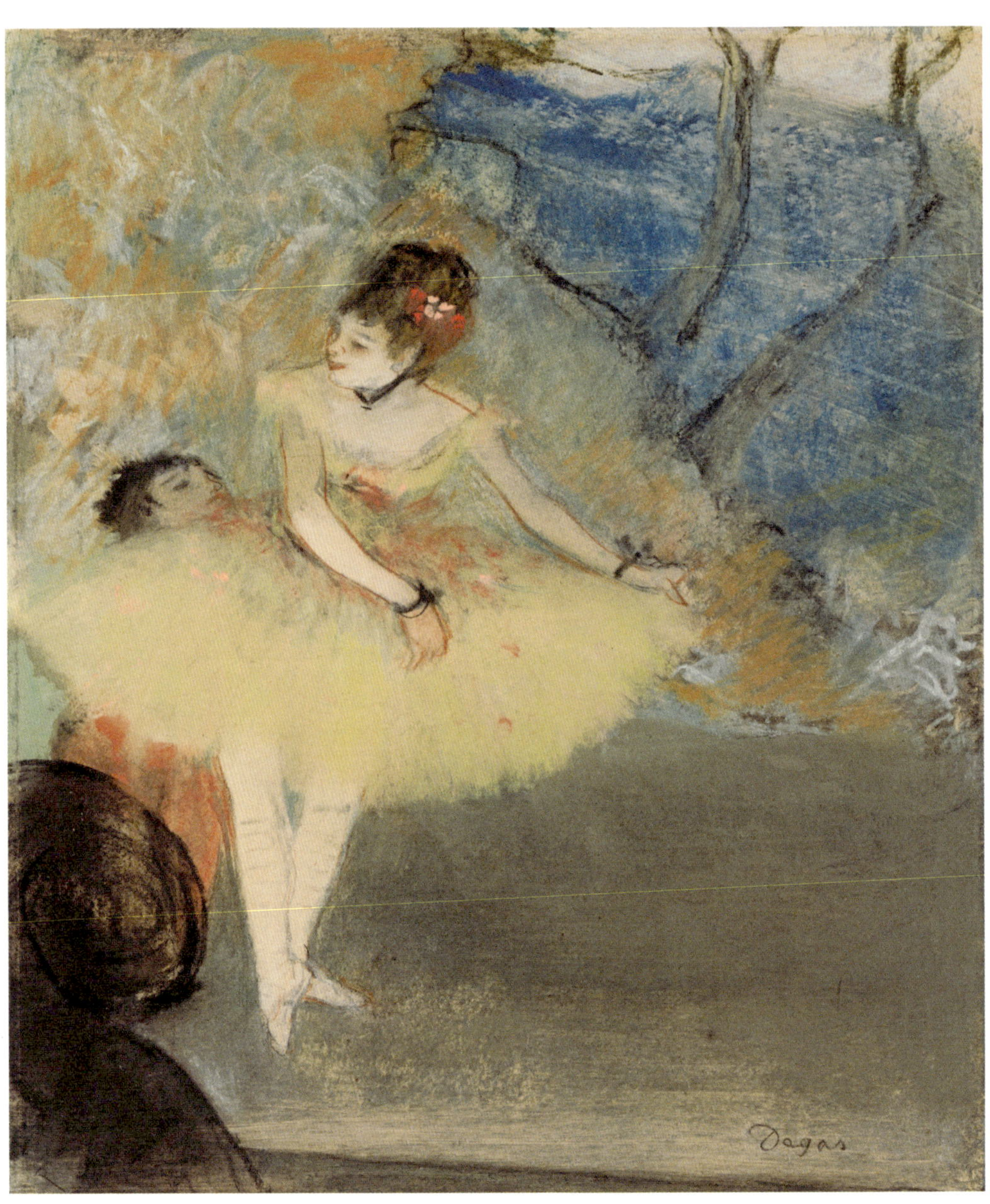

25. *Dancer* (*Danseuse*). c. 1876–77
Pastel and opaque watercolor over monotype on paper
Plate: 8 7/16 × 6 7/8 in. (21.5 × 17.5 cm), sheet: 8 7/16 × 6 7/8 in. (21.5 × 17.5 cm)
Kunstmuseum Winterthur. Anonymous gift

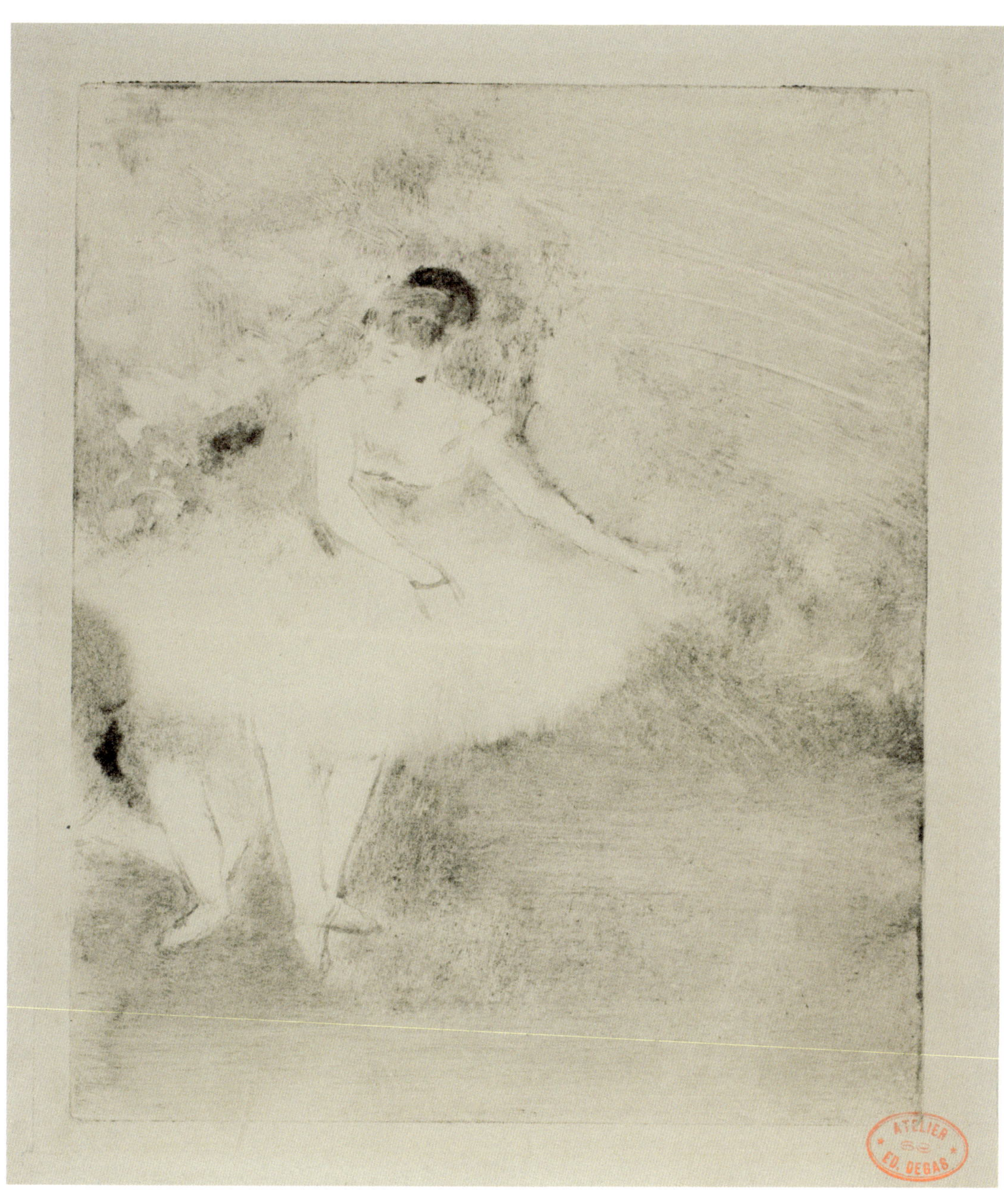

26. *Two Dancers* (*Deux danseuses*). 1877
Monotype on paper
Plate: 8 $\frac{9}{16}$ × 6 $\frac{15}{16}$ in. (21.7 × 17.7 cm)
Statens Museum for Kunst, Copenhagen

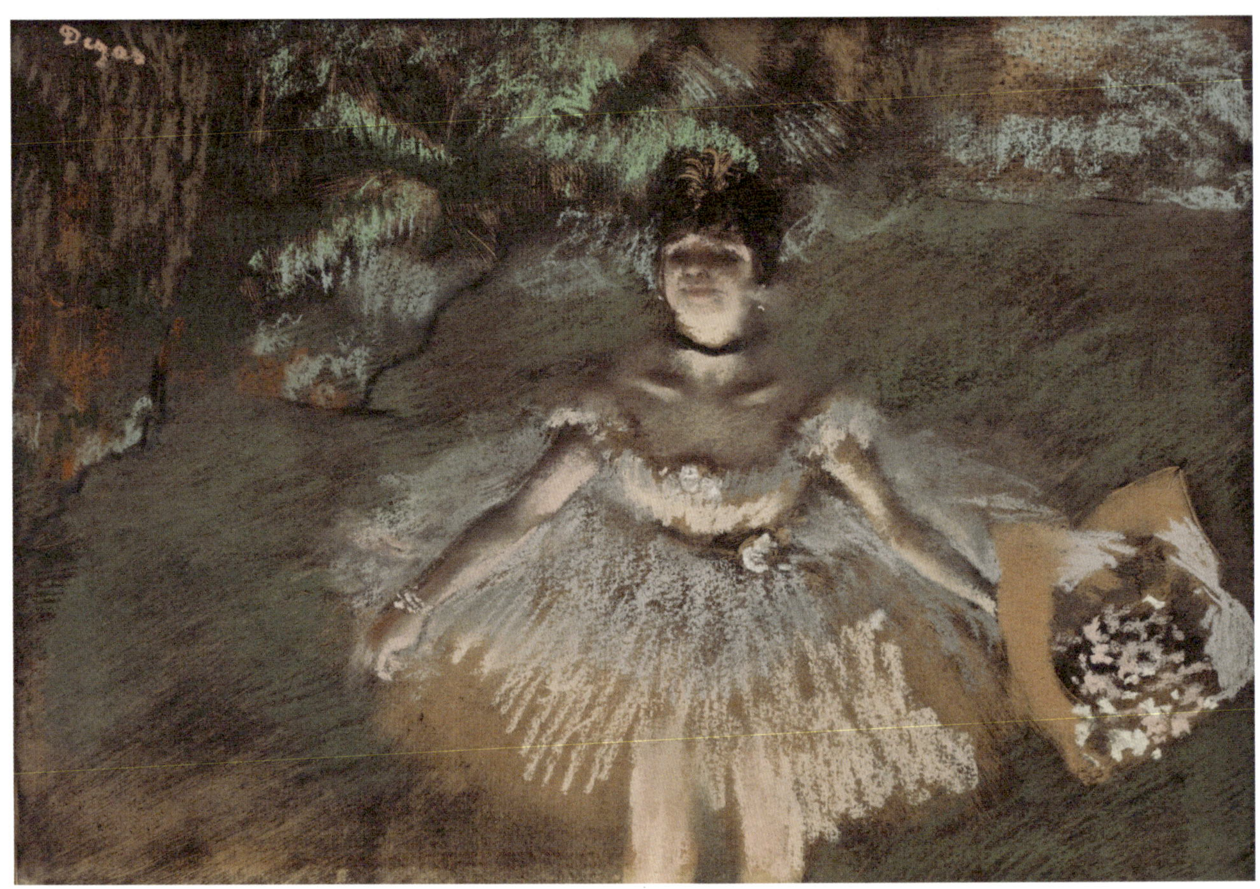

27. *Dancer Onstage with a Bouquet* (*Danseuse saluant*). c. 1876
Pastel over monotype on paper
Plate: 10 ⅝ × 14 ⅞ in. (27 × 37.8 cm)
Private collection

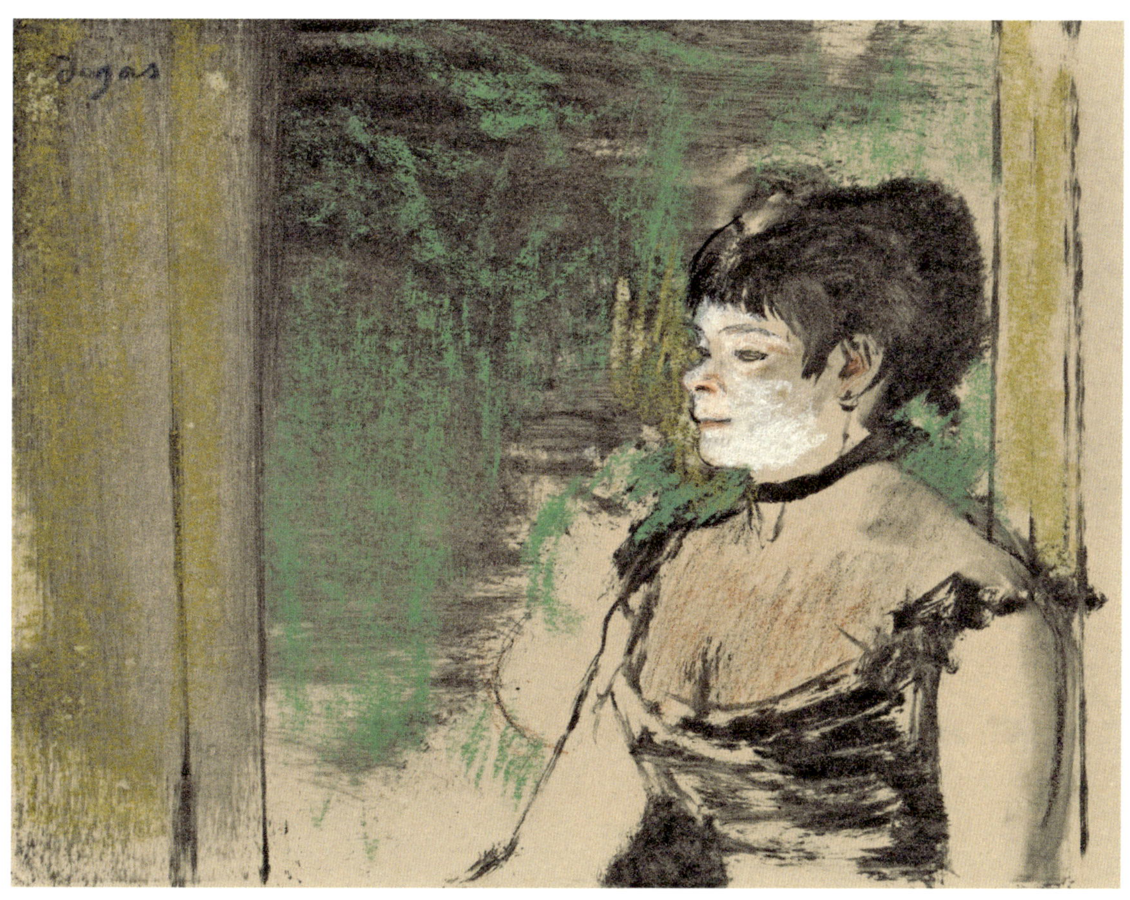

28. *Café-Concert Singer* (*Chanteuse de café-concert*). c. 1875–76
Pastel over monotype on paper
9 ⅛ × 11 3⁄16 in. (23.2 × 28.4 cm)
John and Marine van Vlissingen Foundation

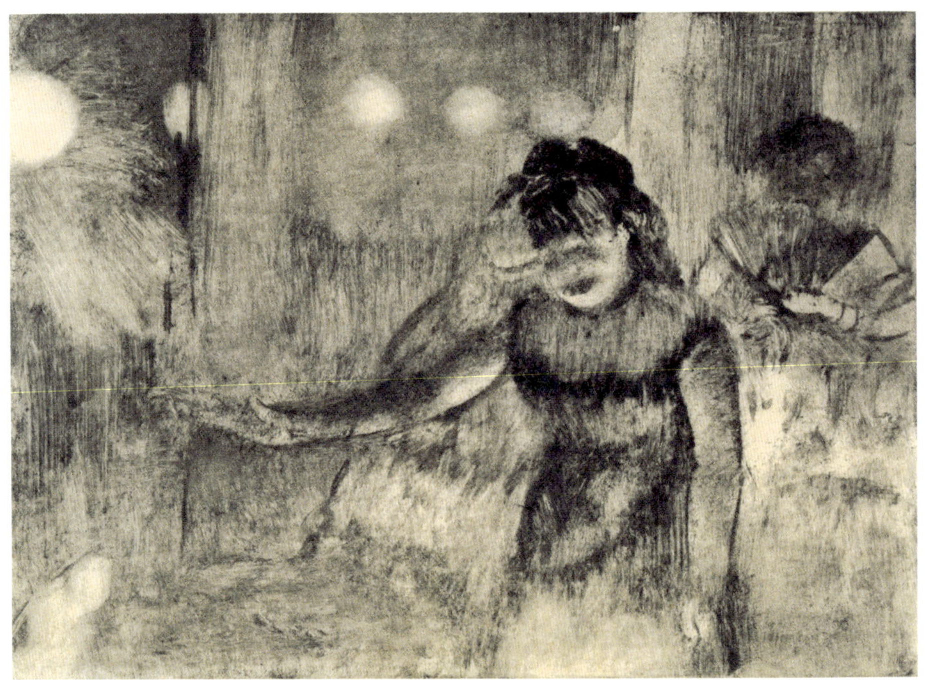

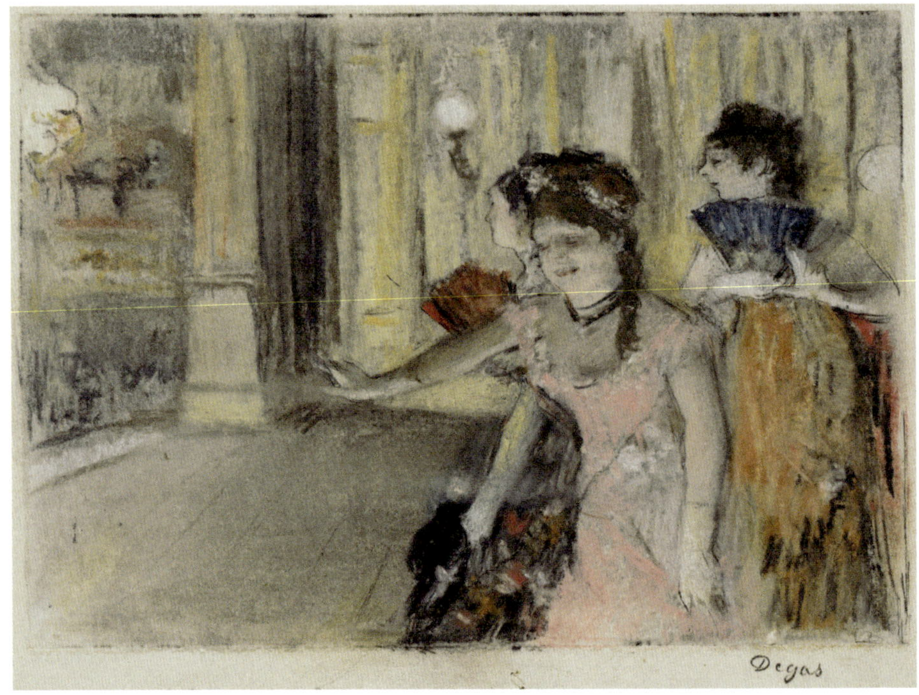

29. *Café Singer* (*Chanteuse du café-concert*). c. 1877–78
Monotype on paper
Plate: 4 ¾ × 6 ⅜ in. (12 × 16.2 cm), sheet: 5 1⁄16 × 6 9⁄16 in. (12.9 × 16.7 cm) (irregular)
Private collection

30. *Singers on the Stage* (*Café-Concert*). c. 1877-79
Pastel over monotype on paper mounted on board
Plate: 4 ¾ × 6 ⅝ in. (12 × 16.9 cm), sheet: 5 7⁄16 × 7 3⁄16 in. (13.8 × 18.2 cm)
The Art Institute of Chicago. Bequest of Mrs. Clive Runnells

Darkness and the Light of Lamps

Hollis Clayson

Innovative lighting was a hallmark of nineteenth-century Paris—a significant component of the City of Light's modernity—and Degas's monotypes *Café Singer* (*Chanteuse du café-concert*, c. 1877–78; plate 29) and *Singers on the Stage* (*Café-Concert*) (1877–79; plate 30) exemplify its entanglement with advanced printmaking.[1] The convergence of printmaking with the visual qualities of artificial light (*éclairage*) linked pictorial modernism to technological modernity, a leitmotif of much of the era's innovative art. Graphic-arts specialists have noted that the first years of electric light's significant presence in Paris were years of consequence for inventive prints, albeit without connecting the two spheres of innovation.[2] I believe that the new *éclairage*, both in the streets and in the spaces of commercial entertainment, helped to foster innovative printmaking in the studios of modernist artists. My essay thus presses "lighting" and "light"—*éclairage* and *lumière*—into intimate association by wagering that Degas repeatedly thought about them concurrently in his prints.

The awareness of lighting in Paris intensified between 1878 and 1882, dynamic years for the industrialization of light in Paris—the period when the city's lights were first electrified, becoming brighter and newsworthy. The era's nonstop march of more radiant and higher-tech lighting into spaces both private and public informed Degas's monochrome light-field-manner prints, which at the fundamental level of syntax consist of darkness and light. Because this silent new glaring light had both an economics and a poetics, it became a figure for the contrary coexistence in modernity of sheltered privacy but also of mechanization, of freedom but also of control, mirroring a fundamental condition of modern life described by Jonathan Crary: "One crucial dimension of capitalist modernity is a constant remaking of the conditions of sensory experience."[3]

In his intaglio prints of the mid-to-late 1870s Degas showed commercial lighting contraptions expertly and often. These preponderantly indoor or threshold pictures use industrialized light as a marker of mechanized urban modernity, and often make women entertainers seem vulgar and brash by juxtaposing and rhyming light fixtures with their heads. The locus classicus of this device is the tiny whimsical etching *Singer's Profile* (*Profil de chanteuse*, c. 1875–78; fig. 1), in which the adjacency of a female performer's profile to four light globes sets up a kinship among spheres; the young woman's winsome expression distinguishes her from the machinic object world, but the quintet of circles is a family of forms nonetheless. The etching's spheres recall a metaphor used in 1882 by Guy de Maupassant in his short story "*Claire de lune*" (Moonlight), later archived by Walter Benjamin:

I reached the Champs-Elysées, where the cafés concerts seemed like blazing hearths among the leaves. The chestnut trees, brushed with yellow light, had the look of painted objects, the look of phosphorescent trees. And the electric globes—like shimmering, pale moons, like moon eggs fallen from the sky, like monstrous, living pearls—dimmed, with their nacreous glow, mysterious and regal, the flaring jets of gas, of ugly, dirty gas, and the garlands of colored glass.[4]

The shared attentiveness to the glow of "moon eggs" is striking: gas globes in Degas, electric orbs in Maupassant.

Degas too wrote about light. In around 1876, for example, he recorded this idea in a notebook: "On evening—infinite variety of subjects in cafés—different tones of the glass globes reflected in the mirrors."[5] A postscript to a letter of 1879 to the artist Félix Bracquemond about plans for the next Impressionist show illustrates Degas's enthusiastic familiarity with the new lights cropping up in his immediate environment: "The Company Jablockof [*sic*] proposes to do the lighting with electric light."[6]

The setting of Degas's monotype *Café Singer* is a largely indistinct café-concert equipped for stage entertainment. The shapes that bracket a dark-haired female performer are essentially human-shaped blurs against which only one gloved hand holding an open fan is clearly defined. The performer herself, the sole legible figure, is by contrast a creature of theatrical illumination: beams of light clearly model her body and head from below. The glare of unseen footlights sculpts her arms in stark darks and lights. The planes of her brightly lit face, on a head that tilts forward dreamily, contrast sharply with her dark smudge of a mouth and barely defined gray eye sockets, which suggest eyes closed against the glare.

The print is chockablock with lamps that shine into view. The rays of a bright-white round globe at the far left form a corona to denote the light's piercing brilliance. It must be a Jablochkoff candle, an electric arc light like the ones Degas mentioned in his letter to Bracquemond and that served as Maupassant's points of departure in 1882; although these lights were in use in some clubs in the later 1870s, this one implies an outdoor space. The three white balls just above the singer's head are surely gas globes, which

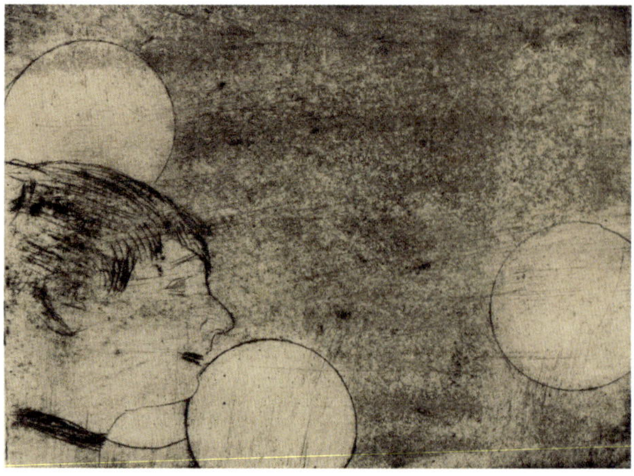

1: Hilaire-Germain-Edgar Degas. *Singer's Profile (Profil de chanteuse).* c. 1875–78. Etching, drypoint, and aquatint on paper, 2 11⁄16 × 3 3⁄8 in. (6.8 × 7.8 cm). Sterling and Francine Clark Art Institute, Williamstown, Massachusetts

Degas often drew, as we have seen, as unmodeled spheres. Following the connotative logic of rhyming things and people, this trio of light fixtures echoes and verifies the presence of three women performers. The identity of a fifth lamp, between this row and the Jablochkoff candle, is less certain, but despite the slight irrationality of its placement, its oval spot of light and dark body suggest a gas streetlight (*un réverbère*). This sheet deserves to be counted among Degas's most virtuosic monochromatic orchestrations of multiple kinds of night light. If complex *éclairage* is a distinguishing feature of this monotype, another is the woman's solitary and striking performance gesture: her expansively extended right arm, a cylindrical pneumatic sausage stretched horizontally across the page. This limb appears distended, as if buoyed up by and floating upon the light that blazes onto its lower surface.

Singers on the Stage, printed from the same plate but significantly modified through the application of pastel, alters the logic of the tonal foundation common to both images. The makeover of both the figures and the spatial setting pushes our belief in the sibling relationship between the two artworks to the breaking point. The transformed mise en scène alters both the axis and the temporality of the routine pursued by the lead performer, who here wears a pink frock: she no longer faces her audience, now obviously off to the left, so she has either finished singing, and is heading toward the wings, or has not yet begun.[7] Her expression too has shifted, from a smile accompanying a gentle melting into the light, ostensibly toward limelight and listeners, to a pinched hesitancy before the onslaught of stage lighting, although that light is mitigated and in places actually erased. This cautious, even worried facial expression, the subtly altered axis of the woman's head, and her swankier hairstyle quite redefine her comportment. And the face of the woman at right, meanwhile, still holding her fan, is now visible but jarringly caricatured.

That a tense demeanor should define an entertainer removed from the space of performance is puzzling. Her right arm still extends right, now toward the audience, but it is shorter, and its distortion and stark modeling are gone. Its straightness, however, augments its sense of strain, not to mention the odd note struck by the eye-catching acute angle it forms with the downward pointing arm of the woman behind the lead performer, previously indistinct but now sharply drawn. This conjunction of two lean arms—as if the hands of a clock were sitting almost at the center of the sheet—is disruptive, and muddies the definition of the space occupied by these two spiky-limbed women.

Another telling modification is the transformation of the lighting. The lamps in the pastel are less numerous, motley, and ferocious; all are powered by gas. A single upmarket sconce (*une applique à gaz*) replaces the naked moon eggs in *Café Singer*. Most significantly, the dazzling electric arc light at the far left of that work, alongside what seems to be a gas streetlight—both markers of the outdoors—are gone, replaced by an elegant multiglobe chandelier (*un lustre à gaz*) suspended over the audience. It secures the room's identity as a theater, a kind of establishment not lit by electricity in Paris in the later 1870s.[8] In moving to this indoor arena, Degas has made a basic change in the nature of the space of two scenes printed from the same plate.

Two extraordinary last details illustrate Degas's abiding interest in the visualities of artificial light. At the top left, to the right of the chandelier, is a sequence of sawtooth gray lines that imply both the rounded shape of an unseen lamp and its sunlike rays, blurred and fragmented illusions that deserve to be called apparitional. These strokes are surrogates for the dazzle shown in the monotype and concealed in the pastel—Degas could not resist experimenting with indications of the brilliance of artificial light. Finally, on the lip of the stage (seen diagonally at far left) is a sequence of bright white marks, which replace an indistinct series of white spheres at the bottom left of the monochrome print. In both cases what is indexed is surely theatrical limelight (a type of gaslight).[9] Might its glare explain the singer's angular gesture, and her pained expression and averted gaze once she is clothed in pink?

1. See Wolfgang Schivelbusch, *Disenchanted Night: The Industrialization of Light in the Nineteenth Century*, trans. Angela Davies (Berkeley: University of California Press, 1988), pp. 133–54.
2. See, e.g., Nicole Minder, *Degas et Pissarro. Alchimie d'une rencontre* (Vevey: Cabinet Cantonal des Estampes, Musée Jenisch, 1998), p. 15.
3. Jonathan Crary, "Attention and Modernity in the Nineteenth Century," in Caroline A. Jones and Peter Galison, eds., *Picturing Science, Producing Art* (New York: Routledge, 1998), p. 476.
4. Walter Benjamin, *The Arcades Project*, 1927–40, trans. Rolf Tiedemann (Cambridge: Belknap Press of Harvard University Press, 1999), p. 570. Guy de Maupaussant's story "Clair de lune" was first published in *Gil Blas* in October 1882.
5. Degas, in Richard Kendall, *Degas by Himself: Drawings, Prints, Paintings, Writings* (Edison, N.J.: Chartwell Books, 1994), p. 112.
6. Ibid., p. 116. "Jablockov" is presumably a misspelling of "Jablochkoff," the name of a Russian engineer, Paul Jablochkoff (or Yablochkov), resident in Paris beginning in the 1870s, who designed an electric arc light that became widely used.
7. Eugenia Parry Janis, *Degas Monotypes: Essay, Catalogue & Checklist*, exh. cat. (Cambridge, Mass.: Fogg Art Museum and Harvard University, 1968), plate 8, and Richard R. Brettell and Suzanne Folds McCullagh, *Degas in The Art Institute of Chicago* (Chicago: The Art Institute of Chicago, and New York: Harry N. Abrams, 1984), p. 86, noted the changed setting years ago.
8. See Frank Géraldy, "L'électricité au théâtre," *La Lumière électrique* 14 (July 1880):284. The first theater to convert entirely to electric light was in San Francisco in 1879; the Savoy in London became the first in Europe in 1881. See Andres Blühm and Louise Lippincott, *Light! The Industrial Age 1750–1900: Art and Science, Technology and Society* (Amsterdam: Van Gogh Museum, and Pittsburgh: Carnegie Museum of Art, 2000), p. 166. In 1877, a new municipal law was passed obliging Paris theaters to electrify.
9. See Blühm and Lippincott, *Light!*, p. 166.

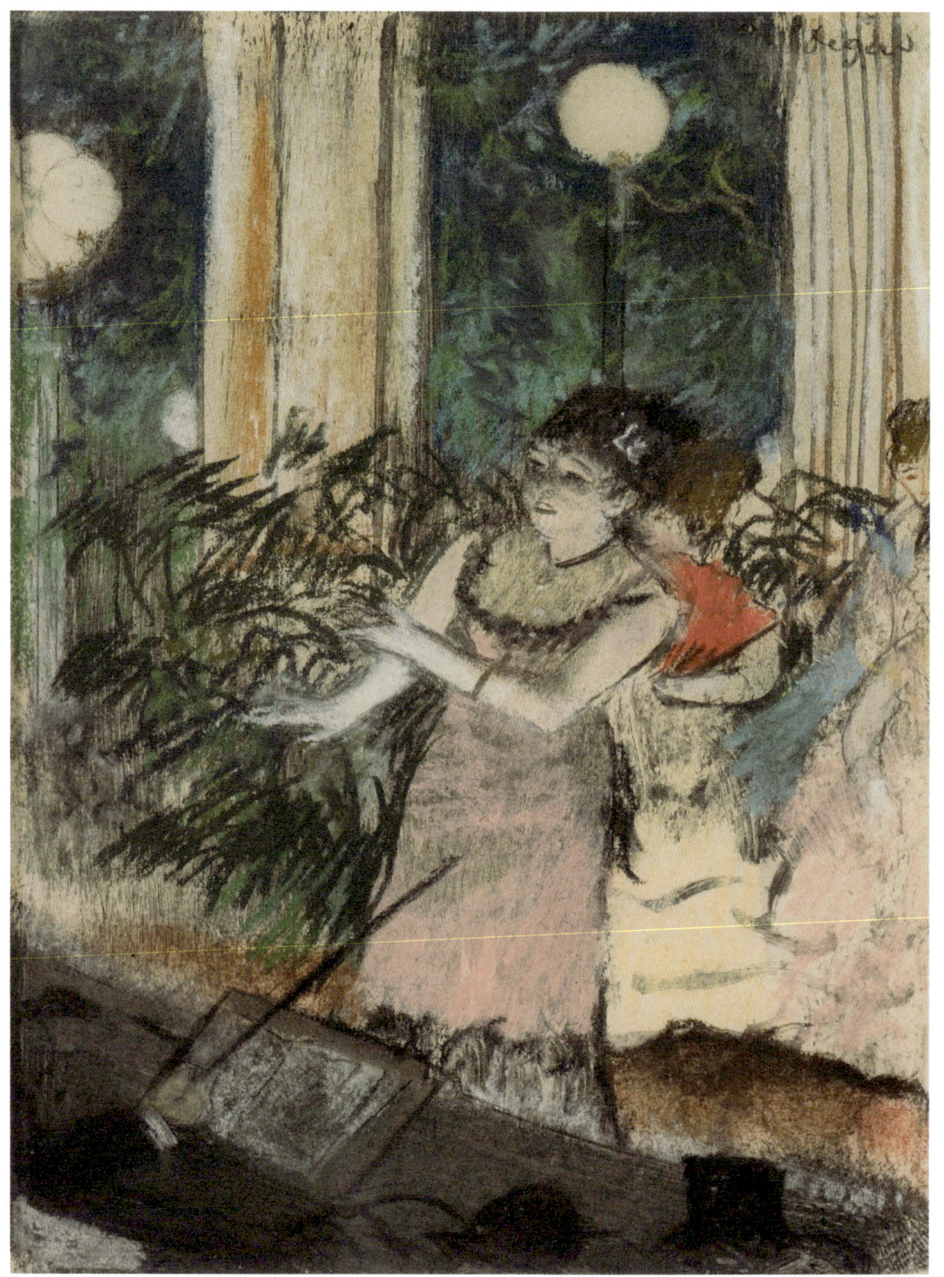

31. *The Café-Concert Singer* (*Chanteuse de café-concert*). 1875–76
Pastel over monotype on paper
Plate: 6 ½ × 4 ¾ in. (16.5 × 12.1 cm)
Private collection

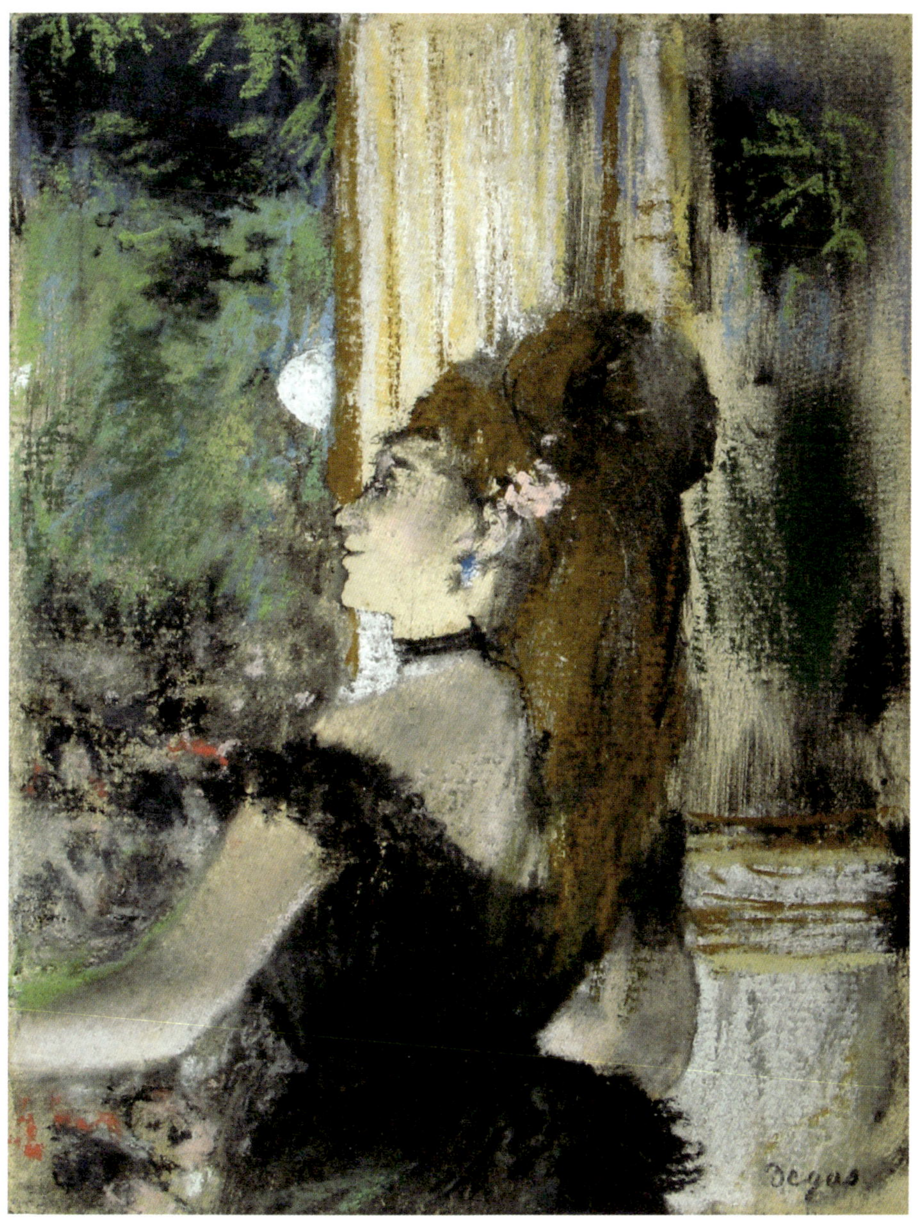

32. *The Singer* (*Chanteuse de café-concert*). 1875–80
Pastel over monotype on paper
Plate: 6 ¼ × 4 ½ in. (15.9 × 11.4 cm)
Reading Public Museum, Reading, Pennsylvania. Gift, Miss Martha Elizabeth Dick Estate

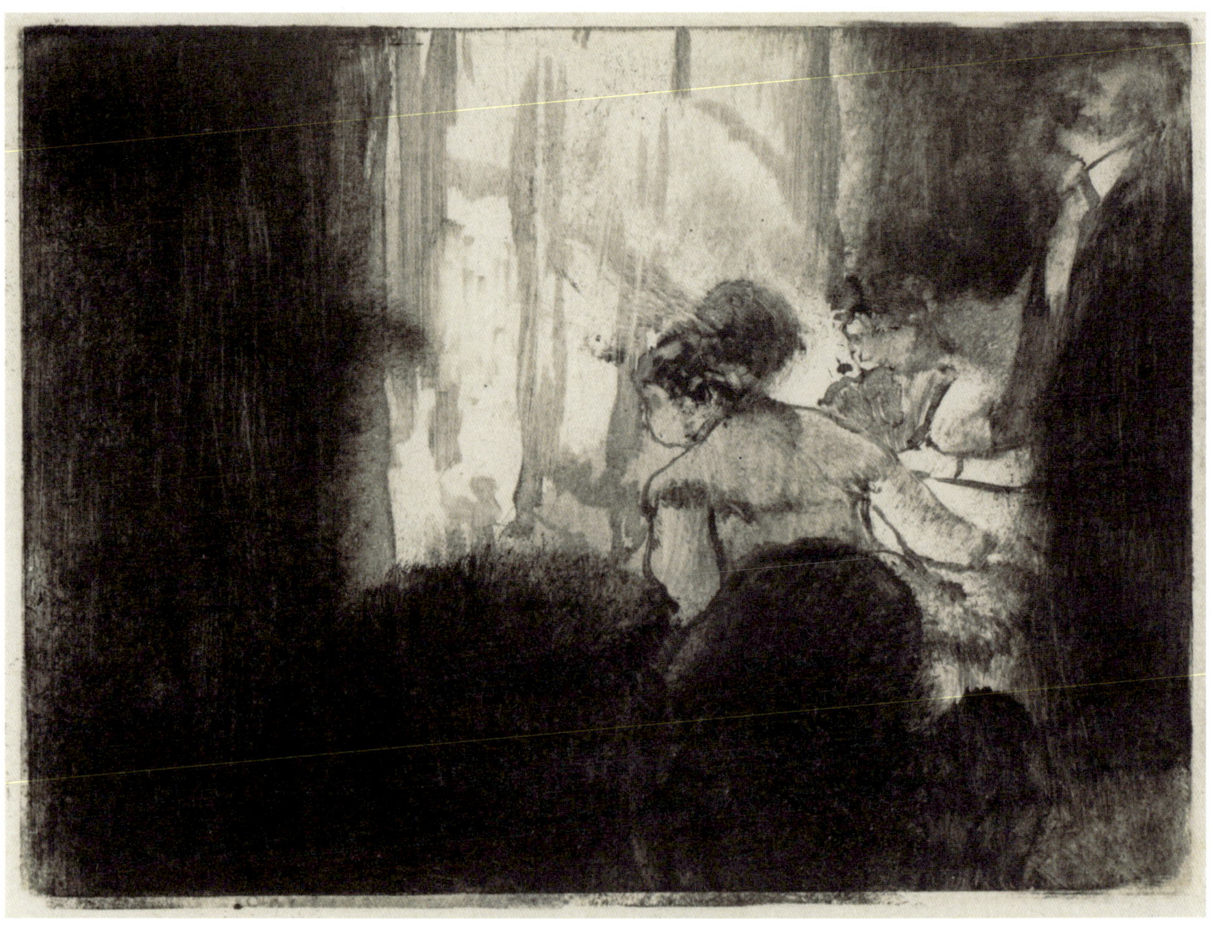

33. *The Loge* (*La Loge*). c. 1878
Monotype on paper
Plate: 4 ¾ × 6 ¼ in. (12.1 × 15.9 cm)
Baltimore Museum of Art. Purchase with exchange funds from Nelson and Juanita Greif Gutman Collection

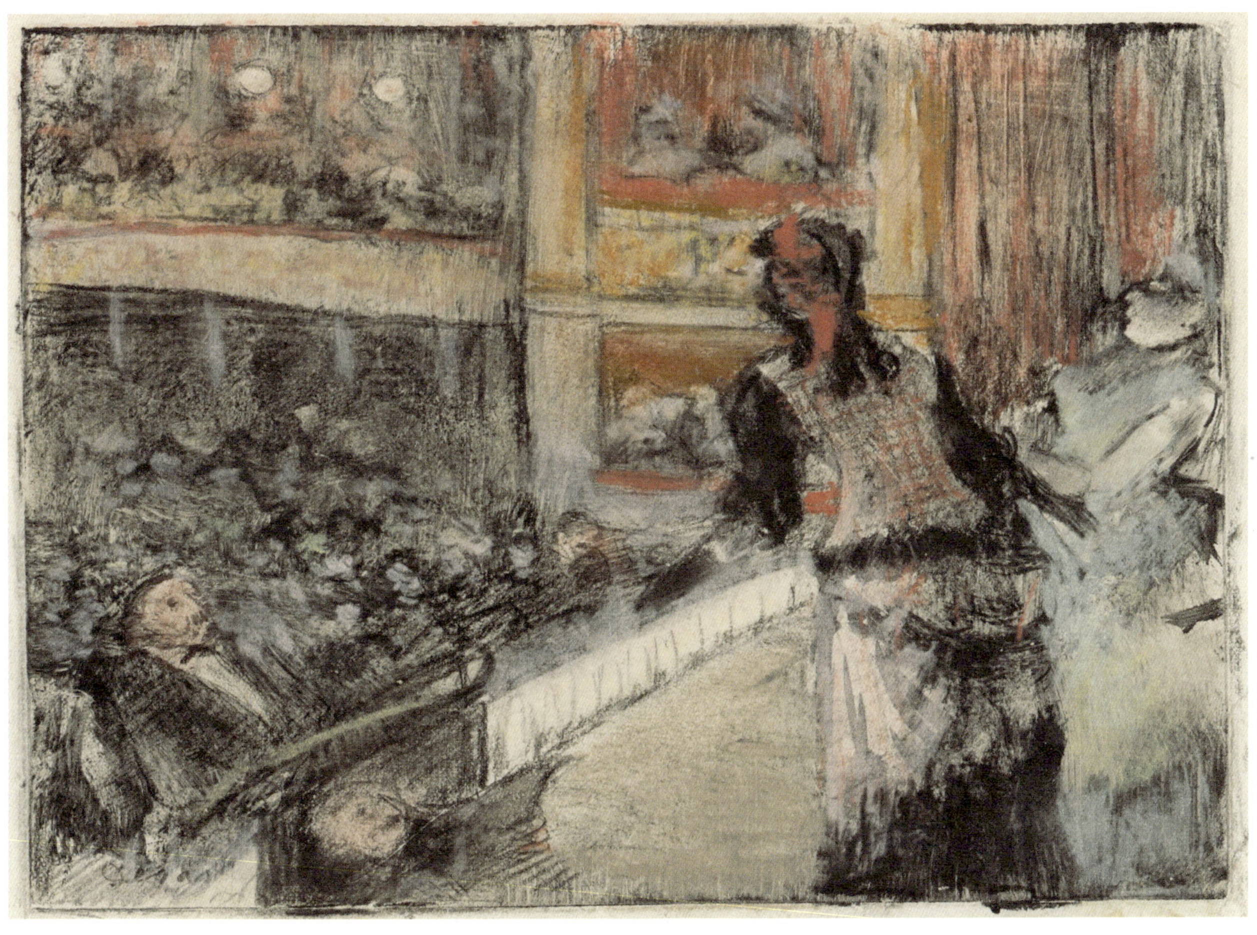

34. *At the Theater: The Duet* (*Le Duo*). 1877–79
Pastel over monotype on paper
Plate: 4 11⁄16 × 6 3⁄8 in. (11.9 × 16.2 cm), sheet: 5 5⁄16 × 7 1⁄16 in. (13.5 × 17.9 cm)
The Morgan Library & Museum, New York. Thaw Collection

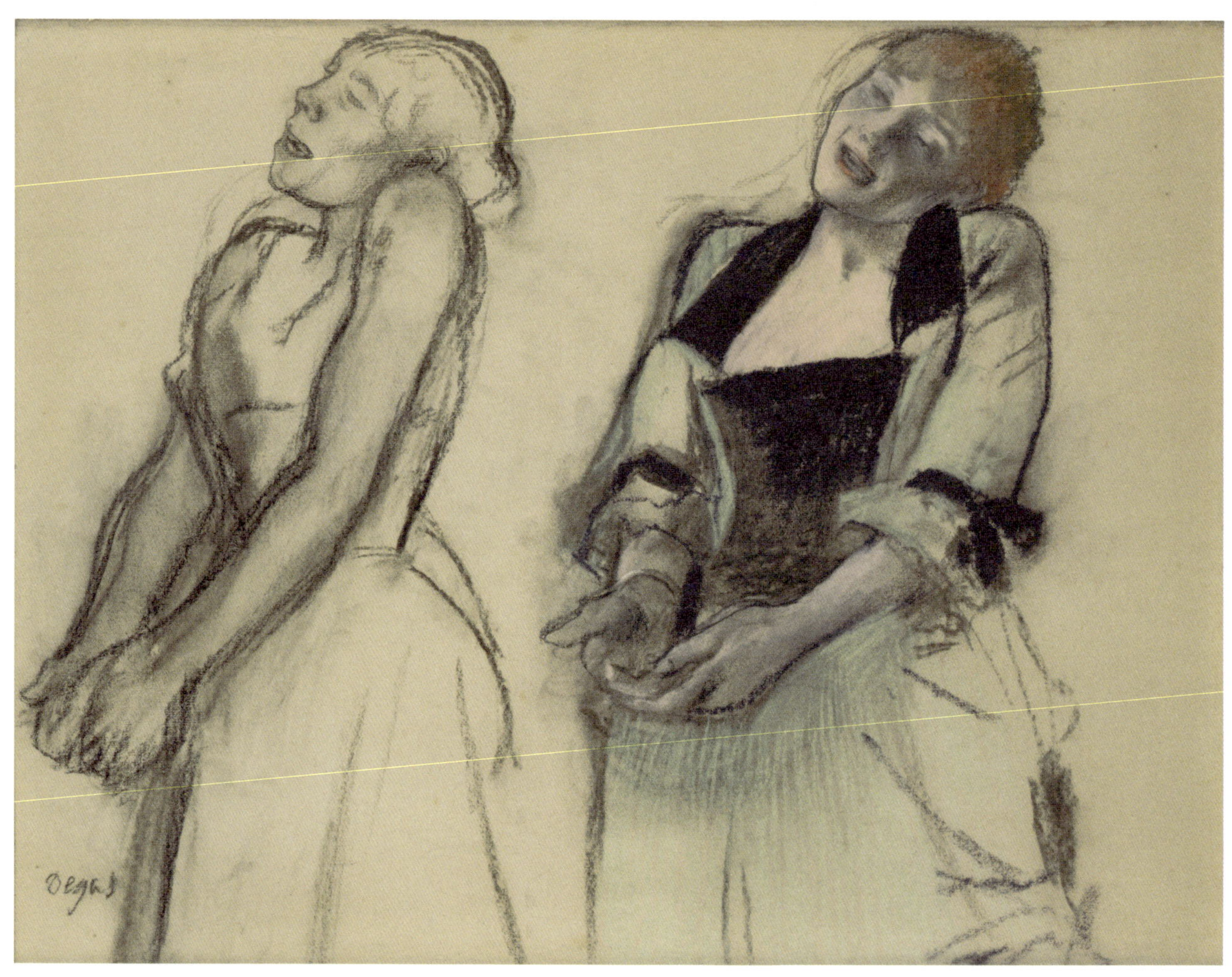

35. *Two Studies for a Music Hall Singer* (*Deux études pour chanteuses de café-concert*). c. 1878–80
Pastel and charcoal on gray paper
17 ½ × 22 7⁄16 in. (44.5 × 57 cm)
Private collection

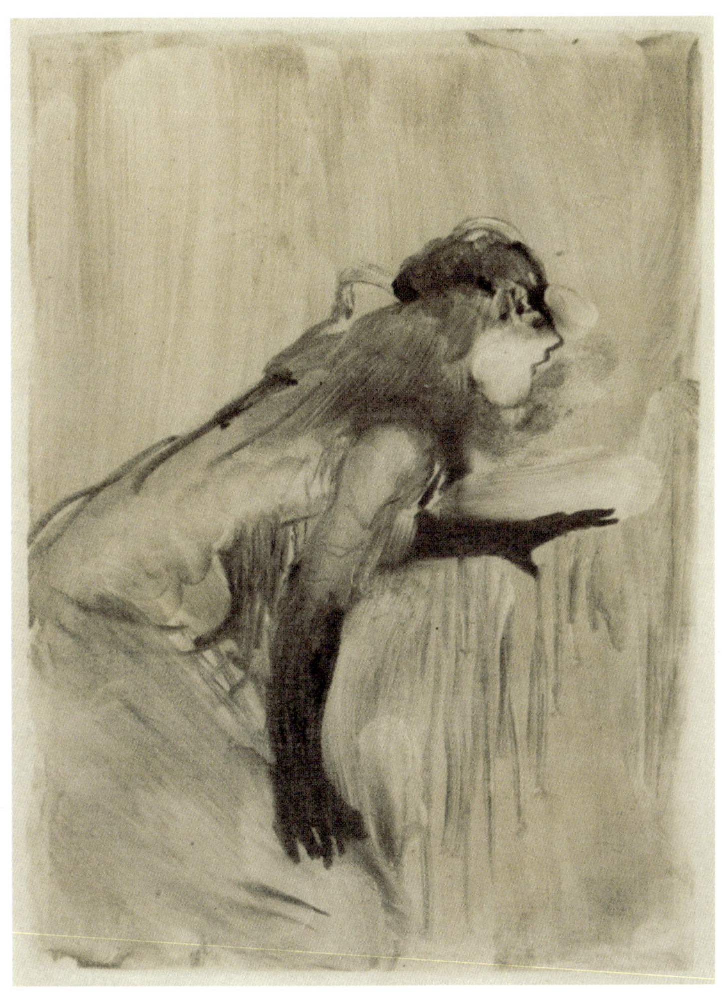

36. *Café-Concert Singer* (*Chanteuse de café-concert*). c. 1877
Monotype on paper mounted on board
Plate: 7 5⁄16 × 5 1⁄16 in. (18.5 × 12.8 cm), sheet: 9 1⁄4 × 7 1⁄16 in. (23.5 × 18 cm)
Private collection

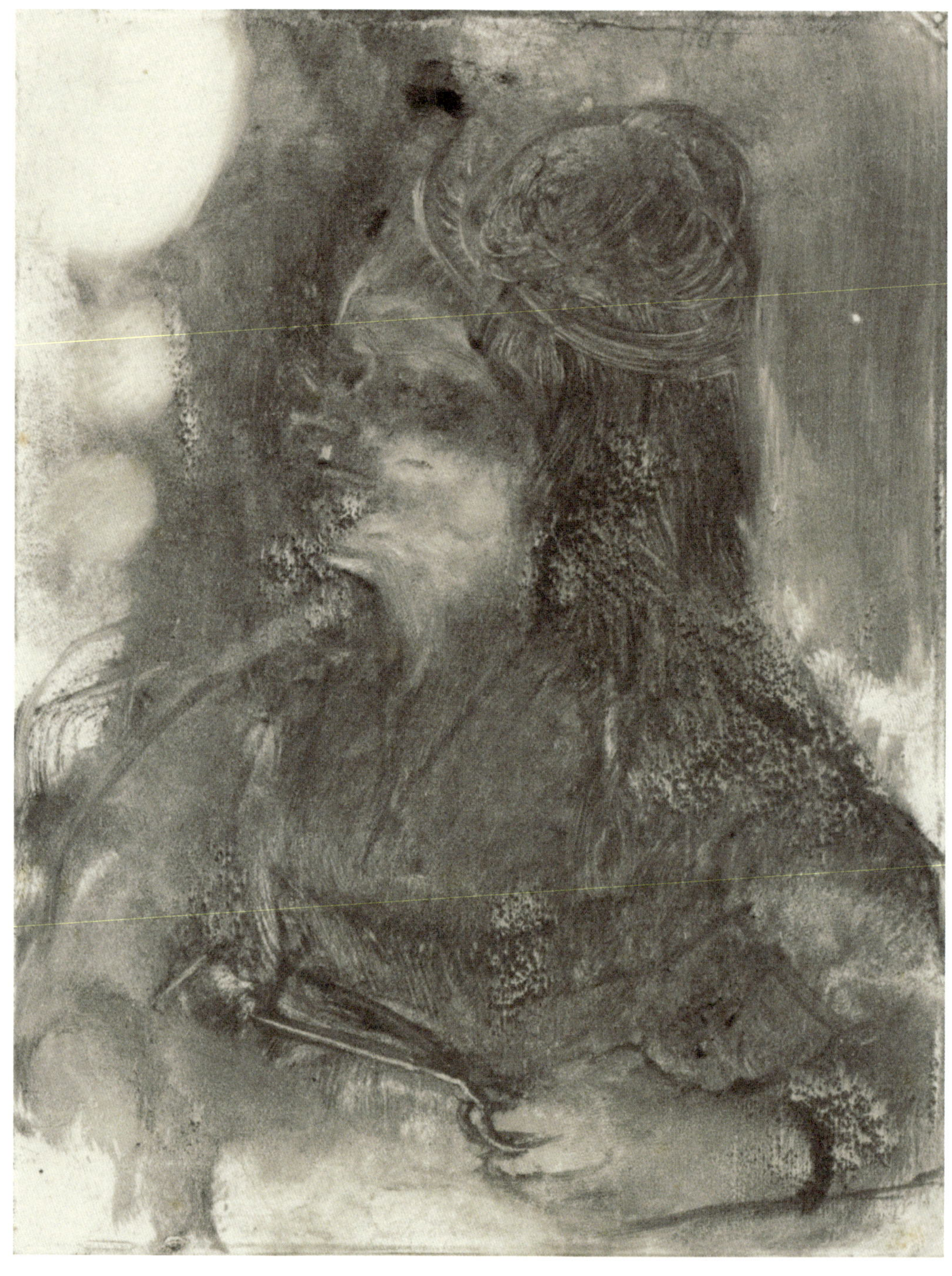

37. *Song of the Scissors* (*La Chanson des ciseaux*). c. 1877–78
Monotype on paper
Plate: 8 ½ × 6 5⁄16 in. (21.6 × 16.1 cm), sheet: 10 5⁄16 × 7 5⁄16 in. (26.2 × 18.5 cm)
Harvard Art Museums/Fogg Museum, Cambridge, Massachusetts. Gift of Henry F. Harrison

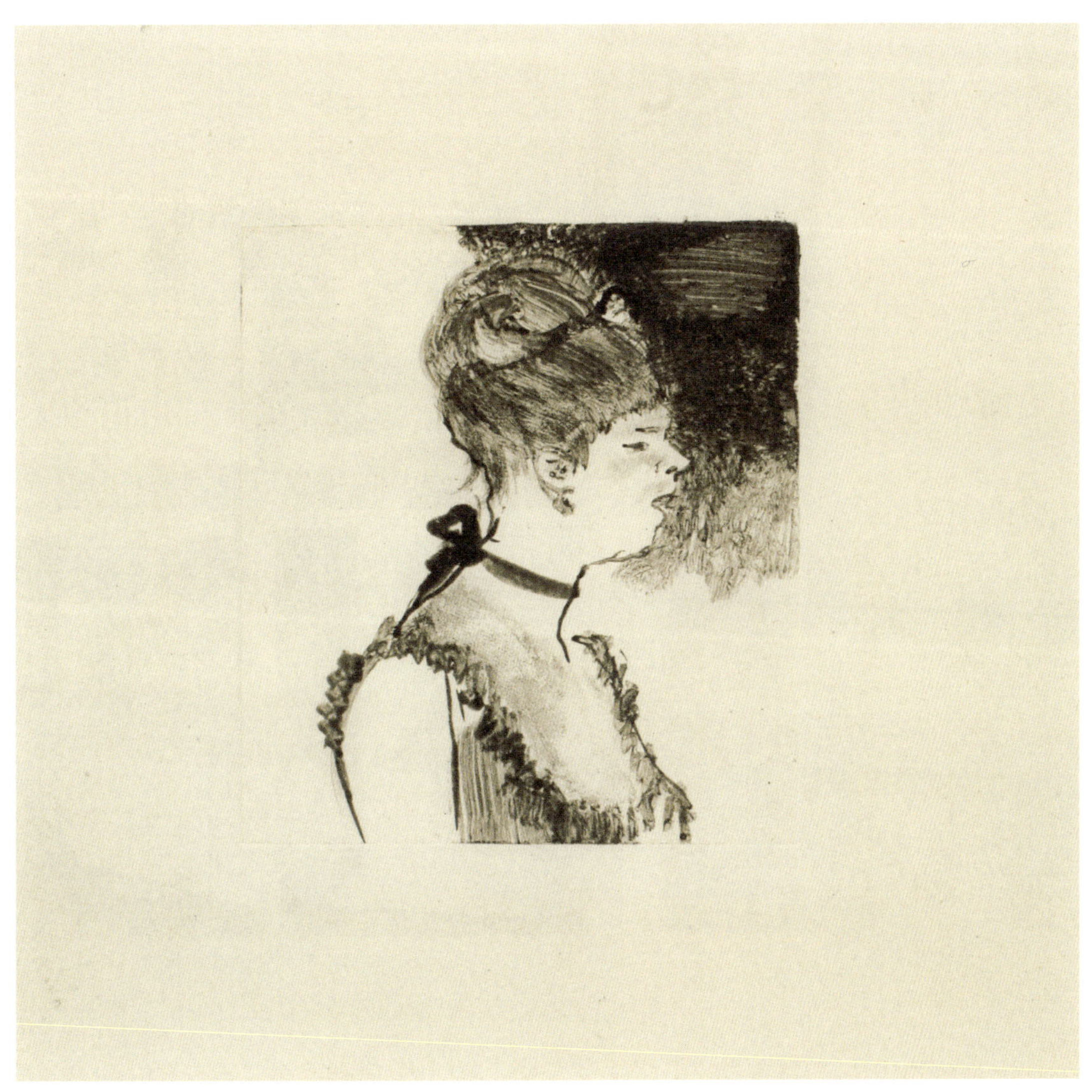

38. *Café-Concert Singer* (*Chanteuse de café-concert, profil droit*). c. 1878–80
Monotype on paper
Plate: 3 ⅛ × 2 13⁄16 in. (8 × 7.2 cm), sheet: 7 ¼ × 6 ⅜ in. (18.4 × 16.2 cm)
The Art Institute of Chicago. Potter Palmer Collection Fund

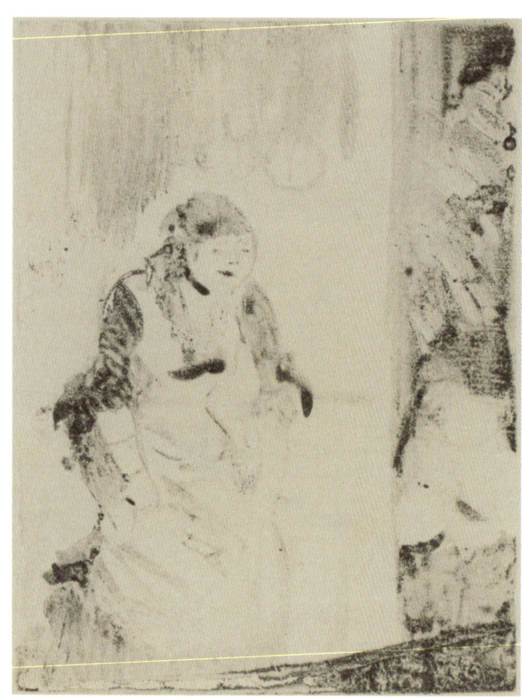

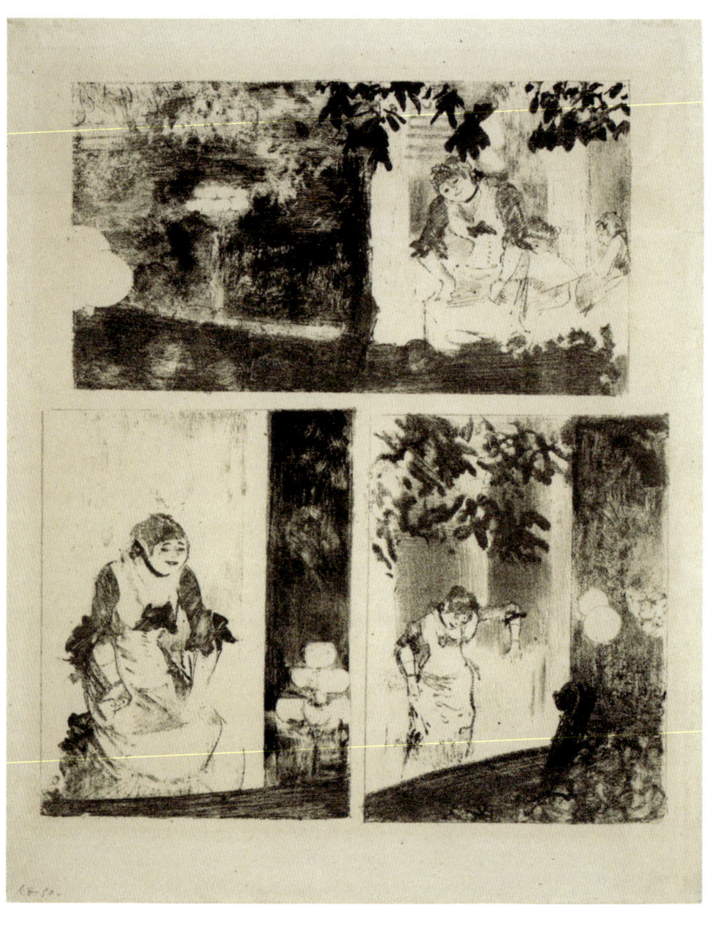

39. *Mlle Bécat*. c. 1877–78
Monotype on paper
Plate: 6 ¼ × 4 11⁄16 in. (15.9 × 11.9 cm)
National Gallery of Art, Washington, D.C.
Rosenwald Collection

40. *Mlle Bécat at the Café des Ambassadeurs: Three Motifs* (*Mlle Bécat aux Ambassadeurs, planche a trois sujets*). c. 1877–78
Lithograph on paper, composition transferred from three monotypes
Sheet: 13 ⅞ × 10 11⁄16 in. (35.2 × 27.2 cm)
Museum of Fine Arts, Boston. Gift of George Peabody Gardner

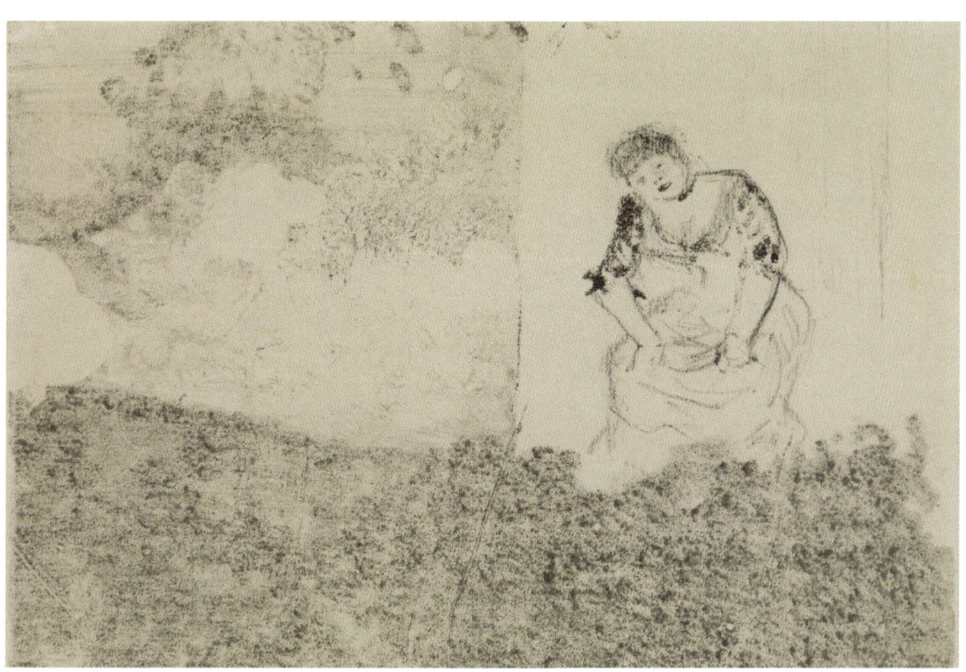

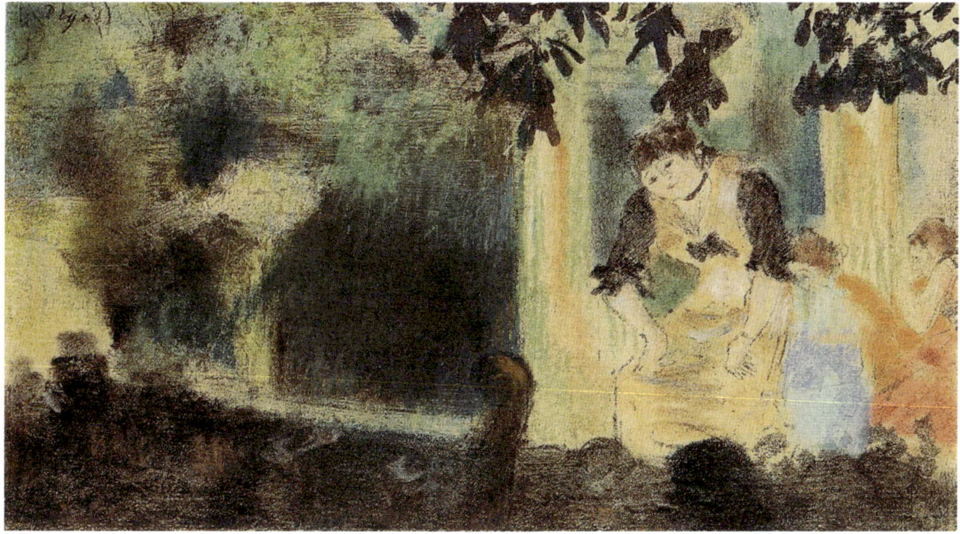

41. *Mlle Bécat at the Café des Ambassadeurs* (*Mlle Bécat aux Ambassadeurs*). c. 1878–80
Monotype on paper
Plate: 5 ⅞ × 8 7⁄16 in. (14.9 × 21.4 cm), sheet: 5 ⅞ × 8 ⅞ in. (14.9 × 22.5 cm)
Statens Museum for Kunst, Copenhagen

42. *Mlle Bécat* (*Mlle Bécat aux Ambassadeurs*). c. 1877–79
Pastel over lithograph on paper
Composition: 4 ⅞ × 8 ⅝ in. (12.4 × 21.9 cm)
Private collection

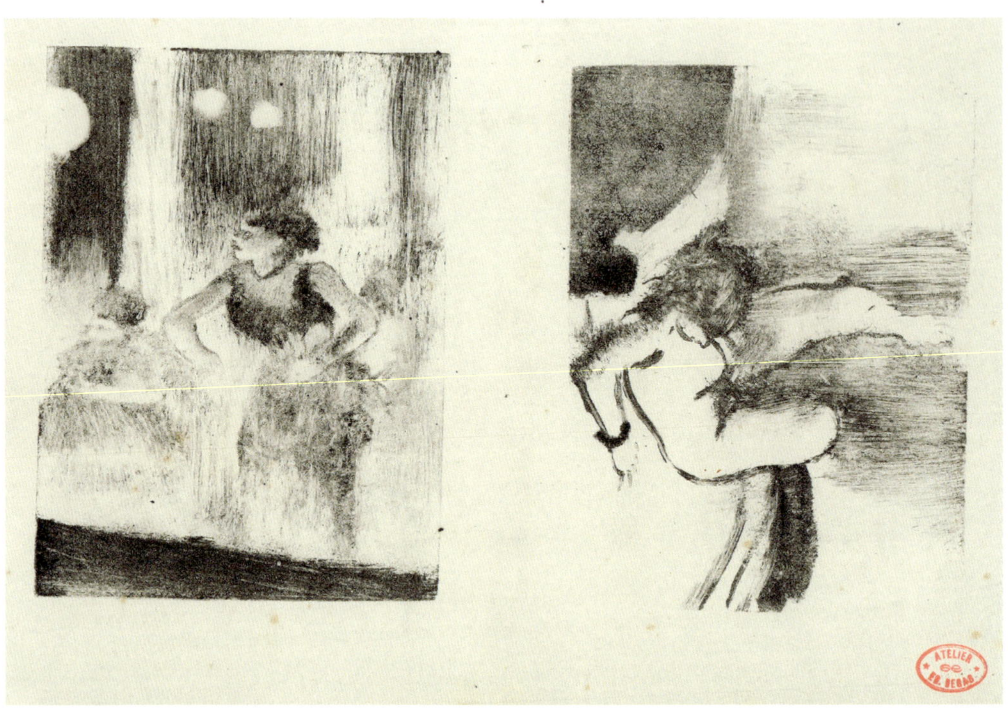

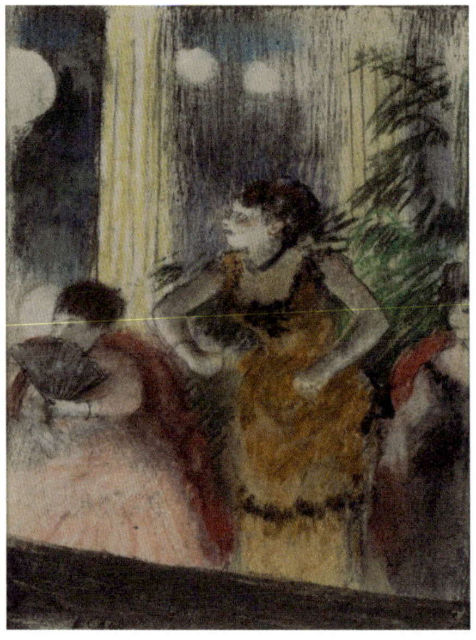

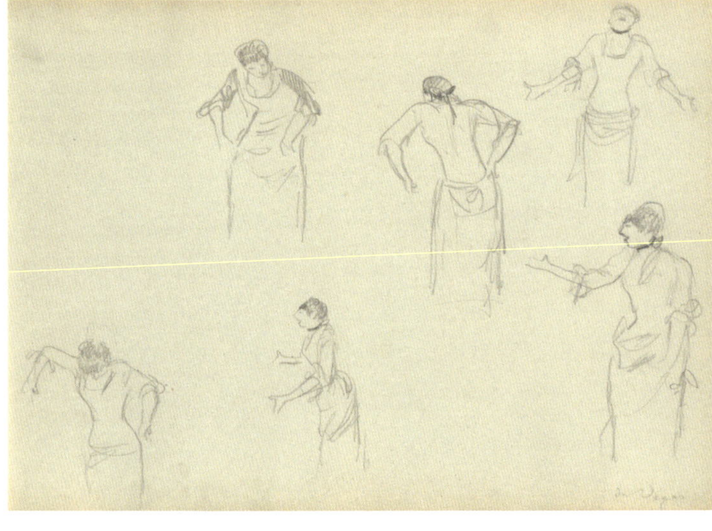

43. *Two Performers at a Café-Concert* and *Morning Frolic* (*Mlle Bécat aux Ambassadeurs* and *Ebats matinal*). 1877–79
Lithograph on paper, composition transferred from two monotypes, only state
Sheet: 9 ⅝ × 12 ⅝ in. (24.5 × 32 cm)
Private collection

44. *Two Performers at a Café-concert* (*Mlle Bécat aux Ambassadeurs [café-concert]*). c. 1877–79
Pastel over lithograph on paper
Composition: 6 ⅜ × 4 13⁄16 in. (16.2 × 12.2 cm)
Private collection

45. Drawings of café singers from a sketchbook. c. 1880
Pencil, charcoal, and blue chalk on paper
Sheet: 9 13⁄16 × 13 ⅜ in. (24.9 × 33.9 cm)
The Morgan Library & Museum, New York. Thaw Collection

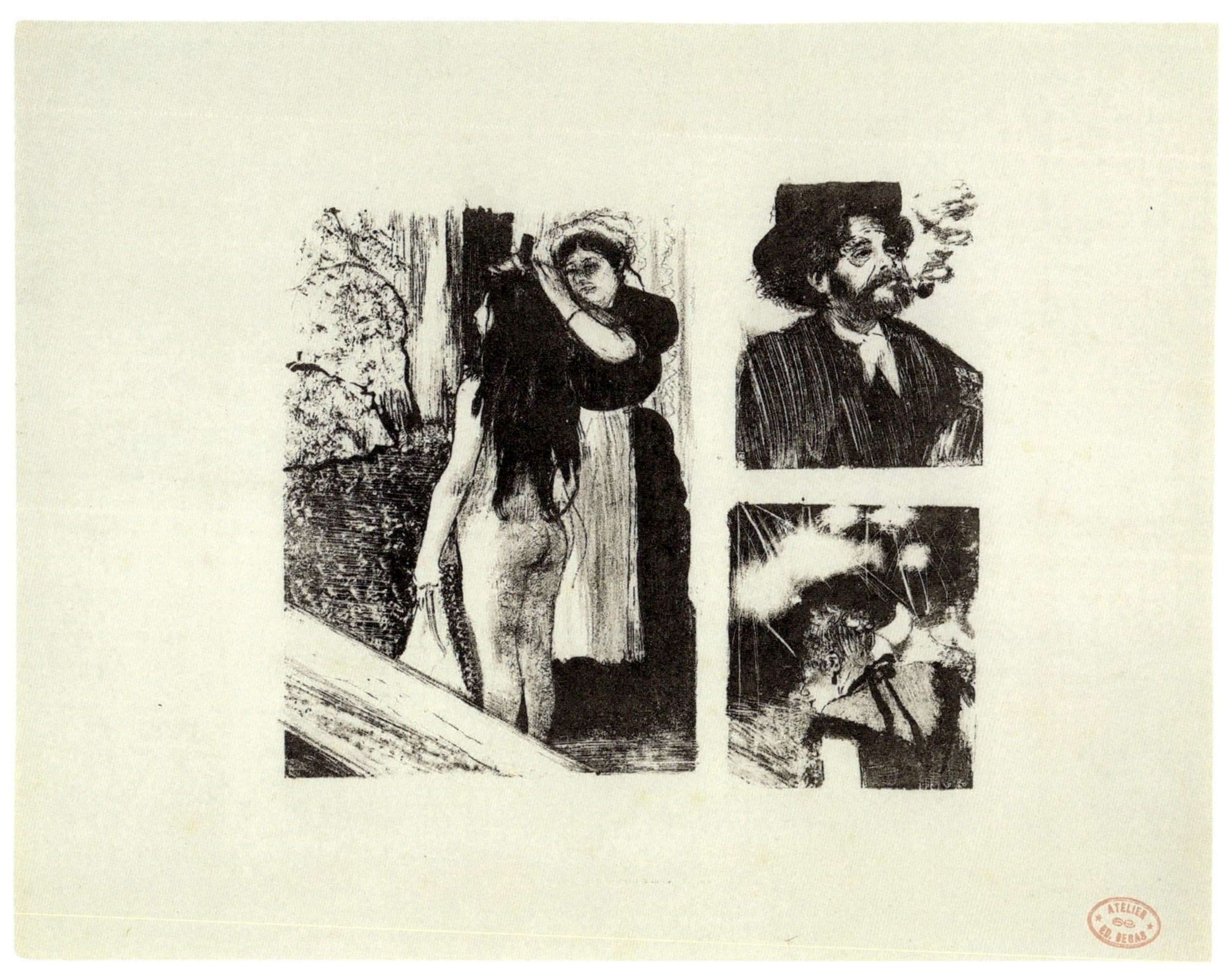

46. *Three Subjects: The Toilette, Marcellin Desboutin, The Café-Concert* (*Planche aux trois sujets: la toilette; Marcellin Desboutin; café-concert*). 1876–77
Lithograph on paper, composition transferred from three monotypes, state I of II
Sheet: $10\frac{9}{16} \times 13\frac{9}{16}$ in. (26.9 × 34.4 cm)
Private collection. Courtesy Nicholas Stogdon

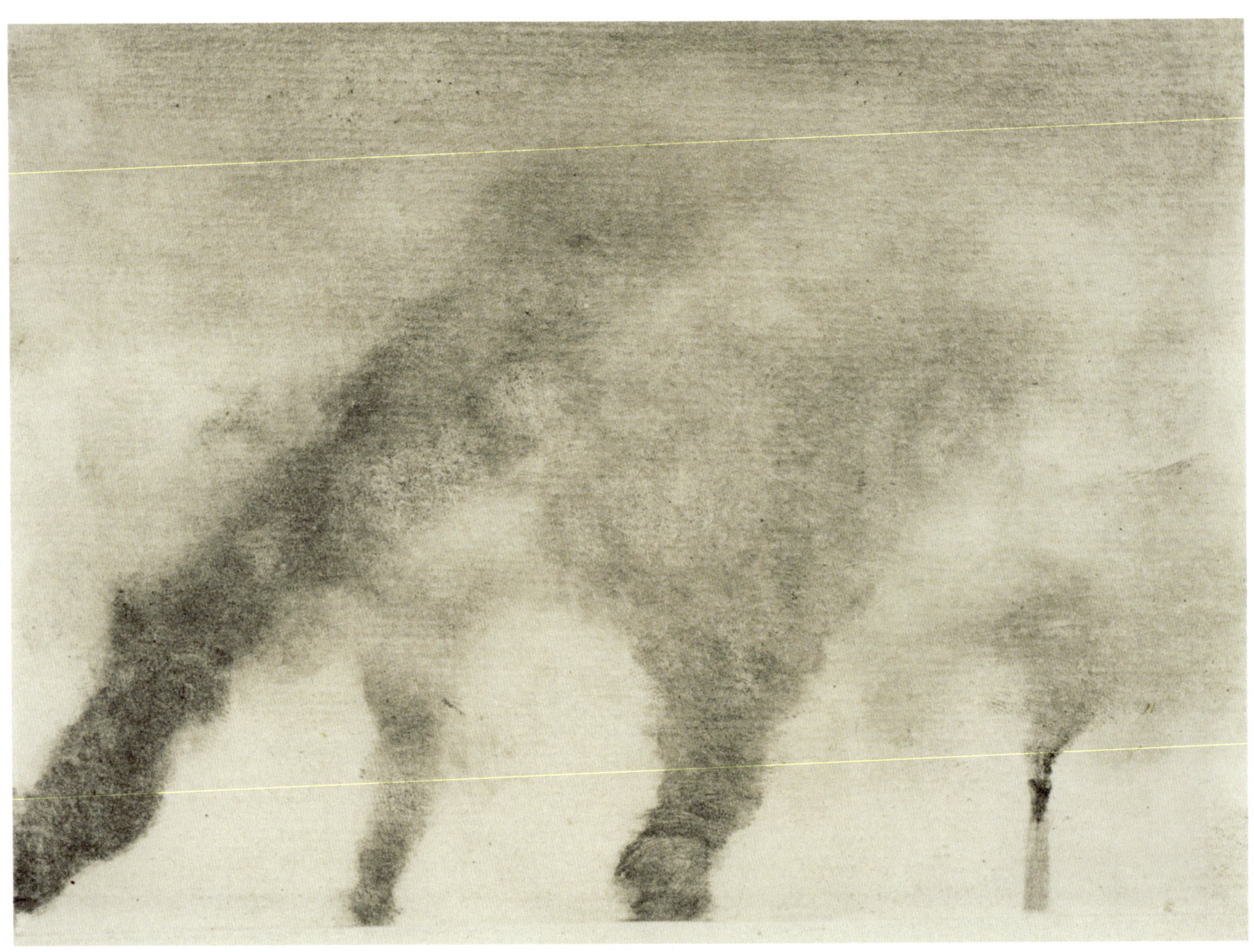

47. *Factory Smoke* (*Fumées d'usines*). 1877–79
Monotype on paper
Plate: 4 11⁄16 × 6 5⁄16 in. (11.9 × 16.1 cm), sheet: 5 13⁄16 × 6 13⁄16 in. (14.7 × 17.3 cm)
The Metropolitan Museum of Art, New York. The Elisha Whittelsey Collection, The Elisha Whittelsey Fund

On Smoke

Samantha Friedman

Four billows of smoke waft into the sky and merge into a single sooty cloud. Three of these plumes lack a clear origin; their chimneys have been cropped out of the frame. But the source of the fourth, rightmost swell makes it into the composition as a tubular funnel, its top sharply defined by a dark triangle of ink—a concrete referent in a scene otherwise dominated by gaseous ambiguity.

That tension—between clear description and hazy suggestion, between solidity and smoke—extends beyond this single monotype, encapsulating a dynamic that is present throughout Degas's work. If our man is a nineteenth-century realist, documenting scenes of modern life with attentive precision, then *Factory Smoke* (*Fumées d'usines*, 1877–79; plate 47) can be read as an emblem of urban industrialization, a picture about iron and carbon and smog. But if Degas is the proto-Symbolist who once told his friend Georges Jeanniot that "a painting demands a certain mystery, vagueness, fantasy," this monotype can be seen as something else: an aesthetic reverie, a Romantic abstraction executed years before the artist's Symbolist affinities are generally acknowledged to have begun.[1]

The dating of *Factory Smoke* derives from its relationship to a passage Degas wrote in around May 1879, in a notebook where he was listing possible subjects: "On smoke—people's smoke, from pipes, cigarettes, cigars; smoke of locomotives, tall chimneys, factories, steamboats, etc.; smoke confined in the space under bridges; steam."[2] If Degas is seen as a realist, this note comes across as a list of observed phenomena, and the artist as a scientist offering a detailed account of the occurrences of a particular visual fact. Read in the context of Symbolism, though, it takes on the character of a Baudelairean chain of associations, one smoky entity triggering the thought of the next. As T. J. Clark writes, describing the effect of a distant puff of factory smoke in Claude Monet's 1874 boating painting *Sailboat at Le Petit Gennevilliers* (*Le Voilier au Petit Gennevilliers*), "The smoke serves to provoke various analogies—between smoke and paint, smoke and cloud, cloud and water."[3]

The relationship between subject and medium is also crucial to Degas's monotype, suggesting, of course, an analogy between smoke and ink. *Factory Smoke* seems to have been executed through a combination of dark-ground technique in the top half of the composition, where passages were wiped away from an ink-covered area of the plate, and light-ground technique in the bottom half, where ink was added to a part of the plate otherwise left clean. The shift between the two zones is subtle, both softened by the texture of the paper and modulated by the ridges of the artist's fingerprints, where he manually blurred any inky edges. The openness of the mono-

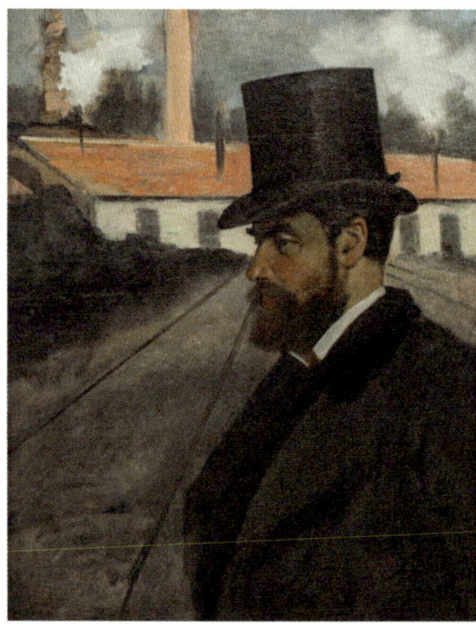

1. Hilaire-Germain-Edgar Degas. *Henri Rouart in front of His Factory (Henri Rouart devant son usine).* c. 1875. Oil on canvas, 25 ¾ × 19 ⅞ in. (65.41 × 50.48 cm). Carnegie Museum of Art, Pittsburgh. Acquired through the generosity of the Sarah Mellon Scaife Family

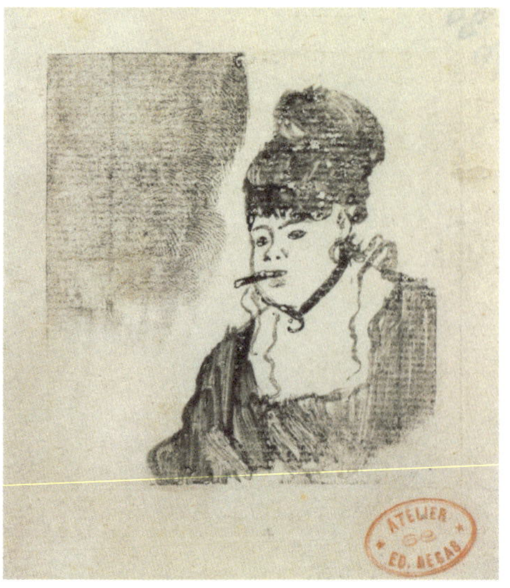

2. Hilaire-Germain-Edgar Degas. *Woman with a Cigarette (Femme à la cigarette).* c. 1880. Monotype on paper, plate: 3 ⅛ × 2 ¾ in. (8 × 7 cm). Private collection. Courtesy Brame & Lorenceau, Paris

type medium to this kind of mutability makes it ideal, both visually and metaphorically, for representing a subject that is itself in flux, and monotype's capacity for nebulous forms makes it well suited to capture smoke's haze. But the medium's connection to its subject also exists on a material level, for lamp black—made from soot—was in Degas's day a major ingredient of black printing ink.[4] It is therefore likely not only that his ink looked and behaved like the stuff it was representing, but also that it may consist of the same compounds that would have chugged out of those factory smokestacks.

Factory smoke had appeared in Degas's work before, in paintings that place him more firmly in the camp of nineteenth-century chroniclers and in the company of contemporaries like Monet and Camille Pissarro, whose Impressionist canvases documented the ways in which modern manufacturing was transforming the French landscape.[5] In *The Gentlemen's Race: Before the Start (Course de gentlemen. Avant le départ*, 1862), distant industrial chimneys dot the horizon beyond a sea of mounted riders, imposing the specter of labor onto a scene of well-bred leisure. And in *Henri Rouart in front of His Factory* (*Henri Rouart devant son usine*, c. 1875; fig. 1), Degas identifies his friend with the site of this factory-owner's industry, placing Rouart's head at the vanishing point where converging railway lines meet a structure spewing smoke. Within the artist's monotype practice, *Beside the Sea* (*Au bord de la mer*, c. 1876–77; plate 59)—with its distant boat emitting a black cloud—has been cited as the work most closely related to *Factory Smoke*, which Eugenia Parry Janis otherwise characterizes as something of an anomaly.[6] But while *Beside the Sea* is linked to *Factory Smoke* by its subject, another monotype—featuring the smoke "from pipes, cigarettes, cigars" also listed in Degas's notebook—is closer in its technique: like *Factory Smoke*, *Woman with a Cigarette* (*Femme à la cigarette*, c. 1880; fig. 2) seems to offer an excuse for Degas to indulge in a formal association between smoke and ink. The upper left quadrant of the composition is dominated by a smudgy cloud, whose texture—embedded with the whorls of Degas's fingerprints—is wholly distinct from the more linear treatment devoted to the monotype's ostensible subject, a portly little *fumeuse*.

No smoke from a volcano is mentioned in Degas's notebook, an absence both suggesting that its entries were indeed based on observation and underscoring the dreamy inventiveness of the pastel-heightened monotype *Vesuvius* (*Le Vésuve*, 1892; plate 148). For while Degas visited the volcano in either 1856 or 1857, on one of his many trips to Naples, the rust-colored drama of an eruption captured in the monotype is pure fancy.[7] Indeed, the print's palette—like that of *Landscape with Smokestacks* (c. 1890; The Art Institute of Chicago), another pastelized monotype whose towers pour out puffs of deep peacock blue—verges on the hallucinogenic. *Factory Smoke*, then, is both chronologically and conceptually situated

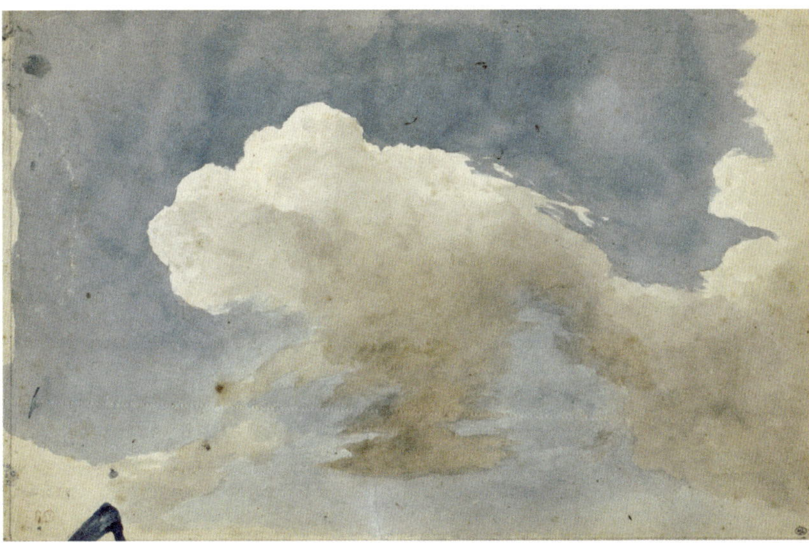

3. Eugène Delacroix. *Cloud Study (Etude de ciel nuageux).* 1849. Watercolor, 10 ¾ × 15 ⅝ in. (27.2 × 39.8 cm). Département des Arts graphiques, Musée du Louvre, Paris

somewhere between Degas's invocations of industry in the 1860s and '70s and his aesthetic inventions of the 1890s. Nonetheless, it remains unique in relinquishing its entire composition to an exploration of its subject's vaporous qualities. In this regard its closest kin may be a work that Degas owned: Eugène Delacroix's *Cloud Study* (*Etude de ciel nuageux*, 1849; fig. 3), which exploits watercolor's capacity for mistily indistinct forms in much the same way that Degas harnessed a similar potential of the monotype.[8] If Delacroix's aqueous medium was uniquely suited to depict clouds, Degas's carbon-based ink was the ideal substance for a devoted description of the effects of smoke.

1. Degas, quoted in Georges Jeanniot, "Souvenirs sur Degas," *Revue Universelle* 55 (1933):281. Both Carol Armstrong and Richard Kendall cite 1886—the year of the final Impressionist exhibition—as the key turning point in Degas's approach. See Armstrong, "Against the Grain: J. K. Huysmans and the 1886 Series of Nudes," in *Odd Man Out: Readings of the Work and Reputation of Edgar Degas* (Chicago and London: The University of Chicago Press, 1991), pp. 157–209, and Kendall, *Beyond Impressionism*, exh. cat. (London: National Gallery, 1996), p. 126.
2. Degas, *The Notebooks of Edgar Degas*, ed. Theodore Reff (Oxford: Clarendon Press, 1976), no. 205, 1:134. Trans. in Jean Sutherland Boggs, *Degas*, exh. cat. (New York: The Metropolitan Museum of Art, 1988), p. 262. Boggs also discusses the dating of the notebook entry, and the notebook entry as the basis for the dating of the print.
3. T. J. Clark, *The Painting of Modern Life: Paris in the Art of Manet and His Followers* (New York: Alfred A. Knopf, 1985), p. 182.
4. Charred vegetable material (vines) and charred bones were other period sources for black printing ink. I am grateful to Assistant Conservator Laura Neufeld for providing this information in conversation, and for pointing me toward an early-twentieth-century book on printers' inks by Louis Edgar Andés, who writes that "the chief pigment used in the manufacture of printing ink is now, as formerly, lampblack, obtained by the incomplete combustion of organic substances rich in carbon." Andés, *Oil Colours and Printers' Inks* (rev. ed. London: Scott, Greenwood & Son, 1918), p. 87. First published as *Oel- und Buchdruckfarben* (Vienna: A. Hartleben, 1889).
5. For an extended discussion of the meanings of factories in the work of these and other artists, including Degas, see James H. Rubin, "Factories and Work Sites: City and Country," in *Impressionism and the Modern Landscape: Productivity, Technology, and Urbanization from Manet to Van Gogh* (Berkeley, Los Angeles, and London: University of California Press, 2008), pp. 121–47.
6. Eugenia Parry Janis, in her catalogue raisonné of Degas's monotypes, lists *Factory Smoke* among those monotypes that "do not belong to any of these [five major] categories and which either fall into minor categories or are more notable as individual works than as members of a group." *Degas Monotypes: Essay, Catalogue & Checklist* (Cambridge, Mass.: Fogg Art Museum, Harvard University, 1968), p. xxvii. The two monotypes are cross-referenced both in Janis's entry for *Beside the Sea* (*Au bord de la mer*; no. 61) and in Boggs's entry on *Factory Smoke*: see Boggs, *Degas*, p. 262, no. 153 (Boggs uses the title *At the Seashore* for *Beside the Sea*). Boggs also discusses this monotype's relationship to *The Gentleman's Race* . . . and *Henri Rouart* . . . , as well as to two other paintings.
7. Degas did not witness an eruption of Vesuvius, as the closest ones to his visit occurred in 1855, 1861, 1868, and 1872. See Richard Kendall, *Degas Landscapes*, exh. cat. (New York: The Metropolitan Museum of Art, in association with Yale University Press, New Haven, 1993), p. 21.
8. For a discussion of this and other works by Delacroix in Degas's collection, and of their influence on his work, see Ann Dumas, Colta Ives, Susan Alyson Stein, et al., *The Private Collection of Edgar Degas*, exh. cat. (New York: The Metropolitan Museum of Art, 1997), pp. 33–41.

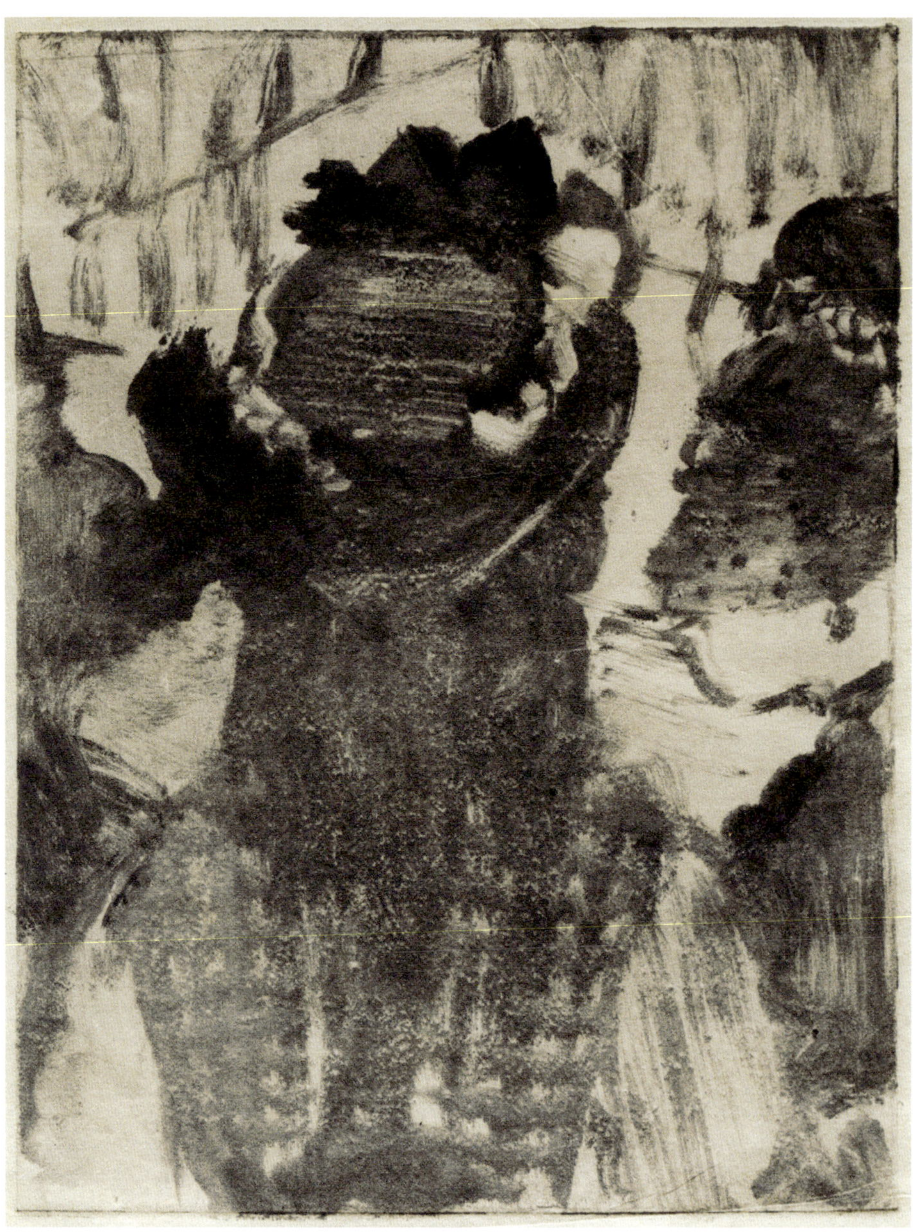

48. *On the Street* (*Dans la rue*). 1876–77
Monotype on China paper
Plate: 6 ⅜ × 4 13⁄16 in. (16.2 × 12.2 cm)
Mrs. Martin Atlas

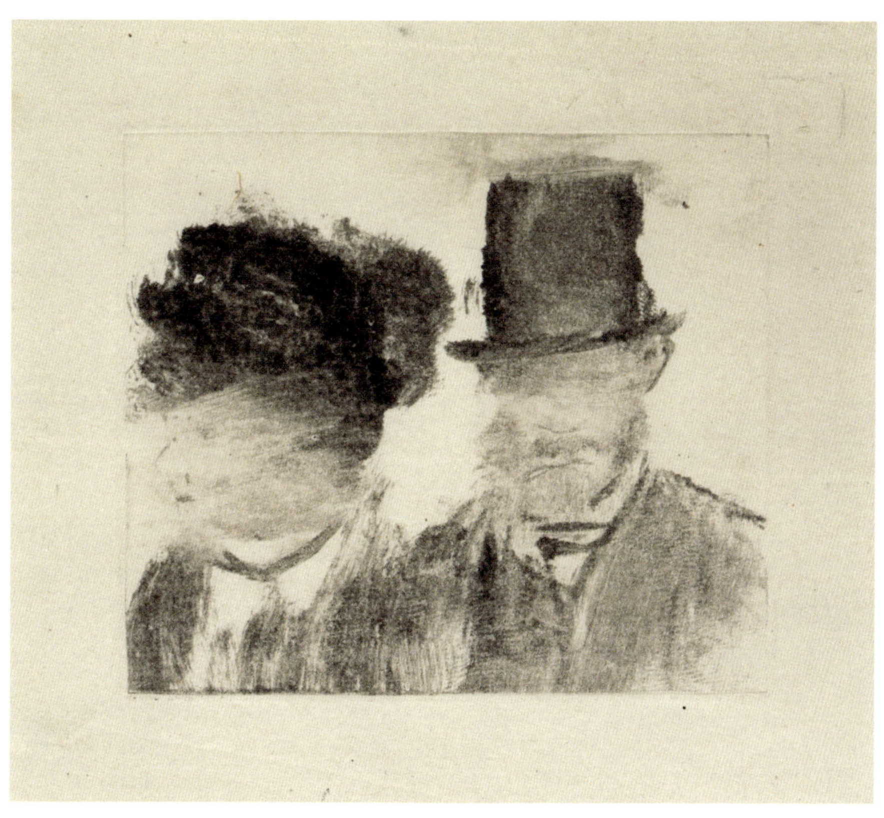

49. *Heads of a Man and a Woman* (*Homme et femme, en buste*). c. 1877–80
Monotype on paper
Plate: 2 13⁄16 × 3 3⁄16 in. (7.2 × 8.1 cm)
British Museum, London. Bequeathed by Campbell Dodgson

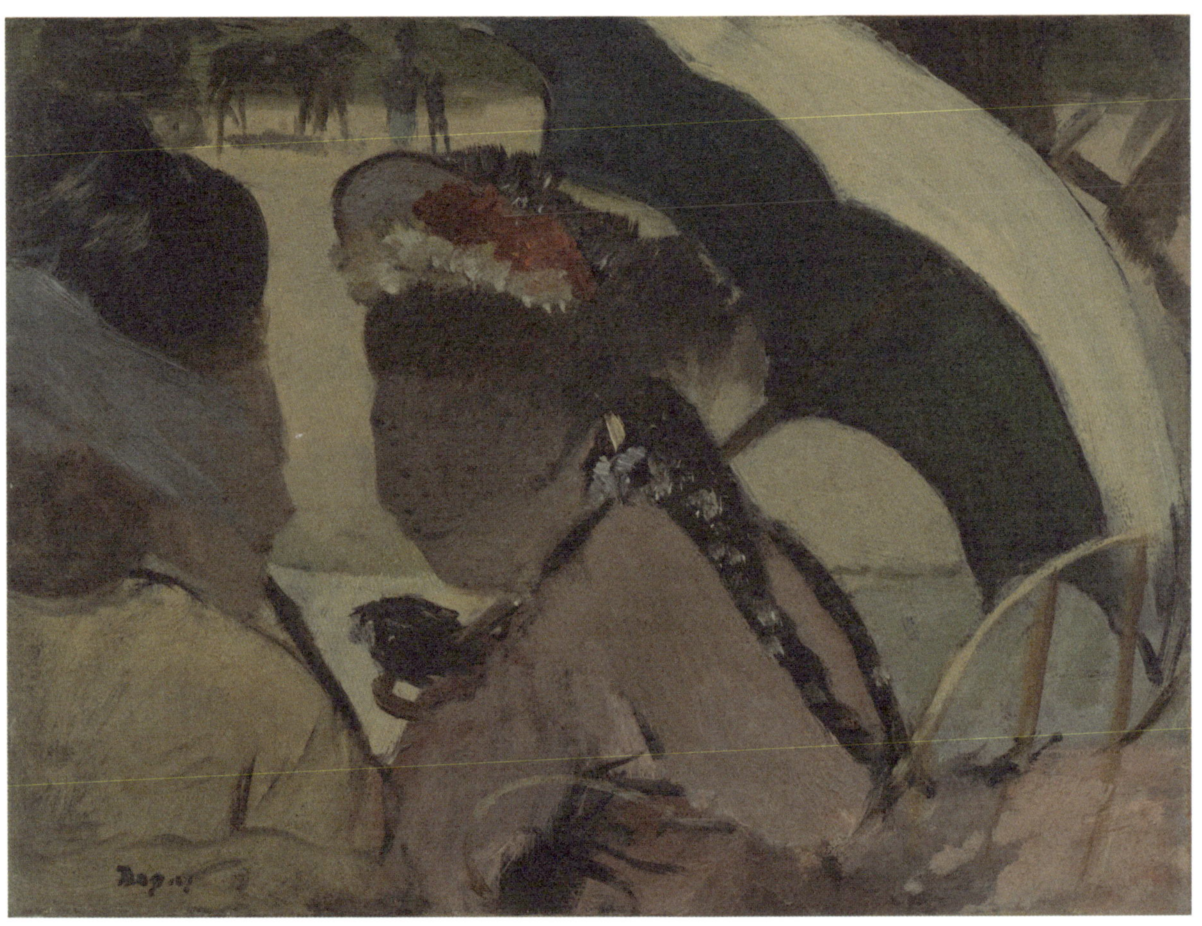

50. *At the Races* (*Aux courses*). c. 1876–77
Oil on canvas
7 ½ × 9 ¹¹⁄₁₆ in. (19.1 × 24.6 cm)
Private collection

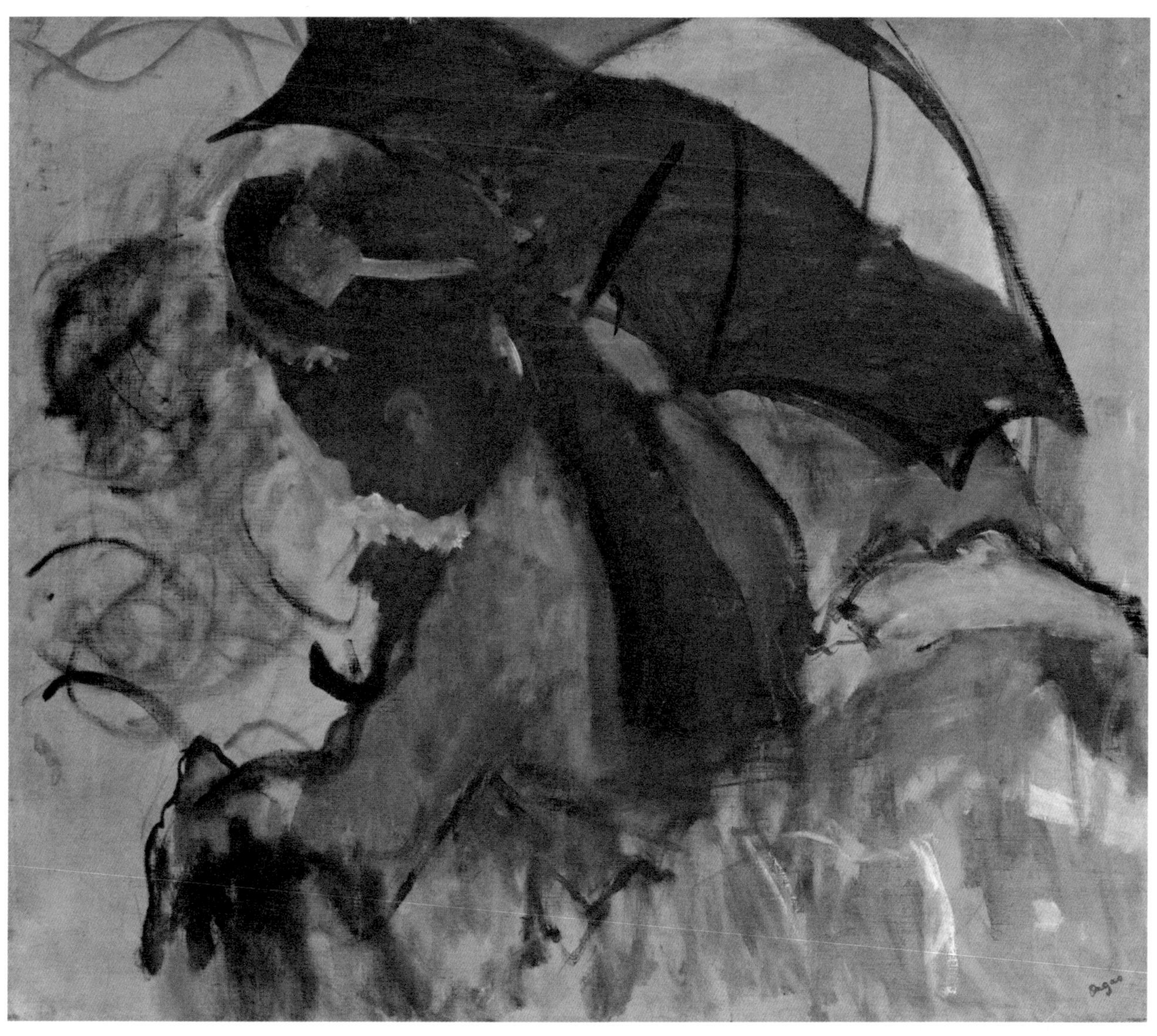

51. *Lady with a Parasol* (*Femme à l'ombrelle*). c. 1870–72
Oil on canvas
29 ⅝ × 33 7⁄16 in. (75.3 × 85 cm)
The Samuel Courtauld Trust, The Courtauld Gallery, London

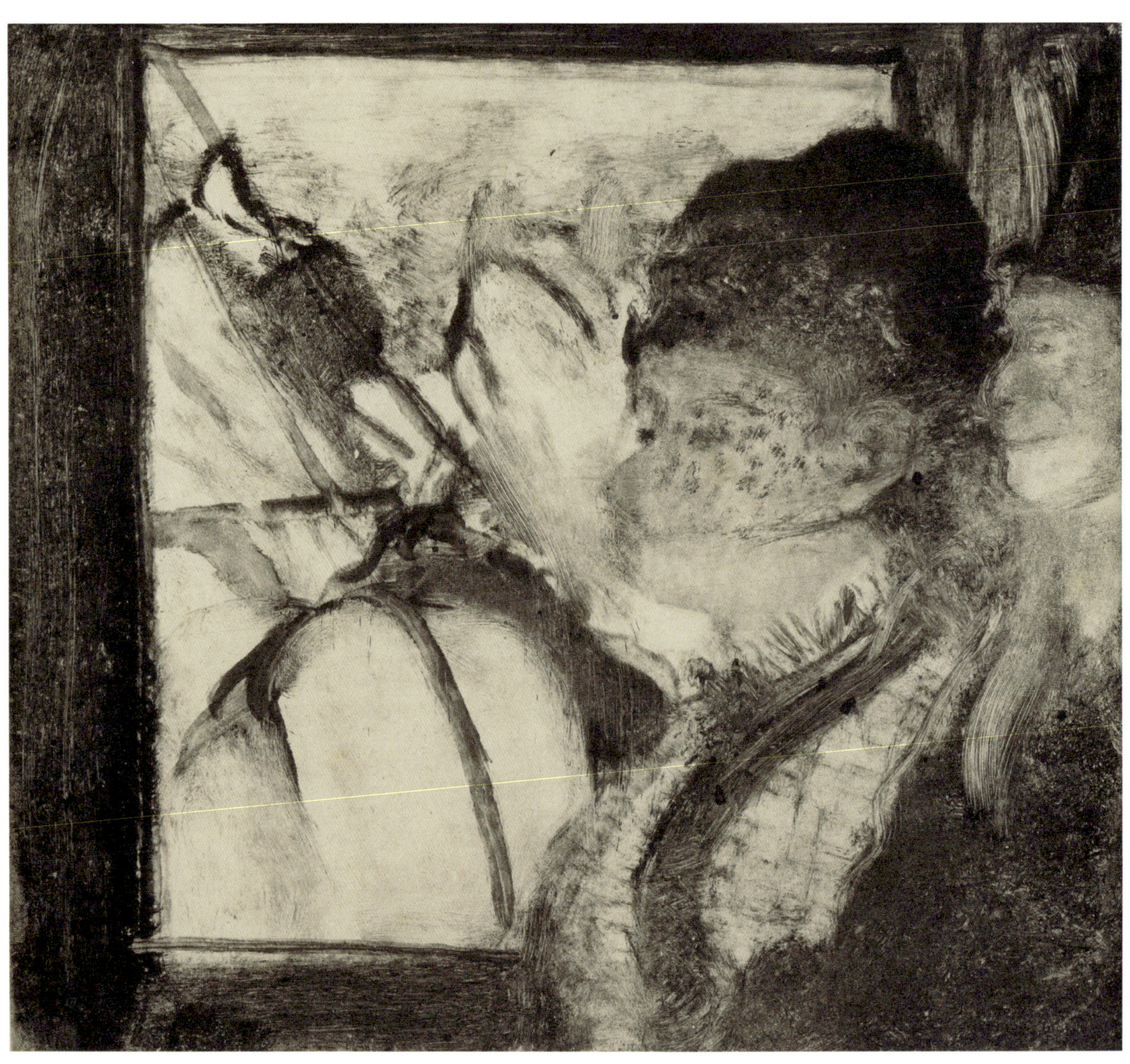

52. *In the Omnibus* (*Dans l'omnibus*). c. 1877–78
Monotype on paper
Plate: 11 × 11 11/16 in. (28 × 29.7 cm)
Musée Picasso, Paris

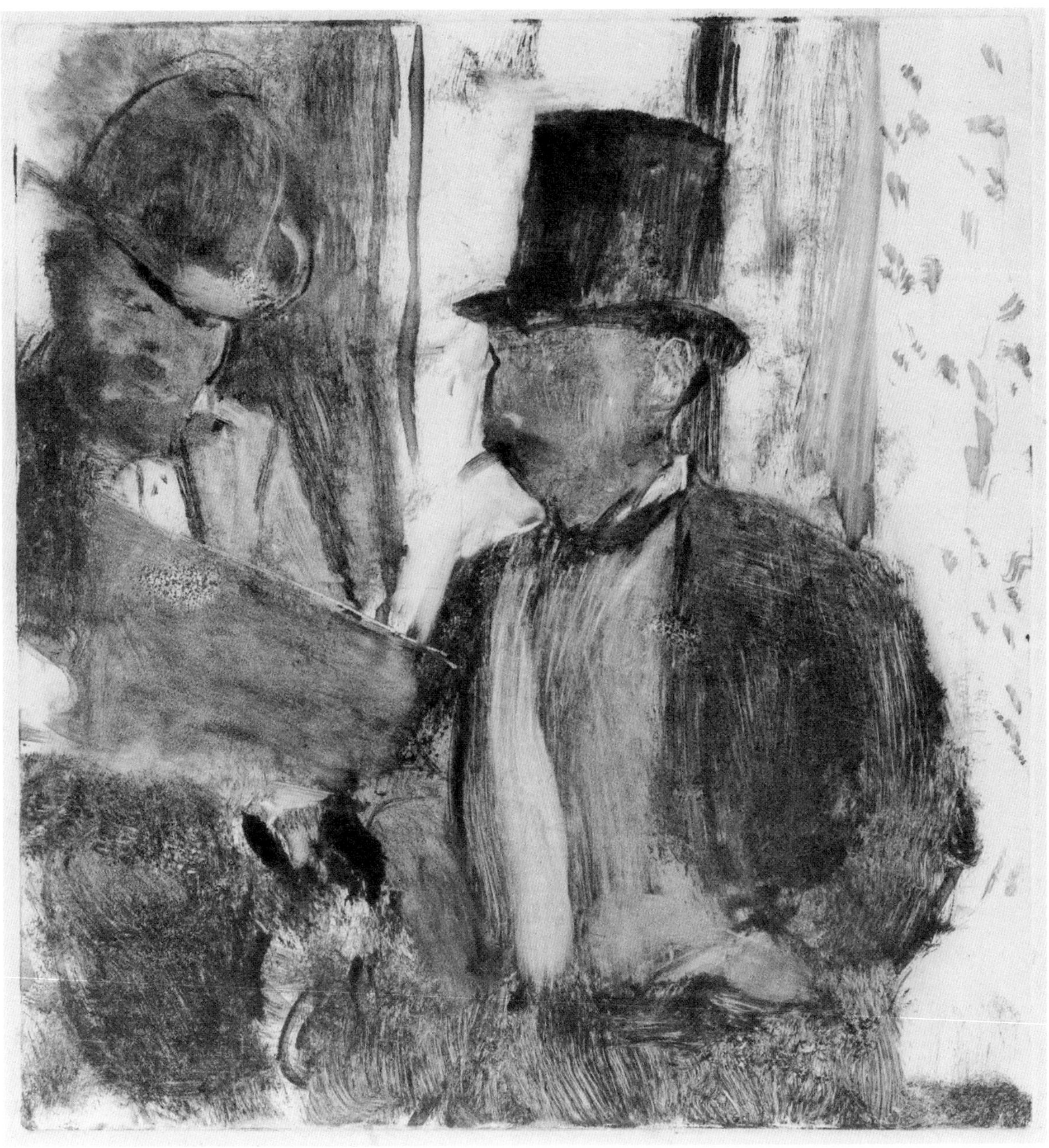

53. *The Two Connoisseurs* (*Les Deux Amateurs*). c. 1880
Monotype on paper mounted on board
Plate: 11 ¾ × 10 ⅝ in. (29.8 × 27 cm), sheet: 13 ⅛ × 12 in. (33.4 × 30.5 cm)
The Art Institute of Chicago. Clarence Buckingham Collection

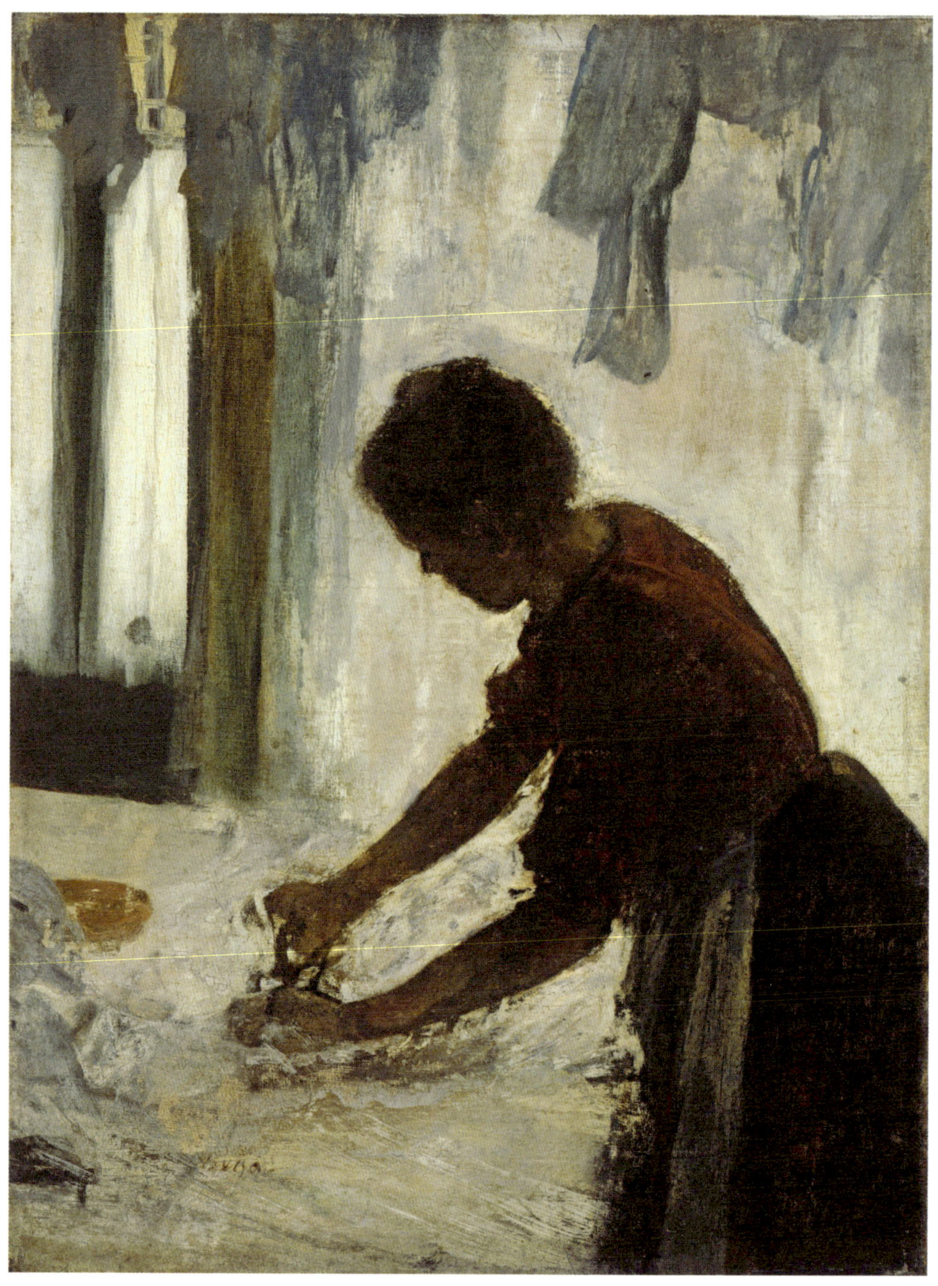

54. *A Woman Ironing* (*Blanchisseuse [Silhouette]*). 1873
Oil on canvas
21 ⅜ × 15 ½ in. (54.3 × 39.4 cm)
The Metropolitan Museum of Art, New York. H. O. Havemeyer Collection, Bequest of Mrs. H. O. Havemeyer

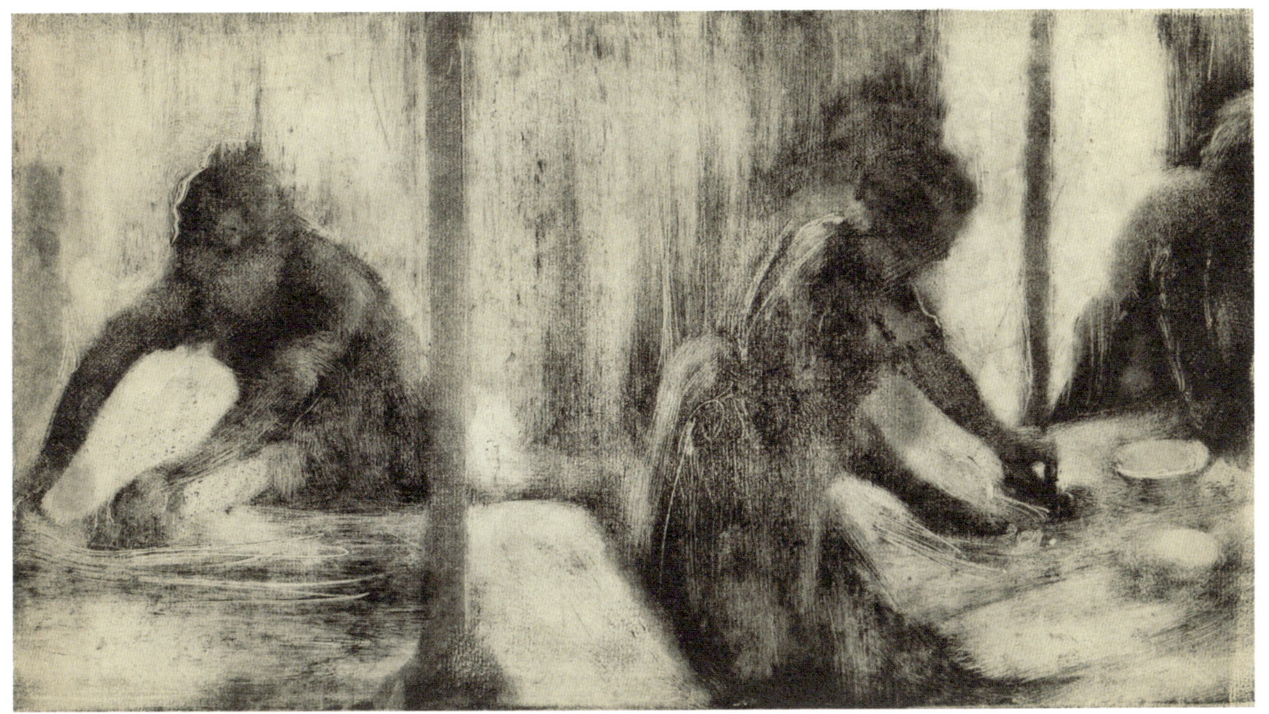

55. *Ironing Women* (*Les Repasseuses*). c. 1877–79
Monotype on paper
Plate: 9 ½ × 17 ½ in. (24.1 × 44.5 cm), sheet: 10 × 17 ½ in. (25.4 × 44.5 cm)
Private collection

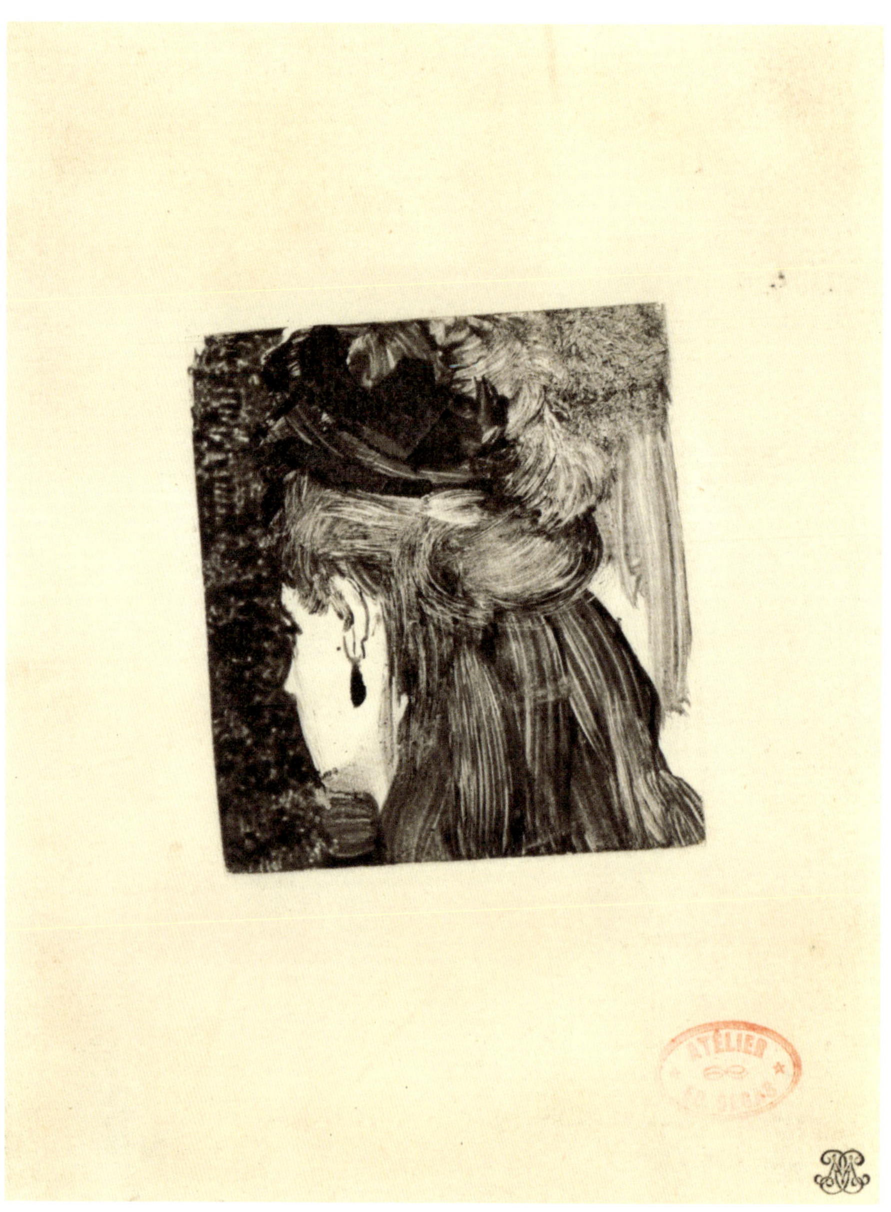

56. *The Jet Earring* (*Profil perdu à la boucle d'oreille*). 1876–77
Monotype on paper
Plate: 3 ¼ × 2 ¾ in. (8.2 × 7 cm), sheet: 7 ¹⁄₁₆ × 5 ³⁄₁₆ in. (18 × 13.2 cm)
The Metropolitan Museum of Art, New York. Anonymous gift, in memory of Francis Henry Taylor

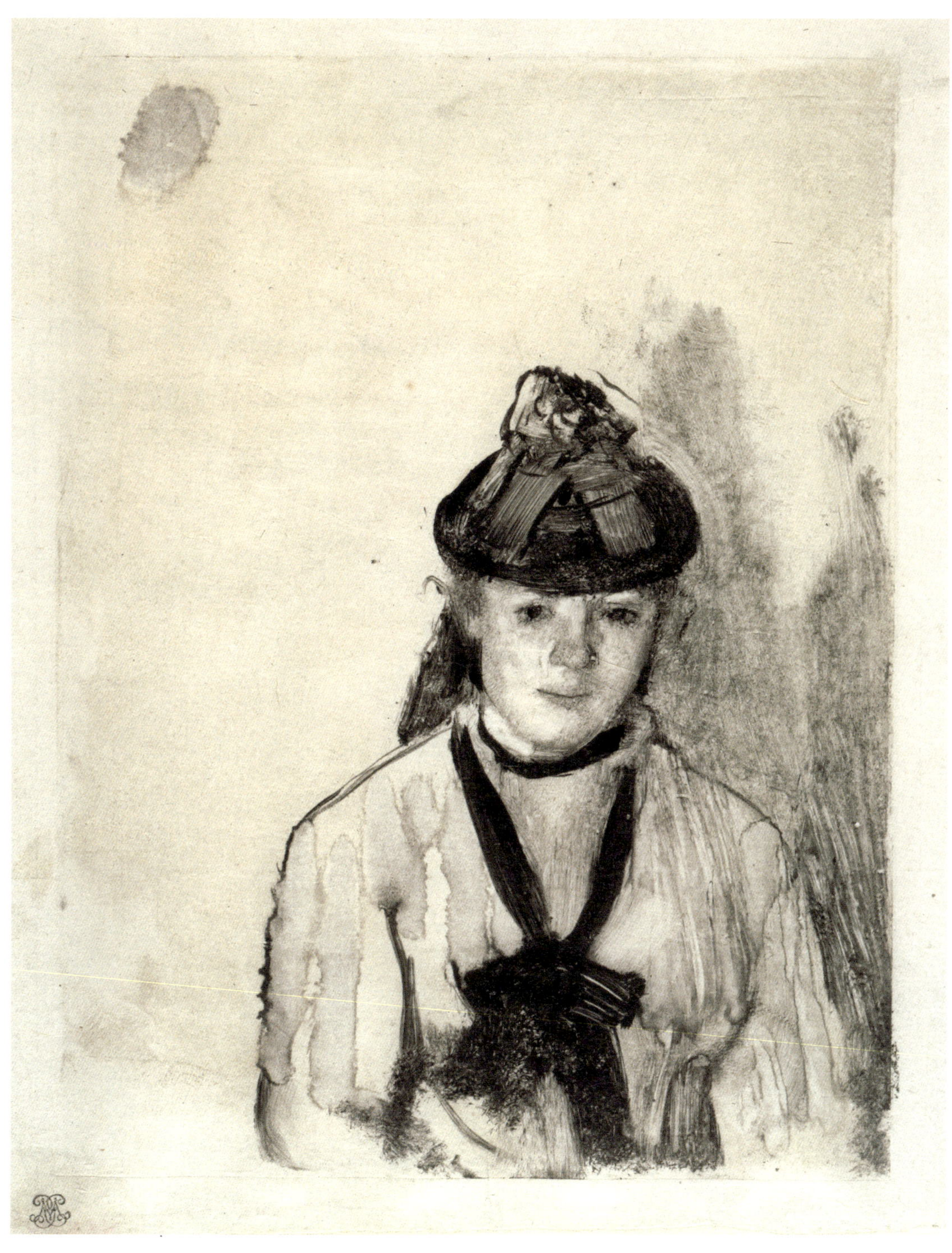

57. *Portrait of Ellen Andrée* (*Portrait de femme*). c. 1876
Monotype on China paper
8 ½ × 6 $^{5}/_{16}$ in. (21.6 × 16 cm)
The Art Institute of Chicago. Potter Palmer Collection

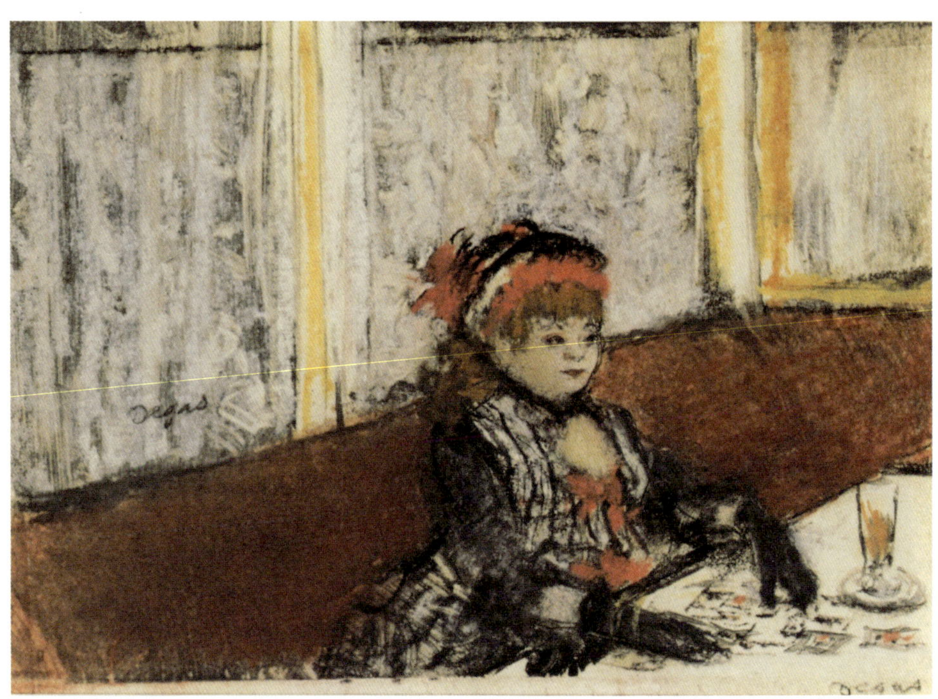

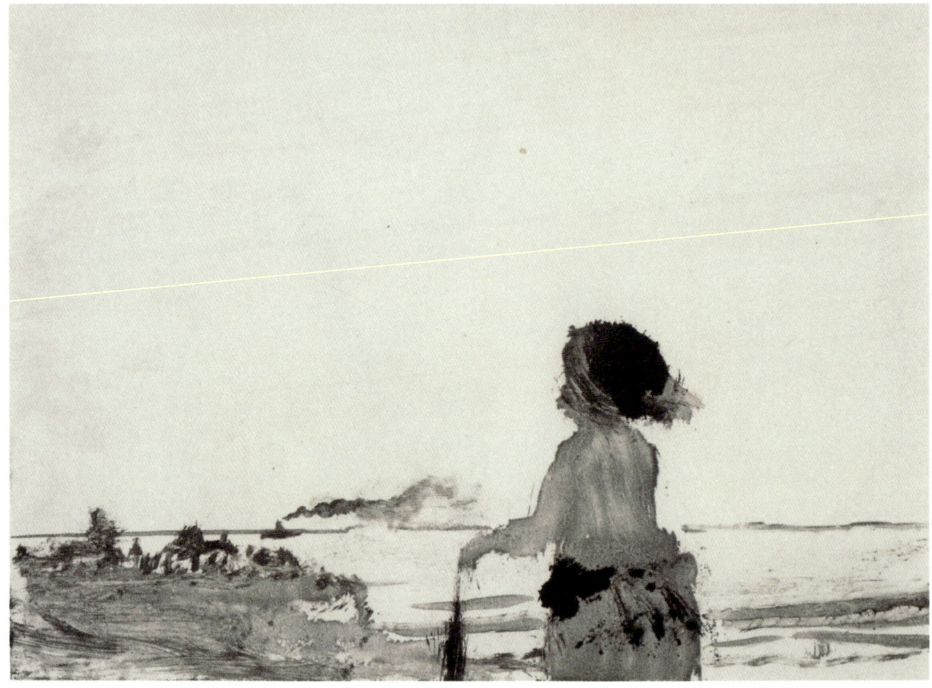

58. *Young Woman in a Café* (*Jeune femme au café*). c. 1877
Pastel over monotype on paper
5 3/16 × 6 3/4 in. (13.1 × 17.2 cm)
Haroche Collection

59. *Beside the Sea* (*Au bord de la mer*). 1876–77
Monotype on paper
Plate: 4 5/8 × 6 3/8 in. (11.8 × 16.2 cm), sheet: 6 3/8 × 6 7/8 in. (16.2 × 17.5 cm)
Museum of Fine Arts, Boston. Gift of Mr. and Mrs. Peter A. Wick

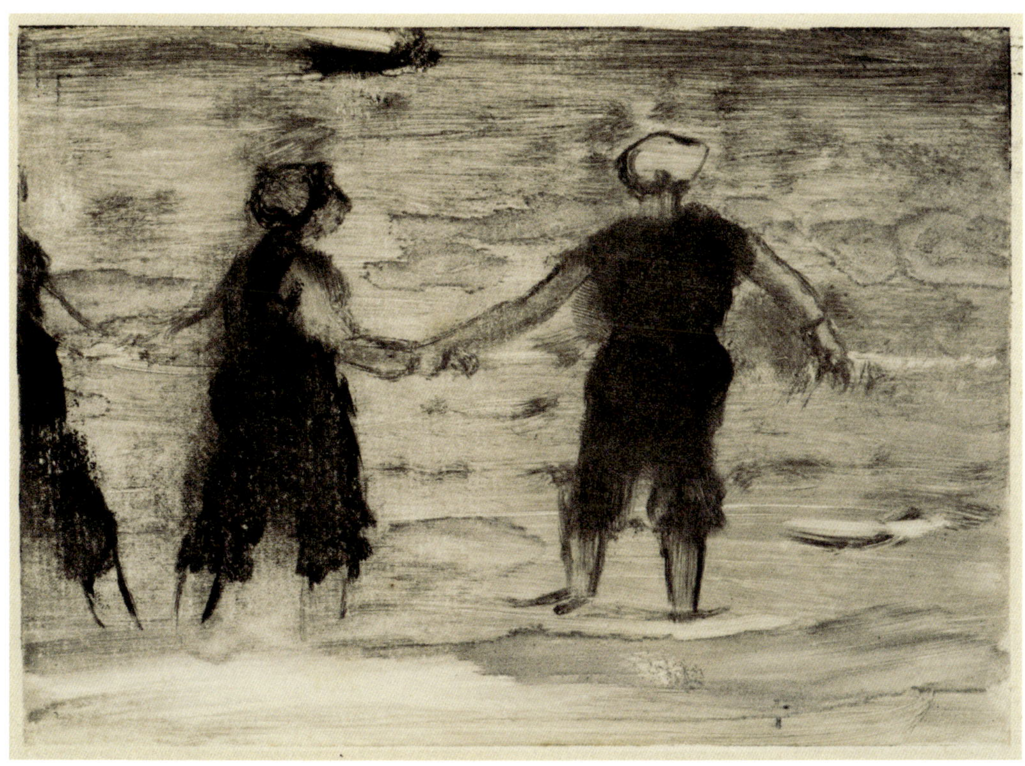

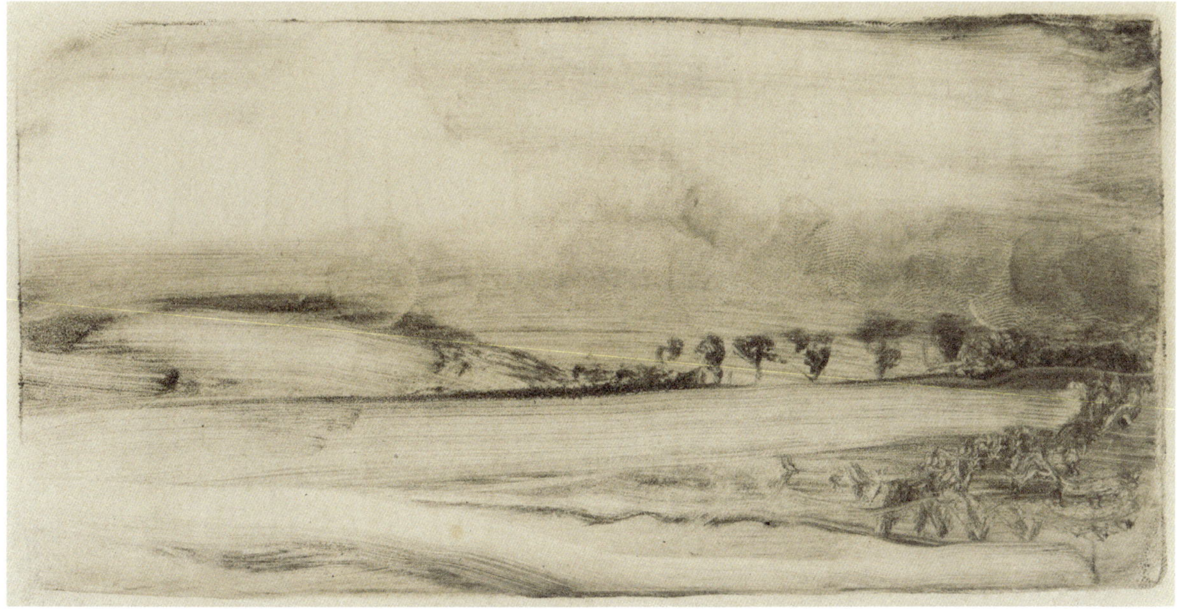

60. *Bathers* (*Les Baigneuses*). c. 1875–80
Monotype on paper
Plate: 4 11⁄16 × 6 3⁄8 in. (11.9 × 16.2 cm),
sheet: 7 3⁄16 × 9 5⁄16 in. (18.2 × 23.7 cm)
Lent by James Bergquist

61. *The River* (*La Rivière*). c. 1877–79
Monotype on paper
Plate: 3 ½ × 6 13⁄16 in. (8.9 × 17.3 cm), sheet: 7 3⁄16 × 9 in. (18.2 × 22.9 cm)
Museum of Fine Arts, Boston. Katherine E. Bullard Fund in memory
of Francis Bullard

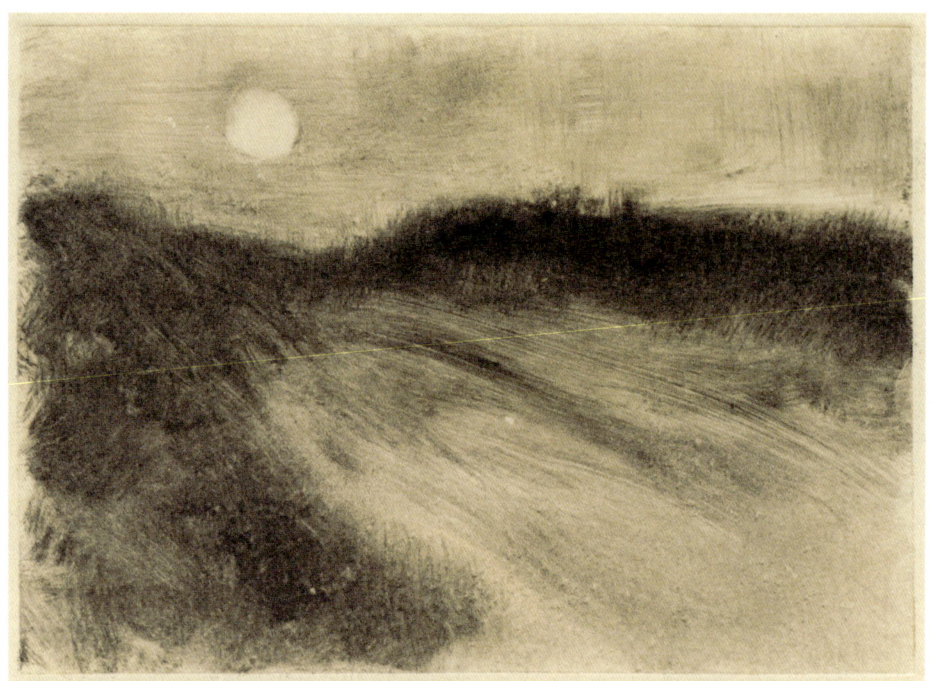

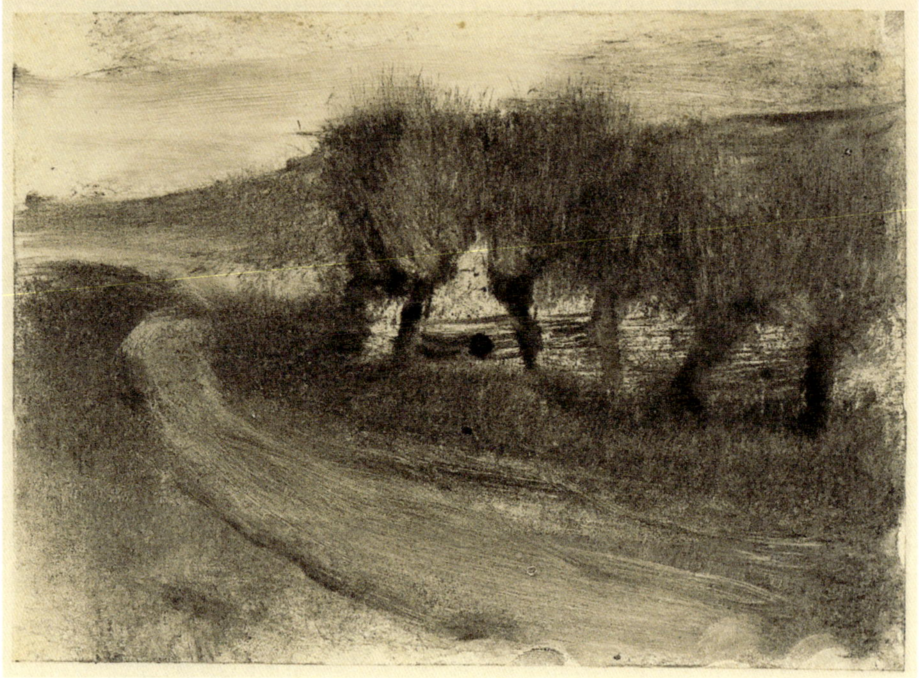

62. *Moonrise* (*Lever de la lune*). c. 1880
Monotype on paper
Plate: 4 ⅝ × 6 5⁄16 in. (11.7 × 16 cm),
sheet: 6 1⁄16 × 9 11⁄16 in. (15.4 × 24.6 cm)
Sterling and Francine Clark Art Institute,
Williamstown, Massachusetts

63. *Willow Trees* (*Les Saules*). c. 1880
Monotype on paper
Plate: 4 ⅝ × 6 5⁄16 in. (11.7 × 16.1 cm),
sheet: 6 9⁄16 × 10 ½ in. (16.7 × 26.7 cm)
Private collection. Courtesy Nicholas
Stogdon

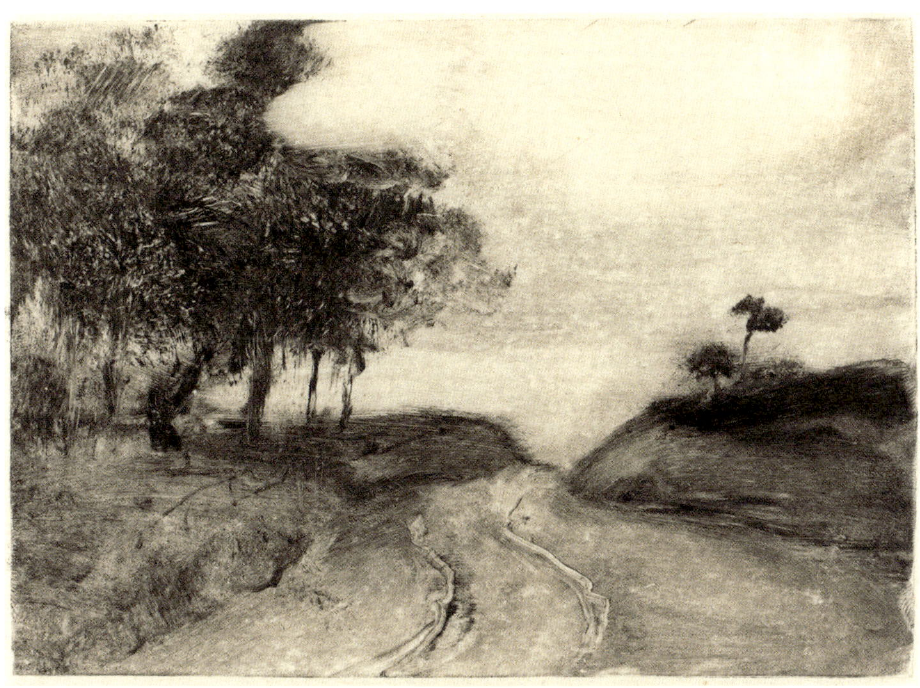

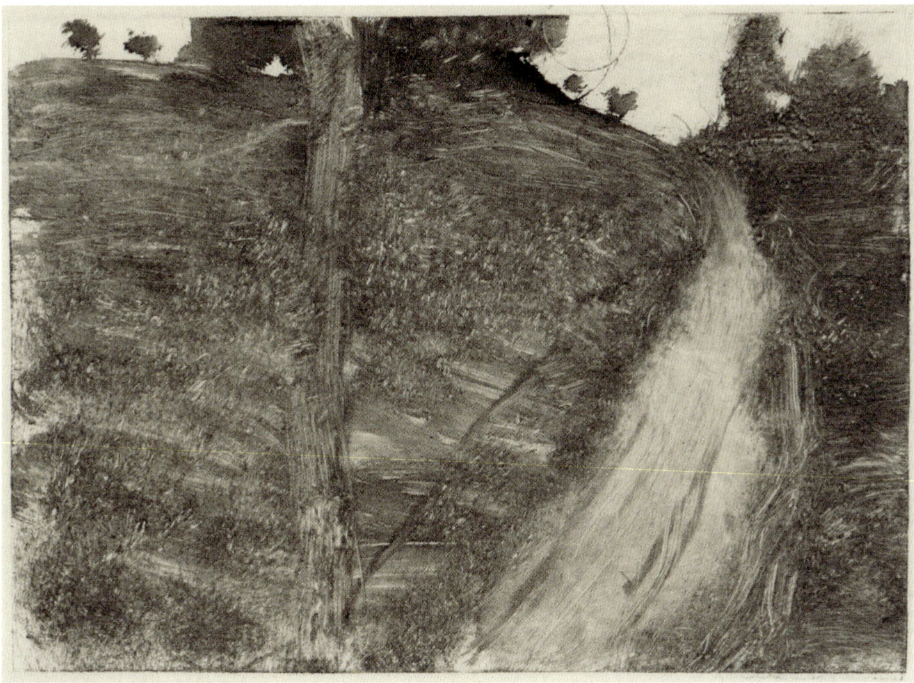

64. *The Road* (*La Route*). c. 1878–80
Monotype on China paper
Plate: 4 ⅝ × 6 5⁄16 in. (11.8 × 16.1 cm), sheet: 6 5⁄16 × 7 ¼ in. (16 × 18.4 cm)
National Gallery of Art, Washington, D.C. Rosenwald Collection

65. *The Path up the Hill* (*Le Chemin montant*). c. 1878–80
Monotype on paper
Plate: 4 11⁄16 × 6 5⁄16 in. (11.9 × 16.1 cm), sheet: 5 13⁄16 × 7 ⅛ in. (14.8 × 18.1 cm)
Museum of Fine Arts, Boston. Fund in memory of Horatio Greenough Curtis

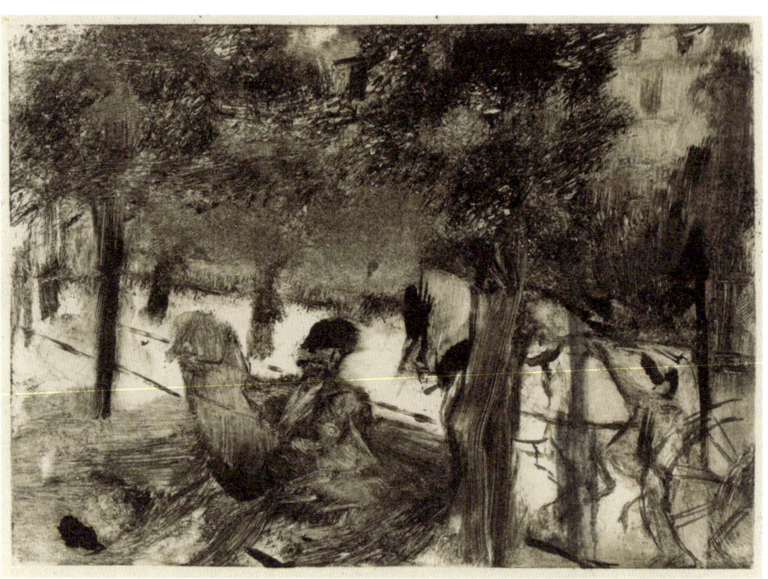

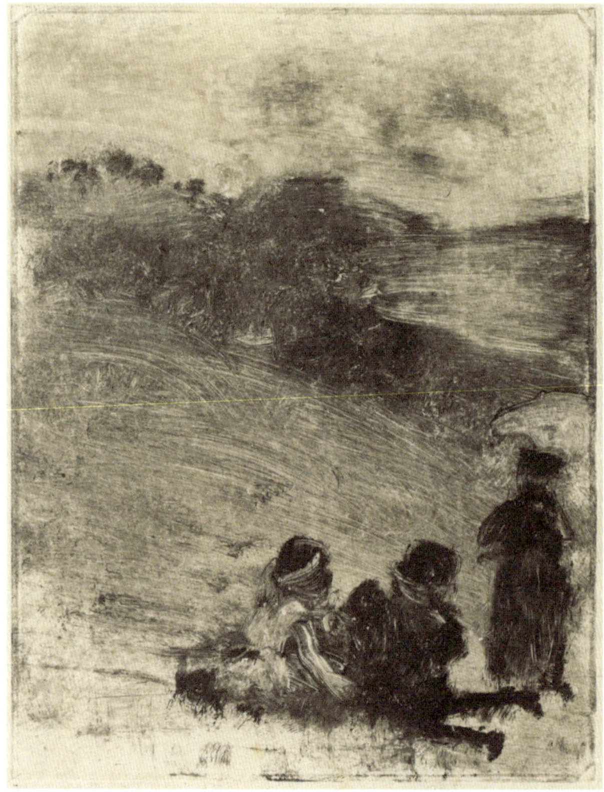

66. *Avenue with Trees* (*L'Avenue du bois*). c. 1880
Monotype on China paper
Plate: 4 ⅝ × 6 5⁄16 in. (11.8 × 16.1 cm),
sheet: 6 ¾ × 8 1⁄16 in. (17.2 × 20.5 cm)
The Syndics of the Fitzwilliam Museum, University of Cambridge.
Bequest of A.S.F. Gow through the National Art Collections Fund

67. *Rest in the Fields* (*Repos dans les champs*). c. 1877–80
Monotype on China paper
Plate: 8 7⁄16 × 6 5⁄16 in. (21.5 × 16 cm),
sheet: 13 ½ × 9 9⁄16 in. (34.3 × 24.3 cm)
Sterling and Francine Clark Art Institute, Williamstown, Massachusetts

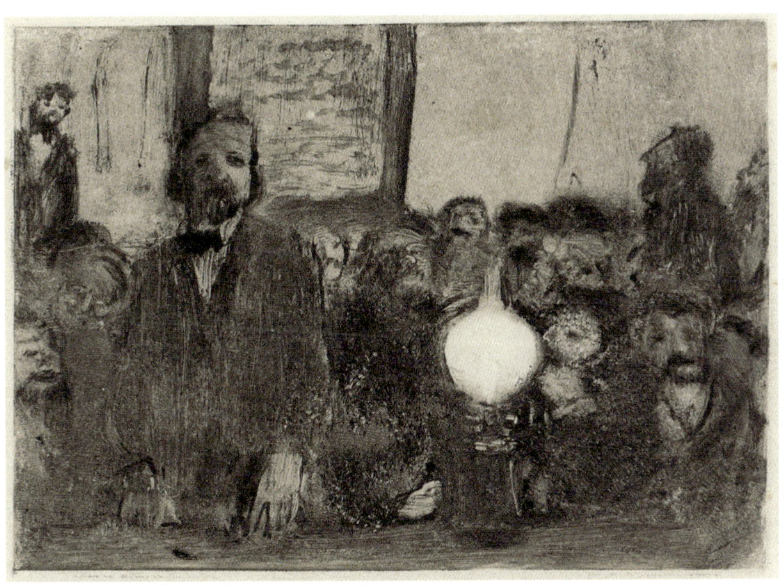

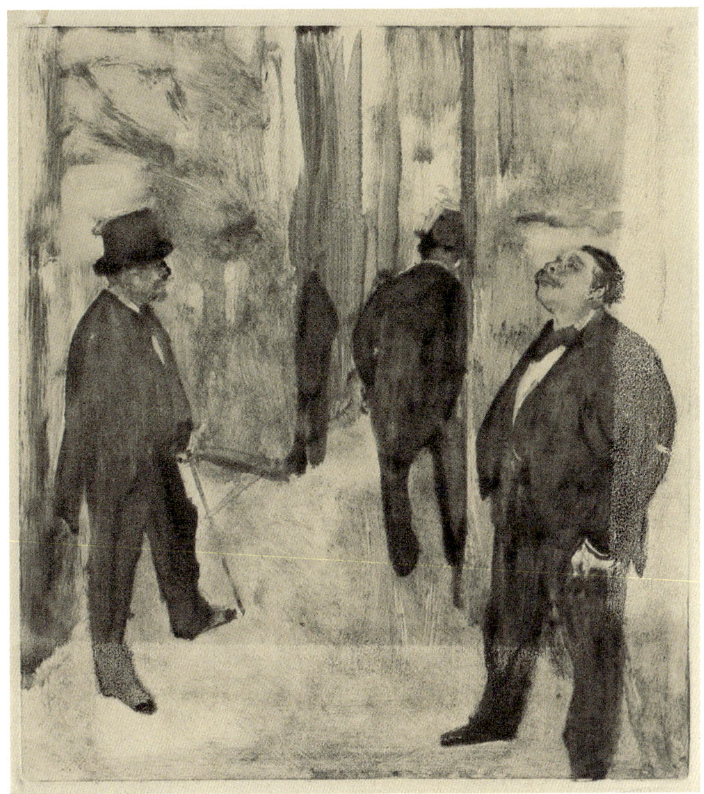

68. *The Public Meeting*
(*La Réunion publique*). c. 1880
Monotype on paper
Plate: 4 ⅝ × 6 ⅜ in. (11.8 × 16.2 cm)
Private collection, Paris

69. *Backstage at the Opera*
(*Dans les coulisses de l'opéra*). c. 1880
Monotype on paper
12 3⁄16 × 10 3⁄16 in. (31 × 27.4 cm)
Private collection, Paris

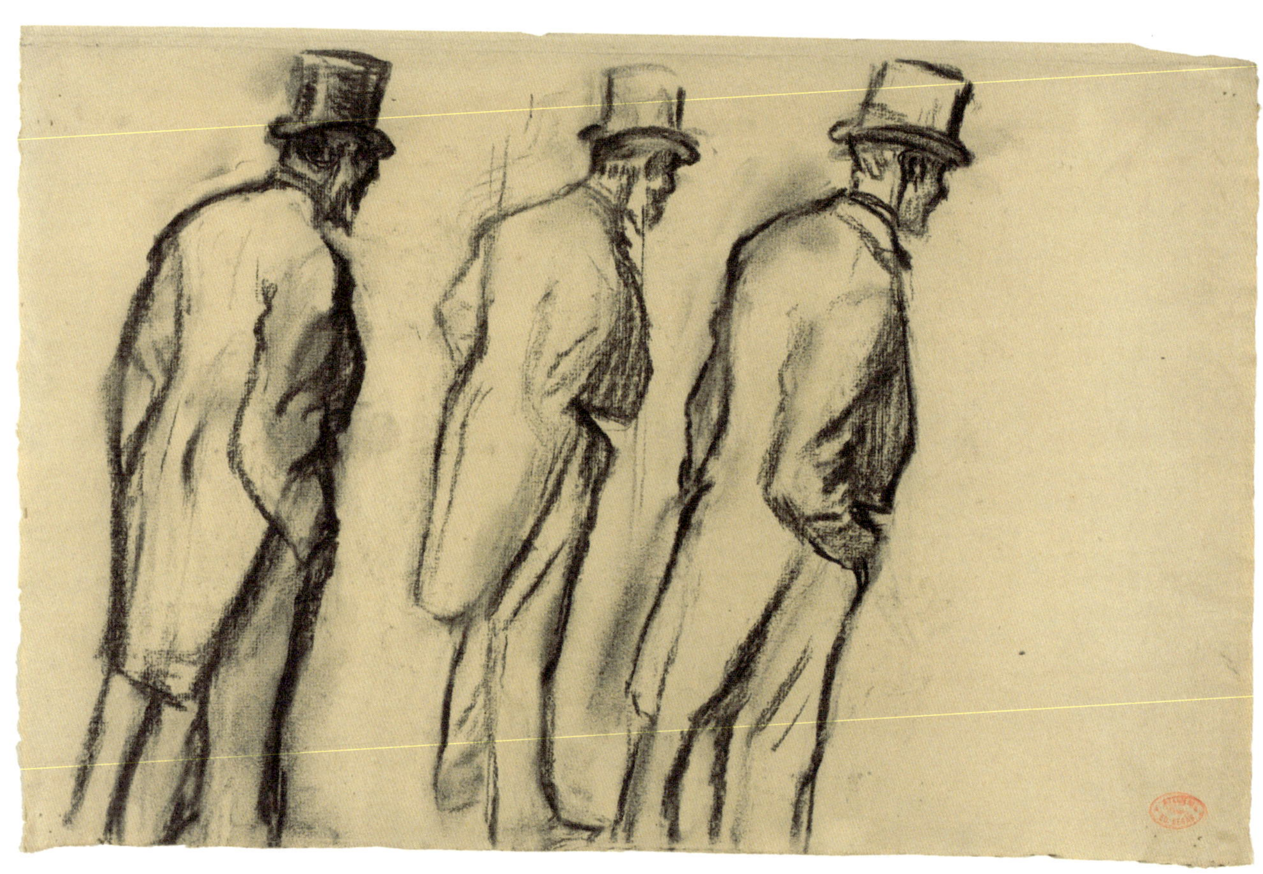

70. Three studies of Ludovic Halévy standing. c. 1876–77
Charcoal on paper
12 ⅝ × 18 ⅞ in. (32 × 48 cm)
National Gallery of Art, Washington, D.C. Collection of Mr. and Mrs. Paul Mellon

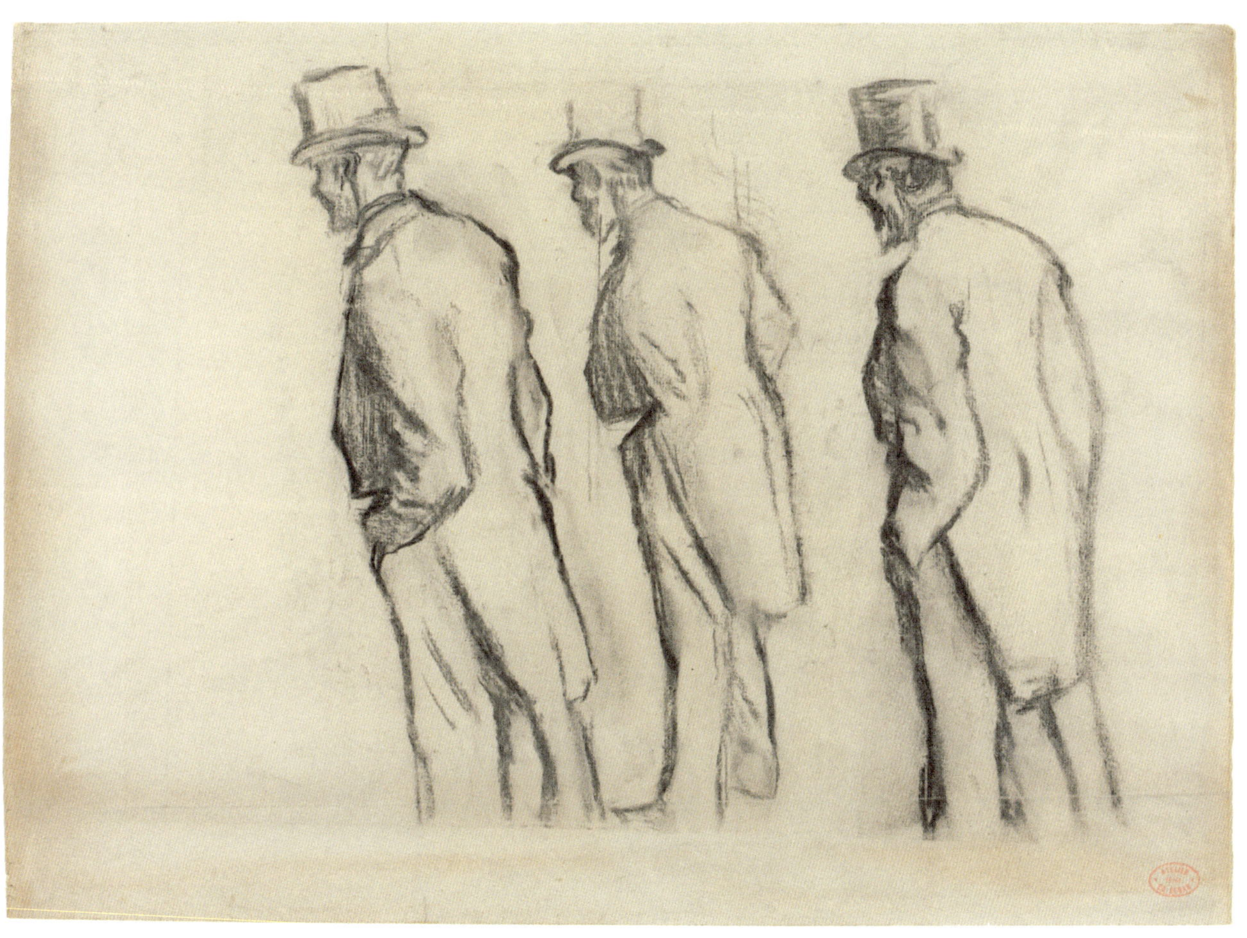

71. Three studies of Ludovic Halévy standing. c. 1876–77
Charcoal on paper, counterproof
14 ⅛ × 19 ¼ in. (35.9 × 48.9 cm)
National Gallery of Art, Washington, D.C. Collection of Mr. and Mrs. Paul Mellon

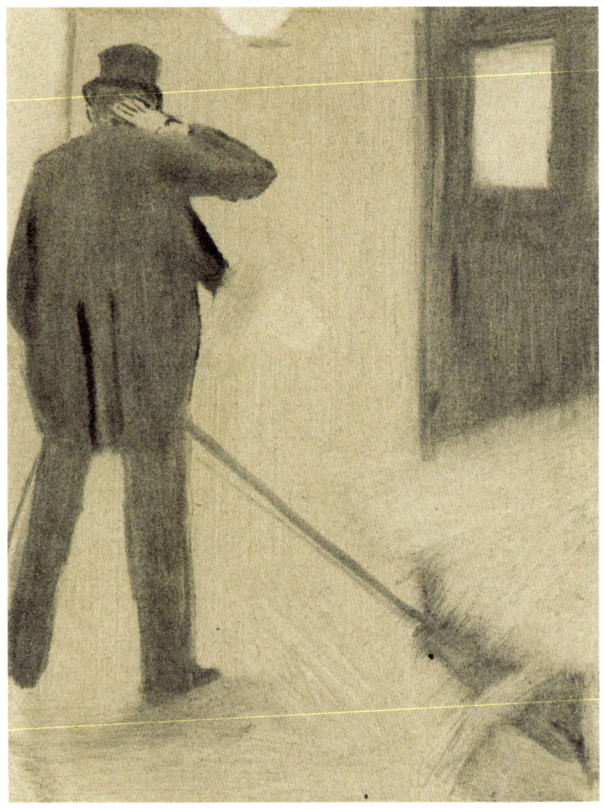

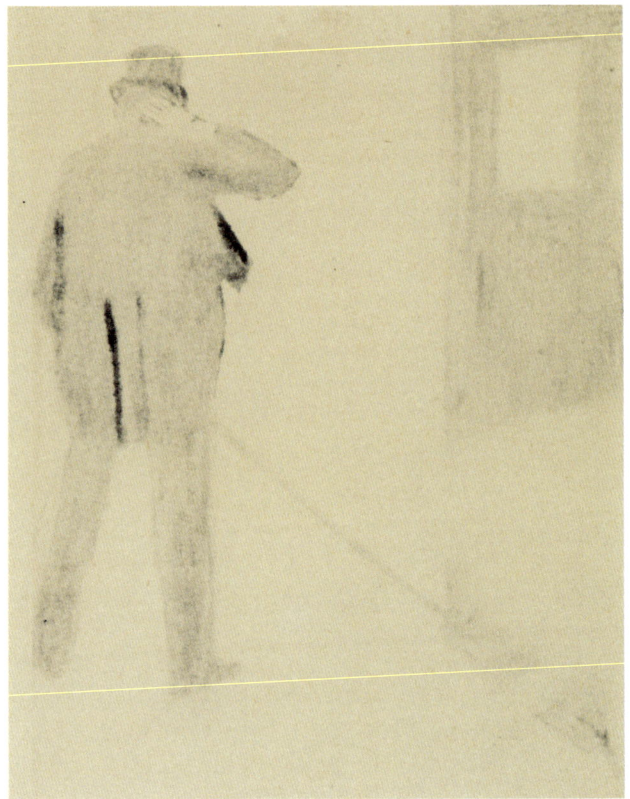

72. *An Admirer in the Corridor* (*Ludovic Halévy dans les coulisses*). c. 1876–77
Proposed illustration for *The Cardinal Family* (*La Famille Cardinal*)
Monotype on paper
Plate: 6 5⁄16 × 4 3⁄4 in. (16.1 × 12 cm), sheet: 9 5⁄16 × 7 1⁄16 in. (23.6 × 17.9 cm)
Staatsgalerie Stuttgart, Graphische Sammlung

73. *Ludovic Halévy in the Wings* (*Ludovic Halévy dans les coulisses*). c. 1876–77
Proposed illustration for *The Cardinal Family* (*La Famille Cardinal*)
Monotype on paper
Plate: 6 3⁄8 × 4 3⁄4 in (16.2 × 12 cm), sheet: 9 3⁄4 × 6 1⁄4 in. (24.7 × 16 cm)
Private collection

An "Anti-spectacular" Art

Kathryn Brown

A well-dressed theatergoer stands awkwardly with his back to us, scratching his head in perplexity (plate 72). A ballerina has just passed behind him, only her legs and the white tulle of her tutu visible as she flees the scene. Perhaps the two have exchanged words, or perhaps the woman has avoided the man altogether—Degas's monotype tells us little about the motivations of its protagonists, their relationship, or the action of the preceding moments. The composition's resistance to narrative exemplifies Degas's pictorial response to the backstage intrigues described in Ludovic Halévy's popular short stories about the Paris Opéra, known collectively as *The Cardinal Family* (*La Famille Cardinal*).

The stories had first appeared in the weekly journal *La Vie parisienne* in the early 1870s. Their success prompted Halévy to revise them for books published under various titles—including *Mme. et M. Cardinal, Les Petites Cardinal*, and *La Famille Cardinal*—from 1872 until his death, in 1908.[1] The narratives describe the lives of Monsieur and Madame Cardinal and their two daughters, Pauline and Virginie, both ballet dancers; through Madame Cardinal's conversations with the narrator, we learn about the young women's amorous adventures and about the social implications of having two female dancers in the family. While Madame Cardinal oversees her daughters' affairs with various wealthy theatergoers, her husband seeks to establish himself in public office. His political ambitions are thwarted, however, by his daughters' reputations (both on- and offstage). In the depiction of Monsieur Cardinal's failed career, Halévy moved his narrative beyond the world of the Opéra and offered his readers a satire on the Third Republic, including its social hierarchy, gender relations, and political leadership.

Degas and Halévy were close for a number of years. Their friendship would eventually collapse in the context of the Dreyfus affair, a scandal of anti-Semitism that began in 1894. In the late 1870s, however, their collaboration on an illustrated edition of a selection of Halévy's *Famille Cardinal* stories must have seemed a natural extension of their relationship, as well as a way for Degas to showcase his skills as a printmaker.[2] Halévy was evidently capable of this kind of collaboration; several of the *Famille Cardinal* anthologies contain images by professional illustrators. Yet his partnership with Degas foundered and the edition went unpublished until well after both men's deaths.

Scholars have proposed various reasons for this. Some suggest that the male protagonist of Degas's images resembled Halévy too closely, and that from the writer's perspective this imbued the stories' sexual intrigues with an autobiographical quality.[3] Others argue that disagreements between the two men

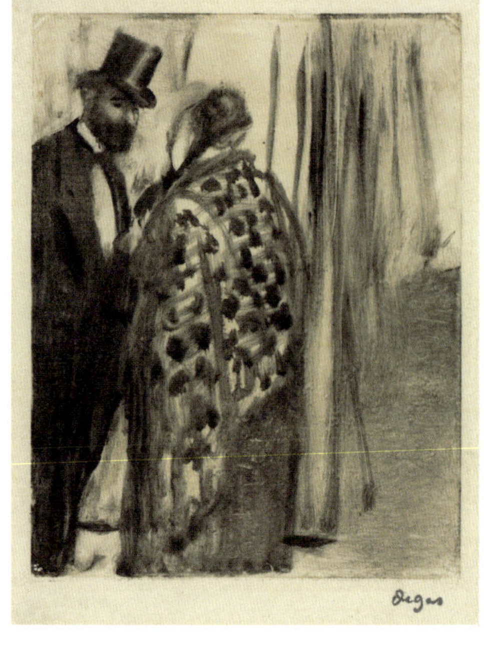

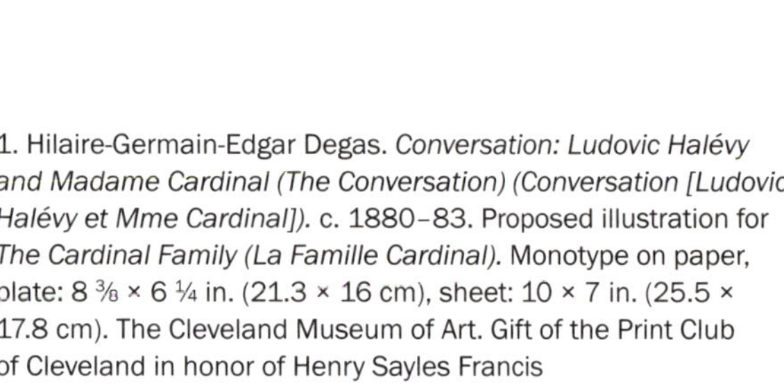

1. Hilaire-Germain-Edgar Degas. *Conversation: Ludovic Halévy and Madame Cardinal (The Conversation) (Conversation [Ludovic Halévy et Mme Cardinal]).* c. 1880–83. Proposed illustration for *The Cardinal Family (La Famille Cardinal).* Monotype on paper, plate: 8 ⅜ × 6 ¼ in. (21.3 × 16 cm), sheet: 10 × 7 in. (25.5 × 17.8 cm). The Cleveland Museum of Art. Gift of the Print Club of Cleveland in honor of Henry Sayles Francis

over the style of the images made a joint production impossible.[4] Degas illustrated Halévy's earliest *Cardinal Family* stories, depicting both backstage encounters and life in the family home. Although his monotypes included scenes and characters familiar from the stories, they diverged from the style of illustration popular in deluxe books of the period: not only do the images unfold in no identifiable sequence, they also question what could be known and communicated about the backstage space of the Paris Opéra, a world restricted to a class of wealthy subscribers (*abonnés*). Throughout Halévy's stories, readers overhear private conversations between the narrator and Madame Cardinal and have access to Madame Cardinal's personal correspondence. The narratives are designed to familiarize readers with the secrets of the Opéra and to draw them into closed conversational networks. In contrast, Degas's images exclude the viewer from such backstage exchanges by repudiating visual detail and resisting integration into narrative both individually and collectively.[5] The monotypes convey fleeting, interstitial moments—swift transitions from the wings to the stage, from private preparation to public performance. Most important, they subvert conventions that typified depictions of theater life in nineteenth-century France.

Degas's paintings and pastels of the ballet have often been associated with the sexualized portrayal of women in nineteenth-century art.[6] Whether facilitating the display of the female body or providing glimpses of an environment in which dancers and their admirers could pursue private liaisons, Degas's ballet scenes have been understood as contributing to visual art's commodification of women for the pleasure of heterosexual male viewers. Yet the *Cardinal Family* monotypes sit uneasily within these conventions in that they deny a voyeuristic gaze. Doors are closed, dressing rooms remain inaccessible, women's bodies are concealed: female presence may be reduced to a glimpse of a costume or body fragment, or the individual may be indistinguishable within a crowd (plate 78). Instead of reinforcing a gendered hierarchy of looking, Degas's monotypes disturb the social legibility of the female body by undermining the visual information provided to the viewer.[7] Subverting the premise of theatrical display, these images are "anti-spectacular" in their privileging of concealment.

Degas's handling of pictorial space complements this effect. The theater depicted in the monotypes is not the Opéra's Palais Garnier—inaugurated in 1875, and a landmark of Baron Haussmann's Paris—but its earlier theater, the Salle Le Peletier, which had been destroyed by fire in 1873. Halévy describes the theater as containing "wonderful old corridors with loads of little corners barely illuminated by smoky oil lamps."[8] Instead of interpreting this literally, Degas isolates features of the building, including a spiral staircase (plate 80), seemingly endless corridors, and recesses that would have facilitated secret conversations (fig. 1). He also keeps these architectural fragments from cohering into a stable form: conventional perspective is abandoned, walls constitute uncertain frames, and corridors tilt in unexpected directions. Just as Degas's images undermine conventional depictions of the female body, the spatial contours of the theater elude any fixed organization.

These adventurous compositional experiments were well suited to the monotype format. As Eugenia Parry Janis shows, Degas applied ink to the plate with brushes and rags, often wiping sections away or adding pigment to create visibly different textures on the printed page.[9] Figures are smudged and scenes lack background detail, leading Clifford Ackley to the observation that Degas's printmaking exploited "restlessness and irresolution."[10] Janis sees Degas's monotypes as transitional compositions that are "resolved" by the application of pastel, but a lack of finish remains crucial to the theme and content of Degas's *Famille Cardinal* monotypes. Like the fleeting moments they depict, these images remain uneasily suspended—permanently hovering on the brink of change.[11]

Degas's images were included in an edition of *La Famille Cardinal* published by Auguste Blaizot & Fils, Paris, in 1938.[12] Comprising a selection of Halévy's stories and heliogravures by Maurice Potin after Degas's monotypes, the book realizes no plan laid down by either the writer or the artist. It nevertheless highlights the innovative features of the monotypes by offsetting them against Halévy's conventional style of storytelling. In their resistance to narrative and unsettling of the gendered hierarchies of looking that typified much nineteenth-century European art, Degas's *Famille Cardinal* monotypes defy categorization as either book illustration or social commentary. This uncompromising interrogation of the limits of the visible anticipated Degas's more radical experiments in the final decades of his career.

1. The publishing history of the stories is discussed in Michael Pantazzi, "Degas, Halévy, and the Cardinals," in Jean Sutherland Boggs, Douglas Druick, Henri Loyrette, et al., *Degas*, exh. cat. (New York: The Metropolitan Museum of Art, 1988), pp. 280–84, and Jonas Beyer, *Zwischen Zeichnung und Druck. Edgar Degas und die Wiederentdeckung der Monotypie im 19. Jahrhundert* (Paderborn: Wilhelm Fink, 2014), pp. 189–203.
2. See Loyrette, "Portrait d'amis sur la scène: Degas et Ludovic Halévy," in Loyrette, ed., *Entre le théâtre et l'histoire. La Famille Halévy (1760–1960)*, exh. cat. (Paris: Fayard and Réunion des Musées Nationaux, 1996), pp. 178–95. On Degas's anti-Semitism and his rupture with Ludovic Halévy see Linda Nochlin, "Degas and the Dreyfus Affair: A Portrait of the Artist as an Anti-Semite," in Nochlin, *The Politics of Vision: Essays on Nineteenth-Century Art and Society* (Boulder: Perseus, 1989), pp. 141–69.
3. See Theodore Reff, "Degas and the Literature of His Time II," *The Burlington Magazine* 112, no. 811 (October 1970):674, 677–88; Nochlin, "A House Is Not a Home: Degas and the Subversion of the Family," in Richard Kendall and Griselda Pollock, eds., *Dealing with Degas: Representations of Women and the Politics of Vision* (New York: Universe, 1992), pp. 43–62; and Beyer, *Zwischen Zeichnung und Druck*, p. 200.
4. See Barbara Stern Shapiro, catalogue entry on *Pauline and Virginie Conversing with Admirers*, in Sue Welsh Reed, Eugenia Parry Janis, Shapiro, David W. Kiehl, Colta Ives, and Michael Mazur, *The Painterly Print: Monotypes from the Seventeenth to the Twentieth Century*, exh. cat. (New York: The Metropolitan Museum of Art, 1980), p. 109; Janis, *Degas Monotypes: Essay, Catalogue & Checklist*, exh. cat. (Cambridge, Mass.: Fogg Art Museum and Garland Publishing, 1968), p. xxi–xxii; and Beyer, *Zwischen Zeichnung und Druck*, p. 178.
5. See the discussion of contrasts between the conversational style of the stories and Degas's aesthetic of exclusion in my essay "Intimacy and Exclusion: Degas's Monotypes for *La Famille Cardinal*," in Kathryn Brown, ed., *Perspectives on Degas* (Farnham: Ashgate, forthcoming in 2016).
6. See, e.g., Tamar Garb, *The Body in Time: Figures of Femininity in Late Nineteenth-Century France*, Murphy Lecture Series (Seattle: Spencer Museum of Art and University of Washington Press, 2008), pp. 22–25; Marilyn R. Brown, "An Entrepreneur in Spite of Himself: Edgar Degas and the Market," in Thomas L. Haskell and Richard F. Teichgraeber III, eds., *The Culture of the Market: Historical Essays* (Cambridge: at the University Press, 1996), pp. 261–92; and Carol Armstrong, *Odd Man Out: Readings of the Work and Reputation of Edgar Degas* (Chicago: at the University Press, 1991), pp. 62–72. See also Laura Mulvey's famous account of "scopophilia" in *Visual and Other Pleasures* (Houndmills: Palgrave, 1989), pp. 16–24.
7. See Beyer's discussion of how Degas's monotypes exploit visual uncertainty in *Zwischen Zeichnung und Druck*, pp. 198–99.
8. Halévy, *La Famille Cardinal* (Paris: Calmann Lévy, 1883), p. 69. Kendall and Jill DeVonyar provide an excellent overview of the history of the Salle Le Peletier, including the social and pictorial background of nineteenth-century theater imagery, in *Degas and the Dance*, exh. cat. (New York: Harry N. Abrams, 2002), pp. 64–65.
9. See Janis's discussion of Degas's technique in *Degas Monotypes*, catalogue entries 46–50, n.p. and Karl Buchberg and Laura Neufeld's essay in the present volume.
10. Clifford Ackley, "The Painter as Printmaker," in Reed and Shapiro, *Edgar Degas: The Painter as Printmaker*, with contributions by Ackley and Roy L. Perkinson and an essay by Druick and Peter Zegers, exh. cat. (Boston: Museum of Fine Arts, 1984), pp. ix–xiv.
11. Janis, "The Role of the Monotype in the Working Method of Degas I" and " . . . II," *The Burlington Magazine* 109, no. 766 (January 1967):20–29, and 109, no. 767 (February 1967):71–81. See the contrasting view in my essay "Touch and Vision in Edgar Degas's Darkfield Monotypes," *Print Quarterly* XXXI, no. 4 (December 2014):395–405.
12. Halévy, *La Famille Cardinal*, with a foreword by Marcel Guérin (Paris: Auguste Blaizot & fils, 1938).

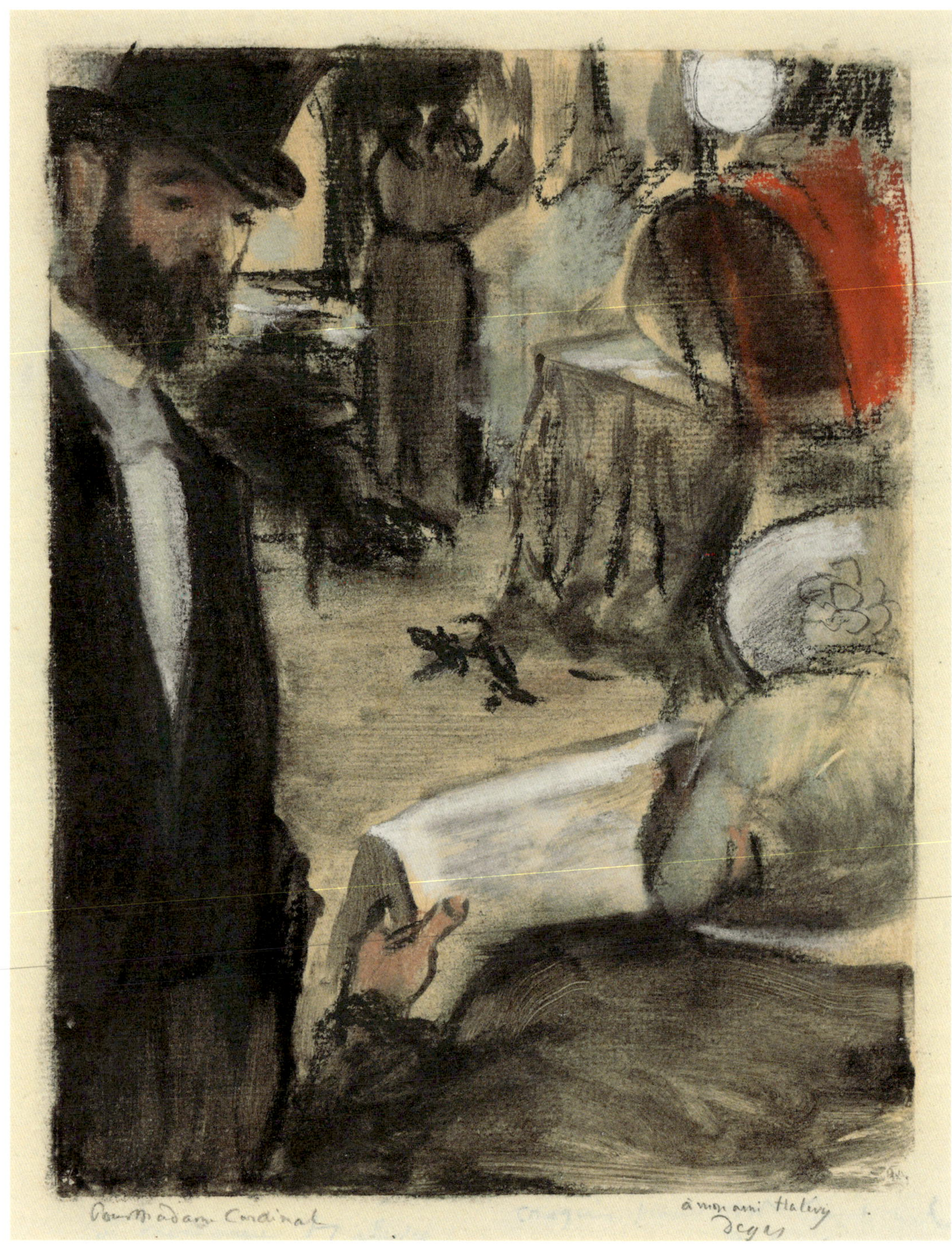

74. *Ludovic Halévy Finds Mme. Cardinal in the Dressing Room*
(*Ludovic Halévy trouve Mme Cardinal dans les loges*). c. 1876–77
Proposed illustration for *The Cardinal Family* (*La Famille Cardinal*)
Pastel and pencil over monotype on paper
Plate: 8 ½ × 6 ¼ in. (21.6 × 15.9 cm), sheet: 10 ½ × 9 in. (26.7 × 22.9 cm)
Private collection

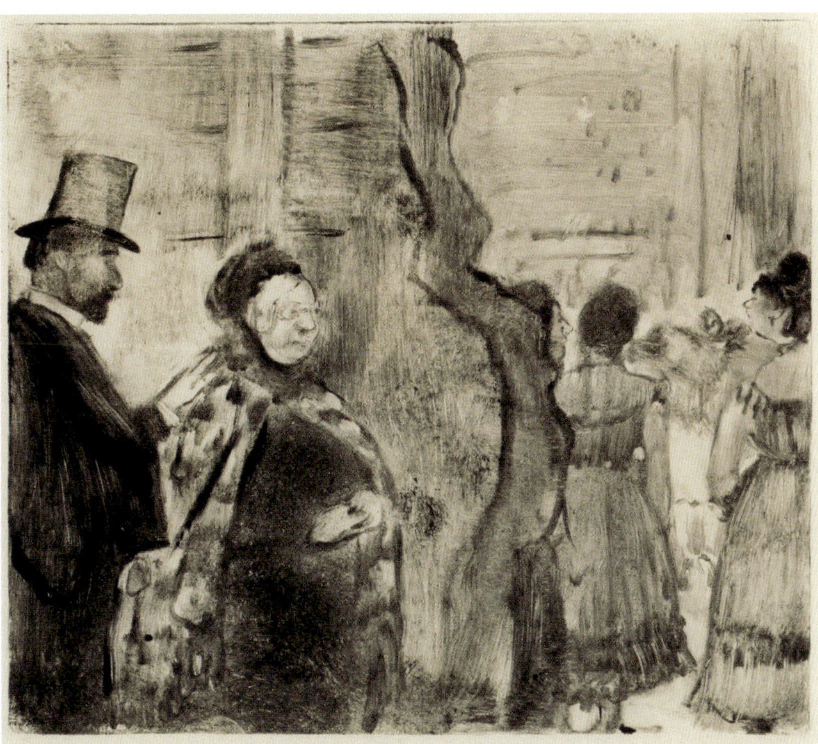

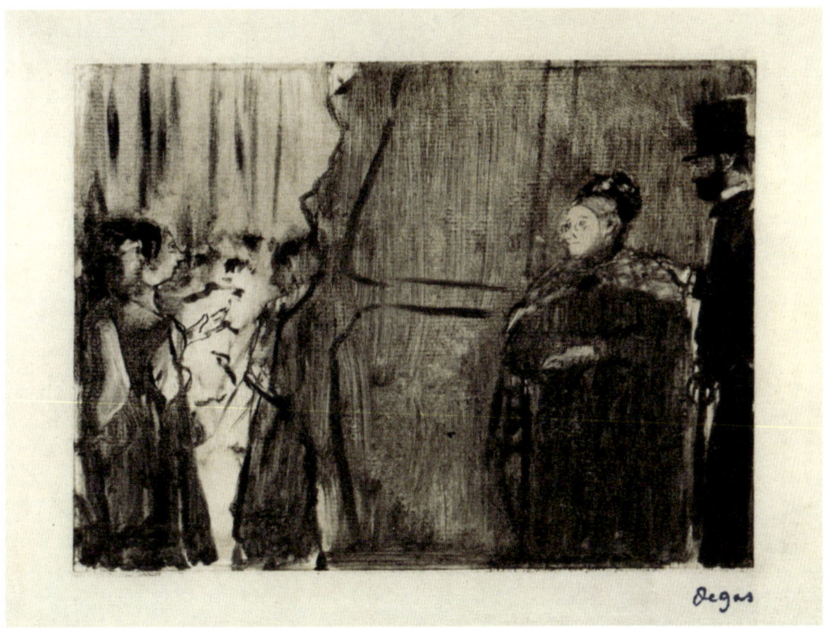

75. *Ludovic Halévy Meeting Mme. Cardinal Backstage* (*Rencontre de Ludovic Halévy et de Madame Cardinal dans les coulisses*). c. 1876–77
Proposed illustration for *The Cardinal Family* (*La Famille Cardinal*)
Monotype on paper
Plate: 10 ¾ × 12 1/16 in. (27.3 × 30.7 cm)
Private collection, Chicago

76. *Ludovic Halévy Meeting Madame Cardinal Backstage* (*Rencontre de Ludovic Halévy et de Madame Cardinal dans les coulisses*). c. 1876–77
Proposed illustration for *The Cardinal Family* (*La Famille Cardinal*)
Monotype on paper
Plate: 6 5/16 × 8 ⅜ in. (16 × 21.3 cm)
Collection André Bromberg

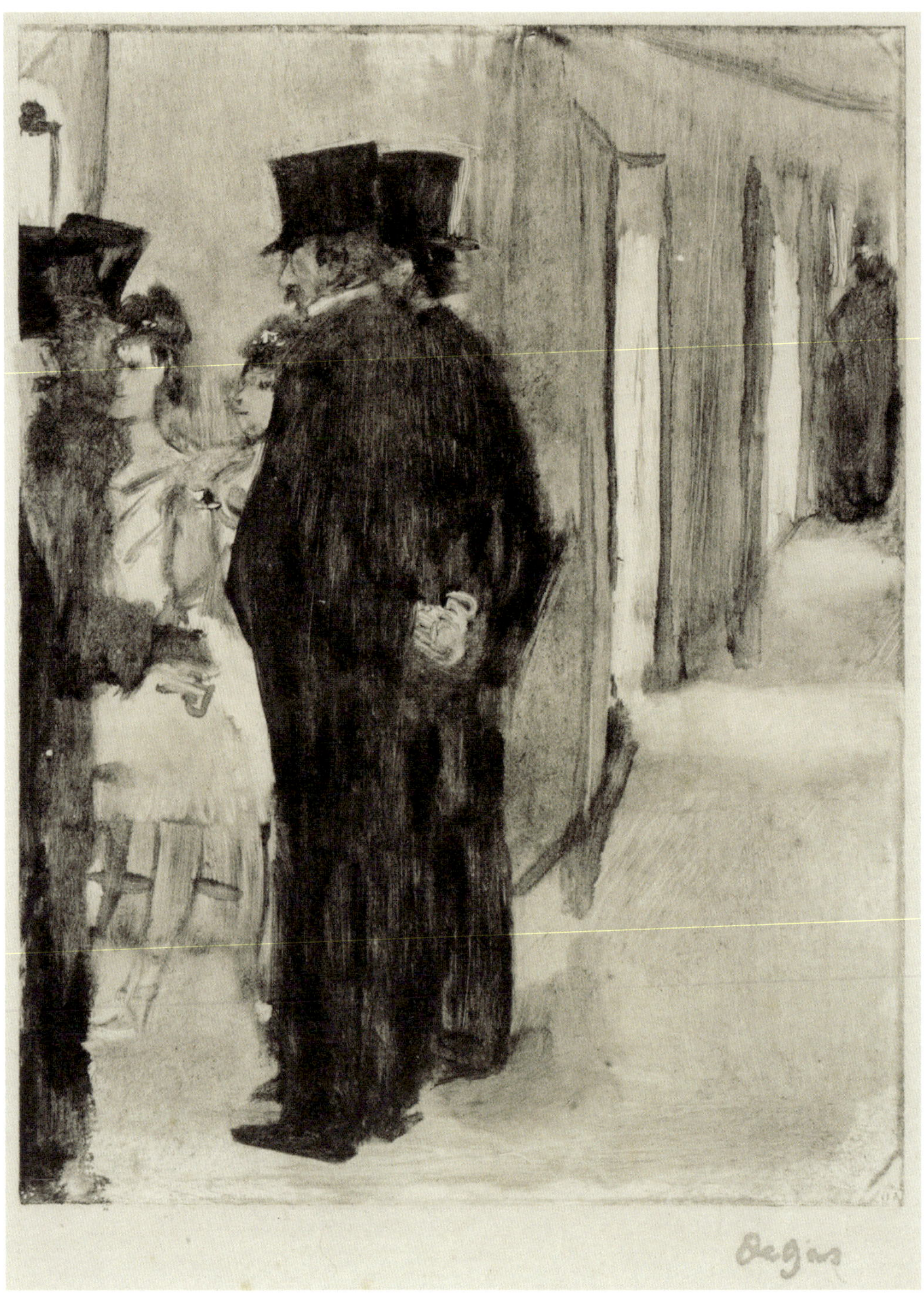

77. *Pauline and Virginie Conversing with Admirers* (*Pauline et Virginie Cardinal bavardant avec des admirateurs*). c. 1876–77
Proposed illustration for *The Cardinal Family* (*La Famille Cardinal*)
Monotype on paper
Plate: 8 7⁄16 × 6 5⁄16 in. (21.5 × 16.1 cm); sheet: 11 3⁄10 × 7 ½ in. (28.7 × 19.1 cm)
Harvard Art Museums/Fogg Museum, Cambridge, Massachusetts. Bequest of Meta and Paul J. Sachs

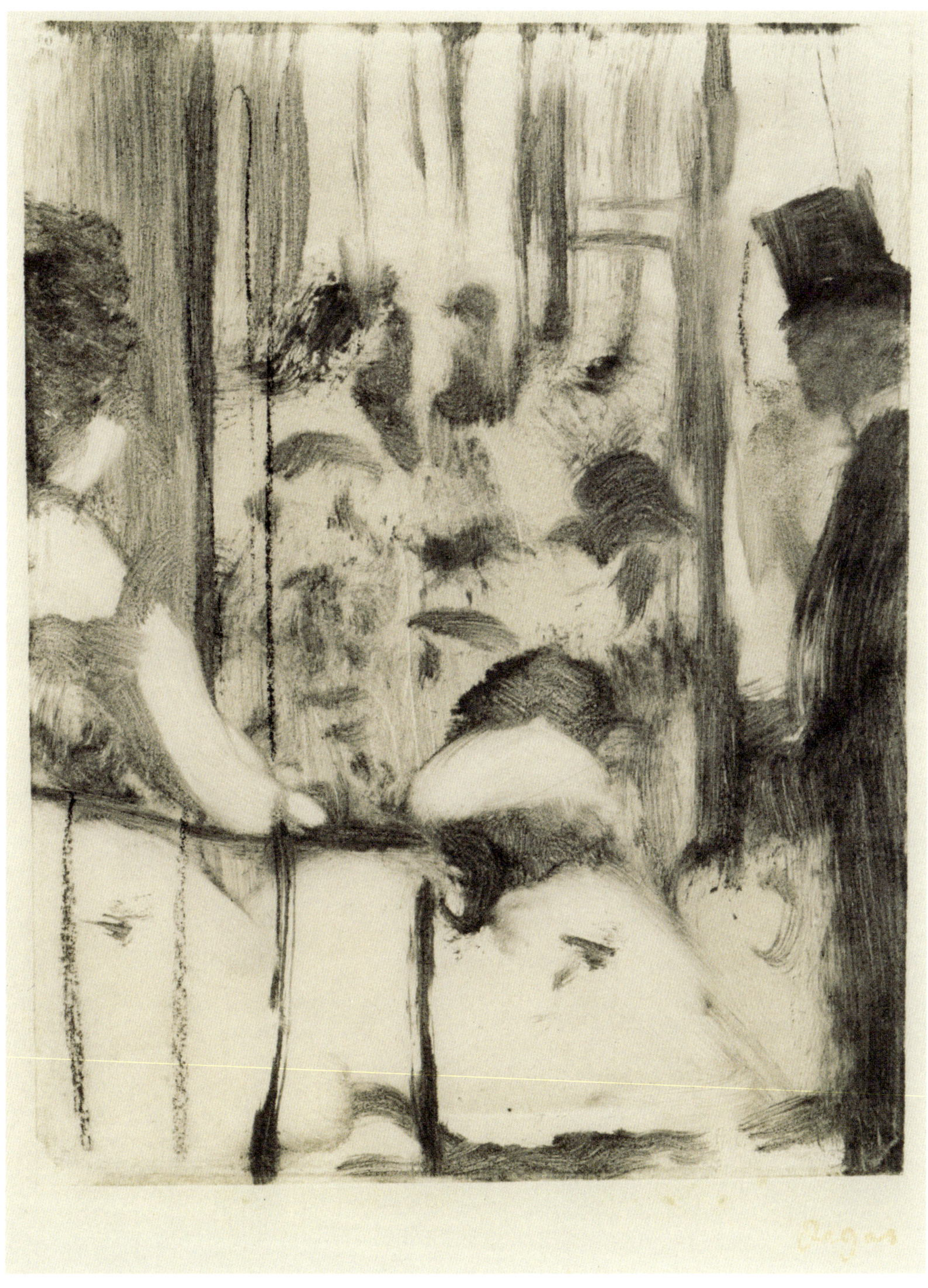

78. *Dancers Coming from the Dressing Rooms onto the Stage* (*Et ces demoiselles frétillaient gentiment devant la glace du foyer*). c. 1876–77
Proposed illustration for *The Cardinal Family* (*La Famille Cardinal*)
Pastel over monotype on paper
Plate: 8 ⅜ × 6 ¼ in. (21.2 × 15.8 cm)
Schorr Collection

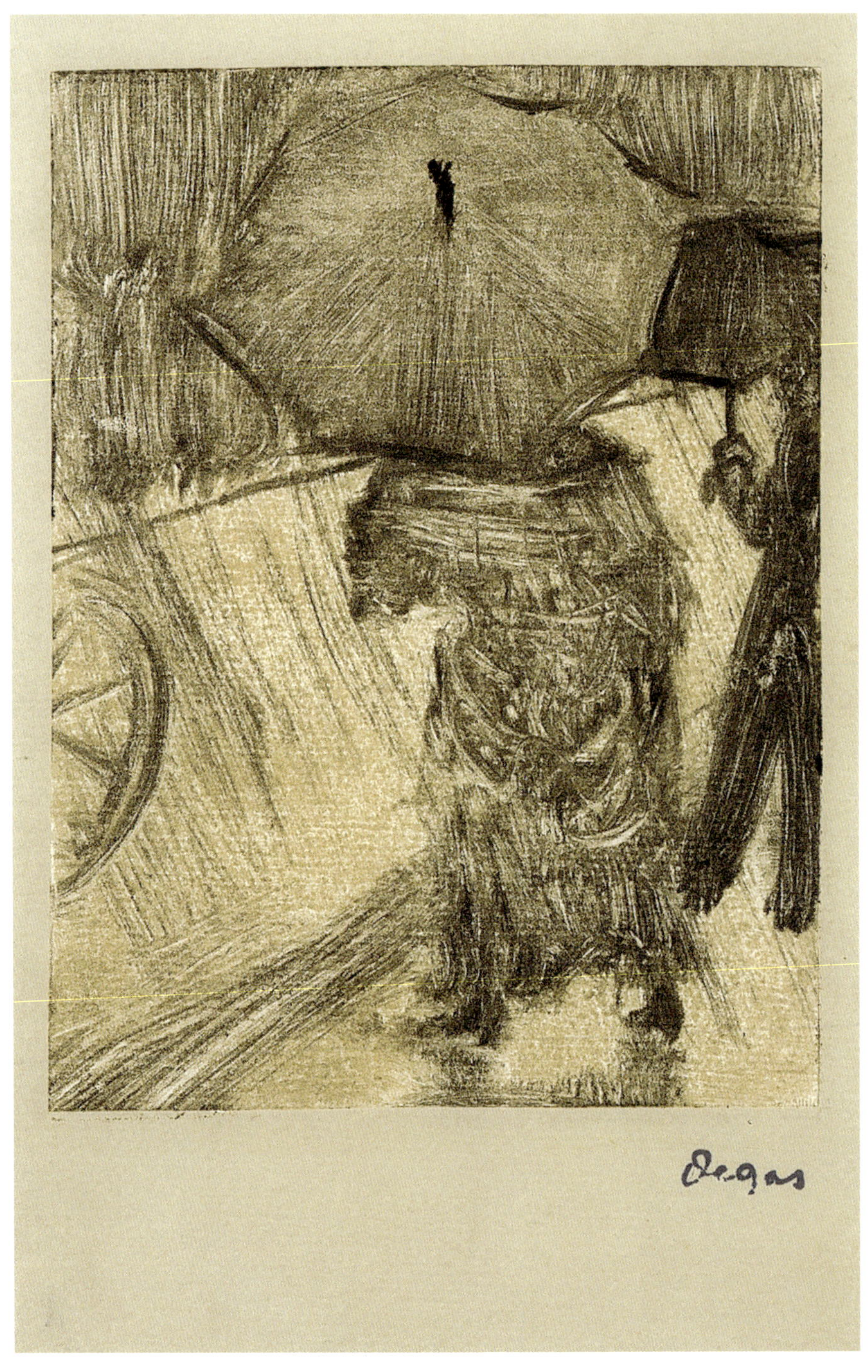

79. *On the Street in the Rain* (*Sous la pluie*). c. 1876–77
Proposed illustration for *The Cardinal Family* (*La Famille Cardinal*)
Monotype on paper
Plate: 6 5⁄16 × 4 5⁄8 in. (16.1 × 11.8 cm), sheet: 10 7⁄16 × 7 1⁄16 in. (26.5 × 17.9 cm)
Private collection. Courtesy Nicholas Stogdon

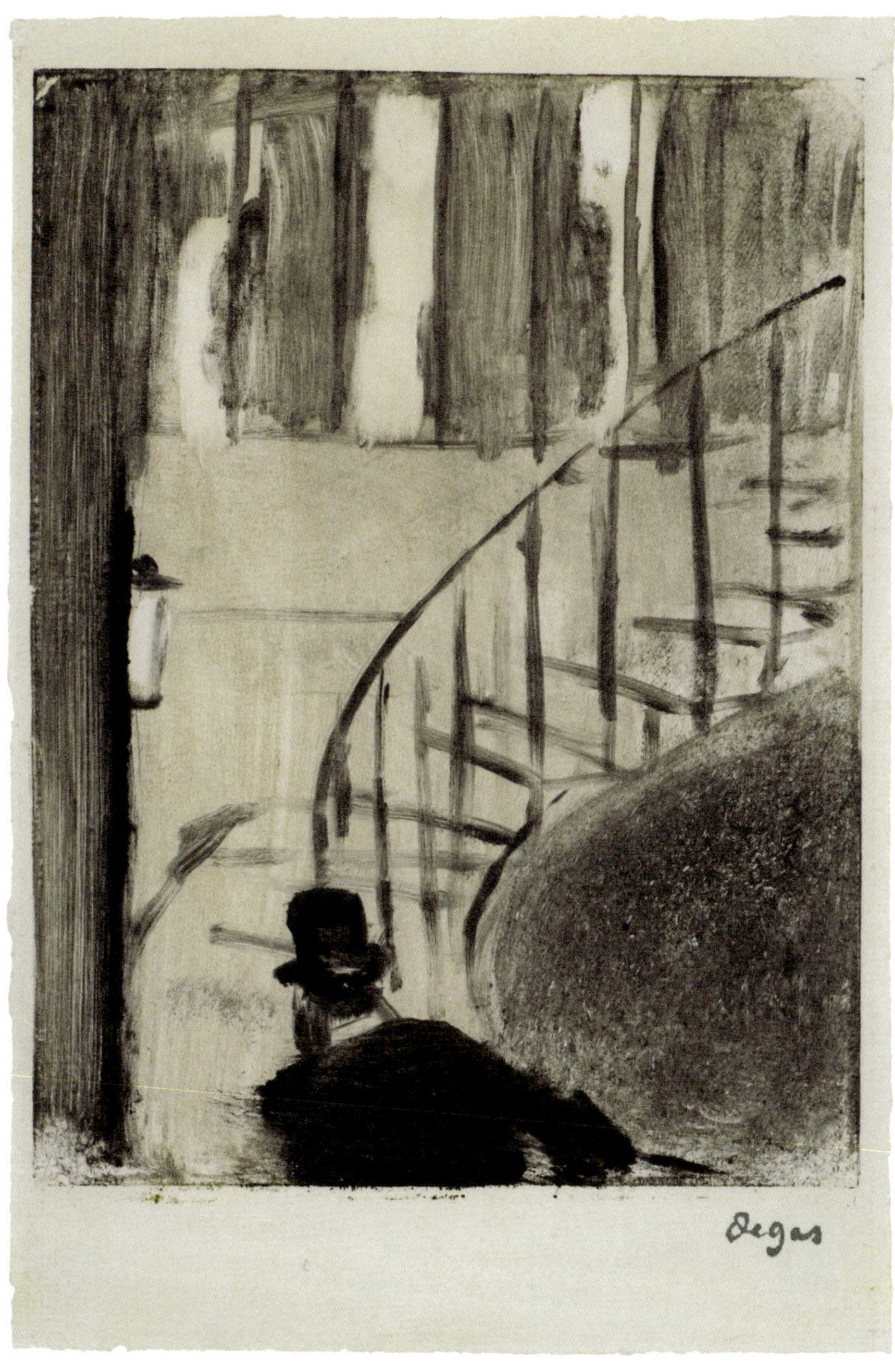

80. *Ludovic Halévy Backstage* (*Ludovic Halévy montant l'escalier*). c. 1876–77
Proposed illustration for *The Cardinal Family* (*La Famille Cardinal*)
Monotype on paper
Plate: 8 ⅜ × 6 ¼ in. (21.3 × 15.9 cm), sheet: 10 × 6 ¾ in. (25.4 × 17.1 cm)
Private collection

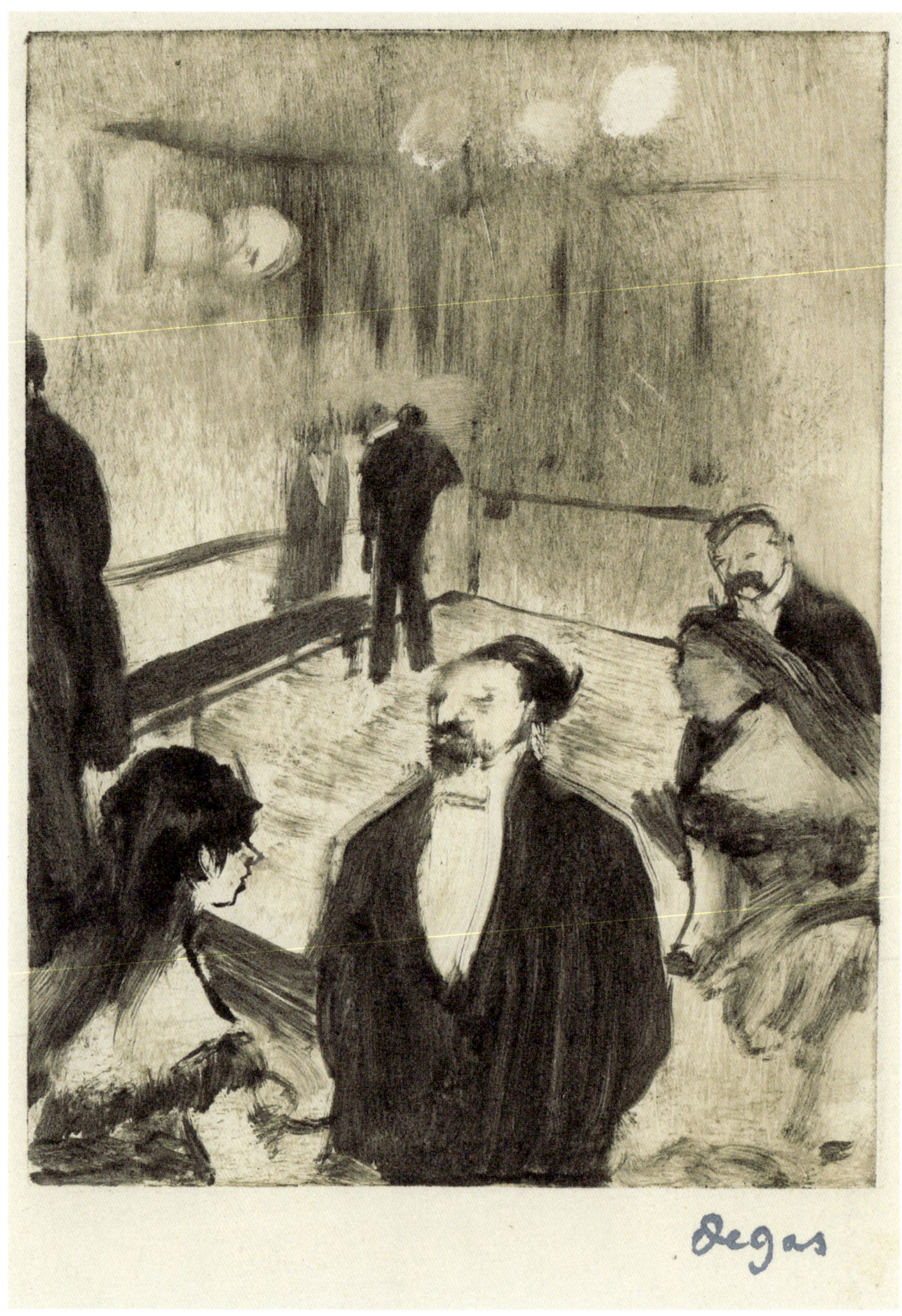

81. *In the Green Room* (*Le Foyer*). c. 1876–77
Proposed illustration for *The Cardinal Family* (*La Famille Cardinal*)
Monotype on paper
Plate: 6 ⅜ × 4 ¹¹⁄₁₆ in. (16.2 × 11.9 cm), sheet: 7 ⅜ × 5 ⅛ in. (18.8 × 13 cm)
Staatsgalerie Stuttgart, Graphische Sammlung

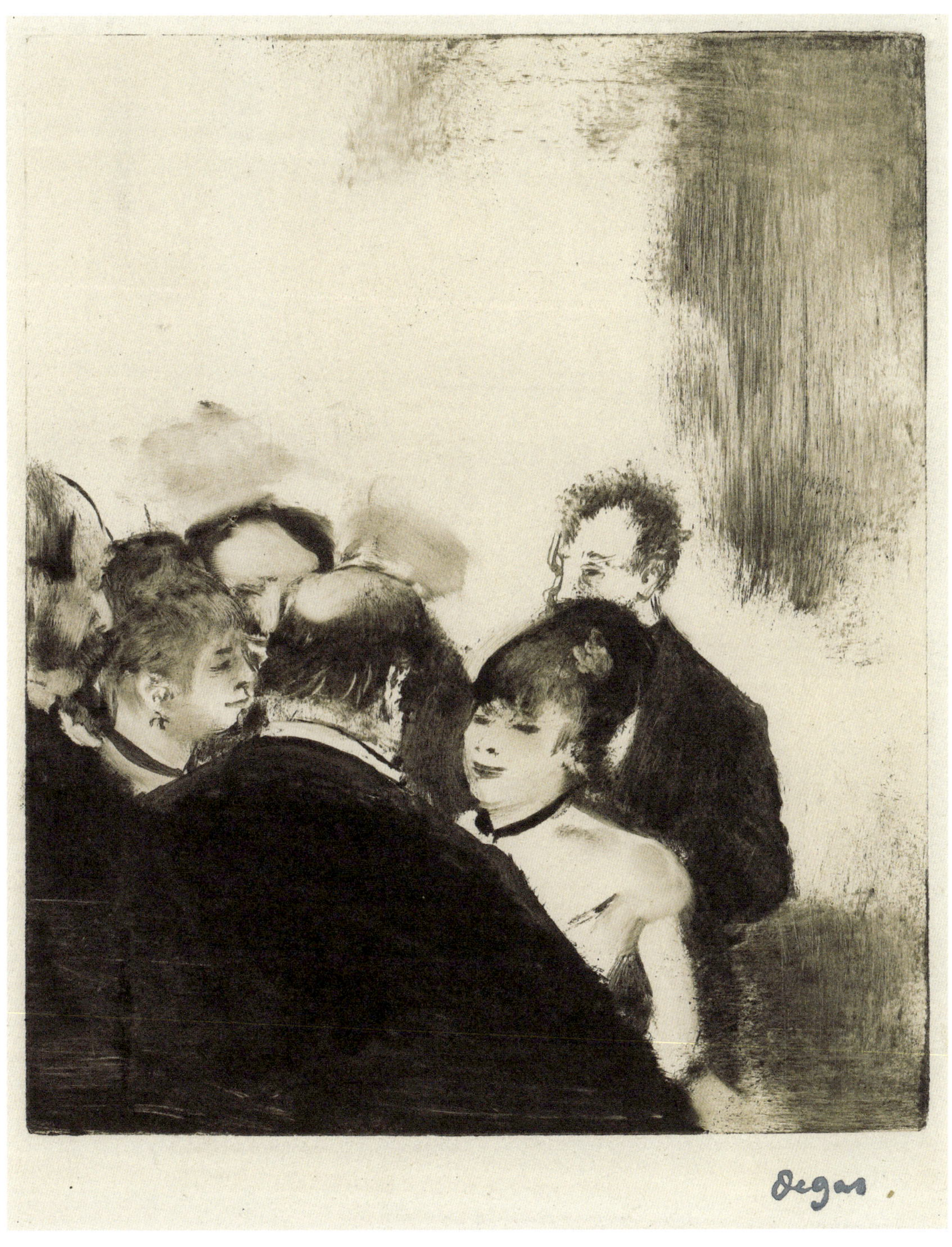

82. *The Cardinal Sisters Talking to Admirers* (*Les Petites Cardinal parlant à leurs admirateurs*). c. 1876–77
Proposed illustration for *The Cardinal Family* (*La Famille Cardinal*)
Monotype on paper
Plate: 8 11⁄16 × 7 in. (22 × 17.8 cm), sheet: 10 5⁄8 × 8 in. (27 × 20.3 cm)
Staatsgalerie Stuttgart, Graphische Sammlung

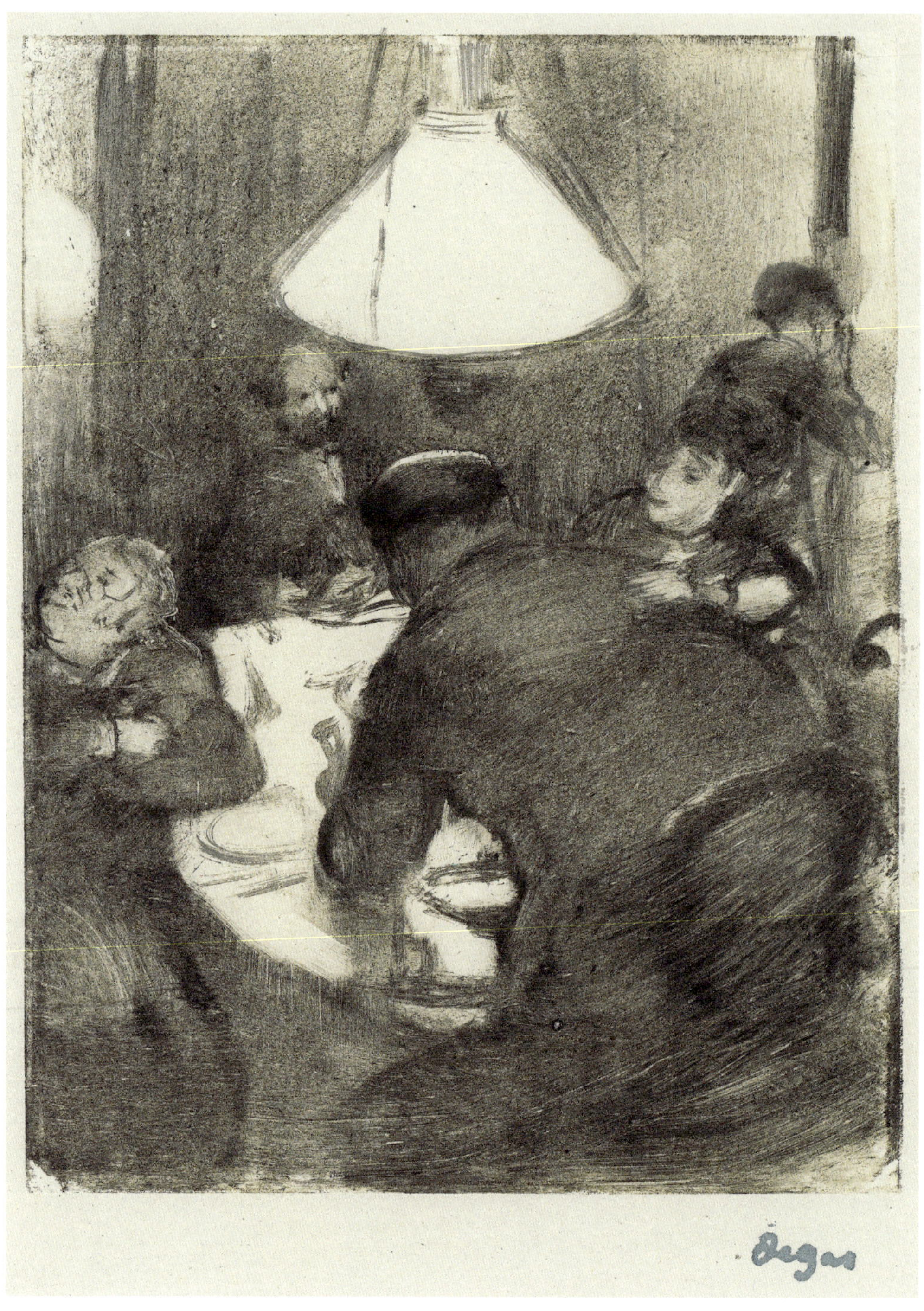

83. *The Famous Good Friday Dinner (An Argument between Virginie's Protector, the Marquis Cavalcanti, and M. Cardinal)* (*Le Fameux Dîner du vendredi*). c. 1876–77
Proposed illustration for *The Cardinal Family* (*La Famille Cardinal*)
Monotype on paper
Plate: 8 ⅜ × 6 5⁄16 in. (21.3 × 16 cm), sheet: 11 ¾ × 8 11⁄16 in. (29.8 × 22 cm)
Staatsgalerie Stuttgart, Graphische Sammlung

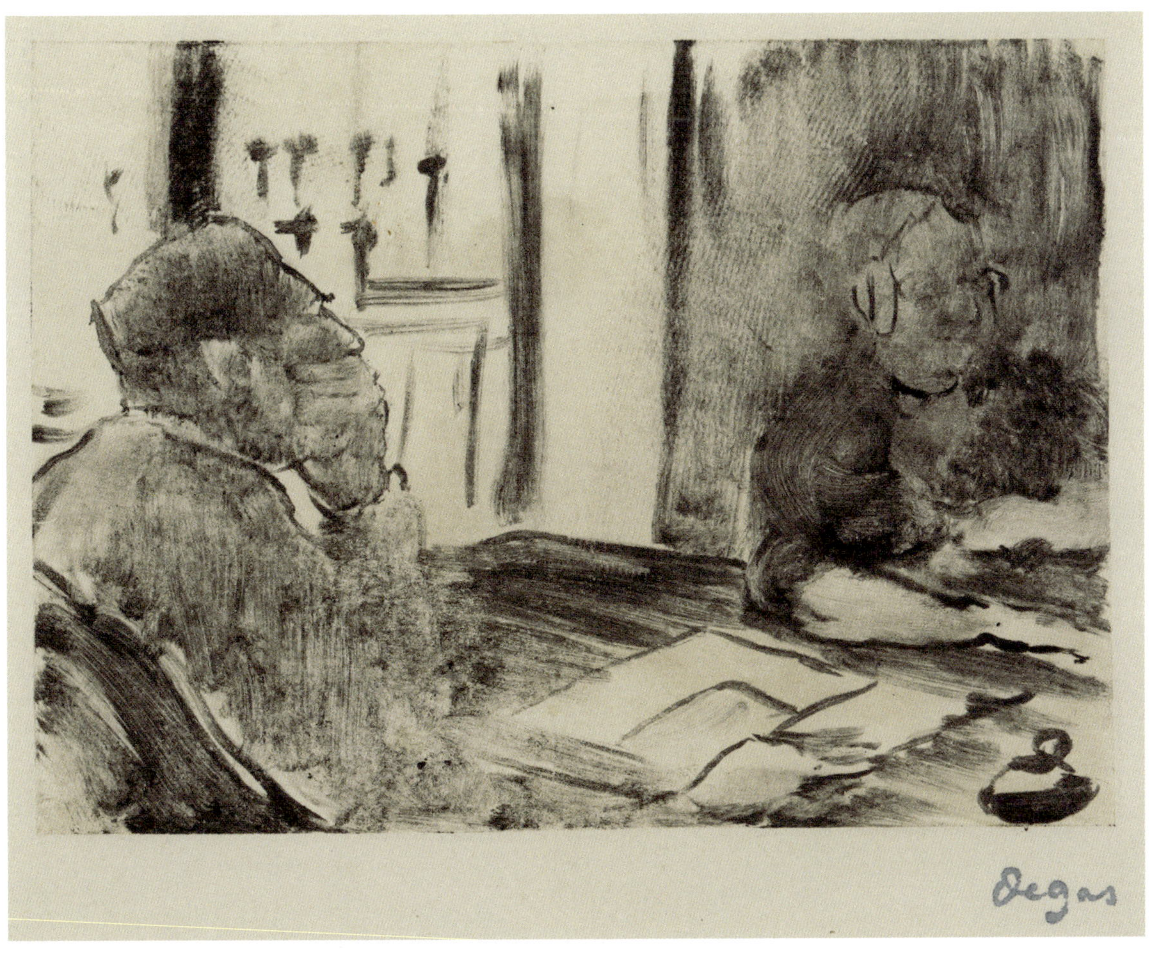

84. *M. Cardinal About to Write a Letter* (*Je ne comprends pas, dit M. Cardinal*). c. 1876–77
Proposed illustration for *The Cardinal Family* (*La Famille Cardinal*)
Monotype on paper
Plate: 4 11/16 × 6 3/8 in. (11.9 × 16.2 cm), sheet: 7 3/8 × 9 1/2 in. (18.7 × 24.2 cm)
Lent by James Bergquist

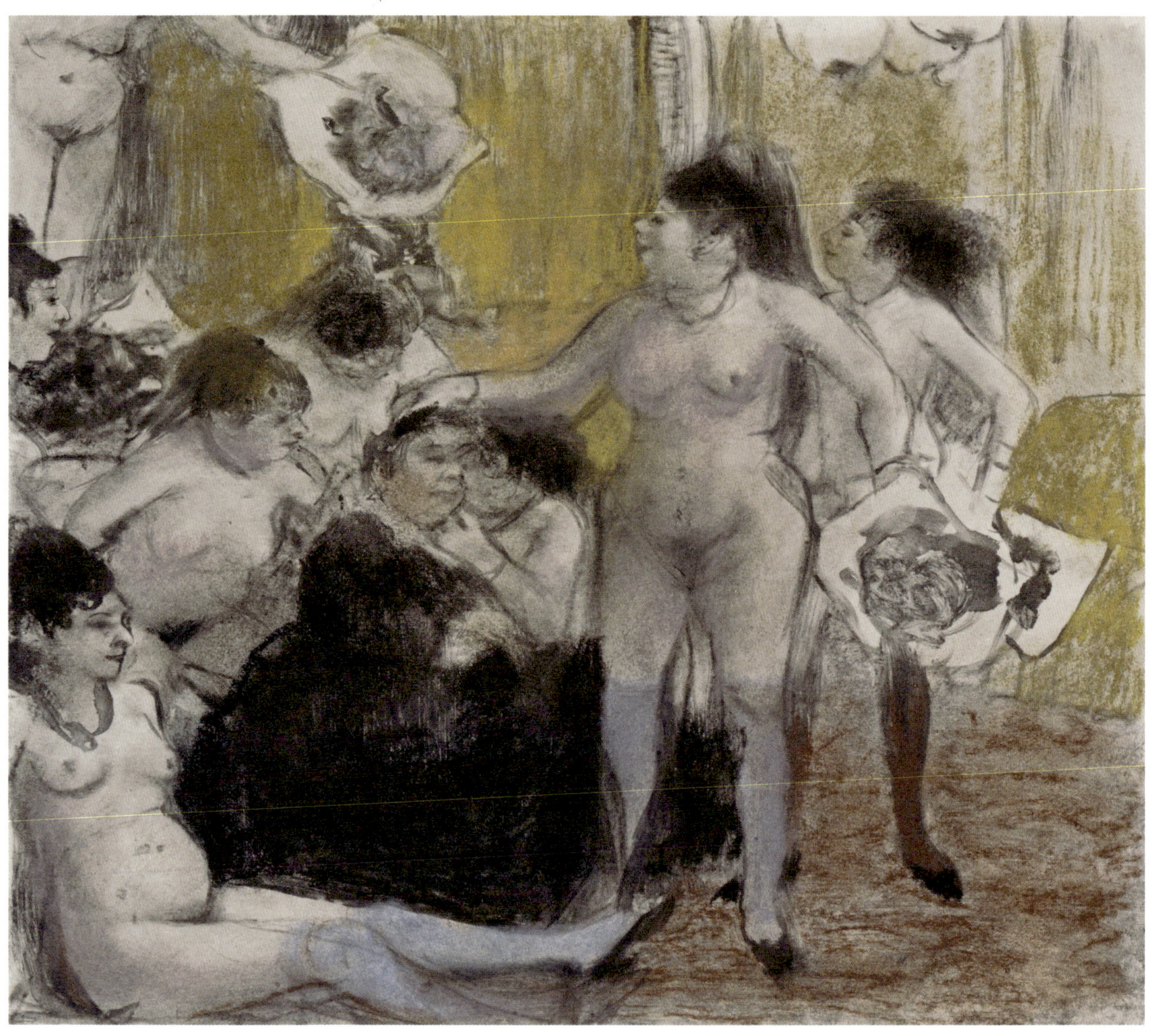

85. *The Name Day of the Madam* (*La Fête de la patronne*). c. 1877–79
Pastel over monotype on paper
10 ½ × 11 ⅝ in. (26.6 × 29.6 cm)
Musée Picasso, Paris

Stockings and Mirrors

Raisa Rexer

More than any other body of Degas's work, the brothel monotypes are a conundrum. Unmentioned in Degas's personal writings, for the most part unremarked by contemporaries and unexhibited until after his death, this series of small-format images left few historical traces to illuminate why or for whom they were produced.[1] With their often severe visual style and casual use of graphic nudity, they seem to lack the "quasi-religious and chaste" quality that, for Pierre-Auguste Renoir, set Degas's prostitutes apart from those of other contemporary artists; indeed Degas's brother René allegedly destroyed another seventy monotypes upon the artist's death because they were too overtly obscene.[2] Yet the monotypes also contain many of Degas's artistic trademarks, opening them to interpretation both as erotic fantasies and as studies in tonal contrast whose controversial content is incidental to their stylistic ingenuity.[3] In the monotypes, subject matter and qualities of execution refuse to align: privilege one and these works look like pornographic indulgence, privilege the other and they look very much like artistic exploration.

There is, however, another iconographic tradition whose shadow presence in the monotypes hints at reconciliation of this standoff between content and form.[4] Almost immediately after the announcement of photography's invention, in 1839, photographic pornography began to appear on the streets of Paris and in the back corners of some of its shops.[5] By the 1880s this new kind of obscenity had become ubiquitous around Europe, and had grown into a large international business generating millions of images.[6] It also introduced a number of representational motifs and conventions that appear in recognizable form in Degas's brothel monotypes, though transformed by his pictorial innovations—his manipulation of perspective and subversive compositional approach. This experimentation with photographic convention is a remarkable testament to his artistic practice, and to the place of the monotypes in that practice, but it is also something else: as this reenvisioning of pornographic tropes deconstructs the visual structures of fantasy at the heart of pornographic photographs, it offers in their place an ultimately sympathetic rendering of the realities of prostitution.

The commercial distribution of all visual and written materials in Second Empire France was governed by a strict system of censorship, one of whose peculiarities was that it allowed for the legal production and sale of academic nude studies for the use of artists.[7] Early photographic nudity accordingly ran the gamut from demure, carefully composed photographic studies that could be sold legally to explicit and illicit pictures of lesbian and heterosexual intercourse. Yet despite this wide variety, a distinctive visual language quickly developed. One of the most

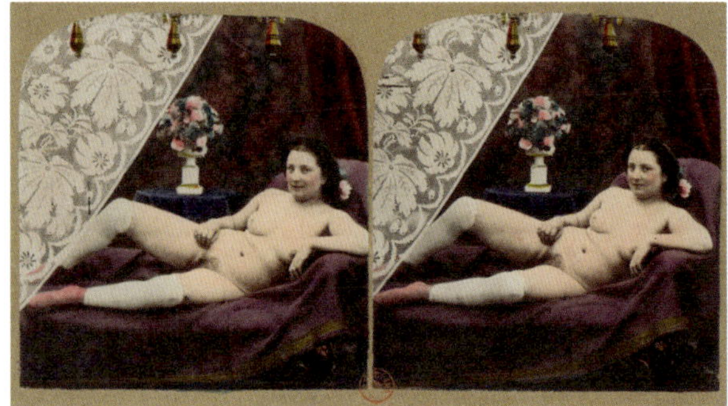

1. Unknown photographer. Erotic scene (*Scéne érotique*). 1860s. Stereoscopic black and white photograph. Bibliothèque nationale de France, Paris

basic characteristics of photographic erotica, distinguishing it immediately from painted and lithographic nudes, was the presence of pubic hair, starkly outlined against the models' light flesh.[8] Alongside this side effect of photography's realism, other props and poses also repeat. Even the earliest nude daguerreotypes of the 1840s and '50s, for instance, manifest a fascination with the erotic potential of the mirror, using its multiplication of perspectives within a single image to offer the viewer the impossible indulgence of possessing the female body from two perspectives at once.[9] Another characteristic trope, identified by the art historian Abigail Solomon-Godeau, is a fetishistic erotics of the stockinged leg, which the models—sometimes naked but for these stockings, sometimes lifting up voluminous skirts to show them—reveal coyly or not so coyly to the viewer (fig. 1).[10] Finally there is the pose that ushers in and defines the era of photographic pornography, the "beaver shot." In these close-up photographs of women spreading their legs, which Solomon-Godeau argues have no precedent in the visual tradition before photography, the model is subsumed into her sexual anatomy, reduced to a physical projection of the viewer's sexual desire.[11]

Many of the prostitutes who lounge in wait for clients in Degas's brothels appear to have stepped right out of these photographs. In the monotypes *Waiting for the Client* (*Attente d'un client*, c. 1877–79; plate 98) and *Resting on the Bed* (*Repos sur le lit*, c. 1877–79; fig. 2), for example, a prostitute in black stockings and shoes opens her legs to the viewer, showing us the taboo locus of her sexual power with the same nonchalant daring as her photographic compatriots. A mirror beside her—a device in so many photographs—reflects a titillating glimpse of her backside.[12] In *Resting on the Bed* she is also framed by decor—chaise, draperies, and upholstered chair off to the side—that is as haphazardly luxurious as the various random pieces of furniture and textiles used by early photographers to evoke the boudoir. Indeed, even the client who lurks in the mirror of *Waiting for the Client* has a counterpart in the viewer (perhaps even the photographer himself) caught in the mirror of at least one photograph (fig. 3). The texture of Degas's gray tones and the crude outlines of the prostitute's body are a far cry from the clarity of pornographic photography, but the pose, the props, and much of the staging could all have been taken directly from photographs.[13]

The monotypes and photographs also share the context of the brothel and the prostitution industry. Few obscene photographs explicitly presented themselves as brothel scenes, but many of the models they show were prostitutes. Moreover, many of these images circulated via prostitutes and in places of prostitution.[14] By the 1870s and '80s, pornographic photography had been integrated into the business models of brothels: enterprising establishments used pornographic photographs to lure clients, putting them on business cards or showing them to prospective clients. Brothels even commissioned photographs.[15] The photographs and Degas's monotypes share an aesthetic of prostitution and of the brothels, one in which a commodified female body is put on display for sexual consumption.

Yet if these photographs and prints share both the reality of a social phenomenon and an aesthetic rooted in that reality, there are also differences between them. As a genre, nineteenth-century pornographic photography uses the camera's privileged relationship to reality to achieve clear depictions of the body characterized by rigid and largely unchanging compositional structures and tone. The subjects usually occupy the center foreground. The camera never retreats farther than is absolutely necessary to capture their bodies, so that extraneous parts are often cut off; the most extreme example of this is the beaver shot, in which the models are sometimes perspectivally decapitated by the short distance between the camera and the body. When their heads are not excised from the image, the women in the photographs may shield their faces or look bored or ashamed, but just as often they smile. In a series of photographs taken in a French brothel in the late nineteenth or early twentieth

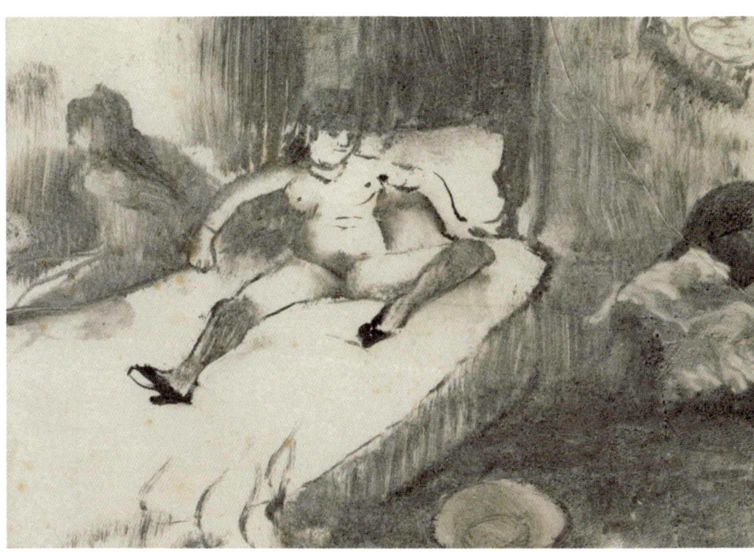

2. Hilaire-Germain-Edgar Degas. *Resting on the Bed* (*Repos sur le lit*). c. 1877–79. Monotype on China paper, plate: 4 11/16 × 6 5/16 in. (11.9 × 16.1 cm). Musée Picasso, Paris

century, for instance, the prostitutes/models look daringly at the camera and contort themselves gleefully, creating the illusion that they are not only willing but delighted to offer their bodies up to the consumer, whether in a photograph or in reality (fig. 4).

Degas's monotypes, on the other hand, categorically reject pornography's defining compositional conventions even as they appropriate its content. Rather than crowding his models as the camera does, Degas distances himself from them, filling that distance with a visual framework that underlines their place in the spaces and system of prostitution. Not only do we see more of the setting of the brothel, we also see the kinds of activities that happen there outside of the sexual transactions. The singular relationship between viewer and model that structures pornography is replaced by a view of prostitution as a collective social activity. If Degas's models lounge in positions reminiscent of pornographic photography, exposing themselves to the viewer, they appear to do so almost accidentally—that is, not for the viewer's benefit. There is neither shame nor a false smile here; instead the models look through, past, and away from the viewer, as if for them he did not exist, shattering any illusion of noncommercial sexual availability.

Perhaps the most formally radical example of this simultaneous appropriation and repudiation of photographic pornography is in a work of an entirely different order from the small-scale images set inside the brothels. For *Naked Woman by a Fireplace* (*Femme se chauffant*, c. 1880–85; plate 103) Degas used a larger plate and what has been called a "dark field" technique: having laid ink across the plate, he drew by removing pigment, creating the figure out of the ink's darkness. The model's awkward pose—facing away from the viewer, with her legs raised and opened toward the fire—is certainly strange, but becomes far more comprehensible if viewed through the conventions of photographic pornography: it would be a paradigmatic beaver shot except that Degas has—quite literally—turned this pornographic exposure of the body on its head, concealing what the photographs reveal. The handworked surfaces of all of the monotypes constitute a rejection of the camera's mechanical exactitude, of its unflinching precision in exposing women's bodies to the observer's scrutiny, but *Naked Woman by a Fireplace* has a hazy, moody visual quality that sets it still farther apart. Furthermore, unlike many of Degas's small-format images of prostitutes, this monotype does not explicitly evoke the interior of a brothel; and the setting that it does evoke—a cocoonlike den of darkness, warmth, and domesticity—constitutes another rejection of the usual reading of her sexualized pose and of the photographs from which it is taken. Strikingly, Degas used a similar perspective in *Woman Reclining on Her Bed* (*Femme étendue sur son lit*, c. 1879–83; plate 100) and its pastelized second impression (plate 101). With no explicit visual link to the space of the brothel, and with the pornographic

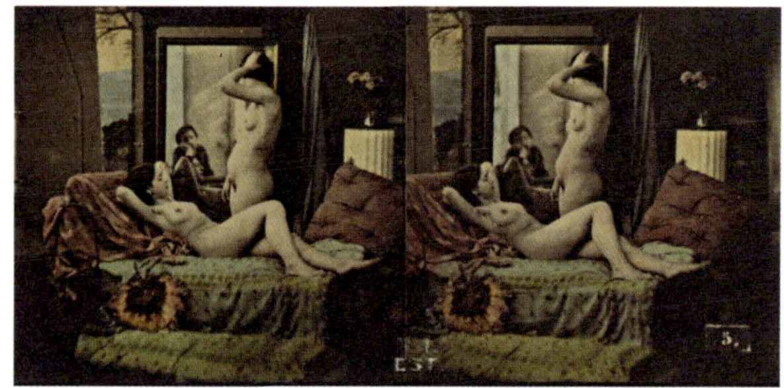

3. Unknown photographer. Two naked women and the reflection of a man in the mirror (*Deux femmes nues et le reflet d'un homme dans le miroir*). 19th century. Stereoscopic photograph. Bibliothèque nationale de France, Paris

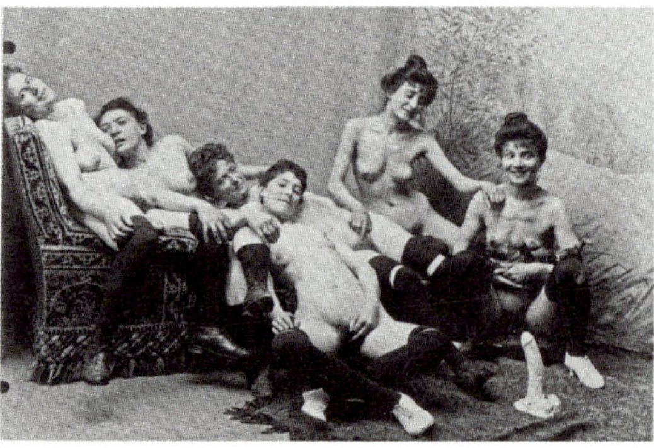

4. Unknown photographer. Erotic scene, 6 nude women (*Scène érotique, 6 femmes nues*). 1906. Bibliothèque nationale de France, Paris

pose further moderated by the model's relaxed legs, these later iterations restore the intimacy and humanity violated by prostitution and pornographic photography alike.[16]

These subversive allusions to the language of photographic pornography have interpretative consequences beyond the realm of aesthetics. Defying the supposed realism of the genre of photographs to which they allude, the monotypes instead reveal the staging of woman-as-consumer-pleasure as another falsehood, a fantasy of all of the shadow presences caught in its mirror: perpetrated by the photographer, the picture is devoured by the viewer and the client alike. In place of these fantasies the monotypes offer a stylized but far "truer" portrait of the body within the context of prostitution—or, in the case of *Naked Woman by a Fireplace* and other dark-field bathers, within the even more radical context of the prostitute's individual human beauty. Where pornographic photographs disguise the economics of sexuality behind an eroticized simulacrum of the body, Degas's appropriation of their conventions exposes and dismantles the visual and social mechanisms of this commodification, showing us just how much the photograph crops out and conceals in order to disseminate its seductions.[17]

In this comparison with pornography, the seeming illegibility of the brothel monotypes, the strange dissonance between their indecent content and their compositional innovations, resolves into clarity. That dissonance is their achievement: a simultaneous evocation and disavowal of pornography, a form whose significance rests on the content it belies. The two qualities that seem so opposed are in fact completely intertwined. Degas's feat is equally remarkable in social and in aesthetic terms; whatever his personal involvement with the prostitution industry may have been, he created images that constitute as much an exposé of the traffic in the female body as they do an artistic revolution.

1. A Degas work that scandalized female viewers at the Impressionist show of 1877 may have been a brothel monotype; see "Beaux-Arts," *Petit Parisien*, April 7, 1877, and Xavier Rey, "The Body Exploited: Degas's Brothel Works," in George Shackelford and Rey, *Degas and the Nude*, exh. cat. (Boston: Museum of Fine Arts, 2011), pp. 69–70, n. 234.
2. Pierre-Auguste Renoir, quoted in Ambroise Vollard, *Degas: 1834–1917* (Paris: Éditions G. Crès, 1924), p. 60. On the alleged destruction of Degas's monotypes see Charles Bernheimer, "Degas's Brothels: Voyeurism and Ideology," *Representations* 20 (Fall 1987):160.
3. Degas's reputation for misogyny has played a role in readings focused on the erotic content of the brothel monotypes, going back to J. K. Huysmans's famous attribution to him of an "attentive cruelty, [and] patient hatred" toward his female subjects; see *Certains. G. Moreau—Degas—Chéret—Whistler—Rops—Le Monstre—Le Fer, etc.* (Paris: Tresse & Stock, 1889), p. 23. Vollard too mentions Degas's reputation for "cruelty" in his representations of women, attributing it not to misogyny but to a Jansenist prudishness and fear. Vollard, *Degas: 1834–1917*, pp. 20–21. For an investigation of Huysmans's assessment of Degas's representations of female subjects, see Carol Armstrong, *Odd Man Out: Readings of the Work and Reputation of Edgar Degas* (Chicago and London: The University of Chicago Press, 1991), pp. 190–91. See also Bernheimer, "Degas's Brothels: Voyeurism and Ideology," pp. 161–62, and Hollis Clayson, *Painted Love: Prostitution in French Art of the Impressionist Era* (New Haven: Yale University Press, 1991), pp. 48–49.
4. This is not to say that the only such possible reconciliation would occur by examining the ghost presence of pornographic photography. I am indebted to Clayson's chapter on the monotypes in *Painted Love*, wherein she aligns the formal qualities of the monotypes and the world of prostitution that is their content, noting, "We can see that a reading of the prints as reports on the modernity of prostitution cannot be undertaken apart from an active discussion of their formal language." P. 33.
5. I discuss the rise and cultural role of photographic pornography in France in my book manuscript *The Art of Exposure: Literature and Nude Photography in Nineteenth-Century France*. Some of these images from the 1850s and '60s are also addressed in Elizabeth McCauley, "Braquehais and the Photographic Nude," *Industrial Madness: Commercial Photography in Paris, 1848–71* (New Haven: Yale University Press, 1994),

pp. 149–94, and Abigail Solomon-Godeau, "The Legs of the Countess" and "Reconsidering Erotic Photography: Notes for a Project of Historical Salvage," *Photography at the Dock: Essays on Photographic History, Institutions, and Practices* (Minneapolis: University of Minnesota Press, 1994), pp. 220–37. The earliest images are discussed in Sylvie Aubenas, "Le nu académique existe-t-il en daguerréotype?," *L'Art du nu au XIXe siècle. Le Photographe et son modèle*, exh. cat. (Paris: Hazan/Editions de la Bibliothèque nationale de France, 1995), pp. 24–29.

6. In 1892, a single French photographer was arrested after producing 800,000 illicit images in three years; see "Tribunaux," *Le Temps*, May 7, 1892. Other contemporary sources indicate a widespread traffic in such images across Europe.

7. See Aubenas, *L'Art du nu au XIXe siècle*.

8. Rey notes the pubic hair in Degas's brothel monotypes as a possible link to the aesthetics of erotic photography. "The Body Exploited," p. 90.

9. With occasional exceptions, the mirror is rare in images that were legally authorized for sale as art nudes, but it is a frequent prop in unauthorized photographic erotica throughout the century. See Aubenas, "Reflets et miroirs," in *L'Art du nu au XIXe siècle*, pp. 130–31.

10. Solomon-Godeau, "The Legs of the Countess," pp. 74–75.

11. Solomon-Godeau, *Photography at the Dock*, p. 233. I take Solomon-Godeau's argument a little farther in arguing that the "beaver shot" *defines* photographic pornography of the period. A number of art historians, including Solomon-Godeau, have noted the similarity between these photographs and Courbet's infamous 1866 painting *L'Origine du monde*. See McCauley, *Industrial Madness*, p. 178; Michel Frizot, "Body of Evidence: The Ethnophotography of Difference," *A New History of Photography* (Cologne: Könemann, 1998), p. 271; and Solomon-Godeau, "The Legs of the Countess," p. 97. Interestingly, Solomon-Godeau reads the painting as an exception to the statement that the photograph "invents" the beaver shot, while I read the arrest of the notorious pornographer Auguste Belloc with a stash of these photographs in 1860, six years before the painting was created, as further evidence of the influence of these photographs on the painter. Courbet probably worked from both legal and illegal photographs in his paintings. See Dominique Font-Réaulx, "Courbet et la photographie: L'Exemple d'un peintre réaliste, entre vérité et réalité," in Aubenas, *L'Art du nu au XIXe siècle*, pp. 84–91. On Belloc see Aubenas, *Obscénités* (Paris: Michel Albin/Bibliothèque nationale de France, 2001).

12. Degas's notebooks offer insight into his use of mirrors to capture objects from multiple perspectives. He wrote, "Enfin étudier à toute perspective une figure ou un objet, n'importe quoi. On peut se servir pour cela d'une glâce—on ne bougerait [pas] de sa place" (Finally, to study a figure or an object, it doesn't matter what, from all perspectives. For this one can use a mirror—one wouldn't move from one's place). Degas, notebook 30, p. 65, late 1870s/early 1880s, in *The Notebooks of Edgar Degas*, ed. Theodore Reff (Oxford: Clarendon Press, 1976), 1:134.

13. For readings of the kinds of gestures and poses that I connect to obscene photography, see, e.g., Clayson, *Painted Love*, p. 46, and Armstrong, *Odd Man Out*, pp. 152–54. For Clayson, *Waiting for the Client* represents the "essence of the brothel prostitute" in its "clumsy and uncontested collapse of the body with the raw obscenity of spreading ones legs for the buyer." Speaking more generally, Armstrong argues that "in the brothel series, the women of Degas's 'public' pictures are stripped naked of their spectacular costumes and their choreography, and reduced to displayed parts, ugly mugs, and masturbatory, scatological, and ablutionary gestures" (p. 152).

14. The social and sexual status of the models in nude photographs was complex; as I discuss in my forthcoming book, not all of them were prostitutes but many of them were—see police register BB3, Archives de la préfecture de police, Paris. For both Solomon-Godeau and McCauley, during the Second Empire in particular, the model's status as a prostitute defined her. See Solomon-Godeau, "The Legs of the Countess," pp. 94–95, 99, and McCauley, *Industrial Madness*, pp. 183–84.

15. See L. Reuss, *La Prostitution au point de vue de l'hygiène et de l'administration en France et à l'étranger* (Paris: Librairie J.-B. Baillière et Fils, 1889), p. 152; Pierre Delcourt, *Le Vice à Paris* (Paris: A. Piaget, 1888), pp. 27–31; Léo Taxil, *La Corruption fin-de-siècle* (Paris: Georges Carré, 1894), pp. 292–93; and Louis Fiaux, *Les Maisons de tolérance, leur fermeture* (Paris: Georges Carré, 1892), pp. 108, 167–69.

16. While the brothel monotypes are perhaps the most socially engaged example of this formal maneuvering, they are not the only place where Degas manipulates a kind of photographic representation of the body. Many of his late nudes (paintings, drawings, and prints) seem to engage in a similar dialogue with both photographic obscenity and other forms of contemporary photographic nudity, such as commercial "academic" nude photographs. This is a dialogue that merits and indeed requires further exploration elsewhere; already, however, Malcolm Daniel has situated Degas's own photographs, including two nudes and some others of female models, in opposition to the conventions of contemporary "art photography." See Daniel, "The Atmosphere of Lamps or Moonlight," in Daniel, Eugenia Parry, and Reff, *Edgar Degas, Photographer*, exh. cat. (New York: The Metropolitan Museum of Art, 1998), pp. 42–45. See also Douglas Crimp, who discusses the monotypes as a precursor to the kinds of visual effects Degas would take up in his photographs in "Positive/Negative: A Note on Degas's Photographs," *October* 5 (Summer 1978):98–99.

17. Here I am in agreement with Bernheimer, who sees Degas's prostitutes as "alienated products of a consumer culture" and argues that the monotypes expose the "commodification of gender relations." He works through a thorough Freudian and Marxist analysis, however, rather than through comparison to pornographic photography. Bernheimer, "Degas Brothels: Voyeurism and Ideology," p. 172.

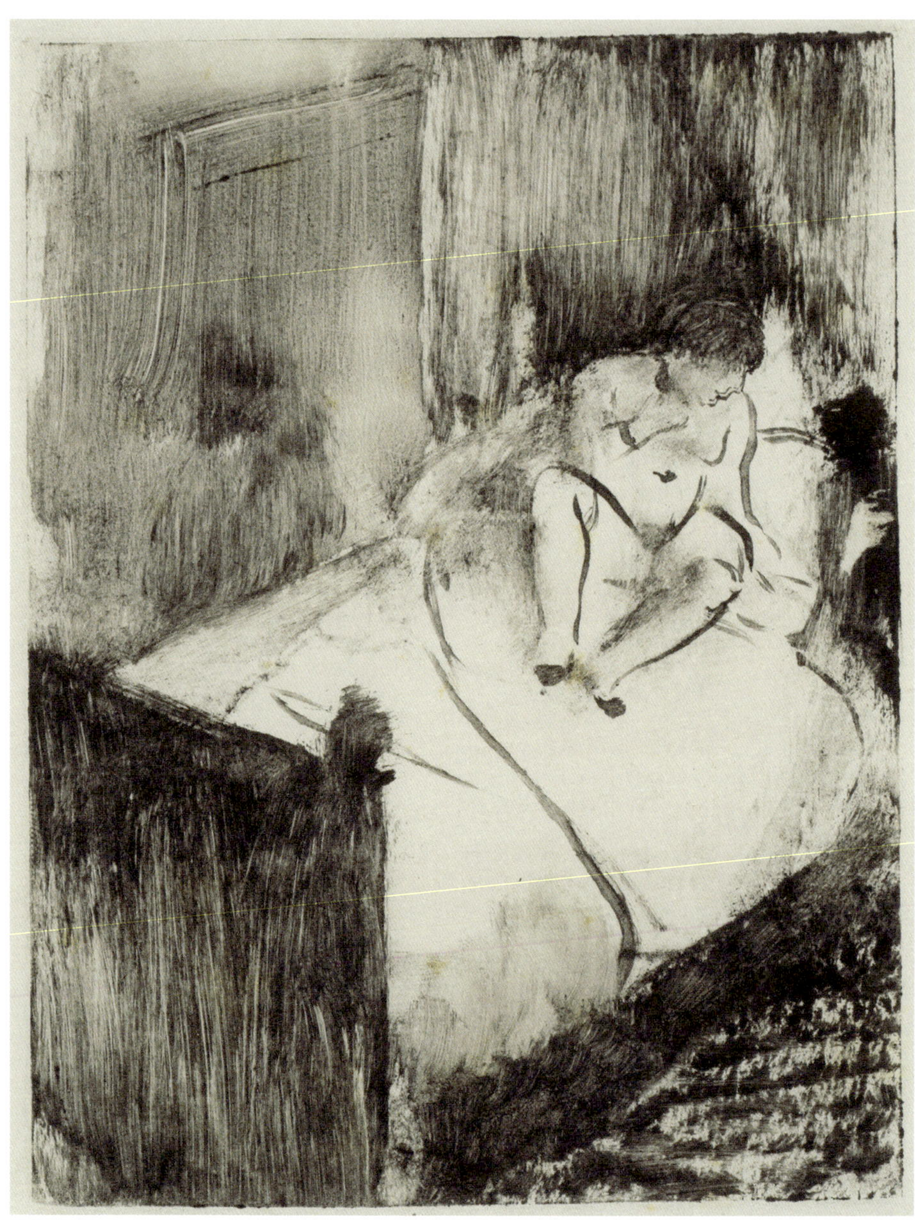

86. *Resting on the Bed* (*Repos sur le lit*). c. 1877–79
Monotype on paper
Plate: 6 5⁄16 × 4 3⁄4 in. (16 × 12 cm), sheet: 8 7⁄8 × 5 7⁄8 in. (22.5 × 15 cm)
Städel Museum, Frankfurt am Main. Property of the Städelscher Museums-Vereins e. V.

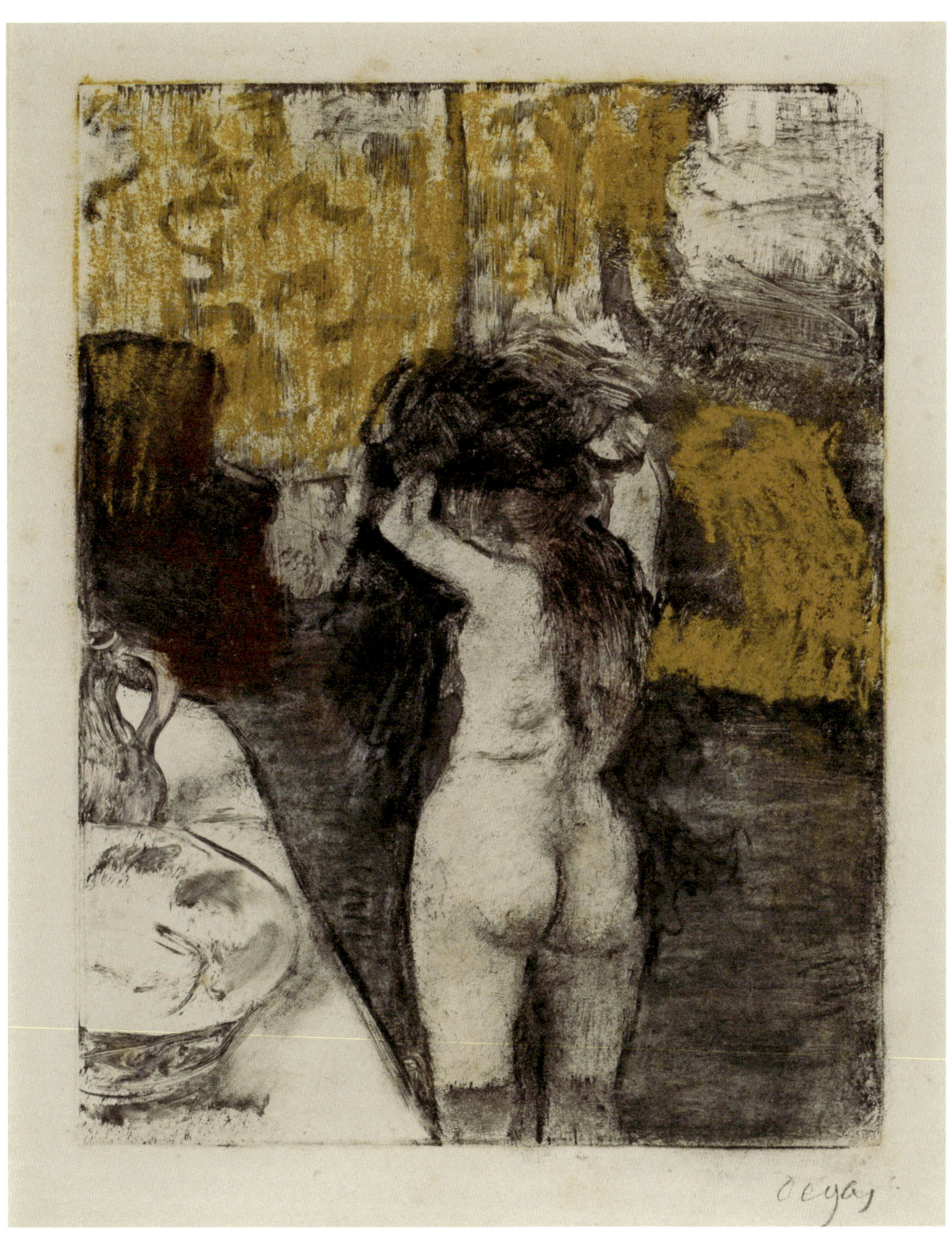

87. *Woman Slipping On Her Dress* (*La Sortie du bain*). c. 1877–79
Pastel over monotype on China paper
8 ¼ × 6 ¼ in. (21 × 15.9 cm)
Private collection, Chicago

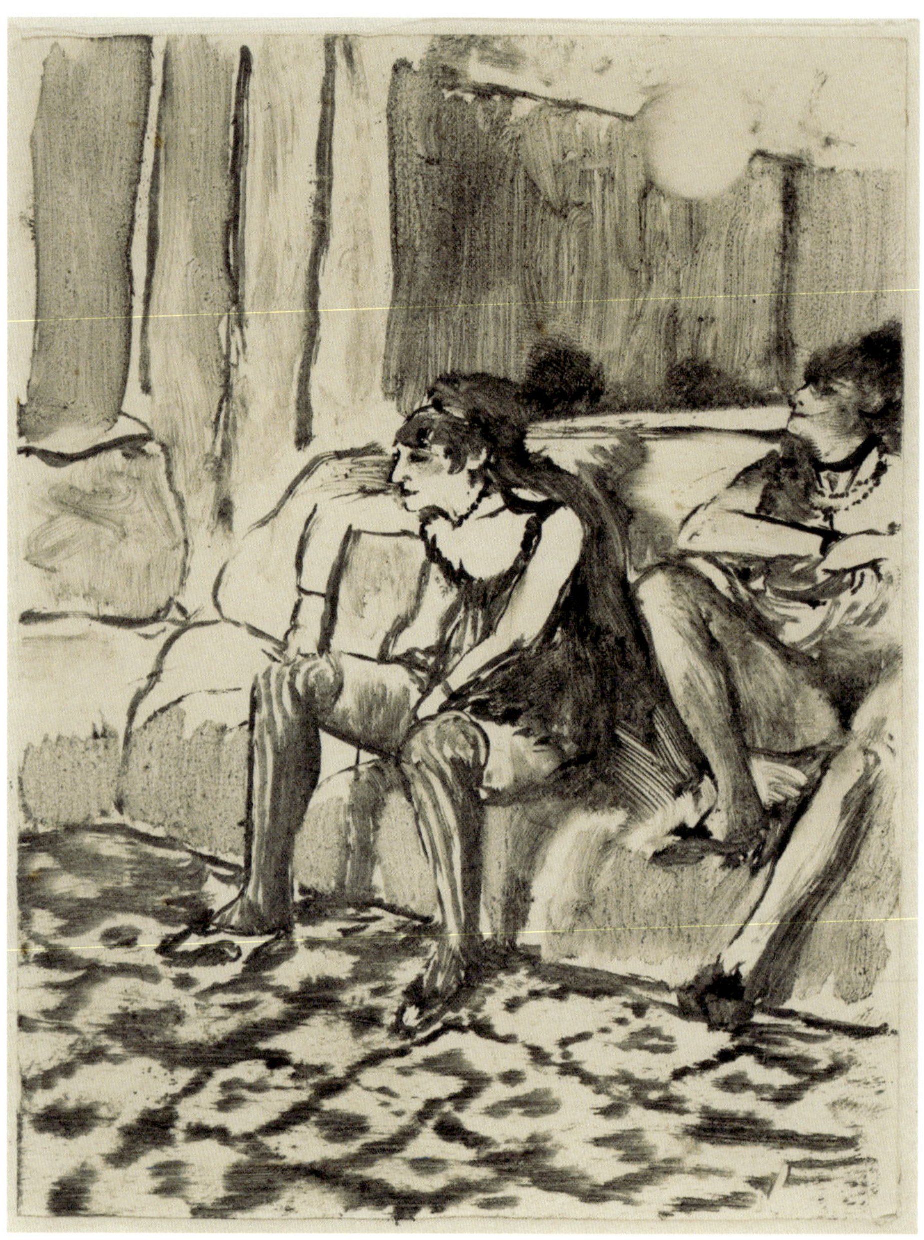

88. *Two Young Girls* (*Deux jeunes filles*). c. 1877–79
Monotype on China paper
Plate: 6 ¼ × 4 ¾ in. (15.9 × 12.1 cm)
Private collection, Chicago

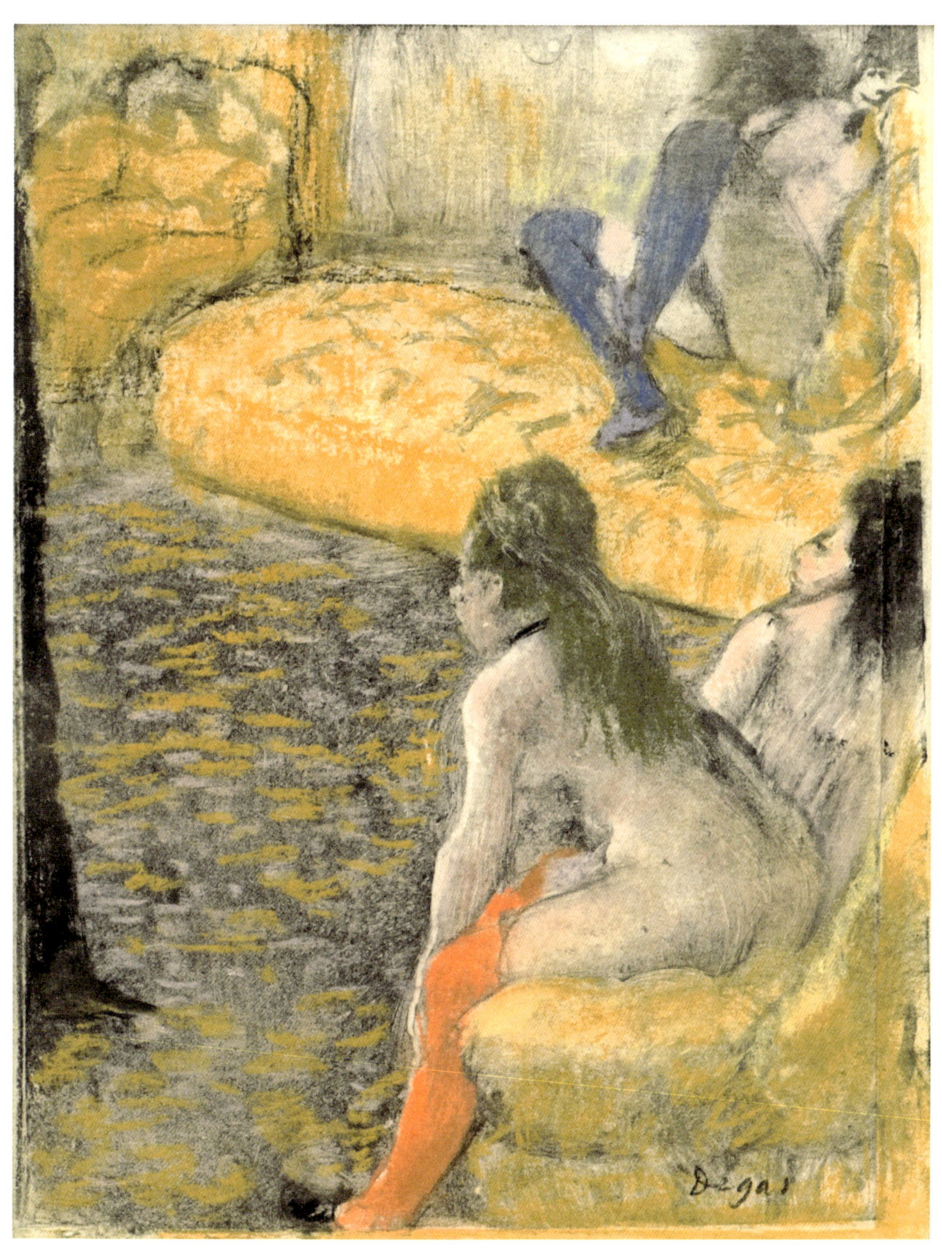

89. *Waiting for the Client* (*Attente d'un client*). c. 1877–79
Pastel over monotype on paper, mounted on paper
Plate: 6 5/16 × 4 15/16 in. (16 × 12.5 cm), sheet: 7 1/2 × 5 5/8 in. (19.1 × 14.3 cm)
Ann and Gordon Getty

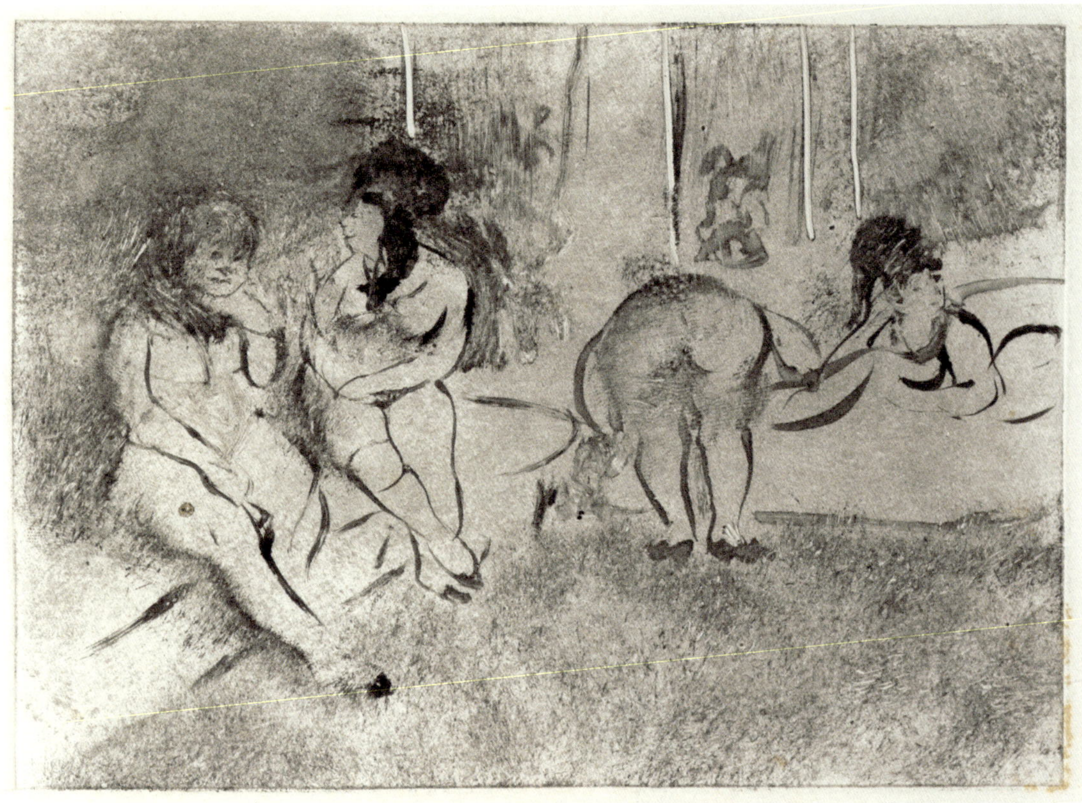

90. *Waiting (first version)* (*L'Attente [première version]*). 1879
Monotype on paper
Plate: 4 ⅝ × 6 5⁄16 in. (11.8 × 16.1 cm)
Musée Picasso, Paris

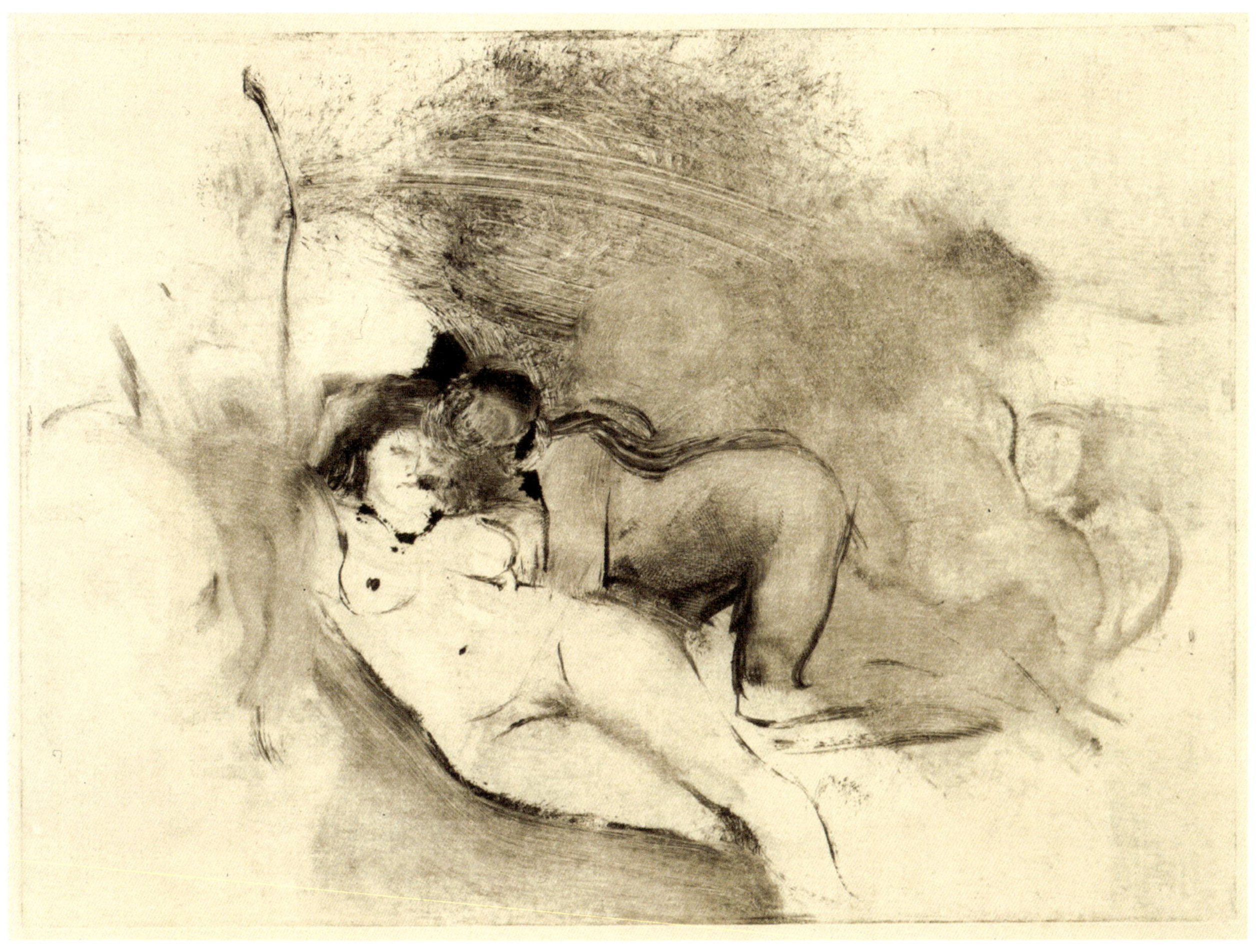

91. *Two Women—Scene from a Brothel* (*Deux femmes [Scène de maison close]*). c. 1877–79
Monotype on paper
Plate: 9 13⁄16 × 11 3⁄8 in. (24.9 × 28.9 cm), sheet: 8 7⁄16 × 6 5⁄16 in. (21.5 × 16 cm)
Museum of Fine Arts, Boston. Katherine E. Bullard Fund in memory of Francis Bullard

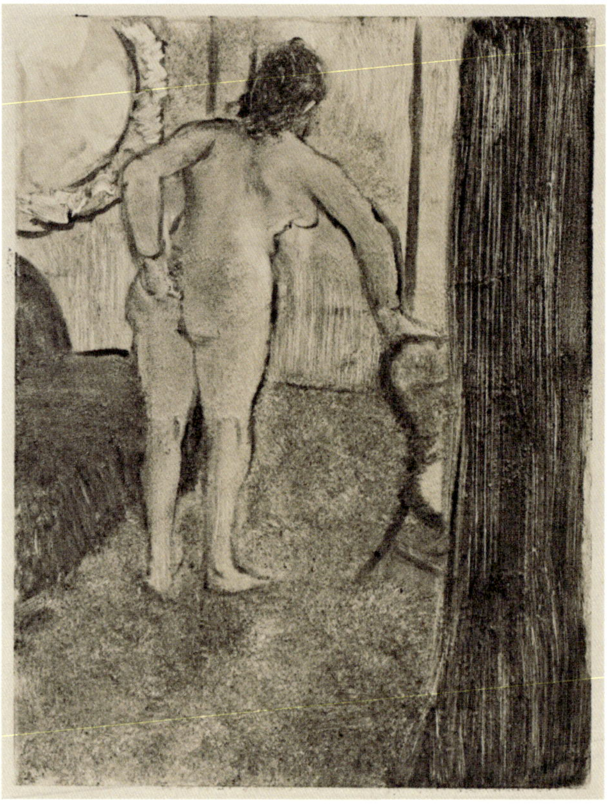

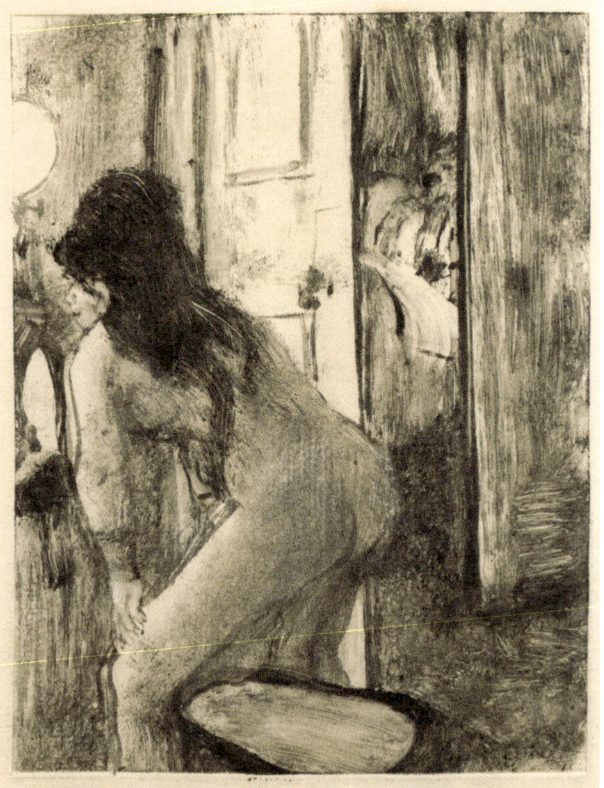

92. *Room in a Brothel* (*Dans le salon d'une maison close*). c. 1877–79
Monotype on paper
Plate: 8 3⁄16 × 6 1⁄4 in. (20.8 × 15.9 cm), sheet: 12 3⁄8 × 9 3⁄16 in. (31.5 × 23.3 cm)
Cantor Arts Center at Stanford University. Mortimer C. Leventritt Fund and Committee for Art Acquisitions Fund

93. *The Bidet* (*Le Bidet*). c. 1877–79
Monotype on paper
Plate: 6 5⁄16 × 4 11⁄16 in. (16 × 11.9 cm), sheet: 9 7⁄16 × 7 7⁄8 in. (24 × 20 cm)
The Saint Louis Art Museum, Missouri. The Marian Cronheim Trust for Prints and Drawings

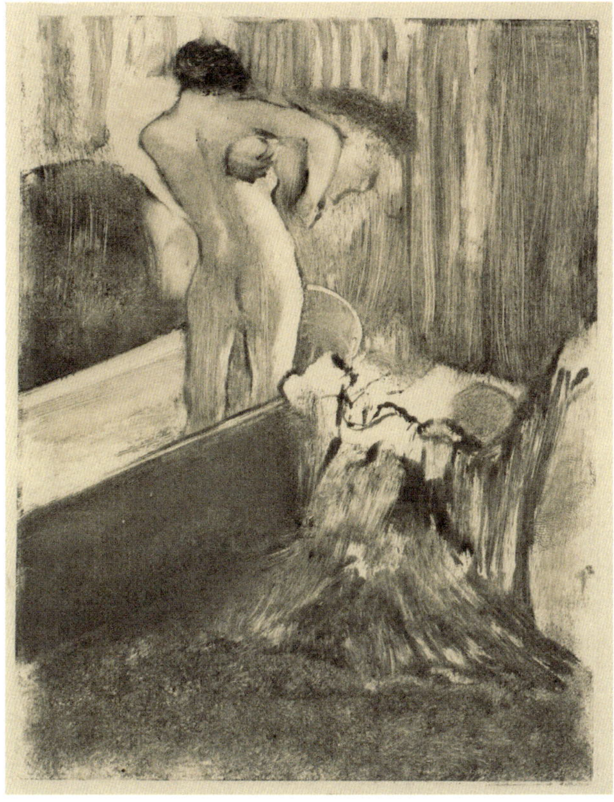

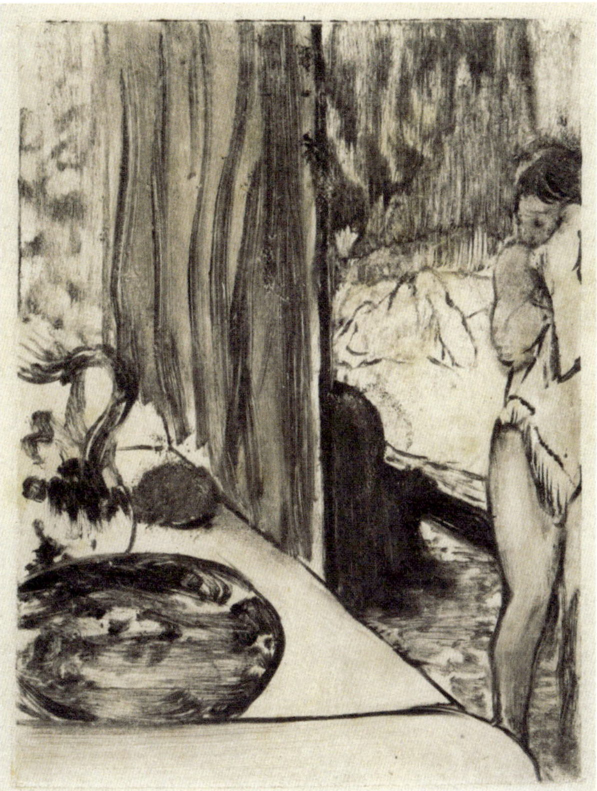

94. *The Bath* (*Le Bain*). 1879–83
Monotype on paper
Plate: 8 ⅜ × 6 ¼ in. (21.3 × 15.9 cm)
Statens Museum for Kunst, Copenhagen

95. *Nude Woman Drying Her Face* (*Femme nue s'essuyant la figure*). c. 1877–79
Monotype on paper
Plate: 6 × 4 ½ in. (15.3 × 11.4 cm), sheet: 7 ½ × 6 7⁄16 in. (19 × 16.3 cm) (irregular)
Private collection

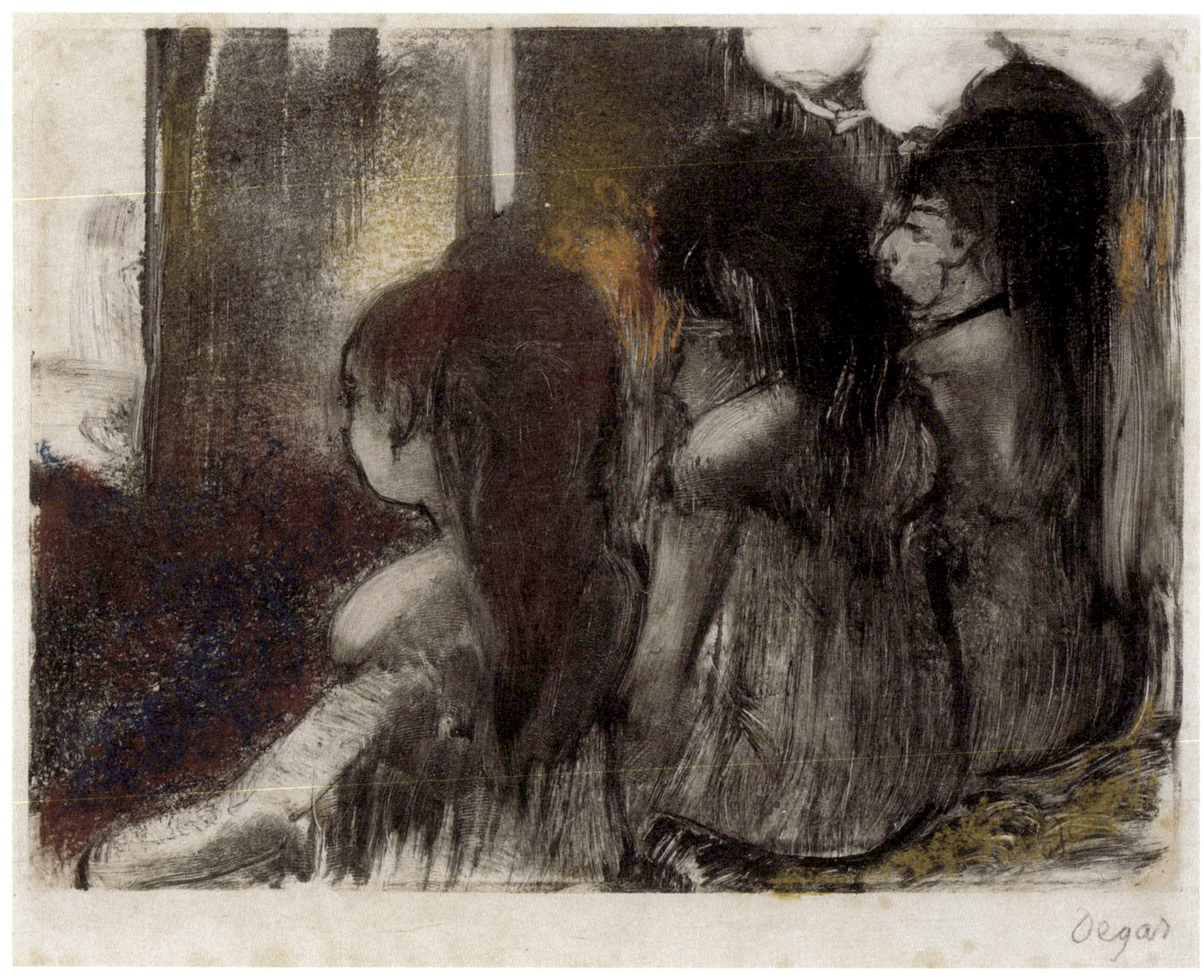

96. *Three Women in a Brothel, Seen from Behind* (*Trois filles assises de dos*). c. 1877–79
Pastel over monotype on paper
6 5⁄16 × 8 7⁄16 in. (16.1 × 21.4 cm)
Musée Picasso, Paris

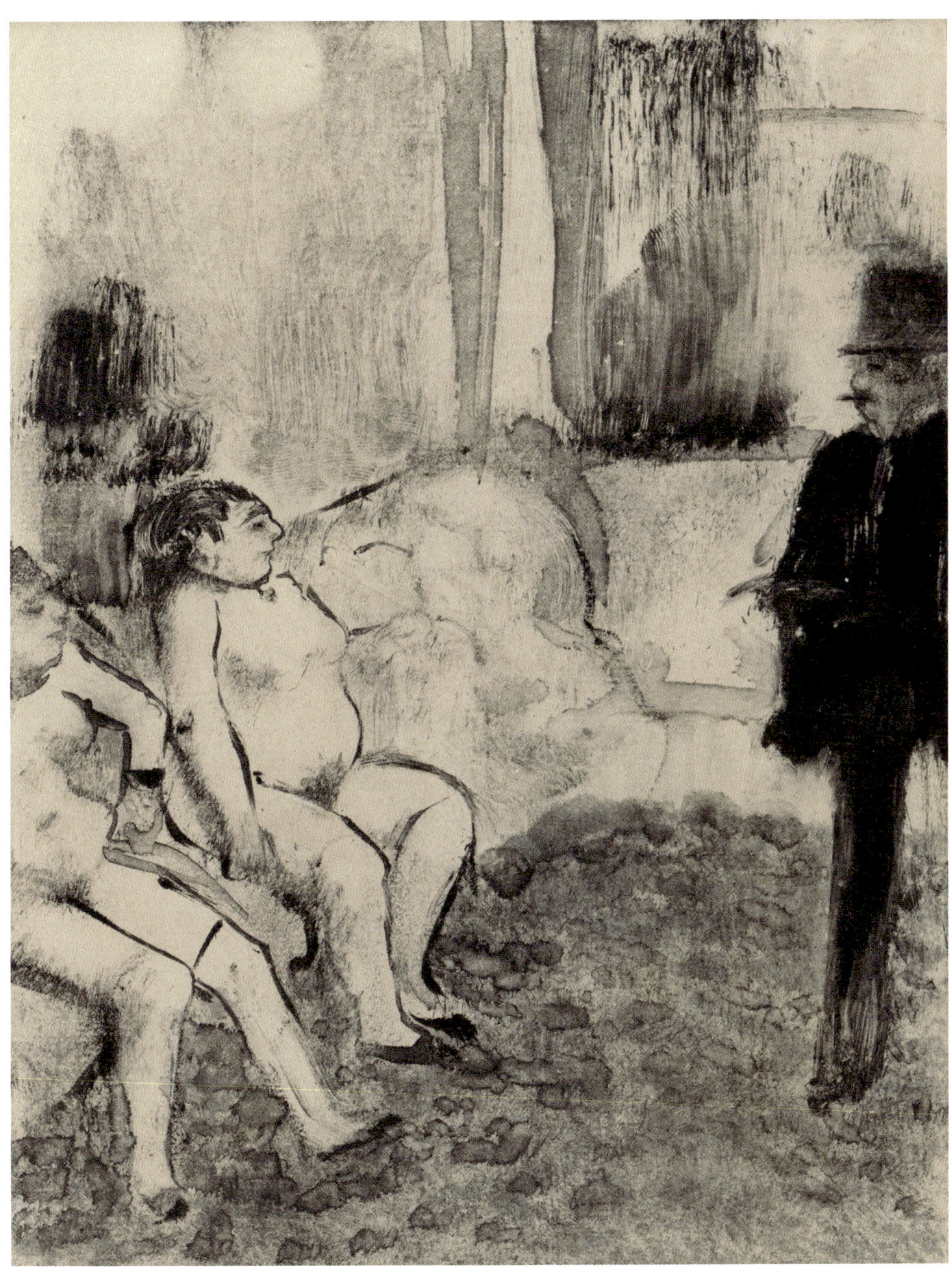

97. *The Client* (*Le Client*). 1879
Monotype on paper
Plate: 8 7⁄16 × 6 ¼ in. (21.5 × 15.9 cm)
Musée Picasso, Paris

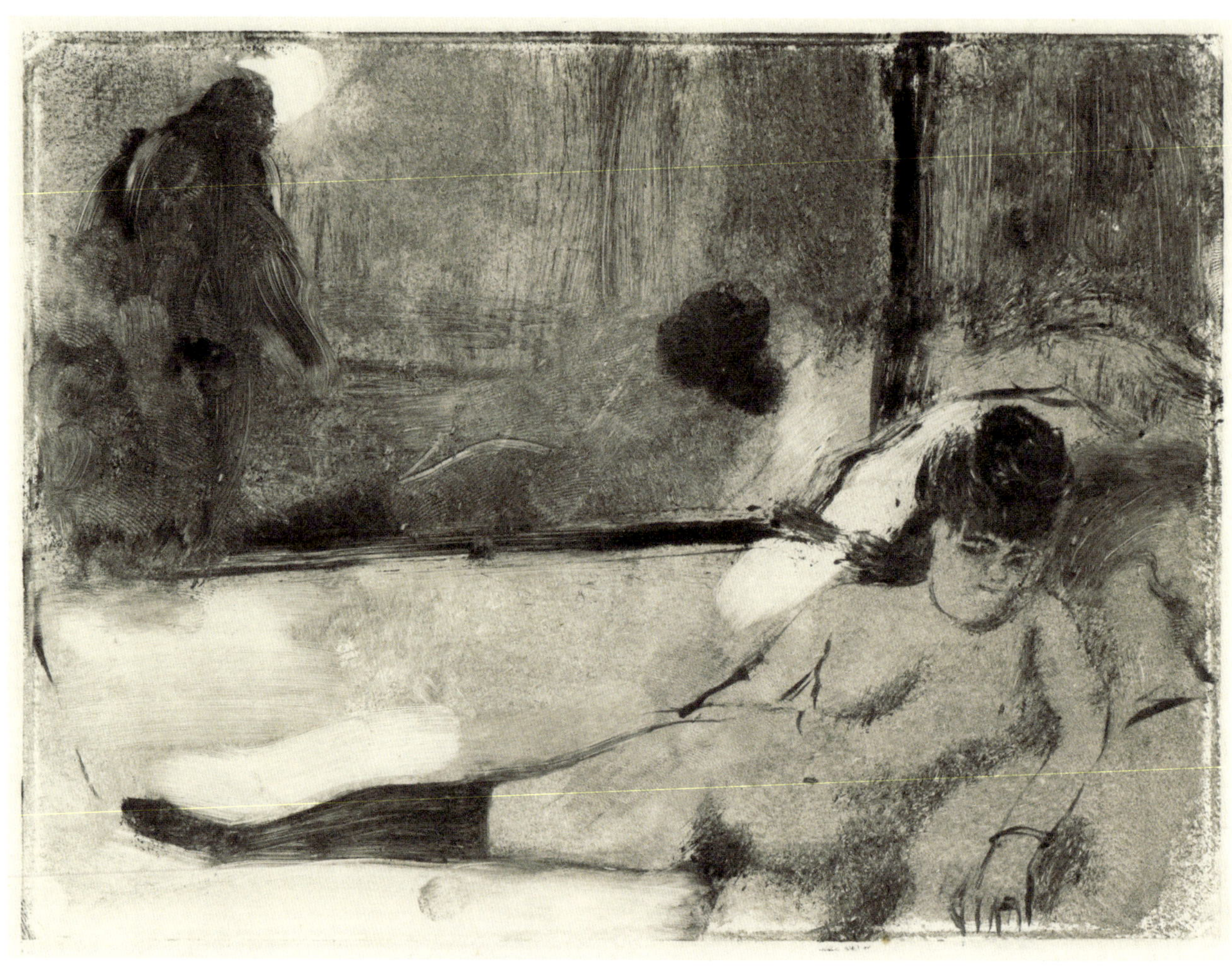

98. *Waiting for the Client* (*En attendant le client*). c. 1877–79
Monotype on paper
Plate: 6 5⁄16 × 8 1⁄4 in. (16 × 21 cm); sheet: 7 1⁄16 × 9 1⁄16 in. (18 × 23 cm)
Private collection. Courtesy Alexander Apsis Fine Art

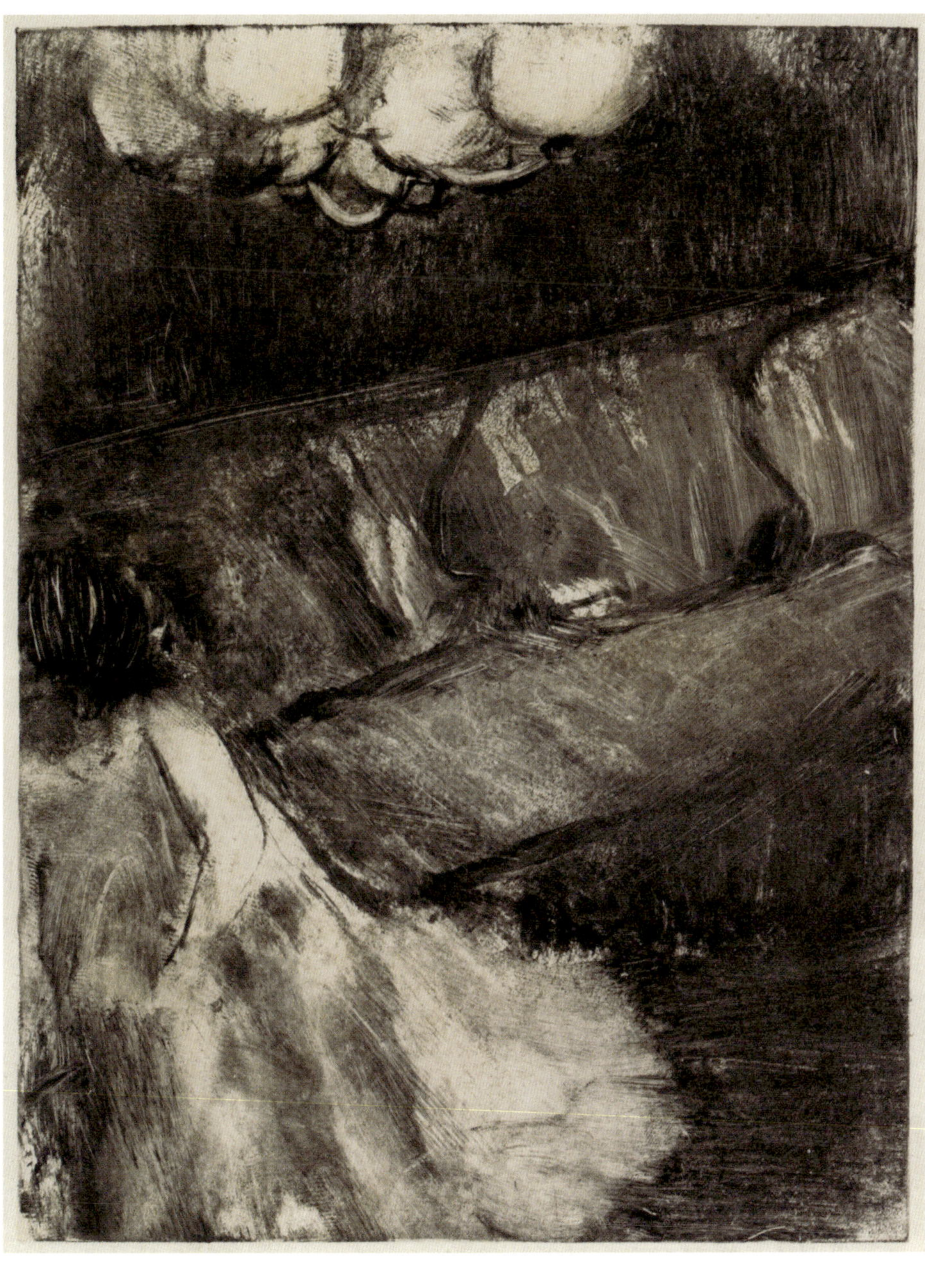

99. *In the Salon* (*Un Coin de salon en maison close*). c. 1877–79
Monotype on China paper
Plate: 6 5⁄16 × 4 5⁄8 in. (16.1 × 11.8 cm), sheet: 11 5⁄8 × 8 1⁄4 in. (29.6 × 20.9 cm)
Private collection, Chicago

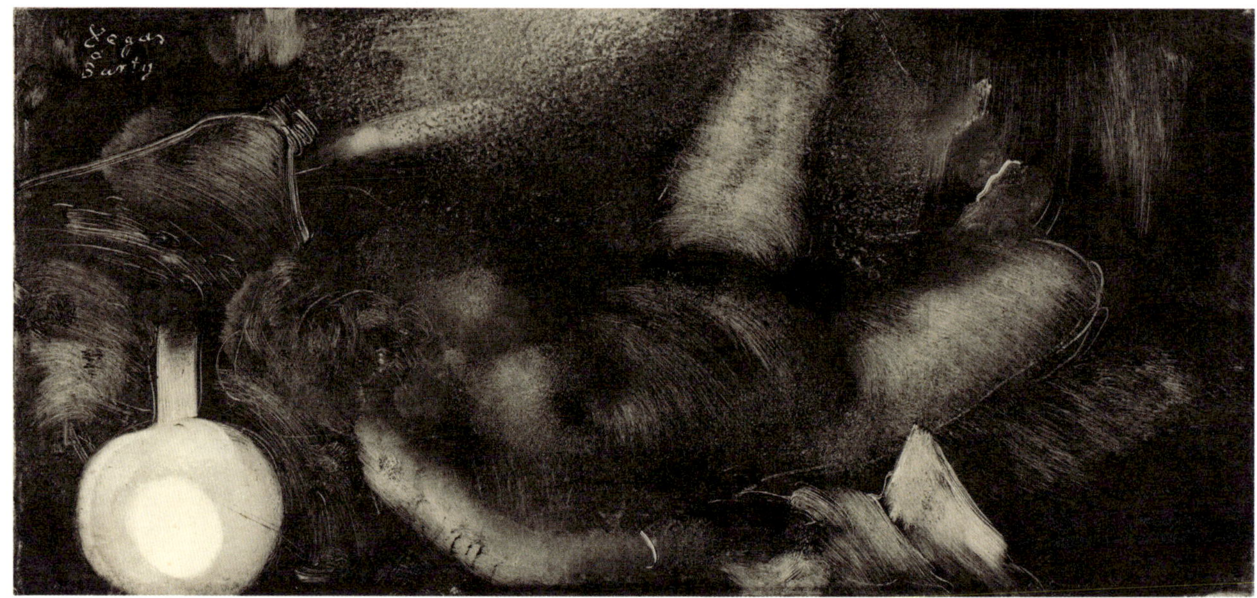

100. *Woman Reclining on Her Bed* (*Femme étendue sur son lit*). c. 1879–83
Monotype on paper
Plate: 7 13⁄16 × 16 5⁄16 in. (19.9 × 41.5 cm), sheet: 8 ¾ × 16 ½ in. (22.2 × 41.9 cm)
The Art Institute of Chicago. Clarence Buckingham Collection

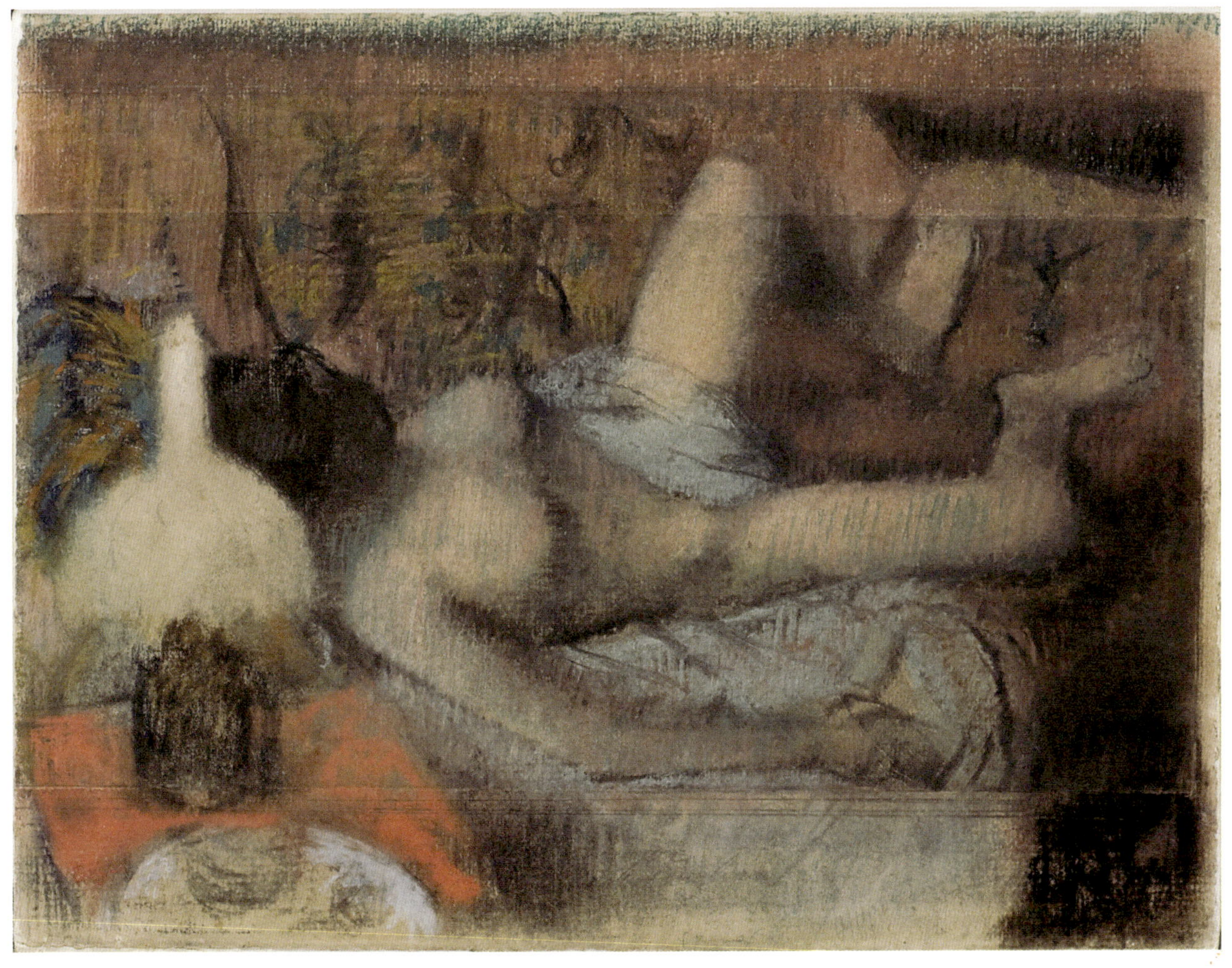

101. *Female Nude Reclining* (*Femme nue couchée*). c. 1888–90
Pastel over monotype
Plate: 7 ¾ × 16 in. (19.7 × 40.6 cm), sheet: 13 × 16 ⅜ in. (33 × 41.6 cm)
Ann and Gordon Getty

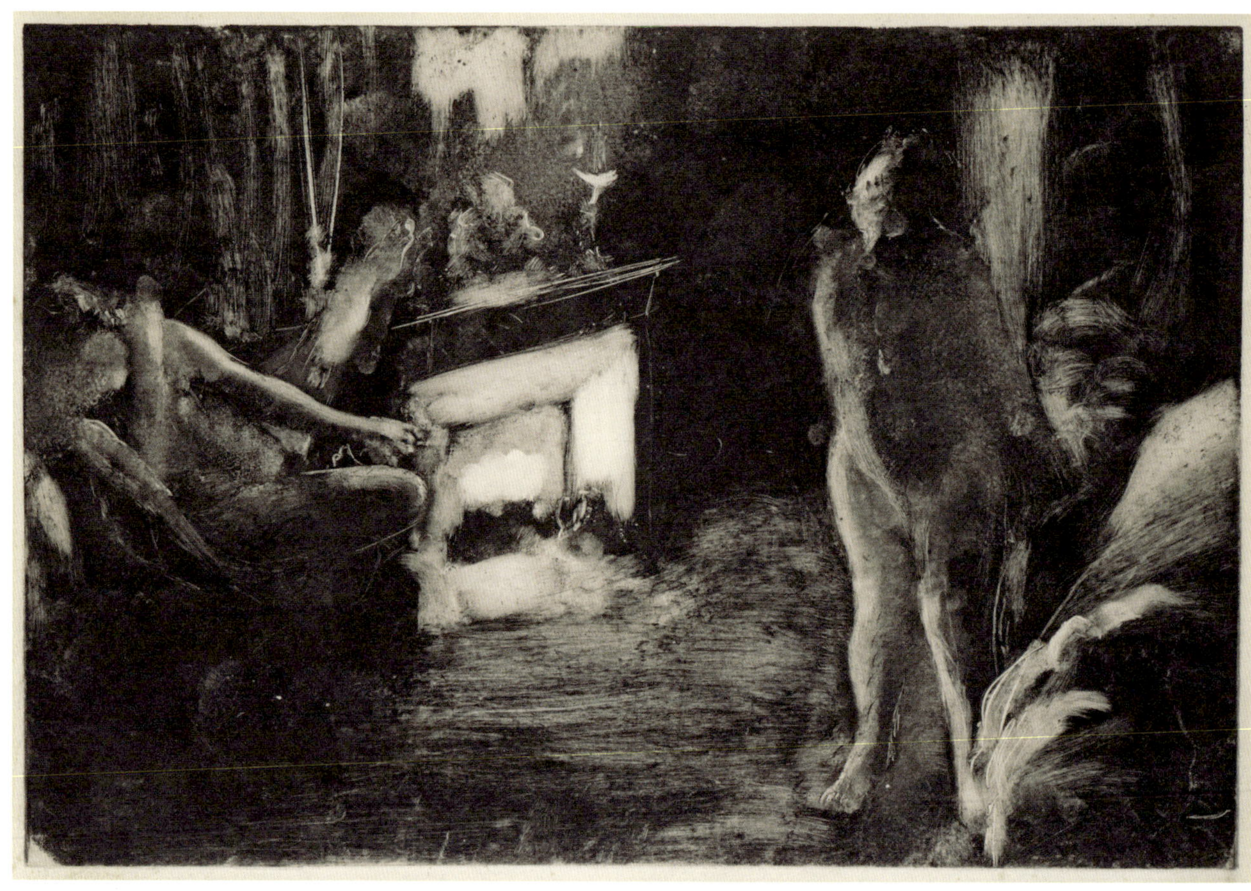

102. *The Fireside* (*Le Foyer [La Cheminée]*). c. 1880–85
Monotype on paper
Plate: 16 ¾ × 23 1/16 in. (42.5 × 58.6 cm), sheet: 19 ¾ × 25 ½ in. (50.2 × 64.8 cm)
The Metropolitan Museum of Art, New York. Harris Brisbane Dick Fund, The Elisha Whittelsey Collection, The Elisha Whittelsey Fund, and C. Douglas Dillon Gift

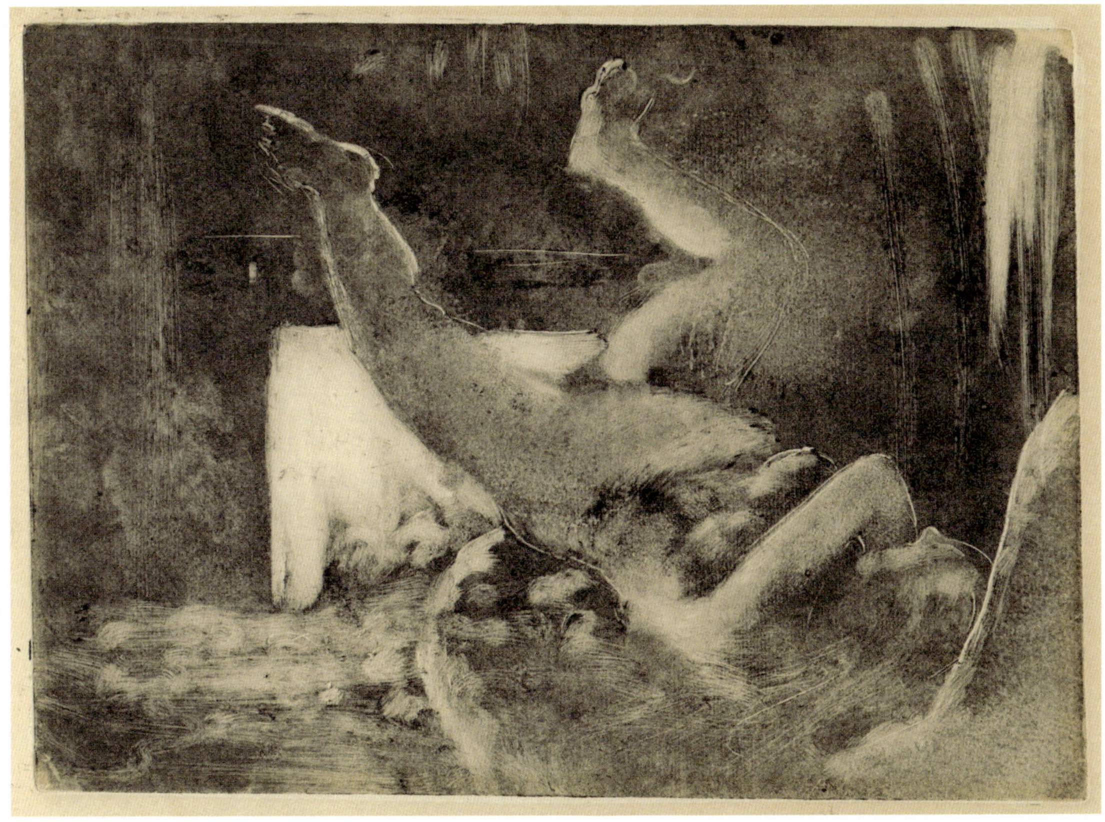

103. *Naked Woman by a Fireplace* (*Femme se chauffant*). c. 1880–85
Monotype on paper
Plate: 10 15⁄16 × 14 15⁄16 in. (27.8 × 37.9 cm), sheet: 14 ¾ × 19 5⁄16 in. (37.5 × 49 cm)
Private collection

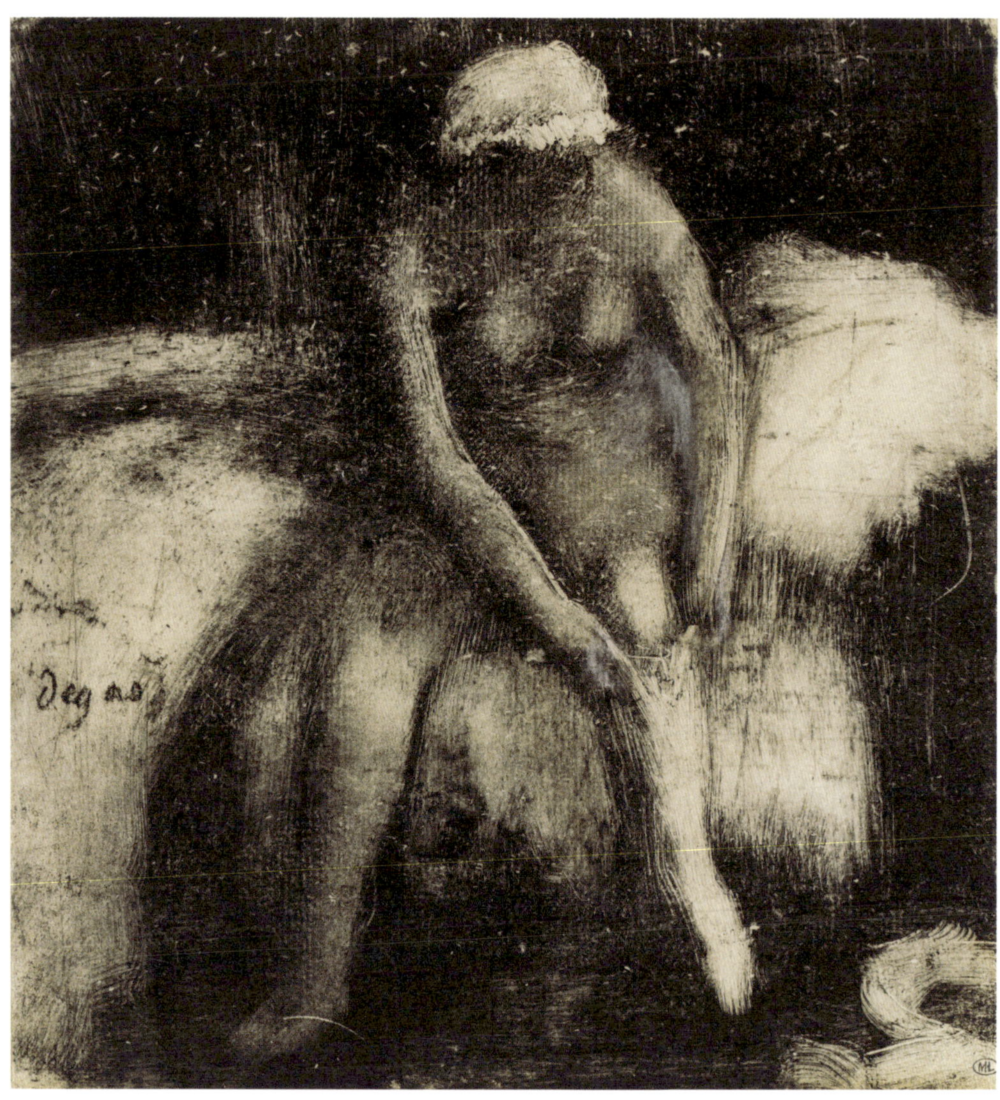

104. *Getting Up: Woman Putting On Her Stockings* (*Le Lever, femme assise mettant ses bas*). c. 1880–85
Monotype on paper
Plate: 9 5/16 × 8 ½ in. (23.7 × 21.6 cm)
Musée d'Orsay, Paris

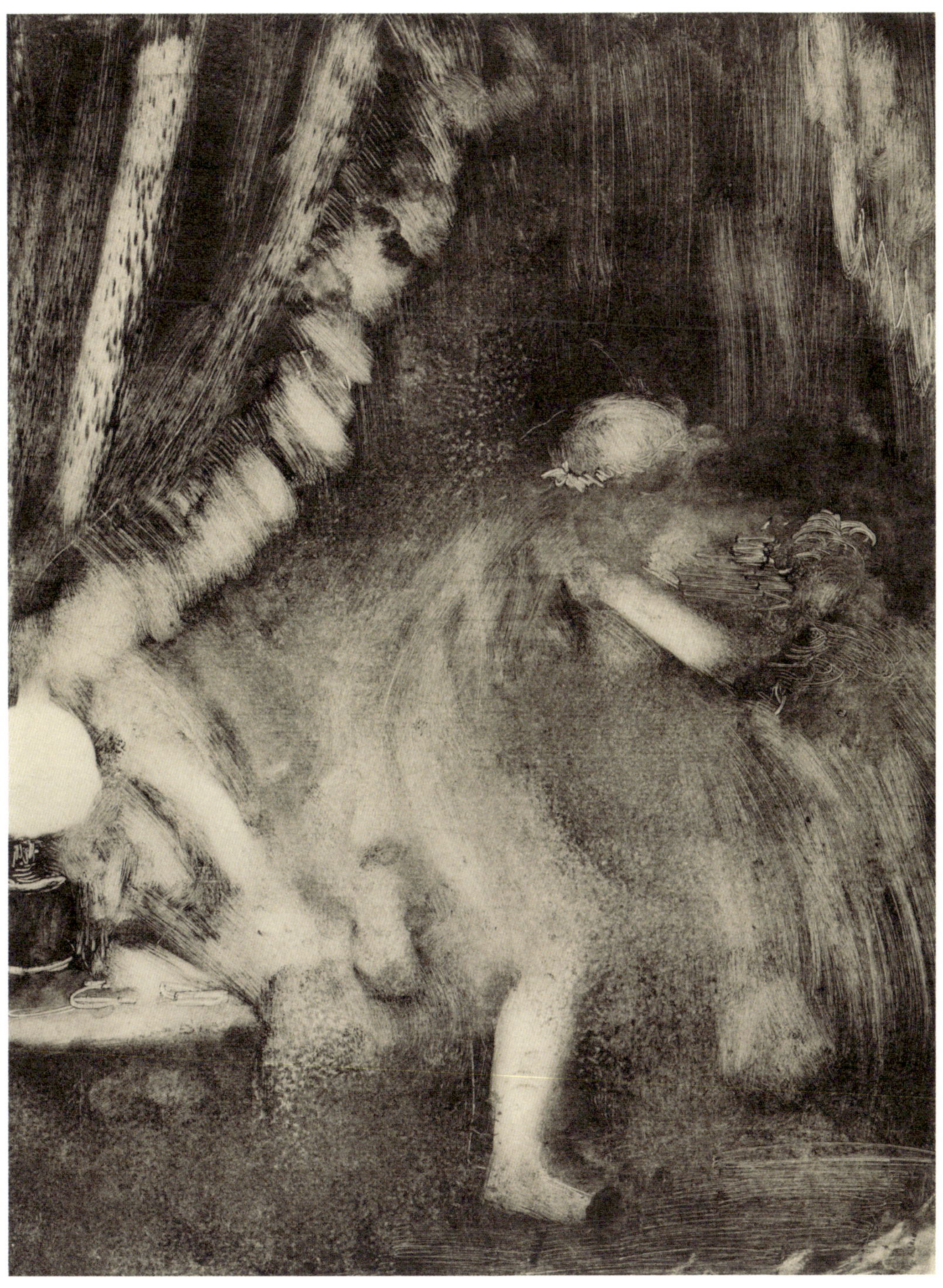

105. *Getting into Bed* (*Le Coucher*). c. 1880–85
Monotype on paper
Plate: 14 ⅞ × 10 ⅞ in. (37.8 × 27.7 cm), sheet: 20 1⁄16 × 13 ¾ in. (51 × 35 cm)
The National Museum of Art, Architecture and Design, Oslo

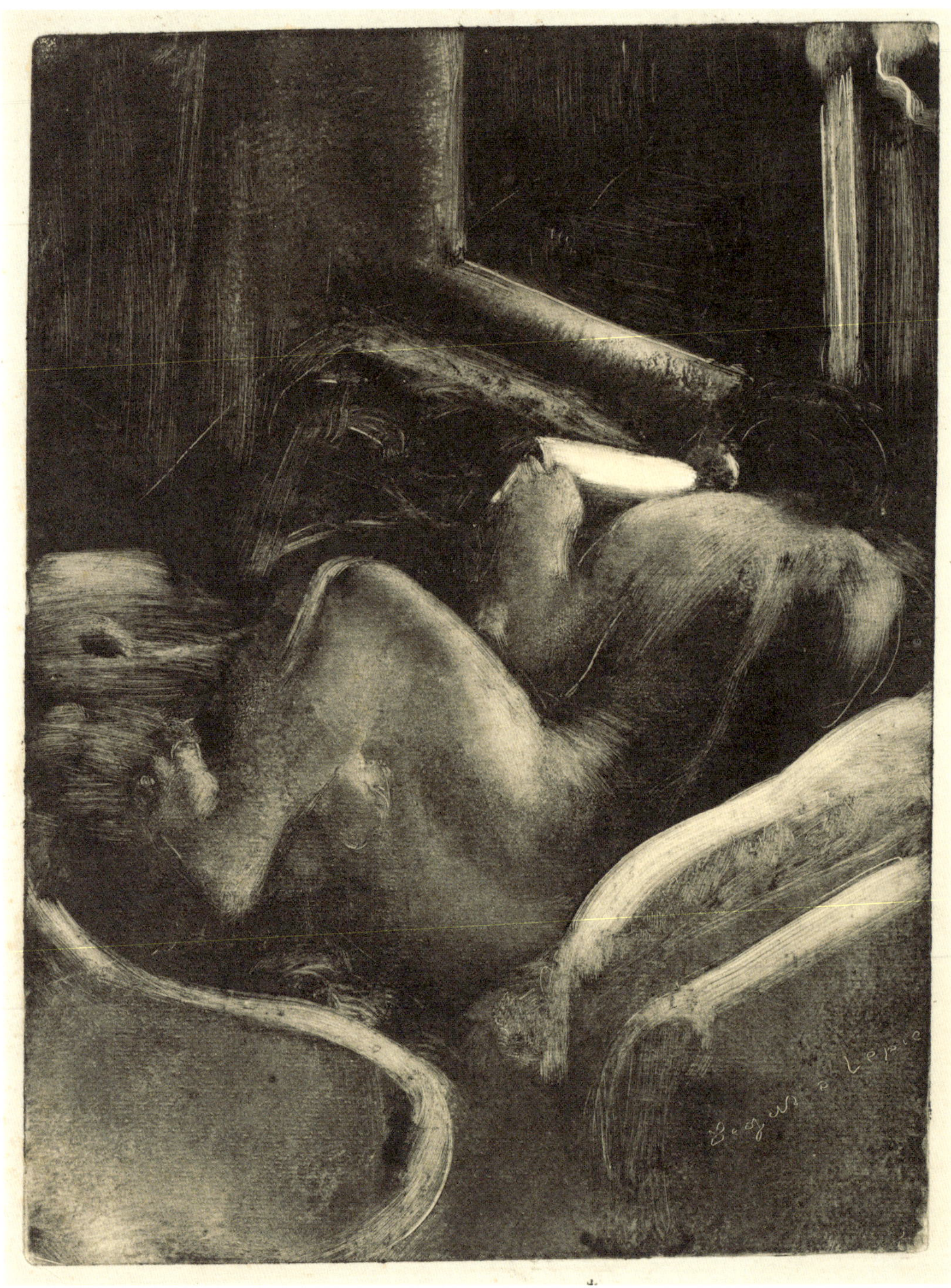

106. *Woman Reading* (*Liseuse*). c. 1880–85
Monotype on paper
Plate: 14 15/16 × 10 7/8 in. (38 × 27.7 cm), sheet: 17 7/16 × 12 13/16 in. (44.3 × 32.5 cm)
National Gallery of Art, Washington, D.C. Rosenwald Collection

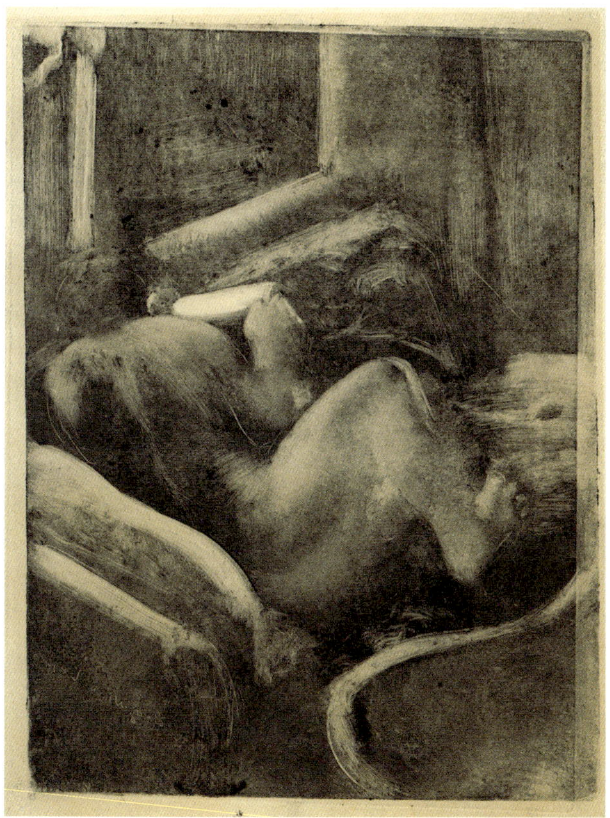

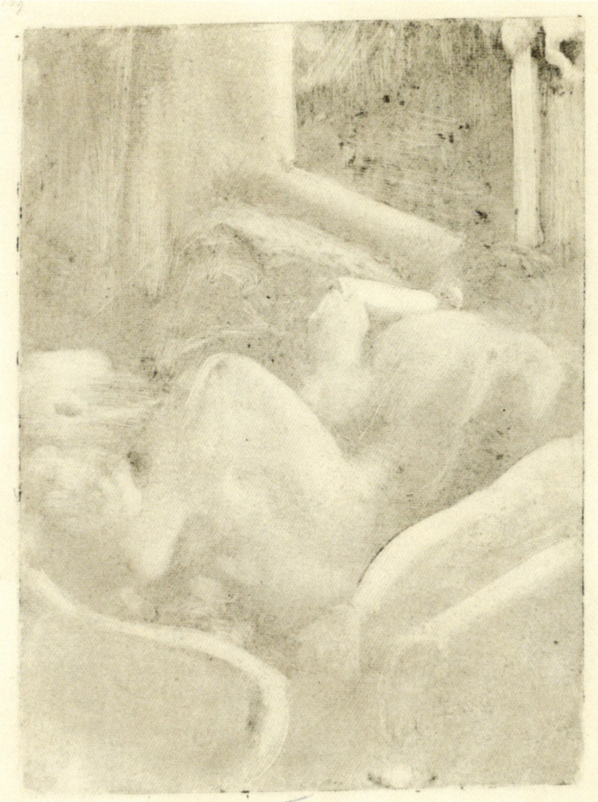

107. *The Reader* (*Le Repos*). c. 1880–85
Recto: monotype on paper, counterproof
Plate: 15 3⁄16 × 11 1⁄4 in. (38.5 × 28.5 cm), sheet: 19 7⁄16 × 13 7⁄8 in. (49.4 × 35.3 cm)
Kunsthalle Bremen. Kupferstichkabinett–Der Kunstverein in Bremen

108. *The Reader* (*Le Repos*). c. 1880–85
Verso: monotype on paper
Plate: 14 15⁄16 × 10 7⁄8 in. (38 × 27.7 cm); sheet: 17 7⁄16 × 12 13⁄16 in. (44.3 × 32.5 cm)
Kunsthalle Bremen. Kupferstichkabinett–Der Kunstverein in Bremen

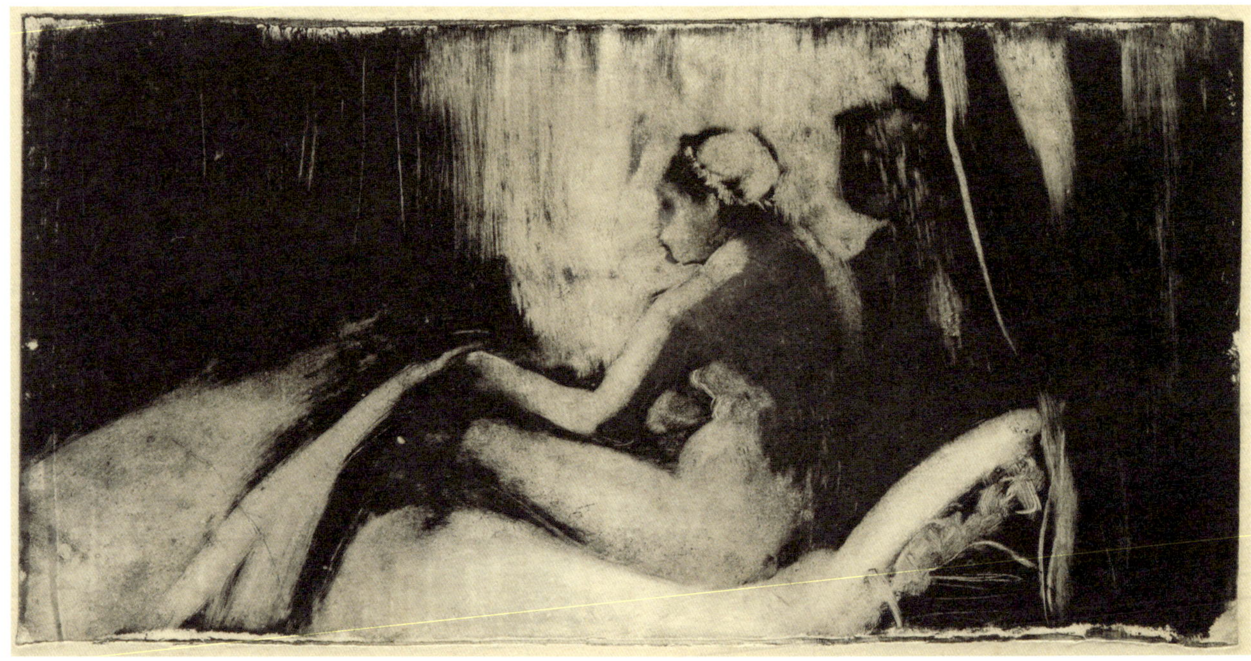

109. *Bedtime* (*Le Coucher*). c. 1880–85
Monotype on paper
Plate: 8 15⁄16 × 17 5⁄16 in. (22.7 × 44 cm)
Private collection

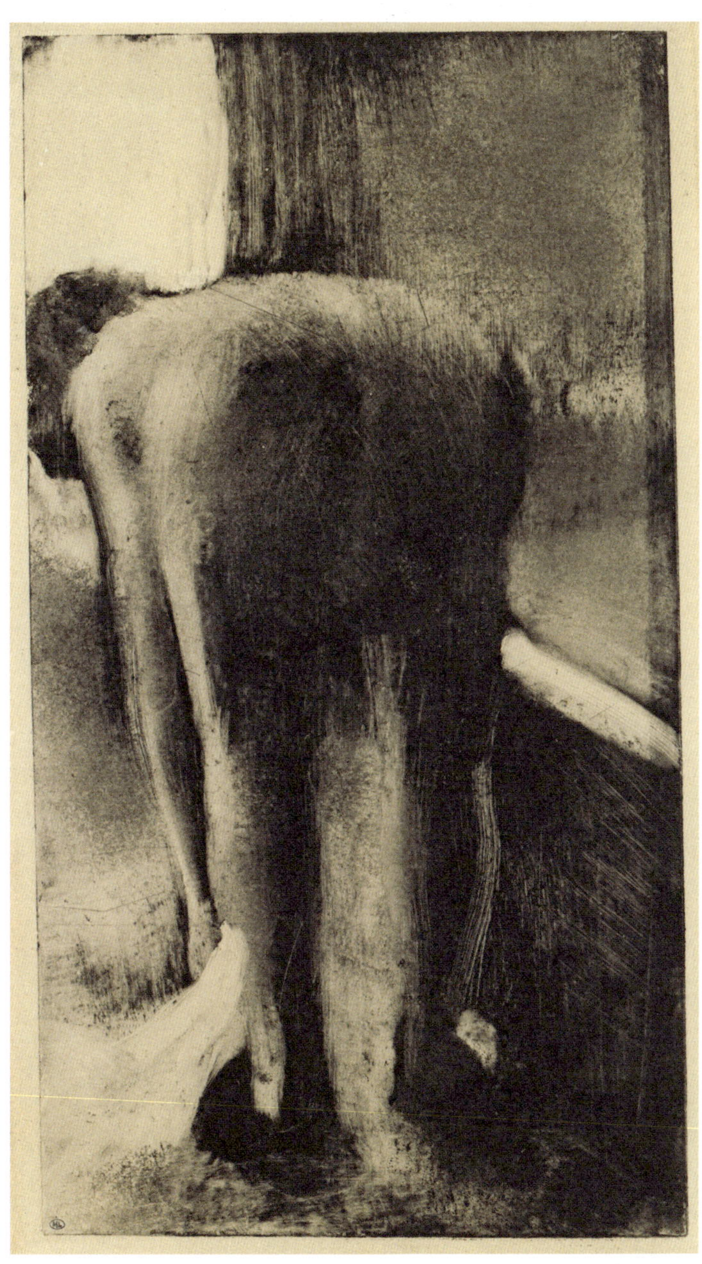

110. *Woman Drying Her Feet* (*Femme s'essuyant les pieds, près de sa baignoire*). c. 1880–85
Monotype on paper
Plate: 17 ¾ × 9 7/16 in. (45.1 × 23.9 cm), sheet: 20 ¼ × 12 ⅝ in. (51.5 × 32 cm)
Musée d'Orsay, Paris

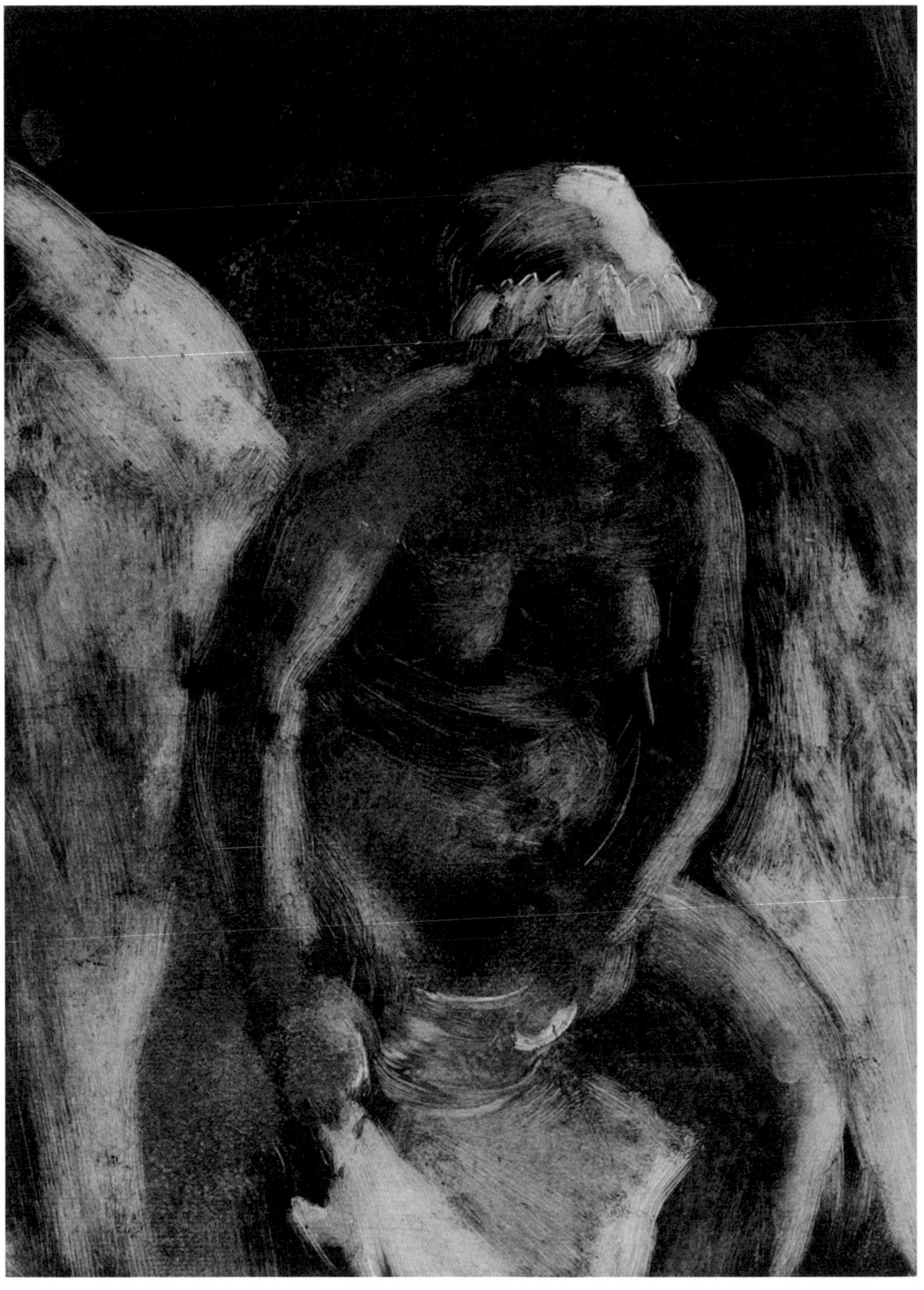

111. *The Toilette* (*The Chamber Pot*) (*La Toilette, la cuvette*). c. 1880–85
Monotype on paper
Plate: 14 15⁄16 × 10 15⁄16 in. (38 × 27.8 cm), sheet: 20 3⁄16 × 13 7⁄8 in. (51.3 × 35.3 cm)
Private collection. Courtesy C. G. Boerner, New York

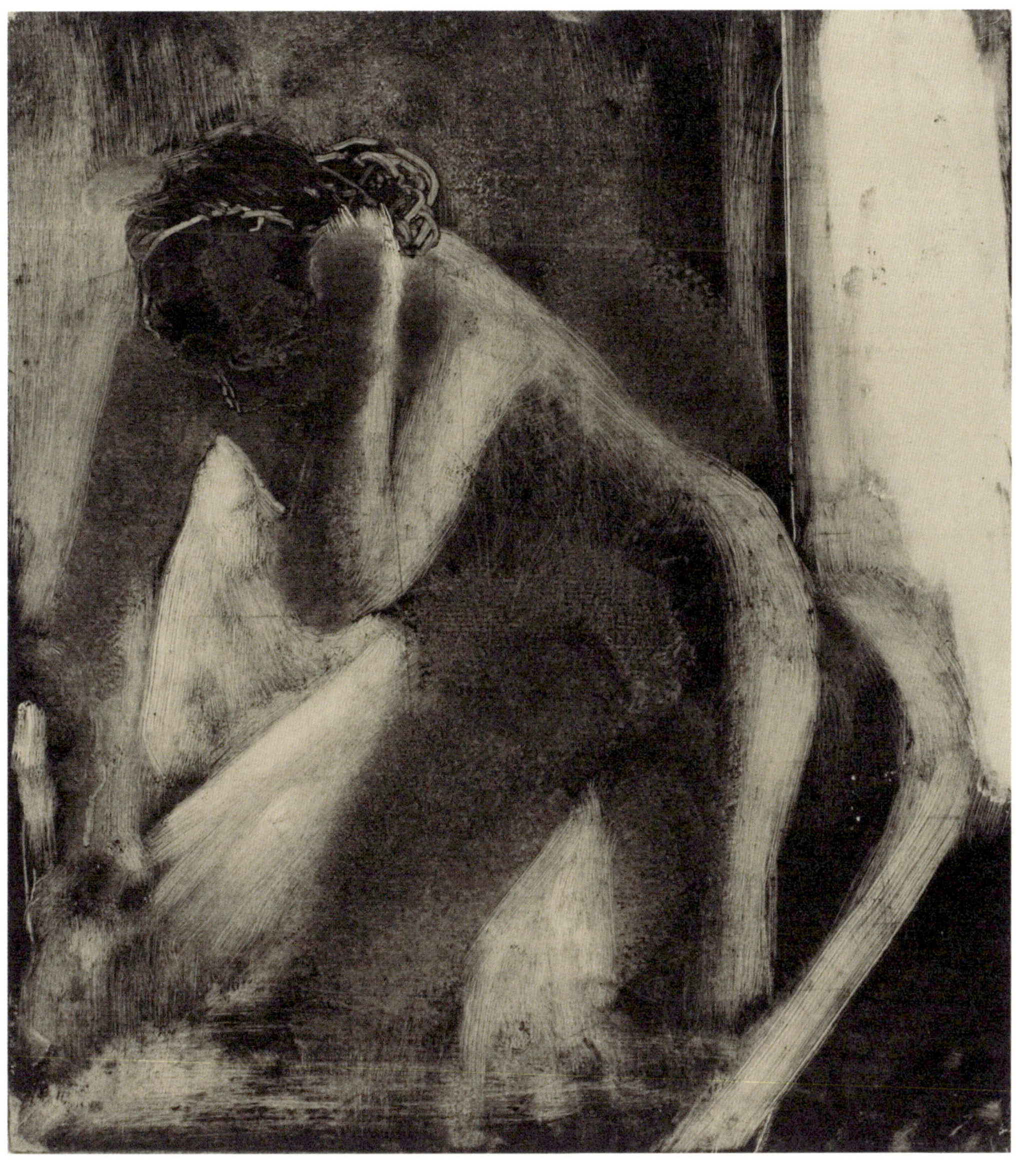

112. *The Bath* (*La Toilette [Le Bain]*). c. 1880–85
Monotype on paper
Plate: 12 ⅜ × 10 15⁄16 in. (31.4 × 27.8 cm), sheet: 20 ¼ × 13 ⅞ in. (51.5 × 35.2 cm)
The Art Institute of Chicago. Clarence Buckingham Collection

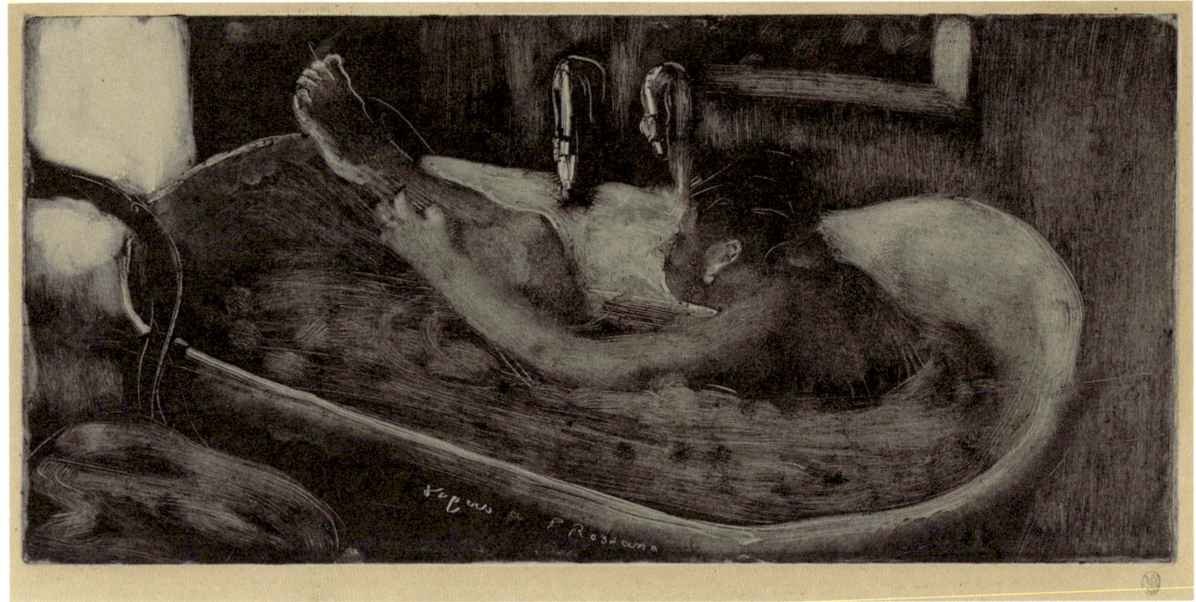

113. *Woman in a Bathtub* (*Femme au bain*). c. 1880–85
Monotype on paper
Plate: 7 ⅞ × 16 ⅞ in. (20 × 41.6 cm)
Private collection

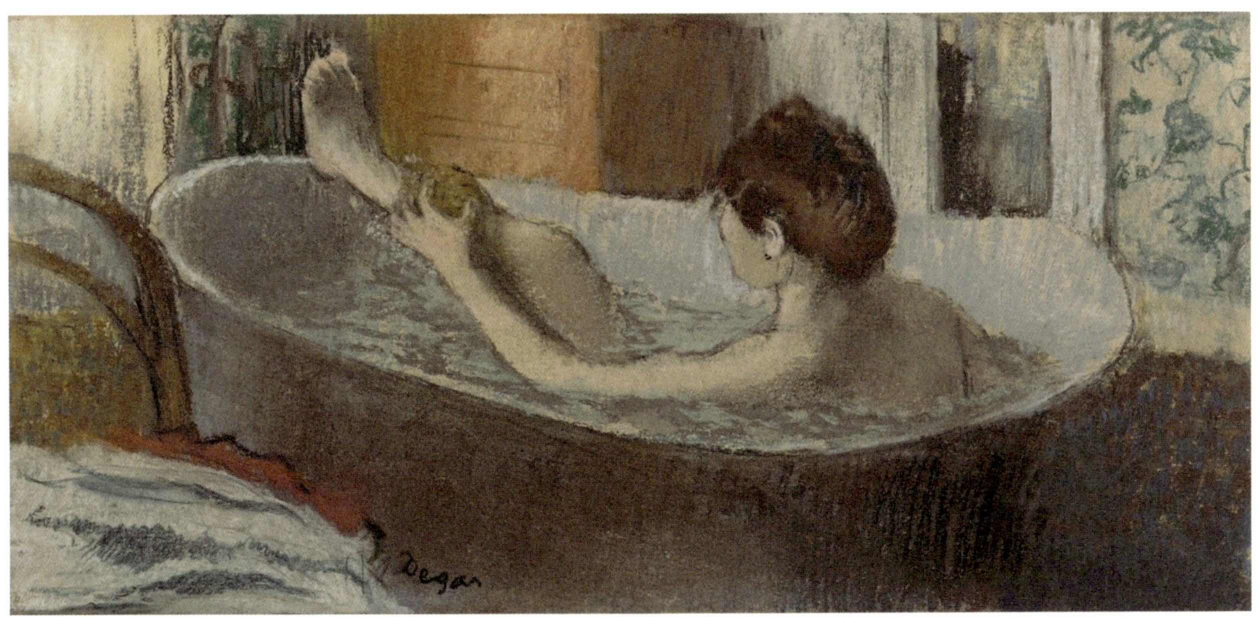

114. *Woman in Her Bath, Sponging Her Leg* (*Femme dans son bain s'épongeant la jambe*). c. 1880–85
Pastel over monotype on paper
7 ¾ × 16 ⅛ in. (19.7 × 41 cm)
Musée d'Orsay, Paris

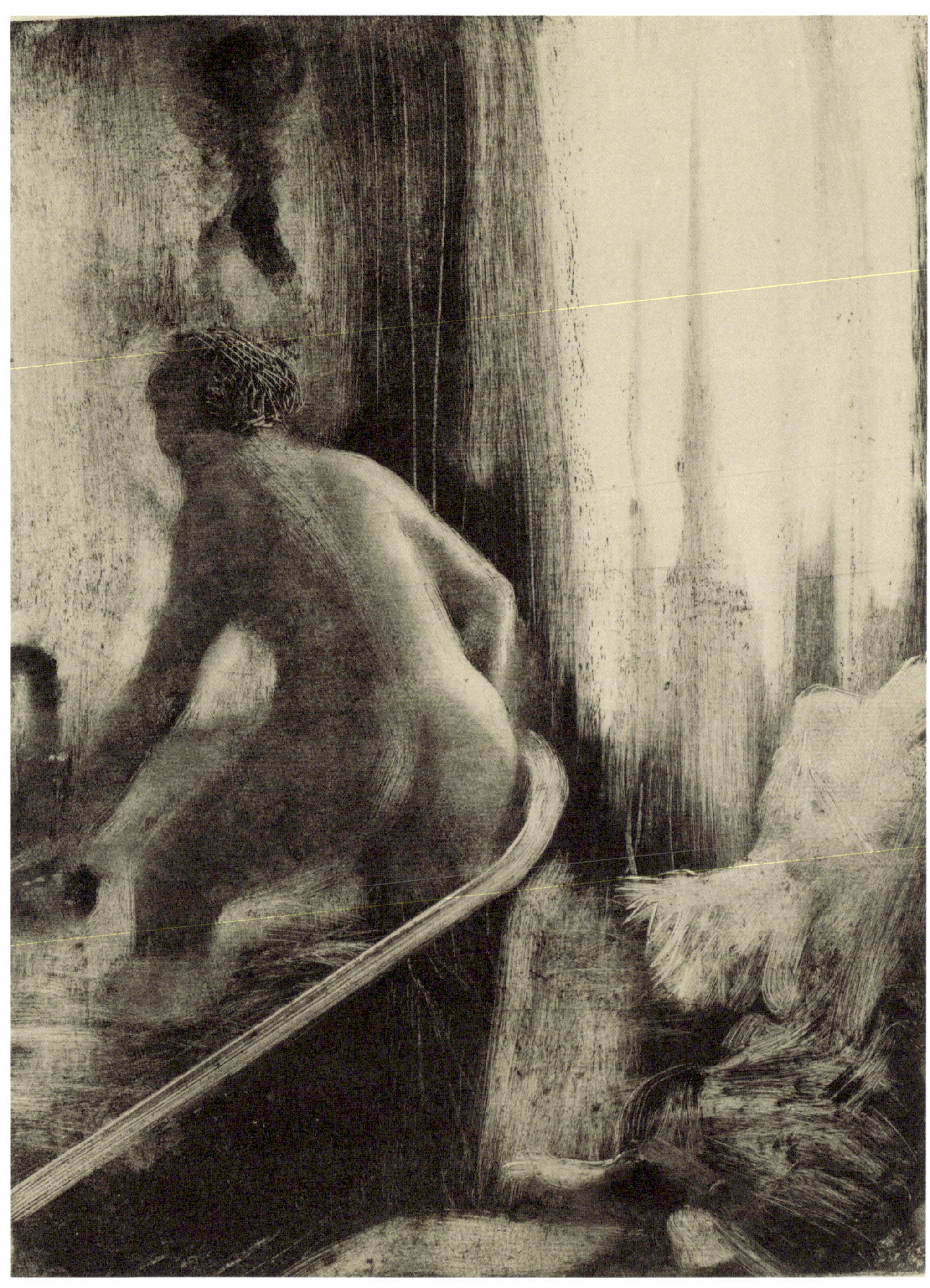

115. *Woman Standing in Her Bath* (*Femme debout dans une baignoire*). c. 1880–85
Monotype on paper
Plate: 14 15⁄16 × 10 5⁄8 in. (38 × 27 cm), sheet: 20 3⁄8 × 13 7⁄8 in. (51.7 × 35.3 cm)
Musée d'Orsay, Paris

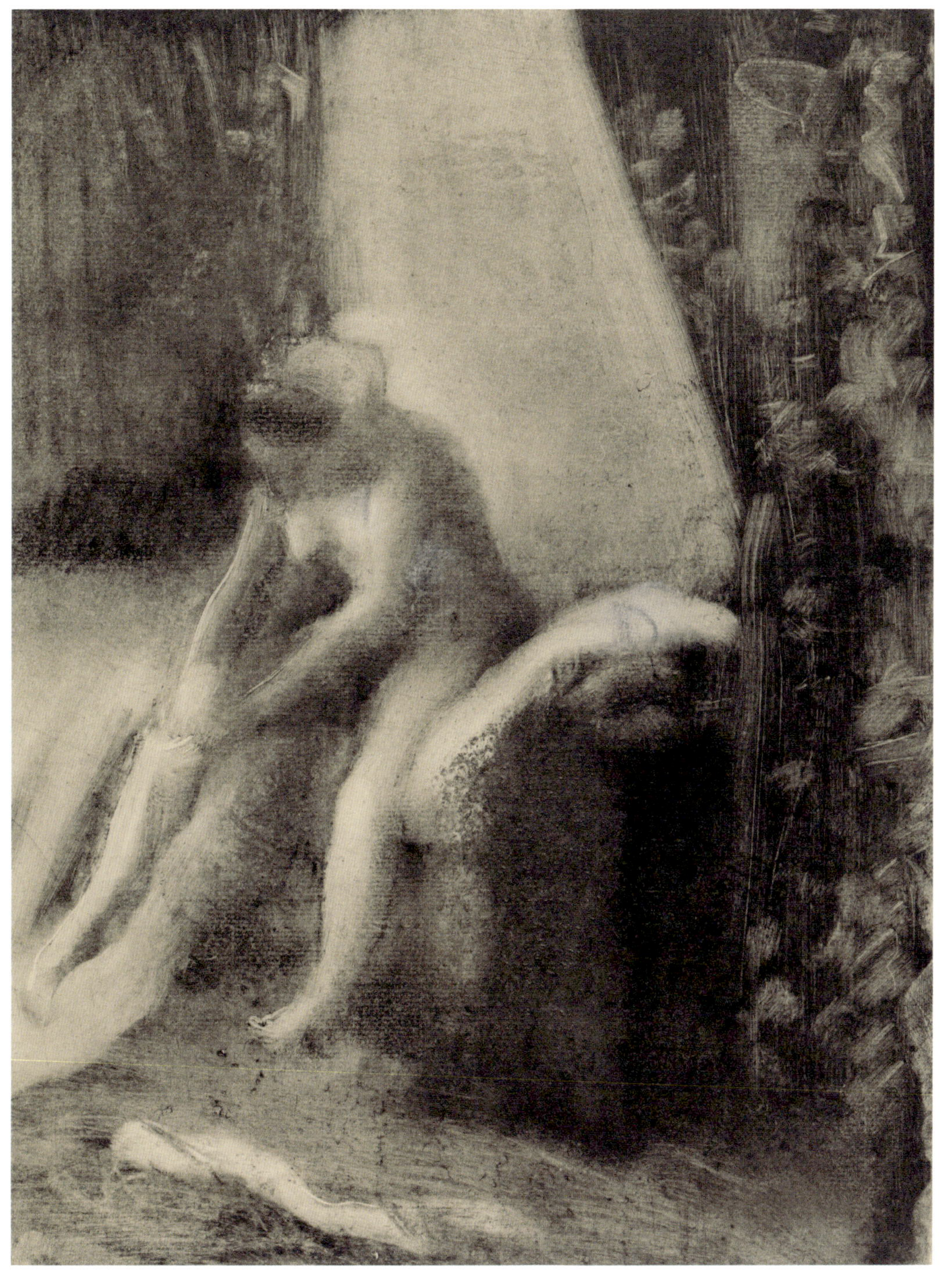

116. *Getting Up—Stockings* (*Le Lever* [*Les Bas*]). c. 1880–85
Opaque watercolor over monotype on paper
Plate: 14 15⁄16 × 10 15⁄16 in. (37.9 × 27.8 cm)
The National Museum of Art, Architecture and Design, Oslo

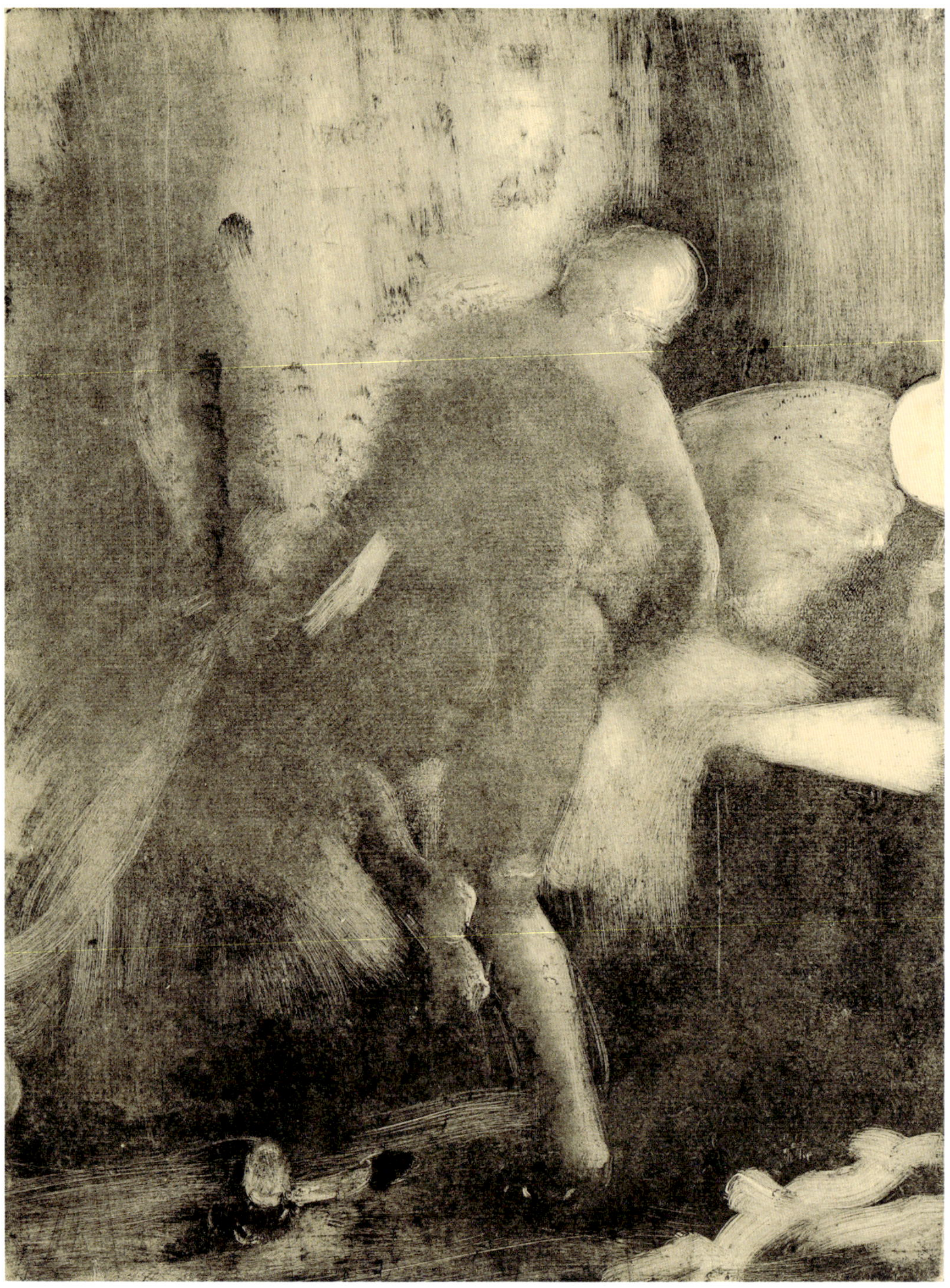

117. *Woman Going to Bed* (*Le Coucher*). c. 1880–83
Monotype on paper
Plate: 14 15⁄16 × 11 in. (38 × 28 cm)
Private collection

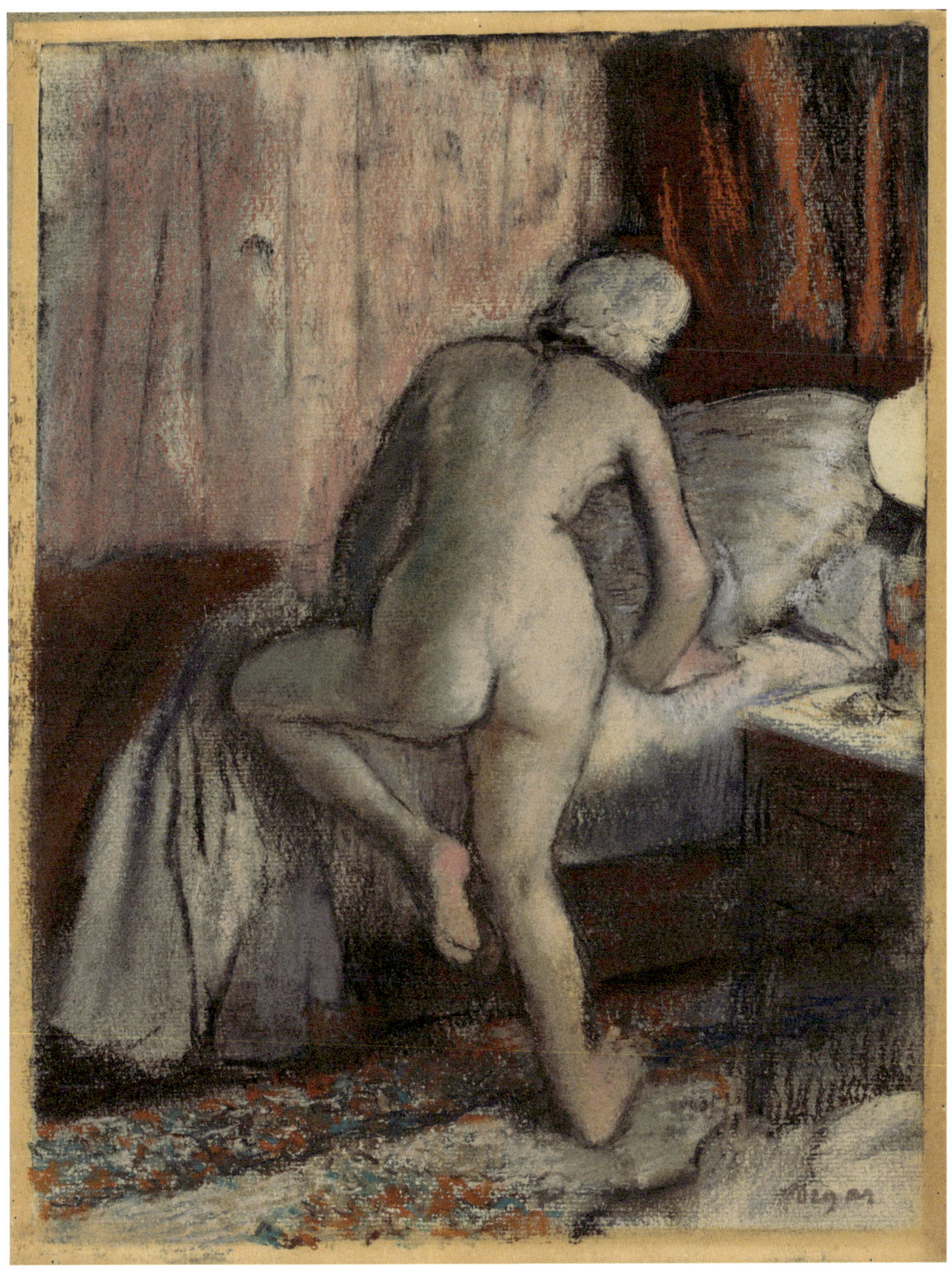

118. *Bedtime* (*Le Coucher*). c. 1883
Pastel over monotype on paper
Plate: 15 × 11 in. (38.1 × 27.9 cm)
Private collection

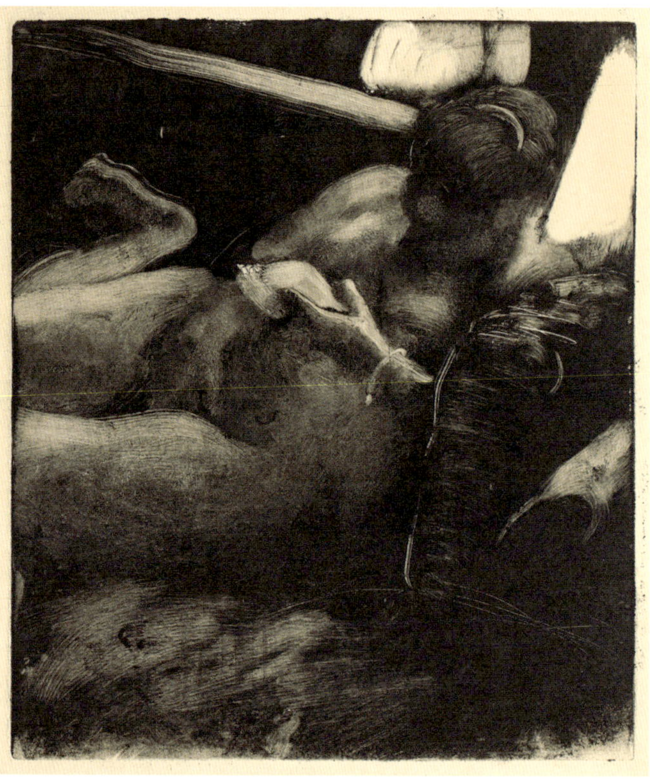

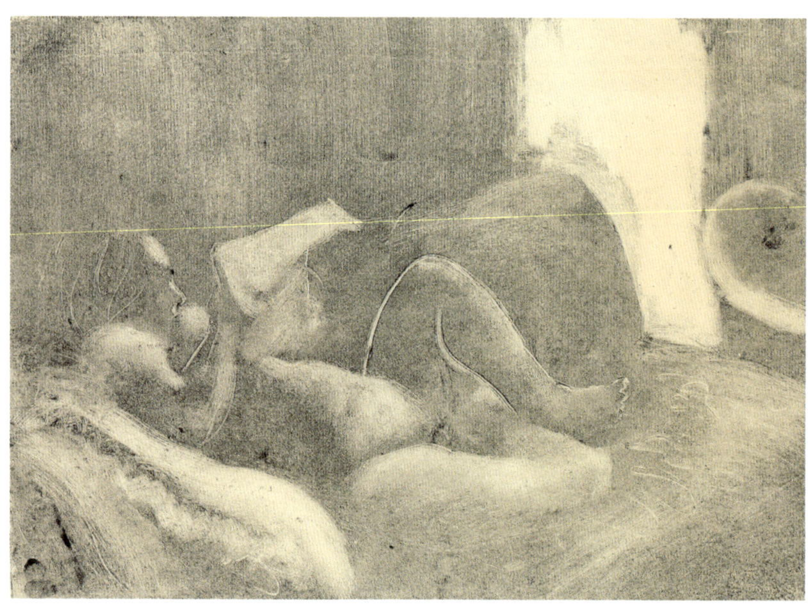

119. *The Letter* (*La Lettre*).
c. 1882–85
Monotype on paper
12 ⅜ × 10 ⅞ in. (31.4 × 27.6 cm)
Collection Marcel Lecomte, Paris

120. *The Toilette (Reading after the Bath)* (*La Toilette [Lecture après le bain]*). c. 1880–85
Monotype on paper
Plate: 10 ⅞ × 14 ⅞ in. (27.7 × 37.8 cm), sheet: 14 × 20 ⅜ in. (35.6 × 51.8 cm)
Private collection. Courtesy Marc Rosen Fine Art Ltd.

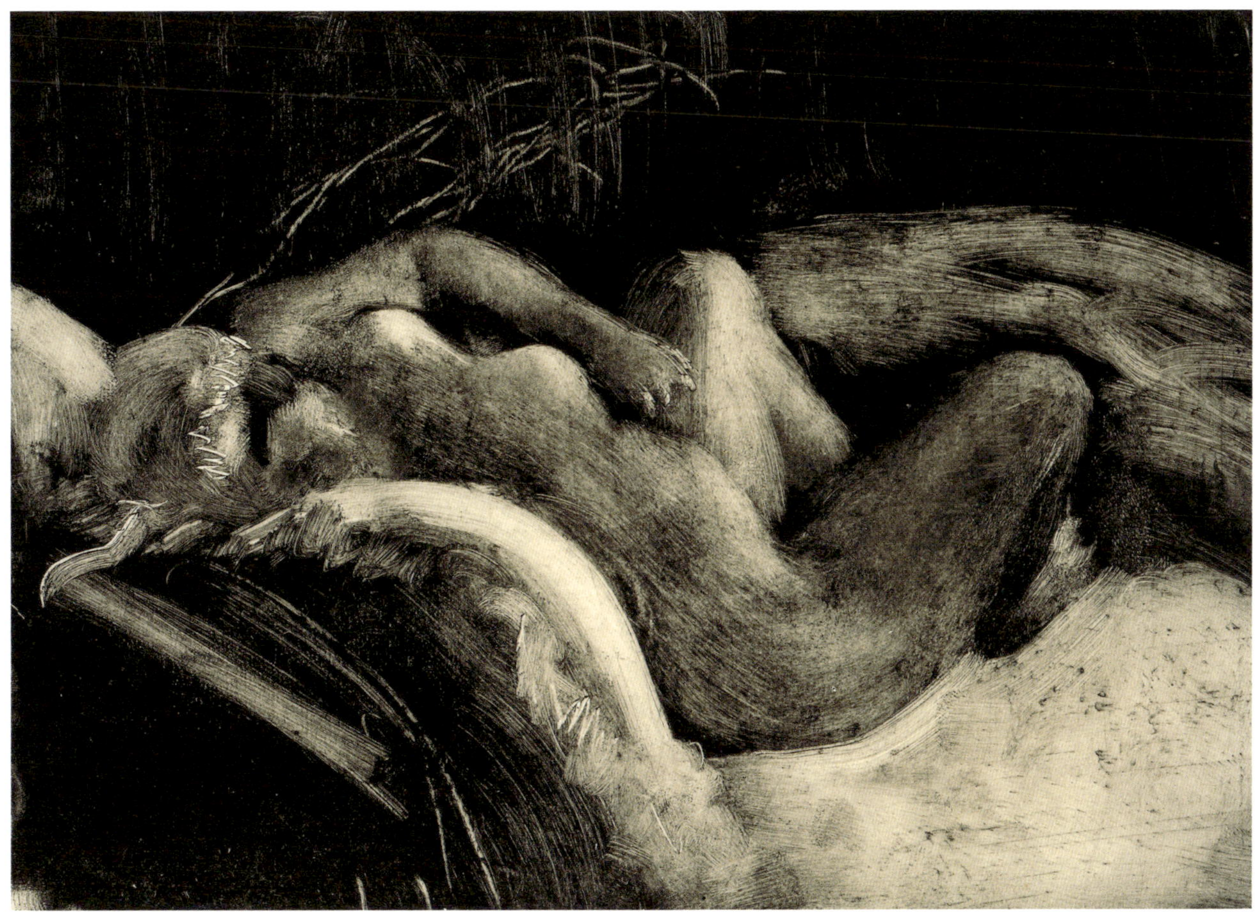

121. *Sleep* (*Le Sommeil*). c. 1880–85
Monotype on paper
Plate: 10 ⅞ × 14 ⅞ in. (27.6 × 37.8 cm)
British Museum, London. Bequeathed by Campbell Dodgson

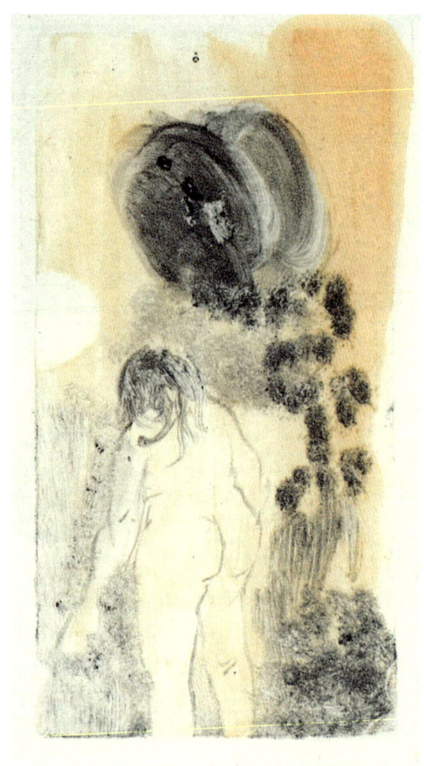

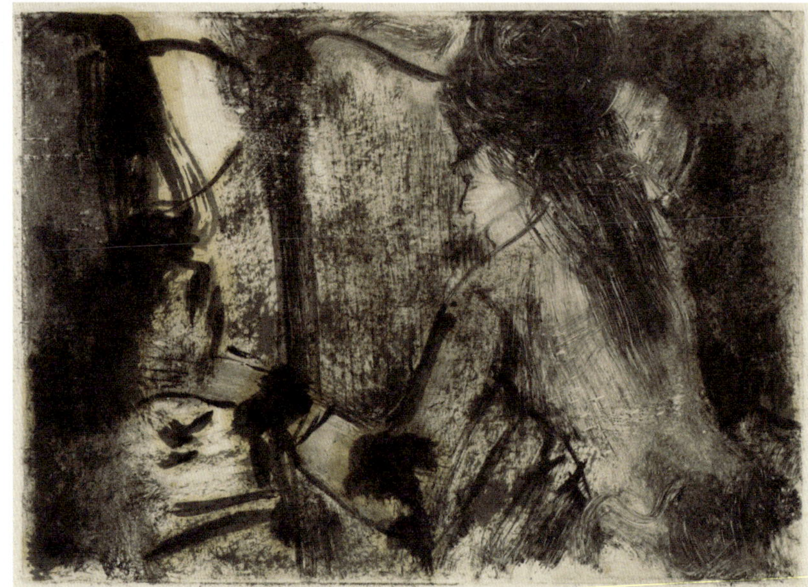

122. *Fantasy, Nude Woman* (*Fantaisie*).
c. 1880–85
Monotype on paper
Plate: 6 ¾ × 3 7⁄16 in. (17.1 × 8.7 cm)
Private collection

123. *Final Touches at the Toilette* (*Dernier préparatifs de toilette*). c. 1880–85
Oil over monotype on paper
Plate: 6 5⁄16 × 8 7⁄16 in. (16 × 21.5 cm)
Fine Arts Museums of San Francisco. Museum Purchase, Achenbach Foundation for Graphic Arts Endowment Fund

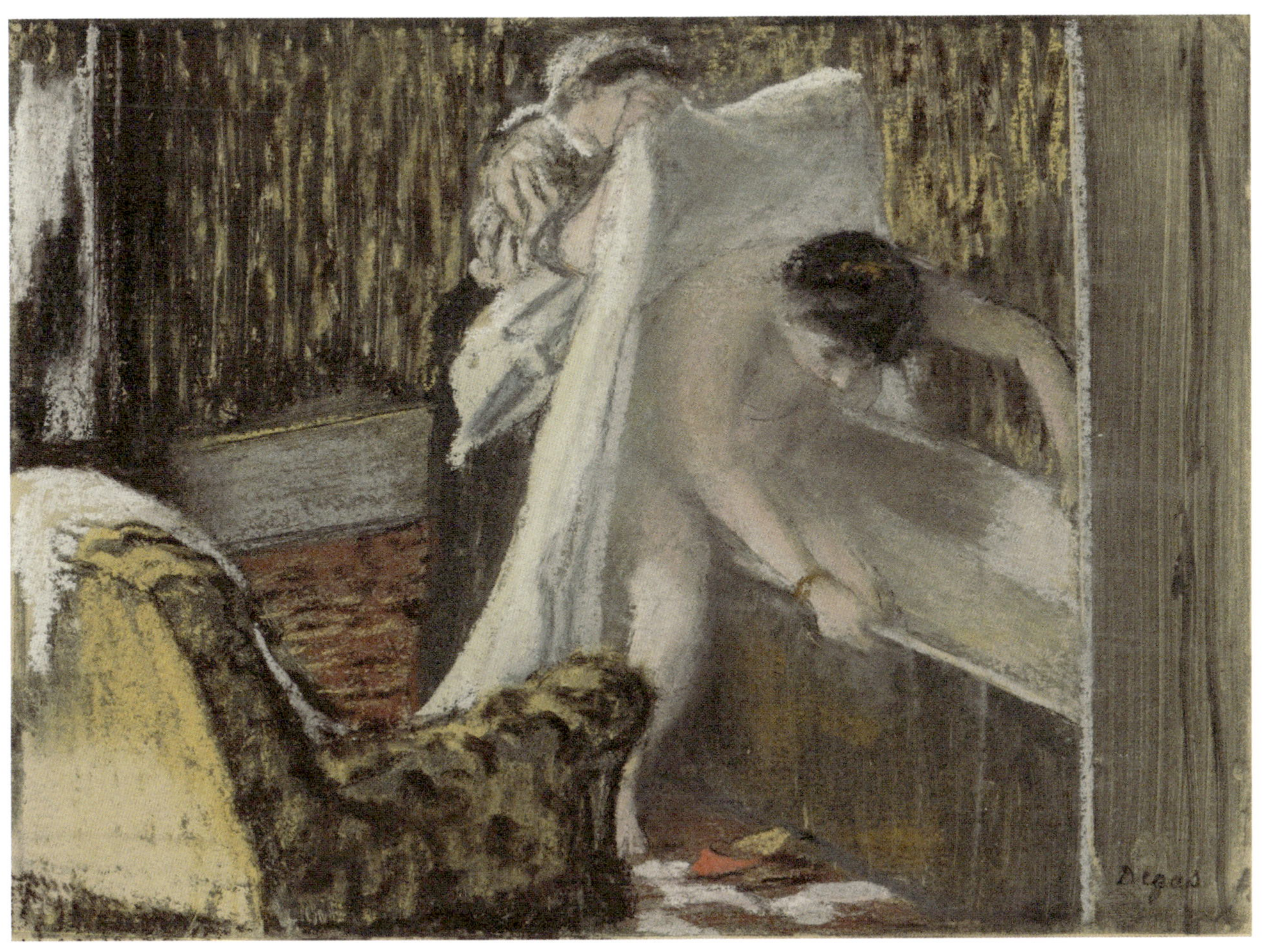

124. *Woman Getting Out of the Bath* (*Femme sortant du bain*). c. 1880–85
Pastel over monotype on paper
6 $\frac{5}{16}$ × 8 $\frac{7}{16}$ in. (16 × 21.5 cm)
Musée d'Orsay, Paris

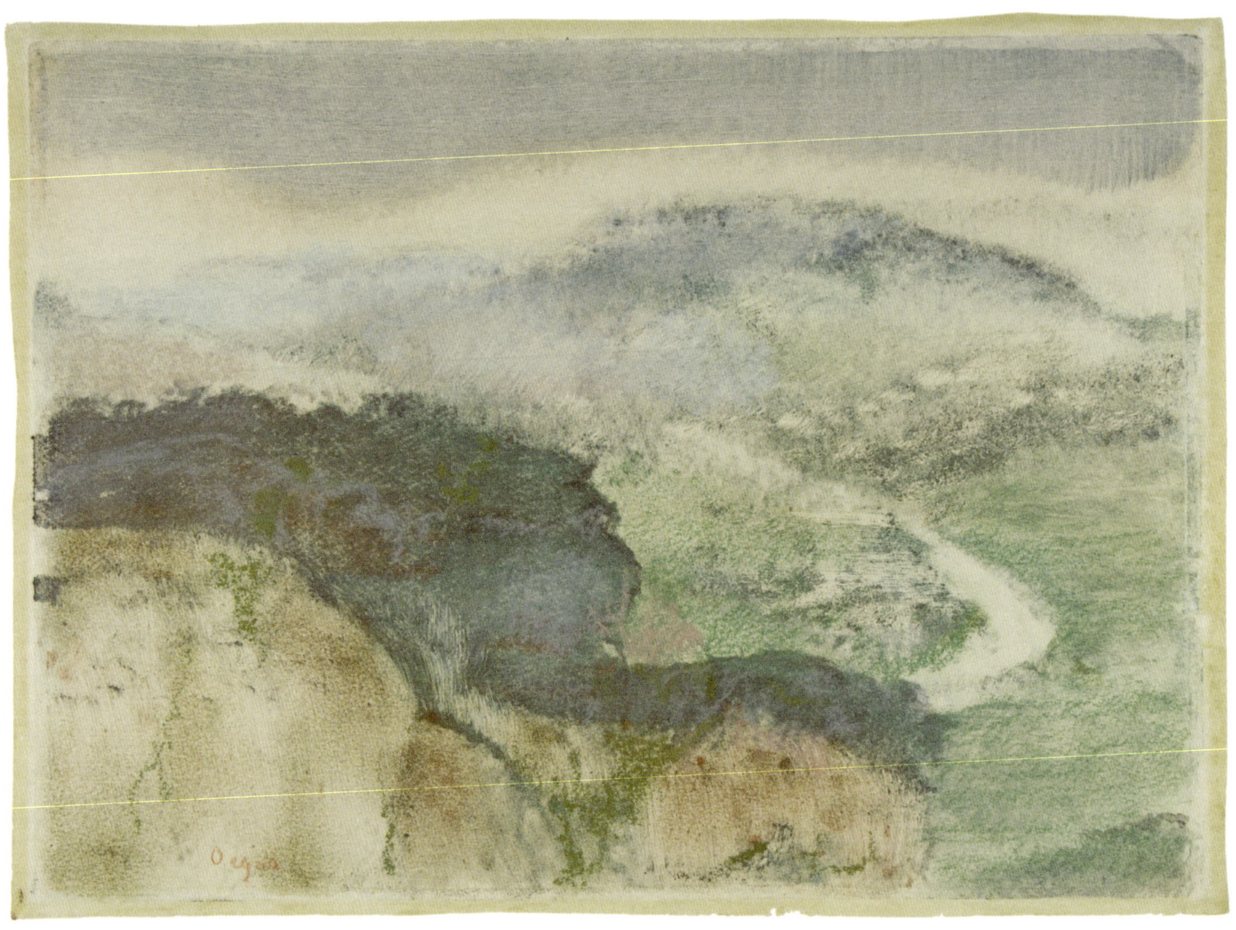

125. *Landscape* (*Paysage*). 1892
Pastel over monotype in oil on blue paper, now faded to off-white, mounted on board
Sheet: 10 × 13 ⅜ in. (25.4 × 34 cm)
The Metropolitan Museum of Art, New York. Purchase, Mr. and Mrs. Richard J. Bernhard Gift

Movement and Landscape

Jonas Beyer

Is it possible to imagine moving through one of Degas's monotype landscapes, such as *Landscape* (*Paysage*; plate 125) of 1892? Can we mentally explore it with confident steps, as Denis Diderot claimed could be done with the landscapes of Claude Joseph Vernet?[1] More likely we would agree with the critic who described the monotypes shown at the Durand-Ruel gallery, Paris, in 1892 as "a series of landscapes by Degas, not studies, but delightfully chimerical scenes, recalled from the imagination."[2] Although a narrow curving road might lead us into the visual depth of *Landscape*, it quickly disappears into vagueness. The other forms too lack hard contours, blending into each other almost seamlessly.

Degas seems to have created this effect of unreality on purpose: before pulling this second proof, he changed the sky from pink to a pale lavender,[3] and he also added pastels to emphasize rather than hide the weakness of the "ghost," as second impressions are sometimes called today. The pastels in the second proof lie on the printed colors like a fine veil, whereas in the first version, in the Museum of Fine Arts, Boston (fig. 1), they match the strength of the original monotype and are distributed vibrantly across the surface. Recent studies show that the colors of the second proof have changed over time: the paper has faded, losing its bluish ground tone.[4] Even when the print was new, though, its forms must have been faint, its colors almost feverishly pale, creating the tentative, dreamlike atmosphere that distinguishes the work to this day.

Another issue too might prevent us from navigating the picture. A clearly defined spatial depth would have brought into play the element of time, which obeys its own quite special laws in Degas's monotype landscapes. What are those laws? Does the sense of time in these images resemble that in landscapes by the artist's Impressionist peers, particularly Claude Monet? The two monotypes in Boston and New York could certainly represent the same landscape at different moments, and it may be worth noting that the artist exhibited his landscapes at Durand-Ruel, where, several months earlier, Monet had shown a number of his Haystack paintings, works that register the visual changes in a single motif with the time of day and the season (fig. 2).[5] But Degas rejects Monet's way of extracting a fleeting moment from a wealth of moments in the encounter with a given subject. The monotype technique prevents that approach, for it requires a printing press; rather than working *sur le motif*, the artist must rely on memory and imagination. Degas's monotype landscapes are based on a sense of time that does not isolate the single moment but merges it into a broader time frame.

We know that Degas produced these landscapes without preliminary studies. Apparently he never stayed long at the sites that inspired them; instead, he appropriated their appearance from a state of motion. The earliest of these prints, mostly made without pastels, date from a trip Degas took through Burgundy in 1890, traveling in a two-wheeled carriage with the artist Paul-Albert Bartholomé (fig. 3). They were traveling to Diénay, to the home of Degas's friend Georges Jeanniot, who had a press in his workshop; it was here that Degas began to make monotypes, astonishing Bartholomé by drawing landscapes on the plate "as if they were still in front of his eyes," even though "he didn't once stop . . . to take a closer look."[6]

A second, later occasion to which we owe a good number of the monotype landscapes was also associated with a mode of transport, this time the train.[7] Few technological innovations have so thoroughly altered humanity's fundamental relationship to time and space. Heinrich Heine may have expressed the new experience most pointedly: "Space is done in by the railroads, and all that remains is time."[8] It was the view from a train compartment in 1892 that

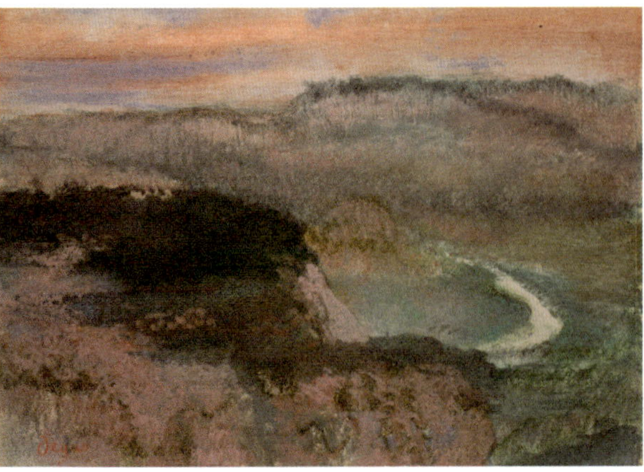

1. Hilaire-Germain-Edgar Degas. *Landscape (Paysage).* 1892. Pastel over monotype in oil on paper, 10 ½ × 14 in. (26.7 × 36.5 cm). Museum of Fine Arts, Boston. Denman Waldo Ross Collection

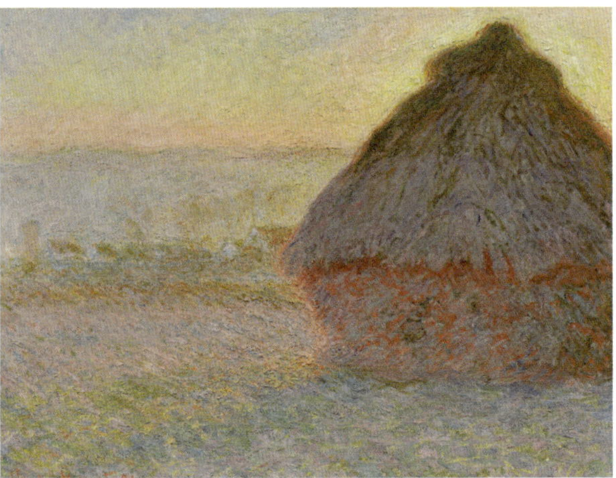

2. Claude Monet. *Grainstack (Sunset) (Meule, soleil couchant).* 1891. Oil on canvas, 28 ⅞ × 36 ½ in. (73.3 × 92.7 cm). Museum of Fine Arts, Boston. Juliana Cheney Edwards Collection

motivated Degas to once again produce monotypes like those he had made in Diénay: "I stood at the door of the railway carriage, and looked around vaguely. That gave me the idea of doing the landscapes."[9]

Landscape probably dates from this later period.[10] One is tempted to relate its vagueness to the circumstances in which Degas saw the view with which it began; the view from the train would have given him at most just a sense of the landscape, hence the relatively undefined forms and their dissolution into an indistinct haze. The monotype technique suited these effects: the element of accident in the colors' search for their way across the paper during the printing process, adhering well here, less well there, enhances the blur of such impressions. Indeed, some of the monotypes in the present exhibition barely do more than suggest a landscape (plates 125, 146).

Other works, though, are heavily reworked with pastels to describe particular details (plates 143, 145), prompting the question of whether we may be overstating the monotypes' tendency toward abstraction: perhaps, for Degas, the almost abstract prints without pastels (plates 127, 128) represented no more than a temporary state, providing basic structures in need of the medium of pastel to clarify their forms. Terms like "finished" and "unfinished" do not properly apply here, however, since in making these prints Degas had allowed time to pass between his encounter with the landscape and its representation. If his memory of a place had faded when he plucked an image of it out of the flow of time, perhaps that was actually helpful: the evocation of landscapes through vague, evanescent forms may reflect his belief in reproducing only what "struck you, that is to say the necessary. That way, your memories and your fantasy are freed from the tyranny of nature."[11]

From this perspective Degas's later use of pastels appears less a necessary step to complete the work than another way for the artist to interrupt the flow of time, a way now based solely on his encounter with the picture on paper itself: thanks to their porous nature, pastels allowed an interaction with each other as well as with the monotype ground. They could also be applied long after the printing of the monotype. One of these landscapes (fig. 4) is even signed three times, suggesting that Degas returned to it again and again, having repeatedly seen new relationships developing among its various layers.[12] Thanks to a fixative developed by the artist Luigi Chialiva, there was no danger of the colors smearing, even with multiple layers of pastel. At least in this sense, some of the monotypes are worked out quite precisely.

Similarly, indistinct visual impressions may only have been part of what Degas worked into his monotypes after his experience on the train. As a passenger he also seems to have developed a new mode of perception. On a train, because of its speed, the eye focuses only selectively. Instead of passing before travelers at a leisurely pace, as it does when they are riding in a horse-drawn carriage, the landscape becomes a kind of staccato succession of images. During his train rides, then, Degas could have imagined the application of this principle to his landscape images, blending one into another. The combination of monotype and pastel was an ideal medium with

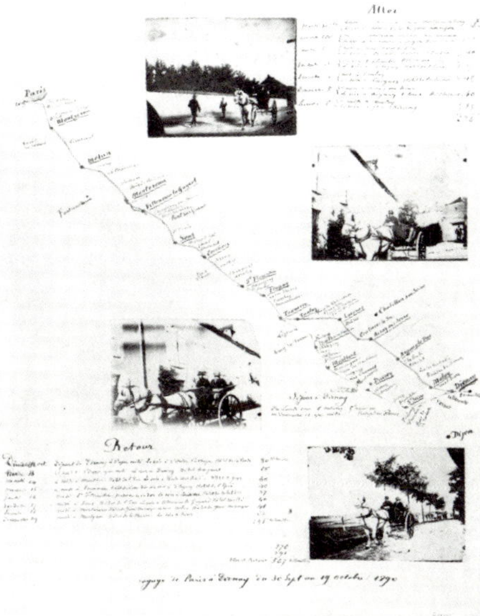

3. Anonymous (Paul-Albert Bartholomé and Charles de Meixmoron?). *Degas's Journey from Paris to Diénay (Voyage de Paris à Diénay).* 1890. Map and photographs, 32 5/16 × 14 ½ in. (82 × 36.8 cm). Bibliothèque nationale de France, Paris

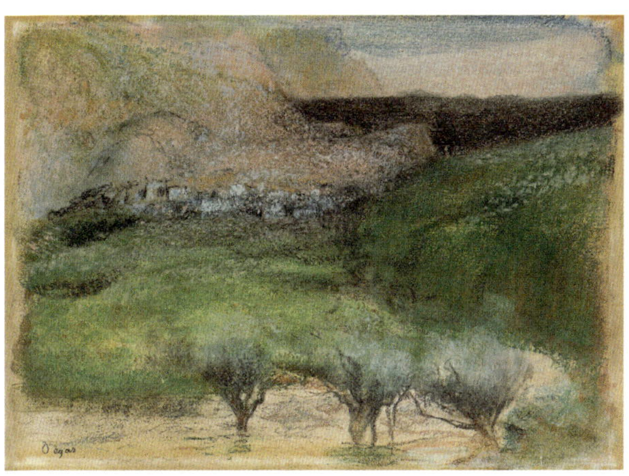

4. Hilaire-Germain-Edgar Degas. *Olive Trees against a Mountainous Background (Oliviers sur fond montagneux).* 1890–92. Pastel over monotype in oil on paper, plate: 10 × 13 ⅝ in. (25.4 × 34.6 cm), sheet: 10 ⅝ × 14 ⅛" (27 × 35.9 cm). The Norton Simon Foundation

which to combine several moments in time in a single image: whether detailed or indistinct, the pastel additions could alienate a landscape from its original form, adding unsuspected elements to it or enriching it with additional recollections.

We should not be misled by the fact that we see no fundamental change in topography between the Boston and the New York versions of *Landscape*. If there is an allusion here to the serial principle of Monet, it is present only to be subverted.[13] Degas's monotype landscapes, no matter how vague, are pictures developed out of other pictures by the artist, and undergoing metamorphoses in the process. Any reference to an actual landscape—various such identifications have been put forward[14]—is only of interest once we see how that setting allowed Degas to engage spontaneous associations, imagined exaggerations, and memories of what had been "truly striking." These are the qualities that make the monotype landscapes distinctive gems, or, as the critic Gustave Geffroy once called them, "precious sapphires in velvet jewelry boxes."[15]

1. Denis Diderot, "Salon de 1767," 1767, Eng. trans. as *Diderot on Art II: The Salon of 1767*, trans. John Goodman (New Haven: Yale University Press, 1995).
2. Remy de Gourmont, "Choses d'art," *Mercure de France*, Série moderne VI (December 1892), p. 374. Eng. trans. from Richard Kendall, *Degas Landscapes*, exh. cat. (New York: The Metropolitan Museum of Art, in association with Yale University Press, New Haven, 1993), p. 226.
3. See Kendall, *Degas Landscapes*, p. 289, n. 46.
4. Investigation of the original by Karl Buchberg and Laura Neufeld of The Museum of Modern Art and Marjorie Shelley of The Metropolitan Museum of Art, New York, has determined that the recto has faded while the verso retains the paper's original bluish tone.
5. Claude Monet exhibited fifteen Haystacks at Durand-Ruel from May 4 to May 18, 1891. The following year, Degas showed about twenty-five monotype landscapes at the same gallery, in his first solo exhibition.
6. Paul-Albert Bartholomé, quoted in Georges Jeanniot, "Souvenirs sur Degas," *La Revue universelle* 55, no. 15 (November 1, 1933):290. Eng. trans. in Kendall, *Degas Landscapes*, p. 149.
7. Degas took several train journeys in 1892, three to Peau, in the Pyrenees, and two more to Switzerland and Belgium. See Kendall, *Degas Landscapes*, p. 210.
8. Heinrich Heine, quoted in Wolfgang Schivelbusch, *Geschichte der Eisenbahnreise. Zur Industrialisierung von Raum und Zeit im 19. Jahrhundert* (Munich and Vienna: Fischer Taschenbuch, 1977), p. 39.
9. Degas, quoted in Daniel Halévy, *Degas parle*, ed. Jean-Pierre Halévy (Paris and Geneva: La Palatine, 1995), p. 132. Eng. trans. in Kendall, *Degas Landscapes*, p. 150.
10. Kendall bases a chronological division of the fifty-five monotype landscapes known at the time of his book on Degas's use of three different plate sizes. See *Degas Landscapes*, pp. 273ff.
11. Degas, quoted in Jeanniot, "Souvenirs sur Degas," *La Revue universelle* 55, no. 14 (October 15, 1933):158. Eng. trans. in Kendall, *Degas Landscapes*, p. 212.
12. See my essay "Degas and Landscape: The Late Monotypes," in Martin Schwander, ed., *Edgar Degas: The Late Work*, exh. cat. (Basel: Fondation Beyeler, and Ostfildern: Hatje Cantz, 2012), p. 218.
13. See my *Zwischen Zeichnung und Druck. Edgar Degas und die Wiederentdeckung der Monotypie im 19. Jahrhundert*, PhD diss., Paderborn, 2014, p. 331.
14. Kendall, *Degas Landscapes*, pp. 154ff.
15. Gustave Geffroy, "Historie de l'impressionisme, Edgar Degas," in *La Vie artistique* (Paris), troisième série, 1894, p. 176. Eng. trans. in Kendall, *Degas Landscapes*, p. 189.

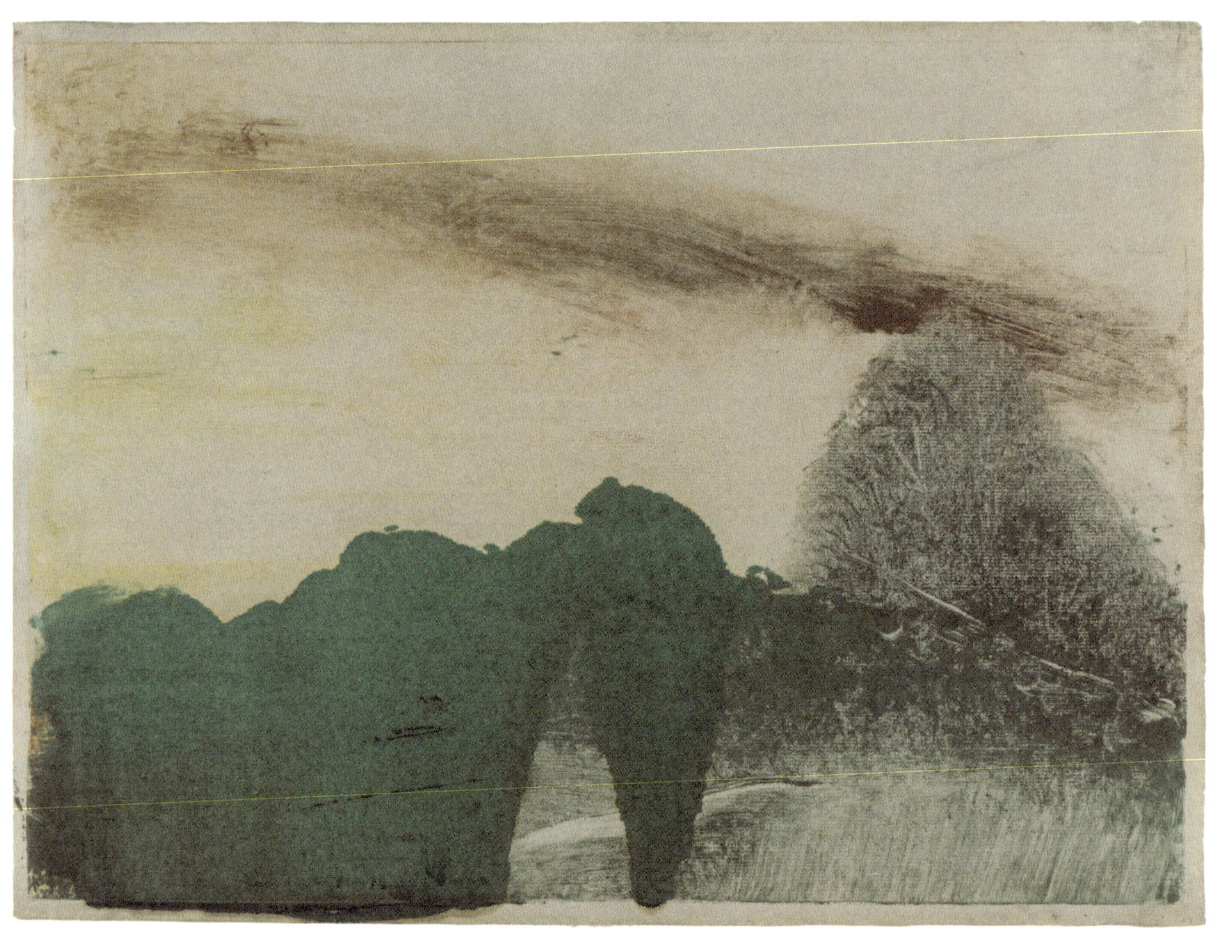

126. *Forest in the Mountains* (*Forêt dans la montagne*). c. 1890
Monotype in oil on paper
Plate: 11 13/16 × 15 3/4 in. (30 × 40 cm), sheet: 12 3/8 × 16 5/16 in. (31.4 × 41.4 cm)
The Museum of Modern Art, New York. Louise Reinhardt Smith Bequest

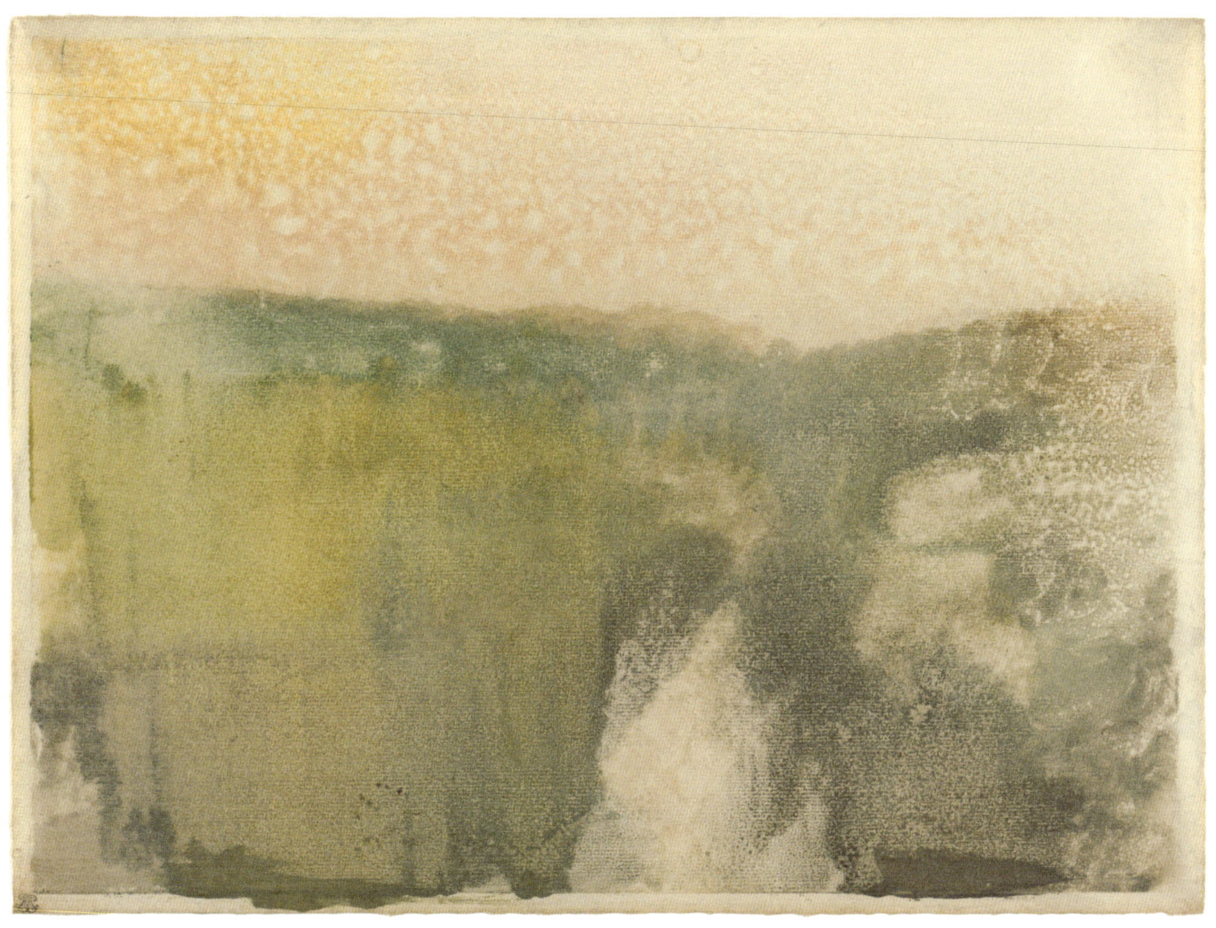

127. *Green Landscape* (*Paysage vert*). 1890
Monotype in oil on paper
Plate: 11 ¾ × 15 ⅝ in. (29.9 × 39.7 cm), sheet: 12 ⅜ × 15 ⅞ in. (31.4 × 40.4 cm)
The Museum of Modern Art, New York. Louise Reinhardt Smith Bequest

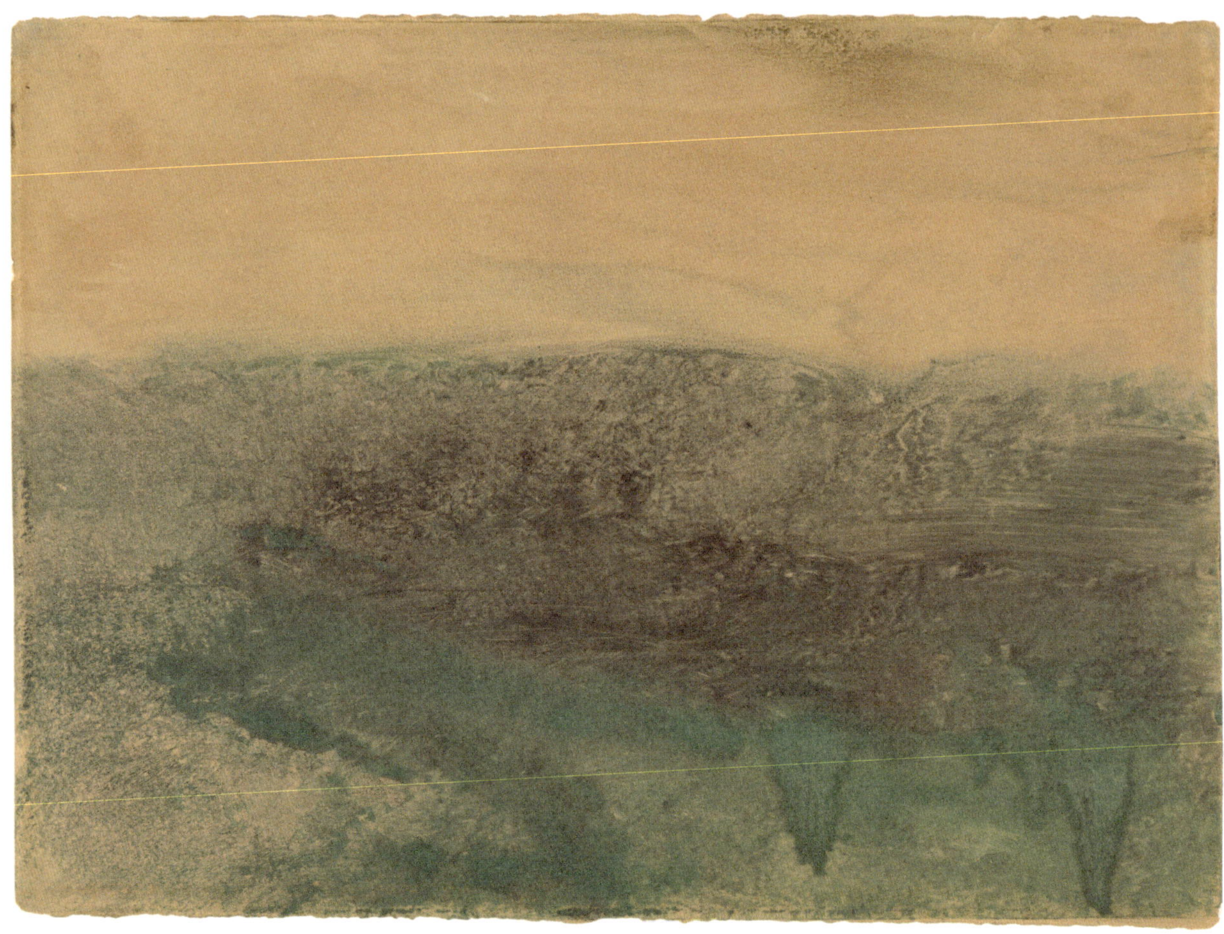

128. *Twilight in the Pyrenees* (*Le Crépuscule dans les Pyrénées*). 1890
Monotype in oil on paper
Plate: 11 ¾ × 15 ¹¹⁄₁₆ in. (29.8 × 39.8 cm)
Collection of the Ackland Art Museum, University of North Carolina at Chapel Hill. Ackland Fund

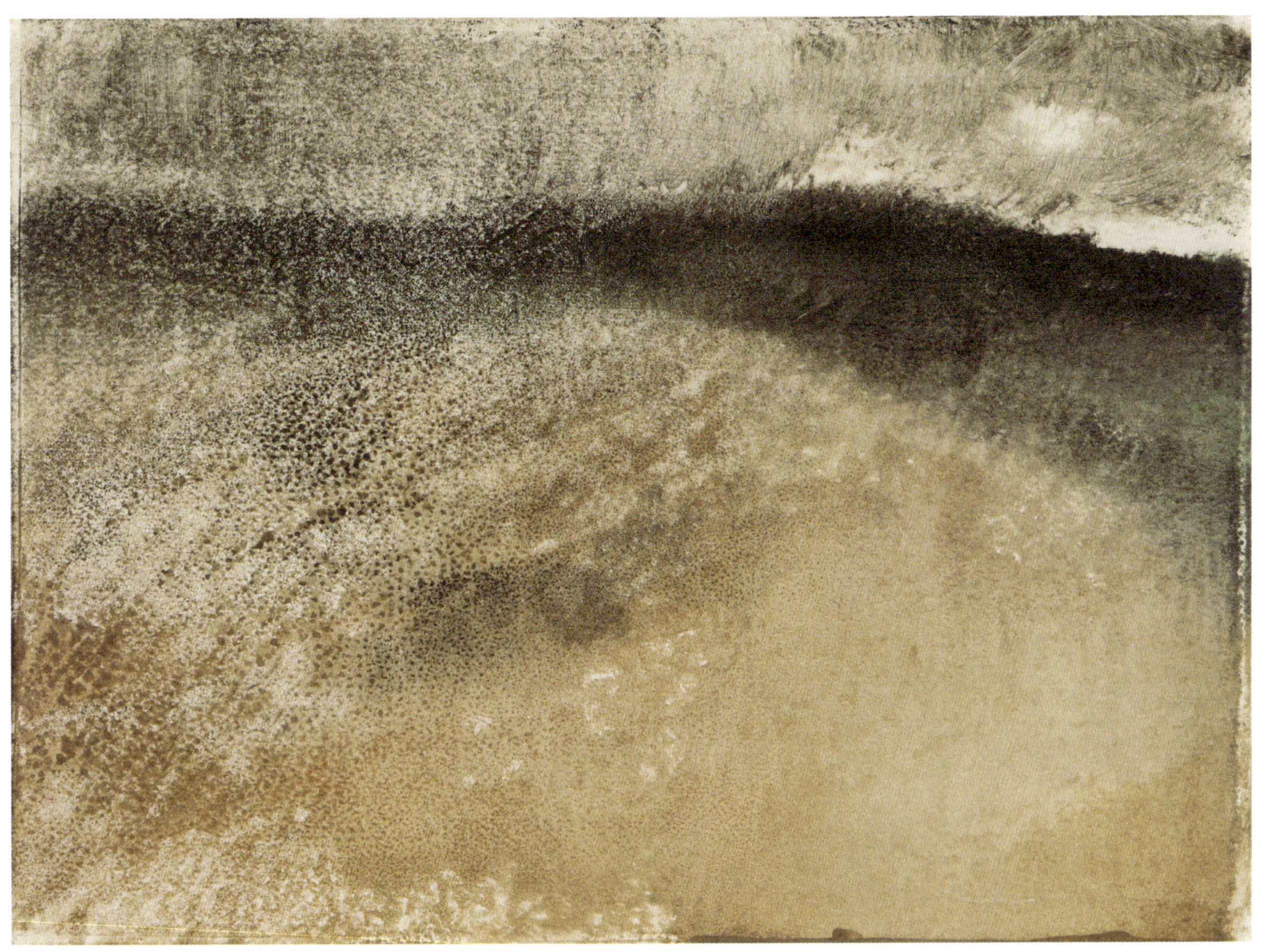

129. *Squall in the Mountains* (*Bourrasque dans la montagne*). 1890
Monotype in oil on paper
Plate: 11 ⅝ × 15 $\frac{9}{16}$ in. (29.5 × 39.5 cm)
Norton Simon Museum, Pasadena, California. Museum Purchase, B. Gerald Cantor Fund

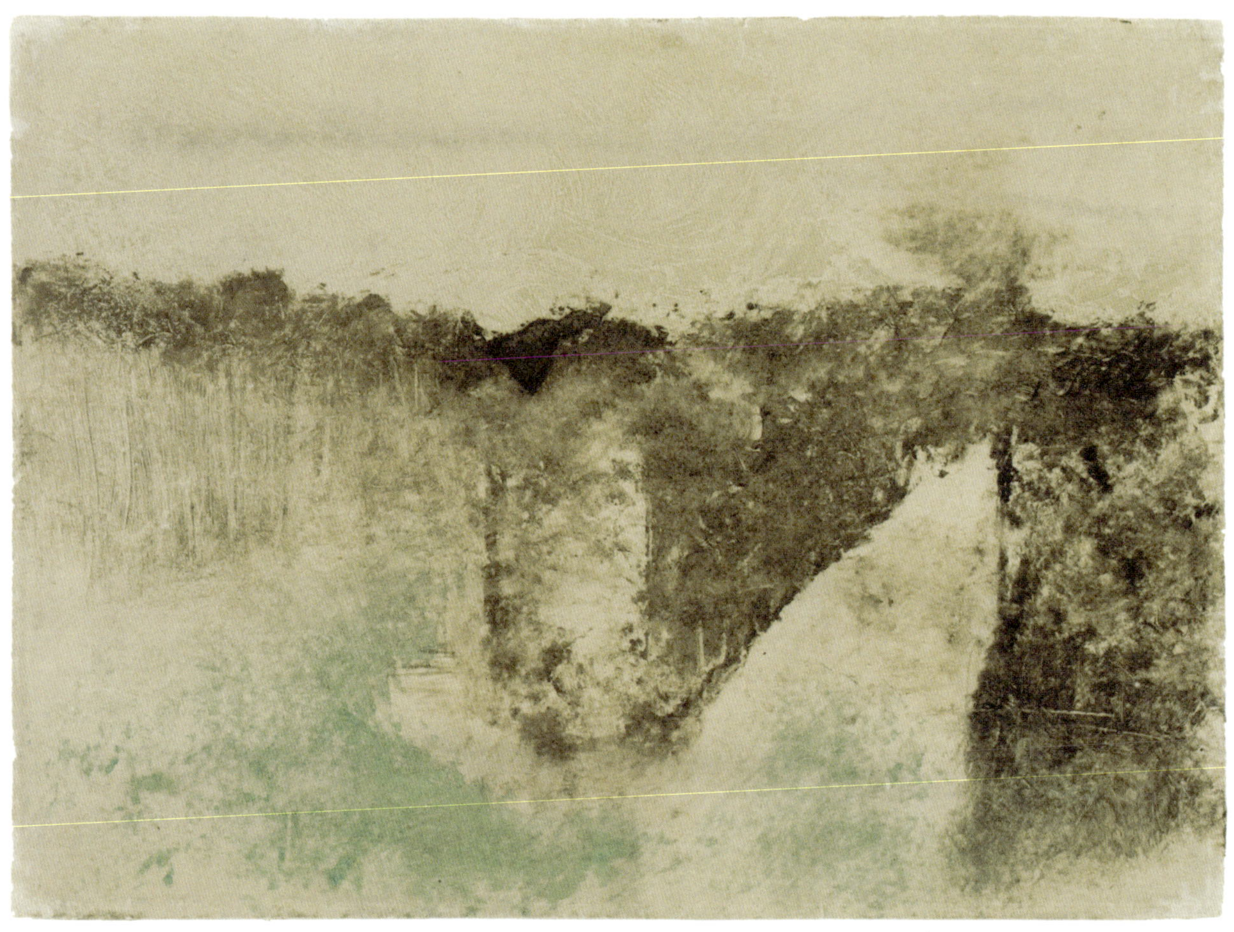

130. *The Road in the Forest* (*La Route dans la forêt*). 1890
Monotype in oil on paper
Plate: 11 13⁄16 × 15 ¾ in. (30 × 40 cm), sheet: 11 13⁄16 × 15 ¾ in. (30 × 40 cm)
Harvard Art Museums/Fogg Museum, Cambridge, Massachusetts. Bequest of Frances L. Hofer

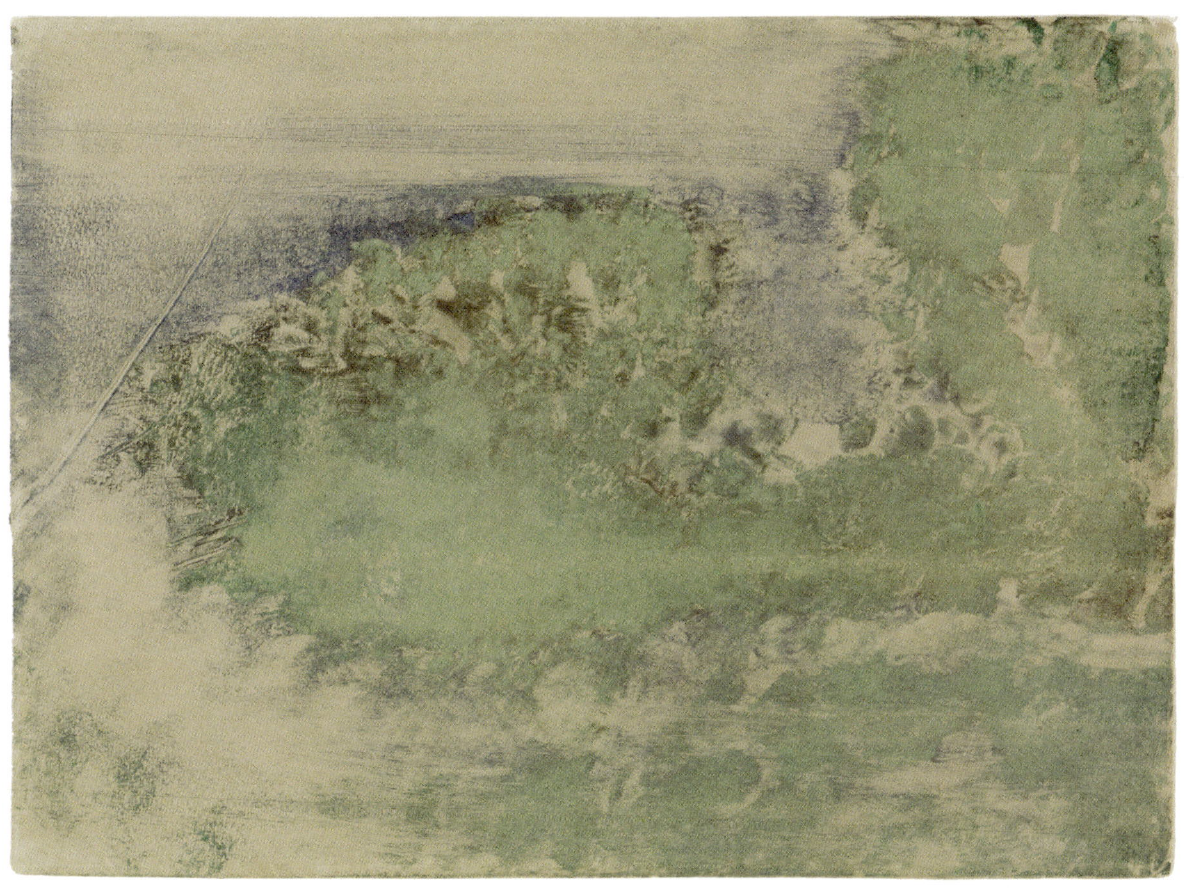

131. *Le Cap Ferrat*. 1892
Monotype in oil on paper
Sheet: 11 11/16 × 15 11/16 in. (29.7 × 39.9 cm)
Staatliche Kunsthalle, Karlsruhe

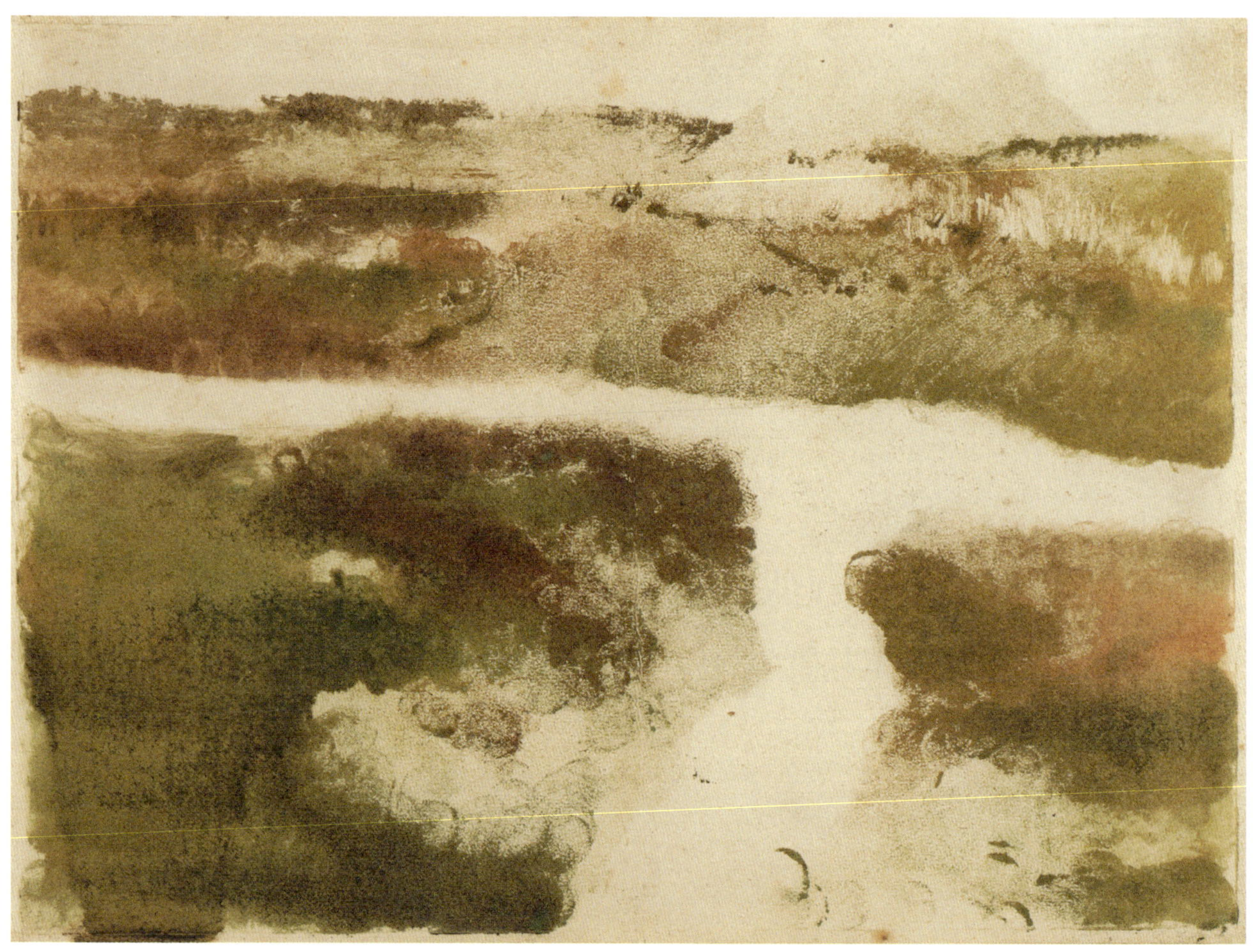

132. *Mountain Landscape* (*Paysage dans la montagne*). 1890
Monotype in oil on paper
Plate: 11 15⁄16 × 15 ¾ in. (30.4 × 40 cm), sheet: 12 ¼ × 16 ⅛ in. (31.1 × 41 cm)
Los Angeles County Museum of Art. Purchased with funds provided
by the Garrett Corporation

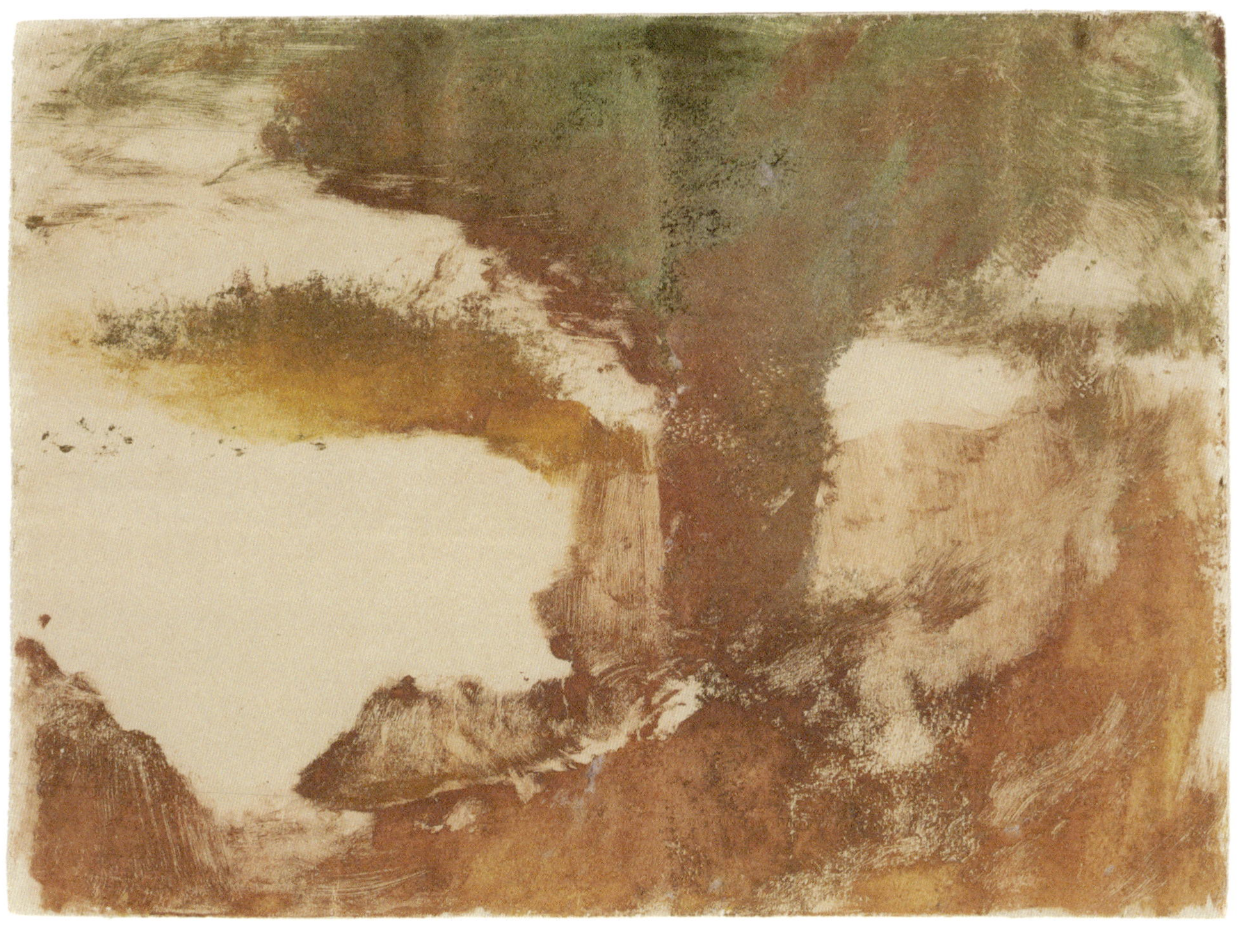

133. *Landscape* (*Paysage*). 1890–92
Monotype in oil on paper
Plate: 11 ½ × 15 ½ in. (29.2 × 39.4 cm)
Harvard Art Museums/Fogg Museum, Cambridge, Massachusetts.
Partial and promised gift of Emily Rauh Pulitzer in honor of Marjorie B. Cohn

134. *Autumn Effect* (*Effet d'automne dans la montagne*), 1890
Monotype in oil on paper
Plate: 11 13⁄16 × 15 13⁄16 in. (30 × 40.2 cm), sheet: 11 13⁄16 × 15 13⁄16 in. (30 × 40.2 cm)
Museum of Fine Arts, Boston. Gift of her children in memory of Elizabeth Paine Metcalf

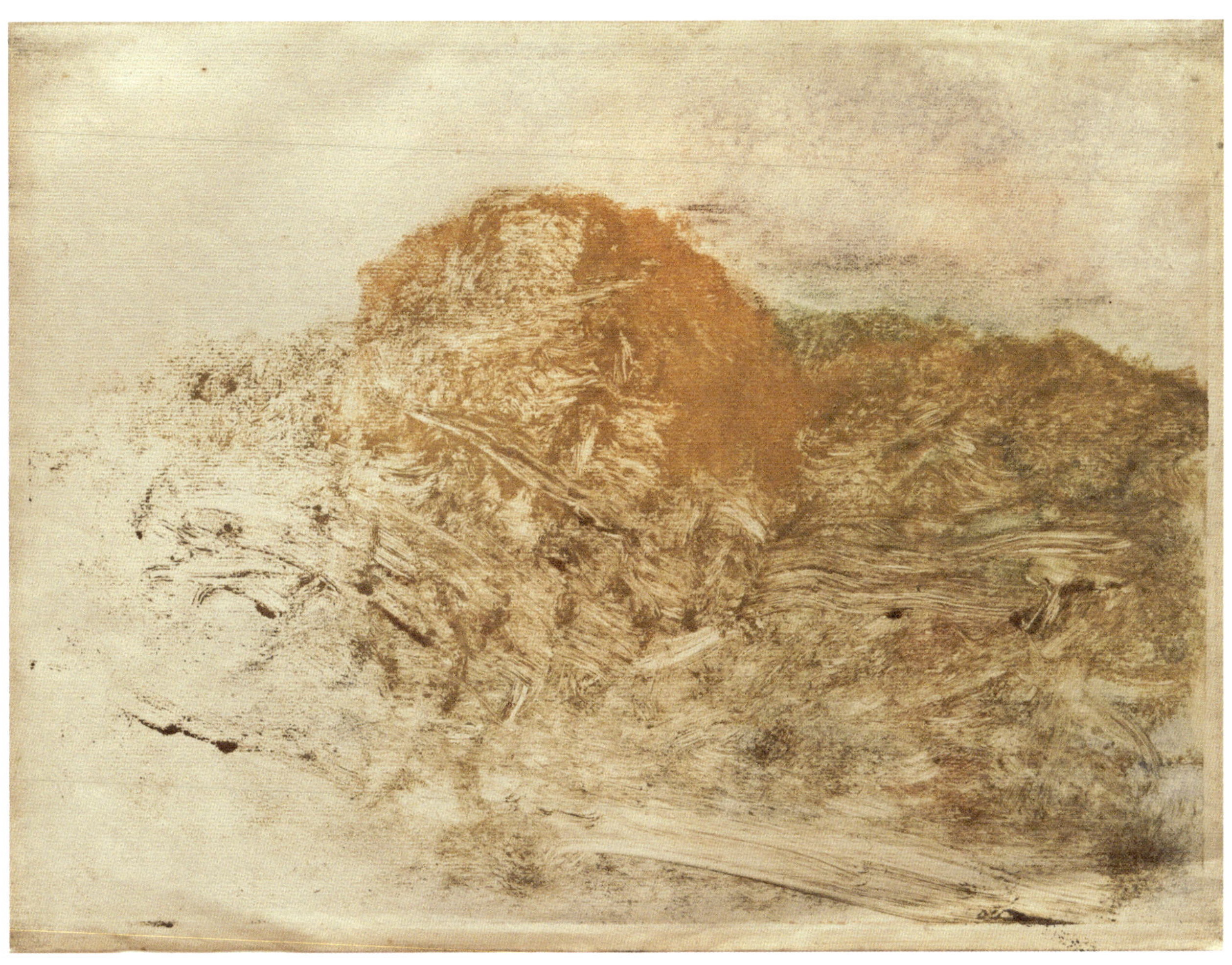

135. *The Ochre Hill* (*Effet de montagne*). 1890
Monotype in oil on paper
Plate: 11 ¾ × 15 9⁄16 in. (29.9 × 39.5 cm)
Private collection

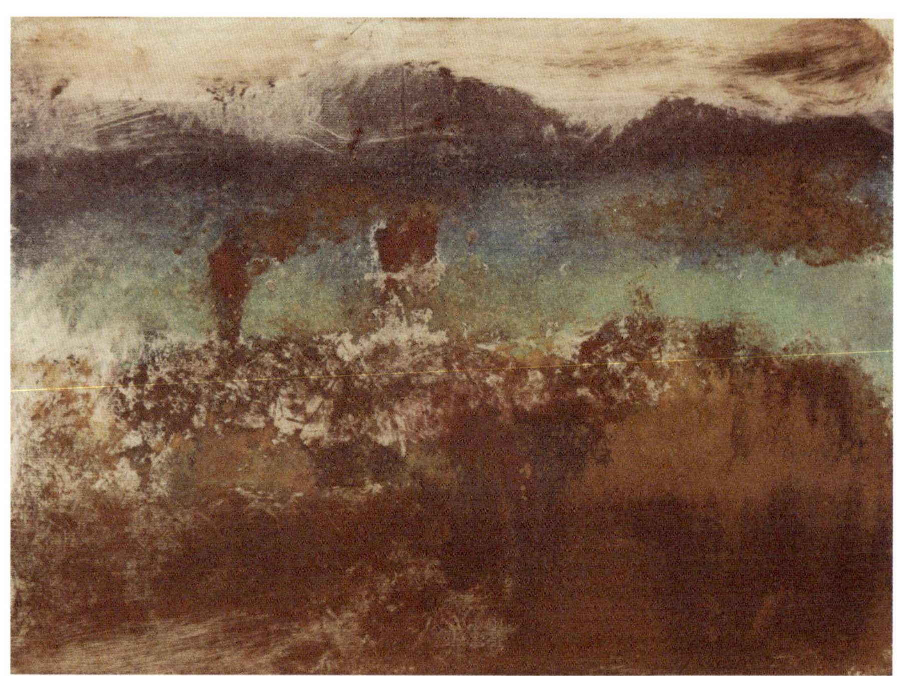

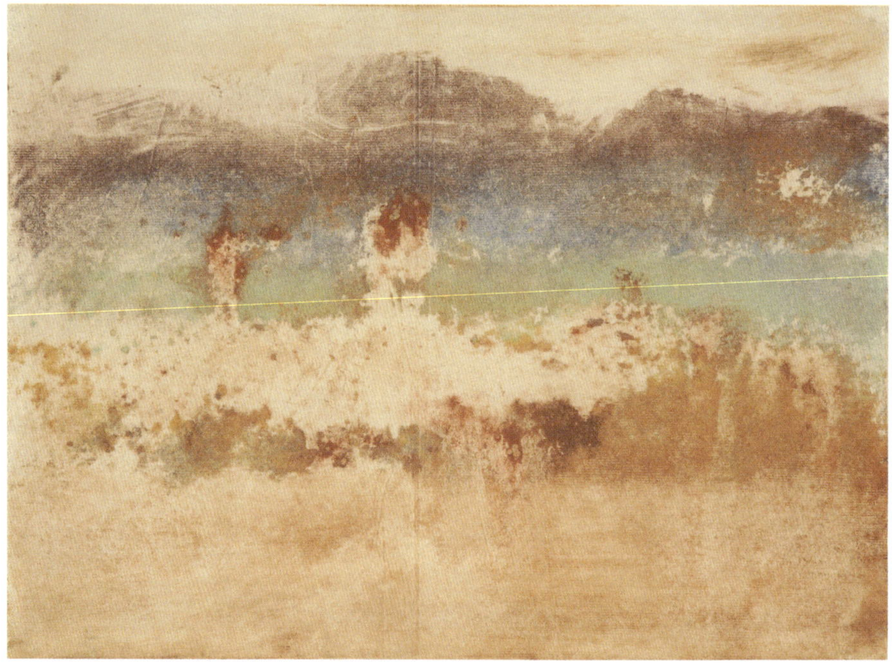

136. *Autumn Landscape* (*L'Estérel*). 1890
Monotype in oil on paper
Plate: 11 ⅞ × 15 ¾ in. (30.2 × 40 cm),
sheet: 12 ½ × 16 ¼ in. (31.8 × 41.3 cm)
Private collection

137. *Autumn Landscape* (*L'Estérel*). 1890
Monotype in oil on paper
Plate: 11 ⅞ × 15 ⅝ in. (30.2 × 39.7 cm),
sheet: 12 ⅛ × 16 ¹⁄₁₆ in. (30.8 × 40.8 cm)
Norton Simon Museum, Pasadena, California.
Museum Purchase, B. Gerald Cantor Fund

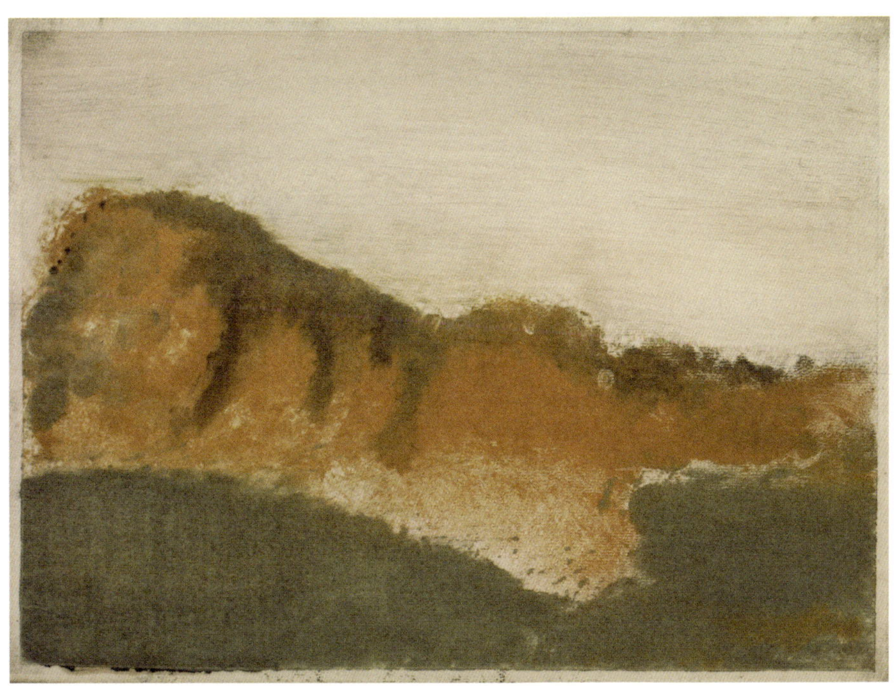

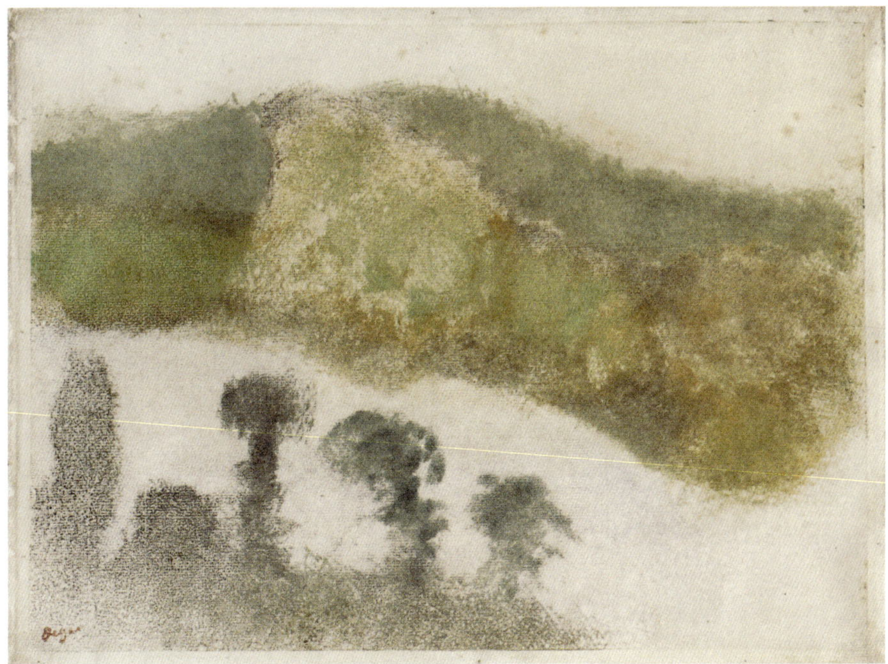

138. *Cap Hornu near Saint-Valery-sur-Somme* (*Le Cap Hornu près Saint-Valery-sur-Somme*). c. 1890–93
Monotype in oil on paper
Plate: 11 ¾ × 15 ¹¹⁄₁₆ in. (29.9 × 39.9 cm)
British Museum, London. Bequeathed by Campbell Dodgson

139. *Mountains and Valley* (*Montagnes et vallon*). 1890
Monotype in oil on paper
Plate: 12 ½ × 16 ⁷⁄₁₆ in. (31.8 × 41.8 cm), sheet: 15 ⅜ × 19 ⁵⁄₁₆ in. (39 × 49 cm)
Private collection, Switzerland

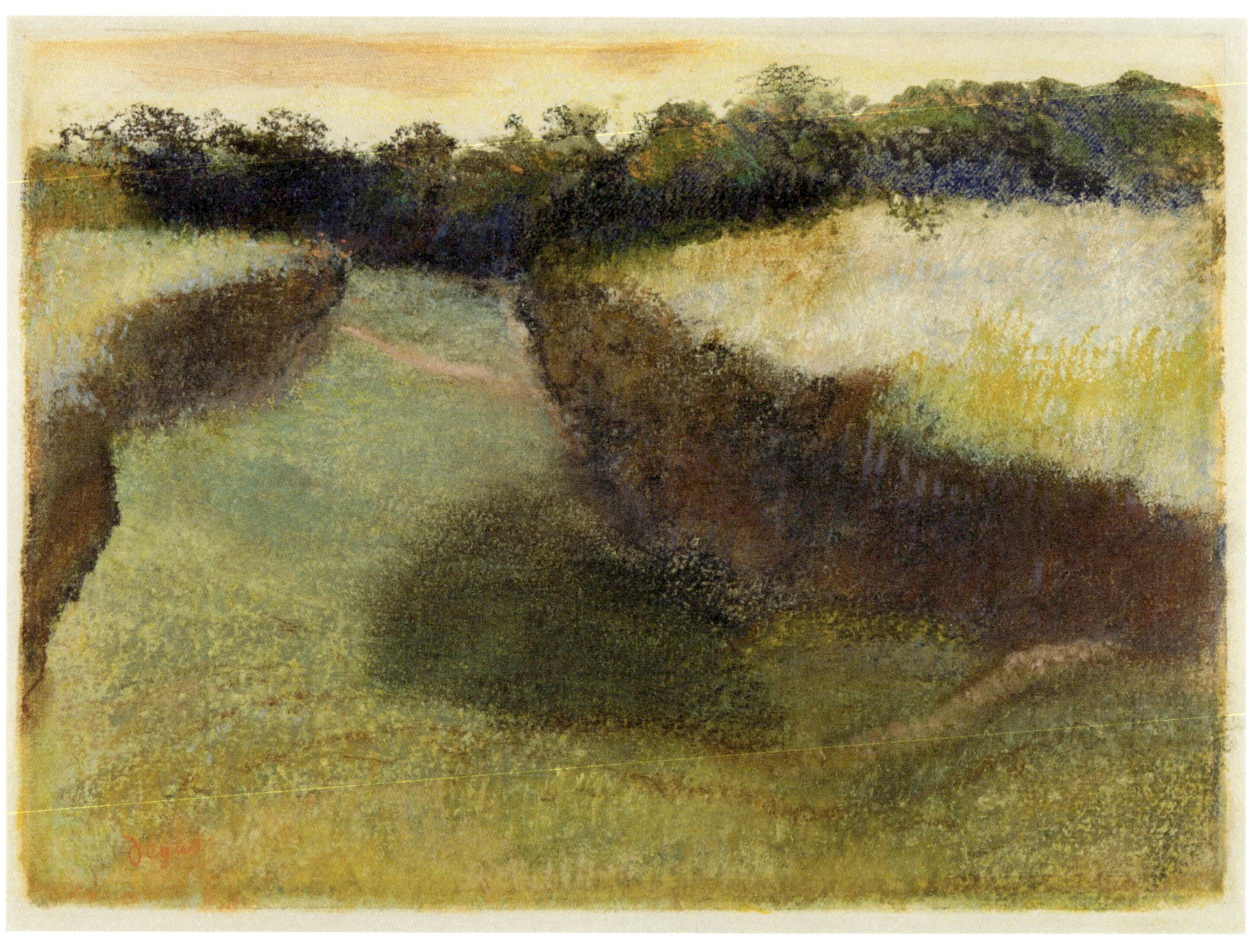

140. *Wheatfield and Line of Trees* (*Champ de blé et ligne d'arbres*). 1890
Pastel over monotype in oil on paper
9 13⁄16 × 13 3⁄8 in. (25 × 34 cm)
Private collection

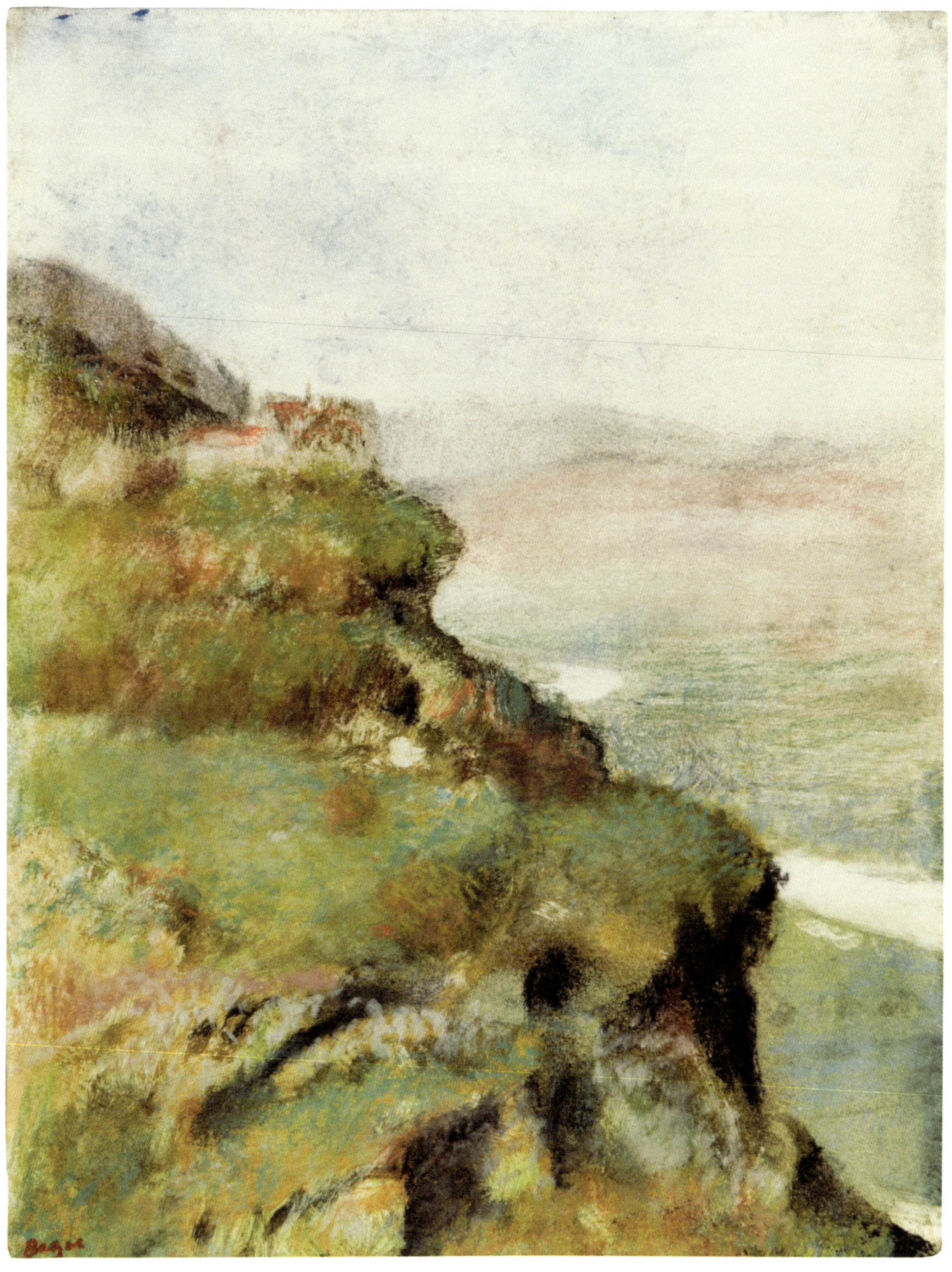

141. *Landscape with Rocky Cliffs* (*Rochers au bord d'une rivière*). 1890
Pastel over monotype in oil on paper
15 ¾ × 11 7/1 in. (40 × 29 cm)
Private collection

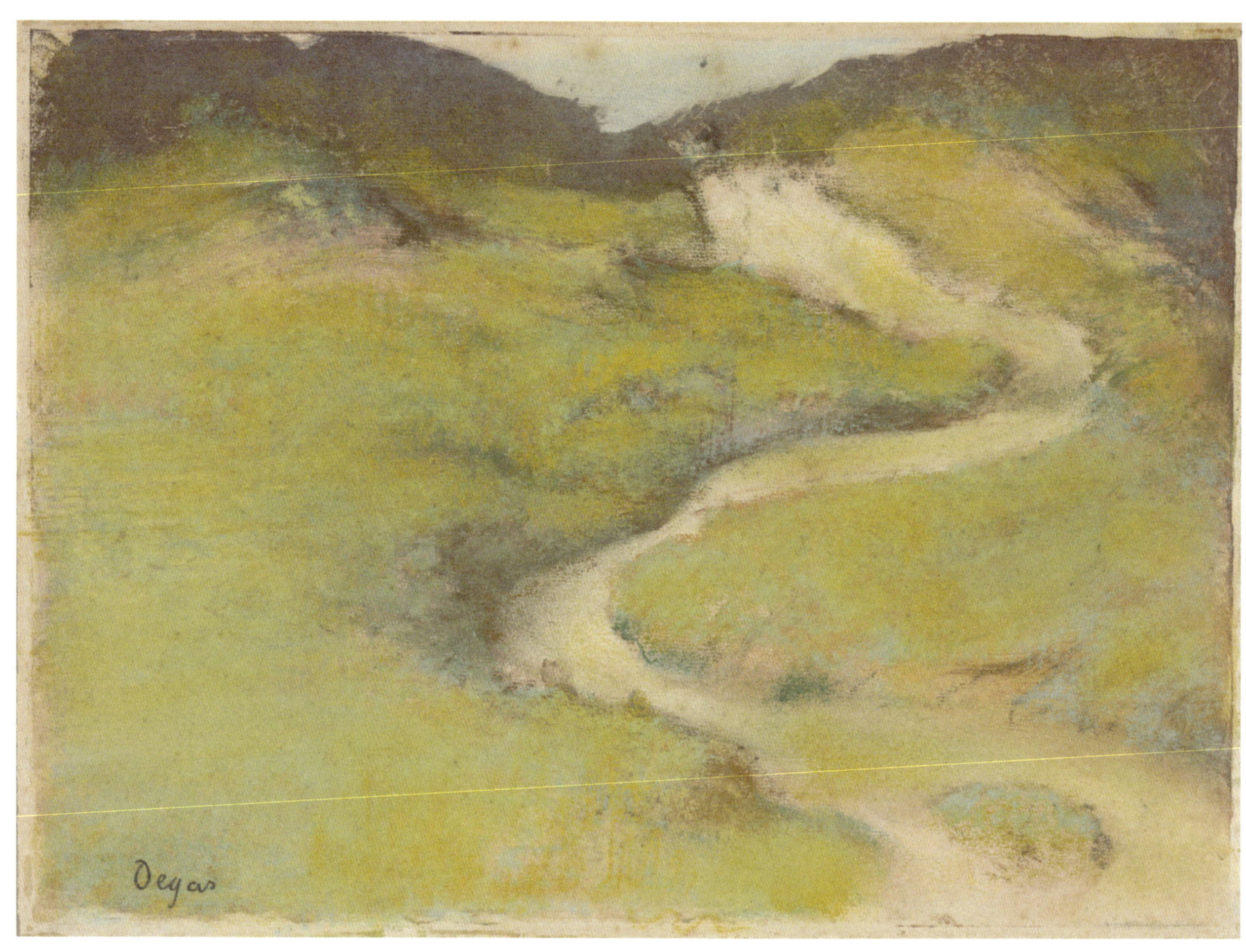

142. *Pathway in a Field* (*Sentier dans la prairie*). 1890
Pastel over monotype in oil on paper
11 13⁄16 × 15 9⁄16 in. (30 × 39.5 cm)
Yale University Art Gallery, New Haven, Connecticut. Katharine Ordway Fund

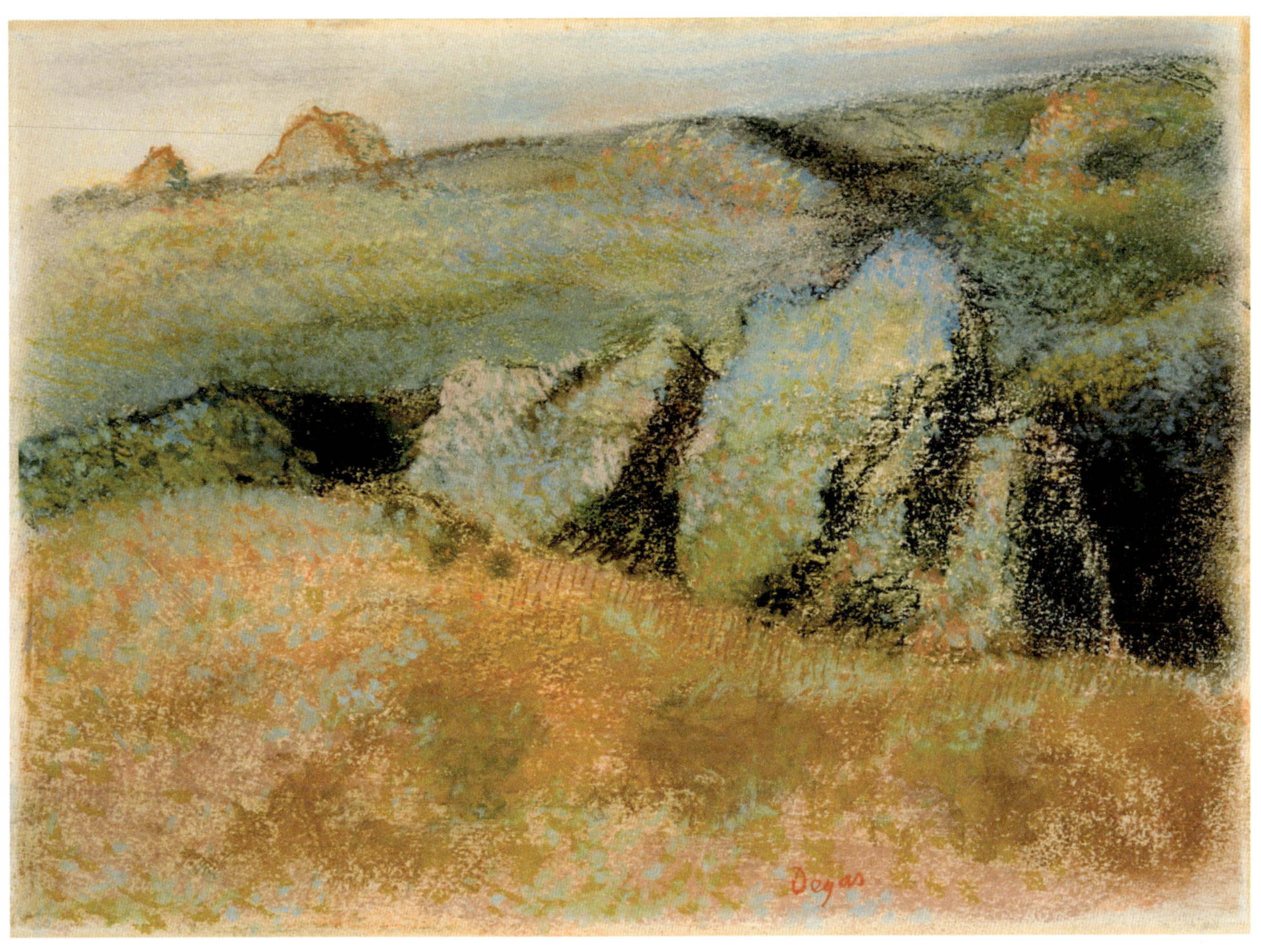

143. *Landscape with Rocks* (*Paysage avec rochers*). 1892
Pastel over monotype in oil on paper
Plate: 9 ¾ × 13 ⅜ in. (24.8 × 34 cm), sheet: 10 ⅛ × 13 9/16 in. (25.7 × 34.4 cm)
High Museum of Art, Atlanta. Purchase with High Museum of Art Enhancement Fund

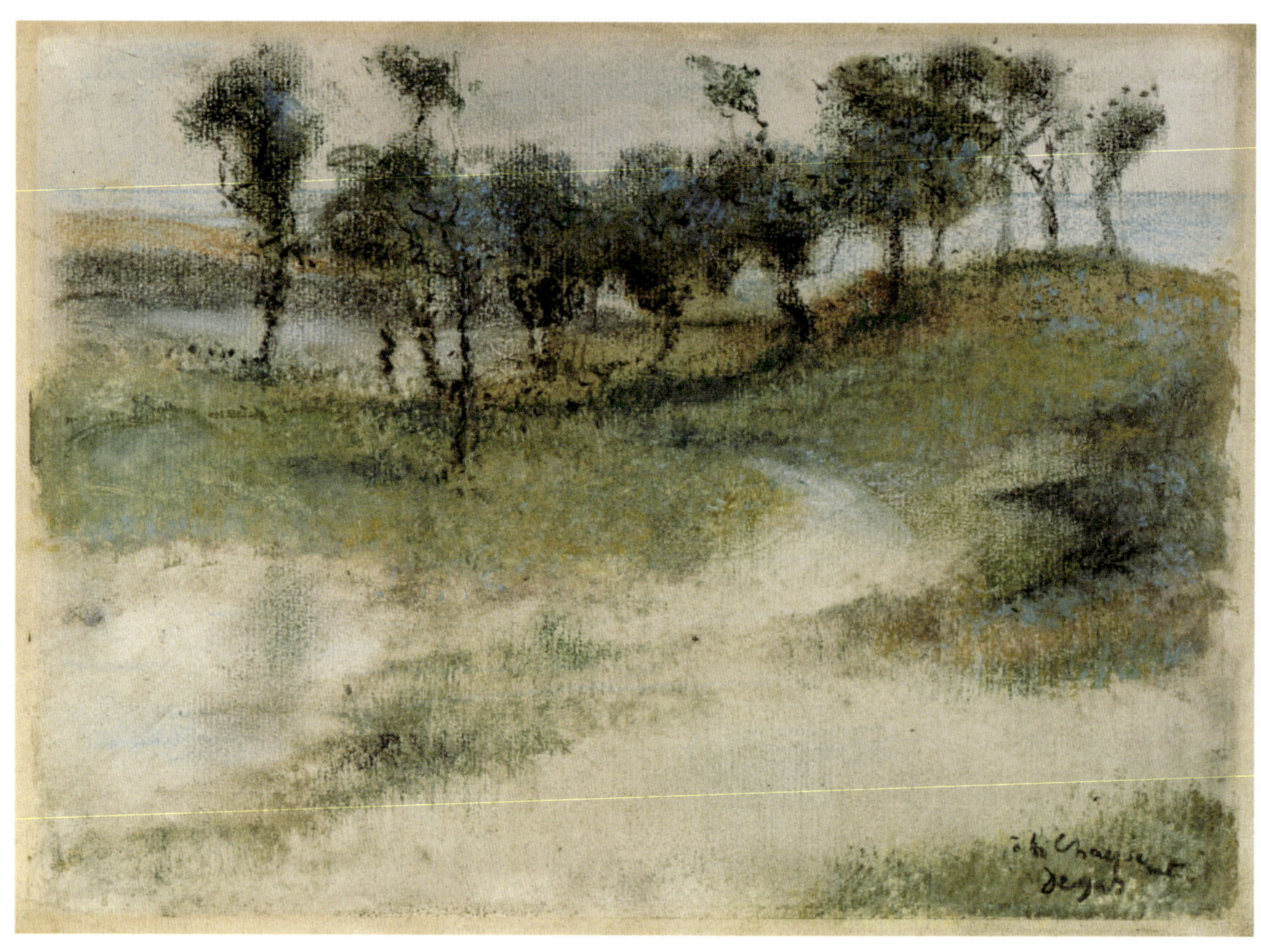

144. *Landscape by the Sea* (*Paysage en bord de mer*). 1892
Pastel over monotype in oil on paper
Plate: 9 15/16 × 13 9/16 in. (25.3 × 34.5 cm), sheet: 10 5/8 × 14 3/16 in. (27 × 36 cm)
Musée d'art et d'histoire, Neuchâtel

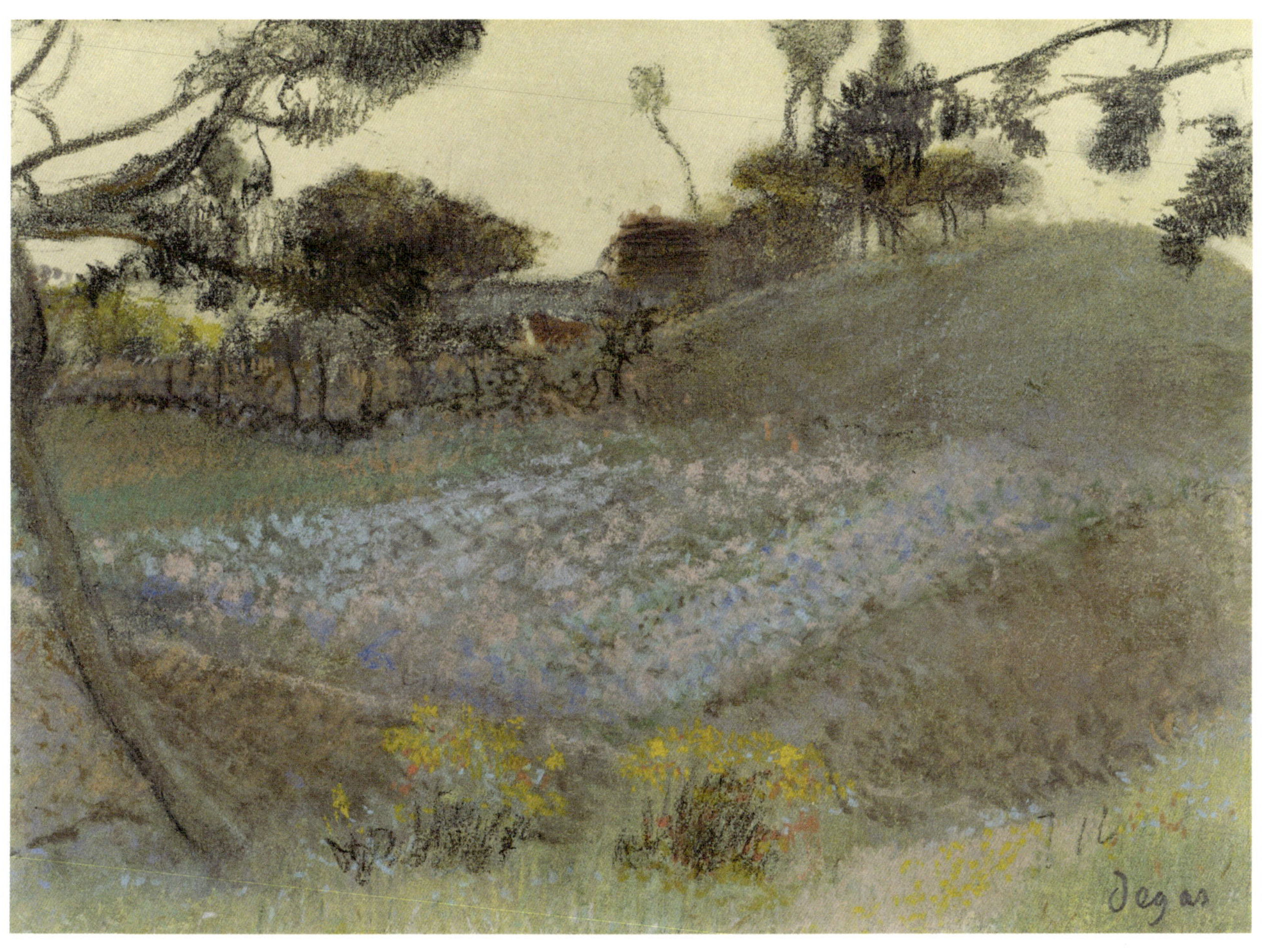

145. *The Field of Flax* (*Le Champ de lin*). 1892
Pastel over monotype in oil on paper
9 13⁄16 × 13 3⁄8 in. (25 × 34 cm)
From the collection of Wendy and Leonard Goldberg

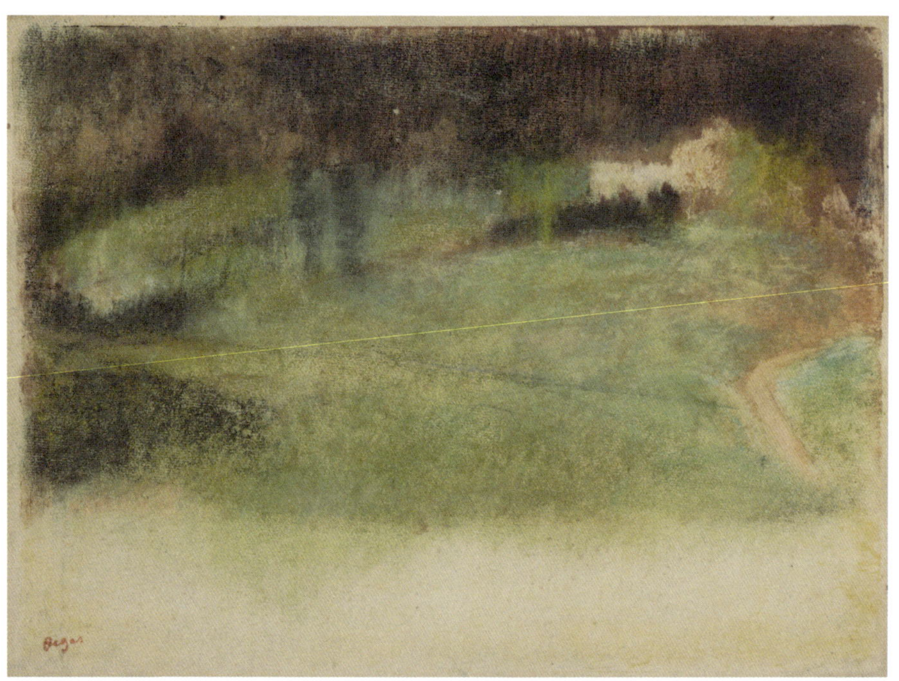

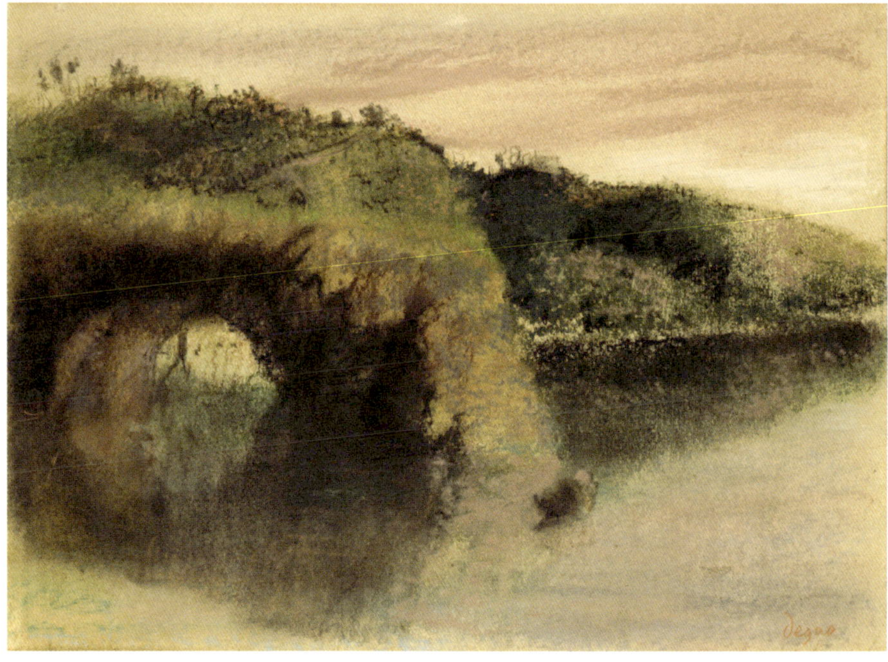

146. *River Banks* (*Bords de rivière*). 1890
Pastel over monotype in oil on paper
11 13⁄16 × 15 ¾ in. (30 × 40 cm)
Private collection, Switzerland.
Courtesy Galerie Fischer, Lucerne

147. *River Banks* (*Bords de rivière*). 1890
Pastel over monotype in oil on paper
11 13⁄16 × 15 ¾ in. (30 × 40 cm)
Private collection

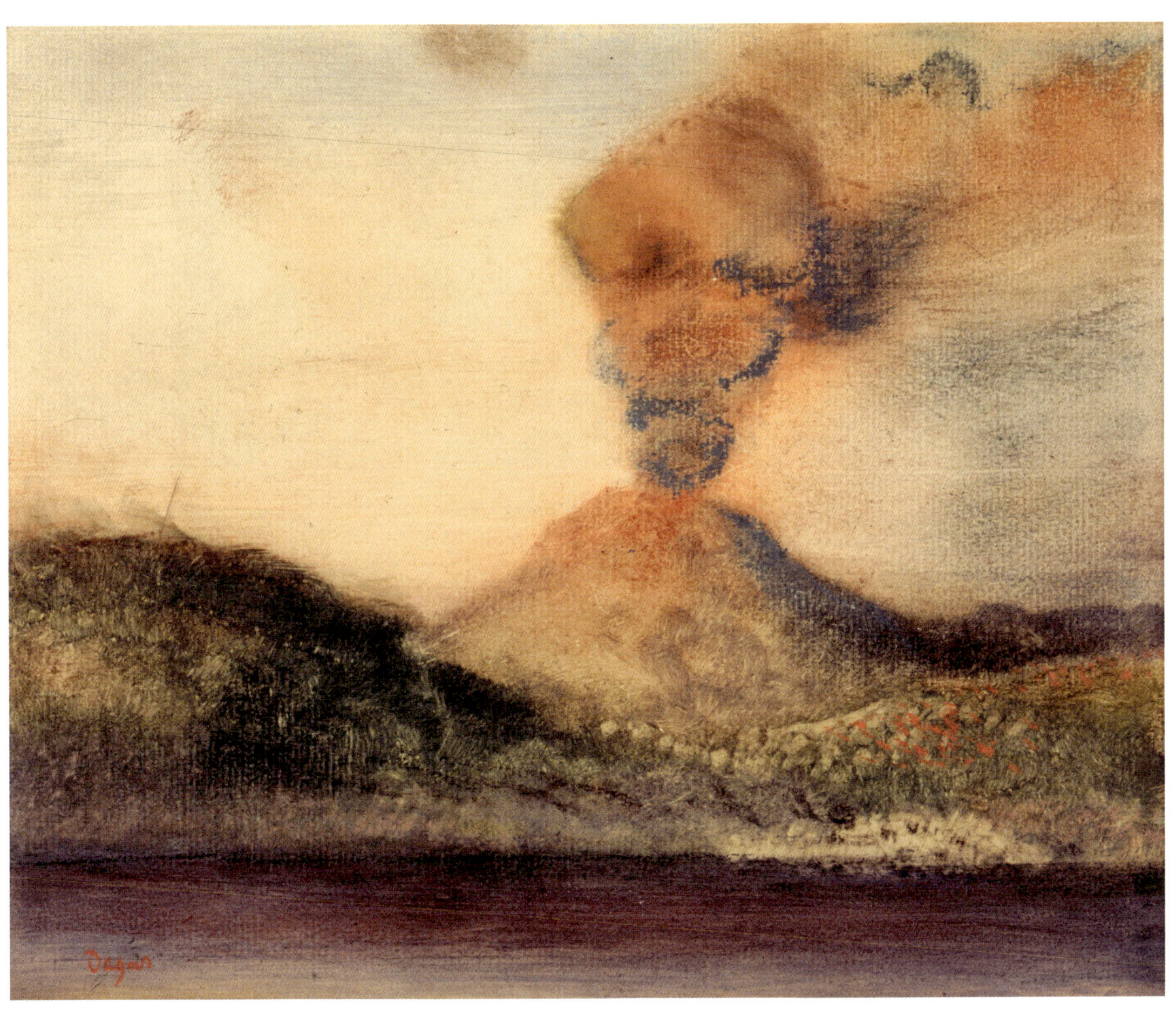

148. *Vesuvius* (*Le Vésuve*). 1892
Pastel over monotype in oil on paper
Plate: 9 13⁄16 × 11 13⁄16 in. (25 × 30 cm), sheet: 10 9⁄16 × 12 ½ in. (26.9 × 31.8 cm)
Private collection

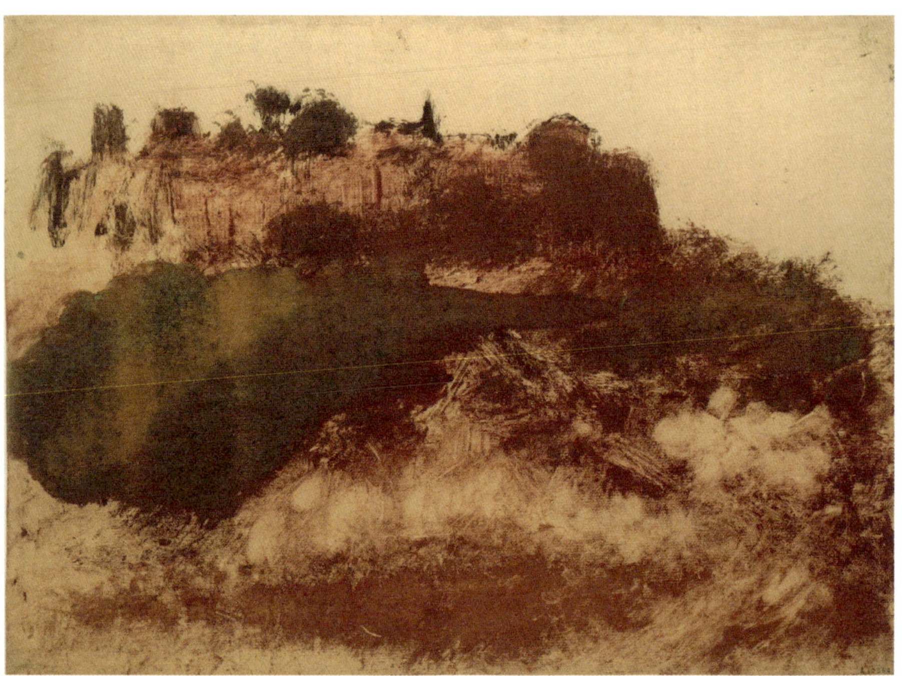

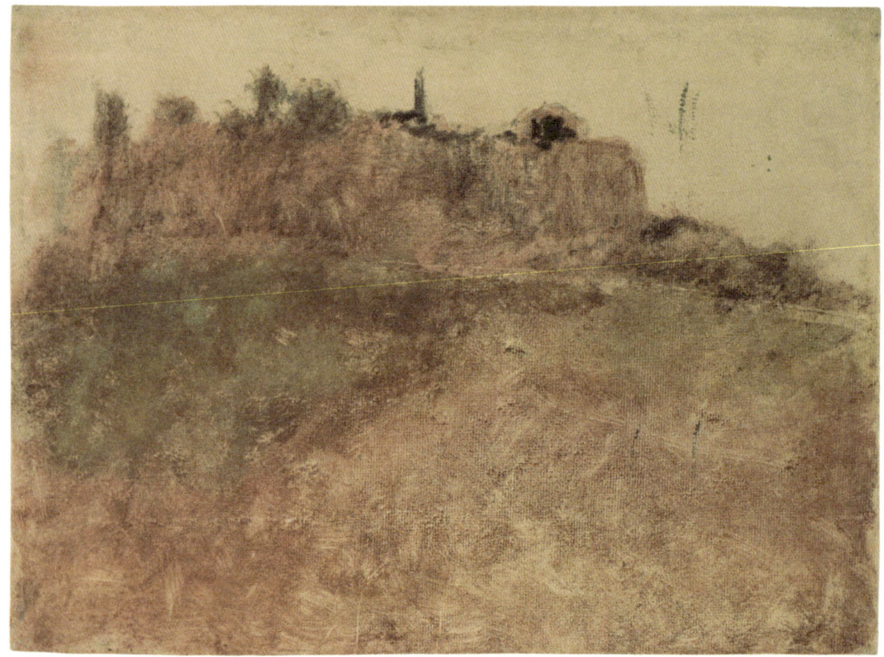

149. *Village in l'Estérel* (*Village dans l'Estérel*). 1890
Monotype in oil on paper
Plate: 11 13⁄16 × 16 ¾ in. (30 × 42.5 cm)
Bibliothèque Nationale de France, Paris

150. *Estérel Village* (*Village dans l'Estérel*). 1890
Monotype in oil on paper
Plate: 11 ¾ × 15 11⁄16 in. (29.9 × 39.9 cm)
The Cleveland Museum of Art. Fiftieth anniversary gift of The Print Club of Cleveland

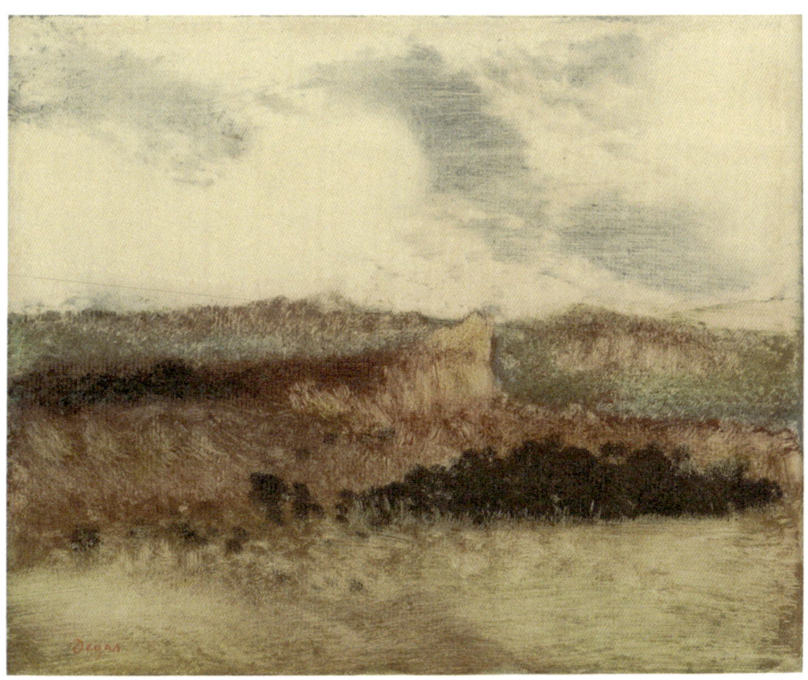

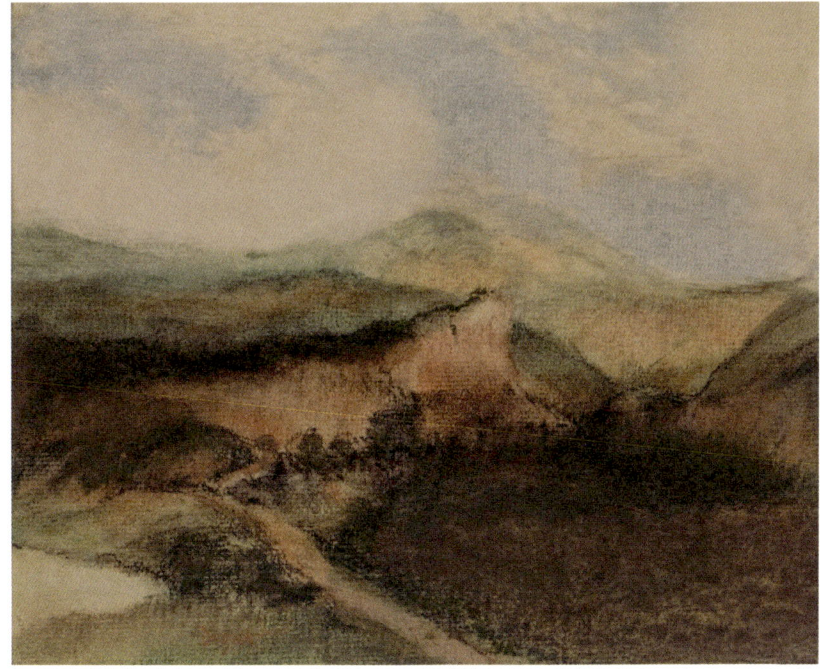

151. *Landscape* (*Paysage*). 1892
Pastel over monotype in oil on paper
Plate: 9 ¾ × 11 ¾ in. (24.8 × 29.9 cm)
Private collection

152. *Landscape* (*Paysage*). 1890–93
Pastel over monotype in oil on paper
Plate: 9 ½ × 11 ½ in. (24.1 × 29.2 cm)
Mottisfont Abbey, The National Trust. The Derek Hill Bequest, through the National Art-Collections Fund

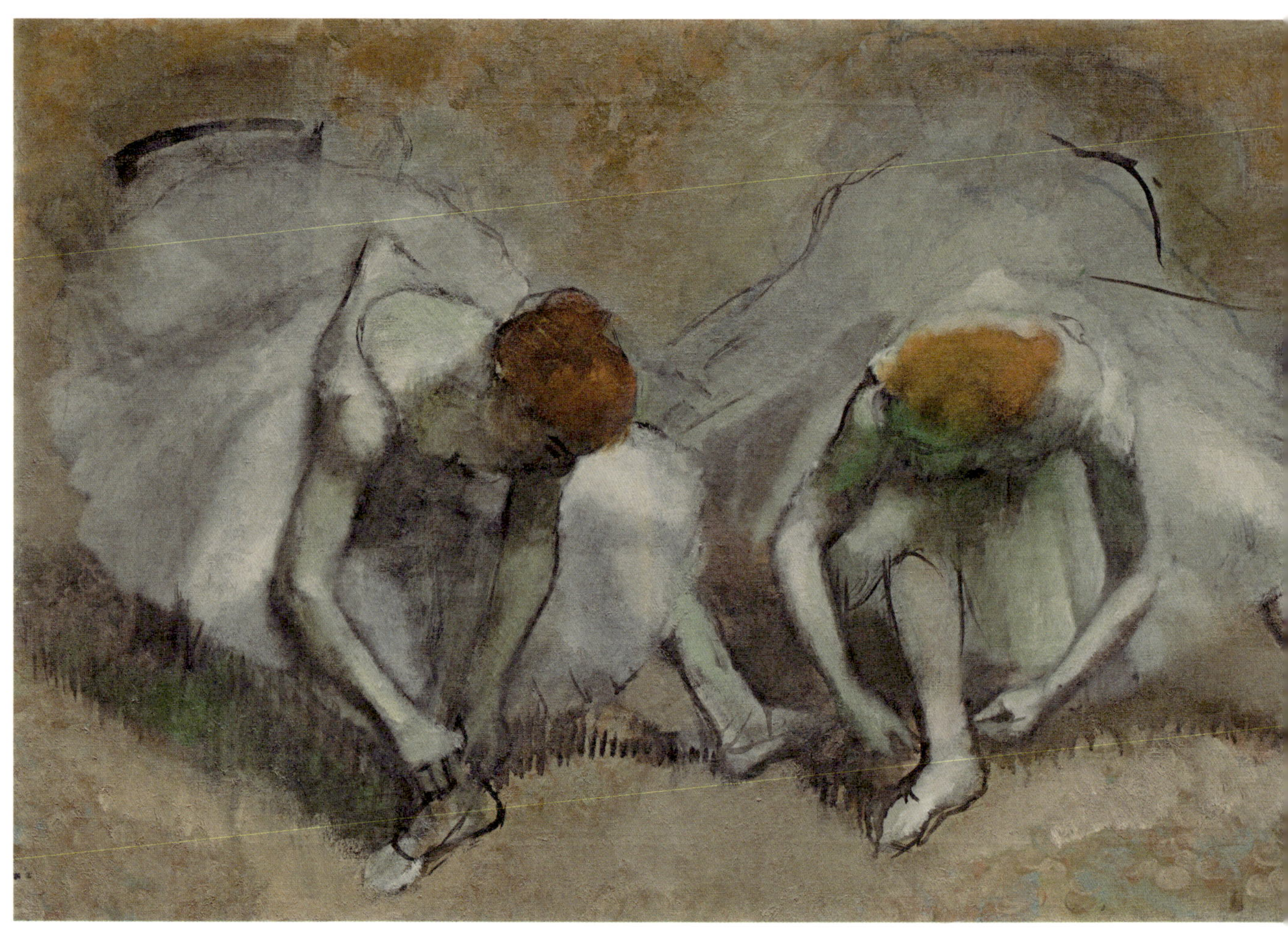

153. *Frieze of Dancers* (*Danseuses attachant leurs sandales*). c. 1895
Oil on canvas
27 9/16 × 78 15/16 in. (70 × 200.5 cm)
The Cleveland Museum of Art. Gift of the Hanna Fund

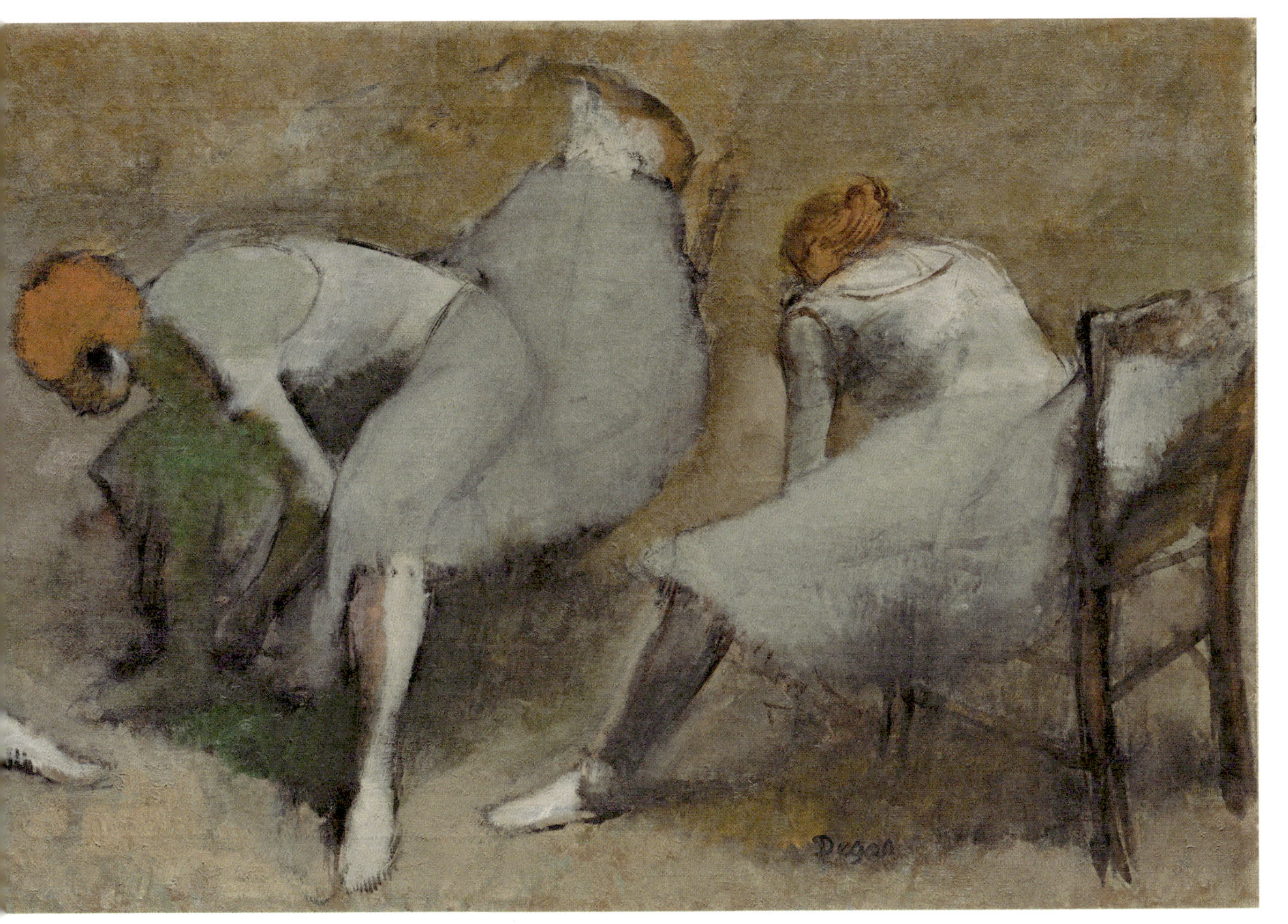
Degas

Frieze of Dancers

Jill DeVonyar

Out of the forming, dissolving and re-forming patterns created by the same set of limbs, as out of the movements which echo each other at equal or harmonious intervals, comes decoration in time, *just as the spatial repetition of motifs, or their symmetry, gives rise to* decoration in space.

—Paul Valéry, *Degas danse dessin*, 1936

Decades after befriending Edgar Degas, Paul Valéry published a series of recollections entitled *Degas danse dessin*. As the narrative unfolds, Valéry's attention shifts between his personal memories of the artist and what he describes as a "variety of ideas" that "crystallized" around Degas in his own mind.[1] Foremost among these ideas were Valéry's meditations on dance and drawing, two of Degas's most enduring preoccupations. The passage cited above forms part of Valéry's eloquent disquisition on dance, but it might also be understood as an evocation of Degas's painting *Frieze of Dancers* (*Danseuses attachant leurs sandales*, c. 1895; plate 153), where the arrangement of billowing tutus creates cadenced "patterns," and the "echoing" shapes of bodies are arranged at "harmonious intervals." Valéry's observation that repetition and inversion are characteristic of dance also applies to much of Degas's oeuvre, where figures mirror each other like photograph and negative, or monotype and counterproof.

The parallels between Valéry's text and Degas's painting can be taken even further. In *Frieze of Dancers*—one of the artist's largest canvases—the poses of the ballerinas are almost identical, and apart from their hair color they are indistinguishable from one another. The most significant difference between them is the direction in which each faces, giving the impression that the four figures represent one dancer pivoted in space. Such a dynamic "repetition of motifs," to borrow Valéry's phrase, occurs nowhere else in Degas's oeuvre on such a monumental scale. From the 1870s onward, Degas made smaller oils and pastels of comparably arranged ballerinas—see, for example, *Three Dancers in the Foyer* (*Trois danseuses au foyer*, 1892–95; plate 167)—but his most concentrated experiment of this kind took the form of drawings: specifically, nine sheets of paper that together contain a total of twenty-six studies of Marie van Goethem, the model for his celebrated sculpture the *Little Dancer Aged Fourteen* (1878–81).[2] The nearly two dozen points of view contained in these drawings constitute an extraordinary two-dimensional account of Marie in the round.[3] Though less thorough in the recording of its subject, *Frieze of Dancers* is a late incarnation of an undertaking Degas had outlined when he began work on the *Little Dancer* in the late 1870s: "Do a suite of movements of arms in dance, or of legs that would not move, turning oneself around," he wrote in a notebook, "study from all perspectives a figure or an object, it doesn't matter which."[4] This strategy yielded sequences of images that appear to depict a subject in movement, much like the figures in action captured

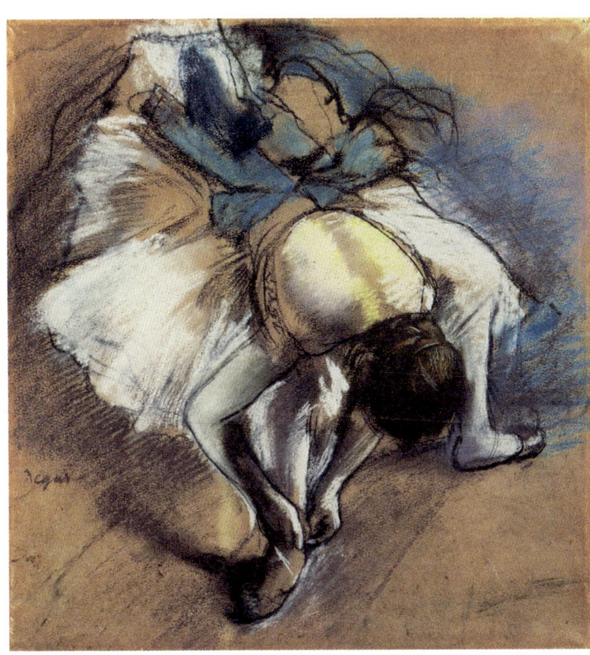

1. Hilaire-Germain-Edgar Degas. *Dancer Adjusting Her Slipper (Danseuse rajustant son chausson).* c. 1885. Pastel and chalk on paper, 18 9⁄16 × 18 9⁄16 in. (47.2 × 43 cm). Private collection

in serial photographs by the artist's contemporaries Eadweard Muybridge and Etienne-Jules Marey.[5] In *Frieze of Dancers* and other pictures by Degas this was achieved through duplication and variation, by reproducing a motif and changing the perspective from which it is viewed.

The frieze also represents a persistent theme in Degas's dance oeuvre: ballerinas adjusting their slippers. They feature in multifigure compositions set in classrooms or theater wings (see, e.g., *Two Dancers [Deux danseuses*, 1905; plate 162), and in focused studies of solitary dancers, such as several pastels from the 1880s showing a ballerina bending over to adjust a shoe. In the four examples illustrated here (figs. 1, 2, plates 154, 155), the gestures, coiffures, and physiques of the women are similar enough for them to be the same person, and as in *Frieze of Dancers* they are observed from a succession of angles.[6] Careful comparison reveals other striking correspondences: all of the ballerinas are seated with legs splayed and leaning forward to tie her right shoe. These resemblances link the painting and the pastels to a larger family of pictures that feature similarly occupied ballerinas; additional relatives include a pair of studies from the 1890s for the two ballerinas at right in the frieze, and several works on paper that were made during the same period as the pastels.[7] In these pictures Degas visits and revisits an integral part of the classical dancer's daily ritual, the tying of shoe ribbons, implicitly highlighting the most distinctive aspect of her craft: pointe work.

Valéry refers to "toe dancing" in an unexpected context in a section of *Degas danse dessin* entitled "Horse, Dancer and Photograph" (*Cheval, danse et photo*). He begins with an analogy that Degas had alluded to in a sonnet many years before: because a "horse walks on its toes," Valéry asserts, "no animal is closer to a première danseuse . . . than a perfectly balanced thoroughbred."[8] Above this statement in Valéry's 1936 book is an illustration of a sketch by Degas, showing not a dancer en pointe but one leaning forward in a chair (fig. 3). This drawing too is part of the "family" of images related to *Frieze of Dancers*, and the ballerina portrayed may well be the model upon whom the figure at far right in the canvas was based.[9] A second drawing—in this case heightened with pastel—exists for the same dancer, and another for the woman seated next to her, and both sheets are nearly the same size as three of the 1880s pastels, suggesting that all derive from the same project.[10] The practice of transporting figures from one composition to another was standard for Degas; the lineage of the pair at right in the frieze can be traced back to works on paper that were made around ten years before it was painted.[11]

Repetitions of motif are evident in pictures by Degas that predate his monotypes, but are especially conspicuous after he began making these technically distinctive prints. As is often pointed out, his monotypes could assume multiple lives: by generating increasingly paler pulls from a single plate; by

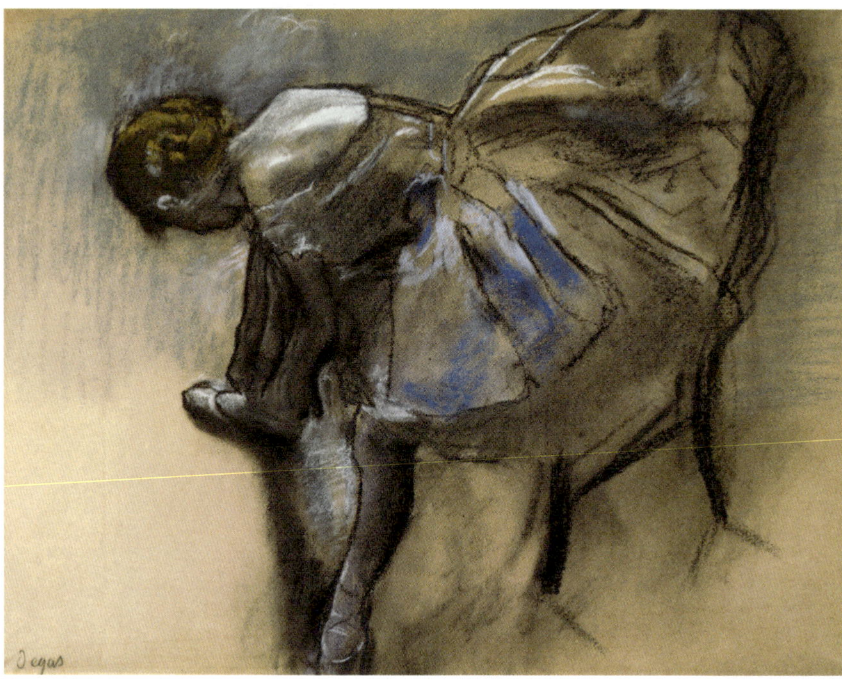

2. Hilaire-Germain-Edgar Degas. *Seated Dancer Tying Her Slipper (Danseuse Attachant son Chausson).* c. 1880. Pastel on paper, 18 ⅛ × 24 ⅛ in. (46.5 × 61.3 cm). Private collection

transforming them to varying degrees with pastel; and by producing monotypes from monotypes, known as counterproofs, yielding reversed images (e.g. plates 106, 107). Equivalents to these printed reiterations proliferate in Degas's late drawings and pastels, but only occasionally appear in paintings such as *Frieze of Dancers*, where the pair of figures at left verge on mirror images of each other, and where changes in viewpoint—ostensibly showing the same individual from front, side, and back—effect a sense of "flipping" that recalls the reversals in counterproofs. Other features of the frieze correspond with certain monotypes heightened with pastel, notably the landscape prints. In the background of the painting, muted earth tones mingle with dull greens, while the figures are rendered in light to medium shades of gray. Over these somber hues Degas applied intense grass green to indicate shadows and a range of coppery hues, including an almost jarring orange, to describe the ballerinas' hair. These additions significantly energize the largely monochromatic frieze, as do the vivid colors that enliven such landscape monotypes as *Landscape with Rocky Cliffs* (*Rochers au bord d'une rivière*, 1890; plate 141).

One of the most unusual aspects of *Frieze of Dancers* is the setting—or, more accurately, the lack of one. In the vast majority of Degas's ballet scenes the action unfolds in a specific space—such as a classroom, the wings, or the stage—described in great detail in some pictures and subtly indicated in others. But in *Frieze of Dancers* the space is indeterminate; only a few shadows, the positions of the dancers' chairs, and the gravity of their bodies suggest where they and the ground might be. The elusiveness of the setting can be accounted for, at least in part, by the artist's handling of his medium: liquid swathes of paint and energetic brushings and daubings animate the ballerinas' surroundings, but they do not illuminate their context. In contrast to the flat and vague *mise en scène*, the figures are clearly three-dimensional: touched with the brightest of whites and defined by emphatic contours, their bodies are fully realized and their skirts float around them like clouds. Again, the relationship of the ballerinas to their environs is reminiscent of the pastelized landscapes made by Degas in the early 1890s, not long before he painted *Frieze of Dancers*.[12] In the canvas, coherent forms emerge from an amorphous background, and in many pastelized monotypes an amorphous ground is given more coherent form (plates 125, 142). Although the two projects differ vastly in terms of process and technique—one involved developing figures and ground in tandem with an oil-based medium, the other generating a print and subsequently transform-

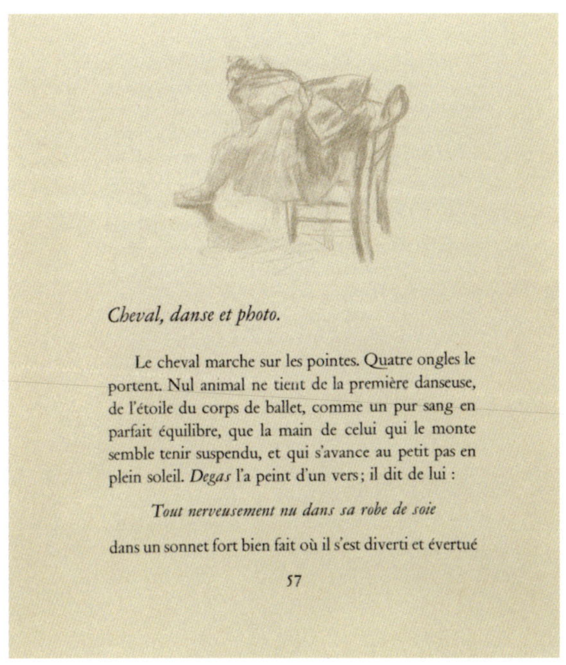

Cheval, danse et photo.

Le cheval marche sur les pointes. Quatre ongles le portent. Nul animal ne tient de la première danseuse, de l'étoile du corps de ballet, comme un pur sang en parfait équilibre, que la main de celui qui le monte semble tenir suspendu, et qui s'avance au petit pas en plein soleil. *Degas* l'a peint d'un vers; il dit de lui :

Tout nerveusement nu dans sa robe de soie

dans un sonnet fort bien fait où il s'est diverti et évertué

57

3. Page from Paul Valéry. *Degas danse dessin.* Paris: Ambroise Vollard, 1936

ing it with chalky pigments—*Frieze of Dancers* and the monotypes represent comparable endeavors: both are a mixture of definition and ambiguity, a combination Degas often pursued in later life.

The title of *Frieze of Dancers* reflects two of the work's most prominent features: the pronounced horizontal format of the canvas and the ballerinas' marked sculptural character. Like processions of figures found in ancient reliefs, the arrangement of dancers is rhythmic and carefully syncopated, and their progress across the scene is sedate. This evocation of "dance" is as compelling as Valéry's, and the resonance between them may be more than coincidental. It is possible that Valéry saw the painting in Degas's studio, where he was a welcome visitor from the mid-1890s and beyond. Perhaps the writer's musings on the dance were inflected by works such as *Frieze of Dancers*, where limbs create lyrical patterns that repeat or mirror each other, and where bodies carve space and mark time.

1. Paul Valéry, "Degas Dance Drawing," in *Degas Manet Morisot*, trans. David Paul (New York: Pantheon Books, 1960), p. 5. The epigraph to this essay appears on p. 16 of this text, which was first published as *Degas danse dessin* by Ambroise Vollard, Paris, in 1936. For excerpts published previously see *Degas Manet Morisot*, p. 235, n. 1.
2. For other works showing identical figures from different perspectives see Paul-André Lemoisne, *Degas et son oeuvre*, 4 vols. (Paris: Paul Brame and C. M. de Hauke, Arts et Métiers Graphiques, 1946), nos. 473, 486, 645, and 704. For drawings related to the *Little Dancer Aged Fourteen* see Lemoisne nos. 586 bis, 586 ter, and 599; Vente III, April 7–9, 1919, *Catalogue des tableaux, pastels, et dessins par Edgar Degas et provenant de son atelier. . .* , (Paris: Galerie Georges Petit, 1919), nos. 149.1, 277, 341.2, and 386; and Vente IV, July 2–4, 1919, *Catalogue des tableaux, pastels, et dessins par Edgar Degas et provenant de son atelier . . .* , (Paris: Galerie Georges Petit, 1919), no. 287.a.
3. See Richard Kendall and Jill DeVonyar, *Degas and the Ballet: Picturing Movement*, exh. cat. (London: Royal Academy Books, 2011), pp. 70-84.
4. Degas, notebook 30, p. 65, in *The Notebooks of Edgar Degas*, ed. Theodore Reff (Oxford: Clarendon Press, 1976), 1:134.
5. On *Frieze of Dancers* in the context of early serial photography see Marta Braun, *Picturing Time: The Work of Etienne-Jules Marey (1830–1904)* (Chicago and London: The University of Chicago Press, 1992), pp. 272–73; Kendall and DeVonyar, *Degas and the Ballet*, pp. 125–27; Aaron Scharf, *Art and Photography*, 1968 (second rev. ed. Harmondsworth: Pelican Books, 1974), pp. 202–4; and Kirk Varnedoe, *A Fine Disregard: What Makes Modern Art Modern* (London: Thames & Hudson, 1990), pp. 109–26.
6. Figs. 1 and 2 are respectively nos. 913 and 600 in Lemoisne. For other works in the series see note 7 below.
7. The similarities of pose between *Frieze of Dancers* and one of the pastels in question, *Dancer Adjusting Her Slipper* (fig. 1), were first noted in George Shackelford, *Degas: The Dancers*, exh. cat. (Washington: The National Gallery of Art, 1984), p. 103. The 1890s studies are Vente II, *Catalogue des tableaux, pastels, et dessins par Edgar Degas et provenant de son atelier....*, (Paris: Galerie Georges Petit, December 11–13, 1918), nos. II:272 and III:332. The 1880s pastels are Lemoisne nos. 599 bis, 600, 906, 907, and 908, and an uncatalogued pastel in the National Gallery of Victoria (Felton Bequest), 1938.
8. Valéry, "Degas Dance Drawing," p. 40. Degas's sonnet is sonnet I, "Pur Sang," in *Huits Sonnets d'Edgar Degas*, with a preface by Jean Nepveu-Degas, (Paris: La Jeune Parque, 1946), p. 26.
9. The picture reproduced is Vente IV, no. 279.
10. Lemoisne 599 bis and 600, respectively.
11. Richard Thomson has pointed out that several of the 1880s pastels are related to a much smaller, earlier frieze-format painting by Degas; see his *Edgar Degas: Waiting* (Malibu: Getty Museum, 1995), pp. 16-21.
12. Although the exact date of *Frieze of Dancers* is unknown, there is a consensus among scholars that it was made in the mid-1890s, a few years after the landscape monotypes.

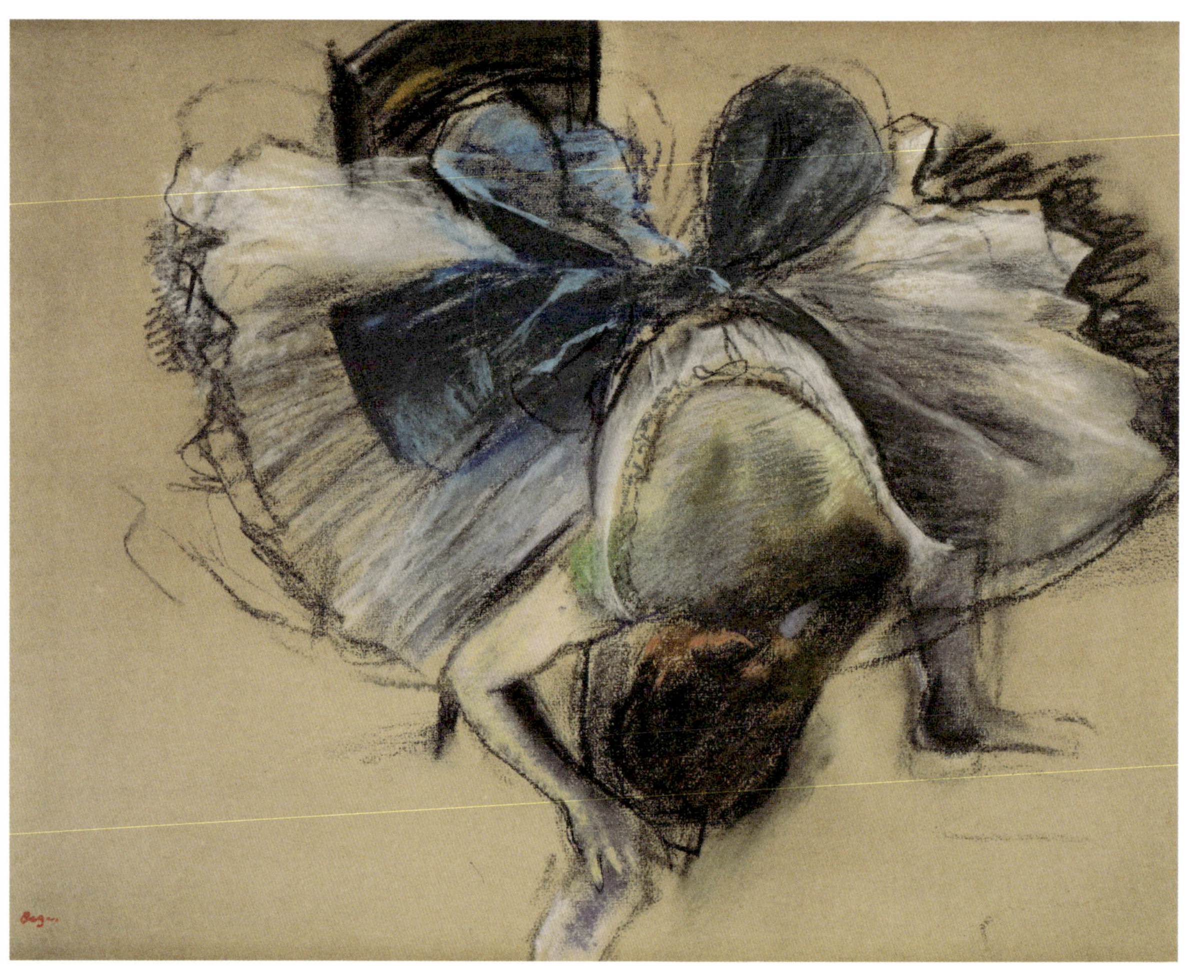

154. *Dancer Adjusting Her Slipper* (*Danseuse rajustant son chausson*). 1887
Pastel on paper
19 ⅝ × 24 ⅝ in. (50 × 62.5 cm)
Frederick Iseman Art Trust

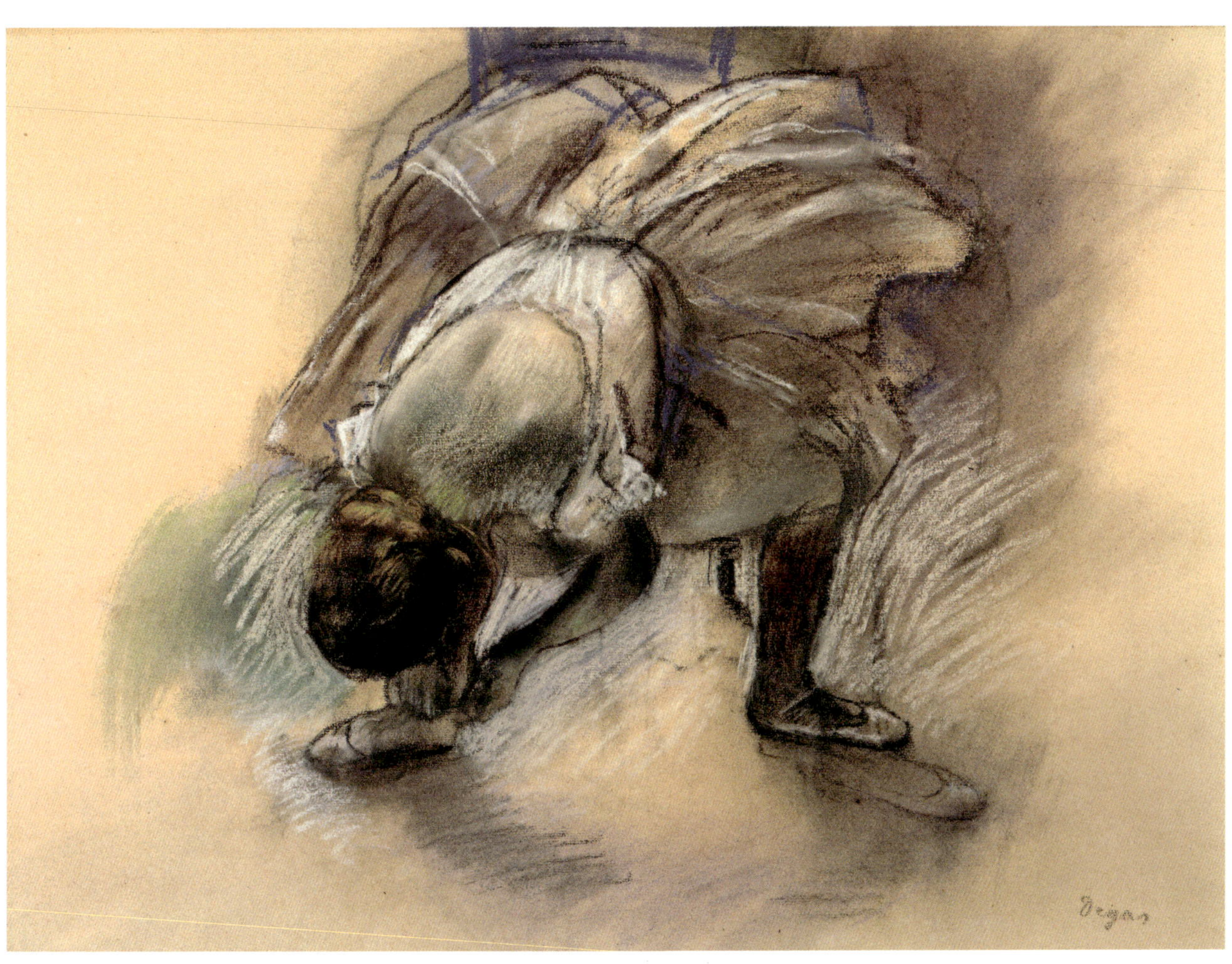

155. *Dancer Adjusting Her Slipper* (*Danseuse rajustant son chausson*). c. 1887
Pastel on paper
18 ¾ × 24 ⅝ in. (47.6 × 62.5 cm)
Private collection

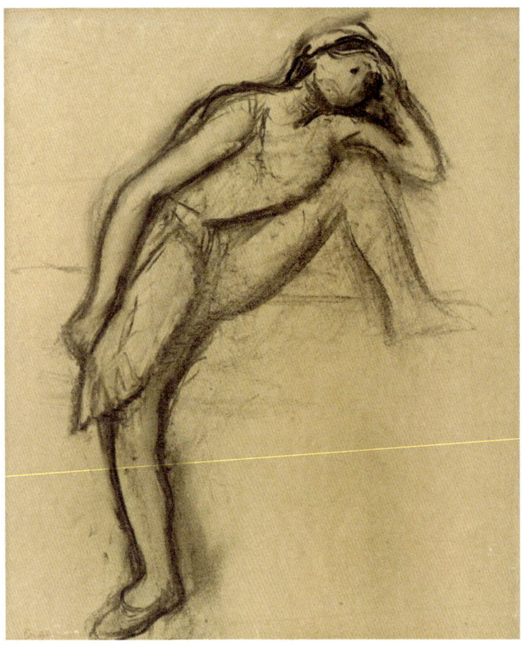

156. *Dancer Holding a Fan* (*Danseuse à l'éventail*). c. 1890
Charcoal on paper mounted on board
17 15⁄16 × 14 in. (45.5 × 35.5 cm)
Courtesy of Marty de Cambiare, Paris

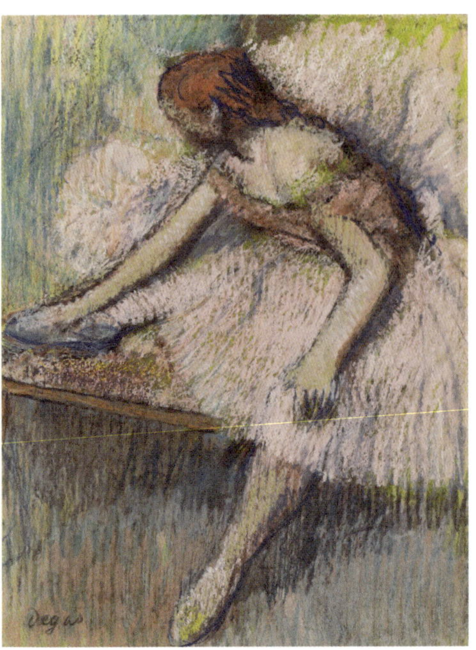

157. *Pink Dancer* (*Danseuse rose*). 1896
Pastel on paper
16 ¾ × 12 3⁄16 in. (42.6 × 31 cm)
Private collection

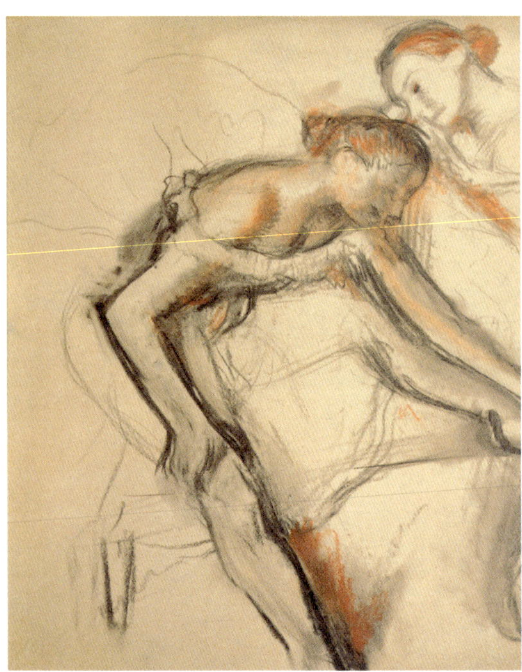

158. *Two Dancers Resting* (*Deux danseuses au repos*). c. 1890–1900
Charcoal and colored chalk or pastel on paper
22 ¼ × 17 ½ in. (56.5 × 44.5 cm)
Philadelphia Museum of Art. The Samuel S. White 3rd and Vera White Collection

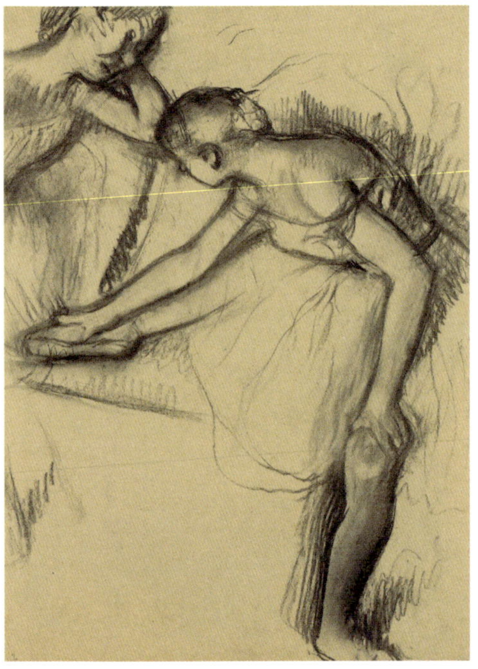

159. *Two Dancers Resting* (*Deux danseuses au repos*). c. 1890–1905
Charcoal on paper
22 ¾ × 16 ⅜ in. (57.8 × 41.6 cm)
Judith and Bernard Briskin. The Briskin Community Property Trust

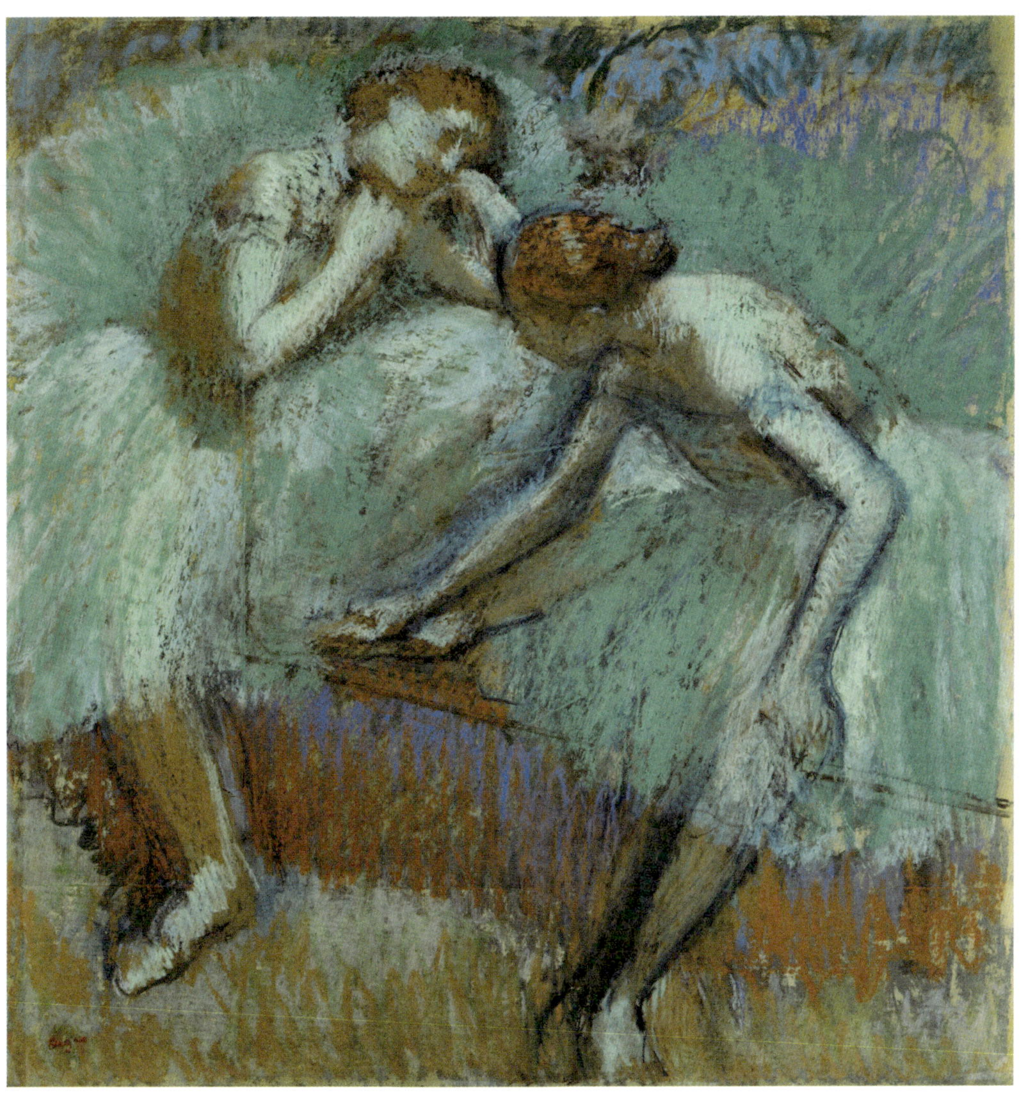

160. *Two Dancers* (*Les Grandes Danseuses vertes*). c. 1898
Pastel on eight sheets of pieced paper
29 ½ × 27 $^{9}/_{16}$ in. (75 × 70 cm)
Ny Carlsberg Glyptotek, Copenhagen

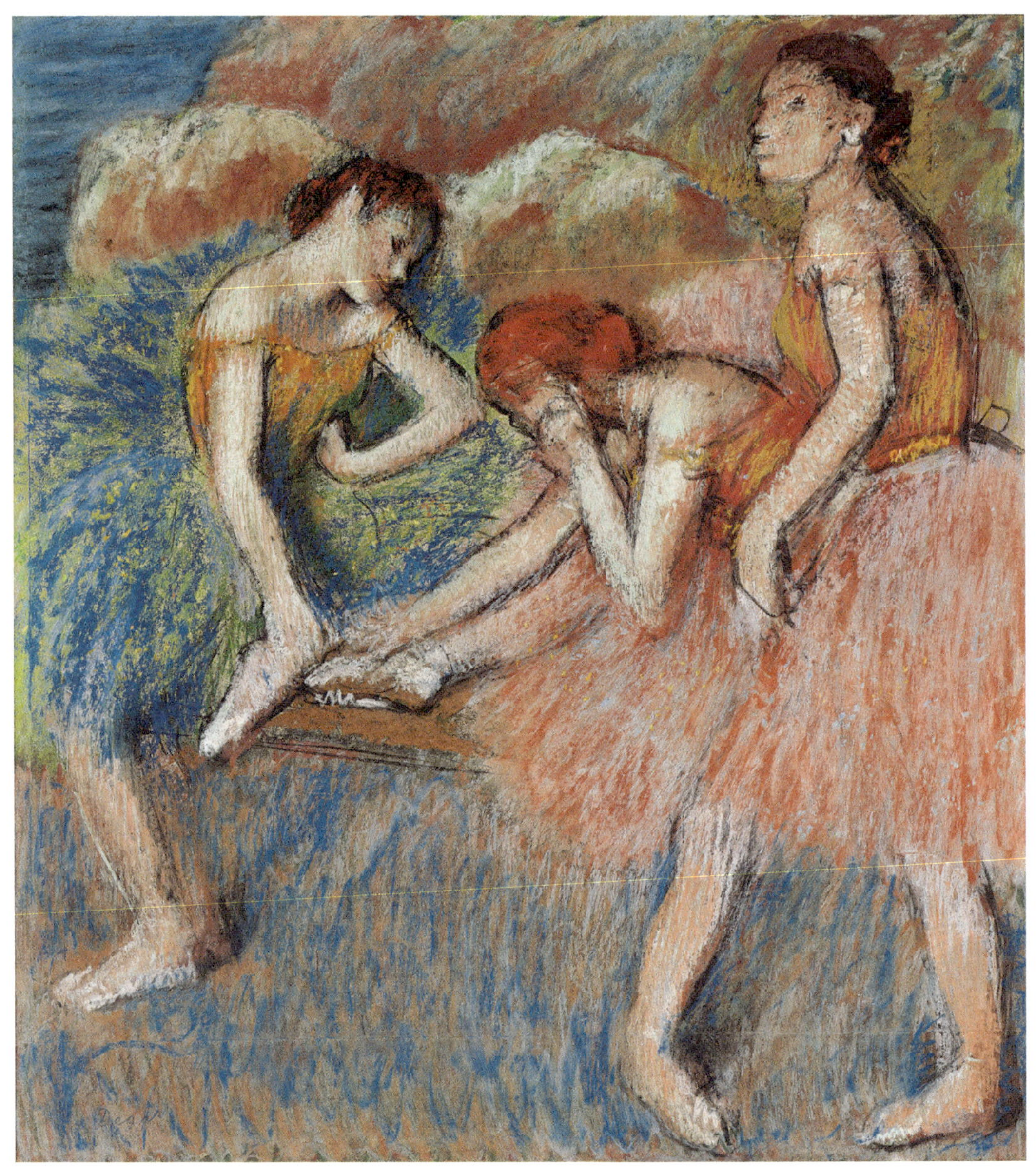

161. *Dancers Resting* (*Danseuses [Danseuses au repos]*). c. 1898
Pastel on five sheets of pieced paper
32 11⁄16 × 28 3⁄8 in. (83 × 72 cm)
Fondation de l'Hermitage, Lausanne. Legs de Lucie Schmidheiny

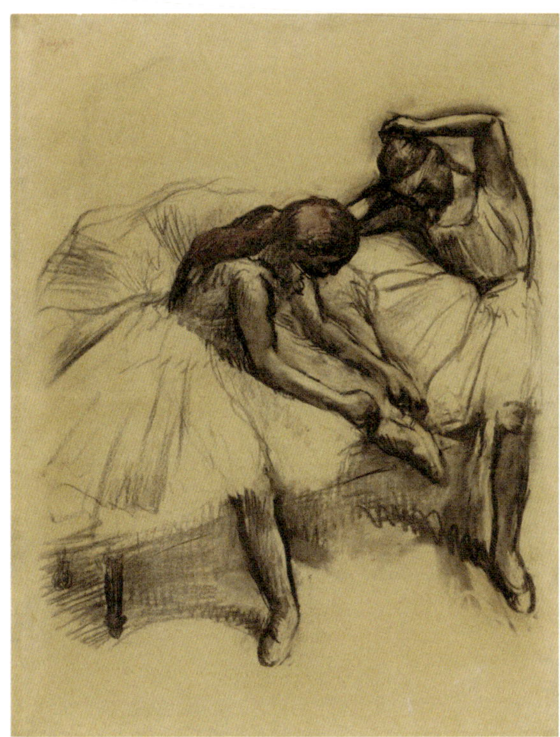

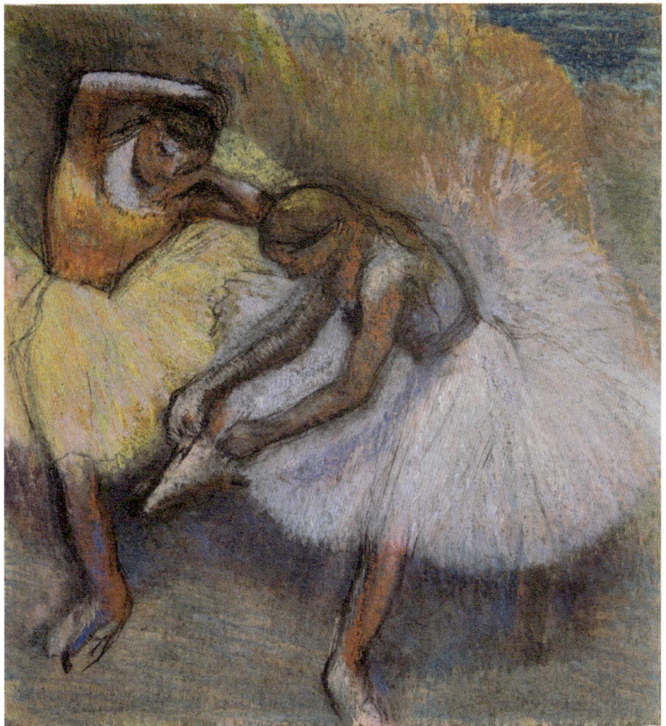

162. *Two Dancers* (*Deux danseuses*). 1905
Charcoal and pastel on tracing paper
43 × 32 in. (109.2 × 81.3 cm)
The Museum of Modern Art, New York.
The William S. Paley Collection

163. *Two Dancers* (*Danseuses*). c. 1898
Pastel on paper
33 ⅜ × 30 ⅜ in. (84.8 × 77.2 cm)
The Saint Louis Art Museum, Missouri. Funds
given by Mrs. Mark C. Steinberg

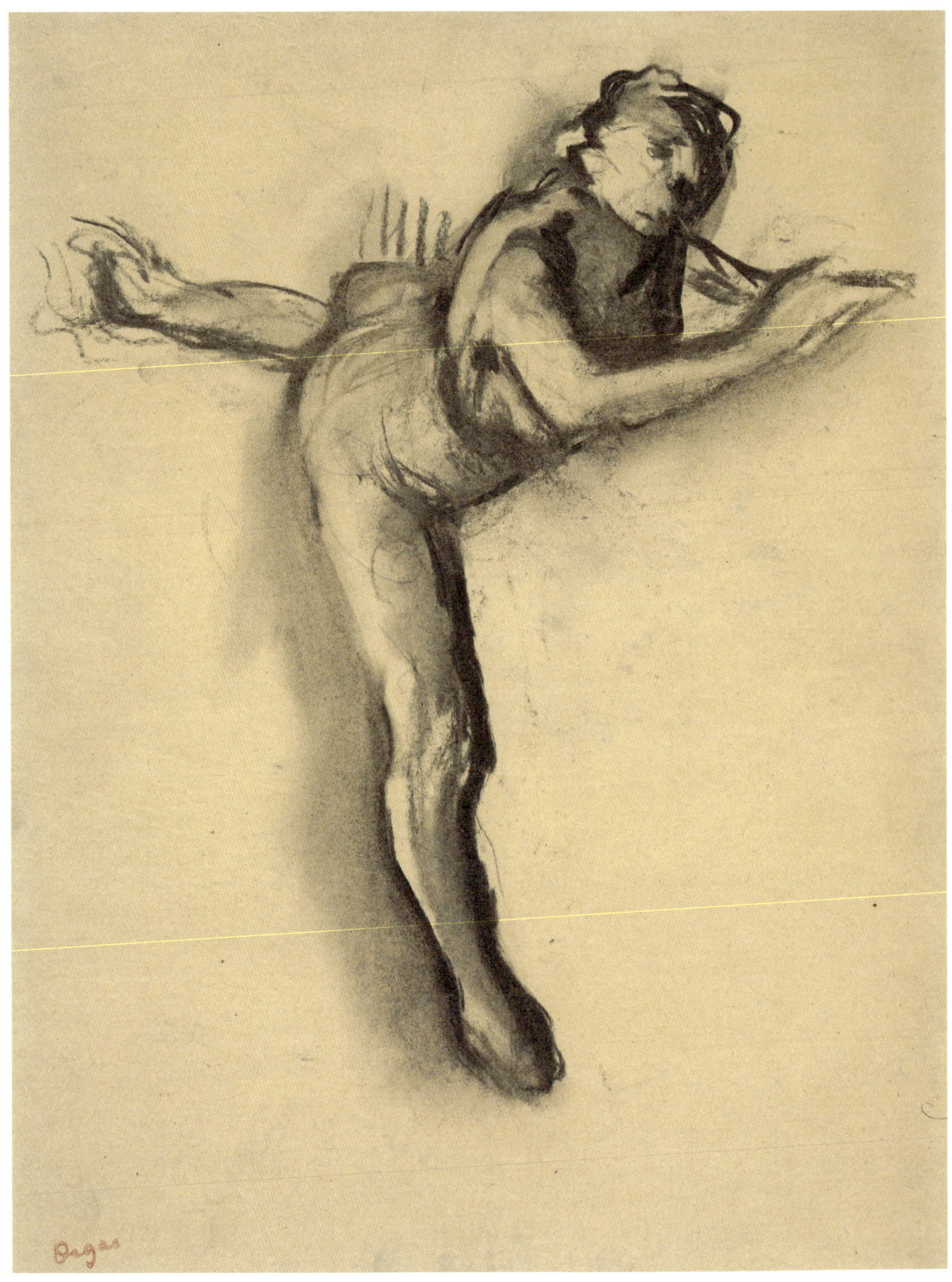

164. *Grand Arabesque, Second Time* (*Grande arabesque, deuxième temps*). 1900–1905
Charcoal on tracing paper
18 ⅛ × 14 $^{3}/_{16}$ in. (46 × 36 cm)
Private collection

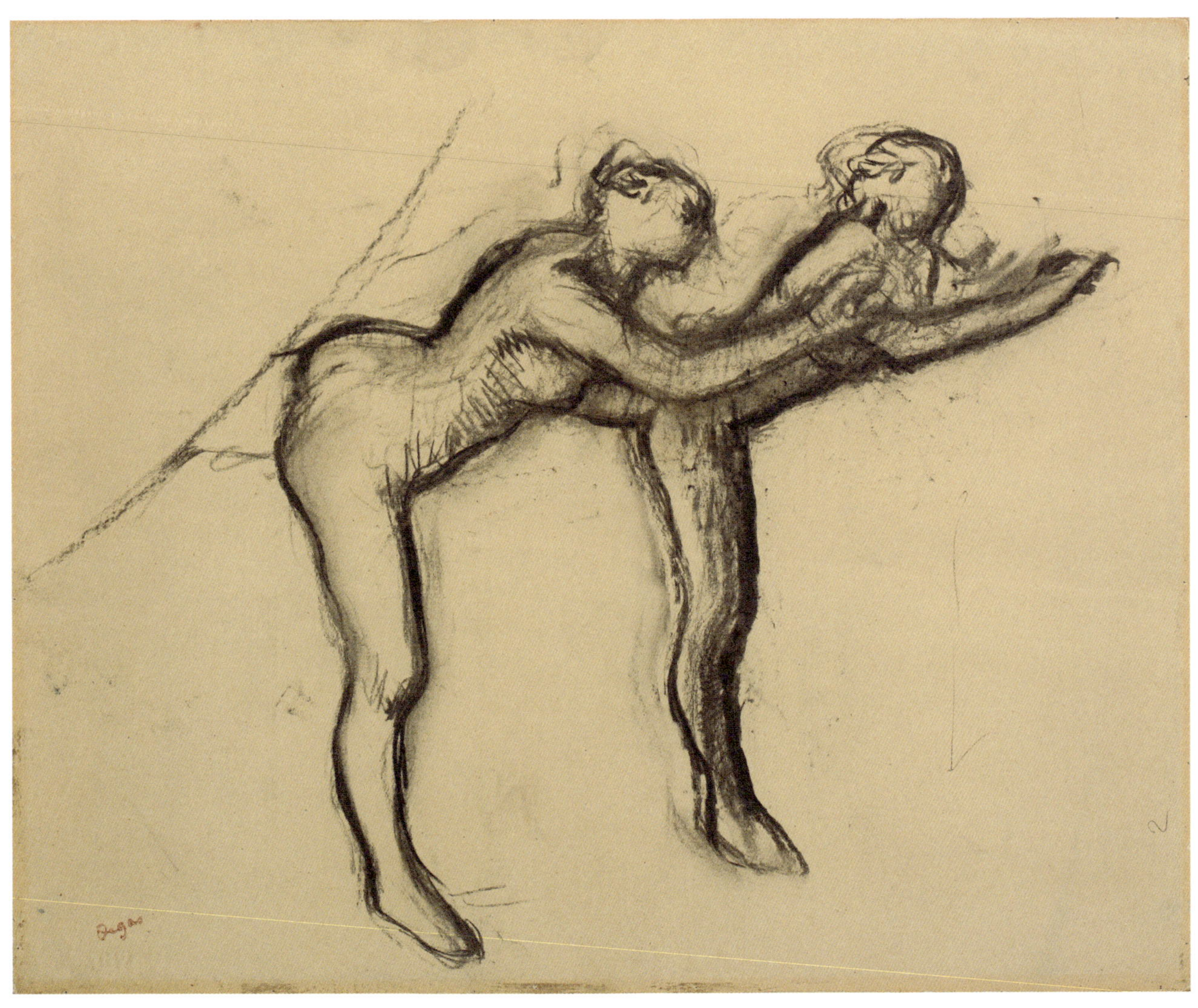

165. *Two Dancers en Arabesque* (*Deux danseuses nues en arabesque*). c. 1885–90
Charcoal on tracing paper
17 11⁄16 × 21 1⁄4 in. (45 × 54 cm)
Galerie Bernard Lecomte, Paris

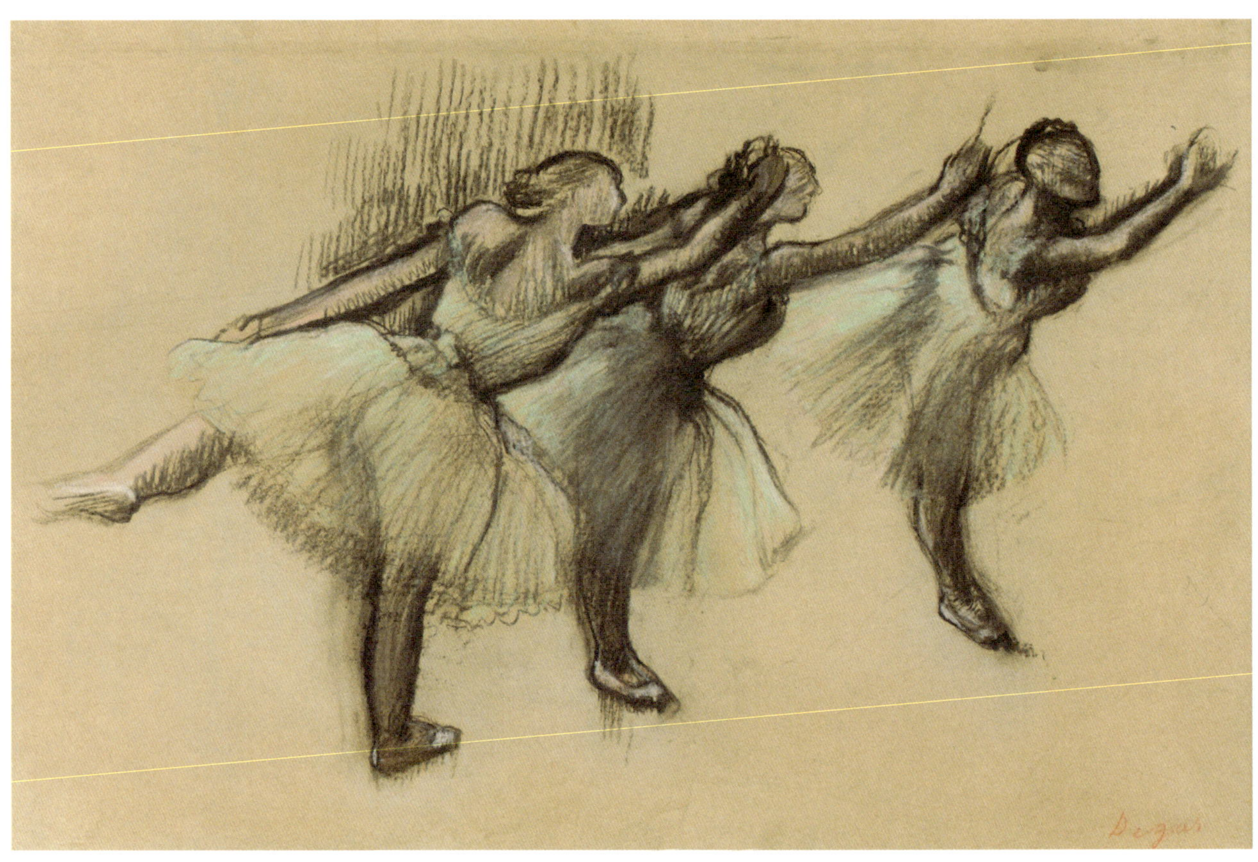

166. *Three Dancers* (*Trois Danseuses*). 1900–1905
Charcoal and pastel on tracing paper
21 ¼ × 30 ⅛ in. (54 × 76.5 cm)
Private collection. Courtesy Halcyon Gallery, London

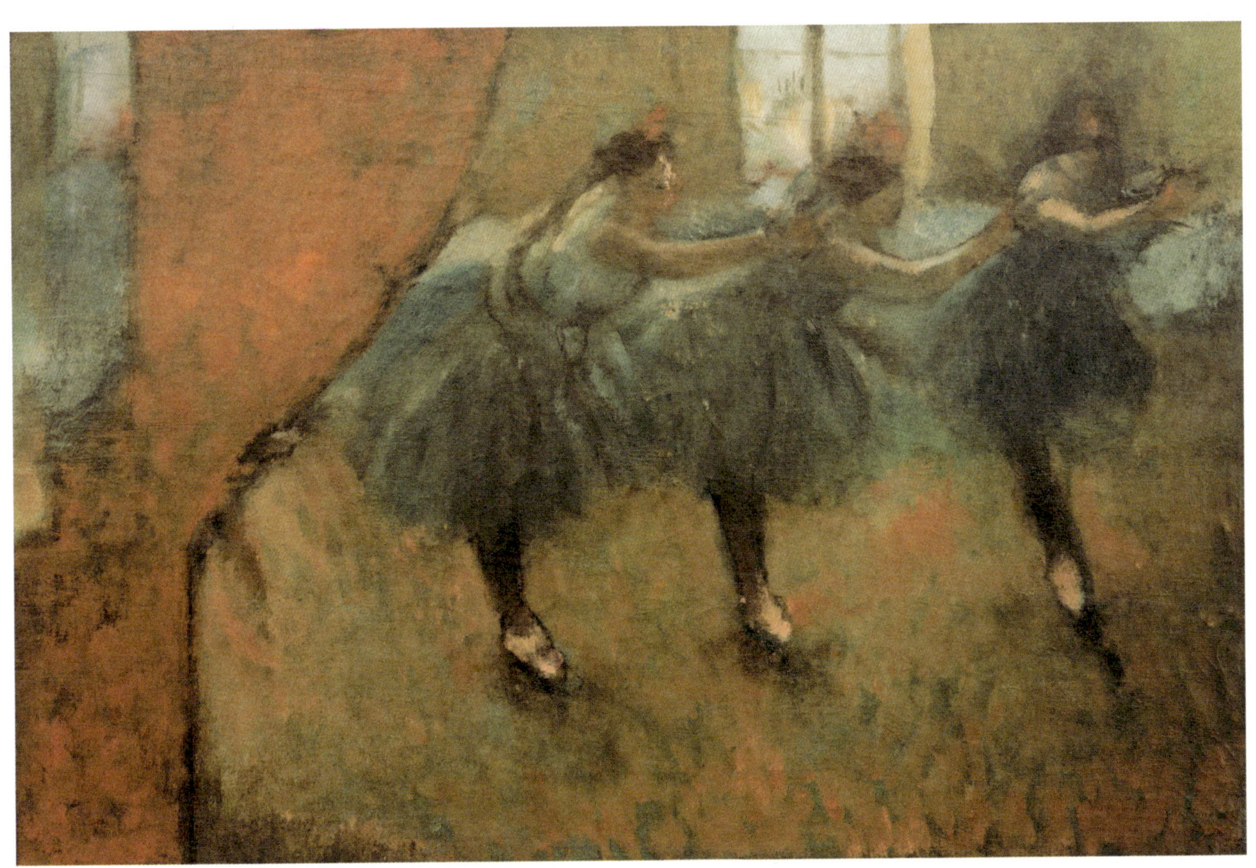

167. *Three Dancers in the Foyer* (*Trois danseuses au foyer*). 1892–95
Oil on canvas
22 ⅛ × 32 ⅛ in. (56.2 × 81.6 cm)
Courtesy of the Larry Ellison Collection

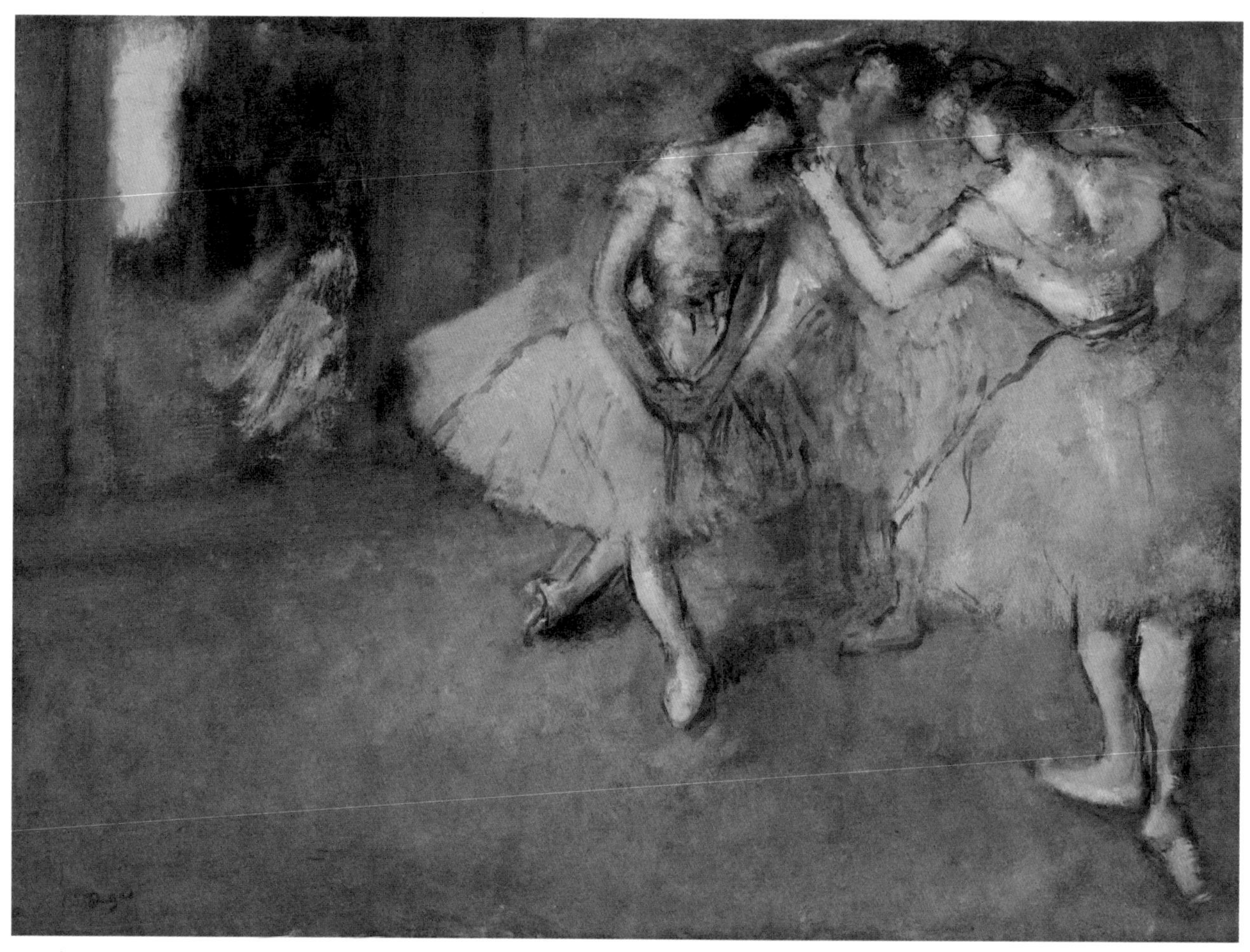

168. *A Group of Dancers* (*Groupe de danseuses*). c. 1898
Oil on paper mounted on canvas
18 ⅛ × 24 ⅛ in. (46 × 61.2 cm)
Scottish National Gallery, Edinburgh

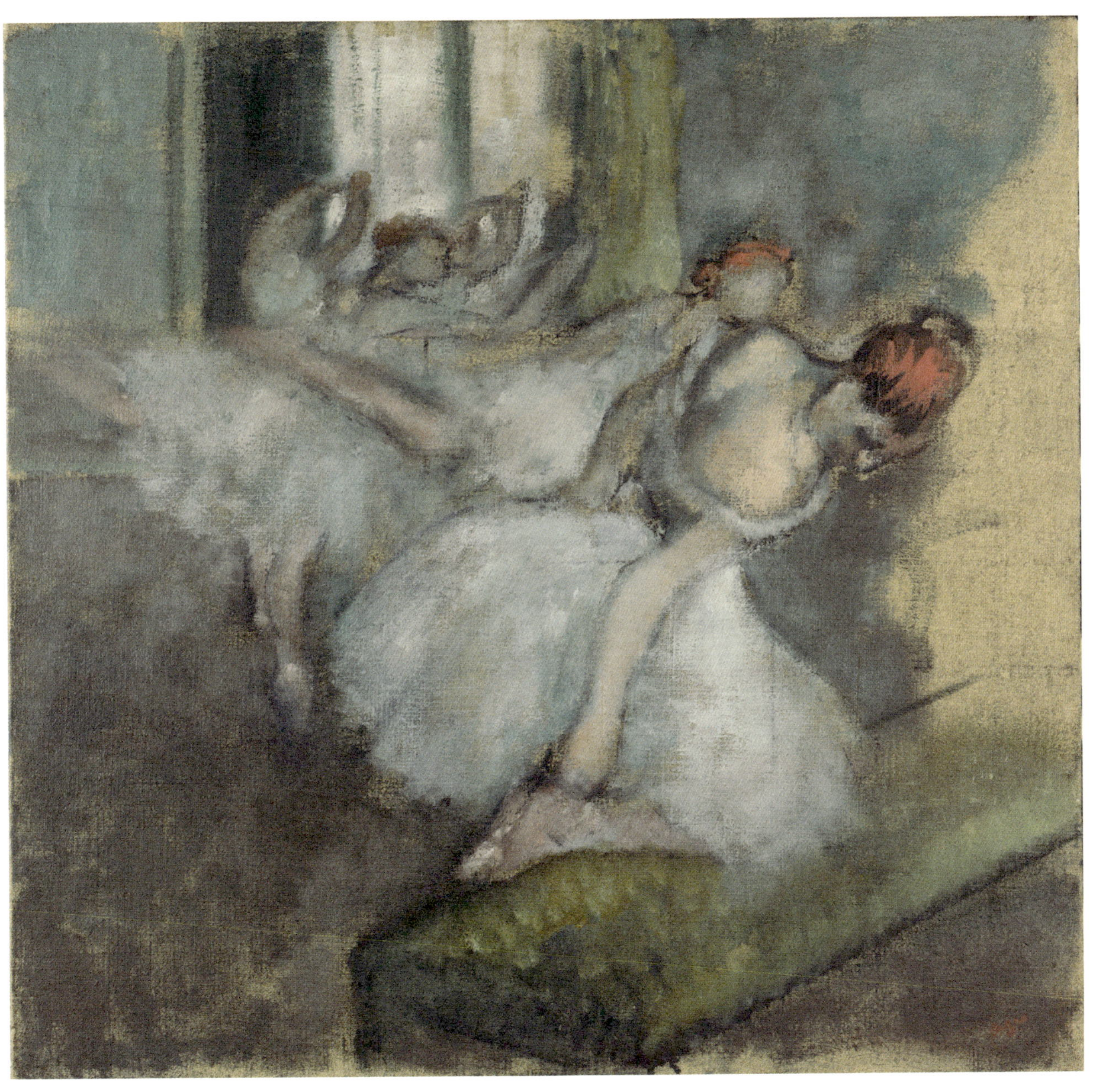

169. *Ballet Dancers* (*Danseuses*). c. 1890–1900
Oil on canvas
28 9⁄16 × 28 ¾ in. (72.5 × 73 cm)
The National Gallery, London. Bought, Courtauld Fund

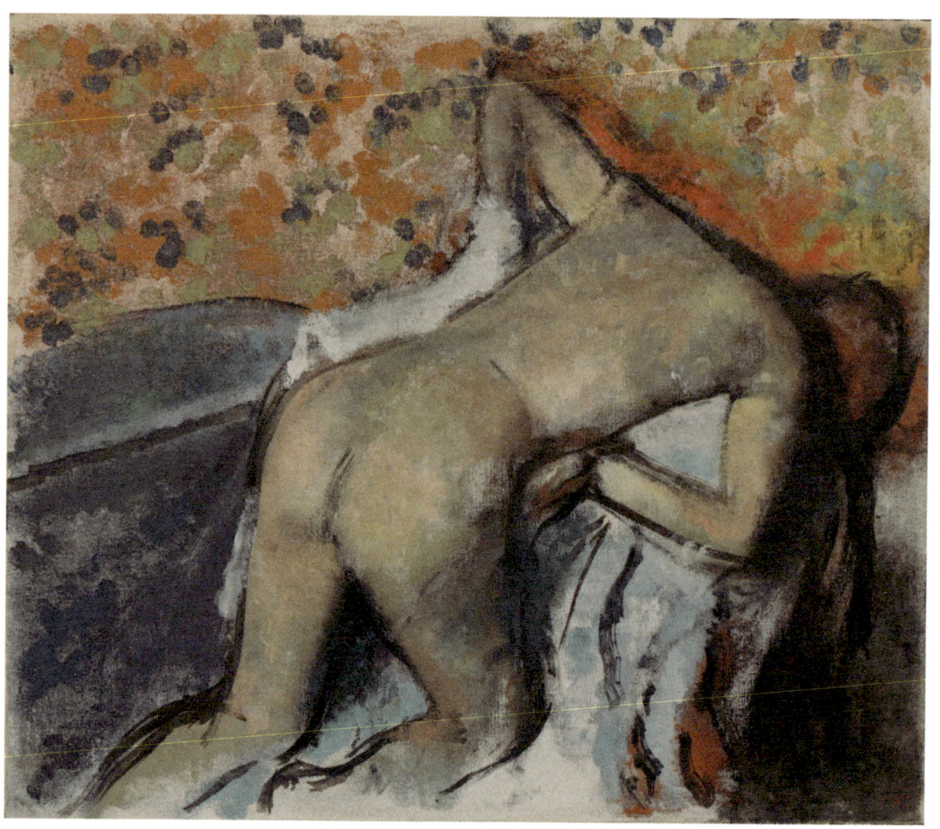

170. *After the Bath, Woman Drying Herself* (*Après le bain, femme s'essuyant*). 1895–1900
Oil on canvas
29 ¾ × 33 ⅞ in. (75.5 × 86 cm)
The Henry and Rose Pearlman Foundation, on long-term loan
to the Princeton University Art Museum

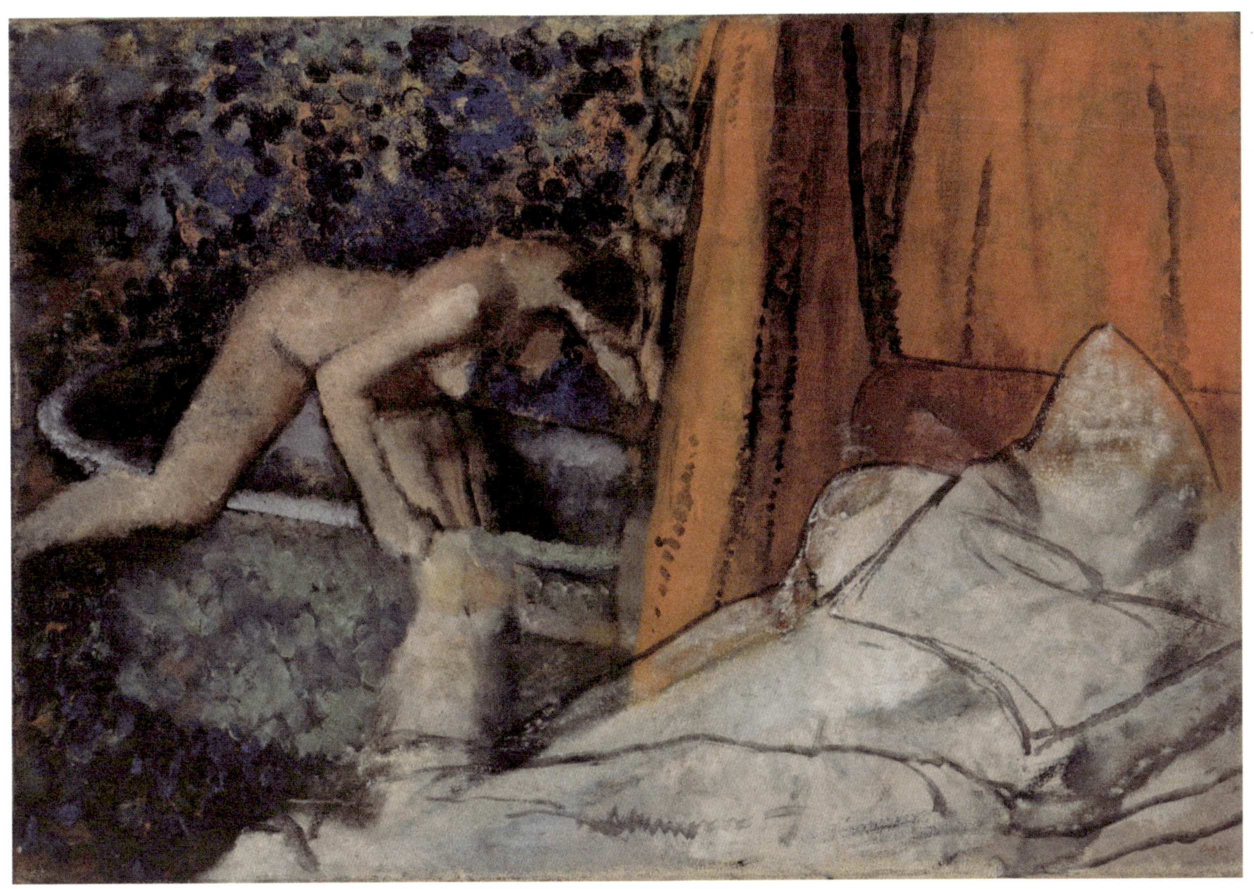

171. *The Bath* (*Le Bain*). c. 1895
Oil on canvas
33 × 45 ¾ in. (83.8 × 116.2 cm)
Carnegie Museum of Art, Pittsburgh, Pennsylvania.
Acquired through the generosity of Mrs. Alan M. Scaife

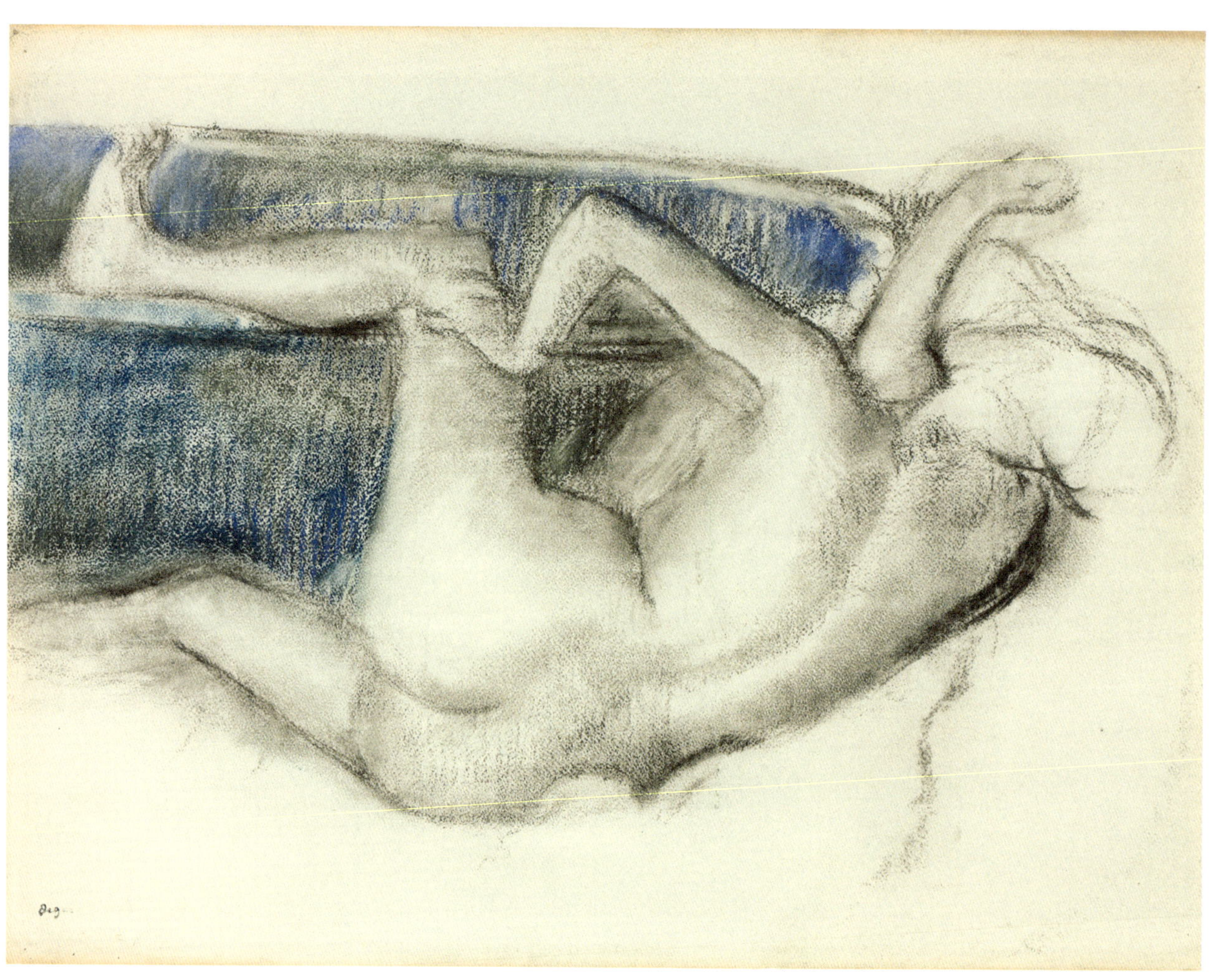

172. *After the Bath* (*Après le bain*). c. 1891
Charcoal and pastel on paper
20 3⁄8 × 26 5⁄16 in. (51.8 × 66.8 cm)
Private collection

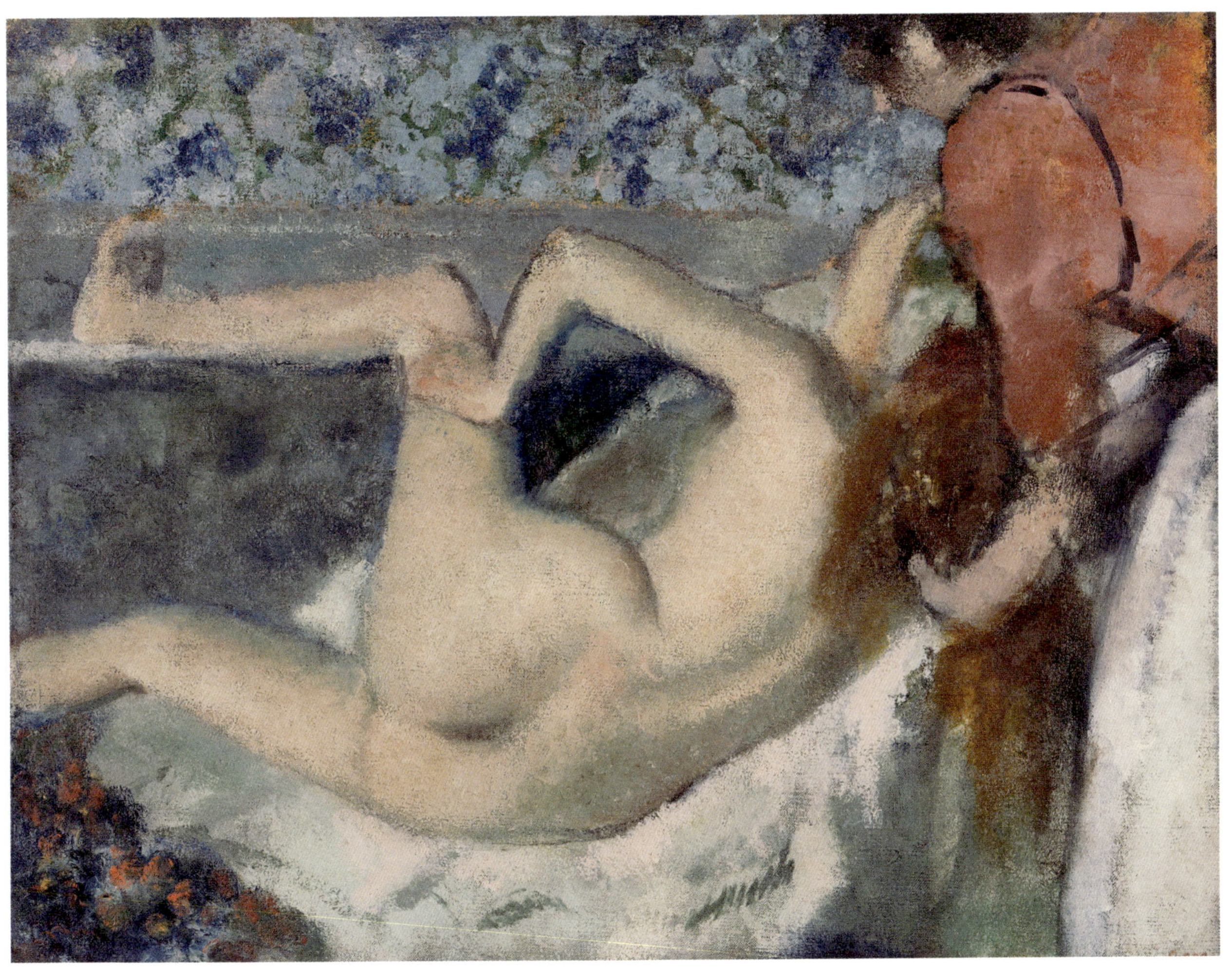

173. *After the Bath* (*Le Bain, femme vue de dos*). c. 1893–98
Oil on canvas
25 ⅞ × 32 ⅜ in. (65.7 × 82.2 cm)
The J. Paul Getty Museum, Los Angeles

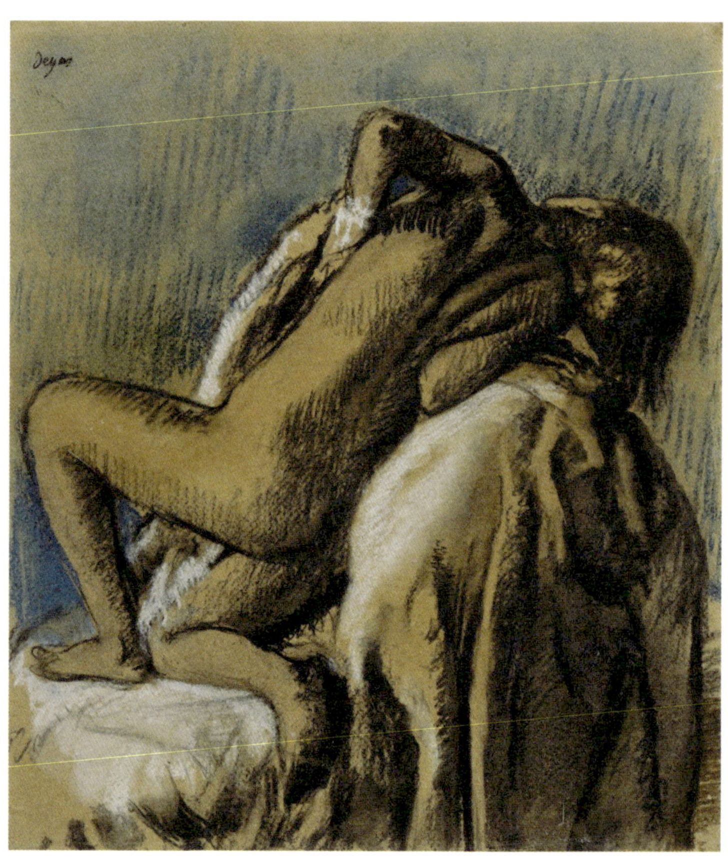

174. *After the Bath* (*Le Repos après le bain*). c. 1896
Charcoal and pastel on paper
15 ⅜ × 13 in. (39 × 33 cm)
Private collection

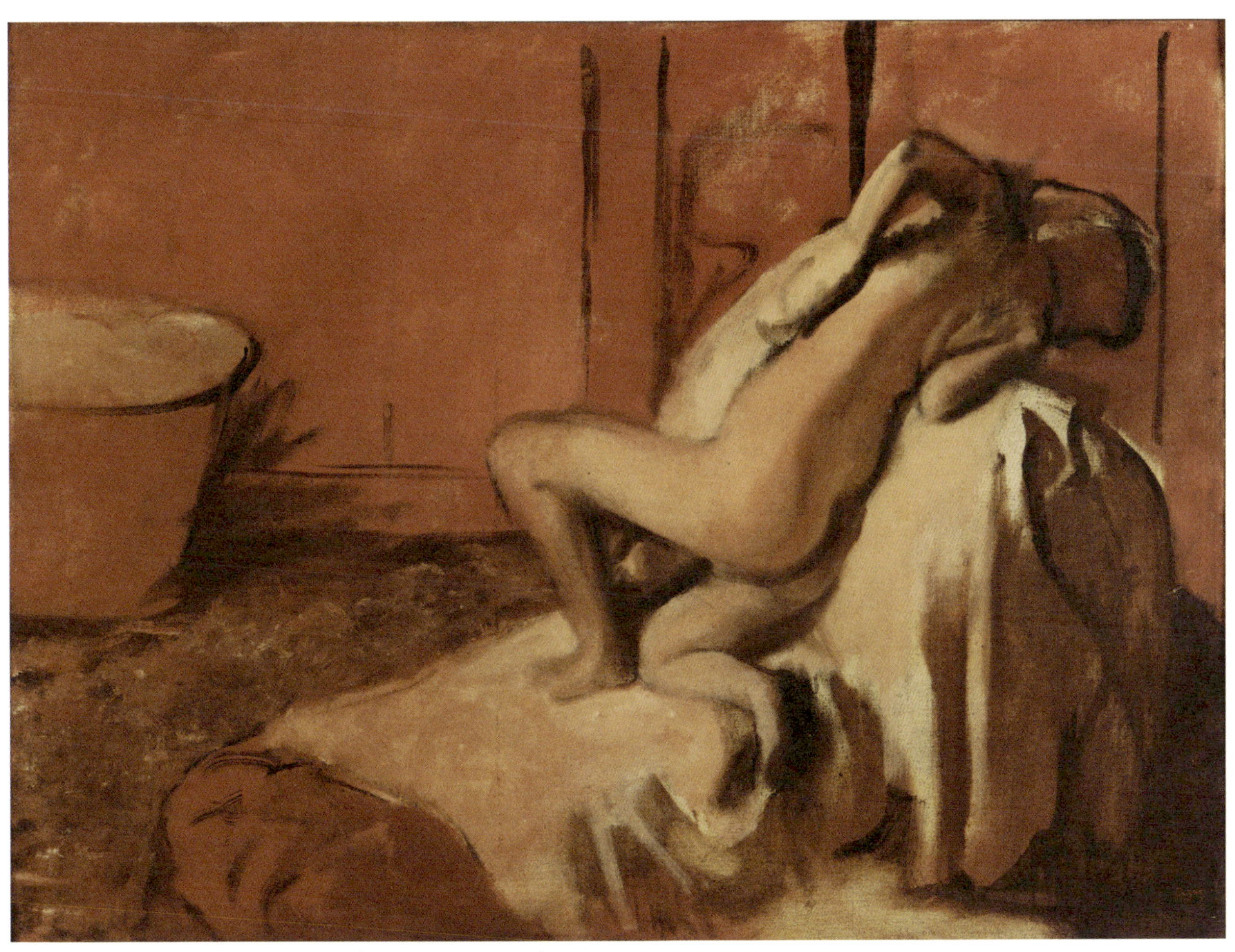

175. *After the Bath (Woman Drying Herself)* (*Après le bain, femme s'essuyant*). c. 1896
Oil on canvas
35 ¼ × 46 in. (89.5 × 116.8 cm)
Philadelphia Museum of Art. Purchased with funds from the estate of George D. Widener

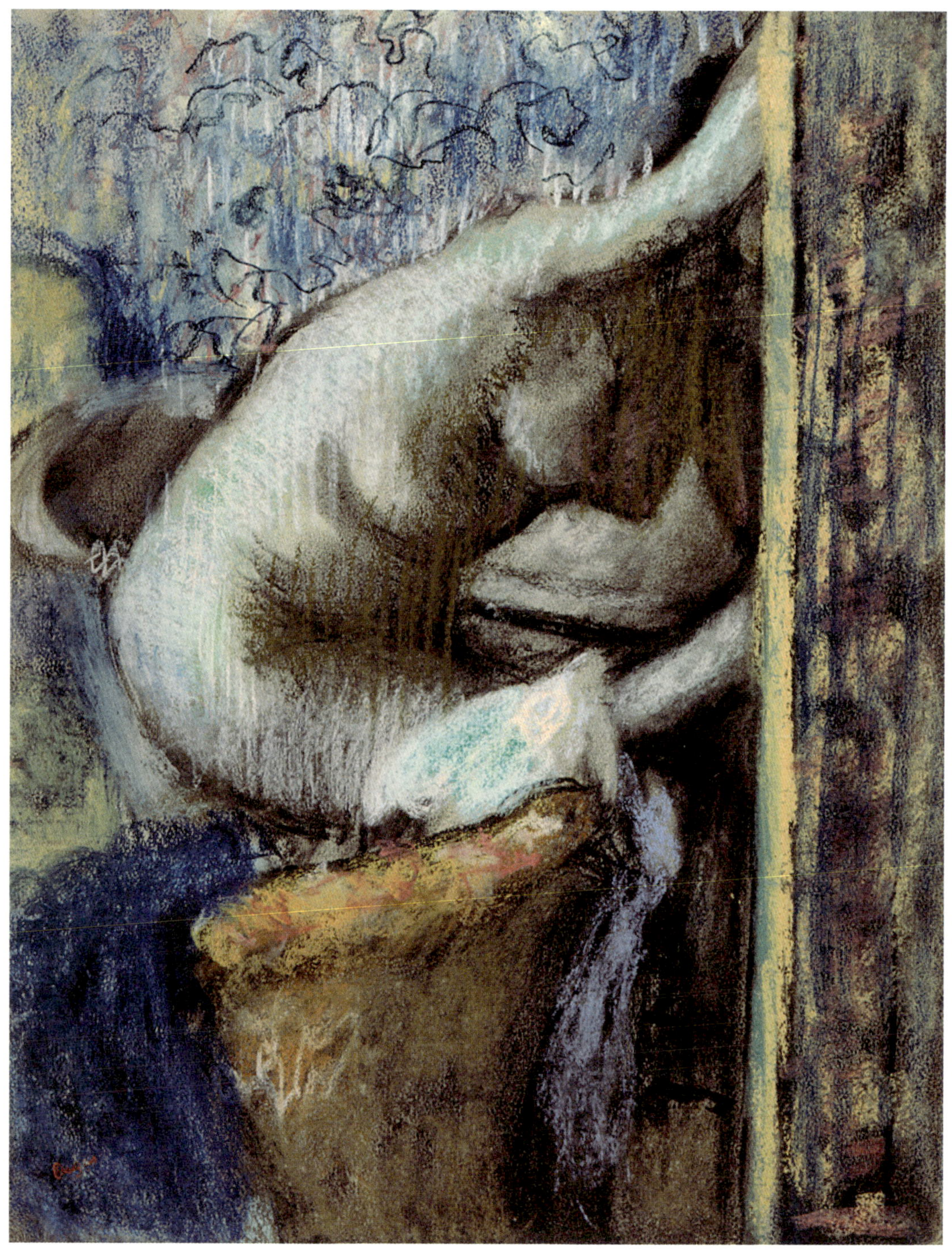

176. *Woman Drying Herself* (*La Toilette après le bain*). After 1888
Pastel on paper
24 ¾ × 18 ½ in. (62.9 × 47 cm)
Los Angeles County Museum of Art, Gift of Jerome K. Ohrbach

Catalogue of the Exhibition

Note to the Reader
All works are by Edgar Degas unless otherwise noted. The works not included in the exhibition are marked by an asterisk; this marking is accurate as of the time of this book's printing.

Titles
Since Degas rarely titled his works himself, most titles are descriptive and were given later. They are provided in both English and French; the translations are not always literal but rather represent how the works are best known in each language. In most cases this means they defer to the catalogues raisonnés indicated below, and to other published sources, including how Degas himself referred to a work if it was exhibited during his lifetime.

Dates
Degas rarely dated his works. The dates given here defer to published sources and outside documentation, including when works were exhibited, inscriptions, letters, or publications. The inability to definitively determine the exact year of a work's completion is indicated by the use of "circa" (c.). Use of a dash in a work's date does not indicate a process of continuous creation during that range of years but creation at some point during it.

Mediums, supports, and dimensions
This information has been provided by the owners or custodians of the works. The monotypes are executed in black printing ink unless otherwise noted. This ink is a mixture of black carbon-based pigments ground with boiled linseed oil and diluted with solvent to a desired consistency. When known, the type of paper and color is provided. The media description of some monotypes includes the notation of a secondary support when the print is mounted onto either a sheet of paper or a board. This information comes from direct examination or from communication with the lender; there may be other examples among works that could not be examined before this book's press date. Dimensions of prints include both plate and full sheet size when possible; in some cases only one of the two measurements was available to us. Measurements are given in inches and centimeters; height precedes width.

Cognates and counterproofs
Degas would often make more than one impression from a single plate; the word "cognate" is used in the literature to describe the resulting related but separate prints. Degas also made counterproofs, prints taken directly from the surface of another print or drawing: to create a counterproof a sheet of damp paper is placed over the still-wet or friable media of the first work, and then both sheets are passed through an etching press. The counterproof will be a mirror image of the work it was printed from, and the intensity of the media will often be diminished. Cognate and counterproof information is provided here only when both works are reproduced.

Stamps
Some of the works show "*vente*" and "*atelier*" stamps. The *vente* stamp imitates Degas's signature and is printed on works that were sold in the sales immediately following the artist's death. "*Atelier Ed. Degas*," in an oval, was stamped on works left in the artist's studio at the time of his death.

Reference numbers
Works catalogued in the key sources listed below are identified by the corresponding abbreviation followed by the reference number assigned in that publication.

A&C: Adhémar, Jean, and Françoise Cachin. *Degas: The Complete Etchings, Lithographs, and Monotypes*. Paris: Arts et Métiers Graphiques, Paris, 1973. Eng. trans. London: Thames & Hudson, 1974.

B&R: Brame, Philippe, and Theodore Reff. *Degas et son œuvre: A Supplement*. New York: Garland, 1984.

J: Janis, Eugenia Parry. *Degas Monotypes*. Cambridge, Mass.: Fogg Art Museum, Harvard University, 1968.

L: Lemoisne, Paul-André. *Degas et son œuvre*. 4 vols. Paris: Paul Brame and C. M. de Hauke, Arts et Métiers Graphiques, 1946.

R: Reff, Theodore, ed. *The Notebooks of Edgar Degas*. Oxford: Clarendon Press, 1976.

R&S: Reed, Sue Welsh, and Barbara Stern Shapiro. *Edgar Degas: The Painter as Printmaker*. Boston: Museum of Fine Arts, 1984.

1. *Self-Portrait* (*Autoportrait*). 1857
Etching and drypoint on paper, state II of IV
Plate: 9 1/16 × 5 11/16 in. (23 × 14.4cm), sheet: 10 3/8 × 6 3/4 in. (26.3 × 17.2 cm)
The Metropolitan Museum of Art, New York. Jacob H. Schiff Fund
A&C 13 (p. 262); R&S 8, second printing

2. *Self-Portrait* (*Autoportrait*). 1857
Etching and drypoint on paper, state III of IV
Plate: 9 1/16 × 5 11/16 in. (23 × 14.4 cm), sheet: 20 1/2 × 13 3/4 in. (52 × 35 cm)
Private collection. Courtesy C. G. Boerner, New York
A&C 13 (p. 262); R&S 8

3. Sketchbook (*Carnet I*). 1859–64
Ink, graphite, charcoal with scrapbook additions including photographs, intaglio printing and pressed flowers
10 × 7 11/16 in. (25.4 × 19.5 cm)
Bibliothèque nationale de France, Paris. Département Estampes et photographie
R 18

4. *The Engraver Joseph Tourny* (*Le Graveur Joseph Tourny*). 1858
Etching on paper
Plate: 9 1/16 × 5 11/16 in. (23 × 14.4 cm)
Princeton University Art Museum. Gift of James H. Lockhart, Jr., Class of 1935
A&C 8A; R&S 5, first printing

5. *The Engraver Joseph Tourny* (*Le Graveur Joseph Tourny*). c. 1865
Etching on paper, only state
Plate: 9 1/16 × 5 11/16 in. (23 × 14.4 cm), sheet: 18 7/8 × 12 3/8 in. (48 × 31.5 cm)
Staatliche Kunsthalle, Karlsruhe
A&C 8B; R&S 5, third printing

6. *The Engraver Joseph Tourny* (*Le Graveur Joseph Tourny*). 1857
Etching on paper
Plate: 9 1/16 × 5 11/16 in. (23 × 14.4 cm), sheet: 18 15/16 × 13 13/16 in. (48.1 × 35.1 cm)
The Metropolitan Museum of Art, New York. Harris Brisbane Dick Fund
A&C 8C; R&S 5, third printing

7. *A Café-Concert Singer* (*Derrière le rideau de fer*). 1877–78
Aquatint and drypoint on paper, only state
Plate: 6 1/4 × 4 5/16 in. (15.9 × 11 cm), sheet: 9 5/16 × 7 1/4 in. (23.6 × 18.4 cm)
Ursula and R. Stanley Johnson Family Collection
A&C 29; R&S 32a

8. *Two Dancers in a Rehearsal Room* (*Deux danseuses*). 1877–78
Aquatint and drypoint on paper, only state
Plate: 6 3⁄16 × 4 9⁄16 in. (15.7 × 11.6 cm), sheet: 11 13⁄16 × 8 7⁄16 in. (30 × 21.4 cm)
Lent by James Bergquist
A&C 37; R&S 33

9. *At the Café des Ambassadeurs* (*Aux Ambassadeurs*). 1879–80
Etching, softground, drypoint, and aquatint on paper, state III of V
Plate: 10 ½ × 11 ⅝ in. (26.6 × 29.6 cm), sheet: 16 ⅛ × 12 ⅜ in. (41 × 31.5 cm)
Sterling and Francine Clark Art Institute, Williamstown, Massachusetts
A&C 30; R&S 49

10. *At the Ambassadeurs* (*Aux Ambassadeurs*). 1879–80
Etching, softground, drypoint, and aquatint on paper, state V of V
Plate: 10 ½ × 11 ⅝ in. (26.6 × 29.6 cm), sheet: 12 5⁄16 × 17 11⁄16 in. (31.3 × 44.9 cm) (irregular)
National Gallery of Canada, Ottawa. Purchase
A&C 30; R&S 49

11. *Actresses in Their Dressing Rooms* (*Loges d'actrices*). 1879–80
Etching and aquatint on paper, state I of V
Plate: 6 5⁄16 × 8 ⅜ in. (16.1 × 21.3 cm), sheet: 7 ⅝ × 10 ¼ in. (19.3 × 26 cm)
Kunsthalle Bremen. Kupferstichkabinett–Der Kunstverein in Bremen
A&C 31; R&S 50

12. *Actresses in Their Dressing Rooms* (*Loges d'actrices*). 1879–80
Etching and aquatint on paper, state V of V
Plate: 6 5⁄16 × 8 7⁄16 in. (16 × 21.5 cm), sheet: 6 11⁄16 × 9 ⅝ in. (17 × 24.5 cm)
Cantor Arts Center at Stanford University. Gift of Marion E. Fitzhugh and Dr. William M. Fitzhugh, Jr., in memory of their mother, Mary E. Fitzhugh
A&C 31; R&S 50

13. *At the Theater: Woman with a Fan* (*Femme a l'éventail, ou loge d'avant-scène*). 1878–80
Lithograph on paper, from transfer paper, only state
Composition: 9 ⅛ × 7 ⅞ in. (23.2 × 20 cm), sheet: 13 ¾ × 10 ⅝ in. (35 × 27 cm)
Private collection
A&C 34; related to R&S 37

14. *Singer at a Café Concert* (*Chanteuse de Café Concert*). 1875
Lithograph on paper, only state
Composition: 10 1⁄16 × 7 9⁄16 in. (25.6 × 19.2 cm), sheet: 13 11⁄16 × 10 11⁄16 in. (34.8 × 27.2 cm)
The Museum of Modern Art, New York. Gift of Abby Aldrich Rockefeller
A&C 33 (p. 265)

15. *Mademoiselle Bécat at the Ambassadeurs* (*Mademoiselle Bécat aux Ambassadeurs*). c. 1877
Lithograph on paper, only state
Composition: 8 ⅛ × 7 ⅝ in. (20.6 × 19.3 cm), sheet: 13 ½ × 10 ¾ in. (34.3 × 27.3 cm)
The Museum of Modern Art, New York. Gift of Abby Aldrich Rockefeller
A&C 42

16. Ludovic-Napoléon Lepic
Views from the Banks of the Scheldt (*Vue des bords de l'Escaut*)
Six works from the series: *Sunrise* (*Lever du soleil*), *Rain* (*La Pluie*), *Willows and Poplars* (*Saules et peupliers*), *The Mill Fire* (*L'Incendie du moulin*), *Snow* (*La Neige*), *The Moon through the Willows* (*Lune dans les saules*). c. 1870–76
Etching with variable inking on paper
Plate: 13 ½ × 29 5⁄16 in. (34.3 × 74.4 cm), sheet: 17 11⁄16 × 31 ⅞ in. (45 × 81 cm), each
The Baltimore Museum of Art. Garrett Collection

17. *The Ballet Master* (*Le Maître de ballet*). c. 1876
White chalk or opaque watercolor over monotype on paper
Plate: 22 ¼ × 27 9⁄16 in. (56.5 × 70 cm), sheet: 24 7⁄16 × 33 7⁄16 in. (62 × 85 cm)
National Gallery of Art, Washington, D.C. Rosenwald Collection
A&C 1; J 1

18. *The Dancing Lesson* (*La Leçon de danse*). c. 1877
Pastel over monotype on paper
Plate: 23 × 28 ⅝ in. (58.4 × 72.7 cm)
The Joan Whitney Payson Collection at the Portland Museum of Art. Gift of John Whitney Payson
L 396

19. *The Dance Lesson* (*La leçon de danse*). c. 1876*
Pastel over monotype on paper mounted on board
Plate: 18 ⅕ × 31 ⅕ in. (43.6 × 79.2 cm)
Private collection

20. *Pas battu*. c. 1879
Pastel over monotype on paper
10 ¾ × 11 ⅝ in. (27.3 × 29.5 cm)
Private collection
J 11; L 569

21. *Three Ballet Dancers* (*Trois danseuses*). c. 1878
Monotype on paper. Cognate of plate 22
Plate: 7 13⁄16 × 16 ⅜ in. (19.9 × 41.6 cm), sheet: 14 × 20 3⁄16 in. (35.6 × 51.3 cm)
Sterling and Francine Clark Art Institute, Williamstown, Massachusetts
A&C 2; J 9

22. *Ballet Scene* (*Scène de ballet*). c. 1879
Pastel over monotype on paper. Cognate of plate 21
Plate: 8 × 16 in. (20.3 × 40.6 cm)
William I. Koch Collection
J 10; L 568

23. Album of forty-five figure studies. c. 1882–85
Black chalk on paper
Sheet: 10 9⁄16 × 8 ⅝ in. (26.8 × 21.9 cm)
The Metropolitan Museum of Art, New York. Fletcher Fund
R 36

24. Study of a ballet dancer (recto). c. 1873
Oil with opaque watercolor on prepared pink paper
17 ½ × 12 ⅜ in. (44.5 × 31.4 cm)
The Metropolitan Museum of Art, New York. Robert Lehman Collection

25. *Dancer* (*Danseuse*). c. 1876–77
Pastel and opaque watercolor over monotype on paper. Cognate of plate 26
Plate: 8 7⁄16 × 6 ⅞ in. (21.5 × 17.5 cm), sheet: 8 7⁄16 × 6 ⅞ in. (21.5 × 17.5 cm)
Kunstmuseum Winterthur. Anonymous gift
Related to A&C 27; J 4

26. *Two Dancers* (*Deux danseuses*). 1877
Monotype on paper. Cognate of plate 25
Plate: 8 9⁄16 × 6 15⁄16 in. (21.7 × 17.7 cm)
Statens Museum for Kunst, Copenhagen
A&C 27; J 4

27. *Dancer Onstage with a Bouquet* (*Danseuse saluant*). c. 1876
Pastel over monotype on paper
Plate: 10 ⅝ × 14 ⅞ in. (27 × 37.8 cm)
Private collection
J 12; L 515

28. *Café-Concert Singer* (*Chanteuse de café-concert*). c. 1875–76
Pastel over monotype on paper
9 ⅛ × 11 3⁄16 in. (23.2 × 28.4 cm)
John and Marine van Vlissingen Foundation
B&R 69; J 36

29. *Café Singer* (*Chanteuse du café-concert*). c. 1877–78
Monotype on paper. Cognate of plate 30
Plate: 4 ¾ × 6 ⅜ in. (12 × 16.2 cm), sheet: 5 1⁄16 × 6 9⁄16 in. (12.9 × 16.7 cm) (irregular)
Private collection
A&C 6; J 29

30. *Singers on the Stage* (*Café-Concert*). c. 1877-79
Pastel over monotype on paper mounted on board. Cognate of plate 29
Plate: 4 ¾ × 6 ⅝ in. (12 × 16.9 cm), sheet: 5 7⁄16 × 7 3⁄16 in. (13.8 × 18.2 cm)
The Art Institute of Chicago. Bequest of Mrs. Clive Runnells
J 30; L 455

31. *The Café-Concert Singer* (*Chanteuse de café-concert*). 1875–76
Pastel over monotype on paper
Plate: 6 ½ × 4 ¾ in. (16.5 × 12.1 cm)
Private collection
B&R 68

32. *The Singer* (*Chanteuse de café-concert*). 1875–80
Pastel over monotype on paper
Plate: 6 ¼ × 4 ½ in. (15.9 × 11.4 cm)
Reading Public Museum, Reading, Pennsylvania. Gift, Miss Martha Elizabeth Dick Estate
J 43; L 462

33. *The Loge* (*La Loge*). c. 1878
Monotype on paper
Plate: 4 ¾ × 6 ¼ in. (12.1 × 15.9 cm)
Baltimore Museum of Art. Purchase with exchange funds from Nelson and Juanita Greif Gutman Collection
A&C 17; J 55

34. *At the Theater: The Duet* (*Le Duo*). 1877–79
Pastel over monotype on paper
Plate: 4 11⁄16 × 6 ⅜ in. (11.9 × 16.2 cm), sheet: 5 5⁄16 × 7 1⁄16 in. (13.5 × 17.9 cm)
The Morgan Library & Museum, New York. Thaw Collection
J 27; L 433

35. *Two Studies for Music Hall Singers* (*Deux études pour chanteuses de café-concert*). c. 1878–80
Pastel and charcoal on gray paper
17 ½ × 22 7⁄16 in. (44.5 × 57 cm)
Private collection
L 504

36. *Café-Concert Singer* (*Chanteuse de café-concert*). c. 1877
Monotype on paper mounted on board
Plate: 7 5⁄16 × 5 1⁄16 in. (18.5 × 12.8 cm), sheet: 9 ¼ × 7 1⁄16 in. (23.5 × 18 cm)
Private collection
A&C 14; J 47

37. *Song of the Scissors* (*La Chanson des ciseaux*). c. 1877–78
Monotype on paper
Plate: 8 ½ × 6 5⁄16 in. (21.6 × 16.1 cm), sheet: 10 5⁄16 × 7 5⁄16 in. (26.2 × 18.5 cm)
Harvard Art Museums/Fogg Museum, Cambridge, Massachusetts. Gift of Henry F. Harrison
A&C 20; J 44

38. *Café-Concert Singer* (*Chanteuse de café-concert, profil droit*). c. 1878–80
Monotype on paper
Plate: 3 ⅛ × 2 13⁄16 in. (8 × 7.2 cm), sheet: 7 ¼ × 6 ⅜ in. (18.4 × 16.2 cm)
The Art Institute of Chicago. Potter Palmer Collection Fund
A&C 13 (p. 272); J 50

39. *Mlle Bécat*. c. 1877–78
Monotype on paper
Plate: 6 ¼ × 4 11⁄16 in. (15.9 × 11.9 cm)
National Gallery of Art, Washington, D.C. Rosenwald Collection
R&S 30b

40. *Mlle Bécat at the Café des Ambassadeurs: Three Motifs* (*Mlle Bécat aux Ambassadeurs, planche a trois sujets*). c. 1877–78
Lithograph on paper, composition transferred from three monotypes
Top: 4 15⁄16 × 8 ⅜ in. (12.5 × 21.3 cm), lower-right: 6 5⁄16 × 4 9⁄16 in. (16.1 × 11.6 cm), lower-left: 6 ⅜ × 4 ¾ in. (16.2 × 12.1 cm), sheet: 13 ⅞ × 10 11⁄16 in. (35.2 × 27.2 cm)
Museum of Fine Arts, Boston. Gift of George Peabody Gardner
A&C 43; R&S 30

41. *Mlle Bécat at the Café des Ambassadeurs* (*Mlle Bécat aux Ambassadeurs*). c. 1878–80
Monotype on paper
Plate: 5 ⅞ × 8 7⁄16 in. (14.9 × 21.4 cm), sheet: 5 ⅞ × 8 ⅞ in. (14.9 × 22.5 cm)
Statens Museum for Kunst, Copenhagen
A&C 4; J 32; R&S 30a

42. *Mlle Bécat* (*Mlle Bécat aux Ambassadeurs*). c. 1877–79
Pastel over lithograph on paper
Composition: 4 ⅞ × 8 ⅝ in. (12.4 × 21.9 cm)
Private collection
L 372; R&S 30c

43. *Two Performers at a Café-Concert and Morning Frolic* (*Mlle Bécat aux Ambassadeurs; Ebats matinal*). 1877–79
Lithograph on paper, composition transferred from two monotypes, only state
Left: 6 5⁄16 × 4 ¾ in. (16 × 12 cm), right: 4 ¾ × 6 ⅜ in. (12 × 16.2 cm), sheet: 9 ⅝ × 12 ⅝ in. (24.5 × 32 cm)
Private collection
R&S 35; Related monotypes: A&C 5, 121; J 33, 34, 94

44. *Two Performers at a Café-concert* (*Mlle Bécat aux Ambassadeurs [café-concert]*). c. 1877–79*
Pastel over lithograph on paper
Composition: 6 ⅜ × 4 13⁄16 in. (16.2 × 12.2 cm)
Private collection
J 34; L 458; R&S 35 fig. 2

45. Drawings of café singers from a sketchbook. c. 1880
Pencil, charcoal, and blue chalk on paper
Sheet: 9 13⁄16 × 13 ⅜ in. (24.9 × 33.9 cm)
The Morgan Library & Museum, New York. Thaw Collection
R 29

46. *Three Subjects: The Toilette, Marcellin Desboutin, The Café-Concert* (*Planche aux trois sujets: la toilette; Marcellin Desboutin; café-concert*). 1876–77
Lithograph on paper, composition transferred from three monotypes, state I of II
Left: 6 7⁄16 × 4 ⅝ in. (16.4 × 11.7 cm), upper-right: 3 ¼ × 2 13⁄16 in. (8.2 × 7.1 cm), lower-right: 3 ¼ × 2 13⁄16 in. (8.2 × 7.1 cm), sheet: 10 9⁄16 × 13 9⁄16 in. (26.9 × 34.4 cm)
Private collection. Courtesy Nicholas Stogdon
A&C 46; R&S 28

47. *Factory Smoke* (*Fumées d'usines*). 1877–79
Monotype on paper
Plate: 4 11⁄16 × 6 5⁄16 in. (11.9 × 16.1 cm), sheet: 5 13⁄16 × 6 13⁄16 in. (14.7 × 17.3 cm)
The Metropolitan Museum of Art, New York. The Elisha Whittelsey Collection, The Elisha Whittelsey Fund
A&C 182; J 269

48. *On the Street* (*Dans la rue*). 1876–77
Monotype on China paper
Plate: 6 ⅜ × 4 13⁄16 in. (16.2 × 12.2 cm)
Mrs. Martin Atlas
A&C 32; J 237

49. *Heads of a Man and a Woman* (*Homme et femme, en buste*). c. 1877–80
Monotype on paper
Plate: 2 13/16 × 3 3/16 in. (7.2 × 8.1 cm)
British Museum, London. Bequeathed by Campbell Dodgson
A&C 47 ("second proof"); J 235

50. *At the Races* (*Aux courses*). c. 1876–77
Oil on canvas
7 ½ × 9 11/16 in. (19.1 × 24.6 cm)
Private collection
L 495

51. *Lady with a Parasol* (*Femme à l'ombrelle*). c. 1870–72
Oil on canvas
29 5/8 × 33 7/16 in. (75.3 × 85 cm)
The Samuel Courtauld Trust, The Courtauld Gallery, London
L 414

52. *In the Omnibus* (*Dans l'omnibus*). c. 1877–78
Monotype on paper
Plate: 11 × 11 11/16 in. (28 × 29.7 cm)
Musée Picasso, Paris
A&C 33 (p. 273); J 236

53. *The Two Connoisseurs* (*Les Deux Amateurs*). c. 1880
Monotype on paper mounted on board
Plate: 11 ¾ × 10 5/8 in. (29.8 × 27 cm), sheet: 13 1/8 × 12 in. (33.4 × 30.5 cm)
The Art Institute of Chicago. Clarence Buckingham Collection
A&C 50; J 234

54. *A Woman Ironing* (*Blanchisseuse [Silhouette]*). 1873
Oil on canvas
21 3/8 × 15 ½ in. (54.3 × 39.4 cm)
The Metropolitan Museum of Art, New York. H. O. Havemeyer Collection, Bequest of Mrs. H. O. Havemeyer
L 356

55. *Ironing Women* (*Les Repasseuses*). c. 1877–79
Monotype on paper
Plate: 9 ½ × 17 ½ in. (24.1 × 44.5 cm), sheet: 10 × 17 ½ in. (25.4 × 44.5 cm)
Private collection
J 258

56. *The Jet Earring* (*Profil perdu à la boucle d'oreille*). 1876–77
Monotype on paper
Plate: 3 ¼ × 2 ¾ in. (8.2 × 7 cm), sheet: 7 1/16 × 5 3/16 in. (18 × 13.2 cm)
The Metropolitan Museum of Art, New York. Anonymous gift, in memory of Francis Henry Taylor
A&C 39; J 243

57. *Portrait of Ellen Andrée* (*Portrait de femme*). c. 1876
Monotype on China paper
8 ½ × 6 5/16 in. (21.6 × 16 cm)
The Art Institute of Chicago. Potter Palmer Collection
A&C 48; J 238

58. *Young Woman in a Café* (*Jeune femme au café*). c. 1877
Pastel over monotype on paper
5 3/16 × 6 ¾ in. (13.1 × 17.2 cm)
Haroche Collection
J 59; L 417

59. *Beside the Sea* (*Au bord de la mer*). 1876–77
Monotype on paper
Plate: 4 5/8 × 6 3/8 in. (11.8 × 16.2 cm), sheet: 6 3/8 × 6 7/8 in. (16.2 × 17.5 cm)
Museum of Fine Arts, Boston. Gift of Mr. and Mrs. Peter A. Wick
A&C 181; J 264

60. *Bathers* (*Les Baigneuses*). c. 1875–80
Monotype on paper
Plate: 4 11/16 × 6 3/8 in. (11.9 × 16.2 cm), sheet: 7 3/16 × 9 5/16 in. (18.2 × 23.7 cm)
Lent by James Bergquist
A&C 169; J 262

61. *The River* (*La Rivière*). c. 1877–79
Monotype on paper
Plate: 3 ½ × 6 13/16 in. (8.9 × 17.3 cm), sheet: 7 3/16 × 9 in. (18.2 × 22.9 cm)
Museum of Fine Arts, Boston. Katherine E. Bullard Fund in memory of Francis Bullard
A&C 180; J 272

62. *Moonrise* (*Lever de la lune*). c. 1880
Monotype on paper
Plate: 4 5/8 × 6 5/16 in. (11.7 × 16 cm), sheet: 6 1/16 × 9 11/16 in. (15.4 × 24.6 cm)
Sterling and Francine Clark Art Institute, Williamstown, Massachusetts
A&C 183; J 270

63. *Willow Trees* (*Les Saules*). c. 1880
Monotype on paper
Plate: 4 5/8 × 6 5/16 in. (11.7 × 16.1 cm), sheet: 6 9/16 × 10 ½ in. (16.7 × 26.7 cm)
Private collection. Courtesy Nicholas Stogdon
A&C 176

64. *The Road* (*La Route*). c. 1878–80
Monotype on China paper
Plate: 4 5/8 × 6 5/16 in. (11.8 × 16.1 cm), sheet: 6 5/16 × 7 ¼ in. (16 × 18.4 cm)
National Gallery of Art, Washington, D.C. Rosenwald Collection
A&C 175; J 266

65. *The Path up the Hill* (*Le Chemin montant*). c. 1878–80
Monotype on paper
Plate: 4 11/16 × 6 5/16 in. (11.9 × 16.1 cm), sheet: 5 13/16 × 7 1/8 in. (14.8 × 18.1 cm)
Museum of Fine Arts, Boston. Fund in memory of Horatio Greenough Curtis
A&C 177; J 267

66. *Avenue with Trees* (*L'Avenue du bois*). c. 1880
Monotype on China paper
Plate: 4 5/8 × 6 5/16 in. (11.8 × 16.1 cm), sheet: 6 ¾ × 8 1/16 in. (17.2 × 20.5 cm)
The Syndics of the Fitzwilliam Museum, University of Cambridge. Bequest of A.S.F. Gow through the National Art Collections Fund
A&C 53; J 260

67. *Rest in the Fields* (*Repos dans les champs*). c. 1877–80
Monotype on China paper
Plate: 8 7/16 × 6 5/16 in. (21.5 × 16 cm), sheet: 13 ½ × 9 9/16 in. (34.3 × 24.3 cm)
Sterling and Francine Clark Art Institute, Williamstown, Massachusetts
A&C 178; J 265

68. *The Public Meeting* (*La Réunion publique*). c. 1880
Monotype on paper
Plate: 4 5/8 × 6 3/8 in. (11.8 × 16.2 cm)
Private collection, Paris
A&C 54; J 256

69. *Backstage at the Opera* (*Dans les coulisses de l'opéra*). c. 1880*
Monotype on paper
12 3/16 × 10 13/16 in. (31 × 27.4 cm)
Private collection, Paris

70. Three studies of Ludovic Halévy standing. c. 1876–77
Charcoal on paper
12 5/8 × 18 7/8 in. (32 × 48 cm)
National Gallery of Art, Washington, D.C. Collection of Mr. and Mrs. Paul Mellon

71. Three studies of Ludovic Halévy standing. c. 1876–77
Charcoal on paper. Counterproof of plate 70
14 1/8 × 19 ¼ in. (35.9 × 48.9 cm)
National Gallery of Art, Washington, D.C. Collection of Mr. and Mrs. Paul Mellon

Plates 72–84 are all proposed illustrations for *The Cardinal Family* (*La Famille Cardinal*)

72. *An Admirer in the Corridor* (*Ludovic Halévy dans les coulisses*). c. 1876–77
Monotype on paper. Cognate of plate 73
Plate: 6 5/16 × 4 ¾ in. (16.1 × 12 cm), sheet: 9 5/16 × 7 1/16 in. (23.6 × 17.9 cm)
Staatsgalerie Stuttgart, Graphische Sammlung
Related to A&C 70; J 224

73. *Ludovic Halévy in the Wings* (*Ludovic Halévy dans les coulisses*). c. 1876–77
Monotype on paper. Cognate of plate 72
Plate: 6 3/8 × 4 3/4 in (16.2 × 12 cm), sheet: 9 3/4 × 6 1/4 in. (24.7 × 16 cm)
Private collection
A&C 70 ("second proof")

74. *Ludovic Halévy Finds Mme. Cardinal in the Dressing Room* (*Ludovic Halévy trouve Mme Cardinal dans les loges*). c. 1876–77
Pastel and pencil over monotype on paper
Plate: 8 1/2 × 6 1/4 in. (21.6 × 15.9 cm), sheet: 10 1/2 × 9 in. (26.7 × 22.9 cm)
Private collection
A&C 65; B&R 96; J 214

75. *Ludovic Halévy Meeting Mme. Cardinal Backstage* (*Rencontre de Ludovic Halévy et de Madame Cardinal dans les coulisses*). c. 1876–77
Monotype on paper
Plate: 10 3/4 × 12 1/16 in. (27.3 × 30.7 cm)
Private collection, Chicago
A&C 56; J 195

76. *Ludovic Halévy Meeting Madame Cardinal Backstage* (*Rencontre de Ludovic Halévy et de Madame Cardinal dans les coulisses*). c. 1876–1877
Monotype on paper
Plate: 6 5/16 × 8 3/8 in. (16 × 21.3 cm)
Collection André Bromberg
A&C 57; J 197

77. *Pauline and Virginie Conversing with Admirers* (*Pauline et Virginie Cardinal bavardant avec des admirateurs*). c. 1876–77
Monotype on paper
Plate: 8 7/16 × 6 5/16 in. (21.5 × 16.1 cm); sheet: 11 3/10 × 7 1/2 in. (28.7 × 19.1 cm)
Harvard Art Museums/Fogg Museum, Cambridge, Massachusetts. Bequest of Meta and Paul J. Sachs
A&C 66; J 218

78. *Dancers Coming from the Dressing Rooms onto the Stage* (*Et ces demoiselles frétillaient gentiment devant la glace du foyer*). c. 1876–77
Pastel over monotype on paper
Plate: 8 3/8 × 6 1/4 in. (21.2 × 15.8 cm)
Schorr Collection
A&C 63; J 209

79. *On the Street in the Rain* (*Sous la pluie*). c. 1876–77
Monotype on paper
Plate: 6 5/16 × 4 5/8 in. (16.1 × 11.8 cm), sheet: 10 7/16 × 7 1/16 in. (26.5 × 17.9 cm)
Private collection. Courtesy Nicholas Stogdon
A&C 52; J 217

80. *Ludovic Halévy Backstage* (*Ludovic Halévy montant l'escalier*). c. 1876–77
Monotype on paper
Plate: 8 3/8 × 6 1/4 in. (21.3 × 15.9 cm), sheet: 10 × 6 3/4 in. (25.4 × 17.1 cm)
Private collection
A&C 60; J 206

81. *In the Green Room* (*Le Foyer*). c. 1876–77
Monotype on paper
Plate: 6 3/8 × 4 11/16 in. (16.2 × 11.9 cm), sheet: 7 3/8 × 5 1/8 in. (18.8 × 13 cm)
Staatsgalerie Stuttgart, Graphische Sammlung
A&C 75; J 230

82. *The Cardinal Sisters Talking to Admirers* (*Les Petites Cardinal parlant à leurs admirateurs*). c. 1876–77
Monotype on paper
Plate: 8 11/16 × 7 in. (22 × 17.8 cm), sheet: 10 5/8 × 8 in. (27 × 20.3 cm)
Staatsgalerie Stuttgart, Graphische Sammlung
Related to A&C 72; J 226

83. *The Famous Good Friday Dinner (An Argument between Virginie's Protector, the Marquis Cavalcanti, and M. Cardinal)* (*Le Fameux Dîner du vendredi*). c. 1876–77
Monotype on paper
Plate: 8 3/8 × 6 5/16 in. (21.3 × 16 cm), sheet: 11 3/4 × 8 11/16 in. (29.8 × 22 cm)
Staatsgalerie Stuttgart, Graphische Sammlung
A&C 81; J 204

84. *M. Cardinal About to Write a Letter* (*Je ne comprends pas, dit M. Cardinal*). c. 1876–77
Monotype on paper
Plate: 4 11/16 × 6 3/8 in. (11.9 × 16.2 cm), sheet: 7 3/8 × 9 1/2 in. (18.7 × 24.2 cm)
Lent by James Bergquist
A&C 79; J 202

85. *The Name Day of the Madam* (*La Fête de la patronne*). c. 1877–79
Pastel over monotype on paper
10 1/2 × 11 5/8 in. (26.6 × 29.6 cm)
Musée Picasso, Paris
J 89; L 549

86. *Resting on the Bed* (*Repos sur le lit*). c. 1877–79
Monotype on paper
Plate: 6 5/16 × 4 3/4 in. (16 × 12 cm), sheet: 8 7/8 × 5 7/8 in. (22.5 × 15 cm)
Städel Museum, Frankfurt am Main. Property of the Städelscher Museums-Vereins e.V.
A&C 105; J 93

87. *Woman Slipping On Her Dress* (*La Sortie du bain*). c. 1877–79
Pastel over monotype on China paper
8 1/4 × 6 1/4 in. (21 × 15.9 cm)
Private collection, Chicago
J 178; L 554

88. *Two Young Girls* (*Deux jeunes filles*). c. 1877–79
Monotype on China paper
Plate: 6 1/4 × 4 3/4 in. (15.9 × 12.1 cm)
Private collection, Chicago
A&C 91; J 81

89. *Waiting for the Client* (*Attente d'un client*). c. 1877–79
Pastel over monotype on paper, mounted on paper
Plate: 6 5/16 × 4 15/16 in. (16 × 12.5 cm), sheet: 7 1/2 × 5 5/8 in. (19.1 × 14.3 cm)
Ann and Gordon Getty
B&R 80; J 84

90. *Waiting (first version)* (*L'Attente [première version]*). 1879
Monotype on paper
Plate: 4 5/8 × 6 5/16 in. (11.8 × 16.1 cm)
Musée Picasso, Paris
A&C 94; J 67

91. *Two Women—Scene from a Brothel* (*Deux femmes [Scène de maison close]*). c. 1877–79
Monotype on paper
Plate: 9 13/16 × 11 3/8 in. (24.9 × 28.9 cm), sheet: 8 7/16 × 6 5/16 in. (21.5 × 16 cm)
Museum of Fine Arts, Boston. Katherine E. Bullard Fund in memory of Francis Bullard
A&C 122; J 117

92. *Room in a Brothel* (*Dans le salon d'une maison close*). c. 1877–79
Monotype on paper
Plate: 8 3/16 × 6 1/4 in. (20.8 × 15.9 cm), sheet: 12 3/8 × 9 3/16 in. (31.5 × 23.3 cm)
Cantor Arts Center at Stanford University. Mortimer C. Leventritt Fund and Committee for Art Acquisitions Fund
A&C 116; J 87

93. *The Bidet* (*Le Bidet*). c. 1877–79
Monotype on paper
Plate: 6 5/16 × 4 11/16 in. (16 × 11.9 cm), sheet: 9 7/16 × 7 7/8 in. (24 × 20 cm)
The Saint Louis Art Museum, Missouri. The Marian Cronheim Trust for Prints and Drawings
J 110

94. *The Bath* (*Le Bain*). 1879–83
Monotype on paper
Plate: 8 3/8 × 6 1/4 in. (21.3 × 15.9 cm)
Statens Museum for Kunst, Copenhagen
A&C 132; J 172

95. *Nude Woman Drying Her Face* (*Femme nue s'essuyant la figure*). c. 1877–79
Monotype on paper
Plate: 6 × 4 ½ in. (15.3 × 11.4 cm), sheet: 7 ½ × 6 7⁄16 in. (19 × 16.3 cm) (irregular)
Private collection
A&C 124; J 113

96. *Three Women in a Brothel, Seen from Behind* (*Trois filles assises de dos*). c. 1877–79
Pastel over monotype on paper
6 5⁄16 × 8 7⁄16 in. (16.1 × 21.4 cm)
Musée Picasso, Paris
J 63; L 548

97. *The Client* (*Le Client*). 1879
Monotype on paper
Plate: 8 7⁄16 × 6 ¼ in. (21.5 × 15.9 cm)
Musée Picasso, Paris
A&C 95; J 85

98. *Waiting for the Client* (*En attendant le client*). c. 1877–79
Monotype on paper
Plate: 6 5⁄16 × 8 ¼ in. (16 × 21 cm); sheet: 7 1⁄16 × 9 1⁄16 in. (18 × 23 cm)
Private collection. Courtesy Alexander Apsis Fine Art
A&C 118; J 104

99. *In the Salon* (*Un Coin de salon en maison close*). c. 1877–79
Monotype on China paper
Plate: 6 5⁄16 × 4 ⅝ in. (16.1 × 11.8 cm), sheet: 11 ⅝ × 8 ¼ in. (29.6 × 20.9 cm)
Private collection, Chicago
A&C 90; J 71

100. *Woman Reclining on Her Bed* (*Femme étendue sur son lit*). c. 1879–83
Monotype on paper. Cognate of plate 101
Plate: 7 13⁄16 × 16 5⁄16 in. (19.9 × 41.5 cm), sheet: 8 ¾ × 16 ½ in. (22.2 × 41.9 cm)
The Art Institute of Chicago. Clarence Buckingham Collection
A&C 163; J 137

101. *Female Nude Reclining* (*Femme nue couchée*). c. 1888–90
Pastel over monotype. Cognate of plate 100
Plate: 7 ¾ × 16 in. (19.7 × 40.6 cm), sheet: 13 × 16 ⅜ in. (33 × 41.6 cm)
Ann and Gordon Getty
J 138; L 752

102. *The Fireside* (*Le Foyer [La Cheminée]*). c. 1880–85
Monotype on paper
Plate: 16 ¾ × 23 1⁄16 in. (42.5 × 58.6 cm), sheet: 19 ¾ × 25 ½ in. (50.2 × 64.8 cm)
The Metropolitan Museum of Art, New York. Harris Brisbane Dick Fund, The Elisha Whittelsey Collection, The Elisha Whittelsey Fund, and C. Douglas Dillon Gift
A&C 167; J 159

103. *Naked Woman by a Fireplace* (*Femme se chauffant*). c. 1880–85
Monotype on paper
Plate: 10 15⁄16 × 14 15⁄16 in. (27.8 × 37.9 cm), sheet: 14 ¾ × 19 5⁄16 in. (37.5 × 49 cm)
Private collection

104. *Getting Up: Woman Putting On Her Stockings* (*Le Lever, femme assise mettant ses bas*). c. 1880–85
Monotype on paper
Plate: 9 5⁄16 × 8 ½ in. (23.7 × 21.6 cm)
Musée d'Orsay, Paris
A&C 136; J 168

105. *Getting into Bed* (*Le Coucher*). c. 1880–85
Monotype on paper
Plate: 14 ⅞ × 10 ⅞ in. (37.8 × 27.7 cm), sheet: 20 1⁄16 × 13 ¾ in. (51 × 35 cm)
The National Museum of Art, Architecture and Design, Oslo
A&C 138; J 166

106. *Woman Reading* (*Liseuse*). c. 1880–85
Monotype on paper. Cognate of plate 108
Plate: 14 15⁄16 × 10 ⅞ in. (38 × 27.7 cm), sheet: 17 7⁄16 × 12 13⁄16 in. (44.3 × 32.5 cm)
National Gallery of Art, Washington, D.C. Rosenwald Collection
A&C 165; J 141

107. *The Reader* (*Le Repos*) (recto). c. 1880–85
Monotype on paper. Counterproof of plate 106
Plate: 15 3⁄16 × 11 ¼ in. (38.5 × 28.5 cm), sheet: 19 7⁄16 × 13 ⅞ in. (49.4 × 35.3 cm)
Kunsthalle Bremen. Kupferstichkabinett–Der Kunstverein in Bremen
J 142

108. *The Reader* (*Le Repos*) (verso). c. 1880–85
Monotype on paper. Cognate of plate 106
Plate: 14 15⁄16 × 10 ⅞ in. (38 × 27.7 cm); sheet: 17 7⁄16 × 12 13⁄16 in. (44.3 × 32.5 cm)
Kunsthalle Bremen. Kupferstichkabinett–Der Kunstverein in Bremen
J 142

109. *Bedtime* (*Le Coucher*). c. 1880–85
Monotype on paper
Plate: 8 15⁄16 × 17 5⁄16 in. (22.7 × 44 cm)
Private collection
A&C 140; J 133

110. *Woman Drying Her Feet* (*Femme s'essuyant les pieds, près de sa baignoire*). c. 1880–85
Monotype on paper
Plate: 17 ¾ × 9 7⁄16 in. (45.1 × 23.9 cm), sheet: 20 ¼ × 12 ⅝ in. (51.5 × 32 cm)
Musée d'Orsay, Paris
A&C 158; J 127

111. *The Toilette (The Chamber Pot)* (*La Toilette, la cuvette*). c. 1880–85
Monotype on paper
Plate: 14 15⁄16 × 10 15⁄16 in. (38 × 27.8 cm), sheet: 20 3⁄16 × 13 ⅞ in. (51.3 × 35.3 cm)
Private collection. Courtesy C. G. Boerner, New York

112. *The Bath* (*La Toilette [Le Bain]*). c. 1880–85
Monotype on paper
Plate: 12 ⅜ × 10 15⁄16 in. (31.4 × 27.8 cm), sheet: 20 ¼ × 13 ⅞ in. (51.5 × 35.2 cm)
The Art Institute of Chicago. Clarence Buckingham Collection
A&C 155; J 123

113. *Woman in a Bathtub* (*Femme au bain*). c. 1880–85
Monotype on paper. Cognate of plate 114
Plate: 7 ⅞ × 16 ⅜ in. (20 × 41.6 cm)
Private collection
J 119

114. *Woman in Her Bath, Sponging Her Leg* (*Femme dans son bain s'épongeant la jambe*). c. 1880–85
Pastel over monotype on paper. Cognate of plate 113
7 ¾ × 16 ⅛ in. (19.7 × 41 cm)
Musée d'Orsay, Paris
J 120; L 728

115. *Woman Standing in Her Bath* (*Femme debout dans une baignoire*). c. 1880–85
Monotype on paper
Plate: 14 15⁄16 × 10 ⅝ in. (38 × 27 cm), sheet: 20 ⅜ × 13 ⅞ in. (51.7 × 35.3 cm)
Musée d'Orsay, Paris
A&C 157; J 125

116. *Getting Up—Stockings* (*Le Lever [Les Bas]*). c. 1880–85
Opaque watercolor over monotype on paper
Plate: 14 15⁄16 × 10 15⁄16 in. (37.9 × 27.8 cm)
The National Museum of Art, Architecture and Design, Oslo
A&C 137; J 167

117. *Woman Going to Bed* (*Le Coucher*). c. 1880–83
Monotype on paper. Cognate of plate 118
Plate: 14 15⁄16 × 11 in. (38 × 28 cm)
Private collection
A&C 139; J 129

118. *Bedtime* (*Le Coucher*). c. 1883
Pastel over monotype on paper. Cognate of plate 117
Plate: 15 × 11 in. (38.1 × 27.9 cm)
Private collection
J 130; L 747

119. *The Letter* (*La Lettre*). c. 1882–85
Monotype on paper
12 3⁄8 × 10 7⁄8 in. (31.4 × 27.6 cm)
Collection Marcel Lecomte, Paris
Related to J 143

120. *The Toilette (Reading after the Bath)* (*La Toilette [Lecture aprés le bain]*). c. 1880–85
Monotype on paper
Plate: 10 7⁄8 × 14 7⁄8 in. (27.7 × 37.8 cm), sheet: 14 × 20 3⁄8 in. (35.6 × 51.8 cm)
Private collection. Courtesy Marc Rosen Fine Art Ltd.
J 140

121. *Sleep* (*Le Sommeil*). c. 1880–85*
Monotype on paper
Plate: 10 7⁄8 × 14 7⁄8 in. (27.6 × 37.8 cm)
British Museum, London. Bequeathed by Campbell Dodgson
A&C 164; J 135

122. *Fantasy, Nude Woman* (*Fantaisie*). c. 1880–85
Monotype on paper
Plate: 6 3⁄4 × 3 7⁄16 in. (17.1 × 8.7 cm)
Private collection
A&C 145; J 183

123. *Final Touches at the Toilette* (*Dernier préparatifs de toilette*). c. 1880–85
Oil over monotype on paper
Plate: 6 5⁄16 × 8 7⁄16 in. (16 × 21.5 cm)
Fine Arts Museums of San Francisco. Museum Purchase, Achenbach Foundation for Graphic Arts Endowment Fund
A&C 134; J 188

124. *Woman Getting Out of the Bath* (*Femme sortant du bain*). c. 1880–85
Pastel over monotype on paper
6 5⁄16 × 8 7⁄16 in. (16 × 21.5 cm)
Musée d'Orsay, Paris
J 175

125. *Landscape* (*Paysage*). 1892
Pastel over monotype in oil on blue paper, now faded to off-white, mounted on board
Sheet: 10 × 13 3⁄8 in. (25.4 × 34 cm)
The Metropolitan Museum of Art, New York. Purchase, Mr. and Mrs. Richard J. Bernhard Gift
J 285; L 1044

126. *Forest in the Mountains* (*Forêt dans la montagne*). c. 1890
Monotype in oil on paper
Plate: 11 13⁄16 × 15 3⁄4 in. (30 × 40 cm), sheet: 12 3⁄8 × 16 5⁄16 in. (31.4 × 41.4 cm)
The Museum of Modern Art, New York. Louise Reinhardt Smith Bequest
A&C 187; J 297

127. *Green Landscape* (*Paysage vert*). 1890
Monotype in oil on paper
Plate: 11 3⁄4 × 15 5⁄8 in. (29.9 × 39.7 cm), sheet: 12 3⁄8 × 15 7⁄8 in. (31.4 × 40.4 cm)
The Museum of Modern Art, New York. Louise Reinhardt Smith Bequest
A&C 199

128. *Twilight in the Pyrenees* (*Le Crépuscule dans les Pyrénées*). 1890
Monotype in oil on paper
Plate: 11 3⁄4 × 15 11⁄16 in. (29.8 × 39.8 cm)
Collection of the Ackland Art Museum, University of North Carolina at Chapel Hill. Ackland Fund
A&C 185; J 307

129. *Squall in the Mountains* (*Bourrasque dans la montagne*). 1890
Monotype in oil on paper
Plate: 11 5⁄8 × 15 9⁄16 in. (29.5 × 39.5 cm)
Norton Simon Museum, Pasadena, California. Museum Purchase, B. Gerald Cantor Fund
A&C 197; J 306

130. *The Road in the Forest* (*La Route dans la forêt*). 1890
Monotype in oil on paper
Plate: 11 13⁄16 × 15 3⁄4 in. (30 × 40 cm), sheet: 11 13⁄16 × 15 3⁄4 in. (30 × 40 cm)
Harvard Art Museums/Fogg Museum, Cambridge, Massachusetts. Bequest of Frances L. Hofer
A&C 195; J 292

131. *Le Cap Ferrat*. 1892
Monotype in oil on paper
Sheet: 11 11⁄16 × 15 11⁄16 in. (29.7 × 39.9 cm)
Staatliche Kunsthalle, Karlsruhe
A&C 184; J 308

132. *Mountain Landscape* (*Paysage dans la montagne*). 1890
Monotype in oil on paper
Plate: 11 15⁄16 × 15 3⁄4 in. (30.4 × 40 cm), sheet: 12 1⁄4 × 16 1⁄8 in. (31.1 × 41 cm)
Los Angeles County Museum of Art. Purchased with funds provided by the Garrett Corporation
A&C 194; J 289

133. *Landscape* (*Paysage*). 1890–92
Monotype in oil on paper
Plate: 11 1⁄2 × 15 1⁄2 in. (29.2 × 39.4 cm)
Harvard Art Museums/Fogg Museum, Cambridge, Massachusetts. Partial and promised gift of Emily Rauh Pulitzer in honor of Marjorie B. Cohn
A&C 190; J 309

134. *Autumn Effect* (*Effet d'automne dans la montagne*), 1890
Monotype in oil on paper
Plate: 11 13⁄16 × 15 13⁄16 in. (30 × 40.2 cm), sheet: 11 13⁄16 × 15 13⁄16 in. (30 × 40.2 cm)
Museum of Fine Arts, Boston. Gift of her children in memory of Elizabeth Paine Metcalf
A&C 189; J 299

135. *The Ochre Hill* (*Effet de montagne*). 1890
Monotype in oil on paper
Plate: 11 3⁄4 × 15 9⁄16 in. (29.9 × 39.5 cm)
Private collection
A&C 188; J 298

136. *Autumn Landscape* (*L'Estérel*). 1890
Monotype in oil on paper. Cognate of plate 137
Plate: 11 7⁄8 × 15 3⁄4 in. (30.2 × 40 cm), sheet: 12 1⁄2 × 16 1⁄4 in. (31.8 × 41.3 cm)
Private collection
A&C 186; J 300

137. *Autumn Landscape* (*L'Estérel*). 1890
Monotype in oil on paper. Cognate of plate 136
Plate: 11 7⁄8 × 15 5⁄8 in. (30.2 × 39.7 cm), sheet: 12 1⁄8 × 16 1⁄16 in. (30.8 × 40.8 cm)
Norton Simon Museum, Pasadena, California. Museum Purchase, B. Gerald Cantor Fund
J 301

138. *Cap Hornu near Saint-Valery-sur-Somme* (*Le Cap Hornu près Saint-Valery-sur-Somme*). c. 1890–93
Monotype in oil on paper. Cognate of plate 139
Plate: 11 3⁄4 × 15 11⁄16 in. (29.9 × 39.9 cm)
British Museum, London. Bequeathed by Campbell Dodgson
A&C 192; J 295

139. *Mountains and Valley* (*Montagnes et vallon*). 1890
Monotype in oil on paper. Cognate of plate 138
Plate: 12 $\frac{1}{2}$ × 16 $\frac{7}{16}$ in. (31.8 × 41.8 cm), sheet: 15 $\frac{3}{8}$ × 19 $\frac{5}{16}$ in. (39 × 49 cm)
Private collection, Switzerland
J 296; L 1057

140. *Wheatfield and Line of Trees* (*Champ de blé et ligne d'arbres*). 1890
Pastel over monotype in oil on paper
9 $\frac{13}{16}$ × 13 $\frac{3}{8}$ in. (25 × 34 cm)
Private collection
J 291; L 1035

141. *Landscape with Rocky Cliffs* (*Rochers au bord d'une rivière*). 1890
Pastel over monotype in oil on paper
15 $\frac{3}{4}$ × 11 $\frac{7}{16}$ in. (40 × 29 cm)
Private collection
J 283; L 1043

142. *Pathway in a Field* (*Sentier dans la prairie*). 1890
Pastel over monotype in oil on paper
Plate: 11 $\frac{13}{16}$ × 15 $\frac{9}{16}$ in. (30 × 39.5 cm)
Yale University Art Gallery, New Haven, Connecticut. Katharine Ordway Fund
J 286; L 1046

143. *Landscape with Rocks* (*Paysage avec rochers*). 1892
Pastel over monotype in oil on paper
Plate: 9 $\frac{3}{4}$ × 13 $\frac{3}{8}$ in. (24.8 × 34 cm), sheet: 10 $\frac{1}{8}$ × 13 $\frac{9}{16}$ in. (25.7 × 34.4 cm)
High Museum of Art, Atlanta. Purchase with High Museum of Art Enhancement Fund
L 1040

144. *Landscape by the Sea* (*Paysage en bord de mer*). 1892
Pastel over monotype in oil on paper
Plate: 9 $\frac{15}{16}$ × 13 $\frac{9}{16}$ in. (25.3 × 34.5 cm), sheet: 10 $\frac{5}{8}$ × 14 $\frac{3}{16}$ in. (27 × 36 cm)
Musée d'art et d'histoire, Neuchâtel
K 6; L 632

145. *The Field of Flax* (*Le Champ de lin*). 1892
Pastel over monotype in oil on paper
9 $\frac{13}{16}$ × 13 $\frac{3}{8}$ in. (25 × 34 cm)
From the Collection of Wendy and Leonard Goldberg
J 321; L 1041

146. *River Banks* (*Bords de rivière*). 1890
Pastel over monotype in oil on paper
11 $\frac{13}{16}$ × 15 $\frac{3}{4}$ in. (30 × 40 cm)
Private collection, Switzerland. Courtesy Galerie Fischer, Lucerne
J 280; L 1056

147. *River Banks* (*Bords de rivière*). 1890
Pastel over monotype in oil on paper
11 $\frac{13}{16}$ × 15 $\frac{3}{4}$ in. (30 × 40 cm)
Private collection
J 281; L 1042

148. *Vesuvius* (*Le Vésuve*). 1892
Pastel over monotype in oil on paper
Plate: 9 $\frac{13}{16}$ × 11 $\frac{13}{16}$ in. (25 × 30 cm), sheet: 10 $\frac{9}{16}$ × 12 $\frac{1}{2}$ in. (26.9 × 31.8 cm)
Private collection
J 310; L 1052

149. *Village in l'Estérel* (*Village dans l'Estérel*). 1890*
Monotype in oil on paper. Cognate of plate 150
Plate: 11 $\frac{13}{16}$ × 16 $\frac{3}{4}$ in. (30 × 42.5 cm)
Bibliothèque Nationale de France, Paris
A&C 191; J 275

150. *Estérel Village* (*Village dans l'Estérel*). 1890
Monotype in oil on paper. Cognate of plate 149
Plate: 11 $\frac{3}{4}$ × 15 $\frac{11}{16}$ in. (29.9 × 39.9 cm)
The Cleveland Museum of Art. Fiftieth anniversary gift of The Print Club of Cleveland
A&C 191a ("second proof" of A&C 191); J 276

151. *Landscape* (*Paysage*). 1892
Pastel over monotype in oil on paper. Cognate of plate 152
Plate: 9 $\frac{3}{4}$ × 11 $\frac{3}{4}$ in. (24.8 × 29.9 cm)
Private collection
J 314; L 1039

152. *Landscape* (*Paysage*). 1890-1893
Pastel over monotype in oil on paper. Cognate of plate 151
Plate: 9 $\frac{1}{2}$ × 11 $\frac{1}{2}$ in. (24.1 × 29.2 cm)
Mottisfont Abbey, The National Trust. The Derek Hill Bequest, through the National Art-Collections Fund
J 278

153. *Frieze of Dancers* (*Danseuses attachant leurs sandales*). c. 1895
Oil on canvas
27 $\frac{9}{16}$ × 78 $\frac{15}{16}$ in. (70 × 200.5 cm)
The Cleveland Museum of Art. Gift of the Hanna Fund
L 1144

154. *Dancer Adjusting Her Slipper* (*Danseuse rajustant son chausson*). 1887
Pastel on paper
19 $\frac{5}{8}$ × 24 $\frac{5}{8}$ in. (50 × 62.5 cm)
Frederick Iseman Art Trust
L 907

155. *Dancer Adjusting Her Slipper* (*Danseuse rajustant son chausson*). c. 1887
Pastel on paper
18 $\frac{3}{4}$ × 24 $\frac{5}{8}$ in. (47.6 × 62.5 cm)
Private collection
B&R 125

156. *Dancer Holding a Fan* (*Danseuse à l'éventail*). c. 1890
Charcoal on paper mounted on board
17 $\frac{15}{16}$ × 14 in. (45.5 × 35.5 cm)
Courtesy of Marty de Cambiare, Paris

157. *Pink Dancer* (*Danseuse rose*). 1896
Pastel on paper
16 $\frac{3}{4}$ × 12 $\frac{3}{16}$ in. (42.6 × 31 cm)
Private collection
L 1245

158. *Two Dancers Resting* (*Deux danseuses au repos*). c. 1890–1900
Charcoal and colored chalk or pastel on paper
22 $\frac{1}{4}$ × 17 $\frac{1}{2}$ in. (56.5 × 44.5 cm)
Philadelphia Museum of Art. The Samuel S. White 3rd and Vera White Collection

159. *Two Dancers Resting* (*Deux danseuses au repos*). c. 1890–1905
Charcoal on paper
22 $\frac{3}{4}$ × 16 $\frac{3}{8}$ in. (57.8 × 41.6 cm)
Judith and Bernard Briskin. The Briskin Community Property Trust

160. *Two Dancers* (*Les Grandes Danseuses vertes*). c. 1898
Pastel on eight sheets of pieced paper
29 $\frac{1}{2}$ × 27 $\frac{9}{16}$ in. (75 × 70 cm)
Ny Carlsberg Glyptotek, Copenhagen
L 1330

161. *Dancers Resting* (*Danseuses [Danseuses au repose]*). c. 1898
Pastel on five sheets of pieced paper
32 $\frac{11}{16}$ × 28 $\frac{3}{8}$ in. (83 × 72 cm)
Fondation de l'Hermitage, Lausanne. Legs de Lucie Schmidheiny
L 1328

162. *Two Dancers* (*Deux danseuses*). 1905
Charcoal and pastel on tracing paper
43 × 32 in. (109.2 × 81.3 cm)
The Museum of Modern Art, New York. The William S. Paley Collection
B&R 149

163. *Two Dancers* (*Danseuses*). c. 1898
Pastel on paper
33 $\frac{3}{8}$ × 30 $\frac{3}{8}$ in. (84.8 × 77.2 cm)
The Saint Louis Art Museum, Missouri. Funds given by Mrs. Mark C. Steinberg
L 1327

164. *Grand Arabesque, Second Time* (*Grande arabesque, deuxième temps*). 1900–1905
Charcoal on tracing paper
18 ⅛ × 14 3/16 in. (46 × 36 cm)
Private collection

165. *Two Dancers en Arabesque* (*Deux danseuses nues en arabesque*). c. 1885–90
Charcoal on tracing paper
17 11/16 × 21 ¼ in. (45 × 54 cm)
Galerie Bernard Lecomte, Paris

166. *Three Dancers* (*Trois Danseuses*). 1900–1905
Charcoal and pastel on tracing paper
21 ¼ × 30 ⅛ in. (54 × 76.5 cm)
Private collection. Courtesy Halcyon Gallery, London

167. *Three Dancers in the Foyer* (*Trois danseuses au foyer*). 1892–95
Oil on canvas
22 ⅛ × 32 ⅛ in. (56.2 × 81.6 cm)
Courtesy of the Larry Ellison Collection
L 1131

168. *A Group of Dancers* (*Groupe de danseuses*). c. 1898
Oil on paper mounted on canvas
18 ⅛ × 24 ⅛ in. (46 × 61.2 cm)
Scottish National Gallery, Edinburgh
L 770

169. *Ballet Dancers* (*Danseuses*). c. 1890–1900
Oil on canvas
28 9/16 × 28 ¾ in. (72.5 × 73 cm)
The National Gallery, London. Bought, Courtauld Fund
L 588

170. *After the Bath, Woman Drying Herself* (*Après le bain, femme s'essuyant*). 1895–1900
Oil on canvas
29 ¾ × 33 ⅞ in. (75.5 × 86 cm)
The Henry and Rose Pearlman Foundation, on long-term loan to the Princeton University Art Museum
L 1117

171. *The Bath* (*Le Bain*). c. 1895
Oil on canvas
33 × 45 ¾ in. (83.8 × 116.2 cm)
Carnegie Museum of Art, Pittsburgh, Pennsylvania. Acquired through the generosity of Mrs. Alan M. Scaife
L 1029

172. *After the Bath* (*Après le bain*). c. 1891
Charcoal and pastel on paper
20 ⅜ × 26 5/16 in. (51.8 × 66.8 cm)
Private collection
L 1106 bis

173. *After the Bath* (*Le Bain, femme vue de dos*). c. 1893–98
Oil on canvas
25 ⅞ × 32 ⅜ in. (65.7 × 82.2 cm)
The J. Paul Getty Museum, Los Angeles
L 1104

174. *After the Bath* (*Le Repos après le bain*). c. 1896
Charcoal and pastel on paper
15 ⅜ × 13 in. (39 × 33 cm)
Private collection
L 1232

175. *After the Bath (Woman Drying Herself)* (*Après le bain, femme s'essuyant*). c. 1896
Oil on canvas
35 ¼ × 46 in. (89.5 × 116.8 cm)
Philadelphia Museum of Art. Purchased with funds from the estate of George D. Widener
L 1231

176. *Woman Drying Herself* (*La Toilette après le bain*). After 1888
Pastel on paper
24 ¾ × 18 ½ in. (62.9 × 47 cm)
Los Angeles County Museum of Art, Gift of Jerome K. Ohrbach
L 948

Selected Bibliography

Compiled by Hillary Reder

Catalogues raisonnés

Adhémar, Jean, and Françoise Cachin. *Degas: The Complete Etchings, Lithographs and Monotypes*. Trans. Jane Brenton, foreword by John Rewald. New York: Viking Press, 1974. First published in French, as *Edgar Degas: gravures et monotypes*. Paris: Arts et Métiers, 1973.

Brame, Philippe, and Theodore Reff. *Degas et son œuvre: A Supplement*. New York and London: Garland Publishing, 1984.

Catalogue des tableaux, pastels et dessins par Edgar Degas et provenant de son atelier. Sales cats., *vente I*, May 6–8, 1918; *vente II*, December 11–13, 1918; *vente III*, April 7–9, 1919; *vente IV*, July 2–4, 1919. Paris: Galeries George Petit, 1918–19.

Catalogue des eaux-fortes, vernis-mous, aqua-tintes, lithographies et monotypes par Edgar Degas et provenant de son atelier. . . . Sale cat., November 22–23, 1918. Paris: Galerie Manzi-Joyant, 1918.

Janis, Eugenia Parry. *Degas Monotypes*. Cambridge, Mass.: Fogg Art Museum, Harvard University, and Greenwich, Conn.: New York Graphic Society, 1968.

Lemoisne, Paul-André. *Degas et son oeuvre*. 4 vols. Paris: Paul Brame and C. M. de Hauke, Arts et Métiers Graphiques, 1946.

The Notebooks of Edgar Degas. Ed. Theodore Reff. 2 vols. Oxford: Clarendon Press, 1976.

Articles, Essays, and Reviews

Adhémar, Jean. "Un Monotype de Degas au cabinet des estampes." *Gazette des beaux-arts* 64 (1964):374–77.

Alexandre, Arsène. "Chroniques d'aujourd'hui." *Paris*. September 9, 1892.

——. "Degas: Graveur et Lithographe." *Les Arts* XV, no. 171 (1918):11–19.

Bernheimer, Charles. "Degas's Brothels: Voyeurism and Ideology." *Misogyny, Misandry, and Misanthropy*. Special issue of *Representations* no. 20 (Autumn 1987):158–86.

Broude, Norma. "Edgar Degas and French Feminism, ca. 1880: 'The Young Spartans,' the Brothel Monotypes, and the Bathers Revisited." *Art Bulletin* 70, no. 4 (December 1988):640–59.

Brown, Kathryn. "Touch and Vision in Edgar Degas's Darkfield Monotypes." *Print Quarterly* 31, no. 4 (December 2014):395–405.

Buchanan, Harvey. "Edgar Degas and Ludovic Lepic: An Impressionist Friendship." *Cleveland Studies in the History of Art* 2 (1997):32–121.

Buerger, Janet, and Barbara Stern Shapiro. "A Note on Degas's Use of Daguerreotype Plates." *The Print Collector's Newsletter* 12, no. 4 (September–October 1981):103–6.

Crimp, Douglas. "Positive/Negative: A Note of Degas's Photographs." *October* 5 (Summer 1978):89–100.

Fletcher, Shelley. "Two Monotype-Pastels by Degas at the National Gallery of Art." *Print Quarterly* 1, no. 1 (March 1984):53–55.

Fletcher, Shelley, and Pia Desantis. "Degas: The Search for His Technique Continues." *Burlington* 131, no. 1033 (April 1989):256–65.

Guérin, Marcel. "Notes sur les monotypes de Degas." *L'Amour de l'Art* 5 (March 1924):77–80.

Harrison, Charles. "Degas' Bathers and Other People." *Modernism/Modernity* 6, no. 3 (September 1999):57–90.

Herbert, Robert. "Degas and Women." *New York Review of Books* 43, no. 7 (April 18, 1996):46–48.

Ives, Colta. "French Prints in the Era of Impressionism and Symbolism." *Metropolitan Museum of Art Bulletin* 46, no. 1 (Summer 1988):8–56, esp. pp. 15–21.

Janis, Eugenia Parry. "The Role of the Monotype in the Working Method of Degas." *The Burlington Magazine* 109, no. 766 (January 1967):20–29 and no. 767 (February 1967):71–81.

——. "Degas and the 'Master of Chiaroscuro.'" *Art Institute of Chicago Museum Studies* 7 (1972):52–71.

Jeanniot, Georges. "Souvenirs sur Degas." *Revue Universelle* LV, no. 14 (October 15, 1933):152–74 and no. 15 (November 1, 1933):280–304.

Kendall, Richard. "'A Little Mystery, Some Vagueness, Some Fantasy . . . ': Degas' Anthropomorphic Landscapes." *Apollo* 139, no. 384 (February 1984):39–45.

Lay, Howard. "Degas at Durand-Ruel, 1892: The Landscape Monotypes." *The Print Collector's Newsletter* 9, no. 5 (November-December 1978):142–47.

Lockhart, Anne L. "Three Monotypes by Edgar Degas." *The Bulletin of the Cleveland Museum of Art* 64, no. 9 (November 1977):299–306.

Nicolson, Benedict. "Degas Monotypes." *The Burlington Magazine* 100, no. 662 (May 1958):172–75.

Raisseur, Tom. "Degas and Hiroshige." *Print Quarterly* 28, no. 4 (December 2011):429–31.

Robins, Anna Gruetzner. "Degas's Method." *Print Quarterly* 31, no. 4 (December 2014):438–41.

Reff, Theodore. "The Technical Aspects of Degas's Art." *Metropolitan Museum Journal* 4 (1971):141–66.

Rouart, Denis. "Degas. Paysages en monotype." *L'Oeil* 117 (September 1964):10–15.

Shapiro, Michael. "Degas and the Siamese Twins of the Café-Concert: The Ambassadeurs and the Alcazar d'Eté." *Gazette des Beaux-Arts* 95 (April 1980):153–64.

Thomson, Richard. "Degas's Torse de Femme and Titian." *Gazette des Beaux-Arts*, pér. 6. XCVIII, nos. 1350–51 (July-August 1981):45–48.

Updike, John. "Degas Out of Doors." *The New York Review of Books* 41, no. 6 (March 24, 1994):16–18.

Books

Armstrong, Carol. *Odd Man Out: Readings of the Work and Reputation of Edgar Degas*. Chicago: at the University Press, 1991.

Berson, Ruth. *The New Painting: Impressionism 1874–1886*. Vol. 1, *Documentation*; vol. 2, *Exhibited Works*. San Francisco: Fine Arts Museums of San Francisco, 1996.

Boggs, Jean Sutherland. *Degas*. Chicago: The Art Institute of Chicago, 1996. Esp. pp 30–37.

Boggs, Jean Sutherland, and Anne F. Maheux. *Degas Pastels*. New York: George Braziller, 1992. Esp. Maheux, "Looking into Degas's Pastel Technique," pp. 19–38.

Bomford, David. *Art in the Making: Degas*. London: National Gallery, 2004.

Brettell, Richard R., and Stephen F. Eisenman. *Nineteenth Century Art in the Norton Simon Museum*. New Haven: Yale University Press, 2006. Esp. Richard Kendall, "Redefining Degas: The Norton Simon Collection," pp. 29–50.

Brettell, Richard R., and Suzanne Folds McCullagh. *Degas in the Art Institute of Chicago*. Chicago: The Art Institute of Chicago, and New York: Harry N. Abrams, 1984.

Browse, Lillian. *Degas Dancers*. London: Faber and Faber, 1949.

Callen, Anthea. *The Spectacular Body: Science, Method, and Meaning in the Work of Degas*. New Haven: Yale University Press, 1995. Esp. chap. 3, "The Invisible Man: Voyeurism and the Narratives of Sexual Conquest," pp. 71–110.

Clayson, Hollis. *Painted Love: Prostitution in French Art of the Impressionist Era*. New Haven: Yale University Press, 1991. Esp. chap. 2, "In the Brothel," pp. 27–46.

Degas, Edgar. *Lettres de Degas*. Ed. Marcel Guérin. Paris: B. Grasset, 1931. Eng. trans. as *Degas Letters*. Oxford: Bruno Cassirer, 1947.

Fourcade, Dominique. *Le Sujet monotype*. Paris: P.O.L., 1997.

Guillaud, Jacqueline and Maurice, eds. *Degas: Form and Space*. Paris: Centre Culturel du Marais, 1984. Esp. Eugenia Parry Janis, "The Monotypes," pp. 397–443.

Halévy, Daniel. *Degas parle*. Paris: La Palatine, 1960. Eng. trans. as *My Friend Degas*. Trans. Mina Curtiss. Middletown, Conn.: Wesleyan University, 1964.

Kendall, Richard, and Griselda Pollock, eds. *Dealing with Degas: Representations of Women and the Politics of Vision*. New York: Universe, 1992. Esp. Linda Nochlin, "A House Is Not a Home: Degas and the Subversion of the Family," pp. 43–65.

Lipton, Eunice. *Looking into Degas: Uneasy Images of Women and Modern Life*. Berkeley: University of California Press, 1986.

Maheux, Anne F. *Degas Pastels*. Ottawa: National Gallery of Canada Ottawa, 1988.

McMullen, Roy. *Degas: His Life, Times, and Work*. Boston: Houghton Mifflin, 1984.

Melot, Michel. *The Impressionist Print*. New Haven: Yale University Press, 1996. Esp. chaps. 26, "Lepic and the Mobile Etching," and 50, "Monotypes of Degas."

Reff, Theodore. *Degas: The Artist's Mind*. New York: The Metropolitan Museum of Art and Harper & Row, 1976. Esp. chap. 7, "The Artist as Technician."

Rouart, Denis. *Degas à la recherche de sa technique*. Paris: Floury, 1945. Eng. trans. as *Degas: In Search of His Technique*. Trans. Pia C. DeSantis, Sarah L. Fisher, and Shelley Fletcher. New York: Rizzoli, 1988. Esp. "Monotypes," pp. 97–106.

——. *E. Degas: Monotypes*. Paris: Quatre chemins, and New York: Shoman Art Co., 1948.

Thomson, Richard. *Degas: The Nudes*. New York: Thames & Hudson, 1988.

——. *Edgar Degas: Waiting*. Malibu: Getty Museum Studies on Art, 1995.

Valéry, Paul. *Degas danse dessin*. Paris: Ambroise Vollard, 1936. Reprint ed. Paris: Gallimard, 1938. Eng. trans. as "Degas Dance Drawing" in *Degas, Manet, Morisot*. Trans. David Paul, with an introduction by Douglas Cooper. Princeton: at the University Press, 1989.

Vollard, Ambroise. *Degas*. Paris: G. Crès, 1924. Eng. trans. as *Degas: An Intimate Portrait*. Trans. Randolph T. Weaver. New York: Greenberg, 1927.

——. *Souvenirs d'un marchand de tableaux*. Paris: Alban Michel, 1937. Eng. trans. as *Recollections of a Picture Dealer*. Trans. Violet M. Macdonald. London: Constable, 1936.

Werner, Alfred. *Degas Pastels*. New York: Watson-Guptill Publications, 1968.

Exhibition Catalogues

Paris 1924. *Exposition Degas. Au profit de la ligue franco-anglo-amèricaine contre le cancer. Peintures, pastels et dessins, sculptures, eaux-fortes, lithographies et monotypes*. Éditions des Galeries Georges Petit. Introduction by Daniel Halévy.

London 1958. *Degas: Monotypes, Drawings, Pastels, Bronzes*. Lefevre Gallery. Foreword by Douglas Cooper.

New York 1964. *Nine Monotypes by Degas: December 1964*. E. V. Thaw & Co.

Paris 1974. *L'Estampe impressionniste*. Bibliothèque nationale. Catalogue by Michel Melot.

New York and Boston 1980–81. *The Painterly Print: Monotypes from the Seventeenth to the Twentieth Century*. The Metropolitan Museum of Art, New York, and the Museum of Fine Arts, Boston. Catalogue by Barbara Stern Shapiro, with essays by Shapiro, Colta Ives, Eugenia Parry Janis, and Michael Mazur. Esp. Shapiro, "Nineteenth-Century Masters of the Painterly Print," pp. 29–39.

Boston 1984–85. *Edgar Degas: The Painter as Printmaker*. Museum of Fine Arts. Catalogue by Sue Welsh Reed and Barbara Stern Shapiro, with essays by Douglas Druick and Peter Zegers.

London 1985. *Degas Monotypes*. Hayward Gallery. Catalogue by Anthony Griffiths, with a foreword by R. B. Kitaj.

San Francisco and Washington, D.C., 1986. *The New Painting: Impressionism 1874–1886*. The M. H. de Young Memorial Museum, San Francisco, and the National Gallery of Art, Washington, D.C. Catalogue by Charles S. Moffett, with essays by Stephen F. Eisenman, Richard Schiff, Paul Tucker, Hollis Clayson, Richard R. Brettell, Ronald Pickvance, Fronia E. Wissman, Joel Isaacson, and Martha Ward. Esp. Brettell, "The Third Exhibition 1877: The 'First' Exhibition of Impressionist Painters," pp. 189–243.

Manchester 1987. *The Private Degas*. Whitworth Art Gallery (catalogue London: Arts Council of Great Britain). Catalogue by Richard Thomson.

Paris, Ottawa, and New York 1988–89. *Degas*. Grand Palais, Paris, National Gallery of Canada, Ottawa, and The Metropolitan Museum of Art, New York (catalogue Ottawa: National Gallery of Canada, and New York: The Metropolitan Museum of Art). General editor Jean Sutherland Boggs. Esp. "First Monotypes," pp. 257–60; "Famille Cardinale" pp. 280–81; "Brothel Scenes," pp. 296–309; "Monotypes of Nudes," pp. 411–12.

Liverpool 1989. *Degas: Images of Women*. Tate Liverpool Gallery. Catalogue by Richard Kendall.

New York and Houston 1993. *Degas Landscapes*. The Metropolitan Museum of Art, New York, and the Museum of Fine Arts, Houston (catalogue New Haven and London: Yale University Press). Catalogue by Richard Kendall.

Copenhagen 1994. *Degas Intime*. Ordrupgaard. Catalogue by Mikael Wivel, introduction by Richard Kendall. Esp. Kendall, "The Impromptu Print: Degas' Monotypes and Their Technical Significance."

Washington, D.C., 2001. *The Unfinished Print*. National Gallery of Art. Catalogue by Peter Parshall, Stacey Sell, and Judith Brodie.

Philadelphia 2003. *Degas and the Dance*. Philadelphia Museum of Art. Catalogue by Richard Kendall and Jill DeVonyar.

London 2004. *Degas: Drawings, Bronzes & Monotypes*. Browse & Darby.

Tübingen 2005. *Bordell und Boudoir. Schauplätze der Moderne*. Kunsthalle Tübingen. Catalogue by Götz Adriani. Esp. "Degas' intimer Blick," pp. 111–57.

New York 2006. *Edgar Degas, 1834–1917: Etchings, Lithographs, Monotypes & Copper Plates*. C. G. Boerner. Catalogue by N. G. Stogdon.

Columbus and Copenhagen 2006. *Edgar Degas: The Last Landscapes*. Columbus Museum of Art, Columbus, and Ny Carlsberg Glyptotek, Copenhagen (catalogue London: Merrell). Catalogue by Ann Dumas, Richard Kendall, Flemming Fribourg, and Line Clausen Pedersen.

Canberra 2008. *Degas the Uncontested Master*. National Gallery of Australia, Canberra. Catalogue by Jane Kinsman with Michael Pantazzi. Esp. Kinsman, "Painterly Prints: The Monotypes," pp. 85–110.

Hamburg 2009. *Degas: Intimität und Pose*. Hamburger Kunsthalle. Catalogue by Hubertus Gaßner, with essays by Patrick Bade, Pablo Jiménez Burillo, Werner Hofmann, Nadia Arroyo Rice, Philippe Saunier, Richard Thomson, and William Tucker. Esp. Bade, "Stage-Brothel-Boudoir," pp. 38–58.

Los Angeles, Washington, D.C., and Chicago 2009–10. *The Darker Side of Light: The Art of Privacy 1950–1900*. Hammer Museum, Los Angeles; National Gallery of Art, Washington, D.C.; Smart Museum of Art, University of Chicago. Catalogue by Peter Parshall, with essays by Hollis Clayson, Christiane Hertel, and Nicholas Penny.

Williamstown and Barcelona 2010–11. *Picasso Looks at Degas*. Sterling and Francine Clark Art Institute, Williamstown, and Museu Picasso, Barcelona. Catalogue by Elizabeth Cowling and Richard Kendall. Esp. Cowling, "'The Best Things He Ever Did': Picasso's and Degas's maisons closes," pp. 211–67.

Boston and Paris 2011–12. *Degas and the Nude*. Museum of Fine Arts, Boston, and Musée d'Orsay, Paris. Catalogue by George T. M. Shackelford and Xavier Rey, with contributions by Lucian Freud, Martin Gayford, and Anne Roquebert. Esp. Rey, "The Body Observed: Degas's Naturalist Nudes," pp. 95–120.

Basel 2012. *Degas: The Late Work*. Fondation Beyeler. Catalogue by Martin Schwander, with essays by Carol Armstrong, Richard Kendall, and Jonas Beyer. Esp. Armstrong, "Degas in the Studio: Embodying Medium, Materializing the Body," pp. 23–33, and Beyer, "Degas and Landscape: The Late Monotypes," pp. 215–22.

Copenhagen 2013. *Degas' Method*. Ny Carlsberg Glyptotek. Catalogue by Line Clausen Pederson, with essays by Daphne Barbour, Flemming Friborg, Edouard Kopp, Josephine Nielsen-Bergqvis, Peter Parshall, Elizabeth Steele, and Shelley Sturman. Esp. Fribourg, "Sapphires in Velvet Jewellery Boxes," pp. 223–54, and Parshall, "Degas and the Closeted Image," pp. 153–72.

Karlsruhe 2014–15. *Degas: Klassik und Experiment*. Staatliche Kunsthalle Karlsruhe. Catalogue by Alexander Eiling, with essays by Margret Stuffmann, MaryAnne Stevens, Anett Göthe, and Bettina Kaufmann.

Paris 2015. *Splendour and Misery. Pictures of Prostitutes in Paris, 1850–1910*. Musée d'Orsay. Catalogue by Nienke Bakker, Mireille Dottin-Orsini, Daniel Grojnowski, Gabrielle Houbre, Isolde Pludermacher, Marie Robert, and Richard Thomson.

Photography Credits

Individual works of art appearing in this publication may be protected by copyright in the United States of America, or elsewhere, and may not be reproduced in any form without the permission of the rights holders. In reproducing the images contained herein, the Museum obtained the permission of the rights holders whenever possible. Should the Museum have been unable to locate a rights holder, notwithstanding good-faith efforts, it requests that any contact information concerning such rights holders be forwarded so that they may be contacted for future editions.

Courtesy the Ackland Art Museum, the University of North Carolina at Chapel Hill: pl. 128.

Courtesy Acquavella Galleries: p. 206 fig. 2; pl. 155.

Photo © Agnew's, London/ Bridgeman Images: p. 205 fig. 1.

Photos © The Art Institute of Chicago: p. 49 fig. 2; p. 65 fig. 3; pls. 30, 38, 53, 57, 100, 112.

Bibliothèque nationale de France, Paris: pp. 22–23 figs. 1, 3, 4; p. 29 fig. 11; p. 44 figs. 9, 10; p. 48 fig. 1; p. 138 fig. 1; p. 140 figs. 3, 4; p. 179 fig. 3; pls. 3, 149. Bibliothèque nationale de France, Paris/Bridgeman Images: p. 26 fig. 7.

© bpk, Berlin/Hamburger Kunsthalle/photo Elke Walford/Art Resource, NY: p. 40 fig. 4.

© bpk, Berlin/Staatliche Kunsthalle, Karlsruhe/photo Heike Kohler/Art Resource, NY: pls. 5, 131.

© The Trustees of the British Museum/Art Resource, NY:pls. 49, 121, 138.

Photo Claude Bornand, Lausanne: pl. 80.

Photos © 2016 Carnegie Museum of Art, Pittsburgh: p. 102 fig. 1; pl. 171.

© The Cleveland Museum of Art: p. 124 fig. 1; pls. 150, 153.

© Editions Gallimard: p. 207 fig. 3.

© Fine Arts Museums of San Francisco: pl. 123.

© Fitzwilliam Museum, Cambridge/Art Resource, NY: pl. 66.

Digital image courtesy the Getty's Open Content Program: p. 24 fig. 5; p. 29 fig. 12; p. 43 figs. 7, 8; pl. 173.

Photo Harry Ransom Center, The University of Texas at Austin: p. 59 fig. 2.

Photo Robert Pettus, Imaging Department; © President and Fellows of Harvard College: p. 51 fig. 5; pls. 37, 77, 130.

Courtesy High Museum of Art, Atlanta: pl. 143.

Photos Mitro Hood: pls. 16, 33.

© Kunsthalle Bremen–Der Kunstverein in Bremen, photos Karen Blindow: pls. 11, 107, 108.

© Erich Lessing/Art Resource, NY: p. 42 fig. 6; pl. 160.

Image copyright © The Metropolitan Museum of Art. Image source: Art Resource, NY: p. 33 fig. 15; p. 38 fig. 2; p. 50 figs. 3, 4; pls. 1, 6, 23, 24, 47, 54, 56, 102, 125.

Image provided by The Metropolitan Museum of Art, New York, Thomas J. Watson Library (Gift of Mrs. J. B. Hoptner, 1989): p. 207 fig. 3.

Digital image © 2016 Museum Associates/LACMA, licensed by Art Resource, NY: pls. 132, 176.

Photo © 2016 Museum of Fine Arts, Boston: p. 178 figs. 1, 2; pls. 40, 59, 61, 65, 91, 134.

Images: The Museum of Modern Art, New York, Department of Imaging and Visual Resources: pls. 14, 126, 127; photo Thomas Griesel: pl. 162; photo Paige Knight: pl. 15.

National Galleries of Scotland, Dist. RMN–Grand Palais/Art Resource, NY: pl. 168.

© The National Gallery, London/ Art Resource, NY: p. 32 fig. 13; pl. 169.

Courtesy National Gallery of Art, Washington, D.C.: pls. 17, 39, 64, 70, 71, 106. National Gallery of Art Library, David K. E. Bruce Fund: p. 64 fig. 1.

© National Trust/Malcolm Smith: pl. 152.

Image © 2016 The Norton Simon Foundation: p. 27 fig. 9; p. 41 fig. 5; p. 64 fig. 2; p. 179 fig. 4; pls. 129, 137.

Photo National Museum of Western Art, Tokyo/DNPartcom: p. 58 fig. 1.

Photo Robert Pettus: pl. 133.

The Philadelphia Museum of Art/ Art Resource, NY: pls. 158, 175.

Courtesy Piasa: pl. 122.

The Pierpont Morgan Library, New York: pls. 33, 45.

Princeton University Art Museum/ Art Resource, NY: pls. 4, 170.

Photo private collection: pl. 172.

Private collection, © Brame & Lorenceau: p. 102 fig. 2.

© Rheinisches Bildarchiv Köln, photo Britta Schlier: p. 34 fig. 16.

Photo Richard Valencia Ltd, London: pl. 103.

© RMN–Grand Palais/Art Resource, NY (Musée d'Orsay): pls. 104, 110, 114, 115, 124. © RMN–Grand Palais/Art Resource, NY (Musée Picasso): p. 139 fig. 2; pls. 52, 90, 97. © RMN–Grand Palais/Art Resource, NY, photo Michele Bellot: p. 103 fig. 3. © RMN–Grand Palais/Art Resource, NY, photo J. G. Berizzi: p. 22 fig. 2. © RMN–Grand Palais/Art Resource, NY, photo Hervé Lewandowski: p. 26 fig. 8; p. 28 fig. 10. © RMN–Grand Palais/Art Resource, NY, photo René-Gabriel Ojéda: pls. 85, 96.

Photo E. G. Schempf: p. 24 fig. 6.

© Giorgio Skory, Romanel-sur-Lausanne: pl. 161.

© SMK Photo: pls. 26, 41, 94.

Photo courtesy Sotheby's: pl. 76. Photo courtesy Sotheby's, Inc., © 1995: pl. 58. Photo courtesy Sotheby's, Inc., © 2013: pl. 154.

Photo Patrick Goetelen Sparte, Geneva: pl. 141.

© and photo Staatsgalerie Stuttgart: pls. 72, 81, 82, 83.

© Städel Museum–U. Edelmann–ARTOTHEK: pl. 86.

Images © Sterling and Francine Clark Art Institute, Williamstown, Mass., photos Michael Agee: p. 86 fig. 1; pls. 9, 21, 62, 67.

© Studio Goedewaagen Fotografie: pl. 28.

Photo Jean Paul Torno: pl. 31.

Trustees of the Museum of Modern Art